Real-World
Functional Programming

Real-World Functional Programming

WITH EXAMPLES IN F# AND C#

TOMAS PETRICEK
with JON SKEET

MANNING
Greenwich
(74° w. long.)

For online information and ordering of this and other Manning books, please visit
www.manning.com. The publisher offers discounts on this book when ordered in quantity.
For more information, please contact

Special Sales Department
Manning Publications Co.
Sound View Court 3B
Greenwich, CT 06830
Email: orders@manning.com

Manning Publications Co.
Sound View Court 3B
Greenwich, CT 06830

Development Editor: Tara Walsh
Copyeditor: Liz Welch
Typesetter: Gordan Salinovic
Cover designer: Leslie Haimes

ISBN 978-1-933988-92-4
Printed in the United States of America
1 2 3 4 5 6 7 8 9 10 – MAL – 14 13 12 11 10 09

brief contents

contents

foreword

For the past couple of decades, object-oriented programming has dominated the industry, its ability to hide complexity and provide structure and intuition providing a major boost to software development.

Not all kinds of complexity submit willingly to the mechanisms of encapsulated shared state and virtual methods. Some domains of computation, analysis, and transformation were not much helped by objects, and, looming bigger every day, the demand for concurrency is placing new pressure on the object-oriented paradigm.

From an obscure existence in academic institutions and research labs, functional and declarative techniques have gradually crept into mainstream languages to counter those challenges. In C#, for instance, we added generics, anonymous functions, and monadic query expressions. But a full-fledged commercial functional programming language with the extensive libraries and tools that are crucial to developer productivity has been lacking. I believe F# is a magnificent milestone: one of those turning points that we will look back on and say *that's* when we turned the corner.

F# reaches back pragmatically over the language divide, comfortably embracing the full object model of the .NET framework. But now, we have to distinguish between functional *programming* and functional programming *languages*. As languages become multi-paradigmatic, what used to be a binary choice up front (object-oriented or functional) morphs into a broadened set of opportunities at every turn in your program. You can use functional programming techniques in C# to great benefit, though it is easier and more natural to do so in F#. You can settle on a preferred flavor in your choice of programming language, but your problem-solving options remain open.

The great genius of this book is how it teases apart the functional mindset from the F# language itself. By showing both the C# and F# embodiments of functional programming patterns, the reader is well served. The developer who wants to embark on coding in F# gets a leg up from seeing the patterns used in a (presumably) familiar language. The programmer with good reasons to stay in C# can appreciate the principles in their pure form from the F# examples.

Functional programming is a state of mind. It is a way of thinking differently about the problem. It is not just a bag of useful tricks (though it is that too), but a perspective from which the gnarliest knots prove to be approachable. In this book, as practical and hands-on as it is, Tomas and Jon gently and bravely insist on stressing the principles underneath. Read it at your own peril; you will never look at your own code the same way again!

MADS TORGERSEN
C# LANGUAGE PROGRAM MANAGER
MICROSOFT CORPORATION

preface

This book is different from many other programming books available today. It doesn't focus only on a specific programming language or library. Instead, it uses the presented languages and libraries to explain a way of thinking—a way of thinking that is becoming increasingly important and has influenced many recent technologies.

You may already know some of the concepts described in this book, because functional ideas appear in many technologies. Examples from the .NET world include C# 3.0 and the LINQ project, Microsoft Parallel Extensions to .NET, and the declarative programming model used in Windows Presentation Foundation (WPF). In this book we'll build on top of your existing .NET and C# experience to explain the functional programming paradigm. We'll introduce F#, Microsoft's new functional programming language, and use it to turn abstract ideas into something more concrete. Where possible we'll also use C#, because functional ideas can help you when designing C# applications.

If we'd been writing a book solely about F#, we could have simply organized it based on the individual language features and explained those features one by one. This book is about functional programming in general, so the structure is loosely based on ideas that form the functional paradigm. This is more difficult, because ideas don't have clear boundaries and often overlap.

We've tried to select the ideas that we believe are the most important for newcomers to functional programming and then shape the book around them. This is particularly important in part 2, where we systematically look at functional values, higher-order functions, and the architecture of functional programs. This means that some examples that can be used to quickly demonstrate functional programming, such as working with collections of data, don't appear in only one place. Instead, they're developed gradually through several chapters after we introduce each new idea. We decided to use this approach because it shows how functional programming elegantly arises from a small set of simple concepts—just as functional programs themselves do.

acknowledgments

The "butterfly effect," a term coined by Edward Lorenz, is based in chaos theory: the idea is that a seemingly minor event such as a flap of butterfly's wings somewhere in Asia can cause a major event such as a hurricane in South America. (The butterfly flapping its wings has been constant in the concept, but the location [Asia or Brazil] and the result [hurricane or tornado] have varied.) This alone would be enough to say that there were many more people (and butterflies), without whom this book would not exist than I can possibly list here. And even if I didn't believe in chaos theory, the number of people I'd want to mention in this section would be enormous.

I would never have become interested in F# and functional programming if I hadn't met Don Syme. Don was my mentor during two internships at Microsoft Research and it was a great pleasure to work with him and participate in long discussions about F# (and life, the universe, and everything else). I'm also grateful to James Margetson from Microsoft Research who taught me many cool functional programming tricks. However, I'd never have met Don and James if I hadn't gained status as an MVP by Microsoft and met Luke Hoban who introduced me to Don later. If I were to continue like this, I'd end up mentioning Michal Bláha, Jan Stoklasa, Božena Mannová, the authors of CodeProject.com, and many others.

The book wouldn't exist without Mike Stephens from Manning who first contacted me, and without Harry Pierson without whose initial involvement we'd never have started working on it. Even though we only worked together briefly, Harry's participation was very important and encouraging.

Now that I've mentioned people without whom the book would never have started, it's also a time to mention those, without whom it would never have been finished.

I'm very grateful to my coauthor Jon for helping me through the long process of turning the initial drafts and sketches into a real book. Jon is also the person to thank if you feel like this book was written exactly for you, because he carefully adjusted everything to be in the right form for our audience. Finally, Jon is a wonderful person to work with, so it was a pleasure to discuss the book with him both online and briefly in person.

At this point, I'd like to mention everyone from Manning who contributed to this book. I already mentioned Mike Stephens who was always helpful in difficult moments. Nermina Miller and Tara McGoldrick Walsh guided me through the everyday jungle of the writing process and Mary Piergies, with Liz Welch and Elizabeth Martin, helped me to find the way out of this jungle to a clear light. I briefly worked with many other great folks at Manning including Gabriel Dobrescu, Steven Hong, Dottie Marsico, Christina Rudloff, Gordan Salinovic, Maureen Spencer, and Karen Tegtmeyer. I would also like to thank publisher Marjan Bace, who provided numerous useful insights.

Folks from Manning also had a lucky hand picking people for the reviews at various points in the writing process. We received a large number of comments, suggestions, and hints, but also exactly the right amount of positive feedback that encouraged me to take as many of these suggestions as possible into account. Aside from our anonymous reviewers, I'd like to thank our two technical reviewers, Matthew Podwysocki and Michael Giagnocavo. I had the role of a technical reviewer in the past, so I can appreciate your hard work! And special thanks to Mads Torgersen, who wrote the foreword

Another group who provided valuable input are readers of the early drafts. First of all, my colleagues Jan Stoklasa and René Stein, but also those who purchased the book through the Manning Early Access Program and shared their feedback in the forums (Dave Novick, Peer Reynders, Vladimir Kelman, and Michiel Borkent to name a few). Other reviewers who had a hand in making this book what it is are Marius Bancila, Freedom Dumlao, Eric Swanson, Walter Myers, Keith J. Farmer, Adam Tacy, Marc Gravell, Jim Wooley, Alessandro Gallo, Lester Lobo, Massimo Perga, Andrew Siemer, Austin Ziegler, Dave McMahon, Jason Jung, Joshua Gan, Keith Hill, Mark Needham, Mark Ryall, Mark Seemann, Paul King, and Stuart Caborn.

I'd, of course, like to thank my friends and my family. To those who don't know them, their question, "When is your book finally going to be finished?" may not sound particularly supportive, but I know them well and I honestly appreciated their encouragement. Last, but not least, I'm grateful to my dearest Evelina, who not only provided invaluable moral support, but also was so kind as to read and review large portions of the manuscript.

TOMAS PETRICEK

I would primarily like to thank Tomas and everyone at Manning for giving me the opportunity to be part of this book. Being a small part of a bigger goal is always interesting, and it's been great fun learning about functional programming "from" a book and "into" a book at the same time. I can only hope that the minor contributions I've made will be useful—I've primarily acted as the voice of a passionate but ignorant reader (and C# enthusiast of course), so in some ways the book you're reading now is tailored toward teaching me functional programming. That in itself is a gift to be grateful for. Tomas has thanked all the editors and other staff at Manning, and I'd like to echo those thanks.

My children are still too young to be programming, and my wife is too...well, normal, basically—but they've always been there for me when higher-order functions have burst my brain. I've been struggling to stay sane and work on more than one book at a time, whereas my wife (who writes children's fiction) seems perpetually up to her ears in proposals, chapter breakdowns, first drafts, copy edits, proofs, and delivered manuscripts, all for different titles and even publishers. Beyond that, she's married to me—how she stays sane is anyone's guess. However, I'm very glad that she does, and I'd like to thank her for being who she is. Tom, Robin, and William show great promise in their love of technology, but it's their smiles and cuddles when I get home from work for which I'm most grateful.

Finally, I'd like to thank all my English teachers, especially Simon Howells. The more I learn about programming languages, the more I believe that the language a software engineer should pay most attention to is the one he uses to communicate with people, not computers. Simon Howells is as passionate about language and literature as I am about computing, and that passion rubs off on his students. It is highly unlikely that he'll ever read a word I've written, but his teaching will be with me for the rest of my life.

JON SKEET

about this book

If you are an existing .NET developer who knows object-oriented technologies and are wondering what this new "functional programming" movement is about and how you can benefit from it, this book is definitely for you.

It's particularly tailored for .NET developers with working knowledge of object-oriented programming and C# 2.0. Of course, you don't need to know either of these for functional programming in general, or even F# in particular. In fact, it's more difficult to learn functional programming if you're already used to thinking in an object-oriented manner, because many of the functional ideas will appear unfamiliar to you. We've written the book with this concern in mind, so we'll often refer to your intuition and use comparisons between OOP and functional programming to explain particular topics.

If you're an existing object-oriented programmer using other languages and tools (for example, Java, Python, or Ruby) with the ability to understand languages quickly, you can also benefit from this book. We're using examples in C#, but many of them would look similar in other object-oriented languages. The C# 3.0 features that aren't available in other languages are briefly explained, so you don't have to worry about getting lost.

This book doesn't focus on academic aspects of functional programming, but if you're a computer science student taking a course on the topic, you can read this book to learn about the real-world uses of functional concepts.

What will this book give you?

If you're still wondering whether this book is right for you, here's what you'll learn by reading it:

- Functional programming concepts. As you read through the book, you'll learn a new way to think about problems. We'll see how complex object-oriented design patterns become one simple concept in functional programming. Functional thinking can be used when programming in any language, so this will be useful regardless of the specific technology you work with.
- Basic functional constructs in practice. Some of the constructs are now available in C# 3.0, so you'll see many of the examples in familiar C# code next to a clean functional F# implementation. We'll also explain recent features in C# 3.0 and how they relate to functional ideas. Understanding the concepts deeply will help you to get the most benefit from the new features.
- Writing real-world F# code. Even though the book isn't only about F#, it will teach you everything you need to know to start. We'll explore areas where F# really shines, including asynchronous programming and creating composable libraries.

We're not claiming this is the perfect book for all purposes: computing isn't a one-size-fits-all field. It's worth knowing what this book *isn't* to avoid disappointment.

What won't this book give you?

This hasn't been written as a reference book. If you haven't been exposed to functional programming, the best way to read the book is to start from the beginning and follow the order of the chapters. That's the way we've assumed it will be read, so later chapters often refer to concepts explained earlier. If you open the book somewhere in the middle, you may find it hard to understand.

This book also isn't a quick guide to F# programming. The only way to become a good F# programmer is to understand functional programming ideas. You could learn all the F# keywords and rewrite your C# code in F#, but it wouldn't do you much good. If you want to write idiomatic F# code, you'll need to learn a different way of thinking that is used in functional programming. That's what you'll get by reading this book. Once you've adapted to thinking in a functional style, there are other books which can help you learn F# in more depth.

Our primary goal is to write a book that can be used by professional programmers to write solutions to real-world business problems. However, that doesn't mean we can offer you a ready-to-use solution for the specific problem you need to solve right now. Instead, we've focused on the relevant concepts and techniques. We've demonstrated those principles with many examples, but it isn't possible to cover all the areas where F# and functional programming can be applied.

Roadmap

This book uses an iterative structure. In part 1 (chapters 1-4) we'll explain a few aspects of the most important topics, so that you can see the motivation and understand what makes functional programming different. Part 2 (chapters 5-8) systematically discusses all the foundations of functional programming. In part 3 (chapters 9-12) we build on these foundations and talk about best practices for functional programming, optimization, and some advanced techniques that most of the functional programmers occasionally need. Part 4 (chapters 13-16) presents more complex examples showing how to use functional programming to develop larger real-world projects.

Chapter 1 discusses the reasons why functional concepts are becoming increasingly important. It gives examples of existing technologies that you may already know and that benefit from some aspects of functional programming. It also shows the first sample application in F#.

Chapter 2 introduces the concepts behind functional programming. Without showing any details and mostly using C#, it'll help you understand how these concepts relate to each other and what they mean for the structure of program.

Chapter 3 finally shows some real functional code. It demonstrates some data types used in F# such as a tuple and a list. We'll see how to work with the types in F#, but we'll also implement them in C# to explain how they work. This chapter introduces the idea of using functions as values, which is essential for functional programming.

Chapter 4 shows our first real-world application implemented in F#. We'll use various .NET and F# libraries to implement a program for drawing pie charts. You'll also see how to efficiently use the tools F# provides during the development process.

Chapter 5 talks about values. Functional programs are written as calculations that take values as arguments and return values as results, so it is easy to see why we have to start the systematic review of functional features by looking at numerous kinds of values.

Chapter 6 describes the most common way of working with values, which is to use higher-order functions. Working with values directly often requires a lot of repetitive code, so this chapter shows how to design and implement reusable operations.

Chapter 7 turns the attention to architectural aspects. The structure of a functional application is determined by the data that it works with. We'll use an application that manipulates and draws simple documents to demonstrate this important principle.

Chapter 8 focuses on the architecture of applications that need to dynamically change their behavior at runtime. This can be done using functions, so we'll talk about them in detail and we'll also explain related topics such as closures.

Chapter 9 shows how to mix object-oriented and functional styles in F#. It demonstrates how you can use functional features like immutability with object-oriented concepts such as encapsulation when writing functional .NET libraries.

Chapter 10 focuses on correctness and efficiency. We'll see how to write functions that can process data sets of arbitrary size and how to write these functions efficiently. You'll also learn how to optimize code using imperative constructs like arrays.

Chapter 11 talks about refactoring, testing and laziness. We'll explain how functional programming makes it easier to understand and improve existing code. We'll also look at unit testing, seeing how composability and strictness remove the need for some types of test.

Chapter 12 starts by showing how we can work with collections of data. We'll introduce F# sequence expressions, which are designed for this purpose. You'll also see that this isn't a built-in feature unlike its closest counterpart in C#—it's an example of a more general ability to change what code means.

Chapter 13 presents a common scenario when working with data in F#. It starts by downloading data using a public web service, then parses it into a structured format. Finally we see how to visualize interesting aspects using Excel.

Chapter 14 shows how to use functional concepts to build applications that are easy to parallelize. It demonstrates this using an image processing application and a simulation featuring animals and predators that hunt them.

Chapter 15 describes how to build declarative functional libraries. The chapter shows that well designed libraries can be elegantly composed. As an example, we'll see how to create a library for creating animations and a library for representing financial contracts.

Chapter 16 shows how to build GUI applications and in general, programs driven by external events. Implementing control flow like this is quite difficult in other languages, so we'll look at tricks that make it much easier in F#.

Typographical conventions

The book contains numerous code examples that are typeset using `fixed-width font`. Longer samples are presented in listings with a heading. Since the book mixes C# and F#, the heading in side-by-side listings also indicates the language used. When showing code in F#, we distinguish between two forms of listing. Code marked as "F#" is plain source code that can be compiled as a whole. Listings marked as "F# Interactive" present snippets in F# entered to an interactive shell. The output produced by the shell is typeset using *italics*. **Bold `fixed-width`** font is used to highlight all C# and F# keywords in all the listings.

Naming conventions

In this book, we're mixing not only two languages, but also a functional programming tradition with the object-oriented tradition. Since we want to use the natural style in both languages, we have to follow different naming conventions in F# and C#.

In C# we follow the usual .NET style. In F#, we use this notation without exceptions when developing classes or when writing components that can be accessed from other .NET languages. When we show F# code that is only a private implementation, we follow the functional naming style. Most notably, we use camelCase for both variable and function names. This is the usual style in F#, because a function declaration is essentially the same thing as a variable declaration.

Occasionally, we use shorter names and abbreviations. There are two reasons for this. First, this style has been often used by functional programmers. With better IDEs there are fewer reasons to use this style, so we've tried to minimize its use. In some cases the shorter name is a common term in functional programming, so we've kept it. The second reason is that sometimes we present two samples side-by-side, which means that we have to use a more compact coding style. Otherwise, the naming mostly follows the .NET style with a few exceptions that are discussed in the text.

StyleCop and FxCop

If you're familiar with tools for code analysis such as StyleCop and FxCop, you may be wondering whether the code in this book follows the rules required by these tools. We follow most—but not all—of the usual .NET conventions. If you run the code through these tools, you'll get numerous warnings, again for two reasons.

- The tools for code analysis were developed for object-oriented languages using the naming and style of the object-oriented tradition. As you'll learn in this book, the functional world is different in many ways and we simply cannot follow all the object-oriented principles. The F# language is successful because it is very different from C# and Visual Basic. This isn't just visible in the language keywords, but in the overall style of programming that it uses and in some ways also in naming conventions that make the code more succinct.
- The limited space we have in the book. We use source code samples to demonstrate important ideas, so we didn't want to include noise that isn't important for the discussion, but would be required to make the code comply with conventions.

Source code downloads

The source code for the examples in the book is available online from the publisher's website at http://www.manning.com/Real-WorldFunctionalProgramming and at a code repository created by the authors http://code.msdn.microsoft.com/realworldfp.

Author Online

The purchase of *Real-World Functional Programming* includes free access to a private web forum run by Manning Publications, where you can make comments about the book, ask technical questions, and receive help from the authors and from other users. To access the forum and subscribe to it, point your web browser to http://www.manning.com/Real-WorldFunctionalProgramming. This page provides information about how to get on the forum once you're registered, what kind of help is available, and the rules of conduct on the forum.

Manning's commitment to our readers is to provide a venue where a meaningful dialogue between individual readers and between readers and the authors can take place. It's not a commitment to any specific amount of participation on the part of the authors, whose contribution to the book's forum remains voluntary (and unpaid). We suggest you try asking them some challenging questions, lest their interest stray!

The Author Online forum and the archives of previous discussions will be accessible from the publisher's website as long as the book is in print.

Other online resources

In addition to Manning's website (http://www.manning/com/Real-WorldFunctional-Programming), we have created a companion website for the book at http://functional-programming.net. It contains additional information that you may find useful, source code for the individual chapters, and material that didn't fit in the book. The page also links to recent articles related to functional programming, so you can look at it to learn more about this topic.

If you're interested in F#, you may also want to check out the official Microsoft's Developer Center available at http://msdn.microsoft.com/fsharp. It contains the most recent information about the language as well as links to articles, videos, and other F# resources. If you want to ask a question about F# and be sure that you'll get a competent answer, you can visit the F# community forums available at http://cs.hubfs.net.

about the cover illustration

The figure on the cover of *Real-World Functional Programming* is captioned "An employee," and it shows an office clerk or civil servant elegantly dressed in suit and top hat and carrying an umbrella. The illustration is taken from a 19th-century edition of Sylvain Maréchal's four-volume compendium of regional dress customs published in France. Each illustration is finely drawn and colored by hand. The rich variety of Maréchal's collection reminds us vividly of how culturally apart the world's towns and regions were just 200 years ago. Isolated from each other, people spoke different dialects and languages. In the streets or in the countryside, it was easy to identify where they lived and what their trade, occupation, or station in life was just by their dress.

Dress codes have changed since then and the diversity by region, so rich at the time, has faded away. It is now hard to tell apart the inhabitants of different continents, let alone different towns or regions. Perhaps we have traded cultural diversity for a more varied personal life—certainly for a more varied and fast-paced technological life.

At a time when it is hard to tell one computer book from another, Manning celebrates the inventiveness and initiative of the computer business with book covers based on the rich diversity of regional life of two centuries ago, brought back to life by Maréchal's pictures.

Part 1

Learning to think functionally

You may have picked up this book for any number of reasons. Perhaps you've heard of functional programming when reading about LINQ and C# 3.0 or another technology that has been largely influenced by it, and you're wondering if it has any other interesting ideas. You may have heard that functional programming makes it simple to write parallel or asynchronous programs. Maybe you've heard about other interesting applications of the functional style—just how *do* you go about writing programs with no mutable state? You may have heard about a new language called F# that's going to be a part of Visual Studio 2010, and you want to learn what it has to offer.

In any case, the first thing you'll learn about functional programming is that it's built on fundamentally different principles than the ones you're probably used to. But that doesn't mean you'll have to throw away any of your existing knowledge, because functional programming on .NET plays nicely with the object-oriented style and existing libraries. The foundations are different, but we can build on top of them and return to familiar areas, looking at them from a different perspective.

In part 1 we'll focus on these fundamental principles. In chapter 1, we'll examine the practical effects of some of these principles, but we won't go into much detail. We'll also write our first F# program so that you can start experimenting with F# on your own while you're reading. In chapter 2, we'll review the ideas behind functional programming more systematically and discuss how they change the way we write programs. We'll use C# for most of the example code in that chapter, because many functional ideas can be used in C# as well.

Chapter 3 gets into F# in more detail, looking at values, function declarations, and several built-in data types. We'll also implement corresponding types and functions in C#. This is the easiest way of explaining how F# works to a C# developer, and we'll be able to reuse some of the types in real-world C# examples later in the book. In chapter 4 we'll use everything we've learned so far to develop a charting application in F#.

Thinking differently

This chapter covers
- Understanding functional programming
- Increasing productivity with functional ideas
- Writing efficient and readable code
- Implementing your first F# application

Functional languages are expressive, accomplishing great feats using short, succinct, and readable code. All this is possible because functional languages provide richer ways for expressing abstractions. We can hide *how* the code executes and specify only the desired *results*. The code that specifies how to achieve the results is written only once. Thanks to the rich abstractions, we can hide all the complexity in libraries.

This different approach to programming has far-reaching implications for real-world applications. This way of expressing logic makes programs readable and easy to reason about, thus making it possible to understand and change previously unknown code. Functional programs are easy to test and refactor. Yet despite these benefits, functional languages have largely been ignored by mainstream developers—until now. Today we're facing new challenges. We need to write programs that process large data sets and scale to a large number of processors We need to deal

3

with ever larger systems, so we have to get a better handle on their complexity. These trends open the door to functional languages. But they are far from being the only reason for using functional programming.

As a result, many mainstream languages now include some functional features. In the .NET world, generics in C# 2.0 were heavily influenced by functional languages. One of the most fundamental features of functional languages is the ability to create function values on the fly, without declaring them in advance. This is exactly what C# 2.0 enables us to do using anonymous methods, and C# 3.0 makes it even easier with lambda expressions. The whole LINQ project is rooted in functional programming.

While the mainstream languages are playing catch-up, truly functional languages have been receiving more attention too. The most significant example of this is F#, which will be an official, fully supported Visual Studio language as of Visual Studio 2010. This evolution of functional languages on .NET is largely possible thanks to the common language runtime (CLR), which allows developers to

- Mix multiple languages when developing a single .NET application
- Access rich .NET libraries from new languages like F#

Sharing of libraries among all .NET languages makes it much easier to learn these new languages, because all the platform knowledge that you've accumulated during your career can still be used in the new context of a functional language.

In this book, we'll explore the most important functional programming concepts and demonstrate them using real-world examples from .NET. We'll start with a description of the ideas, then turn to the aspects that make it possible to develop large-scale real-world .NET applications in a functional way. We'll use both F# and C# 3.0 in this book, because many of these ideas are directly applicable to C# programming. You certainly don't need to write in a functional language to use functional concepts and patterns. But seeing the example in F# code will give you a deeper understanding of how it works, and F# often makes it easier to express and implement the solution.

But we've jumped the gun. This is a book about *functional programming*, after all. Wouldn't it make sense to start off by describing what the term means?

1.1   *What is functional programming?*

Finding a precise definition of functional programming is difficult. Various functional languages exist, and there's no clear set of features that every functional language must have. Nonetheless, functional languages share common properties and support somewhat different styles of expressing solutions to programming problems. It's easiest to describe functional programming by comparing it with the most common alternative option: imperative programming.

FUNCTIONAL LANGUAGES   Functional programming is a style of programming that emphasizes the evaluation of expressions, rather than execution of commands. The expressions in these languages are formed by using functions to combine basic values. [Hutton ed. 2002]

This definition comes from a FAQ of an academic mailing list about functional languages, so it may sound a bit abstract. Believe us, the meaning will soon become clear. The "evaluation of expressions" in the first sentence represents the functional approach, compared with the "execution of commands" style of imperative code. Commands in imperative languages are called *statements,* so we'll use this terminology instead. Let's take a look at these two options in detail:

- *Execution of statements*—The program is expressed as a sequence of commands, which are also called statements. Commands specify how to achieve the end result by creating objects and manipulating them. When using this approach, we typically work with objects that can be changed, and the code describes what modifications we need to perform in order to achieve the desired result. For example, we start by making a cup of black coffee. The object can be modified, so we can change it by adding two sugars to get the desired result.

- *Evaluation of expressions*—In the functional style, the program code is an expression that specifies properties of the object we want to get as the result. We don't specify the steps necessary to construct the object and we can't accidentally use the object before it's created. For example, we say that we want to get a coffee with two packets of sugars. We can't drink it before the sugar is added, because when we get the cup, it already contains the sugar.[1]

This may still sound like a subtle difference, yet it leads to huge changes in the way you design code. The single axiom is that we write code as expressions instead of a sequence of statements, but this approach has many logical consequences. We encapsulate and compose code differently, we use various techniques for writing reusable code, we work with data structures that are more suitable for representing the result of a complex computation...the list goes on.

Providing a definition of functional programming is one thing, but we also need to understand how the concepts can be used together. These two topics form the focus of this book. After you finish reading it, you'll not only have an understanding of our earlier definition, but you'll also get an intuitive feeling for functional programming. This is much more important, and unfortunately, it can't be explained in a few sentences.

So far this may all sound a bit abstract, but this book's title includes the words "Real World" for good reason. Functional programming can offer notable benefits. You may have encountered (just like the authors of this book) these situations where a functional style may be the answer:

- Do you find it hard to predict the results of changing your code, due to hidden dependencies and subtleties?

- Do you find yourself writing the same patterns over and over again, leaving little time for the genuinely different and interesting parts of the problem?

---

[1] The analogy with coffee making was also used by Luca Bolognese in his great talk about F# at TechEd in 2009 [Bolognese, 2009]. This coincidence suggests that by learning functional programming you'll learn to think differently not only about programming problems but also about afternoon breaks.

- Do you find it hard to reason about your code, worrying about whether each statement will execute in the right order and in the right conditions?
- Do you find it hard to express abstractions that hide *how* the code executes and specify only *what* you're trying to achieve?
- Do you struggle with asynchronous control flow, finding that it leads to code that bears more than a passing resemblance to spaghetti?
- Do you find it hard to split tasks into logically independent parts that can be run concurrently on multiple processor cores?
- Does your code behave differently in the real world than it does in unit tests?

Before we look how functional programming can make you more productive, let's briefly talk about its history, which is surprisingly rich.

1.2 *The path to real-world functional programming*

Functional programming is a paradigm originating from ideas older than the first computers. Its history goes as far back as the 1930s, when Alonzo Church and Stephen C. Kleene introduced a theory called lambda calculus as part of their investigation of the foundations of mathematics. Even though it didn't fulfill their original expectations, the theory is still used in some branches of logic and has evolved into a useful theory of computation. To explore the basic principles of functional programming, you'll find a brief introduction to lambda calculus in the next chapter. Lambda calculus escaped its original domain when computers were invented and served as an inspiration for the first functional programming languages.

1.2.1 *Functional languages*

The first functional programming language celebrated its 50th birthday in 2008. LISP, created by John McCarthy in 1958, is based directly on the lambda calculus theory. LISP, an extremely flexible language, pioneered many programming ideas that are still used today, including data structures, garbage collection, and dynamic typing.

In the 1970s, Robin Milner developed a language called ML. This was the first of a family of languages that now includes F#. Inspired by typed lambda calculus, it added the notion of types and even allowed us to write "generic" functions in the same way we do now with .NET generics. ML was also equipped with a powerful type inference mechanism, which is now essential for writing terse programs in F#. OCaml, a pragmatic extension to the ML language, appeared in 1996. It was one of the first languages that allowed the combination of object-oriented and functional approaches. OCaml was a great inspiration for F#, which has to mix these paradigms in order to be a first-class .NET language *and* a truly functional one.

Other important functional languages include Haskell (a language with surprising mathematical purity and elegance) and Erlang (which has become famous for message passing concurrency that we'll discuss in chapter 16). We'll learn more about Haskell and LISP when we focus on topics where those languages have benefits over F#—but first, let's finish our story by looking at the history of F#.

1.2.2 Functional programming on the .NET platform

The first version of .NET was released in 2002, and the history of the F# language dates to the same year. F# started off as a Microsoft Research project by Don Syme and his colleagues, with the goal of bringing functional programming to .NET. F# and typed functional programming in general gave added weight to the need for generics in .NET, and the designers of F# were deeply involved in the design and implementation of generics in .NET 2.0 and C# 2.0.

With generics implemented in the core framework, F# began evolving more quickly, and the programming style used in F# also started changing. It began as a functional language with support for objects, but as the language matured, it seemed more natural to take the best from both styles. As a result, F# is now more precisely described as a multiparadigm language, which combines both functional and object-oriented approaches, together with a great set of tools that allow it to be used interactively for scripting.

MICROSOFT F#   F# is a functional programming language for the .NET Framework. It combines the succinct, expressive, and compositional style of functional programming with the runtime, libraries, interoperability, and object model of .NET. [F# home page]

F# has been a first-class .NET citizen since its early days. Not only can it access any of the standard .NET components but—equally importantly—any other .NET language can access code developed in F#. This makes it possible to use F# to develop standalone .NET applications as well as parts of larger projects. F# has always come with support in Visual Studio, and in 2007 a process was started to turn F# from a research project to a full production-quality language. In 2008 Microsoft announced that F# will become one of the languages shipped with Visual Studio 2010. This alone is a good reason for taking interest in F# and the whole functional paradigm, but let's look at more pragmatic reasons now.

1.3 Being productive with functional programming

Many people find functional programming elegant or even beautiful, but that's hardly a good reason to use it in a commercial environment. Elegance doesn't pay the bills, sad to say. The key reason for coding in a functional style is that it makes you and your team more productive.

In this section, we'll look at the key benefits that functional programming gives you and explain how it solves some of the most important problems of modern software development. Before exploring the specific benefits, we'll consider a higher perspective. Functional programming isn't a strictly delimited technology, because the functional ideas can appear in different forms.

1.3.1 The functional paradigm

Functional programming is a programming paradigm This means that it defines the concepts that we can use when thinking about problems. But it doesn't precisely specify how these concepts should be represented in the programming language. As a result, there are many functional languages, and each emphasizes different features and aspects of the functional style.

We can use an analogy with a paradigm you're already familiar with: object-oriented programming (OOP). In the object-oriented style, we think about problems in terms of objects. Each object-oriented language has some notion of what an object is, but the details vary between languages. For instance, C++ has multiple inheritance and JavaScript has prototypes. Moreover, you can use an object-oriented style in a language that isn't object-oriented, such as C. It's less comfortable, but you'll still enjoy some of the benefits.

Programming paradigms aren't exclusive. The C# language is primarily object-oriented, but in the 3.0 version it supports several functional features, so we can use techniques from the functional style directly. On the other side, F# is primarily a functional language, but it fully supports the .NET object model. The great thing about combining paradigms is that we can choose the approach that best suits the problem.

Learning the functional paradigm is worthwhile even if you're not planning to use a functional language. By learning a functional style, you'll gain concepts that make it easier to think about and solve your daily programming problems. Interestingly, many of the standard object-oriented patterns describe how to encode some clear functional concept in the OOP style.

Now let's focus on the benefits of functional programming. We'll start by looking at the declarative programming style, which gives us a richer vocabulary for describing our intentions.

1.3.2   *Declarative programming style*

In the declarative programming style, we express the logic of programs without specifying the execution details. This description may sound familiar to you because it's quite similar to the definition of functional programming we've seen in section 1.1. But declarative programming is a more general idea that can be realized using different technologies. Functional programming is just one way to achieve that. Let's demonstrate how functional languages make it possible to write declarative code.

When writing a program, we have to explain our goals to the computer using the vocabulary that it understands. In imperative languages, this consists of commands. We can add new commands, such as "show customer details," but the whole program is a step-by-step description saying how the computer should accomplish the overall task. An example of a program is "Take the next customer from a list. If the customer lives in the UK, show their details. If there are more customers in the list, go to the beginning."

NOTE   Once the program grows, the number of commands in our vocabulary becomes too high, making the vocabulary difficult to use. This is where object-oriented programming makes our life easier, because it allows us to organize our commands in a better way. We can associate all commands that involve a customer with some customer entity (a class), which clarifies the description. The program is still a sequence of commands specifying how it should proceed.

Functional programming provides a completely different way of extending the vocabulary. We're not limited to adding new primitive commands; we can also add new control structures—primitives that specify how we can put commands together to create a program. In imperative languages, we were able to compose commands in a sequence or by using a limited number of built-in constructs such as loops, but if you look at typical programs, you'll still see many recurring structures—common ways of combining commands. In fact, some of these recurring structures are very well known and are described by *design patterns*. But in imperative languages, we keep typing the same structure of code over and over again.

In our example we can see a pattern, which could be expressed as "Run the *first command* for every customer for which the *second command* returns true." Using this primitive, we can express our program simply by saying "Show customer details of every customer living in the UK." In this sentence "living in the UK" specifies the second argument and "show customer details" represents the first.

Let's compare the two sentences that we've used to describe the same problem:

- Take the next customer from a list. If the customer lives in the UK, show their details. If there are more customers in the list, go to the beginning.
- Show customer details of every customer living in the UK.

Just like the earlier analogy of making a cup of coffee, the first sentence describes exactly *how* to achieve our goal whereas the second describes *what* we want to achieve.

TIP This is the essential difference between imperative and declarative styles of programming. Surely you'll agree that the second sentence is far more readable and better reflected the aim of our "program."

So far we've been using an analogy, but we'll see how this idea maps to actual source code later in this chapter. This isn't the only aspect of functional programming that makes life easier. In the next section, we'll look at another concept that makes it much simpler to understand what a program does.

1.3.3 *Understanding what a program does*

In the usual imperative style, the program consists of objects that have internal state that can be changed either directly or by calling some method of the object. This means that when we call a method, it can be hard to tell what state is affected by the operation. For example, in the C# snippet in listing 1.1 we create an ellipse, get its bounding box, and call a method on the returned rectangle. Finally, we return the ellipse to whatever has called it.

Listing 1.1 Working with ellipse and rectangle (C#)

```
Ellipse ellipse = new Ellipse(new Rectangle(0, 0, 100, 100));
Rectangle boundingBox = ellipse.BoundingBox;
boundingBox.Inflate(10, 10);                              ❶
return ellipse;
```

How do we know what the state of the `Ellipse` will be after the code runs just by look-ing at it? This is hard, because `boundingBox` could be a reference to the bounding box of the ellipse and `Inflate` ❶ could modify the rectangle, changing the ellipse at the same time. Or maybe the `Rectangle` type is a value type (declared using the `struct` keyword in C#) and it's copied when we assign it to a variable. Perhaps the `Inflate` method doesn't modify the rectangle and returns a new rectangle as a result, so the third line has no effect.

In functional programming, most of the data structures are immutable, which means that we can't modify them. Once the `Ellipse` or `Rectangle` is created, we can't change it. The only thing we can do is create a new `Ellipse` with a new bounding box. This makes it easy to understand what a program does. As listing 1.2 shows, we could rewrite the previous snippet if `Ellipse` and `Rectangle` were immutable. As you'll see, understanding the program's behavior becomes much easier.

Listing 1.2 Working with immutable ellipse and rectangle (C#)

```
Ellipse ellipse = new Ellipse(new Rectangle(0, 0, 100, 100));
Rectangle boundingBox = ellipse.BoundingBox;
Rectangle smallerBox = boundingBox.Inflate(10, 10);      ❶
return new Ellipse(smallerBox);                          ❷
```

When you're writing programs using immutable types, the only thing a method can do is return a result—it can't modify the state of any objects. You can see that `Inflate` returns a new rectangle as a result ❶ and that we construct a new ellipse to return an ellipse with a modified bounding box ❷. This approach may feel a bit unfamiliar the first time, but keep in mind that this isn't a new idea to .NET developers. `String` is probably the best-known immutable type in the .NET world, but there are many exam-ples, such as `DateTime` and other value types.

Functional programming takes this idea further, which makes it a lot easier to see what a program does, because the result of a method specifies fully what the method does. We'll talk about immutability in more detail later, but first let's look at one area where it's extremely useful: implementing multithreaded applications.

1.3.4   *Concurrency-friendly application design*

When writing a multithreaded application using the traditional imperative style, we face two problems:

- It's difficult to turn existing sequential code into parallel code, because we have to modify large portions of the codebase to use threads explicitly.
- Using shared state and locks is difficult. You have to carefully consider how to use locks to avoid race conditions and deadlocks but leave enough space for parallel execution.

Functional programming gives us the answers:

- When using a declarative programming style we can introduce parallelism into existing code. We can replace a few primitives that specify how to combine commands with a version that executes commands in parallel.

- Thanks to the immutability, we can't introduce race conditions and we can write lock-free code. We can immediately see which parts of the program are independent, and we can modify the program to run those tasks in parallel.

These two aspects influence how we design our applications and, as a result, make it much easier to write code that executes in parallel, taking full advantage of the power of multicore machines. The simple fact that we're writing immutable code doesn't mean we'll get parallelization for free. There's work involved, but functional programming minimizes the additional effort we have to put in parallelization.

We haven't finished yet. There are other changes you should expect to see in your design when you start thinking functionally...

1.3.5 *How functional style shapes your code*

The functional programming paradigm no doubt influences how you design and implement applications. This doesn't mean that you have to start all over, because many of the programming principles that you're using today are applicable to functional applications as well. This is true especially at the design level in how you structure the application.

Functional programming can cause a radical transformation of how you approach problems at the implementation level. When learning how to use functional programming ideas, you don't have to make these radical changes right away. In C# you learn how to efficiently use the new features. In F#, you can often use direct equivalents of C# constructs while you're still getting your feet wet. As you become a more experienced functional developer, you'll learn more efficient and concise ways to express yourself.

The following list summarizes how functional programming influences your programming style, working down from a design level to actual implementation:

- Functional programs on .NET still use object-oriented design as a great method for structuring applications and components. A large number of types and classes are designed as immutable, but it's still possible to create standard classes, especially when collaborating with other .NET libraries.

- Thanks to functional programming, you can simplify many of the standard object-oriented design patterns, because some of them correspond to language features in F# or C# 3.0. Also, some of the design patterns aren't needed when the code is implemented in the functional way. You'll see many examples of this throughout the book, especially in chapters 7 and 8.

- The biggest impact of functional programming is at the lowest level, where we encode the algorithms and behavior of the application. Thanks to the combination of a declarative style, succinct syntax, and type inference, functional languages help us concisely express algorithms in a readable way.

We'll talk about all these aspects later in the book. We'll start with the functional values used to implement methods and functions before raising our sights to design and architecture. You'll discover new patterns specific to functional programming, as well as learn whether the object-oriented patterns you're already familiar with fit in with the functional world or are no longer required.

What comes next in the introduction?

So far, we've only talked about functional programming in a general sense. You've seen how functional programming allows you to extend the vocabulary when programming and how this makes your code more declarative. We've also talked about immutable data structures and what they mean for your programs. In the next section, we'll explore four practical aspects of these two basic concepts:

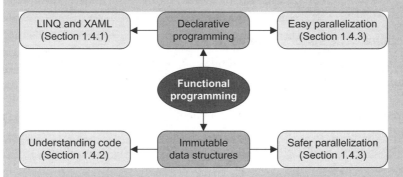

Both declarative programming and immutable data structures affect the readability and clarity of the code in general, and you'll see two examples in sections 1.4.1 and 1.4.2. Then we'll look at a current problem, parallelization, and see how declarative programming helps us parallelize code and how immutable data structures make the process safer.

So far we've concentrated on what makes functional programming different and why it's worth learning, but there's nothing like seeing actual code to bring things into focus. In the next section, we'll look at the source code for the four examples mentioned in the sidebar.

1.4   *Functional programming by example*

The goal of the next examples is to show you that functional programming isn't by any means a theoretical discipline. You'll see that you've perhaps even used some functional ideas in existing .NET technologies. Reading about functional programming will help you understand these technologies at a deeper level and use them more efficiently. We'll also look at a couple of examples from later parts of the book that show important practical benefits of the functional style. In the first set of examples, we'll explore declarative programming.

1.4.1 *Expressing intentions using declarative style*

In the previous section, we described how a declarative coding style makes you more productive. Programming languages that support a declarative style allow us to add new ways of composing basic constructs. When using this style, we're not limited to basic sequences of statements or built-in loops, so the resulting code describes more *what* the computer should do rather than *how* to do it.

We're talking about this style in a general way because the idea is universal and not tied to any specific technology. But it's best to demonstrate using a few examples that you may know already to show how it's applied in specific technologies. In the first two examples, we'll look at the declarative style of LINQ and XAML. If you don't know these technologies, don't worry—the examples are simple enough to grasp without background knowledge. In fact, the ease of understanding code—even in an unfamiliar context—is one of the principal benefits of a declarative style.

WORKING WITH DATA IN LINQ

If you're already using LINQ, this example will be just a reminder. But we'll use it to demonstrate something more important. Here's an example of code that works with data using the standard imperative programming style.

Listing 1.3 Imperative data processing (C#)

```
IEnumerable<string> GetExpenisveProducts() {
  List<string> filteredInfos = new List<string>();              ❶
  foreach(Product product in Products) {                         ❷
    if (product.UnitPrice > 75.0M) {
      filteredInfos.Add(String.Format("{0} - ${1}",
        product.ProductName, product.UnitPrice));                ❸
    }
  }
  return filteredInfos;
}
```

The code, as you can see, is written as a sequence of basic imperative commands. The first statement creates a new list ❶, the second iterates over all products ❷, and a later one adds element to the list ❸. But we'd like to be able to describe the problem at a higher level. In more abstract terms, the code filters a collection and returns information about every returned product.

In C# 3.0, we can write the same code using query expression syntax. This version, shown in listing 1.4, is closer to our real goal—it uses the same idea of filtering and transforming the data.

Listing 1.4 Declarative data processing (C#)

```
IEnumerable<string> GetExpenisveProducts() {
  return from product in Products
         where product.UnitPrice > 75.0M                         ❶
         select String.Format("{0} - ${1}",
           product.ProductName, product.UnitPrice);              ❷
}
```

The expression that calculates the result (filteredInfos) is composed from basic operators such as where or select. These operators take other expressions as an argument, because they need to know what we want to filter or select as a result. Using the previous analogy, these operators give us a new way of combining pieces of code to express our intention with less writing. Note that the whole calculation in listing 1.4 is written as a single expression that describes the result rather than a sequence of statements that constructs it. You'll see this trend repeated throughout the book. In more declarative languages such as F#, everything you write is an expression.

Another interesting aspect in the listing is that many technical details of the solution are now moved to the implementation of the basic operators. This makes the code simpler but also more flexible, because we can change implementation of these operators without making larger changes to the code that uses them. As you'll see later, this makes it much easier to parallelize code that works with data.

LINQ isn't the only mainstream .NET technology that relies on declarative programming. Let's turn our attention to Windows Presentation Foundation and the XAML language.

DESCRIBING USER INTERFACES IN XAML

Windows Presentation Foundation (WPF) is a .NET library for creating user interfaces. The library supports the declarative programming style. It separates the part that describes the UI from the part that implements the imperative program logic. But the best practice in WPF is to minimize the program logic and create as much as possible in the declarative way.

The declarative description is represented as a treelike structure created from objects that represent individual GUI elements. It can be created in C#, but WPF also provides a more comfortable way using an XML-based language called XAML. Nevertheless, we'll see that many similarities exist between XAML and LINQ. Listing 1.5 shows how the code in XAML compares with code that implements the same functionality using the imperative Windows Forms library.

Listing 1.5   Creating a UI using the declarative and imperative styles (XAML and C#)

```
<!-- Declarative user interface in WPF and XAML -->
<Canvas Background="Black">
  <Ellipse x:Name="greenEllipse" Width="75" Height="75"
    Canvas.Left="0" Canvas.Top="0" Fill="LightGreen" />
</Canvas>

// Imperative user interface using Windows Forms
protected override void OnPaint(PaintEventArgs e) {
  e.Graphics.FillRectangle(Brushes.Black, ClientRectangle);
  e.Graphics.FillEllipse(Brushes.LightGreen, 0, 0, 75, 75);
}
```

It isn't difficult to identify what makes the first code snippet more declarative. The XAML code describes the UI by composing primitives and specifying their properties. The whole code is a single expression that creates a black canvas containing a green ellipse. The imperative version specifies how to draw the UI. It's a sequence of statements that specify what operations should be executed to get the required GUI. This example demonstrates the difference between saying *what* using the declarative style and saying *how* in the imperative style.

In the declarative version we don't need as much knowledge about the underlying technical details. If you look at the code, you don't need to know how WPF will represent and draw the GUI. When looking at the Windows Forms example, all the technical details (such as representation of brushes and order of the drawing) are visible in the code. In listing 1.5, the correspondence between XAML and the drawing code is clear, but we can use XAML with WPF to describe more complicated runtime aspects of the program. Let's look at an example:

```
<DoubleAnimation
  Storyboard.TargetName="greenEllipse"
  Storyboard.TargetProperty="(Canvas.Left)"
  From="0.0" To="100.0" Duration="0:0:5" />
```

This single expression creates an animation that changes the `Left` property of the ellipse (specified by the name `greenEllipse`) from the value 0 to the value 100 in 5 seconds. The code is implemented using XAML, but we could've written it in C# by constructing the object tree explicitly. `DoubleAnimation` is a class, so we'd specify its properties. The XAML language adds a more declarative syntax for writing the specification. In either case, the code would be declarative thanks to the nature of WPF. The traditional imperative version of code that implements an animation would be rather complex. It'd have to create a timer, register an event handler that would be called every couple of milliseconds, and calculate a new location for the ellipse.

Declarative coding in .NET

WPF and LINQ are two mainstream technologies that use a declarative style, but many others are available. The goal of LINQ is to simplify working with data in a general-purpose language. It draws on ideas from many data manipulating languages that use the declarative style, so you can find the declarative approach, for example, in SQL or XSLT.

Another area where the declarative style is used in C# or VB.NET is when using .NET attributes. Attributes give us a way to annotate a class or its members and specify how they can be used in specific scenarios, such as editing a GUI control in a designer. This is declarative, because we specify what we expect from the designer when we're working with the control, instead of writing code to configure the designer imperatively.

So far you've seen several technologies that are based on the declarative style and learned how they make problems easier to solve. You may be asking yourself how we use it for solving our own kinds of problems. In the next section, we'll take a brief look at an example from chapter 15 that demonstrates this.

DECLARATIVE FUNCTIONAL ANIMATIONS

Functional programming lets you write your own libraries to solve problems in the declarative style. You've seen how LINQ does that for data manipulation and how WPF does that for UIs, but in functional programming, we'll often create libraries for our own problem domains.

When we mentioned earlier that declarative style makes it possible to ignore implementation details, we left something out. Functional programming doesn't have any mystical powers that would implement the difficult part for us. We need to implement all the technical details when we're designing our own library. But the implementation details can be hidden in the library (just like LINQ hides all the complexity from us), so we can solve the general problem once and for all.

Listing 1.6 uses a declarative library for creating animations that we'll develop in chapter 15. You don't have to fully understand the code to see the benefits of using the declarative style. It's similar to WPF in a sense that it describes how the animation should look rather than how to draw it using a timer.

Listing 1.6 Creating functional animation (C#)

```
var greenCircle = Anims.Circle(
  Time.Forever(Brushes.OliveDrab), 100.0f.Forever());
var blueCircle  = Anims.Circle(
  Time.Forever(Brushes.SteelBlue), 100.0f.Forever());

var movingPoint = Time.Wiggle * 100.0f.Forever();              ❶
var greenMoving = greenCircle.Translate(movingPoint, 0.0f.Forever());  ❷
var blueMoving = blueCircle.Translate(0.0f.Forever(), movingPoint);

var animation = Anims.Compose(greenMoving, blueMoving);        ❸
```

We'll explain everything in detail in chapter 15. You can probably guess that the animation creates two ellipses: a green and a blue one. Later, it animates the location of the ellipses using the `Translate` ❷ method and composes them using the `Compose` method ❸ into a single animation (represented as the `animation` value). If we render this animation to a form, we get the result shown in figure 1.1.

The entire declarative description is based on animated values. There's a primitive animated value called `Time.Wiggle`, which has a value that swings between −1 and +1. Another primitive construct, `x.Forever()`, creates an animated value that always has the same value. If we multiply `Wiggle` by 100, we'll get an animated value that ranges between −100 and +100 ❶. These animated values can be used for specifying animations of graphical objects such as our two ellipses. Figure 1.1 shows them in a state

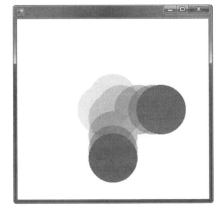

Figure 1.1 The ellipse on the right is moving from the left to the right, and the ellipse on the left is moving from the top to the bottom.

where the X coordinate of the green one and the Y coordinate of the blue one are close to the +100 state.

In listing 1.6, we don't have to know anything about the representation of animated values, because we're describing the whole animation by calculating with the primitive animated value. Another aspect of the declarative style that you can see in the code is that the animation is, in principle, described using a single expression. We made it more readable by declaring several local variables, but if you replaced occurrences of the variable with its initialization code, the animation would remain the same.

Compositionality

An important feature of declarative libraries is that we can use them in a compositional manner. You can see this aspect in the animation library demonstrated in listing 1.6. We can build numerous animated values like `movingPoint` from a few primitives such as `Time.Wiggle` and `x.Forever()`. Similarly, animations can be composed by applying operations such as `Translate` or `Anim.Compose` to simple animated graphical objects. Another example is that in LINQ, you can move a part of a complex query into a separate query and reuse it. We can build our own primitives (let's say for creating orbiting circles) and use them to build our animations (for example, a solar system).

On the last few pages, we looked at declarative programming, which is an approach that we'll use most of the time when programming in a functional language. Listing 1.6 shows how this style can be used in an advanced library for describing animations. In the next section, we'll turn our attention to a more technical, but also very interesting, functional aspect: immutability.

1.4.2 *Understanding code using immutability*

We discussed immutability earlier when describing the benefits of the functional style. We used an example with the bounding box of an ellipse, where it wasn't clear how the code behaved. Once we rewrote the code using immutable objects, it became easier to understand. We'll return to this topic in more detail in later chapters. The purpose of this example is to show how an immutable object looks in practice.

Again, don't worry if you don't grasp everything in detail at this point. Imagine we're writing a game with some characters that are our target. This shows a part of the class that represents the character:

Listing 1.7 Immutable representation of a game character (C#)

```
class GameCharacter {
  readonly int health;          ① Declares all fields
  readonly Point location;         as read-only

  public GameCharacter(int health, Point location) {
    this.health = health;
    this.location = location;    ② Initializes immutable
  }                                fields once and for all
```

```
public GameCharacter HitByShooting(Point target) {
    int newHealth = CalculateHealth(target);
    return new GameCharacter(newHealth, this.location);
}
public bool IsAlive {
    get { return health > 0; }
}
// Other methods and properties omitted
}
```

❸ **Returns game character with updated health**

In C#, we can explicitly mark a field as immutable using the `readonly` keyword. This means that we can't change the value of the field, but we could still modify the target object if the field is a reference to a class that's not immutable. When creating a truly immutable class, we need to make sure that all fields are marked as `readonly` and that the types of these fields are primitive types, immutable value types, or other immutable classes.

According to these conditions, our `GameCharacter` class is immutable. All its fields are marked using the `readonly` modifier ❶. `int` is an immutable primitive type and `Point` is an immutable value type. When a field is read-only, it can be set only when creating the object, so we can set the health and location of the character only in the constructor ❷. This means we can't modify the state of the object once it's initialized. So, what can we do when an operation needs to modify the state of the game character?

You can see the answer when you look at the `HitByShooting` method ❸. It implements a reaction to a shot being fired in the game. It uses the `CalculateHealth` method (not shown in the sample) to calculate the new health of the character. In an imperative style, it would then update the state of the character, but that's not possible because the type is immutable. Instead, the method creates a new `GameCharacter` instance to represent the modified character and returns it as a result.

The class from the previous example represents a typical design of immutable C# classes, and we'll use it (with minor modifications) throughout the book. Now that you know what immutable types look like, let's see some of the consequences.

READING FUNCTIONAL PROGRAMS

You've seen an example that used immutable types in listing 1.1, where we concluded that it makes the code more readable. In this section, we'll consider two snippets that we could use in our functional game.

Listing 1.8 shows two examples, each involving two game characters (`player` and `monster`). The first example shows how we can execute the monster AI to perform a single step and then test whether the player is in danger, and the second shows how we could handle a gunshot.

Listing 1.8   Code snippets form a functional game (C#)

```
var movedMonster = monster.PerformStep();            ❶
var inDanger = player.IsCloseTo(movedMonster);       ❷
(...)

var hitMonster = monster.HitByShooting(gunShot);     ❸
var hitPlayer = player.HitByShooting(gunShot);       ❹
(...)
```

The first part of the code runs one step of the monster AI to move it ❶ to get a new state of the monster, then checks whether the player is close to the newly calculated position of the monster ❷.

The second part processes a shooting in the virtual world. The code creates a value representing an updated monster ❸ and a value representing a new state of the player ❹.

All objects in our functional game are immutable, so when we call a method on an object, it can't modify itself or any other object. If we know that, we can make several observations about the previous examples. In the first snippet, we start by calling the PerformStep method of the monster ❶. The method returns a new monster and we assign it to a variable called movedMonster. On the next line, ❷ we use this monster to check whether the player is close to it and is thus in danger.

We can see that the second line of the code relies on the first one. If we changed the order of these two lines, the program wouldn't compile because movedMonster wouldn't be declared on the first line. If you implemented this in the imperative style, the method wouldn't typically return any result and it'd only modify the state of the monster object.

In that case, we could rearrange the lines and the code would compile, but it'd change the meaning of the program and the program could start behaving incorrectly.

The second snippet consists of two lines that create a new monster ❸ and a new player object ❹ with an updated health property when a shooting occurs in the game. The two lines are independent, meaning that we could change their order. Can this operation change the meaning of the program? It appears that it shouldn't, and when all objects are immutable, it doesn't. Surprisingly, it might change the meaning in the imperative version if gunShot were mutable. The first of those objects could change some property of the gunshot, and the behavior would depend on the order of these two statements.

Listing 1.8 was quite simple, but it already shows how immutability eliminates many possible difficulties. In the next section, we'll see another great example, but first let's review what you'll find later in the book.

Refactoring and unit testing

As you know, immutability helps us understand what a program does and so is helpful when refactoring code. Another interesting functional refactoring is changing when some code executes. The code may run when the program hits it for the first time, but it may as well be delayed and execute when its result is needed. This way of evolving programs is important in F#, and immutability makes refactoring easier in C# too. We'll talk about refactoring in chapter 11.

Another area where immutability proves advantageous is when we're creating unit tests for functional programs. The only thing that a method can do in an immutable world is to return a result, so we only have to test whether a method returns the right result for specified arguments. Again, chapter 11 provides more on this topic.

When discussing how functional programming makes you more productive, we mentioned immutability as an important aspect that makes it easier to write parallel programs. In the next section we'll briefly explore that and other related topics.

1.4.3   *Writing efficient parallel programs*

The fact that functional programming makes it easier to write parallel programs may be the reason you picked up this book. In this section, we'll explore a couple of samples demonstrating how functional programs can be easily parallelized. In the first two examples, we'll use Parallel Extensions to .NET, a new technology from Microsoft for writing parallel applications that ships as part of .NET 4.0. As you might expect, Parallel Extensions to .NET lends itself extremely well to functional code. We won't go into the details—we want to demonstrate that parallelizing functional programs is significantly simpler and, more importantly, less error prone than it is for the imperative code.

PARALLELIZING IMMUTABLE PROGRAMS

First let's take another look at listing 1.8. We've seen two snippets from a game written in a functional way. In the first snippet, the second line uses the outcome of the first line (the state of the monster after movement). Thanks to the use of immutable classes, we can see that this doesn't give us any space for introducing parallelism.

The second snippet consists of two independent lines of code. We said earlier that in functional programming, we can run independent parts of the program in parallel. Now you can see that immutability gives us a great way to spot which parts of the program are independent. Even without knowing any details, we can look at the change that makes these two operations run in parallel. The change to the source code is minimal:

```
var hitMonster = Task.Factory.StartNew(() =>
  monster.HitByShooting(gunShot));
var hitPlayer = Task.Factory.StartNew(() =>
  player.HitByShooting(gunShot));
```

The only thing that we did was wrap the computation in a `Task` type from the Parallel Extensions library. (We'll talk about `Future` in detail in chapter 14.) The benefit isn't only that we have to write less code, but that we have a guarantee that the code is correct. If you did a similar change in an imperative program, you'd have to carefully review the `HitByShooting` method (and any other method it calls) to find all places where it accesses some mutable state and add locks to protect the code that reads or modifies shared state. In functional programming everything is immutable, so we don't need to add any locks.

The example in this section is a form of lower-level *task-based parallelism*, which is one of three approaches that we'll see in chapter 14. In the next section we'll look at the second approach, which benefits from the declarative programming style.

DECLARATIVE PARALLELISM USING PLINQ

Declarative programming style gives us another great technique for writing parallel programs. You know that the code written using the declarative style is composed using primitives. In LINQ, these primitives are query operators such as `where` and `select`. In the declarative style, we can easily replace the implementation of these primitives and that's exactly what PLINQ does: it allows us to replace standard query operators with query operators that run in parallel.

Listing 1.9 shows a query that updates all monsters in our fictitious game and removes those that died in the last step of the game. The change is extremely simple, so we can show you both versions in a single listing.

Listing 1.9 Parallelizing data processing code using PLINQ (C#)

```
var updated =                        var updated =
   from m in monsters                   from m in monsters.AsParallel()    ❶
   let nm = m.PerformStep()             let nm = m.PerformStep()
   where nm.IsAlive select nm;          where nm.IsAlive select nm;
```

The only change that we made in the parallel version on the right side is that we added a call to the `AsParallel` method ❶. This call changes the primitives that are used when running the query and makes the whole fragment run in parallel. You'll see how this works in chapter 12, where we'll discuss declarative computations like this in general, and in chapter 14, which focuses on parallel programming specifically.

You may be thinking that you don't use LINQ queries that often in your programs. This is definitely a valid point, because in imperative programs, LINQ queries are used less frequently. But functional programs do most of their data processing in the declarative style. In C#, they can be written using query expressions whereas F# provides higher-order list-processing functions (as we'll see in chapters 5 and 6). This means that after you've read this book, you'll be able to use declarative programming more often when working with data. As a result, your programs will be more easily parallelizable.

We've explained two ways in which functional programming makes parallelization simpler. This is one of the reasons that makes functional ideas very compelling today and we'll discuss this and related topics in chapters 13 and 14.

Before we can start discussing real functional programs, we need to introduce the F# language. Let's start by looking at classical "Hello world" program as well as at the F# tools. The following section also briefly introduces the typical development process used when developing F# solutions.

1.5   Introducing F#

We'll introduce F# in stages throughout the book, as and when we need to. This section covers the basics, and we'll write a couple of short examples so you can start to experiment for yourself. We'll examine F# more carefully after summarizing important functional concepts in chapter 2. Our first real-world F# application will come in chapter 4. After discussing the "Hello world" sample, we'll talk about F# to explain what you can expect from the language. We'll also discuss the typical development process used by F# developers, because it's quite different from what you're probably used to with C#.

Microsoft PLINQ and Google MapReduce

Google has developed a framework called MapReduce [Dean, Ghemawat, 2004] for processing massive amounts of data in parallel. This framework distributes the work between computers in large clusters and uses the same ideas as PLINQ. The basic idea of MapReduce is that the user program describes the algorithm using two operations (somewhat similar to `where` and `select` in PLINQ). The framework takes these two operations and the input data, and runs the computation. You can see a diagram visualizing the computation in figure 1.2.

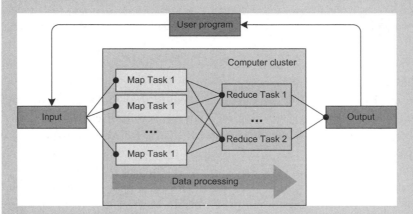

Figure 1.2   **In the MapReduce framework, an algorithm is described by specifying map task and a reduce task. The framework automatically distributes the input across servers and processes the tasks in parallel.**

The framework splits the input data into partitions and executes the map task (using the first operation from the user) on each of the partitions. For example, a map task may find the most important keywords in a web page. The results returned by map tasks are then collected and grouped by a specified key (for example, the name of the domain) and the reduce task is executed for each of the groups. In our example, the reduce task may summarize the most important keywords for every domain.

1.5.1   *Hello world in F#*

The easiest way to start using F# is to create a new script file. Scripts are lightweight F# sources that don't have to belong to a project and usually have an extension of .fsx. In Visual Studio, you can select File > New > File (or press Ctrl+N) and select F# Script File from the Script category. Once we have the file, we can jump directly to the "Hello world" code.

Listing 1.10   Printing hello world (F#)

```
let message = "Hello world!"      ❶
printfn "%s" message              ❷
```

Although this isn't the simplest possible "Hello world" in F#, it would be fairly difficult to write anything interesting about the single-line version. Listing 1.10 starts with a value binding ❶. This is similar to variable declaration, but there's one important difference: the value is immutable and we can't change its value later. This matches with the overall functional style to make things immutable (you'll learn about this in the next two chapters).

After assigning the value `Hello world` to the symbol `message`, the program continues with a call to a `printfn` function ❷. It is important to note that arguments to F# functions are usually only separated by spaces with no surrounding parentheses or commas. We'll sometimes write parentheses when it makes the code more readable, such as when writing `cos(1.57)`, but even in this case the parentheses are optional. We'll explain the convention that we'll use as we learn the core concepts of F# in the next couple of chapters.

The first argument to the `printfn` function is a format string. In our example, it specifies that the function should take only one additional parameter, which will be a string. The type is specified by the `%s` in the format string (the letter *s* stands for *string*) and the types of arguments are even checked by the compiler. Now we'll show you how to run the code (listing 1.11).

TIP   The easiest way to run the code is to use the interactive tools provided by F# tool chain. These tools allow you to use the interactive style of development. This means that you can easily experiment with code to see what it does and verify whether it behaves correctly by running it with a sample input. Some languages have an interactive console, where you can paste code and execute it. This is called read-eval-print loop (REPL), because the code is evaluated immediately.

In F#, we can use a command prompt called F# Interactive, but the interactive environment is also integrated inside the Visual Studio environment. This means that you can write the code with the full IDE and IntelliSense support, but also select a block of code and execute it immediately to test it.

If you're using F# Interactive from the command line, paste in the previous code, and type *;;* and press Enter to execute it.

If you're using Visual Studio, select the code and press Alt+Enter to send it to the interactive window. Let's have a look at the results that we get when we run the code.

Listing 1.11   Running the Hello world program (F# Interactive)

```
Microsoft F# Interactive, (c) Microsoft Corporation, All Rights Reserved
F# Version 1.9.7.4, compiling for .NET Framework Version v2.0.50727

> (...);;
Hello world!                                        ❶
val message : string = "Hello world!"               ❷
```

The first line ❶ is an output from the `printfn` function, which prints the string and doesn't return any value. The second line, ❷ generated by the value binding, reports that a value called `message` was declared and that the type of the value is `string`. We didn't explicitly specify the type, but F# uses a technique called type inference to deduce what the types of values are, so the program is statically typed just as in C#.

Writing something like this "Hello world" example doesn't demonstrate how working with F# looks at the larger scale. The usual F# development process is worth a look because it's quite interesting.

1.5.2   *From simplicity to the real world*

When starting a new project, you don't usually know at the beginning how the code will look at the end. At this stage, the code evolves quite rapidly. But as it becomes more mature, the architecture becomes more solid and you're more concerned with the robustness of the solution rather than with the flexibility. Interestingly, these requirements aren't reflected in the programming languages and tools that you use. F# is appealing from this point of view, because it reflects these requirements in both tools and the language.

> ### F# development process in a nutshell
>
> The F# Interactive tool allows you to verify and test your code immediately while writing it. This tool is extremely useful at the beginning of the development process, because it encourages you to try various approaches and choose the best one. Also, when solving some problem where you're not 100 percent sure of the best algorithm, you can immediately try the code. When writing F# code, you'll never spend a lot of time debugging the program. Once you first compile and run your program, you've already tested a substantial part of it interactively.
>
> When talking about *testing* in the early phase, we mean that you've tried to execute the code with various inputs to interactively verify that it works. In the later phase, we can turn these snippets into unit tests, so the term *testing* means a different thing. When working with a more mature version of our project, we can use tools such as Visual Studio's debugger or various unit-testing frameworks.
>
> F# as a language reflects this direction as well. When you start writing a solution to any problem, you start with only the most basic functional constructs, because they make writing the code as easy as possible. Later, when you find the right way to approach the problem and you face the need to make the code more polished, you end up using more advanced features that make the code more robust, easier to document, and accessible from other .NET languages like C#.

Let's see what the development process might look like in action. We'll use a few more F# constructs, but we won't focus primarily on the code. The more important aspect is how the development style changes as the program evolves.

STARTING WITH SIMPLICITY

When starting a new project, you'll usually create a new script file and try implementing the first prototype or experiment with the key ideas. At this point, the script file contains sources of various experiments, often in an unorganized order. Figure 1.3 shows how your Visual Studio IDE might look like at this stage.

Figure 1.3 shows only the editor and the F# Interactive window, but that's all we need now because we don't have a project yet. As you can see, we first wrote a few value bindings to test how string concatenation works in F# and entered the code in the F# Interactive window to verify that it works as expected. After we learned how to use string concatenation, we wrapped the code in a function. (We'll describe functions in chapter 3.)

Next, we selected the function and pressed Alt+Enter to send it to F# Interactive. If we enter code this way, the shell won't print the source code again: it prints only information about the values and functions we declared. After that, we entered an expression, `sayHello("world")`, to test the function we just wrote. Note that the commands in F# Interactive are terminated with `;;`. This allows you to easily enter multiline commands.

Once we start writing more interesting examples, you'll see that the simplicity is supported by using the functional concepts. Many of them allow you to write the code in a surprisingly terse way, and thanks to the ability to immediately test the code, F# is

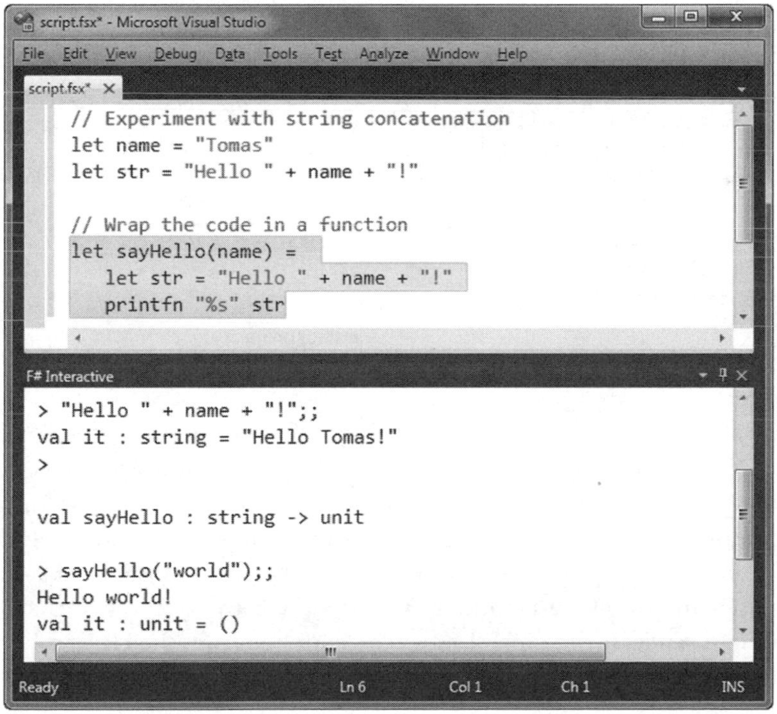

Figure 1.3 Using F# Interactive, we can first test the code and then wrap it into a function.

powerful in the first phase of the development. (Part 2 focuses on the easy-to-use functional constructs.) As the program grows larger, we'll need to write it in a more polished way and integrate it with the usual .NET techniques. Fortunately, F# helps us do that too.

ENDING WITH ROBUSTNESS

Unlike many other languages that are popular for their simplicity, F# lives on the other side as well. In fact, it can be used for writing mature, robust, and safe code. The usual process is that you start with simple code, but as the codebase becomes larger you refactor it in a way that makes it more accessible to other F# developers, enables writing better documentation, and supports better interoperability with .NET and C#.

Perhaps the most important step in order to make the code accessible from other .NET languages is to encapsulate the functionality into .NET classes. The F# language supports the full .NET object model, and classes authored in F# appear just like ordinary .NET classes with all the usual accompaniments, such as static type information and XML documentation.

You'll learn more about F# object types in chapter 9, and you'll see many of the robust techniques in part 4. For now, let's prove that you can use F# in a traditional .NET style as well. Listing 1.12 shows how to wrap the `sayHello` function in a C# style class and add a Windows Forms UI.

Listing 1.12   Object-oriented "Hello world" using Windows Forms (F#)

```
open System.Drawing                              ①
open System.Windows.Forms

type HelloWindow() =                                        ②
  let frm = new Form(Width = 400, Height = 140)
  let fnt = new Font("Times New Roman", 28.0f)
  let lbl = new Label(Dock = DockStyle.Fill, Font = fnt,        Initializes UI
                   TextAlign = ContentAlignment.MiddleCenter)
  do frm.Controls.Add(lbl)

  member x.SayHello(name) =              ③
    let msg = "Hello " + name + "!"
    lbl.Text <- msg                      ◁──┐ Modifies property
  member x.Run() =            ④              │ of .NET type
    Application.Run(frm)
```

Listing 1.12 starts with several `open` directives ① that import types from .NET namespaces. Next, we declare the `HelloWindow` class ②, which wraps the code to construct the UI and exposes two methods. The first method ③ wraps the functionality for concatenating "Hello world" messages that we interactively developed earlier. The second one runs the form as a standard Windows Forms application ④. The class declaration appears just like an ordinary C# class, with the difference that F# has a more lightweight syntax for writing classes. The code that uses the class in F# will look just like your usual C# code:

```
let hello = new HelloWindow()
hello.SayHello("dear reader")
hello.Run()
```

At this stage, we're developing the application in a traditional .NET style, so we'll run it as a standalone application. The interactive style helped us, because we'd already interactively tested the part that deals with string concatenation. You can see how the resulting application looks in figure 1.4.

Figure 1.4   Running our WinForms application created using the OOP style in F#

In this section, you had a taste of what the typical F# development process feels like. We haven't explained every F# construct we've used, because we'll see how everything works later in the book. We started with an example that's simple but that demonstrates how you can use the F# language to write pretty standard .NET programs.

What can F# offer to a C# developer?

F# is well-suited for writing code using simple concepts at the beginning and turning it into a traditional .NET version later, where C# is largely oriented toward the traditional .NET style. If you're a C# developer creating real-world applications, you can easily take advantage of F# in two ways.

The first option is to use F# for rapid prototyping and experimenting with the code as well for exploring how .NET libraries work. As you've seen, using F# interactively is easy, so writing a first sketch of the code can be done in F#. You'll save a lot of time when trying several approaches to a problem or exploring how a new library works. If you require code written in C#, you can rewrite your prototype to C# later and still save a lot of development time.

The second option is to reference a library written in F# from your C# project. F# is a fully compiled .NET language, so there are no technical reasons for preferring C# source code. This means that you can make sure that your library can be easily accessed from C# by turning the code from a simple to a traditional .NET version and use F# for writing parts of a larger .NET solution.

As we close this chapter, it's very likely that you're still finding some of the F# language constructs puzzling, but the purpose of this introduction wasn't to teach you everything about F#; our goal was to show you how F# looks and feels, so you can experiment with it as we explore more interesting examples in the subsequent chapters.

1.6   Summary

This chapter gave you a brief overview of functional programming and what makes it interesting. We introduced the declarative programming style, which we can use when writing applications and libraries in a functional style. The declarative programming style is already used in many successful technologies such as WPF and LINQ, but we can also use it for writing functional solutions to other kinds of problems in C# 3.0.

Parallel programming is a big challenge for modern software development. Using a functional approach makes it significantly easier, thanks to the use of immutability and declarative programming. Immutability helps us write correct and safe code, and declarative programming allows us to hide unnecessary technical details when solving problems.

In the next chapter, you'll see a much broader picture of functional programming. We'll explore the important ideas from a high-level perspective and demonstrate how they relate to one another. Even though we won't look at much real code, the next chapter will give you a solid foundation you can build on in the rest of the book.

Core concepts in
functional programming

This chapter covers

- Understanding concepts and foundations
- Programming with immutable data
- Reasoning about functional code
- Working with functional data types and values

If you ask three functional programmers what they consider the most essential aspect of the functional paradigm, you are likely to get three different answers. The reason is that functional programming has existed for a long time and there's a wide range of diverse programming languages. Every language emphasizes a different set of aspects while giving less importance to others. Most of the concepts are to some extent present in all functional languages.

The central part of this chapter focuses on these common ideas, exploring the basic features and techniques that functional programmers have in their toolset. We'll investigate the concepts from a high-level perspective, and you'll see how they fit together to form one coherent way of tackling problems.

We'll begin by exploring how functional programs represent program state and how they change it. In OOP the state is carried by objects, while in functional programming the key role is played by functions and data types. Next, we'll look at language features that support the declarative programming style we introduced in chapter 1. Finally, we'll talk about types and how they help verify program correctness. This aspect isn't shared by all functional languages, but it's essential for many of them (including OCaml, F#, and Haskell). Their implementation of type checking is advanced and differs in many ways from what you may be used to from C#.

We won't go into much programming yet. Instead you'll get a general understanding of the key concepts and a better feeling about how functional programs look. The sidebar "What comes next in this chapter?" gives an overview of the organization of this chapter. We discussed some of the concepts in chapter 1, but we focused on their consequences. In this chapter we'll analyze their fundamentals.

What comes next in this chapter?

In chapter 1, we focused on two concepts: immutability and declarative style. Here we'll introduce some of the language features that make them possible. We'll also talk about types, another essential concept discussed in this book.

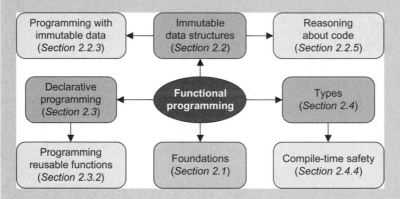

In section 2.1, we'll begin with a brief digression and explore the mathematical background of functional programming. Reading that section isn't necessary, but you may find it interesting, because it demonstrates where many of the concepts come from. After this introduction, we'll return to functional programming in a more concrete form. We'll talk about immutable data structures and in particular, how we can write programs that work with them (section 2.2.3). In section 2.3.2 we'll take a first look at features such as higher-order functions that are essential for writing declarative code in functional languages. We'll show you how types in F# prevent us from making many common programming errors (section 2.4.4).

This chapter focuses on the concepts of functional programming. We'll start by exploring the theoretical foundations, but we'll omit all details and explain the core ideas using a brief example.

2.1 The foundation of functional programming

As you may recall from chapter 1, lambda calculus originated in 1930s as a mathematical theory. Nowadays, it's an important part of theoretical computer science. In logic it's used in tools that assist with the proving and verification of systems (for example, in CPU design). It's also used as a simple formal programming language that can help to explain precisely how other languages behave.

NOTE In the next section, we'll show you a few sample "programs" written in lambda calculus. These programs show the purest and cleanest form of many concepts that we'll see later in this chapter. In lambda calculus, the whole "program" is an expression (section 2.2.4), and functions can take other functions as parameters (2.3.2). We'll get back to these concepts in the context of real programming languages within a few pages.

We've included this background material because it demonstrates some of the ideas in their purest form. Hopefully you'll find it as interesting as we do—but it's not essential in order to understand the rest of the book.

When Alonzo Church introduced lambda calculus in 1932, he attempted to formalize every mathematical construct using the most essential mathematical concept, a function. When you write a mathematical function (let's call it f) which adds 10 to any given argument, you write something like this:

$f(x) = x + 10$

Church wanted to use functions everywhere. In fact, everything in his formalism was a function. Assigning a name to every function would be impractical, because when everything is written as a function, many functions are used only once. He introduced a notation that allowed a function to be written without giving it a name:

$(\lambda x.x + 10)$

This expression represents a function that takes a single parameter, denoted by the Greek letter lambda followed by the variable name (in our case, x). The declaration of the parameter is followed by a dot and by the body of the function (in our case, $x + 10$). In the pure lambda calculus, numerals (such as 10) and mathematical operators (such as +) are also defined using functions, so there's nothing except functions, which is quite surprising. To makes things simple, we'll use standard numbers and operators. Let's continue with our example function. Say we want to set 32 as an argument and see what the result will be:

$(\lambda x.x + 10)\ 32 = 32 + 10 = 42$

Giving an argument to a function (which is called the *application* of a function in lambda calculus) is done by writing the function followed by the argument. When a function is called with some value as an argument, it simply replaces all occurrences of the variable (in our case, *x*) with the value of the argument (*32* in our example). This is the expression that follows the first equal sign. If we look at + as a built-in function, it will be called in the next step, yielding 42 as a result.

The most interesting aspect about lambda calculus—and the cornerstone of functional programming languages—is that any function can take a function as an argument. This means that we can write a function that takes a function (binary operator) and a value as parameter and calls the binary operator with the value as both arguments:

(λop.λx.(op x x))

As you can see, we wrote a function that takes *op* and *x* as arguments. When writing a function with more arguments, we use the lambda symbol multiple times to declare more parameters. In the body of the lambda function, we use *op* to represent a function and *x* to represent the first and second arguments to the *op* function. Let's see what the code does if we give it the plus operator as a first argument and 21 as a second argument:

(λop.λx.(op x x)) (+) 21 = (λx.((+) x x)) 21 = (+) 21 21 = 42

A function with multiple parameters is a function that takes the first argument (in our case, *op*) and returns a lambda expression, which is just another function. This means that in the first step, we apply the function (which takes *op* as an argument) to the argument *(+)*. This yields a result that you can see after the first equal sign: the *op* variable was replaced with a plus sign. The result is still a function with arguments, so we can continue with the evaluation. The next step is to apply the function with *x* as a parameter to a value *21*. The result is an expression, *(+) 21 21*, which is an alternative notation for adding two numbers. It means the same thing as *21 + 21*, so our final result of this calculation is 42. As you can see, the calculation in lambda calculus continues until there's no function application (a function followed by its arguments) that could be evaluated.

Lambda calculus is interesting from a theoretical point of view or to see where the functional ideas came from, but let's turn our attention back to the real world. The first group of concepts that we'll talk about are related to the representation of data in functional programs. These concepts heavily influence how a program works with data.

2.2   *Evaluation of functional programs*

In chapter 1 you learned that functional programs use immutable data structures to represent their state. The functional approach to make things immutable doesn't only influence data structures (or classes in C#), but extends to local variables as well.

We wouldn't be surprised if you were wondering how the program can do anything at all when everything is immutable. The short answer is that functional programs aren't described as a sequence of statements that change the state but rather as computations. In this section, we'll shed some light on how these calculations are written. Let's start with the simple code that works with variables.

2.2.1 Working with immutable values

The first of the common features is that functional programs rarely have typical variables as we know them from other programming languages. The key difference is that functional languages prefer immutable variables, meaning the variable can't change its value once it's initialized. Thus, using the term *variable* is quite inappropriate, and functional programmers prefer the term *value*.

Let's demonstrate with an example. Say we want to write a program that takes an initial value, reads two numbers from the console, adds the first number to the initial value, and multiplies the result by the second number. A typical implementation of something like this in C# would look like this (we'll use the hypothetical methods `GetInitialValue()`, `ReadInt32()`, and `WriteInt32()`, but you could easily implement them if you want to play with this example):

```
int res = GetInitialValue();
res = res + ReadInt32();
res = res * ReadInt32();
WriteInt32(res);
```

We declared a variable `res` to hold the initial value. Then we modified it two times, using an input value read from the console. Now, let's look at the same code implemented without modifying the value of any variables:

```
int res0 = GetInitialValue();
int res1 = res0 + ReadInt32();
int res2 = res1 * ReadInt32();
WriteInt32(res2);
```

Because we couldn't modify the value of the first variable, we declared a new variable every time we wanted to calculate a new value (`res0`, `res1`, `res2`). The key difference is that in the second example, we didn't use the assignment operator (written as an equal sign in C#). The only occurrence of this symbol in a second example is when initializing a variable value, which has a different meaning from the assignment operator. Instead of changing a value of an existing variable, we create a new variable with the specified initial value.

Working with values differs from working with variables in many ways, so using the term *value* isn't just a change in the terminology but a different concept. For this reason we'll use the functional terminology in the rest of the book, but you may sometimes find the analogy between variables and values useful. We'll also use the term *value binding*, which refers to a declaration of a value that assigns (binds) the value to a symbol.

Using immutable values instead of variables requires us to express many problems in a different way. We'll get back to this topic in section 2.2.3. First, let's look at how immutable values relate to the concept of immutable types that we discussed in chapter 1.

2.2.2 Using immutable data structures

When representing data in functional programs, we'll work with data structures. We'll discuss data structures in chapters 5 and 7. For now, keep in mind that we're talking about any composite data type, such as a C# value type or even a class, even though data structures are generally a simpler concept. Recall from chapter 1, in functional programming these data structures are immutable.

The concept of immutable data structures logically follows from the concept of immutable value bindings. A typical data structure contains field declarations. If we extend the idea of immutability from variable declarations to field declarations, we get a world where everything is immutable. In C#, you can write immutable class fields using the readonly modifier, whereas in F# all data structures are immutable by default. F# isn't a *strictly* functional language, so it allows you to create mutable types too.

At this point, you know how to work with immutable data structures and how to create an immutable class in C#. Methods of a class or functions working with the data structure can't modify the state of the structure. The only thing they can do is return something, so all the operations that work with the data structure return a new value as the result. In C# the string type behaves exactly like this. If you write str.Substring(0, 5), you'll get a new string value as the result and the original string remains unchanged.

We mentioned in chapter 1 that functional code is often written as a single expression rather than a sequence of statements. This different understanding of code makes programs more declarative, so using immutable data structures supports this aspect of functional style as well. Say we have a class that represents a functional collection. It'll come with an operation that creates an empty list and an operation that "adds" a number to the list. Because the list is immutable, adding an element can't change the original list. Instead, the operation returns a new list containing the items from the original list and the newly added element. If we want to create a list and add elements to it, we can write something like this:

```
var res = ImmutableList.Empty<int>().Add(1).Add(3).Add(5).Add(7);
```

To do the same thing with a mutable list, we'd have to create it, then modify it by calling the imperative Add method that would modify the list. As a result, we'd write one variable declaration and four statements (perhaps five lines of source code in total). This example shows that the immutable data structures often help you write more succinct code. There are ways to achieve similar benefits in imperative languages, but in the functional style you'll get them without additional effort.

So far, you've seen that functional languages use immutable data structures and immutable values instead of mutable variables. You can imagine how to write some extremely simple programs without using traditional variables and the assignment operator. But once you start thinking about more complicated problems, things become difficult until you change how you look at the world. In the next section, we'll look how to encode more sophisticated calculation in the functional style.

2.2.3   *Changing program state using recursion*

Now, let's see how to write more complicated functions using values. We'll implement a function that sums numbers in a specified range. We could calculate this sum directly, but we'll use it as an example of a calculation that uses a loop. (In section 2.3.1, we'll show you how to change this code into a more generally useful function.)

```
int SumNumbers(int from, int to) {
    int res = 0;
    for (int i = from; i <= to; i++)
        res = res + i;
    return res;
}
```

In this case, we can't directly replace the variable with value bindings, because we need to modify the value during every evaluation of the loop. The program has to keep a certain state, and that state changes on each iteration of the loop. That means we can't declare a new value for every change of the state, as we did in our earlier example. We need to make a fundamental change in the code and use a technique called *recursion* instead of using loops:

```
int SumNumbers(int from, int to) {
    if (from > to) return 0;
    int sumRest = SumNumbers(from + 1, to);
    return from + sumRest;
}
```

As you know, recursion means that a function (SumNumbers in our case) calls itself—in this case, when we calculate the value of the sumRest variable. In this code we're using only value bindings, so it's purely functional. The state of the computation, which was originally stored in a mutable variable, is now expressed using recursion. When we first mentioned that we can't declare a new variable for every change of the state, we were in some sense incorrect, because that's what our new recursive implementation does. Every time the function recursively calls itself, it skips the first number and calculates a sum of the remaining numbers. This result is bound to a variable sumRest, which is declared as a new variable during every execution of the recursive function.

Writing the recursive part of a computation every time would be difficult, so functional languages provide a way for "hiding" the difficult recursive part and expressing most of the problems without explicitly using recursion. We'll get back to this topic in section 2.3.1 after we finish our discussion of calculation in functional programs.

2.2.4 *Using expressions instead of statements*

In imperative languages, an expression is simply a piece of code that can be evaluated and that yields a result. So a method call or any use of a Boolean or integer operator is an expression. A statement is a piece of code that affects the state of the program and doesn't have any result. A call to a method that doesn't return any value is a statement, because it affects the state of the program, depending on whatever the method does. An assignment also changes the state (by changing a value of a variable), but in the simplest version, it doesn't return any value.

NOTE An assignment in C# returns a value, so you can write `a = (b = 42);`. In the simplest form (which we're discussing here), it's a statement that assigns a value to a variable without returning anything (such as `b = 42;`).

Another example of a typical statement is returning from a function using `return` or escaping a loop using `break`. Neither construct has any "return value," and instead, its only purpose is to change the state of the program. `return` and `break` change the currently executing statement of the code (`return` by jumping to back to the code that called the method and `break` by jumping to just after the end of the loop).

As you know, in functional languages the state is represented by what a function returns and the only way to modify a state is to return a modified value. Following this logic, in functional languages everything is interpreted as an expression with a return value. The consequences can be nicely demonstrated with our earlier example that sums numbers in a specified range. Here's the original version of the code, which uses recursion but is still not fully functional because it's written as a series of three statements:

```
int SumNumbers(int from, int to) {
  if (from > to) return 0;
  int sumRest = SumNumbers(from + 1, to);
  return from + sumRest;
}
```

We can turn this into a more functional version using the C# conditional operator (?:). Using this construct, we can rewrite the body as a single expression, which is closer to how functional languages treat all valid code. In C#, this is possible only for relatively simple code samples, because we can't declare local variables in branches of the conditional operator.

To demonstrate how functional languages work, we'll write the same method in a nonexistent "functional C#." As you can see in listing 2.1, the only nonstandard feature of our "functional C#" is that it allows us to place variable declarations inside expressions.

Listing 2.1   Summing numbers in the specified range in a "functional C#"

```
int SumNumbers(int from, int to) {
  return                                          ❶
    (from > to)
      ? 0                                         ❷
      : { var sumRest = SumNumbers(from + 1, to);
          from + sumRest; };                      ❸
}
```

To write the code using only expressions, we have to deal with quite a few restrictions because most of the control flow constructs (such as conditionals or loops) are statements. Even though the example is minimalistic, it gives us useful hints about what we can write in a functional language:

- The whole body of the method is a single expression that returns a value. In C# this means that the body has to start with return ❶. Also, we can't use return anywhere else in the code, because that would require jumping to the end of the method from a middle of an expression, which isn't possible.

- Because if-then-else is a statement, we have to use the conditional operator instead. This also means that we have to provide code for both of the cases (❷ and ❸). Any expression evaluates to a value, but if we omitted the else branch and the condition was false, we wouldn't know what to return!

- The expression in the else branch ❸ is written as a code block that contains a variable declaration followed by a standard expression. It declares a local variable sumRest that will be accessible in the rest of the code block. Variable declarations in F# work exactly this way. The declaration isn't an expression, but a special syntactical construct that can be appended to an expression.

We'll get back to value bindings (an F# equivalent to variable declarations) in chapter 3, so you'll see how this works in F#. Another notable difference in F# is that there's a type that represents nothing. The void keyword in C# isn't an actual type, so you can't declare a variable of type void. The F# type unit is a real type, which has only a single value that doesn't carry any information. All the imperative constructs in F# use this type, so when calling, say, the Console.WriteLine method, F# treats it as an ordinary expression that returns a value of type unit. The fact that everything is an expression makes it easier to reason about the code. We'll take a look at one very interesting technique in the next section.

2.2.5 *Computation by calculation*

The approach discussed in the previous two sections gives us a new way of thinking about program execution. To understand how an imperative program executes, we have to understand how its state changes. In a program written using an object-oriented imperative language, the state is not only the internal state of all the objects, but also the currently executing statement (in each thread!) and the state of all the local variables in every stack frame. The fact that the currently executing statement is part of the state is important, because it makes tracing the state difficult when you're writing the program execution on paper.

In functional programming, we can use an approach called *computation by calculation*. This approach is particularly important for Haskell (see the sidebar "Mathematical purity in Haskell") and is described in more detail in *The Haskell School of Expression* [Hudak, 2000]. Using computation by calculation, we start with the original expression (such as a function call) and perform a single step (like replacing the call with the body of the function or calculating a result of a primitive mathematical operation). By repeating this step several times, we can easily analyze how the program evaluates.

This technique is particularly useful if we want to understand the behavior of a function in corner cases. In listing 2.2 we use it to analyze how SumNumber behaves when it gets the same number as both an upper and a lower bound of the range.

> **Listing 2.2   Functional evaluation of an expression** `SumNumbers(5,5)`

Start evaluating the call `SumNumbers(5, 5)`:

```
SumNumbers(5, 5)
```

Expand the function call using the body of the function. Replace all occurrences of function parameters with the value specified as an argument (`from = 5`, `to = 5`):

```
(5 > 5) ? 0 : {
   var sumRest = SumNumbers(5 + 1, 5);
   5 + sumRest; };
```

Reduce the conditional operator expression. First, evaluate the condition (5 > 5) and then continue evaluating the false branch:

```
var sumRest = SumNumbers(5 + 1, 5);
5 + sumRest;
```

Calculate the value assigned to the `sumRest` variable. To do this, we evaluate values of the function call arguments and expand `SumNumbers(6, 5)`:

```
var sumRest =
   return (6 > 5) ? 0 : {
      var sumRest = SumNumbers(6 + 1, 5);
      6 + sumRest; };
5 + sumRest
```

Continue calculating the value of `sumRest`. Evaluate the condition (6 > 5) and replace the initialization expression with the subexpression from the `then` branch:

```
var sumRest = 0
5 + sumRest
```

After evaluating the value of the variable, we can replace all occurrences of the variable in the rest of the expression with its actual value:

```
5 + 0
```

Evaluate the call to the primitive + operator:

```
5
```

As you can see, this way of writing down the computation of functional code is easy. Even though functional programmers don't spend their lives writing down how their program executes, it's useful to get used to this kind of computation, because it gives us a powerful way of thinking about functional code.

Of course, because this example was so simple, we didn't discuss many important details. Rest assured, we'll get to all of these problems in the next chapter. Another interesting aspect of the computation shown in listing 2.2 is deciding which part of the expression should be evaluated next. In this example we used the innermost subexpression, so we evaluate all arguments of a function call or an operator use (with the exception of conditional operator, which is treated differently). This strategy, called *strict* or *eager*, is how many functional languages, including F#, work, and it's similar to executing the code statement by statement.

> **Mathematical purity in Haskell**
>
> Haskell appeared in 1990 and has been popular in the academic community. In this section you've seen that in functional languages, you work with immutable data structures and use immutable values rather than mutable variables. This isn't strictly true in F# because you can still declare mutable values. This nonstrict approach is particularly useful for .NET interoperability. Most of the .NET libraries rely on mutable state, as it was designed for imperative object-oriented languages such as C# and VB.NET.
>
> On the other hand, Haskell strictly enforces mathematical purity. This means it can be flexible about the order in which programs execute. In our previous example, we mentioned that F# evaluates the innermost part of an expression first. In Haskell, there are no side effects so the order of evaluation doesn't (and can't) matter. As long as we're reordering parts of the code that don't depend on each other, it won't change the meaning of the program. As a result, Haskell uses a technique called *lazy evaluation*, which doesn't evaluate the result of an expression until it's actually needed (for example, to be printed on a console).
>
> The ability to make a change in the program without changing its meaning is important in F# too, and you'll learn how to use it to refactor F# programs in chapter 11. You'll see that lazy evaluation can be used in F# as well and can be a valuable optimization technique.

In the last few sections, we discussed program state and writing calculations using recursion. We promised that you'd learn how to write the difficult part of the code in a reusable way, so that's the main topic of our next section.

2.3 Writing declarative code

In chapter 1, you learned what it means to use a declarative programming style from a high-level perspective. Now, we'll talk about more technical concepts of the functional style that enable declarative programming. From this point of view, two important aspects lead to the declarative style. We just discussed the first one—that every language construct is an expression. This aspect demonstrates that functional languages try to minimize the number of built-in concepts—we don't need any notion of statement, because the whole program can be composed from expressions. Writing every operation using explicit recursion would be difficult. The second aspect addresses this problem, so let's start by seeing how to write a single function that can be used in many variations for different purposes.

2.3.1 Functions as values

The question that motivates this section is "How can we separate the functionality that will vary with every use from the recursive nature of the code that always stays the same?" The answer is simple: we'll write the recursive part as a function with parameters and these parameters will specify the "unique operation" that the function should perform.

Let's demonstrate using the `SumNumbers` method. In section 2.2.3, we wrote a function that takes an initial value, looping through a specified numeric range. It calculates a new "state" of the calculation for each iteration using the previous state and the current number from the range. So far we've used zero as an initial value. We used addition to aggregate the numbers in the range, so a resulting computation for a range from 5 to 10 would look like this: $5 + (6 + (7 + (8 + (9 + (10 + 0)))))$.

What if we decide to modify this function to be more general and allow us to perform computations using different operations? For example, we could multiply all the numbers in the range together, generating the following computation: $5 * (6 * (7 * (8 * (9 * (10 * 1)))))$. If you think about the differences between these two computations, you'll see that there are only two changes: we changed the initial value from 0 to 1 (because we don't want to multiply the result of a call by zero!), and we changed the operator used during the computation from + to *. Let's see how we could write a function like this in C#:

```
int AggregateNumbers(Func<int, int, int> op, int init, int from, int to) {
    if (from > to) return init;
    int sumRest = AggregateNumbers(op, init, from + 1, to);
    return op(from, sumRest);
}
```

We added two parameters to the function—the initial value (`init`) and an operation (`op`) that specifies how to transform the intermediate result and a number from the range into the next result. To specify the second parameter, we're using a delegate, `Func<int, int, int>`, which represents a function that has two parameters of type `int` and returns an `int`. This delegate type is available in .NET 3.5 (we'll talk about it in chapter 3).

In functional languages, we don't have to use delegates, because these languages have a much simpler concept: a function. This is exactly what the term *functions as values* refers to—the fact that we can use functions in the same way as any other data type available in the language. We can write functions that take functions as parameters (as we did in this example), but also return a function as the result or even create a list of functions, and so on. Functions are also useful as a mental concept when approaching a problem.

Thinking about problems using functions

For many people who know functional programming, the most important thing isn't that functional languages have some particular useful features, but that the whole environment encourages you to think differently and more simply about problems that you encounter when designing and writing applications regardless of the language you use.

The idea of using functions as ordinary values is one of these useful concepts. Let's demonstrate using an example. Suppose we have a list of customers and we want to sort it in a particular way.

(continued)

The classical object-oriented way to address this problem is to use a `Sort` method that takes a parameter of some interface type (in .NET this would be `IComparer` `<Customer>`). The parameter specifies how to compare two elements. Now, if we want to sort the list using customer names, we'd create a class that implements this interface and use an instance of that class. To summarize, that means writing an interface that contains a member representing the operation we want to use, creating a class that implements the interface, creating an instance of that class, and passing it as an argument.

In functional programming, we can use the concept of a function. You've seen that C# can represent similar ideas using a delegate—which is definitely simpler than interfaces— but functions are even simpler. They don't have to be declared in advance, and the only thing that matters about them is what arguments they take and what results they return. The generic `Func` delegate in .NET 3.5 is close to the idea of a function, but once you get used to thinking about functions, you'll find places where they are appropriate more often than when thinking about delegates.

The argument of the functional `Sort` method would be a function that takes two customers as arguments and returns an integer. This is a brief way to specify the argument. On the other hand, when using an interface or a delegate, we have to declare some type in advance and then refer to it whenever we want to use the object-oriented `Sort` method. Using a function is more straightforward, because when you look at the functional `Sort` method, you immediately see what argument it expects. The concept of a function is useful even if you end up implementing the code using interfaces. It gives you a terser way to think about the problem, so the number of elements that you'll have to keep in mind will be lower.

In chapter 1, we said that the declarative style gives us a new way for extending the vocabulary we can use to specify a solution to a class of problems. This general goal can be achieved by using functions that take other functions as parameters. We'll talk about these in the next section.

2.3.2 *Higher-order functions*

You know that we can treat functions as values and write functions that take other functions as parameters. There are two important terms that are often used when talking about these kinds of functions:

- *First-class functions*, meaning that a function is a value just like any other, so you can use a function as an argument to another function. As a result, function values also have a type (in C#, this is expressed using a delegate). You can use a function in any place where you can use an integer or a string.
- *Higher-order function*, which refers to a function that takes a function as a parameter or returns it as a result. In the C# examples in this book, we'll often use higher-order functions. For example, the method `AggregateNumbers` from the previous section is a higher-order function.

This kind of parameterization of code is used often in functional languages, so as you'll see, many of the useful functions in the F# library are higher-order functions. Let's look at an example that shows how higher-order functions make our code more declarative.

EXTENDING THE VOCABULARY USING HIGHER-ORDER FUNCTIONS

Working with collections is the best example of how higher-order functions make your code more declarative. You can do so in C# using the extension methods (such as `Where` and `Select`) that are provided as part of LINQ, because everything you can write using a LINQ query can be also written using a method that takes a `Func` delegate as an argument.

In this section we'll look at how to write the same code using lists in F# to demonstrate a few interesting aspects of F#. We haven't yet seen enough from F# to fully explain what the code does, but we know enough to see the high-level picture. The first example in listing 2.3 shows how to filter only odd numbers from a list. The second one filters numbers and then calculates the square of every returned number.

Listing 2.3 Working with lists using higher-order functions (F# Interactive)

```
> let numbers = [ 1 .. 10 ]
  let isOdd(n) = n % 2 = 1        ❶
  let square(n) = n * n           ❷
  ;;
val numbers : int list
val isOdd : int -> bool           ❸
val square : int -> int

> List.filter isOdd numbers;;     ❹
val it : int list = [1; 3; 5; 7; 9]

> List.map square (List.filter isOdd numbers);;   ❺
val it : int list = [1; 9; 25; 49; 81]
```

We first implemented two functions, which we'll use later when working with lists. The first one tests whether a number given as an argument is odd ❶ and the second one returns square of a given integer ❷. Recall from chapter 1, the F# compiler automatically deduces the types of expressions that we enter, so it also deduced the type of those functions ❸. We'll talk about types in F# later in this chapter, and chapter 3 explores in detail the printed type signatures and function declarations.

Listing 2.3 shows how higher-order functions extend our vocabulary when expressing a problem. In the first example, we're using a higher-order function, `List.filter`, which takes a function as the first argument and a list as the second argument ❹. We give it our function that tests whether a number is odd and a list of numbers from 1 to 10. As you can see on the next line, the result is a list containing all odd numbers in that range.

In the usual imperative style, we could implement this using a `for` loop or similar construct. As you learned in the first chapter, imperative languages give us only a limited way to compose basic commands and the `for` loop is one of them. The example we've just seen implements a new control structure for composing commands. The List.filter function is an abstract way for describing certain patterns for working with lists, but makes the pattern reusable, because we can specify the behavior of the filter using a function. Higher-order functions are an essential concept of functional programming, and we'll talk about them again in chapter 6. As you'll see, we can write useful higher-order functions for working with most data structures.

In the second example ❺, we use the entire expression from the first example as an argument to another function. This time we use List.map, which applies the function given as the first argument to all values from the given list. In our example, this means that it calculates squares of all odd numbers. The code is still declarative, but it isn't as readable as it should be. One of the reasons for this is that the first construct of the expression is List.map, but List.map is actually the operation that's performed last. F# is a flexible language and it gives us ways to deal with this problem. Let's see how we can use another feature—*pipelining*—to make the code clearer.

LANGUAGE-ORIENTED PROGRAMMING

Language-oriented programming can be viewed as another programming paradigm, but it is less clearly defined. The principle is that we're trying to write the code in a way that makes it read more naturally. This goal can be achieved in languages that provide more flexibility in how you can write the code.

In this section, we'll see that a relatively simple syntactical change can give us a different point of view when thinking about the code. Listing 2.4 shows the new way of writing the same code—we're still returning squares of odd numbers. The example only demonstrates the idea, so you don't have to fully understand it. We'll talk about language-oriented programming and list processing later in this book. The point of this example is to show a different way of thinking about the task.

Listing 2.4 Elegant way for working with functions (F# Interactive)

```
> let squared =
    numbers
    |> List.filter isOdd
    |> List.map square;;
val it : int list = [1; 9; 25; 49; 81]
```

Instead of nesting function calls, we're now using the *pipelining operator* (|>). This construct allows you to write expressions as a series of operations that are applied to the data. The code is still written in the usual F# language, but if you didn't know that, you could almost believe it was written in a data processing language.

NOTE   From the F# point of view there's nothing special about the code. F# allows you to write custom operators and the pipelining operator is just an operator that we can define ourselves. The rest of the code is written using the appropriate parameterized higher-order functions.

We can look at the set of list processing constructs (such as |>, List.map, and others) as if it were a separate list processing language embedded in F#. This is what the term *language-oriented programming* refers to. Even though the code is implemented as a completely standard F# library, it looks like a language designed for this particular problem, which makes the code more readable. In fact, many well-designed functional libraries look like declarative languages.

The fact that functional libraries look like declarative languages for solving problems in some specific area is a critical aspect of the declarative style. Its great benefit is that it supports division of work in larger teams. You don't have to be an F# guru to understand how to use the list processing "language" or any other library that's already available. This means that even novice F# programmers can quickly learn how to solve problems using an existing library. Implementing the library is more difficult, so this is a task that would be typically handled by the experienced F# developers on the team.

This book aims to train functional masters, so we'll talk about this problem in upcoming chapters. In chapter 6, we'll look at writing higher-order functions for working with lists and other basic types. Using higher-order functions is a basic technique used when designing functional libraries, but as we've seen in this section, it makes the code look natural. In chapter 15, we'll take the next step and design a library for creating animation with the goal of making the syntax as natural as possible.

Language-oriented programming in LISP

LISP appeared in 1958 and is the oldest high-level language still in common use (other than FORTRAN). There are also some popular LISP dialects, including Common Lisp and Scheme. The languages from this family are widely known for their extremely flexible syntax, which allows LISP to mimic many advanced programming techniques. This includes OOP, but also some less widely known approaches, like aspect-oriented programming (AOP). AOP is available today in languages like AspectJ or libraries such as PostSharp or prototype-based object systems (also seen in JavaScript).

Anything you write in LISP is either a list or a symbol, so you can write `(- n 1)`. This is a list containing three symbols: `-`, `n`, and `1`. LISP can be viewed as program code: a call to the function `-` (the binary minus operator) with two arguments: `n` and `1`. This makes the code a bit difficult to read if you're not used to the syntax, but we wanted to show it here to demonstrate how far the idea of making the language uniform can be taken. When solving some difficult problem in LISP, you almost always create your own language (based on LISP syntax), which is designed for solving the problem. You can simply define your own symbols with a special meaning and specify how the code written using these symbols executes.

You saw something similar when we discussed declarative animations in chapter 1, so you know that we can use a language-oriented approach even when writing the code in C#. We'll talk about this example in chapter 15, where you'll learn how language-oriented programming looks in both C# and F#.

In the declarative programming style, we're extending the vocabulary, which we can use to express our intentions. We also need to make sure that the primitives we're adding will be used in a correct way. In the next section, we'll look at types, which serve as "grammar rules" for these primitives.

2.4 Functional types and values

The C# language is a statically typed programming language;[1] every expression has a type known during compilation. The compiler uses static typing to verify that when the program runs, it will use values in a consistent way. For example, it can guarantee that the program won't attempt to add a `DateTime` with an integer, because the + operator can't be used with these two types.

In C#, we have to specify the types explicitly most of the time. When writing a method, we have to specify what the types of its parameters are and what the return type is. In F# we don't typically write any types. F# language is also statically typed. In F#, every expression has types as well, but F# uses a mechanism called *type inference* to deduce the types automatically at compile-time. Static typing in a functional language such as F# guarantees even more than it does in C#. We'll see an example in chapter 5 when we discuss the `option` type, which can be used to avoid using uninitialized references.

Types in functional programming

Because functional languages treat any piece of code as an expression, saying that every expression has a type is a very strong statement. It means that any syntactically correct piece of F# code has some type. The type says what kind of results we can get by evaluating the expression, so the type gives us valuable information about the expression.

Types can be viewed as grammar rules for composing primitives. In functional languages, a function (such as the `square` function from the previous example) has a type. This type specifies how the function can be used—we can call it with an integer value as an argument to get an integer as the result.

More importantly, the type also specifies how we can compose the function with higher-order functions. For example, we couldn't use `square` as an argument for `List.filter`, because filtering expects that the function returns a Boolean value and not an integer. This is exactly what we mean by a grammar rule—the types verify that we're using the functions in a meaningful way.

We'll talk about values and their types primarily in chapter 5. In chapter 6, you'll learn how types of higher-order functions help you to write correct code. You'll also see that type information can often give you a good clue about what the function does. In the

---

[1] C# 4.0 adds support for some of the dynamic language features, but even with these features, C# is still a mostly statically typed language.

next section, we'll look at the mechanism that allows us to use types without writing them explicitly.

2.4.1 Type inference in C# and F#

When most of the types have a simple name such as int or Random, there's only a small need for type inference, because writing the type names by hand isn't difficult. C# 2.0 supports generics, so you can construct more complicated types. The types in functional languages like F# are also quite complicated, particularly because you can use functions as a value, so there must also be a type that represents a function.

A simple form of type inference for local variables is now available in C# 3.0. When declaring a local variable in earlier versions of C#, you had to specify the type explicitly. In C# 3.0 you can often replace the type name with a new keyword, var. Let's look at a couple of basic examples:

```
var num = 10;
var str = "Hello world!";
```

The first line declares a variable called num and initializes its value to 10. The compiler can easily infer that the expression on the right-hand side is of type int, so it knows that the type of the variable must also be int. Note that this code means exactly the same thing as if you had written the type explicitly. During the compilation, the C# compiler replaces var with the actual type, so there is no additional work done at runtime. As we have mentioned, this is particularly useful when working with complex generic types. For example, we can write the following:

```
var dict = new Dictionary<string, List<IComparable<int>>>();
```

Without the var keyword, you'd have to specify the type twice on a single line:

- When declaring the variable
- When creating the instance of Dictionary class

The type inference in C# is limited to local variable declarations. In F# you often don't write any types at all. If the F# type inference fails to deduce some type, you can specify the type explicitly, but this is a relatively rare occurrence.

To give you a better idea of how this works, listing 2.5 shows a simple function that takes two parameters, adds them, and formats the result using the String.Format method. The listing first shows valid F# code, then how you could write it in C# if implicit typing were extended to allow you to use the var keyword in other places.

Listing 2.5   Implementing methods with type inference

```
let add a b =            ❶
  let res = a + b          ❷
  String.Format("{0} + {1} = {2}", a, b, res)      ❸

var Add(var a, var b) {
  var res = a + b;                                    ❹
  return String.Format("{0} + {1} = {2}", a, b, res);
}
```

As you can see, the F# syntax is designed in a way that you don't have to write any types at all in the source code ❶. In the pseudo-C# version ❹, we used the var keyword instead of any types, and this is (in principle) what the F# compiler sees when you enter the code. If you paste the code for this function into F# Interactive, it will be processed correctly and F# Interactive will report that the function takes two integers as arguments and returns a string. Let's look how the F# compiler can figure this out.

The first hint that it has is that we're adding the values a and b ❷. In F#, we can use + to add any numeric types or to concatenate strings, but if the compiler doesn't know anything else about the types of values, it assumes that we're adding two integers. From this single expression, the compiler can deduce that both a and b are integers. Using this information, it can find the appropriate overload of the String.Format method ❸. The method returns string, so the compiler can deduce that the return type of the add function is also a string.

Thanks to the type inference, we can avoid many errors and use all other benefits of static typing (like hints to developers when writing the code) and at almost no price, as the types are inferred automatically in most of the cases. When using F# in Visual Studio, the type inference is running in the background, so when you hover over a value with a mouse pointer, you'll instantly see its type. The background compilation also reports any typing errors instantly, so you'll get the same experience as when writing C# code.

If you're accustomed to using types from other programming languages, you probably already know that there are primitive types (like integers, characters, or floating-point numbers) and more complicated types composed from these primitive types. Functional languages have a slightly different set of composed types. We'll talk about all these types in detail in chapter 5, but first let's explore one particularly interesting type.

2.4.2 *Introducing the discriminated union type*

In this section, we'll focus on the discriminated union type, one of the basic functional types. Let's begin with a sample that illustrates its usefulness. Imagine that you're writing an application that works with graphical shapes. We'll use a simple representation of shape, so it will be a rectangle, an ellipse (defined by the corners of a bounding rectangle), or a shape composed from two other shapes.

If you think about this problem using the object-oriented concepts, you'll probably say that we need an abstract class to represent a shape (let's call it Shape) and three derived classes to represent the three different cases (Ellipse, Rectangle, and Composed). Using the object-oriented terminology, we now have in mind four classes that describe the problem. Also, we don't yet know what we'll want to do with shapes. We'll probably want to draw them, but we don't know yet what arguments we'll need to do the drawing, so we can't yet write any abstract method in the Shape class.

Our original idea was simpler than this full-blown class hierarchy: we just needed to have a representation of a shape with three different cases. We want to define a simple data structure that we can use to represent the shape—and F# allows us to do exactly that:

```
type Shape =
  | Rectangle of Point * Point
  | Ellipse of Point * Point
  | Composed of Shape * Shape
```

This code creates a discriminated union type called Shape, which is closer to the original intention we had when describing the problem to start with. As you can see, the type declaration contains three cases that cover three possible representations of the shape. When working with values of this type in F#, we'll write code such as Rectangle(pt1, pt2) to create a rectangle. Unlike with unions in the C language, the value is tagged, which means that we always know which of the options it represents. As we'll see in the next section, this fact is quite important for working with discriminated union values.

The usual development process in F# starts by designing data structures needed to keep the program data. We'll explore this problem in greater detail in chapters 7 through 9. In the next section, we'll introduce pattern matching, a concept that makes many typical functional programming tasks easy. Even though pattern matching doesn't look like a concept related to types, you'll see that there are some important connections. Among other things, we can use pattern matching for implementing functions that work with discriminated unions.

2.4.3   *Pattern matching*

When using functional data types, we know much more about the structure of the type that we're working with. A nice demonstration of this property is a discriminated union—when working with this type, we always know what kind of values we can expect to get (in our previous example, it could be a rectangle, an ellipse, or a composed shape).

When writing functions that work with discriminated unions, we must specify what the program should do for each of the cases. The construct that makes this possible is in many ways similar to the switch statement from C#, but several important differences exist. First let's see how we can use the switch statement to work with a data structure mimicking a discriminated union in C#. Listing 2.6 shows how we could print information about the given shape.

Listing 2.6   Testing cases using the switch statement (C#)

```
switch(shape.Tag) {          1
  case ShapeType.Rectangle:
    var rc = (Rectangle)shape;
    Console.WriteLine("rectangle {0}-{1}", rc.From, rc.To);
    break;
  case ShapeType.Composed:
    Console.WriteLine("composed");
    break;
}
```

Listing 2.6 assumes that the shape type has a property Tag ❶, which specifies what kind of shape it represents. This corresponds to F# discriminated unions, where we can also test which of the possible cases the value represents. When the value is a rectangle, we want to print some information about the rectangle. To do this in C#, we first have to cast the shape (which has a type of the abstract base class Shape) to the type of the derived class (in our example, it's Rectangle), and then we can finally access the properties that are specific for the rectangle. In functional programming we use this type of construct more often than in regular C#, so we'll need an easier and safer way for accessing properties of the specific cases.

A final thing worth noting about listing 2.6 is that it contains code for only two of the three cases. If the shape represents an ellipse, the switch statement won't do anything. This may sometimes be the right behavior in C#, but it's not appropriate for functional programs. We said that everything is an expression in functional programming, so we could return some value from the functional version switch. In that case, we definitely need to cover all cases, because otherwise the program wouldn't know what value to return.

In listing 2.7, we'll look at the F# alternative to the C# switch statement. The construct is called match; we'll use it to calculate the area occupied by the shape.

> **Listing 2.7 Calculating the area using pattern matching (F#)**

```
match shape with
| Rectangle(pfrom, pto) ->
    rectangleArea(pfrom, pto)          ❶
| Ellipse(pfrom, pto) ->
    ellipseArea(pfrom, pto)
| Composed(Rectangle(from1, to1), Rectangle(from2, to2))       ❷
     when isNestedRectangle(from2, to2, from1, to1) ->
    rectangleArea(from1, to1)
| Composed(shape1, shape2) ->          ❸
    let area1 = shapeArea(shape1)
    let area2 = shapeArea(shape2)
    area1 + area2 - (intersectionArea(shape1, shape2))
```

The first important difference from the C# switch construct is that in F#, we can deconstruct the value that we're matching against the patterns. In listing 2.7, it is used in all the cases. The different cases (denoted using the | symbol) are usually called *patterns* (or *guards*).

When calculating area of a rectangle ❶, we need to get the two points that specify the rectangle. When using match, we can just provide two names (pfrom and pto) and the match construct assigns a value to these names when the shape is represented as a rectangle and the branch is executed. Listing 2.7 is simplified, so it just uses a utility function to calculate the actual number.

The second case is for an ellipse, and it's very similar to the first one. The next case is more interesting ❷. The pattern that specifies conditions under which the branch should be followed (which is specified between the bar symbol and the arrow [->]) is quite complicated. The pattern only matches when the shape is of type Composed, *and* both of the shapes that form the composed shape are rectangles. Instead of giving names for values inside the Composed pattern, we specify another two patterns (Rectangle, twice). This is called a *nested pattern* and it proves very useful. Additionally, this pattern contains a when clause, which allows us to specify any arbitrary condition. In our example, we call the isNestedRectangle function, which tests whether the second rectangle is nested inside the first one. If this pattern is matched, we get information about two rectangles. We also know that the second one is nested inside the first one, so we can optimize the calculation and return the area of the first rectangle.

The F# compiler has full information about the structure of the type, so it can verify that we're not missing any case. If we forgot the last one ❸ it would warn us that there are still valid shapes that we're not handling (for example, a shape composed from two ellipses). The implementation of the last case is more difficult, so if our program often composes two rectangles, the optimization in the third case would be quite useful. Similar to first-class functions, discriminated unions and pattern matching are other functional concepts that let us think about problems in simple terms.

> ## Thinking about problems using functional data structures
>
> Even though there's no simple way to create a discriminated union type in C#, the concept is still valuable even for C# developers. Once you become more familiar with them, you'll find that many of the programming problems you face can be represented using discriminated unions.
>
> If you know the object-oriented design pattern called *composite*, you may recognize it in our earlier example. We can create a more complicated shape by composing it from two other shapes. In functional programming, we'll use discriminated unions more often to represent program data, so in many cases the composite design pattern will disappear.
>
> If you end up implementing the problem in C#, you can encode a discriminated union as a class hierarchy (with a base class and a derived class for every case). Mentally you can still work with the simple concept, which makes thinking about the application architecture easier. In functional programming, this kind of data structure is used frequently, which also explains why functional languages support more flexible pattern matching constructs. Listing 2.7 demonstrated that the F# match expression can simplify implementation of rather sophisticated constructs. We'll see this type of simplification repeatedly throughout the book: an appropriate model and a bit of help from the language can go a long way to keeping code readable.

We mentioned that the F# compiler can verify that we don't have any missing cases in the pattern matching. This is one of the benefits that we get thanks to the static typing of the F# language, but there are many other areas where it helps too. In the next section, we'll review the benefits and look at one example that highlights the goals of compile-time checking in F#.

2.4.4 *Compile-time program checking*

Well-known benefits of using compile-time typing are that it prevents many common mistakes and the compiled code is more efficient. In functional languages there are several other benefits. Most importantly, types are used to specify how functions can be composed with each other. The types are not only useful for writing correct code, but serve as valuable information:

- For the developer, as part of the documentation
- For the IDE, which can use types to provide useful hints when writing the code

Types in functional languages tell us even more than they do in imperative languages such as C#, because the functional code uses generics more often. In fact, most of the higher-order functions are generic. We've seen that, thanks to type inference, the types can be nonintrusive and you often don't have to think about them when coding.

In the next section, we'll show one example of a feature that nicely demonstrates the purpose of types and compile-time program checking in F#. The goal is to make sure that your code is correct as early as possible and to provide useful hints when writing it.

UNITS OF MEASURE

In 1999 NASA's Climate Orbiter was lost because part of the development team used the metric system and another part used imperial units of measure. A part of the team expected that distances were measured in meters and weight in kilograms, while the other part provided data in inches and pounds. This incident was one of the motivations for a new F# feature called *units of measure*, which allows us to avoid this kind of issue. We'll talk about units of measure in chapter 13; here we want to use units of measure to demonstrate how type checking helps when writing F# code. We chose this example because it's easy to explain, but the compile-time checking is present when writing any F# code.

Listing 2.8 shows a brief session from F# Interactive. The calculation tests whether the speed of a car is violating a specified maximum speed.

Listing 2.8 Calculating speed using units of measure (F# Interactive)

```
> let maxSpeed = 50.0<km/h>
  let actualSpeed = 40.0<mile/h>       ←── Actual speed in mph       Maximal allowed
  ;;                                                                  speed in km/h
val maxSpeed : float<km/h>             ❶
val actualSpeed : float<mile/h>

> if (actualSpeed > maxSpeed) then     ❷
    printfn "Speeding!";;
Error FS0001: Type mismatch.
Expecting a float<mile/h> but given a float<km/h>.                    ❸
The unit of measure 'mile/h' does not match the unit of measure 'km/h'

> let mphToKmph(speed:float<mile/h>) =
    speed * 1.6<km/mile>;;             ❹
val mphToKmph : float<mile/h> -> float<km/h>
```

```
> if (mphToKmph(actualSpeed) > maxSpeed) then       ❺
    printfn "Speeding!";;
Speeding!
```

Listing 2.8 starts by declaring two values (`maxSpeed` and `actualSpeed`). The declaration annotates these values with units, so you can see that the first is in kilometers per hour and the second is in miles per hour. This information is captured in the type ❶, so the type of these two values isn't just a `float` but a `float` with additional information about the units.

Once we have these values, we try to compare the actual speed with the speed limit ❷. In a language without units of measure, this comparison would be perfectly valid and the result would be `false` (because 40 is less than 50), so the driver would escape without a penalty. The F# compiler reports ❸ that we can't compare these numbers, because the type `float<km/h>` is a different than `float<mile/h>`.

To solve the problem, we have to implement a function that converts the speed from one type to another ❹. The function takes an argument of type `float<mile/h>`, which means that the speed is measured in miles per hour and returns a float representing speed in kilometers per hour. Once we use this conversion function in the condition ❺, the code compiles correctly and reports that the actual speed is in fact larger than the allowed speed. If we implemented this as a standalone application (without using F# Interactive), we'd get an error complaining about units during the compilation. Additionally, you can see the units in Visual Studio, so it helps you verify that your code is doing the right thing. If you see that a value that should represent the speed has a type `float<km^2>`, you quickly realize that something is wrong with the equation. Note that there's a zero runtime penalty for units of measure in F#. The verification of the code correctness is done at compile-time as part of type checking.

While static type checking isn't present in all functional languages, it's extremely important for F#. In the last few sections, we looked at the concepts that are important for functional languages, and you've seen how some functional constructs differ from similar constructs in the common imperative and object-oriented languages. Some of the features may still feel a bit unfamiliar, but we'll discuss every concept in detail later in the book, so you may return to this overview to regain the "big picture" after you learn more about functional programming details.

2.5 *Summary*

In this chapter, we talked about functional programming in general terms, including its mathematical foundation in lambda calculus. You've learned about the elements that are essential for functional programming languages such as immutability, recursion, and using functions as values. We briefly introduced the ideas that influenced the design of these languages and that are to some extent present in almost all of them. These ideas include making the language extensible, writing programs using a declarative style, and avoiding mutable state. Even though all of the languages we've discussed are primarily "functional," there are still important differences between them. This is because each of these languages puts emphasis on a slightly different combination of the essential concepts. Some of the languages are extremely simple and extensible, while others give us more guarantees about the program execution.

In the next chapter, we'll see how some of the functional concepts look in practice in F# and how the same ideas can be expressed in C#, so you can see familiar C# code with a functional F# equivalent side by side. In particular, we'll describe functional data structures and look at the tuple, a basic F# immutable data structure, as well as its equivalent in C#. We'll also look at collections of data (called *lists* in functional languages) and how you can work with them using recursion. You've seen that a single recursive function can be used for various purposes when it takes another function as an argument, so we'll use this technique for writing universal list-processing code.

Meet tuples, lists, and functions in F# and C#

3

This chapter covers

- Declaring functions and values
- Working with immutable tuples and lists
- Processing lists using recursion
- Parameterizing processing functions

In chapter 2, we explored the most important concepts of functional programming, but we did this from a high-level perspective. We haven't shown you any *real* functional code, aside from quick examples to demonstrate our ideas. Our goal so far has been to illustrate how concepts relate to one another and how the result is a very different approach to programming.

In this chapter you'll finally get to write functional F# code, but we'll focus on examples that can be nicely explained and demonstrated using C#. We won't yet delve into the details; you'll learn more about those in part 2.

Here's a brief look at this chapter's topics:

- *Value bindings*—The F# feature that unifies function and value declarations; we'll also look at constructs that aren't familiar from C#, such as nested function declarations.
- *Immutability*—A general principle saying that values can't change after they've been initialized; we'll demonstrate it using the simplest functional data type: a tuple.
- *Lists*—A humble, but very useful, functional data type; just like the tuple, it's *immutable*, but it's also *recursive*, which is another important aspect; most importantly, we'll look at how to write recursive computations that process lists.
- *Pattern matching*—A feature used for checking the structure and content of data types; we'll introduce it when we'll talk about tuples and lists.
- *Functions as values*—Using function values as parameters of other functions, we can hide the difficult part of a computation. We'll see how to implement this idea in both F# and C#.

As you can see, we have a quite a few features to go through! After the introduction from chapter 2, you have a good idea about most of the features, so understanding them in practice won't be a problem for you. We'll also use C# examples to demonstrate how the F# code works, which is often more useful than numerous paragraphs of written text.

3.1 Value and function declarations

You've already seen several examples of value binding (written using the `let` keyword in F#) in chapter 1. As you'll see, value binding isn't just a value declaration—it's a powerful and common construct, used for declaring both local and global values as well as functions. Before we explore examples using functional programming in F#, let's look at other uses for value binding.

3.1.1 Value declarations and scope

As we already know, you can use the `let` keyword to declare immutable values. We haven't yet talked about a scope of the value, but it's easier to explain with a concrete example. Listing 3.1 is extremely simple, but we think you'll agree it's amazing how many nuances can hide in just four lines of code.

Listing 3.1 The scope of a value (F#)

```
let number = 42          ❶
printfn "%d" number
let message = "Answer: " + number.ToString()      ❷
printfn "%s" message
```

Listing 3.1 is quite straightforward: it declares two values—the second ❷ is calculated using the first ❶—then prints them to the console. What's important for us is the *scope* of the values—that is, the area of code where the value can be accessed. As you'd expect, the value `number` is accessible after we declared it on the first line, and the value `message` is accessible only on the last line. You can look at the code and verify that we're using the values only when they're in scope, so our code is correct.

We'll use this code to demonstrate one more thing. The example in listing 3.1 looked a lot like C# code, but it's important to understand that F# treats the code differently. We touched on this topic in chapter 2 (section 2.2.4), where we attempted to write code in C# using only expressions. We've seen that value bindings have to be treated specially, if we want every valid F# code to be an expression. Indeed, if you wrote code to do the same thing as listing 3.1 in C#, the compiler would see it as a sequence of four statements. Let's now see how F# understands the code. To demonstrate, we've made a few syntactical changes (see listing 3.2).

Listing 3.2   Example of `let` binding with explicit scopes (F#)

```
let number = 42 in
(
  printfn "%d" number;       ❷
  let message =
    "Answer: " + number.ToString() in       ❶          ❸
  (
    printfn "%s" message
  )
)
```

Listing 3.2 sports several obvious changes to the layout, but it's also worth noting the introduction of the `in` keyword after every `let` binding. Adding the `in` keyword is required if you turn off the default syntax where whitespace is significant.[1] The other change is that a block of the code following the `let` binding is enclosed in parentheses. Doing so is optional, but it's closer to how the F# compiler understands the code we wrote. Interestingly, the code in listing 3.2 is still valid F# code with the same meaning as earlier—because sometimes you may want to be more explicit about the code, and using `in` keywords and additional parentheses to wrap expressions enables you to do that.

What becomes more obvious in listing 3.2 is that the `let` binding assigns a value to a symbol and specifies that the symbol can be used inside an expression. The first `let` binding states that the symbol `number` refers to the value 42 in the expression following the `in` keyword, which is enclosed in parentheses ❶. The whole `let` binding is treated as an expression, which returns the value of the inner expression. For example, the `let` binding that defines the value `message` ❸ is an expression that returns a result of `printfn`. This function has `unit` as a return type, so the result of the whole expression will be a `unit`.

NOTE   A single line starting with `let` and ending with the `in` keyword wouldn't alone be a valid expression, because it would be missing the body part of the `let` binding. You always have to specify some expression as the body.

---

[1]   The default setting is sometimes called *lightweight syntax*. F# also supports OCaml-compatible syntax, which is more schematic and which we'll use in the example. We won't use it in the rest of the book, but in case you want to experiment with this syntax, you can turn it on by adding the directive `#light "off"` to the beginning of F# source file.

The next interesting thing is the sequencing of expressions. The expression ❸ is preceded by another expression ❷, and as you can see, we added a semicolon between these two. The semicolon works as a sequencing operator in F#. It specifies that the expression preceding the semicolon should be evaluated before the one following it. In our example, that means ❷ will be evaluated before ❸. The expression preceding the sequencing operator should also return a unit, because otherwise the returned value would be lost.

NOTE When using the lightweight syntax, we don't have to include the semicolon and can use a line break instead. The compiler uses the indentation in the code to figure out which lines are expressions and automatically inserts semicolons at the end of the line.

So far we've seen only ordinary bindings that declare an ordinary value, but the same let binding is also used for declaring functions and for nested bindings, as you'll learn next.

3.1.2 Function declarations

As noted earlier, we can use let bindings to declare functions. Let's demonstrate this on a fairly simple function that multiplies two numbers given as the arguments. This is how you'd enter it in F# Interactive:

```
> let multiply num1 num2 =
    num1 * num2;;
val multiply : int -> int -> int
```

To write a function declaration, you must follow the name of the symbol with one or more parameter names. In our example, we're writing a function with two parameters, so the name of the function (multiply) is followed by two parameters (num1 and num2). Let's now look at the body of the function. We can view the body simply as an expression that's bound to the symbol representing a name of the function (multiply in our case), with the difference being that the symbol doesn't represent a simple value but rather represents a function with several arguments.

In chapter 2, you learned that functions in F# are also values. This means that when using the let construct, we're always creating a value, but if we specify arguments, we declare a special type of value: a function. From a strictly mathematical point of view, an ordinary value is a function with no arguments, which also sheds more light on the F# syntax. If you omit all the arguments in a function declaration, you'll get a declaration of a simple value.

When writing a function, be sure to indent the body of the function properly. That way, you don't have to use other, more explicit ways to specify where the function declaration ends, as you would using the OCaml-compatible syntax.

FUNCTION SIGNATURES

One part of the previous example that we haven't discussed yet is the output printed by F# Interactive. It reports that we declared a new value and its inferred type. Because we're declaring a function, the type is a function type written as int -> int -> int.

This type represents a function that has two arguments of type int (two ints before the last arrow sign) and returns a result of type int (the type after the last arrow sign). We've already seen that F# uses type inference to deduce the type, and in this example, F# used the default type for numeric calculations (an integer). We'll get back to function types in chapter 5, where we'll also explain why parameters are separated using the same symbol as the return value.

NESTED FUNCTION DECLARATIONS

Let's now examine a slightly more complicated function declaration in listing 3.3, which also demonstrates another interesting aspect of let bindings: the fact that they can be nested.

Listing 3.3   Nested let bindings (F# Interactive)

```
> let printSquares message num1 num2 =
    let printSquareUtility num =
      let squared = num * num                    ❸
      printfn "%s %d: %d" message num squared     ❹        ❷        ❶
    printSquareUtility(num1)
    printSquareUtility(num2)
  ;;
val printSquares : string -> int -> int -> unit

> printSquares "Square of" 14 27;;
Square of 14: 196
Square of 27: 729
```

Listing 3.3 shows an implementation of a function named printSquares. As you can see from its signature (string -> int -> int -> unit), this function takes a string as its first argument (message) and two numbers (num1 and num2) as the second and third arguments. The function prints squares of the last two arguments using the first argument to format the output. It doesn't return any value, so the return type of the function is unit.

The body of the printSquares function ❶ contains a nested declaration of the function printSquareUtility. This utility function takes a number as an argument, calculates its square, and prints it together with the original number. Its body ❷ contains one more nested let binding, which declares an ordinary value called squared ❸. This value is assigned the square of the argument, to make the code more readable. The utility function ends with a printfn call that prints the message, the original number, and the squared number. The first argument specifies the format and types of the arguments (%s stands for a string, and %d stands for an integer).

One more important aspect about nested declarations can be demonstrated with this example. We've mentioned that the parameters of a function are in scope (meaning that they can be accessed) anywhere in the body of a function. For example, the parameter message can be used anywhere in the range ❶. This also means that it can be used in the nested function declaration, and this is exactly what we do inside printSquareUtility on the fourth line ❹ when we output the numbers using the message value. The nested declarations are, of course, accessible only inside the scope where they're declared—you can't use `printSquareUtility` directly from other parts of the program, for example. Correct scoping of values also guarantees that the `message` parameter will always have a value.

One last aspect of value declarations in F# is that they can be used for declaring mutable values. Even though we usually work with immutable values in functional programs, it's sometimes useful to be able to create a mutable value as well.

3.1.3 Declaring mutable values

In section 3.1.1, we declared a value of type integer by writing `let number = 10`. If you were curious and tried to modify it, you may have attempted to write something like `number = 10`. This doesn't work because a single equal sign outside a `let` binding is used to compare values in F#. It would be *valid* code, but it'd probably return `false` (unless `num` happened to have the value 10). It would seem that modifying an existing value in F# isn't even possible.

That isn't true, since F# is pragmatic and sometimes you may need to use mutable values in F#. This situation is most likely to occur when you're optimizing code or using mutable .NET objects. Listing 3.4 shows how immutable and mutable values can be used in F# and what the operator for mutating values looks like.

> **Listing 3.4 Declaring mutable values (F# Interactive)**

```
> let n1 = 22;;           ❶
val n1 : int

> n1 <- 23;;                                    ❷
error FS0027: This value is not mutable.

> let mutable n2 = 22;;    ❸
val mutable n2 : int

> n2 <- 23;;                       ❹
> n2;;
val it : int = 23
```

All values in F# are immutable by default, so when we declare a value using the usual `let` binding syntax ❶ and then attempt to modify it using the assignment operator (`<-`) we get a compile-time error message ❷. To declare a mutable variable, we have to explicitly state it using the `mutable` keyword ❸. We can later change this value using the assignment operator, and when we print it, we can see that the value has changed ❹.

NOTE You should get into the habit of using immutable values wherever possible in F#—only use mutable values when you *really* have to, not because they're necessarily *wrong*, but they're not idiomatic. Thinking functionally will lead to more concise code, which will be easier to read and reason about. Don't expect this to happen overnight, but the more you work *with* the language instead of fighting its normal idioms, the more you're likely to get out of it.

You've learned quite a lot from a section that focused on such a basic concept, but that was all we need to cover before moving to the core parts of the chapter. As we mentioned in chapter 1, the default use of immutability doesn't only influence local value declarations but also extends to data structures. In the next section, we'll look at the most basic immutable types that we use in functional programming.

3.2 Using immutable data structures

An immutable data structure (or object) is a structure whose value doesn't change after it's created. When you declare a data structure that contains some values, you store these values in *slots*, such as a field or value declaration. In functional programming, all these slots are immutable, which leads to the use of immutable data structures. In this section, we'll demonstrate the simplest built-in immutable data type. You'll see more common functional data structures in the upcoming chapters.

3.2.1 Introducing tuple type

The simplest immutable data structure in F# is a *tuple*[2] type. Tuple is a simple type that groups together several values of (possibly) different types. The following example shows how to create a value, which contains two values grouped together:

```
> let tp = ("Hello world!", 42);;
val tp : string * int
```

Creating a tuple value is fairly easy: we write a comma-separated list of values enclosed in parentheses. But let's look at the code in more detail. On the first line, we create a tuple and assign it to a tp value. The type inference mechanism of the F# language is used here, so you don't have to explicitly state what the type of the value is. The F# compiler infers that the first element in the tuple is of type string, and the second is an integer, so the type of the constructed tuple should be something like *a tuple containing a string as the first value and an integer as the second value.* Of course, we don't want to lose any information about the type, and if we represented the result using only some type called, for example, Tuple, we wouldn't know that it contains a string and an integer.

The inferred type of the expression is printed on the second line. You can see that in F# a type of a tuple is written as string * int. In general, a tuple type is written as types of its members separated by an asterisk. In the next few sections, you'll see how tuples can be used in F#, but we'll also show you how to use the same functionality in C#. If you don't immediately understand everything after reading the F# code, don't worry; continue with the C# examples, which should make everything clearer.

In C#, we can use a type that's already available in .NET 4.0, but we'll also look how to implement it to better understand the internal workings of tuples. Representing tuples in C# is possible thanks to generics. We can use them to implement a type that

---

[2]   The *u* in the word *tuple* is pronounced as the same as in *cup*.

can store different values in a type-safe fashion. Using generics, the C# equivalent of the F# type string * int will then be Tuple<string, int>. We'll get to the C# version shortly after discussing one more F# example.

WORKING WITH TUPLES IN F#

Let's look at more complicated F# code that uses tuples. In listing 3.5, we use tuples to store information about a city. The first member is a string (the name of the city) and the second is an integer, containing a number of people living there. We implement a function printCity, which outputs a message with the city name and its population, and finally we create and print information about two cities.

Listing 3.5   Working with tuples (F# Interactive)

```
> let printCity(cityInfo) =
    printfn "Population of %s is %d."
            (fst cityInfo) (snd cityInfo)
  ;;
val printCity : string * int -> unit

> let prague  = ("Prague", 1188126)
  let seattle = ("Seattle", 594210)
  ;;
val prague : string * int
val seattle : string * int

> printCity(prague)
  printCity(seattle);;
Population of Prague is 1188126.
Population of Seattle is 594210.
```

❶ Shows type of function

❷ Creates two tuple values

❸

Listing 3.5 shows a session from F# Interactive, so you can easily try it for yourself. The first piece of code ❶ declares a function printCity, which takes information about the city as an argument and prints its value using the standard F# printfn function. The formatting string specifies that the first argument is a string and the second is an integer. To read the first and second element of the tuple, we use two standard F# functions, fst and snd, respectively (which obviously represent *first* and *second*).

The next line shows the type of the function deduced by the F# type inference. As you can see, the function takes a tuple as an argument (denoted using an asterisk: string * int) and doesn't return any value (denoted as the unit type on the right side of the arrow symbol). This is exactly what we wanted.

Next, we create two tuple values ❷ that store population information about Prague and Seattle. After these lines are entered, the F# Interactive shell prints the types of the newly declared values, and we can see that the values are of the same tuple type that the printCity function takes as an argument. That means we can pass both values as an argument to our printing function and get the expected result ❸.

We promised that we'd implement exactly the same code as the previous example in C# as well, so now it's time to fulfill this promise.

Type checking when using tuples

The fact that types of the tuple match the parameter type of the function is important, because otherwise the two types would be incompatible and we wouldn't be able to call the function. To demonstrate this, you can try entering the following code in the F# Interactive console:

```
let newyork = ("New York", 7180000.5)
printCity(newyork)
```

We're not sure how New York could have 7,180,000.5 inhabitants, but if this were the case, the type of the tuple `newyork` wouldn't be `string * int` anymore and would instead be `string * float`, as the type inference would correctly deduce that the second element of the tuple is a floating-point number. If you try it, you'll see that the second line isn't valid F# code, and the compiler will report an error saying that the types are incompatible.

WORKING WITH TUPLES IN C#

As we mentioned, if we use .NET 4.0, we can work with an existing generic type, `Tuple<T1, T2>`, from the `System` namespace. We'll look how to implement a type like that shortly.

In any case, the type we'll work with will have a single constructor with two parameters of types `T1` and `T2` respectively. It'll also have two properties for accessing the values of its members, so unlike in F# where we accessed the elements using the functions `fst` and `snd`, in C# we'll use the properties `Item1` and `Item2`. Listing 3.6 has the same functionality as listing 3.5, but it's written in C#.

Listing 3.6   Working with tuples (C#)

```
void PrintCity(Tuple<string, int> cityInfo) {          ❶
  Console.WriteLine("Population of {0} is {1}.",
    cityInfo.Item1, cityInfo.Item2);                   ❷
}

var prague  = new Tuple<string, int>("Prague", 1188000);   ❸
var seattle = new Tuple<string, int>("Seattle", 582000);

PrintCity(prague);          ❹
PrintCity(seattle);
```

The translation from F# code to C# is straightforward once we have an equivalent for the F# tuple type in C#. The `PrintCity` method takes a tuple of `string` and `int` as an argument. In C# we have to specify the types of method arguments explicitly, so you can see that the type of the `cityInfo` parameter is `Tuple<string, int>` ❶. The method prints the information using the .NET `Console.WriteLine` method and uses properties of the tuple type (`Item1` and `Item2`) to read its value ❷. Next, we initialize two tuples that store information about the cities using a constructor with two arguments ❸, and we use the `PrintCity` method to show the information ❹.

The code is slightly more verbose, mainly because we have to explicitly specify the type several times; in the F# example, the type inference mechanism was able to infer the type everywhere. In a moment you'll see that we can minimize the number of explicitly stated types in the C# code a bit. So far, we've only used a new C# 3.0 feature (the var keyword), which at least lets us use type inference when declaring the prague and seattle variables ❸, because we're initializing the variables and C# can automatically infer the type from the right-hand side of the assignment.

Just like in the F# code, if we declared a tuple with an incompatible type (for example, Tuple<string, double>) we wouldn't be able to use it as an argument to the PrintCity method. This restriction is more obvious in C#, because we have to explicitly state what the type arguments for the generic parameters of the Tuple type are.

3.2.2 *Implementing a tuple type in C#*

The actual Tuple<T1, T2> type available in the System namespace is a bit more complicated, but we can quite easily implement the features that we need in this chapter. We'll follow the same naming as the .NET type, so if you're not using .NET 4.0, you can use our implementation in all the examples. The complete code is shown in listing 3.7.

Listing 3.7 Implementing the tuple type (C#)

```
public sealed class Tuple<T1, T2> {
  private readonly T1 item1;
  private readonly T2 item2;                        ❶

  public T1 Item1 { get { return item1; } }
  public T2 Item2 { get { return item2; } }

  public Tuple(T1 item1, T2 item2) {
    this.item1 = item1;                             ❷
    this.item2 = item2;
  }
}
```

The most notable thing is that the type is immutable. We've already seen how to create an immutable class in C# in the first chapter. In short, we mark all fields of the type using the readonly modifier ❶ and provide only a getter for both of the properties. Interestingly, this is somewhat the opposite of F#, where you have to explicitly mark values as mutable. Read-only fields can be set only from the code of the constructor ❷, which means that once the tuple is created, its internal state can't be mutated as long as both of the values stored in the tuple are immutable as well.

BETTER TYPE INFERENCE FOR C# TUPLES

Before moving forward, we'd like to show you one C# trick that makes our further examples that use tuples much more concise. In the earlier examples, we had to create instances of our tuple type using a constructor call, which required explicit specification of type arguments. We used the new C# 3.0 var keyword, so that the C# compiler inferred the type of variables for us, but we can do even better.

There's one more place where C# supports type inference: when calling a generic method. If you're calling a generic method and its type parameters are used as types of the method parameters, then the compiler can use the compile-time types of the method arguments when the method is called to infer the type arguments.[3] To clarify this, let's look at listing 3.8.

Listing 3.8   Improved type inference for tuples (C#)

```
public static class Tuple {
  public static Tuple<T1, T2> Create<T1, T2>(T1 item1, T2 item2) {
    return new Tuple<T1, T2>(item1, item2);
  }
}

var prague  = Tuple.Create("Prague", 1188000);        ❶
var seattle = Tuple.Create("Seattle", 582000);
```

Listing 3.8 implements a static method `Create`, which has two generic parameters and creates a tuple with values of these types. We need to place this method in a nongeneric class, because otherwise we'd have to specify the generic parameters explicitly. Luckily, C# allows us to use the name `Tuple`, because types can be overloaded by the number of their type parameters (`Tuple` and `Tuple<T1, T2>` are two distinct types). It probably won't surprise you that this class is available in the `System` namespace as well, so if you're using .NET 4.0, you don't have to implement it yourself.

The body of the method is simple: its only purpose is to make it possible to create a tuple by calling a method instead of calling a constructor. This allows the C# compiler to use type inference ❶. The full syntax for calling a generic method includes the type arguments, so using the full syntax we'd have to write `Tuple.Create<string, int>(...)`. In the next section, we'll look at writing code that calculates with tuples. Since we've just implemented the tuple type in C#, we'll start with the C# version of the code and then move on to the F# alternative.

3.2.3   *Calculating with tuples*

In the examples so far, we've created several tuples and printed the values, so let's perform some calculation now. We might want to increment the number of inhabitants by adding a number of newborns for the last year.

As you know, the tuple type is immutable, so we can't set the properties of the C# tuple class. In F#, we can read the values using two functions (`fst` and `snd`), but there are no functions for setting the value, so the situation is similar. This means that our calculation will have to follow the usual functional pattern and return a new tuple formed by the original name of the city copied from the initial tuple and the incremented size of population.

---

[3] My sincere apologies for the mess of "type arguments," "method arguments," and so forth in this sentence. Sometimes the terminology defined in specifications doesn't allow for elegant prose.

Listing 3.9 shows how this can be done in C#. Rather than adding the method to the Type<T1, T2> class from listing 3.7, we implement it as an extension method. This way, we can use the method with the sealed tuple type that exists in the .NET 4.0 library.

Listing 3.9   Incrementing the population of a city (C#)

```
static class TupleExtensions {
  public static Tuple<T1, T2> WithItem2<T1, T2>
      (this Tuple<T1, T2> tuple, T2 newItem2) {          ❶
    return Tuple.Create(tuple.Item1, newItem2);
  }
}

var pragueOld = Tuple.Create("Prague", 1188000);
var pragueNew = pragueOld.WithItem2(pragueOld.Item2 + 13195);   ❷
PrintCity(pragueNew);
```

The WithItem2 method ❶ takes a new value of the second element as an argument and uses the Tuple.Create method to create a new tuple with the first element copied from the current tuple (this.item1) and the second element set to the new value newItem2. The listing also shows how to use the method. We create city information about Prague and increment it by 13195 ❷ to get a new value representing the population in the next year.

Now we'd like to do the same thing in F#. We'll write a function withItem2 (listing 3.10), which will do exactly the same thing as the WithItem2 method from our earlier C# example.

Listing 3.10   Incrementing the population of a city (F#)

```
let withItem2 newItem2 tuple =
  let (originalItem1, originalItem2) = tuple          ❶
  (originalItem1, newItem2)                           ❷

let pragueOld = ("Prague", 1188000)
let pragueNew = withItem2 (snd(pragueOld) + 13195) pragueOld
printCity(pragueNew)
```

Listing 3.10 first shows an implementation of the function withItem2. We could implement it simply using the fst function, which reads a value of the first element in the tuple, but we wanted to demonstrate one more F# feature that can be used with tuples: *pattern matching*. You can see that inside the function, we first decompose the tuple given as the argument into two separate values ❶. This is where the pattern matching occurs; on the left-hand side of the equal sign you can see a language construct called a *pattern*, and on the right-hand side we have an expression that's matched against the pattern. Pattern matching takes the value of an expression and decomposes it into values used inside the pattern.

On the next line ❷, we can use originalItem1 extracted from the tuple using pattern matching. We reconstruct the tuple using the original value of the first element and the new value of the second element given as an argument (newItem2). (We'll look at more examples of pattern matching on tuples in the next section.) Aside from using pattern matching, the code doesn't show us anything new, but pattern matching is an important topic and F# provides other ways of using it with tuples, too. Let's take a closer look.

3.2.4   *Pattern matching with tuples*

In the previous example, we decomposed a tuple using pattern matching in a `let` binding. We can slightly improve the code in listing 3.10. Since we didn't actually *use* the second element of the tuple, we only need to assign a name to the first one. To do this, we can write an underscore for the second value in the pattern like this:

```
let (originalItem1, _) = tuple
```

The underscore is a special pattern that matches any expression and ignores the value assigned to it. Using pattern matching in `let` bindings is often very useful, but there are other places you can use it too. In fact, patterns can occur almost anywhere an expression is assigned to some value. Another place where pattern matching is extremely useful is when we're specifying the parameters of a function. Instead of parameter names, we can use patterns. This makes our `withItem2` function even simpler:

```
let withItem2 newItem2 (originalItem1, _) = (originalItem1, newItem2)
```

Now we've shortened our declaration from three lines to one. The result doesn't use any unnecessary values and clearly shows how the data flows in the code. Just from looking at the code, you can see that the first element of the original tuple is copied (by tracing the use of the symbol `originalItem1`) and that the second function argument is used as a second element of the returned tuple (by following the use of `newItem2`). This is the preferred way of working with tuples in most of the F# functions that we'll write.

One other common use for pattern matching is in an F# `match` expression, which we saw in section 2.4.3. We could rewrite our `withItem2` function to use a `match` expression like this:

```
let withItem2 newItem2 tuple =
  match tuple with
  | (originalItem1, _) -> (originalItem1, newItem2)
```

The `match` construct lets us match the specified expression (`tuple`) against one or more patterns starting with the bar symbol. In our example, we have only one pattern, and because any tuple with two elements can be deconstructed into two values containing its elements, the execution will always follow this single branch. The F# compiler analyzes the pattern matching to deduce that the argument `tuple` is a tuple type containing two elements.

NOTE Keep in mind that you can't use pattern matching to determine whether a tuple has two or three elements. This would lead to a compile-time error, because the pattern has to have the same type as the expression that we're matching against the pattern and the type of a tuple with three elements (such as int * int * int) isn't compatible with a tuple that has two elements (such as int * int). Pattern matching can be used only for determining runtime properties of values; the number of elements in a tuple is specified by the type of the tuple, which is checked at compile time. If you're wondering how to represent some data type that can have several distinct values, you'll have to wait until chapter 5, where we'll look at discriminated unions.

In the previous example we used a pattern that can't fail, because all tuples of two elements can be deconstructed into individual elements. This is called a *complete pattern* in F#. The match construct is particularly useful when working with patterns that aren't complete and can fail, because we can specify several different patterns (every pattern on a new line, starting with the bar symbol); if the first pattern fails, the next one is tried until a successful pattern is found.

What would be an incomplete pattern for tuples? Well, we could write a pattern that matches only when the first element (a city name) is some specific value. Let's say there are 100 people in New York who are never counted by any statistical study, so when setting the second element of a tuple (the population of the city) we want to add 100 when the city is New York. You could write this using an if expression, but listing 3.11 shows a more elegant solution using pattern matching.

Listing 3.11 Pattern matching with multiple patterns (F# Interactive)

```
> let setPopulation tuple newPopulation =
    match tuple with
    | ("New York", _) -> ("New York", newPopulation + 100)     ❶
    | (cityName, _) -> (cityName, newPopulation)               ❷
  ;;
val setPopulation : string * 'a -> int -> string * int

> let prague = ("Prague", 123)
  setPopulation prague 10;;                          Shows the
val it : string * int = ("Prague", 10)    ◁─┘       expected result

> let ny = ("New York", 123)
  setPopulation ny 10;;                              Returns
val it : string * int = ("New York", 110)  ◁─┘      incremented value
```

In listing 3.11, the match expression contains two distinct patterns. The first contains a tuple with a string "New York" as the first element and an underscore as a second ❶. This means that it only matches tuples with a first element set to "New York" and with any value for the second element. When this pattern is matched, we return a tuple representing New York, but with a population that's 100 more than the given argument. The second pattern ❷ is the same as in previous examples, and it sets the second element of the tuple.

The examples following the function declaration show the code behaving as expected. If we try to set a new population of Prague, the new value of population is used, but when we try to do this for New York, the new value of population is incremented by 100.

Tuples are used particularly often during the early phase of development, because they're so simple. In the next section, we'll look at another elementary immutable data type: a list. We've seen that a tuple represents a known number of elements with diverse types. Lists work the other way around: a list represents an unknown number of elements of the same type.

3.3 Lists and recursion

A tuple is a very good example of an immutable functional data type, but there's one more property of many functional data types that's worth discussing in this chapter: recursion. Let's start with a classic programming joke: what's the dictionary definition of recursion? "Recursion. See recursion."

Recursion appears in functional programming in different forms. It can be present in the structure of the type, such as lists. The type that represents functional lists is either an empty or is composed from an element and a list. You can see that the type list that we're describing is recursively used in its definition. The second form of recursion is probably more widely know and is used when writing recursive functions. Let's start by looking at one example of the second form; then we'll focus on lists to demonstrate the first form.

3.3.1 Recursive computations

The most common example of a recursive function is calculating the factorial of a number. If you're not already familiar with it, here's a short definition: the factorial of a non-negative number n is 1 if n is one or zero; for larger n, the result is factorial of $n - 1$ multiplied by n. This function can be implemented essentially in two ways. In C# you can do it using a `for` loop, which iterates over numbers in the range between 2 and n and multiplies some temporary variable by the number in each iteration:

```
int Factorial(int n) {
  int res = 1;
  for(int i = 2; i <= n; i++)
    res = res * i;
  return res;
}
```

This is a correct implementation, but it isn't easy to see that it corresponds to the mathematical definition of the function. The second way to implement this function is to use recursion and write a method in C# or a function in F# that recursively calls itself. These two implementations are surprisingly similar, so you can see both of them side by side in listing 3.12.

Listing 3.12   Recursive implementation of factorial in C# and F#

C#	F#

```
int Factorial(int n) {        ❶
    if (n <= 1)
        return 1;             ❷
    else
        return n * Factorial(n - 1);    ❸
}
```

```
let rec factorial(n) =        ❶
    if (n <= 1) then
        1                     ❷
    else
        n * factorial(n - 1)    ❸
```

Declaration of recursive function or method ❶; in F# we have to explicitly declare that it's recursive by using the let rec binding instead of an ordinary let.

The pattern matching contains two cases. The first case terminates the recursion and returns 1 immediately ❷. The second one performs the recursive call to a factorial function or Factorial method ❸.

The C# version of the code is straightforward. The F# version is also quite clear, but we have to explicitly state that the function is recursive using the rec keyword. This keyword specifies that the let binding is recursive, making it possible to refer to the name of the value (factorial) within the declaration of the function.

In general, every recursive computation should have at least two branches: a branch where the computation performs a recursive call and a branch where the computation terminates. You can see both marked in listing 3.12. Usually, the recursive calculation performs the recursive call several times until a termination condition occurs (in our case, when we're calculating the factorial of 1) and returns some constant value or calculates the result using nonrecursive code. If the termination condition is incorrect, the code can keep looping forever or can eventually crash with a stack overflow exception.

Since recursion is absolutely essential for functional programming, functional languages have developed several ways for avoiding stack overflows even for very deep recursive calls and some other optimization mechanisms. This and other advanced topics will be discussed in chapter 10.

3.3.2   Introducing functional lists

Now that we're more comfortable with the general principle of recursion, we can look at functional lists in some detail. Earlier we mentioned that a list is either empty or composed from an element and another list. This means that we need a special value to represent an empty list, and a way of constructing a list by taking an existing list and prepending an element at the beginning. The first option (an empty list) is sometimes called *nil*, and the second option produces a *cons cell* (short for *constructed list cell*). You can see a sample list constructed using an empty list and cons cells in figure 3.1.

Figure 3.1   A functional list containing 6, 2, 7, and 3. Rectangles represent cons cells, which contain a value and a reference to the rest of the list. The last cons cell references a special value representing an empty list.

As you can see in figure 3.1, every cons cell stores a single value from the list (called the *head*) and a reference to the rest of the list (called the *tail*), which can be either another cons cell or an empty list (*nil*). Let's now look at several ways that F# offers for creating lists:

```
> let ls1 = []
val ls1 : 'a list = []

> let ls2 = 6::2::7::3::[]
val ls2 : int list = [6; 2; 7; 3]

> let ls3 = [6; 2; 7; 3]
val ls3 : int list = [6; 2; 7; 3]

> let ls4 = [1 .. 5]
val ls4 : int list = [1; 2; 3; 4; 5]

> let ls5 = 0::ls4
val ls5 : int list = [0; 1; 2; 3; 4; 5]
```

At first, we created an empty list, which is written as [] in F#. If you look at the result, you can see that F# created a value containing no elements. The type of the list is a bit unclear, because we don't yet know the type of values contained in the list, so F# infers that the type is a list of "something." This is called a generic value, and we'll talk about it in chapter 5.

The second example is much more interesting. You can see how lists are created under the covers: we take an empty list and use a syntax for creating a cons cell ::. Unlike operators such as +, the :: construct is right associative, which means that it composes values from the right to the left. If you read the expression in that direction, you can see that we construct a list cell from a value of 3 and an empty list, then use the result together with a value of 7 to construct another cell, and so on. After entering the expression, F# Interactive reports that we created a list of type int list. This means that the type of the ls2 value is a list that contains integers. This is again done using generic types that you may know from C# (and you'll see how to use them in F# in detail later).

In the next two examples, we use a piece of syntactic sugar F# provides for creating lists. The first one uses square brackets with list elements separated by a semicolon, and the second uses dot-dot to create a list containing a sequence of numbers.

The last example shows how we can use cons cells to create a list by appending values at the beginning of another list. You can see that ls5 contains 0 at the beginning and then all elements from the ls4 list.

An important fact about functional lists is that they're immutable. This means that we can construct a list (as in the previous example) but we can't take an existing list and modify it; we can't add or remove an element. Functions that need to add new elements or remove existing ones always return a new list without modifying the original one, because modifying a list is in fact impossible. We'll see more examples of these functions in chapters 5, 6, and 10, but for now, let's look at processing the elements in an existing list.

When working with lists in functional languages, the typical code for processing a list contains two branches:

- A branch that performs something when the given list is an empty list
- A branch that performs an operation when the argument is a cons cell

The latter branch generally performs a calculation using the head value and recursively processes the tail of the list. We'll see all these common patterns later in this chapter, but first let's explore how to write code that chooses between these two branches using pattern matching.

DECOMPOSING LISTS USING PATTERN MATCHING

When discussing pattern matching on tuples in section 3.2.4, we saw two distinct ways for using it. One method was to write the pattern directly in the `let` binding, either when assigning the result of an expression to a value or in the declaration of function parameters. The other method was using the `match` keyword. The important difference between these two is that using `match` we can specify multiple patterns with multiple branches. For lists, we'll need to use the second option, because we have to specify two distinct branches every time we write list processing code (one for an empty list and one for a list that was created using cons cell).

The following code demonstrates pattern matching on lists and prints a message with the value of the first element or "Empty list" when the list is empty:

```
match list with
| []        -> printfn "Empty list"
| head::tail -> printfn "Starting with %d" head
```

You can see the pattern that matches an empty list on the second line and a pattern that extracts a head (the value of the first element) and a tail (the list appended after the head) on the third line. Both of these patterns are written with exactly the same syntax that we used earlier for creating the list. An empty list is matched using `[]` and a cons cell is deconstructed using the `::` pattern. The second case is much more interesting, because it assigns a value to two new symbols, `head` and `tail`. These will contain a number and the rest of the list obtained by decomposing the first cons cell. An empty list doesn't carry any value, so the first pattern doesn't bind a value to any symbol; it only informs us that the original list was empty.

If you refer to figure 3.1, you can see that the first pattern corresponds to the nil ellipse, which doesn't contain any value. The second pattern matches the cons cell rectangle and takes out the contents of its two parts.

As in the example with tuples, the list of patterns is complete, meaning that it can't fail to choose a branch for any given list. Let's now see what happens if we try using an incomplete pattern.

> **Listing 3.13 An incomplete pattern matching on lists (F# Interactive)**

```
> let squareFirst list =
    match list with
    | head::_ -> head * head
```

```
;;
Warning FS0025: Incomplete pattern matches on this
expression. The value '[]' will not be matched.
val sqareFirst : int list -> int

> squareFirst [4; 5; 6];;
val it : int = 16

> squareFirst []
Exception of type 'Microsoft.FSharp.Core.
  MatchFailureException' was thrown.
(...)
```

① Takes list, returns integer

②

③ Throws exception at runtime

We start by declaring a function called squareFirst, which contains a pattern match that matches a cons cell and returns a square of the first element from the list. However, this pattern doesn't handle the situation when a list is empty. We can see that the F# compiler is quite smart, and when we write a pattern match that can possibly fail it detects this situation and even gives us an example when the match will fail **①**. You shouldn't ignore this warning unless you're absolutely sure that the situation can never occur. Even if the function doesn't have any reasonable meaning for empty lists, it's better to add a handler for the remaining case (you can use an underscore character as a pattern that matches any value) and either throw an exception with additional information or just do nothing. Of course, if the function's return type is anything other than unit, you'll have to work out a suitable value to return if you do nothing. Throwing an exception is generally a better idea if the function really shouldn't be called with an empty list.

Even though there was a warning, F# Interactive is willing to crunch the function, so we can try calling it. First, we try a case that should work **②**, and we can see that it behaves as expected. If we call the function with an empty list as an argument **③**, the match construct doesn't contain any matching pattern, so it throws an exception. This is a normal .NET exception and can be caught using the try construct in F#.

You should have some idea what we can expect from functional lists, so in the next section we'll turn our attention to C# and use it to explain lists in detail. We'll also write our first list-processing code.

3.3.3   *Functional lists in C#*

To show how a functional list type works, let's look at how we can implement the same functionality in C#. There are several ways for representing the fact that a list can be either empty or have a *head* and a *tail*. The object-oriented solution would be to write an abstract class FuncList<T> with two derived classes for representing the two cases—for example, EmptyList<T> and ConsCellList<T>. To make the code as simple as possible, we'll use a single class, with a property IsEmpty that will tell us whether or not the instance contains a value. Note that every instance of the FuncList<T> type contains at most one value. When the instance represents an empty list, it doesn't contain any value and when it's a cons cell, it stores exactly one value. Listing 3.14 shows the implementation.

Listing 3.14   A functional list (C#)

```
public class FuncList<T> {
  public FuncList() {              ❶
    IsEmpty = true;
  }
  public FuncList(T head, FuncList<T> tail) {     ❷
    IsEmpty = false;
    Head = head;
    Tail = tail;
  }
  public bool IsEmpty { get; private set; }       ◁────  Represents whether
  public T Head { get; private set; }                    list is empty
  public FuncList<T> Tail { get; private set; }          Stores properties
}                                                        of cons cell

public static class FuncList {                    ❸
  public static FuncList<T> Empty<T>() {
    return new FuncList<T>();
  }
  public static FuncList<T> Cons<T>(T head, FuncList<T> tail) {
    return new FuncList<T>(head, tail);
  }
}
```

The FuncList<T> class is a generic C# class, so it can store values of any type. It has a property called IsEmpty, which is set to true when we're creating an empty list using the parameter-less constructor ❶. The second constructor ❷ takes two arguments, creates a cons cell, and sets IsEmpty to false. The first argument (head) is a value that we're storing in the cons cell. The second argument (tail) is a list following the cons cell that we're creating. The tail has the same type as the list we're creating, which is written as FuncList<T>. The first constructor corresponds to the F# empty list (written as []), and the second one creates a cons cell in the same way as the double colon operator (head::tail).

As already mentioned, functional lists are immutable, so all properties of the class are read only. We're implementing all of them using C# 3.0 *automatic properties*, which generate a getter and setter of the property for us, but we're specifying that the setter should be private, so they can't be modified from outside. To make the type truly read only, we set the values of the properties only in constructors, so once a list cell is created, none of its properties can change. The fact that there are many different implementation strategies for declaring immutable types demonstrates that immutability is a concept that we can use in different ways and not a language feature. When using automatic properties, we're losing the checking that the C# compiler can do when we use fields marked using readonly as a trade-off for a more convenient syntax.

Just as in our previous tuple example, we've included a nongeneric utility class FuncList ❸ with static methods that simplify creation of generic lists by providing methods for creating an empty list (Empty) and one for creating a cons cell (Cons). The advantage of using this class is that C# can infer the type arguments for a method call, so we don't have to specify the type of values carried by the list if it's obvious from the context. Now that we have a C# implementation of the list, we can write code that uses lists to perform computation.

3.3.4   *Functional list processing*

So far we've discussed what the functional list type looks like and how it can be implemented in C#. Now it's time to write code that actually does something with functional lists. For our example, we want to implement a method `SumList` in C# (or a `sumList` function in F#) that sums all the numbers in a list.

SUMMING NUMBERS IN A LIST WITH C#

If you're used to imperative programming in C# and have worked with the standard .NET array or the `List<T>` class from `System.Collections.Generic`, you'd probably create a variable called `total` initialized to zero and write a `for` loop that iterates over all the elements, adding every element to the `total` (something like `total +=` `list[i]`). (Alternatively, you could do this using a `foreach` loop, which is syntactic sugar that makes this a bit easier to write, but the idea is still the same.)

But how can we do this using our functional list, which won't let us access elements by index and that doesn't support `foreach`?[4] To do this, we can use recursion and write a method with code for the two cases: when the list is empty and when the list is a cons cell. You can see the code for the C# version of `SumList` in listing 3.15.

Listing 3.15   Summing list elements (C#)

```
int SumList(FuncList<int> numbers) {
  return numbers.IsEmpty ? 0 :          ❶
    numbers.Head + SumList(numbers.Tail);    ❷
}

var list = FuncList.Cons(1, FuncList.Cons(2,    │ Creates list
  FuncList.Cons(3, FuncList.Cons(4,             │ with 1, 2, 3, 4, 5
  FuncList.Cons(5, FuncList.Empty<int>()))))));

int sum = SumList(list);        │ Calculates sum,
Console.WriteLine(sum);         │ prints 15
```

The `SumList` method first checks whether the list is empty. If the list is nonempty, the branch that matches the cons cell ❷ is executed. It recursively calls `SumList` to calculate the sum of elements in the tail (which is a list) and adds this result to the value stored in the head. This recursive call is performed until we reach the end of the list and find an empty list as a tail. For an empty list ❶, the function terminates and returns zero.

Next, we create a list using the utility methods `Cons` and `Empty` from the nongeneric `FuncList` class. The creation is a bit cumbersome, but you could make it less so by implementing a method that creates a functional list from a normal .NET collection.

---

[4] We could add support for the `foreach` statement to our code, and it would be desirable to do so for a real-world `FuncList<T>` type.

SUMMING NUMBERS IN A LIST WITH F#

Now that you know how the code looks in C#, let's try implementing the same functionality in F#. Listing 3.16 shows an F# function sumList and a few F# Interactive commands for testing it.

> **Listing 3.16 Summing list elements (F# Interactive)**

```
> let rec sumList list =
    match list with
    | []         -> 0                              ① ── ◁── ┐ Matches list
    | head::tail -> head + sumList(tail)   ②       │ against patterns
  ;;
val sumList : int list -> int        ③

> let list = [ 1 .. 5 ];;      ◁── Creates list for testing
val list : int list

> sumList(list);;      ◁── Calculates, prints sum
val it : int = 15
```

If you compare the code with the previous C# implementation, you'll find many similarities. As in the previous case, there are two branches, one for an empty list ① and one for a cons cell ②. The second branch is again implemented using recursion. The notable difference is that in F# we can use pattern matching for selecting an execution path. Pattern matching also extracts values from the cons cell, so once the execution enters the second branch, head and tail values are already available. This adds to the robustness of the code: you can't use values that haven't been matched by a pattern. It sounds trivial, but it prevents the code from accidentally trying to access the (nonexistent) elements of an empty list. Pattern matching is a natural construct in functional languages and there's no corresponding feature in C#, so we had to use the conditional operator (?:) to implement the same behavior.

Also, F# type inference was helpful once again: we didn't have to specify the types explicitly anywhere in the code. As you can see, it correctly inferred that the function takes a list of integers and returns an integer ③. The inference algorithm used the fact that we're testing whether list value is an empty list or a cons cell to deduce that the type of the value is a list. Because one branch returns zero, it knows that the whole function returns an integer. Because we're adding elements of the list together, it deduces that the argument is a list containing integers.

The recursion that we used in this section is important, but writing everything using recursion explicitly would be difficult. In the next section we'll introduce a mechanism that allows you to hide the difficult recursive parts of the code.

3.4 *Using functions as values*

In the previous section, we talked about immutable lists and you learned how to write a function that processes a list recursively. In this section, we'll look at one more essential concept of functional programming: treating functions as values. You'll see why it's so useful to work with functions in this way and what it means to treat a function as a value. More information about functions will follow in chapter 5.

3.4.1   Processing lists of numbers

Imagine that we want to write a method similar to SumList but that multiplies the numbers rather than adding them. Making this change looks quite easy: we can copy the SumList method and tinker with it. There are only two changes in the modified method:

```
int MultiplyList(FuncList<int> numbers) {
  if (numbers.IsEmpty) return 1;                                    ❶
  else return numbers.Head * MultiplyList(numbers.Tail);           ❷
}
```

The first change is that we're using multiplication instead of addition in the branch that does the recursive call ❷. The second change is that the value returned for an empty list is now 1 instead of 0 ❶. As we mentioned in chapter 2, this solution works, but copying blocks of code is a bad practice. Instead, we'd like to write a parameterized method or function that can do both adding and multiplying of the list elements depending on the parameters. This allows us to hide the difficult recursive part of the list processing routine in a reusable function, and writing SumList or MultiplyList will become a piece of cake.

This example is similar to one we discussed in chapter 2 (section 2.3.1). The solution is to write a method or a function that takes two arguments: the initial value and the operation that should be performed when aggregating the elements. Let's see how we can implement this idea in C#.

PASSING A FUNCTION AS AN ARGUMENT IN C#

You've seen that in C#, passing a function as an argument can be done using delegates, in particular the Func delegate. In listing 3.17, the delegate will have two arguments of type int and will return an int as a result. The code shows how we can implement the aggregation as a recursive method that takes a delegate as a parameter.

Listing 3.17   Adding and multiplying list elements (C#)

```
int AggregateList(FuncList<int> list, int init, Func<int,int,int> op) {
  if (list.IsEmpty)
    return init;                                        ❶
  else {
    int rest = AggregateList(list.Tail, init, op);      ❷
    return op(rest, list.Head);
  }
}

static int Add(int a, int b) { return a + b; }     │ Declares methods
static int Mul(int a, int b) { return a * b; }     │ for testing

var list = FuncList.Cons(1, FuncList.Cons(2,       │
  FuncList.Cons(3, FuncList.Cons(4,                │ Initializes
  FuncList.Cons(5, FuncList.Empty<int>()))))));    │ sample list

Console.WriteLine(AggregateList(list, 0, Add));    │ Prints 15 as sum,
Console.WriteLine(AggregateList(list, 1, Mul));    │ 120 as product
```

Let's look at the `AggregateList` method first. It takes the input list to process as the first parameter. The next two parameters specify what should be done with the input. The second parameter is the initial value, which is an integer. It's used when a list is empty ❶ and we want to return the initial value from the method.

The last parameter is a delegate and is used in the other branch ❷. Here we first recursively calculate the aggregate result for the rest of the list and call the `op` delegate to calculate the aggregate of that result and the head of the list. In our later examples, it would either add or multiply the given parameters. The delegate type that we're using here is the generic `Func<T1, T2, TResult>` delegate from .NET 3.5, which is further discussed in chapter 5. Briefly, it allows us to specify the number and types of the arguments as well as the return type using .NET generics. This means that when we call `op` ❷ the compiler knows we should provide two integers as arguments and it will return an integer as a result.

Later in the code, we declare two simple methods that are compatible with the delegate type: one for adding two numbers and one for multiplying them. The rest of the code shows how to call the `AggregateList` method to get the same results as those returned by `SumList` and `MultiplyList` in our earlier examples.

Of course, writing the helper methods this way is a bit tedious, because they aren't used anywhere else in the code. In C# 2.0, you can use anonymous methods to make the code nicer, and in C# 3.0 we have an even more elegant way for writing this code using lambda expressions. Lambda expressions and the corresponding feature in F# (called lambda functions) are used almost everywhere in a real functional code, so we'll discuss them much more fully in chapter 5. In the next section, we're going to look at the last code example in this chapter and see how to implement the same behavior in F#.

PASSING A FUNCTION AS AN ARGUMENT IN F#

The function `aggregateList` in F# will be quite similar to the method that we've already implemented. The important distinction is that F# supports passing functions as arguments to other functions naturally, so we don't have to use delegates for this.

The function is a special kind of type in F#. Similarly to tuples, the type of a function is constructed from other basic types. With a tuple, the type was specified in code using an asterisk between the types of the elements (e.g., `int * string`). In the case of functions, the type is specified in terms of the types of arguments and the return type. This provides type safety in the same way delegates do in C#. A function that takes a number and adds 1 to it would be of type `int -> int`, meaning that it takes an integer and returns an integer. The type of a function that takes two numbers and returns a number would be of type `int -> int -> int`, and this is exactly the type of the first parameter in our `aggregateList` function. Listing 3.18 shows the F# version of our example.

Listing 3.18 Adding and multiplying list elements (F# Interactive)

```
> let rec aggregateList (op:int -> int -> int) init list =        ⟵┐ Takes function
    match list with                                                │ as argument
    | []     -> init        ❶
```

```
    | hd::tail ->
       let resultRest = aggregateList op init tail        ❷
       op resultRest head
  ;;
val aggregateList : (int -> int -> int) -> int -> int list -> int      ❸
> let add a b = a + b
  let mul a b = a * b
  ;;
val add : int -> int -> int      | Shows type compatible
val mul : int -> int -> int      | with op parameter

> aggregateList add 0 [ 1 .. 5 ];;      | Tests function
val it : int = 15                       | immediately
> aggregateList mul 1 [ 1 .. 5 ];;
val it : int = 120
```

Just like in the C# version, the first two parameters of the function specify how the elements in the list are aggregated. The second parameter is the initial value, and the first one is an F# function. In this example, we wanted to make the function work only with integers to make the code more straightforward, so we added a type annotation for the first parameter. It specifies that the type of the op function is a function taking two integers and returning an integer.

Next we see the familiar pattern for list processing: one branch for an empty list ❶ and one for a cons cell ❷. After entering the code for the aggregateList function in F# Interactive, it prints a signature of the function ❸. This kind of signature may look a bit daunting the first time you see it, but you'll soon become familiar with it. In figure 3.2 you can see what each part of the signature means.

Finally, we write two simple functions (add and mul) that both have a signature corresponding to the type of the first parameter of aggregateList and verify that the function works as expected. We wrote these two functions just to make the sample look exactly like the previous C# version, but F# allows us to take any binary operator and work with it as if it were an ordinary function. This means that we don't need to write the add function and can instead just use the plus symbol directly:

```
Function taking two numbers                List to be processed
   and returning a number
             |                                       |
(int -> int -> int)  ->  int  ->  int list  ->  int
             |                 |                  |
   Initial value of type int    Returns the aggregated value
```

Figure 3.2   The type signature of the `aggregate-List` function in detail. The first argument specifies how two numbers are aggregated, the second is an initial value, and the third is an input list.

```
> aggregateList (+) 0 [ 1 .. 5 ];;
val it : int = 15
```

This feature is often quite helpful, and working with operators makes F# code very succinct. Note that when using an operator in place of a function, we have to enclose it in parentheses, so instead of just writing +, we have to write (+).

You may be thinking that aggregateList isn't a particularly useful function and that there aren't many other uses for it other than adding and multiplying elements in a list, but the next section shows one surprising example.

3.4.2 *Benefits of parameterized functions*

Let's look at one additional example that will use this function for another purpose—something that at first glance seems very different from adding or multiplying the elements of a list. Let's see if we can work out the largest value:

```
> aggregateList max (-1) [ 4; 1; 5; 2; 8; 3 ];;
val it : int = 8
```

The function that we used as a first argument (`max`) is a built-in F# function that returns the larger from two numbers given as arguments. We used −1 as an initial value, because we expect that the list contains only positive numbers. The program first compares −1 with 3 and returns the larger of these two. In the next iteration it takes the current value (the result of the previous comparison, which is 3), compares it with 8, and returns the larger. In the next step, 8 is compared with 2, then with 5, and so on. Similarly, you could easily find the smallest element in a list by using `min` as a first argument and some large number (such as `Int32.MaxValue`) as the second argument.

   In fact, the function can be made even more useful by allowing the caller to use something other than an integer during the aggregation. You can see that the body of `aggregateList` function doesn't state anywhere that the aggregated value should be integer; the only place where this is specified is in the type annotation for the `op` parameter. It specifies that the function returns an integer, so F# knows that the aggregated value will be an integer, but we could simply remove the type annotation and make the code more general. This powerful feature of the F# language is called automatic generalization and we'll see how to use it in chapter 6.

3.5 *Summary*

In this chapter we explored essential functional constructs and techniques in practice. We started with value and function declarations using `let` bindings, and you learned how F# minimizes the number of concepts that you have to work with—from a strictly mathematical point of view, an immutable value is just a function with no arguments.

   Next, we looked at the simplest immutable data structure used in functional languages: the tuple. We used it to demonstrate how you can work with immutable data structures. When you perform a calculation with an immutable data structure, you can't modify the existing instance, but you can create a new instance by copying the original values and replacing those that were newly calculated. The next interesting immutable data type that we encountered was a list. Working with lists helped us to explore recursion, both in terms of how to construct one list from another and in using pattern matching to process a list recursively.

   Writing the same recursive processing whenever we want to perform an operation on lists would be inconvenient, so we looked at a mechanism that allows us to make the code general, so that it can be used for a broader range of similar use cases. In the previous chapter, we called this mechanism higher-order functions. It means that a function can be simply parameterized by another function that's given to it as an argument.

This chapter served as a sneak preview showing some of the most important functional techniques in action in their most simplistic form. Most of them can be quite well written in C# too. Now that you have an idea of the look and feel of functional programming, we'll examine the F# language and tools in more detail, so that you can play with them and try writing some code on your own.

The examples from this chapter are just an overview, and we'll get back to all the concepts mentioned here later in the book. Other common functional data types will be discussed in chapter 5, and in chapter 6 we'll talk mostly about higher-order functions that can be used for working with them. In these two chapters, we'll also see how to make the code more general by using not only generic types but generic functions as well.

Exploring F# and
.NET libraries by example

This chapter covers

- Working with common .NET and F# libraries
- Implementing our first real-world application in F#
- Developing code using F# Interactive
- Loading data from file and drawing charts

Even though we've looked at only the most basic F# language features so far, you should already know enough to write a simple application. In this chapter we won't introduce any new functional language constructs; instead we'll look at practical aspects of developing .NET applications in F#. You probably know how to write a similar application in C#, so all code in this chapter will be in F#.

As we write our first real-world application in F#, we'll explore several functions from the F# library and also see how to access .NET classes. The .NET platform contains many libraries and all of them can be used from F#. In this chapter we'll look at several examples, mainly in order to work with files and create the UI for our application. We'll come across several other .NET libraries in the subsequent chapters, but after reading this one you'll be able to use most of the functionality provided by .NET from your F# programs, because the technique is often the same.

4.1   *Drawing pie charts in F#*

We'll develop an application for drawing pie charts, as shown in figure 4.1. The application loads data from a comma-separated value (CSV) file and performs preprocessing in order to calculate the percentage of every item in the data source. Then it plots the chart and allows the user to save the chart as a bitmap file. We could use a library to display the chart (and we'll do that in chapter 13), but by implementing the functionality ourselves, we'll learn a lot about F# programming and using .NET libraries from F# code.

We'll implement the application in three parts:

- Section 4.2—We'll implement loading information from a file and perform basic calculations on the data. We'll use the tuple and list types that we introduced in the previous chapter.
- Section 4.3—We'll add simple console-based output, so we can see the results of the calculations in a human-readable form.
- Section 4.4—We'll add a graphical user interface (GUI), drawing charts of the data. We'll use the standard .NET Windows Forms library to implement the UI and the `System.Drawing` namespace for drawing.

Even though you're only a quarter of the way through this book, the code that we'll write will be very close to what you'd do if you wanted to develop an application like this after reading the entire book. This is because F# code is developed in an iterative way: you start with the simplest possible way to solve the problem and later refine it to fit your advanced needs. Many people prefer developing F# code like this because it allows you to get interesting results as soon as possible, and because F# makes it easy to refactor code later to improve its organization and readability. The ability to quickly write a working prototype for a problem is extremely useful.

One benefit of iterative development is that you can interactively test your application when writing the first version, as you'll see in this chapter. In the early phase, you

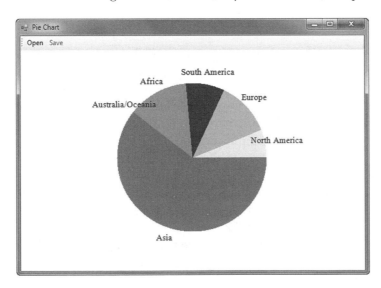

Figure 4.1
Running the F# application for drawing pie charts developed in this chapter. The chart shows distribution of the world population among continents.

can also easily author unit tests (learn more in chapter 11). Another benefit is that it's easier to correctly design the whole application if you already know how the core parts look in the prototype. Also, F# and Visual Studio are perfect tools for this kind of development. You can start writing the code in Visual Studio and execute it using F# Interactive to see whether it works as you expected and later start wrapping this experimental code in modules or types.

4.2 Writing and testing code in FSI

From the description in section 4.1, you should have a good idea of what kind of data we'll be using. The application works with a series of elements containing a title to be displayed in the chart and a number. It will load the data from a simplified CSV file, which contains a single element per line. Listing 4.1 shows a sample file with world population distribution in millions.

Listing 4.1 Our CSV file with population information

```
Asia,3634
Australia/Oceania,30
Africa,767
South America,511
Europe,729
North America,307
```

CSV files like this one are supported by many spreadsheet editors, including Microsoft Excel, so if you save the file with the .csv extension, you can easily edit it. Our application will only support basic files, so we'll assume that values are separated using commas and that there are no commas or quotation marks in the titles. Those extra elements would make the file format more complicated, leading to more complex parsing code.

Let's start by writing F# functions to read the file and perform basic calculations on the loaded data. We'll develop the code interactively, which will allow us to test every single function immediately after writing it.

4.2.1 Loading and parsing data

As a first step, we'll implement a function called convertDataRow, which takes a single row from the CSV file as a string and returns two components from the row in a tuple. Immediately after implementing the function, we test it by giving it a sample input that should be correctly parsed (a string "Testing reading,1234"). You can see the code for this function and the result of our test in listing 4.2.

Listing 4.2 Parsing a row from the CSV file (F# Interactive)

```
> open System;;
> let convertDataRow(csvLine:string) =              ❶
    let cells = List.ofseq(csvLine.Split(','))       ❷
    match cells with
    | title::number::_ ->        <-- Should have two or more cells
```

```
        let parsedNumber = Int32.Parse(number)
        (title, parsedNumber)
    | _ -> failwith "Incorrect data format!"     ◁——  Reports an error
  ;;
val convertDataRow : string -> string * int

> convertDataRow("Testing reading,1234");;          ❸
val it : string * int = ("Testing reading", 1234)
```

After starting F# Interactive, we import functionality from the System namespace. We need to open the namespace because the code uses the Int32.Parse method. This has to be imported explicitly, whereas the functions from the core F# libraries, such as List.ofseq, are available implicitly.

The function convertDataRow ❶ takes a string as an argument and splits it into a list of values using a comma as a separator. We're using the standard .NET Split method to do this. When invoking an instance method on a value, the F# compiler needs to know the type of the value in advance. Unfortunately, the type inference doesn't have any other way to infer the type in this case, so we need to use type annotation to explicitly state that the type of csvLine is a string ❷.

The Split method is declared using the C# params keyword and takes a variable number of characters as arguments. We specify only a single separator: the comma character. The result of this method is an array of strings, but we want to work with lists, so we convert the result to a list using the ofseq function from the F# List module. We'll talk about arrays and other collection types in chapters 10 and 12.

Once we have the list, we use the match construct to test whether it's in the correct format. If it contains two or more values, it will match the first case (title::number::_). The title will be assigned to a value title, the numeric value to number, and the remaining columns (if any) will be ignored. In this branch we use Int32.Parse to convert a string to an integer and return a tuple containing the title and the value. The second branch throws a standard .NET exception.

If you look at the signature, you can see that the function takes a string and returns a tuple containing a string as the first value and an integer as the second value. This is exactly what we expected: the title is returned as a string and the numeric value from the second column is converted to an integer. The next line demonstrates how easy it is to test the function using F# Interactive ❸. The result of our sample call is a tuple containing "Testing reading" as a title and "1234" as a numeric value.

Working with .NET strings in F#

When working with strings in F#, you'll usually use the normal .NET methods. Let's see how we can use them in F#, starting with a few selected static methods available in the String class. We can use these as if they were ordinary F# functions (using the String class name). The arguments to these functions must be specified in parentheses as a comma-separated tuple. In the type signatures, tuples are written using asterisks:

(continued)

- `String.Concat` (overloaded)—Accepts a variable number of arguments of type string or object and returns a string obtained by concatenating all of them:

```
> String.Concat("1 + 3", 3);;
val it : string = "1 + 33"
```

- `String.Join (sep:string * strs:string[]) : string`—Concatenates an array of strings supplied as the `strs` parameter using a separator specified by `sep`; we can use the `[| ... |]` syntax to construct an array literal:

```
> String.Join(", ", [| "1"; "2"; "3" |]);;
val it : string = "1, 2, 3"
```

Strings in .NET are also objects and they also have instance members too. These can be used in F# using the typical dot notation. We've already seen this in the previous example when splitting a string using `str.Split`. The following examples assume that we have a string value `str` containing `"Hello World!"`:

- `str.Length`—Property that returns the length of the string; properties are accessed in F# the same way as in C#, so the call reading the property isn't followed by braces:

```
> str.Length;;
val it : int = 12
```

- `str.[index:int]`—Indexing into a string, which can be written using square braces; returns the character at the location specified by the `index` value. Note that you still need the dot before the opening brace, unlike in C#:

```
> str.[str.Length - 1];;
val it : char = '!'
```

We can also use functions available in the FSharp.PowerPack.dll library. Most of the string processing code in F# can be implemented using .NET methods.

In the previous listing we implemented the `convertDataRow` function, which takes a string containing a line from the CSV file and returns a tuple containing a label and a numeric value. As a next step we'll implement a function that takes a list of strings and converts each string to a tuple using `convertDataRow`. Listing 4.3 shows the function—and a test immediately afterward, parsing a sample list of strings.

Listing 4.3   Parsing multiple lines from the input file (F# Interactive)

```
> let rec processLines(lines) =
    match lines with
    | [] -> []                              ❶
    | currentLine::remaining ->             ❷          Processes
      let parsedLine = convertDataRow(currentLine)      head of list
      let parsedRest = processLines(remaining)    ⟵   Recursively
      parsedLine :: parsedRest                          processes tail
```

```
;;
val processLines : string list -> (string * int) list

> let testData = processLines ["Test1,123"; "Test2,456"];;        ❸
val testData : (string * int) list =
  [("Test1", 123); ("Test2", 456)]
```

This function is in many ways similar to those for processing lists that we implemented in the previous chapter. As you can see, the function is declared using the
let rec keyword, so it's recursive. It takes a list of strings as an argument (lines)
and uses pattern matching to test whether the list is an empty list or a cons cell. For
an empty list, it directly returns an empty list of tuples ❶. If the pattern matching
executes the branch for a cons cell ❷, it assigns a value of the first element from the
list to the value currentLine and list containing the remaining elements to the value
remaining. The code for this branch first processes a single row using the convert-
DataRow function from listing 4.2 and then recursively processes the rest of the list.
Finally the code constructs a new cons cell: it contains the processed row as a head
and the recursively processed remainder of the list as a tail. This means that the
function executes convertDataRow for each string in the list and collects the results
into a new list.

To better understand what the processLines function does, we can also look at
the type signature printed by F# Interactive. It says that the function takes a list of
strings (string list type) as an argument and returns a list containing tuples of type
string * int. This is exactly the type returned by the function that parses a row, so it
seems that the function does the right thing. We verify this by calling it with a sample
list as an argument ❸. You can see the result of the call printed by F# Interactive: it's a
list containing two tuples with a string and a number, so the function works well.

Now we have a function for converting a list of strings to a data structure that we'll
use in our chart-drawing application. Before we can implement the key data processing part, we need to look at one simple utility.

4.2.2   Calculating with the data

In the first version of the application, we'll simply print labels together with the proportion of the chart occupied by each item (as a percentage).

To calculate the percentage, we need to know the sum of the numeric values of all
the items in the list. This value is calculated by the function calculateSum in listing 4.4.

Listing 4.4   Calculating a sum of numeric values in the list (F# Interactive)

```
> let rec calculateSum(rows) =
    match rows with                         Returns zero
    | [] -> 0                    ◁──────    for empty list
    | (_, value)::tail ->                        ❶
      let remainingSum = calculateSum(tail)   ◁──   Recursively sums
      value + remainingSum                          elements of tail
  ;;
val calculateSum : ('a * int) list -> int
```

```
> let sum = calculateSum(testData);;
val sum : int = 579
> 123.0 / float(sum) * 100.0;;        ❷
val it : float = 21.24352332
```

This function exhibits the recurring pattern for working with lists yet again. Writing code that follows the same pattern over and over may suggest that we're doing something wrong (as well as being boring—repetition is rarely fun). Ideally, we should only write the part that makes each version of the code unique without repeating ourselves. This objection is valid for the previous example, and we can write it in a more elegant way. We'll learn how to do this in upcoming chapters. You'll still need both recursion and pattern matching in many functional programs, so it's useful to look at one more example and become familiar with these concepts.

For an empty list, the function `calculateSum` simply returns 0. For a cons cell, it recursively sums values from the tail (the original list minus the first element) and adds the result to a value from the head (the first item from the list). The pattern matching in this code demonstrates one interesting pattern that's worth discussing. In the second branch ❶, we need to decompose the cons cell, so we match the list against the `head::tail` pattern. The code is more complicated than that, since at the same time, it also matches the head against pattern for decomposing tuples, which is written as `(first, second)`. This is because the list contains tuples storing the title as the first argument and the numeric value as the second argument. In our example, we want to read the numeric value and ignore the title, so we can use the underscore pattern to ignore the first member of the tuple. If we compose all these patterns into a single one, we get `(_, value)::tail`, which is what we used in the code.

If we look at the function signature printed by F# Interactive, we can see that the function takes a list of tuples as an input and returns an integer. The type of the input tuple is `'a * int`, which means that the function is generic and works on lists containing any tuple whose second element is an integer. The first type is not relevant, because the value is ignored in the pattern matching. The F# compiler makes the code generic automatically in situations like this using a feature called *automatic generalization*. You'll learn more about writing generic functions and automatic generalization in chapters 5 and 6.

The last command ❷ from listing 4.3 prepared the way for the test in listing 4.4: why enter test data more than once? Having calculated the sum to test the function, we finally calculate the percentage occupied by the record with a value 123. Because we want to get the precise result (21.24 percent), we convert the obtained integer to a floating point number using a function called `float`.

Converting and parsing numbers

F# is a .NET language, so it works with the standard set of numeric types available within the platform. The following list shows the most useful types that we'll work with. You can see the name of the .NET class in italics and the short name used in F# in parentheses:

(continued)

- *Int32, UInt32* (int, uint32)—Standard 32-bit integer types; literals are written in F# as 42 (signed) or 42u (unsigned); there are also 16- and 64-bit variants written as 42s and 42us for 16-bit (int16, uint16) and 1L or 1UL for 64-bit (int64, uint64).

- *Double, Single* (float, float32)—Represent a double-precision and a single-precision floating-point number; the literals are written as 3.14 and 3.14f, respectively. Note the difference between F# and C# here—double in C# is float in F#; float in C# is float32 in F#.

- *SByte, Byte* (sbyte, byte)—Signed and unsigned 8-bit integers; the literals are written as 1y (signed) and 1uy (unsigned).

- *Decimal* (decimal)—Floating decimal point type, appropriate for financial calculations requiring large numbers of significant integral and fractional digits. Literals are written as 3.14M.

- *BigInteger* (bigint)—A type for representing integers of arbitrary size. This is a new type in .NET 4.0 and is available in the System.Numerics namespace; earlier versions of F# contain their own implementation of the type, so you can use it when targeting earlier versions of the .NET Framework in Visual Studio 2008. In F#, the literals of this type are written as 1I.

Unlike C#, the F# compiler doesn't insert automatic conversions between distinct numeric types when precision can't be lost. F# also doesn't use a type-cast syntax for explicit conversions, so we have to write all conversions as function calls. The F# library contains a set of conversion functions that typically have the same name as the F# name of the target type. The following list shows a few of the most useful conversion functions:

- *int*—Converts any numeric value to an integer; the function is polymorphic, which means that it works on different argument types. We can, for example, write (int 3.14), for converting a float value to an integer, or (int 42uy), for converting a byte value to an integer.

- *float, float32*—Converts a numeric value to a double-precision or a single-precision floating-point number; it's sometimes confusing that float corresponds to .NET Double type and float32 to .NET Single type.

These functions can be also used when converting strings to numbers. If you need more control over the conversion and specify for example the culture information, you can use the Parse method. This method is available in a .NET class corresponding to the numeric type that can be found in a System namespace. For example, to convert a string to an integer you can write Int32.Parse("42"). This method throws an exception on failure, so there's also a second method called TryParse. Using this method, we can easily test whether or not the conversion succeeded. The method returns the Boolean flag and gives us the parsed number via an out parameter, but it can be accessed in a simpler way in F#. We'll talk about the details in chapter 5, but as you can see, the usage is straightforward:

(continued)

```
let (succ, num) = Int32.TryParse (str)
if succ then Console.Write("Succeeded: {0}", num)
else Console.Write("Failed")
```

This is by no means a comprehensive reference for working with numbers in F# and .NET. We've discussed only the most commonly used numeric types and functions. To learn more, refer to the standard .NET reference or the F# online reference [F# website].

In listing 4.4 we ended with an equation that calculates the percentage of one item in our test data set. This is another example of iterative development in F#, because we'll need exactly this equation in the next section. We tried writing the difficult part of the computation to make sure we could do it in isolation: now we can use it in the next section. We'll start by writing code to read the data from a file and then use this equation as a basis for code to print the data set to the console.

4.3   Creating a console application

Writing a simple console-based output for our application is a good start, because we can do it relatively easily and we'll see the results quickly. In this section, we'll use several techniques that will be important for the later graphical version as well. Even if you don't need console-based output for your program, you can still start with it and later adapt it into a more advanced, graphical version as we'll do in this chapter.

We've already finished most of the program in the previous section by writing common functionality shared by both the console and graphical versions. We have a function, processLines, that takes a list of strings loaded from the CSV file and returns a list of parsed tuples, and a function, calculateSum, that sums the numerical values from the data set. In listing 4.4, we also wrote the equation for calculating the percentage, so the only remaining tasks are reading data from a file and printing output to a console window. You can see how to put everything together in listing 4.5.

Listing 4.5   Putting the console-based version together (F# Interactive)

```
> open System.IO;;

> let lines = List.ofseq(File.ReadAllLines(@"C:\Ch03\data.csv"));;      ❶
val lines : string list
                                          ┌  Converts lines
> let data = processLines(lines);;    ◄───┘  to list of tuples
val data : (string * int) list =
  [("Asia", 3634); ("Australia/Oceania", 30); ("Africa", 767);
   ("South America", 511); ("Europe", 729); ("North America", 307)]

> let sum = float(calculateSum(data));;    ◄─┐ Sums numeric
val sum : float = 5978.0                      │ values

> for (title, value) in data do      ❷
```

```
let percentage = int((float(value)) / sum * 100.0)        Calculates
Console.WriteLine("{0,-18} - {1,8} ({2}%)",                percentage, prints it
                  title, value, percentage)
;;
Asia                - 3634 (60%)
Australia/Oceania   -   30 (0%)
Africa              -  767 (12%)
South America       -  511 (8%)
Europe              -  729 (12%)
North America       -  307 (5%)
```

Listing 4.5 starts by opening the System.IO namespace, which contains .NET classes for working with the filesystem. Next, we use the class File from this namespace and its method ReadAllLines ❶, which provides a simple way for reading text content from a file, returning an array of strings. Again we use the ofseq function to convert the array to a list of strings. The next two steps are fairly easy, because they use the two functions we implemented and tested in previous sections of this chapter—we process the lines and sum the resulting values.

Let's now look at the last piece of code ❷. It uses a for loop to iterate over all elements in the parsed data set. This is similar to the foreach statement in C#. The expression between keywords for and in isn't just a variable; it's a pattern. As you can see, pattern matching is more common in F# than you might expect! This particular pattern decomposes a tuple into a title (the value called title) and the numeric value (called value). In the body of the loop, we first calculate the percentage using the equation that we tested in listing 4.4 and then output the result using the familiar .NET Console.WriteLine method.

Formatting strings in F# and .NET

String formatting is an example of a problem that can be solved in two ways in F#. The first option is to use functionality included in the F# libraries. This is compatible with F# predecessors (the OCaml language), but it's also designed to work extremely well with F#. The other way is to use functionality available in the .NET Framework, which is sometimes richer than the corresponding F# functions. The printfn function, which we've used in earlier examples, represents the first group, and Console.WriteLine from the last listing is a standard .NET method.

When formatting strings in .NET, we need to specify a *composite format string* as the first argument. This contains placeholders that are filled with the values specified by the remaining arguments. The placeholders contain an index of the argument and optionally specify alignment and format. Two of the most frequently used formatting methods are Console.WriteLine (for printing to the console) and String.Format (which returns the formatted string):

```
> let name, date = "Tomas", DateTime.Now;;
> let s = String.Format("Hello {0}! Today is: {1:D}", name, date);;
val s : string = "Hello Tomas! Today is: Sunday, 15 March 2009"
```

(continued)

The *format string* is specified after the colon; for example, {0:D} for a date formatted using the long date format, {0:e} for the scientific floating point, or {0:x} for a hexadecimal integer. In the last listing, we also specified alignment and padding of the printed value, which is done by adding a number after the comma:

```
> Console.WriteLine("Number with spaces: {0,10}!", 42);;
Number with spaces:         42!
> Console.WriteLine("Number with spaces: {0,-10}!", 42);;
Number with spaces: 42        !
```

Aside from the specification of alignment and padding, the .NET libraries are frequently used from F# when formatting standard .NET data types (such as the DateTime type or the DateTimeOffset type, which represents the time relatively to the UTC time zone). The following example briefly recapitulates some of the useful formatting strings. Note that the output is culture-sensitive, so it can vary depending on your system settings:

```
> let date = DateTimeOffset.Now;;
val date : DateTimeOffset = 03/15/2009 16:37:53 +00:00
> String.Format("{0:D}", date);;
val it : string = "Sunday, 15 March 2009"
> String.Format("{0:T}", date);;
val it : string = "16:36:09"
> String.Format("{0:yyyy-MM-dd}", date);;
val it : string = "2009-03-15"
```

The F#-specific functions for formatting strings are treated specially by the compiler, which has the benefit that it can check that we're working correctly with types. Just like in .NET formatting, we specify the format as a first argument, but the placeholders in the format specify the type of the argument. There's no index, so placeholders have to be in the same order as the arguments. In F#, you'll often work with printf and printfn to output the string to the console (printfn adds a line break) and sprintf, which returns a formatted string:

```
printfn "Hello %s! Today is: %A" name date
let s = sprintf "Hello %s! Today is: %A" name date
```

The following list shows the most common types of placeholders:

- %s—The argument is of type string.
- %d—Any signed or unsigned integer type (e.g., byte, int, or ulong)
- %f—A floating-point number of type float or float32
- %A—Outputs the value of any type using a combination of F# reflection and .NET ToString method. This prints the most readable debug information about any value.

Choosing between the .NET and F# approach is sometimes difficult. In general, it's usually better to use the F# function, because it has been designed to work well with F# and checks the types of arguments based on the format string. If you need functionality that isn't available or is hard to achieve using F# functions, you can switch to .NET formatting methods, because both can be easily used in F#.

Instead of running everything in F# Interactive, we could turn the code from listing 4.5 into a standard console application. If you're writing the code in Visual Studio and executing it in F# Interactive by pressing Alt+Enter, you already have the complete source code for the application. The only change that will make it more useful is the ability to read the filename from the command line. In F#, we can read command-line arguments using the standard .NET `Environment.GetCommandLineArgs` method. Alternatively, you can write an entry-point function that takes a string array as an argument and mark it using the `EntryPoint` attribute. The first element of the array is the name of the running executable, so to read the first argument, we can write `args.[1]`.

In this section, we added a simple console-based output for our data processing application. Now it's time to implement the GUI using the Windows Forms library and then draw the pie chart using classes from the `System.Drawing` namespace. Thanks to our earlier experiments and the use of F# Interactive during the development, we already know that a significant part of our code works correctly. If we were to write the whole application from scratch, we'd quite possibly already have several minor, but hard-to-find, bugs in the code. Of course, in a later phase of the development process, we should turn these interactive experiments into unit tests. We'll talk about this topic in chapter 11.

4.4   *Creating a Windows Forms application*

Windows Forms is a standard library for developing GUI applications for Windows and is nicely integrated with functionality from the `System.Drawing` namespace. These two libraries allow us, among other things, to draw graphics and display them on the screen. The .NET ecosystem is quite rich, so we could use other technologies as well. We can use Windows Presentation Foundation (WPF), which is part of .NET 3.0, for creating visually attractive UIs that use animations, rich graphics, or even 3D visualizations.

4.4.1   *Creating the user interface*

For this chapter we're using Windows Forms, which is in many ways simpler, but using other technologies from F# shouldn't be a problem for you. The UI in Windows Forms is constructed using components (like `Form`, `Button`, or `PictureBox`), so we're going to start by writing code that builds the UI controls. This task can be simplified by using a graphical designer, but our application is quite simple, so we'll write the code by hand. In some UI frameworks (including WPF), the structure of controls can be described in an XML-based file, but in Windows Forms, we're going to construct the appropriate classes and configure them by specifying their properties.

Before we can start, we need to configure the project in Visual Studio. By default, the F# project doesn't contain references to the required .NET assemblies, so we need to add references to `System.Windows.Forms` and `System.Drawing`. We can do this using the Add Reference option in Solution Explorer. Also, we don't want to display the console window when the application starts. You can open the project properties and select the Windows Application option from the Output Type drop-down list.

After configuring the project, we can write the first part of the application, as shown in listing 4.6.

Listing 4.6   Building the user interface (F#)

```
open System
open System.Drawing
open System.Windows.Forms

let mainForm = new Form(Width = 620, Height = 450, Text = "Pie Chart")   ❶

let menu = new ToolStrip()
let btnOpen = new ToolStripButton("Open")
let btnSave = new ToolStripButton("Save", Enabled = false)
ignore(menu.Items.Add(btnOpen))
ignore(menu.Items.Add(btnSave))

let boxChart =
  new PictureBox
     (BackColor = Color.White, Dock = DockStyle.Fill,
      SizeMode = PictureBoxSizeMode.CenterImage)

mainForm.Controls.Add(menu)
mainForm.Controls.Add(boxChart)

// TODO: Drawing of the chart & user interface interactions

[<STAThread>]      ❷
do
  Application.Run(mainForm)
```

Constructs application menu

Constructs control to display pie chart

Starts application with main form

The listing starts by opening .NET namespaces that contain classes used in our program. Next, we start creating the controls that represent the UI. We start with constructing the main window (also called the *form*). We're using an F# syntax that allows us to specify properties of the object directly during the initialization ❶. This makes the code shorter, but also hides side effects in the code. Internally, the code first creates the object using a constructor and then sets the properties of the object specified using this syntax, but we can view it as single operation that creates the object. When creating the form, we're using a parameterless constructor, but it's possible to specify arguments to the constructor too. You can see this later in the code when we create btnSave, whose constructor takes a string as an argument. A similar syntax for creating objects is now available in C# 3.0 as well and has an interesting history on the .NET platform (for more information, see the sidebar "Constructing classes in F#, C# 3.0, and Cω").

When adding the toolbar buttons to the collection of menu items, we call the Add method, which returns an index of the added item. In C#, you can call this method and ignore the return value, but F# is stricter. In functional programming, return values are much more important, so it is usually a mistake to ignore them. For this reason, F# compiler reports a warning when we ignore a return value. Fixing the code is quite easy, we can wrap the call inside a call to the ignore function. The function takes any value as an argument and returns unit (representing no return value) so that the compiler stops complaining.

The listing continues by constructing the menu and `PictureBox` control, which we'll use for showing the pie chart. We're not using F# Interactive this time, so there's a placeholder in the listing marking the spot where we'll add code for drawing the charts and for connecting the drawing functionality to the UI.

The final part of listing 4.6 is a standard block of code for running Windows Forms applications ❷. It starts with a specification of threading model for COM technology, which is internally used by Windows Forms. This is specified using a standard .NET attribute (`STAThreadAttribute`) so you can find more information about it in the .NET reference. In C# we'd place this attribute before the `Main` method, but in F# the source can contain code to be executed in any place. Since we need to apply this attribute, we're using a `do` block, which groups together the code to be executed when the application starts.

Constructing classes in F#, C# 3.0, and Cω

We already mentioned that some GUI frameworks use XML to specify how the controls should be constructed. This is a common approach, because constructing objects and setting their properties is similar to constructing an XML node and setting its attributes. This similarity was a motivation for researchers working on a language Cω [Meijer, Schulte, and Bierman, 2003] in Microsoft Research in 2003, which later motivated many features that are now present in C# 3.0. In Cω, we could write a code to construct `ToolStripButton` control like this:

```
ToolStripButton btn = <ToolStripButton>
                        <Text>Save</Text>
                        <Enabled>True</Enabled>
                        <Image>{saveIco}</Image>
                      </ToolStripButton>
```

In Cω, the XML syntax was integrated directly in the language. The elements nested in the `ToolStripButton` node specify properties of the object, and the syntax using curly braces allows us to embed usual non-XML expressions in the XML-like code. The ease of constructing objects in this way probably inspired the designers of XAML, which is an XML-based language used in WPF for describing UIs. On the language side, it motivated C# 3.0 feature called *object initializers*:

```
var btn = new ToolStripButton("Save"){ Enabled = false, Image = saveIco };
```

It no longer uses XML-based syntax, but the general idea to construct the object and specify its properties is essentially the same. We can also specify arguments of the constructor using this syntax, because the properties are specified separately in curly braces. Listing 4.6 shows that the same feature is available in F# as well:

```
let btn = new ToolStripButton("Save", Enabled = false, Image = saveIco)
```

The only difference from C# 3.0 is that in F# we specify properties directly in the constructor call. The arguments of the constructor are followed by a set of key-value pairs specifying the properties of the object.

> **(continued)**
> Another way to parameterize construction of a class, but also any ordinary method call, is to use named arguments. The key difference is that names of the parameters are part of the constructor or method declaration. Named parameters can also be used to initialize immutable classes, because they don't rely on setting a property after the class is created. This feature is available in F#, and you can find more information in the F# documentation. In C#, named arguments are being introduced in version 4.0 and the syntax is similar to specification of properties in F#. However, it's important to keep in mind that the meaning is quite different.

So far, we've implemented a skeleton of the application, but it doesn't *do* anything yet—at least, it doesn't do anything with our data. In the next section, we're going to fill in the missing part of the code to draw the chart and display it in the existing `PictureBox` called `boxChart`.

4.4.2 Drawing graphics

The application will draw the pie chart in two steps: it will draw the filled pie and it will add the text labels. This way, we can be sure that the labels are never covered by the pie.

A large part of the code that performs the drawing can be shared by both steps. For each step, we need to iterate over all items in the list to calculate the angle occupied by the segment of the pie chart. The solution to this problem is to write a function that performs the shared operations and takes a drawing function as an argument. The code calls this function twice. The drawing function in the first step fills segments of the pie chart, and the one in the second step draws the text label.

CREATING RANDOM COLOR BRUSHES

Let's start by drawing the pie. We want to fill specified segments of the pie chart using random colors, so first we'll write a simple utility function that creates a randomly colored brush that we can use for filling the region, as shown in listing 4.7.

Listing 4.7   Creating brush with random color (F#)

```
let rnd = new Random()
let randomBrush() =
  let r, g, b = rnd.Next(256), rnd.Next(256), rnd.Next(256)
  new SolidBrush(Color.FromArgb(r,g,b))
```

The code declares two top-level values. The first is an instance of a .NET class `Random`, which is used for generating random numbers. The second is a function `randomBrush`. It has a `unit` type as a parameter, which is an F# way of saying that it doesn't take any meaningful arguments. Thanks to this parameter, we're declaring a function that can be run several times giving a different result. If we omitted it, we'd create a value that would be evaluated only once when the application starts. The only possible unit value is (), so when calling the function later in the code, we're actually giving it `unit` as an argument, even though it looks like a function call with no arguments at all. The `randomBrush` function uses the `rnd` value and generates `SolidBrush` object, which can be used for filling of specified regions. It has side effects and as you already know, we should be careful when using side effects in functional programs.

Hiding the side effects

The function `randomBrush` is an example of a function with side effects. This means that the function may return a different result every time it's called, because it relies on some changing value, other than the function arguments. In this example, the changing value is the value `rnd`, which represents a random number generator and changes its internal state after each call to the `Next` method. Listing 4.7 declares `rnd` as a global value despite the fact that it's used only in the function `randomBrush`. Of course, this is a hint that we should declare it locally to minimize the number of global values. We could try rewriting the code as follows:

```
let randomBrush() =
  let rnd = new Random()
  let r, g, b = rnd.Next(256), rnd.Next(256), rnd.Next(256)
  new SolidBrush(Color.FromArgb(r,g,b))
```

But this code doesn't work! The problem is that we're creating a new `Random` object every time the function is called and the change of the internal state isn't preserved. When created, `Random` initializes the internal state using the current time, but since the drawing is performed quickly the "current time" doesn't change enough and we end up with the whole chart being drawn in the same color.

Not surprisingly, there's a way to write the code without declaring `rnd` as a global value, but that allows us to keep the mutable state represented by it between the function calls. To write this, we need two concepts that will be discussed in chapter 5: a closure and a lambda function. We'll see a similar example showing a frequent pattern for hiding side effects like this one in chapter 8.

Now that you know how to create brushes for filling the chart, we can take a look at the first of the drawing functions.

DRAWING THE PIE CHART SEGMENTS

Listing 4.8 implements a function called `drawPieSegment`. It fills the specified segment of the chart using a random color. This function will be used from a function that performs the drawing in two phases later in the application. The processing function will call it for every segment, and it will get all the information it needs as arguments.

Listing 4.8   Drawing a segment of the pie chart (F#)

```
let drawPieSegment(gr:Graphics, title, startAngle, occupiedAngle) =
  let br = randomBrush()
  gr.FillPie
```

```
  (br, 170, 70, 260, 260,
    startAngle, occupiedAngle)
  br.Dispose()
```

Specifies center
and size of pie

The function parameters are written as one big tuple containing four elements, because this helps to make the code more readable. The first argument of the function is written with a type annotation specifying that its type is `Graphics`. This is a `System.Drawing` class, which contains functionality for drawing. We use its `FillPie` method within the function, but that's all that the compiler can tell about the `gr` value. It can't infer the type from that information, which is why we need the type annotation. The next three tuple elements specify the title text (which isn't used anywhere in the code but will be important for drawing labels), the starting angle of the segment, and the total angle occupied by the segment (in degrees). Note that we also dispose of the brush once the drawing is finished. F# has a nicer way to do this, and we'll talk about it in chapter 9.

Choosing a syntax when writing functions

We've seen two ways for writing functions with multiple arguments so far: we can write the function arguments either as a comma-separated list in parentheses or as a list of values separated by spaces. Note that the first style isn't really special in any way:

```
let add(a, b) = a + b
```

This is a function that takes a tuple as an argument. The expression `(a, b)` is the usual pattern, which we used for deconstructing tuples in chapter 3. The question is which option is better. Unfortunately there isn't an authoritative answer and this is a personal choice. The only important thing is to use the choice consistently.

In this book, we'll usually write function arguments using tuples, especially when writing some more complicated utility functions that work with .NET libraries. This will keep the code consistent with the syntax you use when calling .NET methods. We'll use spaces when writing simple utility functions that deal primarily with F# values.

We'll write parentheses when calling or declaring a function that takes a single argument, so for example we'll write `sin(x)` even though parentheses are optional and we could write `sin x`. This decision follows the way functions are usually written in mathematics and also when calling .NET methods with multiple arguments. We'll get back to this topic in chapters 5 and 6, when we discuss functions in more detail and also look at implementing and using higher-order functions.

The `drawPieSegment` function from the previous listing is one of the two drawing functions that we'll use as an argument to the function `drawStep`, which iterates over all the segments of the pie chart and draws them. Before looking at the code for `drawStep`, let's look at its type. Even though we don't need to write the types in the code, it's useful to see the types of values used in the code.

DRAWING USING FUNCTIONS

The first argument to the drawStep function is one of the two drawing functions, so we'll use a name DrawingFunc for the type of drawing functions for now and define what it is later. Before discussing the remaining arguments, let's look at the signature of the function:

```
drawStep : (DrawingFunc * Graphics * float * (string * int) list) -> unit
```

We're again using the tuple syntax to specify the arguments, so the function takes a single big tuple. The second argument is the Graphics object for drawing, which will be passed to the drawing function. The next two arguments specify the data set used for the drawing—a float value is the sum of all the numeric values, so we can calculate the angle for each segment, and a value of type (string * int) list is our familiar data set from the console version of the application. It stores the labels and values for each item to be plotted.

Let's look at the DrawingFunc type. It should be same as the signature of the drawPieSegment function from listing 4.8. The second drawing function is drawLabel, which we'll see shortly has exactly the same signature. We can look at the signatures and declare the DrawingFunc type to be exactly the same type as the types of these two functions:

```
drawPieSegment : (Graphics * string * int * int) -> unit
drawLabel      : (Graphics * string * int * int) -> unit

type DrawingFunc = (Graphics * string * int * int) -> unit
```

The last line is a type declaration that declares a *type alias*. This means that we're assigning a name to a complicated type that could be written in some other way. We're using the DrawingFunc name only in this explanation, but we could use it, for example, in a type annotation if we wanted to guide the type inference or make the code more readable.

As I mentioned earlier, we don't need to write these types in the code, but it will help us understand what the code does. The most important thing that we already know is that the drawStep function takes a drawing function as a first argument. Listing 4.9 shows the code of the drawStep function.

Listing 4.9   Drawing items using specified drawing function (F#)

```
let drawStep(drawingFunc, gr:Graphics, sum, data) =
  let rec drawStepUtil(data, angleSoFar) =                    ❶
    match data with
    | [] -> ()                          ❷
    | [title, value] ->                           ❸
      let angle = 360 - angleSoFar              <──┐  Calculates angle
      drawingFunc(gr, title, angleSoFar, angle)    │  to add up to 360
    | (title, value)::tail ->                           ❹
      let angle = int(float(value) / sum * 360.0)
      drawingFunc(gr, title, angleSoFar, angle)
      drawStepUtil(tail, angleSoFar + angle)    <──┐  Recursively
  drawStepUtil(data, 0)                          │  draws the rest
                                        <── Runs utility function
```

To make the code more readable, we implement the function that does the actual work as a nested function ❶. It iterates over all items that should be drawn on the chart. The items are stored in a standard F# list, so the code is quite like the familiar list processing pattern. There is one notable difference, because the list is matched against three patterns instead of the usual two cases matching an empty list and a cons cell.

The first branch in the pattern matching ❷ matches an empty list and doesn't do anything. As we've already seen, "doing nothing" is in F# expressed as a unit value, so the code returns a unit value, written as (). This is because F# treats every construct as an expression and expressions always have to return a value. If the branch for the empty list were empty, it wouldn't be a valid expression.

The second branch ❸ is what makes the list processing code unusual. As you can see, the pattern used in this branch is [title, value]. This is a nested pattern composed from a pattern that matches a list containing a single item [it] and a pattern that matches the item with a tuple containing two elements: (title, value). The syntax we're using is shorthand for [(title, value)], but it means the same thing. The first pattern is written using the usual syntax for creating lists, so if you wanted to write a pattern to match lists with three items, you could write [a; b; c]. We included this special case, because we want to correct the rounding error: if we're processing the last item in the list, we want to make sure that the total angle will be exactly 360 degrees. In this branch we simply calculate the angle and call the drawingFunc function, which was passed to us as an argument.

The last branch processes a list that didn't match any of the previous two patterns. The order of the patterns is important in this case, because any list matching the second pattern ❸ would also match the last one ❹ but with an empty list as the tail. The order of the patterns in the code guarantees that the last branch won't be called for the last item.

The code for the last branch calculates the angle and draws the segment using the specified drawing function. This is the only branch that doesn't stop the recursive processing of the list, because it's used until there's a last element in the list, so the last line of the code is a recursive call. The only arguments that change during the recursion are the list of remaining elements to draw and the angleSoFar, which is an angle occupied by all the already processed segments. Thanks to the use of local function, we don't need to pass along the other arguments that don't change. Only one thing is done in the drawStep function itself: it invokes the utility function with all the data and the argument angleSoFar set to 0.

DRAWING THE WHOLE CHART

Before looking at the second drawing function, let's see how to put things together. Figure 4.2 shows each of the layers separately: the code that we've already written draws the left part of the figure; we still need to implement the function to draw the labels shown on the right part.

The code that draws the chart first loads data from a file, then processes it is the same as in the console application. Instead of printing data to the console, we now use

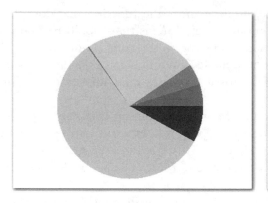
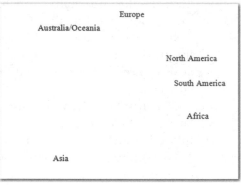

Figure 4.2   Two phases of drawing the chart: the first phase using `drawPieSegment` (left) and the second using the `drawLabel` function (right). The chart shows distribution of the world population in 1900.

the functions described earlier to draw the chart. You can see the function `drawChart` that does the drawing in listing 4.10.

Listing 4.10   Drawing the chart (F#)

```
let drawChart(file) =
  let lines = List.ofSeq(File.ReadAllLines(file))       Loads,
  let data = processLines(lines)                        processes data
  let sum = float(calculateSum(data))

  let pieChart = new Bitmap(600, 400)                   Creates bitmap and
  let gr = Graphics.FromImage(pieChart)                 object for drawing
  gr.Clear(Color.White)
  drawStep(drawPieSegment, gr, sum, data)        ❶
  drawStep(drawLabel, gr, sum, data)        ❷

  gr.Dispose()     ⟵── Finalizes drawing
  pieChart
```

The function takes a name of the CSV file as an argument and returns an in-memory bitmap with the pie chart. In the code, we first load the file and process it using our existing `processLines` and `calculateSum` functions. We then draw the chart, and on the last line we return the created bitmap as a result of the function.

To draw anything at all, we first need to create a `Bitmap` object and then an associated `Graphics` object. We've used `Graphics` for drawing in all the previous functions, so once it's created we can fill the bitmap with a white background and draw the chart using the `drawStep` function. The first call ❶ draws the pie using `drawPieSegment`, and the second call ❷ draws the text labels using `drawLabel`. You can try commenting out one of these two lines to draw only one of the steps and get the same results shown in figure 4.2. We haven't implemented the `drawLabel` function yet, because we wanted to show how the whole drawing works first, but now we're ready to finish this part of the application.

When we specify the first argument (a function for calculating the date) to the map-Schedule function, we get a function of type Schedule -> Schedule. This is exactly what the List.map operation expects as the first argument, so we don't have to write lambda function explicitly. This example shows another reason why many higher-order functions take the original value as the last argument. That way, we can use both pipelining *and* partial application when processing a list of values.

Another option would be to use *sequence expressions* that are similarly succinct, but probably more readable for a newcomer. We'll look at sequence expressions in chapter 12, but now let's see how we could implement the same functionality in C#.

6.3.2 *Processing schedules in C#*

In C# we'll build a MapSchedule method that should be similar to the mapSchedule function in F#. Again, this will have two parameters: a function for calculating the new date and the original schedule. As we're working with alternative values in C#, we'll use a switch block and the Tag property as you saw in chapter 5. Listing 6.9 shows the complete implementation.

Listing 6.9 Map operation for schedule type (C#)

```
public static Schedule MapSchedule
    (this Schedule schedule, Func<DateTime, DateTime> rescheduleFunc) {      ◁─┐
  switch(schedule.Tag) {                                        Uses this     │
    case ScheduleType.Never:                                    modifier    ➊
      return new Never();
    case ScheduleType.Once:                                    ┌ Calculates
      var os = (Once)schedule;                                 │ new date
      return new Once(rescheduleFunc(os.EventDate));     ◁─────┘
    case ScheduleType.Repeatedly:                              ┌ Move the first
      var rs = (Repeatedly)schedule;                          │ occurrence
      DateTime newStart = rescheduleFunc(rs.StartDate);  ◁────┘
      return new Repeatedly(newStart, rs.Interval);
    default:                                             ┌ Unreachable
      throw new InvalidOperationException();        ◁───┘ code!
  }
}
```

The method provides a branch for each of the possible representations and returns a new value in each branch. When the option carries a date that can be processed (Once and Repeatedly), it first casts the argument to the appropriate type, then uses the rescheduleFunc argument to calculate the new date.

The method is implemented as an extension method inside a ScheduleUtils class (for simplicity, the listing doesn't include the class declaration). This means that we can call it as a static method, but also more readably using dot notation on any instance of the Schedule class. The following snippet shows how we can move every schedule in a list by one week:

```
schedules.Select(schedule =>
    schedule.MapSchedule(dt => dt.AddDays(7.0)) )
```

This is similar to our earlier F# code. We're using the LINQ `Select` method (instead of the `List.map` function) to calculate a new schedule for each schedule in the original list. Inside a lambda function, we call `MapSchedule` on the original schedule, passing it an operation that calculates the new date.

When we have several similar operations that we need to perform with the value, it would be tedious to use the schedule type directly, because we'd have to provide the same unwrapping and wrapping code multiple times for each of the operations. In this section, we've seen that a well-designed higher-order function can simplify working with values quite a lot. Now, let's look at writing higher-order functions for another alternative value that we introduced in chapter 5: the `option` type.

6.4   *Working with the option type*

One of the most important alternative values in F# is the `option` type. To recap what we've seen in the previous chapter, it gives us a safe way to represent the fact that value may be missing. This safety means that we can't easily write code that would assume that the value is present and would fail if the `option` type represents a missing value. Instead, we have to use pattern matching and write code for both of the cases. In this section, we'll learn about two useful functions for working with the `option` type.

NOTE   The functions we saw earlier for working with tuples aren't part of the F# library, because they're extremely simple and using tuples explicitly is usually easy enough. However, the functions we'll see in this section for working with the `option` type are part of the standard F# library.

First, let's quickly look at an example that demonstrates why we need higher-order operations for working with the `option` type. We'll use the `readInput` function from the previous chapter, which reads user input from the console and returns a value of type `int option`. When the user enters a valid number, it returns `Some(n)`; otherwise it returns `None`. Listing 6.10 shows how we could implement a function that reads two numbers and returns a sum of them or `None` when either of the inputs wasn't a valid number.

Listing 6.10   Adding two options using pattern matching (F#)

```
let readAndAdd1() =
  match (readInput()) with
  | None    -> None
  | Some(n) ->
    match (readInput()) with
    | None    -> None
    | Some(m) ->
      Some(n + m)
```

The function calls `readInput` to read the first input, extracts the value using pattern matching, and repeats this for the second input. When both of the inputs are correct, it adds them and returns `Some`; in all other branches it returns `None`. Unfortunately, the explicit use of pattern matching makes the code rather long. Let's now look at two operations that will help us rewrite the code more succinctly.

6.4.1 *Using the map function*

We'll work with two operations that are already available in the F# library, so we'll start by looking how we can use them. Later we'll discuss their implementation and how we can use them from C#. As we've already seen, the best way to understand what a function does in F# is often to understand its type signature. Let's look at `Option.map`:

```
> Option.map;;
val it : (('a -> 'b) -> 'a option -> 'b option) = (...)
```

Map operations usually apply a given function to values carried by the data type and wrap the result in the same structure. For the `option` type, this means that when the value is `Some`, the function given as the first argument (`'a -> 'b`) will be applied to a value carried by the second argument (`'a option`). The result of type `'b` will be wrapped inside an `option` type, so the overall result has type `'b option`. When the original `option` type doesn't carry a value, the `map` function will return `None`.

We can use this function instead of the nested match. When reading the second input, we want to "map" the carried value to a new value by adding the first number:

```
match (readInput()) with
| None        -> None
| Some(first) -> readInput() |> Option.map (fun second -> first + second
```

On the third line we already have a value from the first number entered by the user. We then use `readInput()` to read the second option value from the console. Using `Option.map`, we project the value into a new option value, which is then returned as the result. The lambda function used as an argument adds the first value to a number carried by the option value (if there is one).

6.4.2 *Using the bind function*

As a next step, we'd like to eliminate the outer pattern matching. Doing this using `Option.map` isn't possible, because this function always turns input value `None` into output value `None` and input value `Some` into output `Some` carrying another value. In the outer pattern matching, we want to do something quite different. Even when the input value is `Some`, we still may return `None` when we fail to read the second input. This means that the type of the lambda function we specify as an argument shouldn't be `'a -> 'b`, but rather `'a -> 'b option`.

An operation like this is called `bind` in the functional programming terminology, and it's provided by the standard F# library. Let's explore the signature and see what this function does:

```
> Option.bind;;
val it : (('a -> 'b option) -> 'a option -> 'b option) = (...)
```

The difference in the type signature of `bind` and `map` lies only in the type of the function parameter, as we discussed earlier. Understanding a behavior of a function using only the type is a very important skill of functional programmers. In this case, the type gives us a good clue of what the function does if we assume that it behaves reasonably. We can analyze all the cases to infer the specification of the function's behavior:

- When the input value is None, bind can't run the provided function, because it can't safely get the value of type 'a and thus immediately returns None.
- When the input value is Some carrying some value x of type 'a, bind can call the provided function with x as an argument. It could still return None, but a more reasonable behavior is to call the function when possible. There are two different cases depending on what the function given as the argument returns:
  - If the function returns None, the bind operation doesn't have a value of type 'b, so it has to return None as the overall result.
  - If the function returns Some(y), then bind has a value y of type 'b and only in this case can it return Some as the result, so the result is Some(y).

Using bind we can now rewrite the outer pattern matching, because it gives us a way to return an undefined value (None) even when we successfully read the first input. Listing 6.11 shows the final version of readAndAdd.

Listing 6.11   Adding two options using bind and map (F#)

```
let readAndAdd2() =
  readInput() |> Option.bind (fun num ->     ❶
    readInput() |> Option.map ((+) num) )     ❷
```

After reading the first input, we pass it to the bind operation ❶, which executes the given lambda function only when the input contains a value. Inside this lambda function, we read the second input and project it into a result value ❷. The operation used for projection adds the first input to the value. In this listing, we've written the operation using the plus operator and partial application instead of specifying the lambda function explicitly. If you compare the code with listing 6.10, you can see that it's definitely more concise. Let's now analyze how it works in some more detail.

6.4.3   *Evaluating the example step-by-step*

It can take some time to become confident with higher-order functions like these, especially when they're nested. We're going to examine how the code from the previous listing works by tracing how it runs for a few sample inputs. Moving from the abstract question of "What does this code do in the general case?" to the concrete question of "What does this code do in this particular situation?" can often help clarify matters.

Let's see what happens if we enter an invalid value as the first input. In that case, the first value returned from readInput() will be None. To see what happens, we can use computation by calculation and show how the program evaluates step by step. You can see how the calculation proceeds in listing 6.12.

Listing 6.12 Evaluation when the first input is invalid

Start evaluating the body of the readAndAdd2 function:

```
readInput() |> Option.bind (fun num ->
  readInput() |> Option.map ((+) num) )
```

Read the first input from the user. Then we can replace the readInput() call with the returned value None:

```
None |> Option.bind (fun num ->
  readInput() |> Option.map ((+) num) )
```

Evaluate the Option.bind call. The lambda function isn't called and None is returned as the overall result:

```
None
```

In the first step, we replace the call with the None value that the function returns when we enter some invalid input (such as an empty string). The second step is more interesting. Here, the Option.bind function gets None as its second argument. However, None doesn't carry any number, so bind can't call the specified lambda function; the only thing it can do is immediately return None.

Now, how would the function behave if we entered *20* as the first input? Obviously, there will be two different options: one when the second input is correct and one when it's invalid. Listing 6.13 shows what happens if the second input is *22*.

Listing 6.13 Evaluation when both inputs are valid

Start evaluating the body of the readAndAdd2 function:

```
readInput() |> Option.bind (fun num ->
  readInput() |> Option.map ((+) num) )
```

Read the first input from the user. Then we can replace the readInput() call with the first input. In this case, it carries a value:

```
Some(20) |> Option.bind (fun num ->
  readInput() |> Option.map ((+) num) )
```

Evaluate the Option.bind call. It calls the lambda function and gives it 20 as the argument. In the code, we replace all occurrences of num with the actual value:

```
readInput() |> Option.map ((+) 20)
```

Read the second input from the user. Read the second input value

```
Some(22) |> Option.map ((+) 20)
```

Next, we evaluate the Option.map call. It calls the provided function and wraps the result of the call in the Some discriminated union case:

```
Some( (+) 20 22 )
```
❷

Finally, evaluate the + operator. We calculate 20 + 22 and keep the result wrapped in the Some case:

```
Some(42)
```

The first step is similar to the previous case, but this time, we call `Option.bind` with `Some(20)` as an argument. This option value carries a number that can be passed as the `num` argument to the lambda function we provided. `Option.bind` returns the result that it gets from this function, so the result in the next step will be the body of this function ❶. We also replace all occurrences of `num` with the actual value, which is 20.

We then read the next input value with `readInput()`, which returns `Some(22)`. Having replaced `readInput()` with `Some(22)`, we can evaluate the `Option.map` function. This operation evaluates the function it gets as an argument and in addition wraps the result in the `Some` discriminator. So our next step ❷ shows that we need to calculate the addition next and wrap the result in `Some`. After calculating the addition, we finally get the result: `Some(42)`.

After following this step-by-step explanation, you should have pretty good idea how `Option.bind` and `Option.map` work. Equipped with this information, we can look at the implementation of these two operations in both F# and C#.

6.4.4   *Implementing operations for the option type*

The implementations of both `bind` and `map` have a similar structure, because they're both higher-order functions that pattern-match against an option value. We'll take a look at both F# and C# implementations, which are good examples of encoding functional ideas in C#. Let's start with listing 6.14, which shows the implementation of the `map` operation.

Listing 6.14   Implementing the `map` operation in F# and C#

F# Interactive	C#

```fsharp
> let map f input =
    match input with
    | None -> None
    | Some(value) ->
        Some(f(value));;
val map :
  ('a -> 'b) ->
  'a option -> 'b option
```

```csharp
Option<R> Map<T, R>(this Option<T>
        input, Func<T, R> f) {
    T v;
    if (input.MatchSome(out v))
        return Option.Some(f(v));
    else
        return Option.None<R>();
}
```

The implementation first examines the option value given as an argument. When the value is `None`, it immediately returns `None` as the result. Note that we can't return the `None` value that we got as an argument, because the types may be different. In the C# version this is more obvious. The type of the result is `Option<R>`, but the type of the argument is `Option<T>`.

When the value of the argument matches the discriminated union case `Some`, we get the value of type `T` and use the provided function (or `Func` delegate) to project it into a value of type `R`. Since the value returned from the operation should have a type `Option<R>`, we need to wrap this value using the `Some` constructor again.

The source code of `map` and `bind` operations is quite similar, but there are some important differences. Let's now look at the second couple of operations in listing 6.15.

Listing 6.15 Implementing the `bind` operation in F# and C#

F# Interactive	C#

```
> let bind f input =
    match opt with
    | None -> None
    | Some(value) -> f(value)
  ;;
val bind :
   ('a -> 'b option)
   -> 'a option -> 'b option
```

```
Option<R> Bind<T, R>(this Option<T>
     input, Func<T, Option<R>> f) {
  T value;
  if (input.MatchSome(out value))
    return f(value);
  else
    return Option.None<R>();
}
```

The `bind` operation starts similarly by pattern-matching on the `option` value given as the argument. When the option value is `None`, it immediately returns `None` just like in the previous case. The difference is when the option carries actual value. We again apply the function that we got as an argument, but this time we don't need to wrap the result inside a `Some` constructor. The value returned from the function is already an option, and as you can see from the type signature, it has exactly the type that we want to return. This means that even in the `Some` case, the `bind` operation can still return `None`, depending on the function provided by the user.

As usual, the F# version takes the original value as a last argument to enable pipelining and partial application, while the C# version is an extension method. Let's now look how to rewrite the previous example in C# using the newly created methods.

USING THE OPTION TYPE IN C#

Extension methods give us a way to write the code that uses `Bind` and `Map` in a fluent manner. As the number of parentheses can be confusing, note that the call to `Map` is nested inside a lambda function that we give as an argument to `Bind`:

```
Option<int> ReadAndAdd() {
  return ReadInput().Bind(n =>
    ReadInput().Map(m => m + n));
}
```

In C# the difference between using higher-order functions and working with option types explicitly is even more significant. C# doesn't directly support types like discriminated unions, but if we supply our types with appropriate processing functions, the code becomes readable. This is the important point to keep in mind when writing functional-style programs in C#: some of the low-level constructs may feel unnatural, but thanks to lambda functions, we can write elegant functional code in C# too.

So far, we've seen how to use higher-order functions to work with multiple values and alternative values. The last kind of value we talked about in the previous chapter was the function. In the next section, we'll see that we can write surprisingly useful higher-order functions for working with function values as well.

6.5   *Working with functions*

All the higher-order functions we've discussed so far in this chapter have had a similar structure. They had two parameters: one was a value to be processed and the second was a function that specified how to process the value. When working with functions, the value parameter will be also a function, so our higher-order functions will take two functions as arguments.

6.5.1   *Function composition*

The most important operation for working with functions is composition. Let's start by looking at an example where this will be helpful. We'll use the example where we stored a name and population using a tuple. In listing 6.16 we create a function to determine whether the place is city, town, or village based on the size of the population. We also test it by determining the status of several places stored in a list.

Listing 6.16   Working with city information (F# Interactive)

```
> let places = [ ("Grantchester", 552);
                 ("Cambridge", 117900);              Creates list
                 ("Prague", 1188126); ];;       ◄──  with test data
val places : (string * int) list
                                                     Returns status
                                                     based on population
> let statusByPopulation(population) =     ◄──
    match population with
    | n when n > 1000000 -> "City"
    | n when n >    5000  -> "Town"
    | _                   -> "Village";;
val statusByPopulation : int -> string
                                               ❶ Iterates over places,
                                                 reads population info
> places |> List.map (fun (_, population) ->   ◄──
    statusByPopulation(population));;          ◄──
val it : string list = ["Village"; "Town"; "City"]   ❷ Calculates status
```

The first parts of listing 6.16 (creating a list of test data and the declaration of the statusByPopulation function) are quite straightforward. The interesting bit comes in the last few lines. We want to obtain the status of each place using List.map. To do this we pass it a lambda function as an argument. The lambda function first extracts the second element from the tuple using pattern matching ❶ and then calls our statusByPopulation function ❷.

The code works well but it can be written more elegantly. The key idea is that we have to perform two operations in sequence. We first need to access the second element from a tuple, then perform the calculation using the returned value. Since the first operation can be done using the snd function, we need to compose these two functions. In F#, this can be written using the function composition operator (>>) like this:

```
snd >> statusByPopulation
```

The result of this operation is a function that takes a tuple, reads its second element (which has to be an integer), and calculates the status based on this number. We can understand how the functions are composed by looking at table 6.1, which shows their type signatures.

Function value	Type
snd	('a * 'b) -> 'b
snd (after specification)	('a * int) -> int
statusByPopulation	int -> string
snd >> statusByPopulation	('a * int) -> string

Table 6.1
Type signatures of snd, statusByPopulation, **and a function obtained by composing these two functions using the** >> **operator**

On the second line, the table shows a specific type of the snd function after the compiler figures out that the second element of the tuple has to be an integer. We can get this type if we substitute type parameter 'b from the first row with a type int. Now we have two functions that can be composed, because the return type on the second row is the same as the input type on the third row. Using composition, we join the functions together and get a function that calls the first one and passes the result of this call as an input to the second one. The resulting function has the same input type as the function on the second row and the same return type as the function on the third row. Listing 6.17 shows how we can rewrite the original code using function composition.

> **Listing 6.17   Using the function composition operator (F# Interactive)**

```
> places |> List.map (fun x -> (snd >> statusByPopulation) x);;     ❶
val it : string list = ["Village"; "Town"; "City"]

> places |> List.map (snd >> statusByPopulation);;     ❷
val it : string list = ["Village"; "Town"; "City"]
```

On the first line ❶, we call the composed function explicitly by giving it the tuple containing the city name and population as an argument. This is to demonstrate that a result of composition is a function that can be called using the usual syntax. However, the reason for using function composition is that we can use the composed function as an argument to other functions. In this case, the composed function takes a tuple and returns a string, so we can immediately use it as an argument to List.map to get a list of the statuses of the sample places ❷.

The implementation of the function composition operator is remarkably simple. Here's how we could define it if it didn't already exist in the F# library:

```
> let (>>) f g x = g(f(x))
val (>>) : ('a -> 'b) -> ('b -> 'c) -> 'a -> 'c
```

In this declaration, the operator has three parameters. When we were working with it earlier, we only specified the first two parameters (the functions to be composed). We'll get better insight into how it works by looking at the two possible interpretations of the type signature in figure 6.2.

The operator can be used for composing functions thanks to the partial application. If we specify just the first two arguments, the result is a composed function. When the operator receives the third argument, it uses that argument to call the first

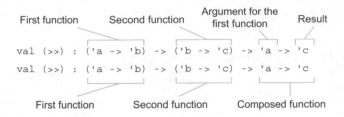

Figure 6.2 Type signature of the function composition operator. If we specify three arguments (annotations above), it returns the result of calling them in sequence. If we specify only two arguments (annotations below), it returns a composed function.

function and then calls the second function using the result. Clearly, specifying all three arguments to it isn't typically very useful—we could just call the functions directly, without using the operator!

Now that we've seen how function composition works in F#, let's look at what it might look like in C#.

6.5.2 Function composition in C#

Function composition in C# is possible, but it has only a very limited use. This is partly because a partial application can't be used as easily in C#, but more importantly because most of operations are written as members instead of functions. We can at least demonstrate the same idea in C#. Listing 6.18 shows an implementation of the Compose method as well as an example of using it.

Listing 6.18 Implementing and using the Compose method (C#)

```
static Func<A, C> Compose<A, B, C>(this Func<A, B> f, Func<B, C> g) {
  return (x) => g(f(x));                          ❶
}

// Using function composition in C#
Func<double, double> square = (n) => n * n;
Func<double, string> formatNum = (n) => n.ToString("E");    ❷

var data = new double[] { 1.1, 2.2, 3.3 };
var sqrs = data.Select(square.Compose(formatNum));          ❸

// Prints: "1.210000E+000"; "4.840000E+000"; "1.089000E+001"
foreach (var s in sqrs) Console.Write(s);
```

Function composition is implemented as an extension method for the Func<T, R> delegate, so we can call it on function values that take a single argument using dot notation. In F# it was written as a function with three parameters, even though it's usually used just with two arguments. In C# we have to implement it as a method with two arguments that returns a Func delegate explicitly. We construct a lambda function that takes an argument and calls functions that we're composing ❶, and return this function as a delegate.

To test the method, we create two functions that we want to compose ❷. We use the composed function when processing numbers in a collection using Select. Instead of specifying an explicit lambda function as the argument, we call Compose to create a composed function value and pass it to the Select method ❸.

Over the last few sections, we've seen that many of the useful processing functions are generic, some of them having even three type parameters. Writing functions like this in F# has been easy because we haven't had to write the types explicitly: type inference has figured out the types automatically. It's time to take a closer look at how this mechanism works.

6.6 Type inference

We have talked about type inference for values. We've seen it in C# 3.0 with the `var` keyword and in F# with `let` bindings. We'll start this section with another aspect that's shared by both C# and F#. When calling a generic method, such as `Option.Some` (listing 5.9) or `Option.Map` (listing 6.13) in C#, we *can* specify the type arguments explicitly like this:

```
var dt = Option.Some<DateTime>(DateTime.Now);
var nt = dt.Map<DateTime, int>(d => d.Year);
```

That's very verbose, and we've almost never written code in this style in the previous examples, because C# performs type inference for generic method calls. This deduces type arguments automatically, so in the previous example we could have written just `dt.Map(d => d.Year)`.

The process of type inference in C# is quite complicated, but it works well and it usually isn't important to understand it at an intimate level. If you really need the details, you can find complete documentation in the C# Language Specification [ECMA 2006] or in *C# in Depth* [Skeet 2008]. Type arguments are inferred from the normal method arguments, with anonymous functions getting special treatment to make the whole process more streamlined. Also note that in C# 3.0, the order of parameters doesn't matter.

6.6.1 Type inference for function calls in F#

Even though it's possible to specify type arguments in F# using angle brackets in the same way as in C#, this approach is used only rarely. The reason is that when the compiler can't infer all the information and needs some aid from the programmer, we can add type annotation to the particular location where more information is needed. Let's demonstrate this using an example:

```
> Option.map (fun dt -> dt.Year) (Some(DateTime.Now));;
error FS0072: Lookup on object of indeterminate type.

> Option.map (fun (dt:DateTime) -> dt.Year) (Some(DateTime.Now));;
val it : int option = Some(2008)
```

Unlike in C#, the order of arguments matters in F#, so the first case fails. The reason is that the F# compiler doesn't know that the value `dt` is of type `DateTime` until it reaches the second argument, and so it doesn't know whether the `Year` property exists when processing the first argument. To correct this, we added a type annotation in the second case, which specifies the type of the `dt` value explicitly. This is one more interesting aspect of the pipelining operator: if we use pipelining to write the previous code snippet, we don't need type annotations:

```
> Some(DateTime.Now) |> Option.map (fun dt -> dt.Year);;
val it : int option = Some(2008)
```

This works because the `option` value, which contains the `DateTime` value, appears earlier so it's processed before the lambda function. When processing the lambda function, the compiler already knows that the type of `dt` has to be `DateTime`, so it can find the `Year` property with no trouble.

So far, we've looked at the similarities between C# and F#, but type inference goes further in F#. Let's see how the F# compiler can help us when we write higher-order functions.

6.6.2 *Automatic generalization*

We've implemented several higher-order functions in F# in this chapter and we've seen a few side-by-side implementations in F# and C# as well. The interesting fact about the F# implementations is that we didn't need to specify the types at all. This is thanks to *automatic generalization*, which is used when inferring the type of a function declaration. We'll explain how this process works using an implementation of the `Option.bind` function as an example:

```
let bind func value =          ❶
  match value with             ❷
  | None    -> None            ❸
  | Some(a) -> func(a)         ❹
```

1 We describe the type inference process for this function step by step. It begins with the most general possible type and adds constraints as it processes the code, so the listing shows steps that are made while processing the function body.

2 Use the declaration signature ❶ to infer that `bind` is a function with two arguments and assign a new type parameter to each of the arguments and to the return type:

```
func  : 't1
value : 't2
bind  : 't1 -> 't2 -> 't3
```

3 Use the pattern matching ❷ to infer that `value` is an `option` type, because it's matched against `Some` and `None` patterns. Use ❸ to infer that the result of `bind` is also an `option` type, because it can have `None` as a value:

```
func  : 't1
value : option<'t4>
bind  : 't1 -> option<'t4> -> option<'t5>
```

4 Use ❹ to infer that `func` is a function, because we're calling it with a single parameter:

```
func  : ('t6 -> 't7)
value : option<'t4>
bind  : ('t6 -> 't7) -> option<'t4> -> option<'t5>
```

5 From ❹ we know that the parameter to the function has type `'t4` and that the result has the same type as the result of `bind` function, so we add two following constraints:

```
't6 = 't4
't7 = option<'t5>
```

6 Now, we can replace types `'t6` and `'t7` using the constraints obtained in the previous step:

```
func  : ('t4 -> option<'t5>)
value : option<'t4>
bind  : ('t4 -> option<'t5>) -> option<'t4> -> option<'t5>
```

7 We rename the type parameters according to the usual F# standards:

```
bind  : ('a -> option<'b>) -> option<'a> -> option<'b>
```

Even though implementing the F# type inference algorithm using this description would be difficult, it should show you what kind of information F# can use when deducing a type of a higher-order function. Probably the most interesting step in the process was the deduction of the type of a function (`func`) used as a parameter. This is an important step, because functions given as parameters represent operations that can be used on values. As we've seen earlier, these are in some sense similar to methods, but thanks to the type inference, writing code like this in F# doesn't require any additional type specification and still makes the code completely type-safe.

After that short interlude about type inference and automatic generalization, we'll get back to writing and using higher-order functions. We've discussed most of the types from chapter 5, but we're still missing one important functional value. In the next section we'll tackle more familiar territory with a look at higher-order functions for working with lists.

6.7   *Working with lists*

We talked about lists in chapter 3 where we learned how to process lists explicitly using recursion and pattern matching. We also implemented a functional list type in C#. In the sample application in chapter 4, we used lists in this way, but noted that writing list processing explicitly isn't very practical.

This is a recurring pattern of this chapter, so you probably already know what we're going to say next. Instead of using pattern matching explicitly in every case, we can use higher-order functions for working with lists. We've already seen some functions for working with F# lists such as `List.map` and similar methods for working with C# collections (`Select`). In this section, we'll look at these in more detail, examining their type signatures and seeing how they can be implemented.

6.7.1   *Implementing list in F#*

Even though we've been working with functional lists in F# and implemented the same functionality in C#, we haven't explored how we might implement the list type in F#.

When we discussed lists earlier, we saw that a list is represented as either a nil value (for an empty list) or a cons cell containing an element and a reference to the rest of the list.

Now, if we look at our gallery of values from the previous chapter, this is exactly like an alternative value with two options. There's one slight wrinkle: the list type is recursive, which means that a cons cell contains a value of type list itself. Listing 6.19 shows a type definition that creates a similar list type to the one in the F# standard library.

Listing 6.19 Definition of a functional list type (F#)

```
> type List<'T> =          ❶
    | Nil                   ❷
    | Cons of 'T * List<'T>    ❸
type List<'T> = (...)

> let list = Cons(1, Cons(2, Cons(3, Nil)));;    ◁—┐ Creates list
val list : List<'T>                                 │ containing I, 2, 3
```

The type is written as a generic type with a single type parameter ❶. The type parameter represents the type of the values stored in the list. Alternatives in F# are represented using discriminated unions, and this particular union has two discriminators. The first one ❷ represents an empty list, and the second one ❸ is a list with an element (of type 'T) and a reference to the rest of the list, whose type is written recursively as List<'T>.

The last line in the code sample shows how we can create a list with three elements. The first argument to the Cons constructor is always a number, and the second argument is a list, which in turn is constructed using another Cons or the Nil discriminator. The built-in F# list type is declared in exactly this way. Earlier we worked with lists using two primitives. The :: constructor corresponds to Cons in our definition, and [] represents the same value as Nil.

In general, creating a recursive discriminated union type is a common way to represent program data, as we'll see in the next chapter. The list type lies somewhere between simple values and complex program data. It can be interpreted in both ways, depending how it's used in the program. We'll also see how recursive unions can express many of the standard design patterns, but for now let's get back to the higher-order functions that make it easier to work with lists.

6.7.2 *Understanding type signatures of list functions*

As I mentioned earlier, we were already using functions for filtering and projecting lists, but we were using them quite intuitively. In this section, we'll look at their type signature and see how we can deduce what a higher-order function does just using this information.

Of course, you can't tell what a function does by looking at its type in general, but for generic and higher-order functions, such as those for working with lists, this is often possible. As we've seen earlier, functions for working with generic values can't do much with the value alone, because they don't know anything about it. As a result, they usually take a function as an extra argument and use it to work with the value.

The type of the function gives some clues as to how the result will be used. Let's demonstrate this using type signatures displayed in listing 6.20.

Listing 6.20   Types of functions and methods for working with lists (F# and C#)

```
// F# function signatures
List.map    : ('a -> 'b)    -> 'a list -> 'b list
List.filter : ('a -> bool) -> 'a list -> 'a list

// C# method declarations
List<B> Select<A, B> (List<A>, Func<A, B>)
List<A> Where<A>     (List<A>, Func<A, bool>)
```

Let's first look at projection ❶. As you can see, the input parameter is a list of values of type 'a and the result is a list of values of type 'b. The operation doesn't know what 'b is and so it can't create values of this type alone. The only way to create a value of type 'b is to use a function given as an argument that turns a value of type 'a into a value of type 'b. This suggests that the only reasonable way for the operation to work is to iterate over the values in the input list, call the function for each of the values, and return a list of results. Indeed, this is exactly what the projection operation does.

It is worth noting that in this case the types of the input list and output list can differ. In chapter 5 we were adding a number 10 to a list of integers, so the input list had the same type as the output list. We could use a function that created a string from a number as an argument. In this case the input list would be a list of integers and the result will be a list of strings.

The second operation is filtering ❷. Here the input and the resulting lists have the same type. The function given as an argument is a predicate that returns true or false for a value of type 'a, which is the same type as the elements in the input list. This gives us a good hint that the operation probably calls the function for each of the list elements and uses the result to determine whether the element should be copied to the returned list.

WORKING WITH LISTS

Let's look at a larger example showing the use of filtering and projection. Both of them are available in the F# library for various collection types, but we'll use lists as we're already familiar with them. In C#, these methods are available for any collection implementing IEnumerable<T>, so we'll use the generic .NET List<T> class. Listing 6.21 shows initialization of the data that we'll be working with.

Listing 6.21   Data about settlements (C# and F#)

```
// C# version using a simple class
class CityInfo {                                            ❷
  public CityInfo(string name, int population) {
    Name = name; Population = population;
  }
  public string Name { get; private set; }
  public int Population { get; private set; }
}
```

```
var places = new List<CityInfo> { new CityInfo("Seattle", 594210),    ❸
  new CityInfo("Prague", 1188126), new CityInfo("New York", 7180000),
  new CityInfo("Grantchester", 552), new CityInfo("Cambridge", 117900) };
```

```
// F# version using tuples
> let places =                                                          ❶
    [ ("Seattle", 594210); ("Prague", 1188126); ("New York", 7180000);
      ("Grantchester", 552); ("Cambridge", 117900) ];;
val places : (string * int) list
```

In F#, we'll use our usual example—a list with information about cities with name and population ❶. Even though we could convert the F# tuple into the `Tuple` class that we've implemented, we'll use a more typical C# representation this time. We declare a class `CityInfo` ❷ and use it to create a list containing city information ❸.

In C#, we can work with the data using the `Where` and `Select` methods that are available in .NET 3.5. Both are extension methods, so we can call them using the usual dot notation:

```
var names =
  places.Where(city => city.Population > 1000000)
        .Select(city => city.Name);
```

Again, this shows the benefits of using higher-order operations. The lambda functions given as arguments specify what the condition for filtering is (in the first case), or the value to return for each city (in the second case). This is all we have to specify. We don't need to know the underlying structure of the collection, and we're not specifying how the result should be obtained. This is all encapsulated in the higher-order operations.

Let's perform the same operation in F#. We want to filter the data set first, then select only the name of the city. We can do this by calling `List.filter` and using the result as the last argument to the `List.map` function. As you can see, this looks quite ugly and hard to read:

```
let names =
  List.map fst
          (List.filter (fun (_, pop) -> 1000000 < pop) places)
```

Of course, F# can do better than this. The previous C# version was elegant because we could write the operations in the same order in which they're performed (filtering first, projection second), and we could write each of them on a single line. In F#, we can get the same code layout using pipelining:

```
let names =
  places |> List.filter (fun (_, pop) -> 1000000 < pop)
         |> List.map fst
```

In this case, the pipelining operator first passes the value on the left side (`places`) to the filtering function on the right side. In the next step, the result of the first operation is passed to the next operation (here projection). Even though we've been using this operator for quite some time, this example finally shows why it is called "pipelining." The data elements are processed in sequence as they go through the "pipe," and the pipe is created by linking several operations using the pipelining operator.

Note that sometimes the order of operations is important and sometimes not. In this case we have to perform the filtering first. If we did the projection in the first step, we'd obtain a list containing only city names and we wouldn't have the information about population, which is needed to perform the filtering.

When writing list processing in F#, you can combine pipelining with other functional techniques such as partial function application and function composition. Let's briefly look at the next step that we could make when writing the processing code:

```
let names =
  places |> List.filter (snd >> ((<) 1000000))
         |> List.map fst
```

Instead of specifying the filtering function explicitly using a lambda expression, we're building it using function composition. The first function is `snd`, which returns the second element of a tuple. In our case, this is the number representing population. The second function used in the composition is a partially applied operator. We're specifying only the first argument, so we'll get a function that returns `true` when the second argument is larger than the given number.

TIP When writing code (not only in the functional style), you should always consider how difficult it will be to understand the code when you'll need to modify it later. In the previous example, the version written using function composition isn't particularly shorter and it doesn't look more elegant. In fact, we think it's less readable than the version written using an explicit lambda function, so in this case we'd prefer using lambda notation. There are many situations where function composition can significantly simplify the code. Unfortunately, there's no simple rule to follow. The best advice we can give you is to use common sense and imagine someone else trying to understand the code.

Processing collections of data is a task we do often, so programming language designers try to make it as easy as possible. Both C# and F# now provide an easier way that lets you solve the same task we just implemented using higher-order functions. Understanding how higher-order functions work is essential, because you can use them for working with any data structures, not just lists.

C# 3.0 queries and F# sequence expressions

You've probably seen examples of data queries written in C# using *query expressions*. Using this feature, our previous code would look like this:

```
var names = from p in places
            where 1000000 < p.Population
            select p.Name
```

This is often demonstrated as a key new feature, but it wouldn't exist without the underlying machinery, such as lambda functions and higher-order operations. We've focused on using these explicitly, because when you learn to use them explicitly, you can use a similar functional approach for working with any data and not just collections.

(continued)

The simplified syntax is quite useful and a similar feature called *sequence expressions* is available in F# too. We'll talk about this in chapter 12, but just for the curious, here's the same query written in F#:

```
let names =
   seq { for (name, pop) in places do
            if (1000000 < pop) then yield name }
```

It looks almost like ordinary code enclosed in a block and marked with the word seq. This is the intention, because in F#, it's a more general language construct and can be used for working with other values as well. In chapter 12 we'll see how to use it when working with option values, but we'll also see how C# query expressions can sometimes be used for similar purposes.

Having looked at how we can use the two most common list processing functions and seen how useful they are, let's take a deeper look at a third such function and implement it ourselves.

6.7.3   *Implementing list functions*

Instead of showing how to implement the functions for filtering and projection that we've just seen, we'll look at a function that we started creating in chapter 3. Since all list processing functions have a similar structure, you'll probably be able to implement any of the others after looking at the following example.

In chapter 3, we wrote a function that could either sum or multiply all elements in a list. We later realized that it's more useful than it first appeared: we saw that it could be used to find the minimum or maximum elements as well. We hadn't covered generics at that point, so the function worked only with integers. In listing 6.22, we look at a similar function without the type annotations that originally restricted automatic generalization.

Listing 6.22   Generic list aggregation (F# Interactive)

```
> let rec fold f init list =
    match list with
    | [] -> init
    | head::tail ->
      let state = f init head
      fold f state tail
  ;;
val fold : ('a -> 'b -> 'a) -> 'a -> 'b list -> 'a
```
❶ Shows type signature

The implementation is very much like the one in chapter 3. More importantly, we removed type annotations, so the inferred signature is more general ❶. The function now takes a list with values of type 'b, and the value produced by aggregation can have a different type (type parameter 'a). The processing function takes the current aggregation result (of type `'a`) and an element from the list (`'b`) and returns a new aggregated result.

As we'll see very soon, the use of generics makes the aggregation far more useful. It's also available in the F# library. The version that works with the immutable F# list type is located in the `List` module. The following snippet shows our original use from chapter 3, where we multiplied all the elements in a list together:

```
> [ 1 .. 5 ] |> List.fold (*) 1
val it : int = 120
```

As we're working with generic functions, the compiler had to infer the types for the type parameters first. In this case, we're working with a list of integers, so parameter `'b` is int. The result is also an integer, so `'a` is int too. Listing 6.23 shows some other interesting examples using `fold`.

Listing 6.23   Examples of using `fold` (F# Interactive)

```
> places |> List.fold (fun sum (_, pop) -> sum + pop) 0;;         ❶
val it : int = 9080788

> places |> List.fold (fun s (n, _) -> s + n + ", ") "";;         ❷
val it : string =
  "Seattle, Prague, New York, Grantchester, Cambridge, "

> places
    |> List.fold (fun (b,str) (name, _) ->                        ❸
         let n = if b then name.PadRight(20) else name + "\n"
         (not b, str+n)
       ) (true, "")           ◁── Specifies initial tuple value
    |> snd              ❹
    |> printfn "%s";;          ◁── Prints formatted string
Seattle             Prague
New York            Grantchester
Cambridge
```

In all the examples, we're working with our collection of city information, so the type of the list is always the same. This means that the actual type of parameter `'b` is always the (`string * int`) tuple. However, the result of aggregation differs. In the first case ❶, we're just summing population, so the type of the result is int. In the second example ❷, we want to build a string with names of the cities, so we start the aggregation with an empty string. The lambda function used as the first argument appends the name of the currently processed city and a separator.

In the last example ❸ we implement a version with improved formatting—it writes the city names in two columns. This means that the lambda function performs two alternating operations. In the first case, it pads the name with spaces (to fill the first column), and in the second case it adds a newline character (to end the row). This is done using a temporary value of type `bool`, which is initially set to `true`, then inverted in every iteration. The aggregation value contains this alternating temporary value and the resulting string, so at the end, we need to drop the temporary value from the tuple ❹.

IMPLEMENTING FOLD IN C#

An operation with the same behavior as fold is available in the .NET library as well, although it has the name Aggregate. As usual, it's available as an extension method working on any collection type and we can use it in the same way as the F# function. Let's rewrite the last example from listing 6.21 in C# 3.0. In F# we used a tuple to store the state during the aggregation. As you'll recall from previous chapters, we mentioned that C# 3.0 anonymous types can be sometimes used for the same purpose. This is an example of where they're a really good fit:

```
var res =
  places.Aggregate(new { StartOfLine = true, Result = "" },
  (r, pl) => {
    var n = r.StartOfLine ? pl.Name.PadRight(20) : (pl.Name + "\n");
    return new { StartOfLine = !r.StartOfLine, Result = r.Result + n };
  }).Result;
```

In C#, the initial value is specified as the first argument. We create an anonymous type with a flag StartOfLine (used as a temporary value) and the property Result, which stores the concatenated string. The lambda function used as the second argument does the same thing as in our previous F# example, but returns the result again as an anonymous type, with the same structure as the initial value. To make the code more efficient, we could also use the StringBuilder class instead of concatenating strings, but we wanted to show the simplest possible example.

Now that you know how to use the function in C#, we should look to see how it's implemented. In listing 6.24 you can see two implementations. One is a typical functional implementation for the functional list from chapter 3, and the other is an imperative implementation for the generic .NET List type, which is in principle the same as the Aggregate extension method in .NET library.

> **Listing 6.24   Functional and imperative implementation of Fold (C#)**

```
// Functional implementation using 'cons list'
R Fold<T, R>(this FuncList<T> list, Func<R, T, R> func, R init) {    ❶
  if (list.IsEmpty)
    return init;         ❷
  else {
    var state = func(init, list.Head)                    ❸
    return list.Tail.Fold(func, state);
  }
}

// Imperative implementation using 'List<T>'
R Fold<T, R>(this List<T> list, Func<R, T, R> func, R init) {    ❹
  R temp = init;
  foreach(var item in list)
    temp = func(temp, item);         ❺
  return temp;
}
```

Aside from using different type of collection, the signature of both methods ❶ ❹ is the same. It corresponds to the earlier declaration in F#, although we have to write the type parameters explicitly. In both cases, we're using list as the first parameter and the methods are implemented as extensions for the collection type.

In the functional version, we have two branches. The first one processes the empty list case ❷. The second branch recursively processes a cons cell and aggregates the result using the func parameter ❸. The imperative version declares a local mutable value to store the current result during the aggregation. The aggregated value is calculated by iterating over all the elements and updating the value in each iteration ❺.

As we've mentioned, implementing the other operations is quite a similar process. In the functional version of map or filter, you'd return an empty list in ❷ and in the imperative version, you'd use mutable list as a temporary value. The other change would be on lines ❹ and ❺. When performing a projection, we'd just call the given function, while for filtering we'd decide whether to append the current element.

To conclude our discussion of higher-order functions, we'll highlight a few interesting relationships between the functions that we've used for manipulating lists and the functions available for working with option values.

6.8 Common processing language

We've seen a few recurring patterns over the course of this chapter, such as an operation called map that's available for both option values and lists. We also used it when we were working with tuples and implemented the mapFirst and mapSecond functions.

Many different values share a similar set of processing functions, so it makes sense to think about these operations as a common language. However, the name of the operation can vary for different values: similarities in type signatures are often better clues than similarities in names.

6.8.1 Mapping, filtering, and folding

The most common operations in functional programming are map, filter, and fold. We've used them when working with functional lists, but they're supported by all other collection types (we'll talk about some of them in chapters 10 and 12). These operations aren't limited to collections. All of them can also be used when working with the option type.

Listing 6.25 shows signatures of the map, filter, and fold functions for several types. The listing includes the functions Option.filter and Option.fold, which we haven't discussed yet.

Listing 6.25 Signatures of filter and map functions (F#)

```
// map operation
val mapFirst    : ('a -> 'b) -> 'a * 'c   -> 'b * 'c
val List.map    : ('a -> 'b) -> 'a list   -> 'b list
val Option.map  : ('a -> 'b) -> 'a option -> 'b option

// filter operation
val List.filter   : ('a -> bool) -> 'a list   -> 'a list
val Option.filter : ('a -> bool) -> 'a option -> 'a option
```

```
// fold operation
val List.fold    : ('a -> 'b -> 'a) -> 'a -> 'b list   -> 'a
val Option.fold : ('a -> 'b -> 'a) -> 'a -> 'b option -> 'a
```

The map operation can perform the function given as the first argument on any elements that are somehow enclosed in the composed value. For tuples, it's used exactly once; for an option value it can be called never or once; for a list it's called for each element in the list. In this light, an option value can be viewed as a list containing zero or one element.

This also explains what the new Option.filter could do. For an option value with no elements it would return None; for an option with a single value it would test whether it matches the predicate and returns either Some or None depending on the result. This function is used quite rarely, so it isn't part of the core F# library. Using the information from this chapter you should be able to easily implement it yourself. Then you might write code like this to filter option values containing even numbers:

```
> Some(5) |> Option.filter (fun n -> n%2 = 0);;
val it : int option = None
```

If we use the analogy between lists and options, this code filters a list containing one value and the result is an empty list. The next new function in the listing is Option.fold. It takes three parameters: an aggregation function, the initial state, and an option value. When the value is None, it returns the initial state. On the other hand, when the option carries some value, the fold operation uses an aggregation function to combine it with the specified initial value.

This is again similar to the way the fold operation works for lists, so the analogy between lists and options is again quite useful. The analogy can work the other way around as well—we've already seen the bind operation for options, and we can apply the same concept to lists.

6.8.2 *The bind operation for lists*

We've only discussed the bind operation for option values, but as we'll see in chapter 12, it is an extremely important functional operation in general. Listing 6.26 shows the type signature of the bind operation for option values and also what it would look like if we defined it for lists.

Listing 6.26   Signatures of bind operations (F#)

```
Option.bind :  ('a -> 'b option) -> 'a option -> 'b option
List.bind   :  ('a -> 'b list)   -> 'a list   -> 'b list
```

The function List.bind is available in the F# library under a different name, so let's try to figure out what it does using the type signature. The input is a list, and for each element, it can obtain a list with values of some other type. A list of this type is also returned as a result from the bind operation.

In practice, this means that the operation calls the given function for each element and concatenates the lists returned from this function. In the F# library the function is called `List.collect`. A similar operation is also available in LINQ and is very important for one special kind of query. We'll talk about it in more details in chapter 12.

We can use the `List.collect` function to get a list of all files from a given list of directories. Note that a single directory usually contains a list of files. Listing 6.27 shows how we can list all source files for this chapter.

Listing 6.27   Listing files using collect (F# Interactive)

```
> open System.IO;;
> let directories =
    [ "C:\Source\Chapter06\Chapter06_CSharp";
      "C:\Source\Chapter06\Chapter06_FSharp";
      "C:\Source\Chapter06\FunctionalCSharp" ];;
val directories : string list

> directories |> List.collect (fun d ->
    d |> Directory.GetFiles
      |> List.ofSeq                        Gets list of filenames
      |> List.map Path.GetFileName );;     for given directory
val it : string list =
  [ "Chapter06_CSharp.csproj"; "Program.cs"; "Chapter06_FSharp.fsproj";
    "Script.fsx"; "FunctionalCSharp.csproj"; "List.cs";
    "Option.cs"; "Tuple.cs" ]
```

The `collect` operation calls the given lambda function for each of the directory in the input list. The lambda function then gets all files from that directory, converts them from an array into a list, and uses `List.map` to get the filename from the full path. The results are then collected into a single list that's returned as the overall result. You probably won't be surprised to hear that this operation is also available in .NET 3.5, where it's represented by the `SelectMany` method. This is the method used when you specify multiple `from` clauses in a C# 3.0 query expression.

6.9   *Summary*

This chapter, together with chapter 5, covered functional values. As we saw in the previous chapter, values are important for controlling the flow of the program, and they allow us to write code in a functional way—composing it from functions that take values as an argument and return values as the result. In this chapter we've seen a more convenient way for working with values. Instead of directly using the structure of the value, we used a set of higher-order functions that are defined in the F# library. We've seen how they are implemented and also how we can implement similar functionality for our own types.

In particular, we talked about functions that allowed us to perform an operation on the values carried by standard F# types such as tuples and `option` types, and also our type for representing schedules. You learned how to construct a function from two functions using function composition and seen how all these features, together with partial application and the pipelining operator, can be used to write elegant and readable code that works with values.

Finally, we looked at several functions for working with lists and observed similarities between some of the higher-order functions acting on different types. We saw that the map operation is useful for many distinct kinds of values and that the bind operation for an option type looks similar to the collect function for working with lists. We'll talk more about this relationship in chapter 12.

When we began talking about using values in chapter 5, we made a distinction between *local values* and *program data*. In the next chapter, we'll turn our attention to program data, which represent the key information that the program works with. For example, this could be the structure of shapes in a vector graphics editor or the document in a text editor. In this chapter we introduced a convenient way for working with local values, and we'll see that same ideas can be used for working with program data as well. We've already taken a step in this direction when we talked about lists, because many programs represent their data as a list of records.

Designing
data-centric programs

This chapter covers

- Representing and processing documents
- Designing immutable data structures
- Converting between data representations
- Using records and recursive discriminated unions

When designing a functional program, first think about the data that the program works with. Because nontrivial programs use data, this phase is extremely important in application design. When implementing a program in a functional language, we also begin with the data structures that we'll use in the code, then write operations to manipulate the data as the second step.

This is different from object-oriented design, where data is encapsulated in the state of the objects; processing is expressed as methods that are part of the objects and interact with other objects involved in the operation. Most functional programs are data-centric, which means that data is clearly separated from operations. Adding a new operation to work with the data is a matter of writing a single function.

NOTE *Data-centric and behavior-centric programs* Even though most functional programs are data-centric, there are some applications and components where we can't think only about the data, because the primary concern is behavior. In an application that allows batch processing of images using filters, the primary data structure would be a list of filters, and from a functional point of view, a filter is a function.

　　This shows that we have two primary ways of looking at functional code. These approaches are often combined in different parts of a single application, but we'll talk about them separately. In this chapter, we'll look at data-centric programs and in chapter 8 we'll discuss behavior-centric programs.

The primary aim of this chapter is to teach you how to think about application design in a functional way. We'll demonstrate the ideas in the context of an application that works with simple documents containing text, images, and headings. In this chapter, we'll use F# as our primary language. Although we can program in C# in a functional style, designing the whole structure of the application in a functional way would be somewhat inconvenient, because functional data structures rely heavily on data types like discriminated unions. We'll mention several related object-oriented design patterns, and we'll also consider how we'd work with immutable types in C#.

Using data representations

In functional programming, it's common to use multiple data structures to represent the same program data. This means that we design different data structures, then write transformations between the representations. These transformations usually compute additional information about the data.

Different operations can be more easily implemented using different data representations. In this chapter we'll work with two representations of documents. In section 7.2, we'll implement a flat data structure, which is suitable for drawing of the document. In section 7.3 we'll add structured representation, which is more appropriate for storing and processing of the document. This approach also supports sharing work, because operations working on different representations can be developed and maintained to some extent independently by different developers.

We'll start by talking about one more F# type that's important for representing program data, then we'll turn our attention to the example application.

7.1 *Functional data structures*

In functional programming, the data that the program manipulates is always stored in data structures. The difference between data structures and objects is that data structures expose the structure of the data representation they use (as the name suggests). Knowing the structure of the data makes it easier to write code that manipulates it, but as we'll see in chapter 9, F# also gives us a way to encapsulate the structure, just like in

OOP, when we want to export the F# data structures from a library or make it available to C#. As we mentioned when we talked about functional concepts in chapter 2, these data structures are immutable.

We'll look at two of the most common representations of program data in this chapter:

- A list of composed values such as tuples or discriminated unions
- A more general recursive data structure such as a tree

In chapter 4 we used a list of tuples to draw a pie chart, where each tuple contained a title and a value. Using tuples is simple, but impractical for more complicated data. In this section we'll look at the F# *record* type, which is the one remaining core F# data type left to discuss.

7.1.1 Using the F# record type

Records are "labeled tuples." They store multiple different elements in a single value; in addition, each element has a name that can be used to access it. In F#, the names of the elements are *fields*. This is in many ways similar to records or struct constructs from C or to anonymous types in C#. Unlike anonymous types, records have to be declared in advance. Similar to anonymous types, records in their basic form contain only properties to hold data; listing 7.1 shows one such declaration to represent a rectangle.

> **Listing 7.1 Representing a rectangle using a record type (F# Interactive)**

```
> type Rect =
    { Left   : float32
      Top    : float32          Declares fields
      Width  : float32          of record
      Height : float32 };;
type Rect = (...)

> let rc = { Left = 10.0f; Top = 10.0f;              ❶
             Width = 100.0f; Height = 200.0f; };;
val rc : Rect = (...)                                ❷

> rc.Left + rc.Width;;       ⟵── Accesses fields using name
val it : float32 = 110.0f
```

When declaring a record type, we have to specify the types of the fields and their names. In this example, we're using the `float32` type, which corresponds to `float` in C# and the .NET `System.Single` type, because we'll need rectangles of this type later. To create a value of an F# record, we specify values for all its fields in curly braces ❶. Note that we don't have to write the name of the record type: this is inferred automatically using the names of the fields, and as you can see, in our example the compiler correctly inferred that we're creating a value of type `Rect` ❷. This is different compared to how anonymous types in C# work. If the compiler couldn't find any appropriate record type based on the names of the fields, it would report an error.

When working with records we'll need to read their fields, but we'll also need to "change" values of the fields—for example, when moving the rectangle to the right. Since a record is a functional data structure and it's immutable, we'll instead have to create a record with the modified value. Moving a rectangle record to the right could be written like this:

```
let rc2 = { Left = rc.Left + 100.0f; Top = rc.Top;
            Width = rc.Width; Height = rc.Height }
```

Writing all code like this would be awkward, because we'd have to explicitly copy values of all fields stored in the record. In addition, we may eventually need to add a new field to the record declaration, which would break all the existing code. F# lets us express the idea of "copy an existing record with some modifications" in a succinct manner:

```
let rc2 = { rc with Left = rc.Left + 100.0f }
```

Using the with keyword, we can specify a value of the fields that we're going to change and all the remaining fields will be copied automatically. This has the same meaning as the previous code, but it's much more practical.

So far we've seen how to write "primitive" operations on records—but of course we're trying to write code in a functional style, so we really want to be able to manipulate records with functions.

WORKING WITH RECORDS

We'll use the Rect type later in this chapter and we'll need two simple functions to work with rectangles. The first function deflates a rectangle by subtracting the specified width and height from all its borders, and the second one converts our representation to the RectangleF class from the System.Drawing namespace. You can see both in listing 7.2.

Listing 7.2   Functions for working with rectangles (F# Interactive)

```
> open System.Drawing;;
> let deflate(original, wspace, hspace) =
    { Left = original.Left + wspace
      Top = original.Top + hspace                   Creates, returns
      Width = original.Width - (2.0f * wspace)      deflated rectangle
      Height = original.Height - (2.0f * hspace) };;
val deflate : Rect * float32 * float32 -> Rect      ❶

> let toRectangleF(original) =
    RectangleF(original.Left, original.Top,         Returns new instance
          original.Width, original.Height);;        of RectangleF class
val toRectangleF : Rect -> RectangleF               ❷

> { Left = 0.0f; Top = 0.0f;
    Width = 100.0f; Height = 100.0f; };;
val it : Rectangle = (...)

> deflate(it, 20.0f, 10.0f);;                        ❸
val it : Rectangle = { Left = 20.0f;  Top = 10.0f;
                Width = 60.0f; Height = 80.0f;}
```

As you can see from the type signatures (❶, ❷), the F# compiler correctly deduced that the type of the `original` parameter is of type `Rect`. The compiler uses the names of the fields accessed in the function body. If we had two record types and used only fields shared by both of them, we'd have to specify the type explicitly. We could use type annotations and write `(original:Rect)` in the function declaration. As usual when working with F# Interactive, we immediately test the function ❸. We didn't use a `let` binding when creating the value, so later we access it using the automatically created value called `it`.

To summarize, F# records are immutable and can be easily cloned using the `{ x with ... }` construct. If we were designing a functional data structure like this in C#, we'd use classes or occasionally structs, but we'd write them in a special way. In the next section, we'll look how to do that.

7.1.2 *Functional data structures in C#*

We've implemented several functional immutable data types in C# such as `FuncList` or `Tuple`. In C#, we do this by writing a class in a particular way. Most importantly, all its properties have to be immutable. This can be done either by using the `readonly` field or by declaring a property that has a private setter and is set only in the constructor of the class. In listing 7.3, we use the first approach to implement a class similar to the `Rect` type from listing 7.1.

Listing 7.3 Immutable `Rect` type (C#)

```
public sealed class Rect {
  private readonly float left, top, width, height;

  public float Left   { get { return left; } }
  public float Top    { get { return top; } }       Returns value of
  public float Width  { get { return width; } }      read-only property
  public float Height { get { return height; } }

  public Rect(float left, float top, float width, float height) {     Constructs
    this.left = left; this.top = top;                                  rectangle
    this.width = width; this.height = height;
  }

  public Rect WithLeft(float left) {                             ❶
    return new Rect(left, this.Top, this.Width, this.Height);       Creates copy
  }                                                                  of object
  // TODO: WithTop, WithWidth and WithHeight
}
```

The class contains fields marked using the `readonly` modifier that are initialized in the constructor. This is the right way of implementing a truly immutable class or value type in C#. You could also use C# 3.0 automatic properties with private setter. In that case, it's your responsibility to ensure that the properties are set only in the constructor, but it makes the code slightly shorter.

The more interesting part is the `WithLeft` method ❶, which can be used to create a clone of the object with a modified value of the `Left` property. We've omitted similar methods for other properties, because they're all easy to implement. These methods correspond to the `with` keyword that we've seen earlier for F# records. You can see the similarity yourself:

```
let moved = { rc with Left = 10.0f }
var moved = rc.WithLeft(10.0f);
```

The important thing is that we don't have to explicitly read all properties of the `Rect` class and we just mention the property that we want to change. This syntax is actually quite elegant even if we want to modify more than one of the properties:

```
var moved = rc.WithLeft(10.0f).WithTop(10.0f);
```

Just as we've seen in this example, you'll often need to set two related properties at the same time. If this happens frequently, it's more convenient to add a new method that creates a clone and modifies all the related properties. In our example, we'd likely also add methods `WithPosition` and `WithSize`, because they represent common operations. This can also be necessary if each individual change would otherwise create an object in an invalid state but the combined operation represents a valid state transition.

That's all we need to know about F# record types for now. We'll get back to functional data types in .NET in chapter 9. In the next section, we'll start working on a larger sample application, which is the heart of this chapter, and we'll talk about one usual way of representing program data.

7.2   *Flat document representation*

We'll develop an application for viewing documents in this chapter. Let's begin by designing a representation of the document that's suitable for drawing it on the screen. In this representation, the document will be a list of elements with some content (either text or an image) and a specified bounding box in which the content should be drawn. You can see an example of a document with three highlighted elements in figure 7.1.

Let's look at the data structures that represent the document in F#. Listing 7.4 introduces a new discriminated union to represent the two alternative kinds of elements and a new record type for text elements. It uses the `Rect` type we defined earlier.

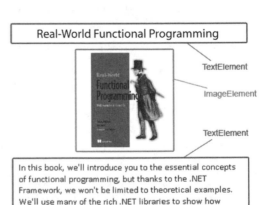

Figure 7.1 **Sample document that consists of three elements; two display text with different fonts and one shows an image.**

Listing 7.4   Flat document representation (F#)

```
open System.Drawing                          Contains
                                             Font class
type TextContent =          ❶
  { Text : string
    Font : Font }

type ScreenElement =                    ❷
  | TextElement  of TextContent * Rect            Stores image
  | ImageElement of string * Rect                 filename
```

In this sample, we're defining two types. First, we define a record type called `TextContent` ❶ that represents text and the font that should be used to draw it. The second type, called `ScreenElement` ❷, is a discriminated union with two alternatives. The first alternative stores text content and the second one contains the filename of an image. Both also have a `Rect` to define the bounding box for drawing. Listing 7.5 shows the code to represent the sample document from figure 7.1 using our new data types.

Listing 7.5   Sample document represented as a list of elements (F#)

```
let fntText = new Font("Calibri", 12.0f)     Create fonts for heading
let fntHead = new Font("Calibri", 15.0f)     and for usual text

let elements =                                       Create a list of
  [ TextElement                                      ScreenElement values
      ({ Text = "Functional Programming for the Real World"
         Font = fntHead },
       { Left = 10.0f; Top = 0.0f; Width = 410.0f; Height = 30.0f });
    ImageElement
      ("cover.jpg",
       { Left = 120.0f; Top = 30.0f; Width = 150.0f; Height = 200.0f });
    TextElement
      ({ Text = "In this book, we'll introduce you to the essential " +
          "concepts of functional programming, but thanks to the .NET " +
          "Framework, we won't be limited to theoretical examples. " +
          "We'll use many of the rich .NET libraries to show how " +
          "functional programming can be used in the real world."
         Font = fntText },
       { Left = 10.0f; Top = 230.0f; Width = 400.0f; Height = 400.0f }) ]
```

First we define fonts for the two different text elements, then we construct a list containing the elements. When creating elements, we create several F# record type values using the syntax discussed earlier. This way of constructing structured documents is a bit impractical, and we'll design a different representation, more suitable for creating documents, in section 7.3. Before that, we'll implement a function to draw a document stored using this representation.

7.2.1   Drawing elements

Just like in chapter 4 when we drew a pie chart, we'll use the standard .NET `System.Drawing` library. The point of this example is to demonstrate that using the previous representation, drawing is extremely simple, so the core function in listing 7.6 has only a few lines of code. It iterates over all elements in a list and contains drawing code for the two different kinds of elements.

Listing 7.6   Drawing document using flat representation (F# Interactive)

```
> let drawElements elements (gr:Graphics) =
    for p in elements do                              ❶
      match p with
      | TextElement(text, boundingBox) ->
        let boxf = toRectangleF(boundingBox)                    Converts Rect to
        gr.DrawString(text.Text, text.Font, Brushes.Black, boxf)   .NET RectangleF
      | ImageElement(imagePath, boundingBox) ->
        let bmp = new Bitmap(imagePath)         <── Loads image
        let wspace, hspace =
          boundingBox.Width / 10.0f, boundingBox.Height / 10.0f
        let rc = toRectangleF(deflate(boundingBox, wspace, hspace))   ❷
        gr.DrawImage(bmp, rc);;
val drawElements : seq<ScreenElement> -> Graphics -> unit
```

The function draws the specified list of elements to the given `Graphics` object. The type of the first parameter is `seq<ScreenElement>`, which represents any collection containing values of type `ScreenElement`. So far we've been working with lists, but you'll see some other collections (such as arrays) in chapters 10 and 12. In the code, we only need to iterate over the elements in the collection using a `for` loop ❶, so the compiler inferred the most general type for us. The type `seq<'a>` corresponds to the generic `IEnumerable<T>`, so in C# the type of the parameter would be `IEnumerable<ScreenElement>`.

The code also uses the functions from the previous section to work with the `Rect` values. We use `toRectangleF` to convert our `Rect` value to the type that the `DrawString` method needs, and `deflate` to add space around the image ❷.

Our drawing function takes the `Graphics` object as an argument, so we need some way of creating one. As a final step, we'll write some code to create a form and draw the document onto it.

7.2.2   *Displaying a drawing on a form*

The drawing will be similar to the example from chapter 4. Because the drawing can take some time, we'll create an in-memory bitmap, draw the document there, then display the bitmap on a form rather than drawing the document every time the form is invalidated. Let's first look at one very useful functional programming pattern that we'll use in this section.

The "Hole in the Middle" pattern

One common situation when writing a code is that you perform some initialization, then the core part of the function, and then some clean-up at the end. When you repeat similar operations in multiple places of the program, the initialization and clean-up don't change and only the core part is different. A sample that draws on an in-memory bitmap written in C# would look like this:

> **(continued)**
> ```
> var bmp = new Bitmap(width, height)
> using(var gr = Graphics.FromImage(bmp)) {
>     (...)
> }
> ```
>
> Here, the core part of the code is the placeholder on the third line of code where we would draw using the `gr` value. The problem is that using only OOP concepts, you can't simply wrap the code that performs the initialization and finalization into a subroutine and share it between all the places that do different drawing. The C# language supports this pattern for some well-known and often used kinds of initialization and cleanup. The `using` construct is exactly this case. How can we achieve similar things for our own code patterns?
>
> In functional programming, the solution is trivial. You can write a higher-order function and wrap the core part into a lambda function and use it as an argument:
>
> ```
> var bmp = DrawImage(width, height, gr => {
>     (...)
> });
> ```
>
> From a functional point of view, this is an uninteresting example of using a higher-order function, but the case where we need to perform some initialization followed by the core part and then clean-up is very common, so it deserves a special name. The name was first used by Brian Hurt in his blog post "The 'Hole in the Middle' Pattern" [Hurt, 2007]. It nicely describes the fact that only the middle part needs to be filled in with a different functionality in every use of the code.

Listing 7.7 shows an F# implementation of a function similar to the `DrawImage` from the sidebar "The "Hole in the Middle" pattern." In addition to the two parameters that specify the size of the created bitmap, it allows us to specify margins from the border of the image.

Listing 7.7   Function for drawing images (F# Interactive)

```
> let drawImage (width:int, height:int) space coreDrawingFunc =
    let bmp = new Bitmap(width, height)
    use gr = Graphics.FromImage(bmp)        ❶
    gr.Clear(Color.White)                              ┐ Shifts all
    gr.TranslateTransform(space, space)    ◄─┘ drawing
    coreDrawingFunc(gr)                          ❷
    bmp
  ;;
val drawImage : int * int -> float32 -> (Graphics -> unit) -> Bitmap        ❸
```

When we use this function to draw an image, the core part of the drawing will be specified in a function given as the last argument. The type signature ❸ shows that the function takes a `Graphics` as an argument and doesn't return a result. It's invoked in the middle of the code ❷ after the bitmap and the `Graphics` object are created. We also call `TranslateTransform` in the initialization phase, to provide padding for the drawing.

The `Graphics` object that we're creating implements `IDisposable`, so we need to dispose it after we finish drawing. In C#, we'd use the well-known `using` construct. In F#, we can do similar things thanks to the `use` keyword ❶. In listing 7.7, it'll automatically dispose of the graphics object before returning the bitmap as a result. The `use` keyword works a bit differently than `using`, and we'll discuss that in chapter 9.

Finally we have everything we need to see our code in action. For now, we'll create and test the form interactively. Listing 7.8 shows how to draw the screen elements from listing 7.5 and display the document on a form.

Listing 7.8   Drawing the document using WinForms (F# Interactive)

```
> let docImage = drawImage (450, 400) 20.0f (drawElements elements)     ❶
val docImg : Bitmap

> open System.Windows.Forms
  let main = new Form(Text = "Document", BackgroundImage = docImage,       Creates
                  Width = docImage.Width, Height = docImage.Height)        form with
  main.Show();;                                                            document
```

The line where we draw the bitmap ❶ may require explanation. We're calling `drawImage`, which takes a function specifying the core part of the drawing as the last argument. Since we've already implemented this in the `drawElements` function, you might expect us to be able to pass it directly as the last argument. However, `drawElements` has two parameters, but `drawImage` expects a function with only one (the `Graphics` object to draw on). We use a partial function application to specify the list with `ScreenElement` values. The result of the partial application is a function that takes a `Graphics` object and draws the document, which is exactly what we need (figure 7.2).

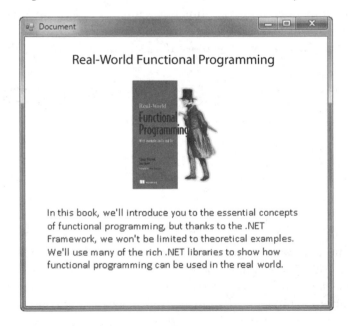

Figure 7.2 Sample document stored as a list of screen elements, drawn using the `drawElements` function on a form.

Our previous representation of the document allowed us to implement drawing easily although the code we had to use to create the document was somewhat awkward. In functional programming, you'll often find that different contexts suggest different data structures: the desired usage determines the ideal representation to some extent. It's not uncommon for a functional program to have different representations for the same information in a single program. Now that we've got a suitable form for drawing, let's design one that's suitable for construction and processing, then write a transformation function to get from one representation to the other.

7.3 *Structured document representation*

The data structure that we'll design in this section is inspired by the HTML format, the familiar and successful language for creating documents. Just like HTML, our representation will have several types of content, and it will be possible to nest some parts in appropriate ways. Figure 7.3 shows an annotated sample document, which should give you an idea of what the format will include.

There are two different kinds of parts. Simple parts like `TextPart` and `ImagePart` contain content, but can't contain nested parts. On the other side, `TitledPart` contains one nested part and adds a title, while `SplitPart` consists of one or more nested parts and specification of an orientation. As you may have guessed, we'll represent the different parts using a discriminated union. Because two of the parts can contain nested parts, the type will be recursive. Listing 7.9 shows the type declaration, giving us something more concrete to discuss in detail.

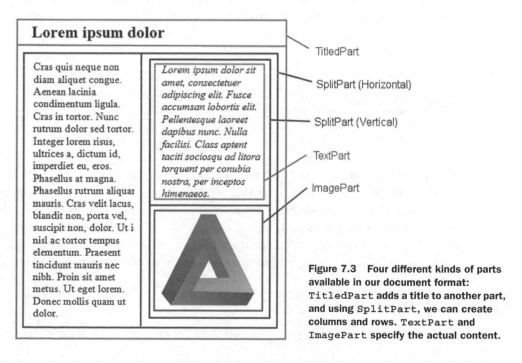

Figure 7.3 Four different kinds of parts available in our document format: `TitledPart` adds a title to another part, and using `SplitPart`, we can create columns and rows. `TextPart` and `ImagePart` specify the actual content.

Listing 7.9   Hierarchical document representation (F#)

```
type Orientation =            ❶
  | Vertical
  | Horizontal

type DocumentPart =                                   ❷
  | SplitPart  of Orientation * list<DocumentPart>
  | TitledPart of TextContent * DocumentPart
  | TextPart   of TextContent
  | ImagePart  of string
```

❷ Contains other parts in columns or rows

Represents part with a title

Stores primitive content

The transcription of our informal specification from the previous paragraph to F# code is very straightforward. This is definitely one of the most attractive aspects of the standard F# type declarations. We first declare a simple discriminated union with two options to represent an orientation for split parts ❶ and then declare the Document-Part type ❷ with four alternative options.

Two of the options recursively contain other document parts. SplitPart contains several other parts in a list and an orientation to determine how the area should be divided; TitledPart consists of a single other part and a title to decorate it with. The text is stored using the TextContent type from the previous section, which is a record containing a string, together with a font.

The DocumentPart type represents the document as a whole. Because the type is recursive, we can nest any number of content parts inside a single document part. This is different from the previous approach, where we created a type for an element and then represented the document as a list of elements. In that representation, the list served as a "root" of the data structure and the elements weren't further nested. Using the new data types, we can write the document from section 7.2 like this:

```
let doc =
  TitledPart({ Text = "Functional Programming for the Real World";
             Font = fntHead },
    SplitPart(Vertical,
      [ ImagePart("cover.jpg");
        TextPart({ Text = "..."; Font = fntText }) ]
    )
  )
```

We omitted the content of the TextPart located below the image, but you can still see that the representation is terser, because we don't need to calculate bounding rectangles ourselves. However, we don't have an implementation of drawing for this data type. We aren't going to write one, either—why would we, when we've already got a perfectly good drawing function for the earlier representation? All we need to do is provide a translation from the "designed for construction" form to the "designed for drawing" one.

7.3.1   Converting representations

Two key differences exist between the data types that we've just implemented:

1 In the new representation, the document is a single (recursive) value, while in the first case it's a list of elements.

2 The data type from section 7.2 explicitly contains the bounding boxes specifying the location of the content.

3 The second data type, which only indicates how the parts are nested.

This means that when we translate the representation, we'll need to calculate each location based on the nesting of the parts.

These differences affect the signature of the translation function looks, so let's analyze that before we study the implementation:

```
val documentToScreen : DocumentPart * Rect -> ScreenElement list
```

The function takes the part of the document to translate as the first argument and returns a list of `ScreenElement` values from section 7.2. This means that both the input argument and the result can represent the whole document. The function has also a second argument, which specifies the bounding rectangle of the whole document. During the translation, we'll need it to calculate positions of the individual parts. Listing 7.10 shows the implementation, which is (not surprisingly) a recursive function.

Listing 7.10 Translation between document representations (F#)

```
let rec documentToScreen(doc, bounds) =
  match doc with
  | SplitPart(Horizontal, parts) ->                              ❶ Calculates size of
    let width = bounds.Width / (float32(parts.Length))              individual parts
    parts
      |> List.mapi (fun i part ->
          let left = bounds.Left + float32(i) * width
          let bounds = { bounds with Left = left; Width = width }  ❷
          documentToScreen(part, bounds))
      |> List.concat                             ❸

  | SplitPart(Vertical, parts) ->                ❹
    let height = bounds.Height / float32(parts.Length)           Calculates
    parts                                                        bounding
      |> List.mapi (fun i part ->                                box of row
          let top = bounds.Top + float32(i) * height
          let bounds  = { bounds with Top = top; Height = height }
          documentToScreen(part, bounds))                      Processes
      |> List.concat                                           element
  | TitledPart(tx, content) ->                   ❺              recursively
    let titleBounds = { bounds with Height = 35.0f }
    let restBounds  = { bounds with Height = bounds.Height - 35.0f;
                                    Top = bounds.Top + 35.0f }
    let convertedBody = documentToScreen(content, restBounds)    Translates
    TextElement(tx, titleBounds)::convertedBody                  body,
                                                                 appends
  | TextPart(tx)  -> [ TextElement(tx, bounds) ]     ❻          title
  | ImagePart(im) -> [ ImageElement(im, bounds) ]
```

Let's start from the end of the code. It's easy to process parts that represent content ❻ because we only return a list containing a single screen element. We can use the rectangle that we've been provided as an argument to indicate the position and size. No further calculation is required.

The remaining parts are composed from other parts. In this case, the function calls itself recursively to process all the subparts that form the larger part. This is where we have to perform layout calculations, because when we call documentTo-Screen again, we give it a subpart and the bounding box for the subpart. We can't copy the bounds parameter, or all the subparts would end up in the same place! Instead we have to divide the rectangle we've been given into smaller rectangles, one for each subpart.

TitledPart ❺ contains a single subpart, so we need to perform one recursive call. Before that, we calculate one bounding box for the title (35 pixels at the top) and one for the body (everything except the top 35 pixels). Next, we process the body recursively and append a TextElement representing the title to the returned list of screen elements.

We process a SplitPart using a separate branch for each of the orientations (❶, ❹). We calculate the size of each column or row and convert all its parts. We use the List.mapi function ❷, which is just like List.map, but it also gives us an index of the part that we're currently processing. We can use the index to calculate the offset of the smaller bounding rectangle from the left or from the top of the main rectangle. The lambda function then calls documentToScreen recursively and returns a list of screen elements for every document part. This means that we get a list of lists as the result of the projection using List.mapi. The type of the result is list<list<ScreenElement>> rather than the flat list we need to return, so we use the standard F# library function List.concat ❸, which turns the result into a value of type list<ScreenElement>.

NOTE   The translation between different representations of the document is the most difficult part of this chapter, so you may want to download the source code and experiment with it to see how it works. The most interesting (and difficult) part is calculating the bounding rectangle for each recursive call. It's worth making sure you understand the list returned by the function and how it's built from each of the deep recursive calls. You may find it useful to work through an example with a pencil and paper, keeping track of the bounding rectangles and the returned screen elements as you go.

Translation between representations is often the key to the simplicity of a functional program, as it allows us to implement each of the other operations using the most appropriate data structure for the situation. We've seen that the first representation is perfect for drawing the document but that the second makes construction simpler. The second form also makes manipulation easier, as we'll see in section 7.4. Before that, we'll introduce one more representation: XML.

7.3.2 *XML document representation*

The XML format is very popular and is a perfect fit for storing hierarchical data such as our document from the previous section. Working with XML is important for many real-world applications, so in this section we'll extend our application to support loading documents from XML files. We'll use the .NET 3.5 *LINQ to XML* API to do most of the hard work—there's no point in writing yet *another* XML parser. LINQ to XML is a good example of how functional concepts are being used in mainstream frameworks: although it isn't a purely functional API (the types are generally mutable), it allows objects to be constructed in a recursive and declarative form. This can make the structure immediately apparent from the code, so it's much easier to read than typical code using the DOM API.

In some sense, this is another translation from one representation of the data into another. In this case the source representation is a structure of LINQ to XML objects, and the target is our document data type from section 7.3.1. The translation is a lot easier this time because both of the data structures are hierarchical. Listing 7.11 demonstrates the XML-based format that we'll use for representing our documents.

Listing 7.11 XML representation of a sample document (XML)

```xml
<titled title="Functional Programming for the Real World"
        font="Cambria" size="18" style="bold">
  <split orientation="vertical">
    <image filename="C:\Writing\Functional\Cover.jpg" />    Stores subparts as
    <text>In this book, we'll introduce you (...)</text>    nested XML elements
  </split>
</titled>
```

Before looking at the core part of the translation, we need to implement some utility functions that parse the attribute values shown in the XML. In particular, we need a function for parsing a font name and the orientation of the `SplitPart`. Listing 7.12 shows these functions and introduces several objects from the LINQ to XML library.

Listing 7.12 Parsing font and orientation using LINQ to XML (F#)

```fsharp
open System.Xml.Linq

let attr(node:XElement, name, defaultValue) =          ❶
  let attr = node.Attribute(XName.Get(name))               Returns default
  if (attr <> null) then attr.Value else defaultValue  ◄─┘  value if missing

let parseOrientation(node) =                           ❷
  match attr(node, "orientation", "") with
  | "horizontal" -> Horizontal
  | "vertical" -> Vertical                               Throws
  | _ -> failwith "Unknown orientation!"  ◄─┘            exception

let parseFont(node) =                                  ❸
  let style = attr(node, "style", "")
  let style =
    match style.Contains("bold"), style.Contains("italic") with
```

```
      | true,  false  -> FontStyle.Bold
      | false, true   -> FontStyle.Italic
      | true,  true   -> FontStyle.Bold ||| FontStyle.Italic    <---|
      | false, false  -> FontStyle.Regular
   let name = attr(node, "font", "Calibri")
   new Font(name, float32(attr(node, "size", "12")), style)
```

Combines two
options of .NET
enumeration

This code will only work with a reference to System.Xml.dll and System.Xml.Linq.dll assemblies. In Visual Studio, you can use the usual Add Reference command from Solution Explorer. In F# Interactive you can use the #r "(...)" directive and specify the path to the assembly as the argument, or just the assembly name if it's in the Global Assembly Cache (GAC).

The listing starts with the attr function ❶ that we use for reading attributes. It takes an XElement (the LINQ to XML type representing an XML element) as the first argument and then the name of the attribute. The final parameter is the default value to use when the attribute is missing. The next function ❷ uses attr to read the value of the orientation attribute of an XML node that's passed into it. If the attribute contains an unexpected value, the function throws an exception using the standard F# function failwith.

parseFont ❸ is used to turn attributes of an XML tag like title in listing 7.11 into a .NET Font object. The most interesting part is the way that we parse the style attribute. It tests whether the attribute value contains two strings ("bold" and "italic") as substrings and then uses pattern matching to specify a style for each of the four possibilities. The function also converts a string representation of the size into a number using the float32 conversion function and creates an instance of the Font.

Now that we have all the utility functions we need, loading the XML document is quite easy. Listing 7.13 shows a recursive function loadPart, which performs the complete translation.

Listing 7.13 Loading document parts from XML (F#)

```
let rec loadPart(node:XElement) =
  match node.Name.LocalName with      ❶
  | "titled" ->
    let tx = { Text = attr(node, "title", ""); Font = parseFont node}
    let body = loadPart(Seq.head(node.Elements()))    <---| Recursively loads
    TitledPart(tx, body)                                    first child element
  | "split" ->
    let orient = parseOrientation node
    let nodes = node.Elements() |> List.ofSeq |> List.map loadPart   <---|
    SplitPart(orient, nodes)                                              Recursively
  | "text"  ->                                                           loads all
    TextPart({Text = node.Value; Font = parseFont node})                 children
  | "image" ->
    ImagePart(attr(node, "filename", ""))
  | name -> failwith("Unknown node: " + name)      ❷
```

The function takes an XML element as an argument, and we'll give it the root element of the XML document when we use it later. Its body is a single match construct ❶ that tests the name of the element against the known options and throws an exception if it encounters an unknown tag ❷.

Loading image and text parts is easy because we only need to read their attributes using our utility functions and create appropriate `DocumentPart` values. The remaining two document part types involve recursion, so they're more interesting.

To create a `TitledPart` from a `titled` element, we first parse the attributes for the title text, then recursively process the first XML element inside the part. To read the first child element, we call the `Elements()` method, which returns all the child elements as a .NET `IEnumerable` collection. `IEnumerable<T>` is abbreviated as `seq<'a>` in F#, and we can work with it using functions from the `Seq` module that are similar to functions for working with lists. In our example, we use `Seq.head`, which returns the first element (the head) of the collection. If we were writing this code in C#, we could call `Elements().First()` to achieve the same effect.

To create a `SplitPart` from a `split` element, we need to parse *all* the children, so again we call the `Elements()` method, but this time we convert the result to a functional list of `XElement` values. We recursively translate each one into a `DocumentPart` value using a projection with the `loadPart` function as an argument.

The function is very straightforward because it provides a few lines of code that parse the XML node for each of the supported tags. A lot of the simplicity is due to the fact that the XML document is hierarchical in the same way as the target representation. This lets us use recursion when a part has nested subparts.

We can finally see how the application displays a larger document: designing the document in an XML editor is easier than creating values in F#. Listing 7.14 shows the final piece of plumbing used to combine all the code that we've developed so far into a normal Windows Forms application.

Listing 7.14 Putting the parts of the application together (F#)

```fsharp
open System.Windows.Forms

[<System.STAThread>]
do
  let doc = loadPart(XDocument.Load(@"..\..\document.xml").Root)
  let bounds = { Left = 0.0f; Top = 0.0f; Width = 520.0f; Height = 630.0f }
  let parts = documentToScreen(doc, bounds)
  let img = drawImage (570, 680) 25.0f (drawElements parts)
  let main = new Form(Text = "Document", BackgroundImage = img,
                      ClientSize = Size(570, 680))
  Application.Run(main)
```

The code starts by loading the document from an XML file using the `XDocument` class. We pass the document's root element to our `loadPart` function, which converts it into the hierarchical document representation. Next, we convert this into the flat representation using `documentToScreen`, then draw and display the document using the code we saw in listing 7.8. We've also added the `STAThread` attribute, which is needed for a standalone Windows Forms application. The final line starts the application with the `Application.Run` method. Figure 7.4 shows the result.

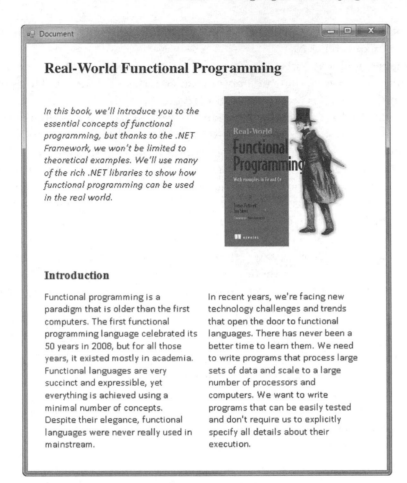

Figure 7.4   Finished application displaying a more complex document with all four kinds of document parts

We mentioned that the hierarchical representation is useful for manipulating the document as well as performing the initial construction. Let's take a look at that now.

7.4   *Writing operations*

There are many kinds of operations that we could perform with a document. We could capitalize all the titles in the document or merge text in multiple columns into a single column. All these operations have something in common, and you may see a similarity between them and the map operation from the previous chapter. Just like mappings, each of these operations examines the document, performs some transformation with certain parts of it, and returns a new document.

Another kind of operation would return only a single value of a different type. We could implement a function to count the words in the document or return all the document text as a single string. This should sound familiar: the fold function from section 6.7.3 does the same job, but working with lists instead of documents.

As you learned in the previous chapter, writing a separate function for each operation would be impractical, and we can get better results if we write a single higher-order function that can be reused for different purposes. We'll start by implementing the function discussed in the first paragraph: the one reminiscent of the map operation.

7.4.1 *Updating using a map operation*

Even though the operation is similar to map, we need to make an important design choice about the implementation. The split part can recursively contain more than one part, so the document structure is a tree. We need to decide in which order we want to process the nodes:

1 Start from the root part and recursively call the map operation on all its nested parts.
2 Start from leafs and process the most deeply nested parts first, then return to parts that contain them.

When processing lists, the order doesn't matter, but for tree structures it's quite important. Imagine that we had a document containing one vertical split part containing two horizontal split parts with text. What would happen if we run the mapping function for merging split parts that contain only text?

- If we start from the root part, we'd call the merging function on the vertical split part. The function wouldn't be able to merge the columns, because each of them contains another split part. Then it would recursively process both of the horizontal split parts. These contain only text parts, so the function would merge them. As a result we'd get document with two rows of text.
- If we start from leafs, we first call the function on the primitive text parts that would remain unchanged. Next it would process both of the horizontal split parts. Each of them contains only text, so the function would merge it. Finally, we'd call it on the root vertical split part, which now contains only two text parts. As a result we'd get only a single text part.

The second behavior is more desirable, because we merged all parts containing only text. For the implementation, it means that we'll first recursively process all subparts of the given part and after that run the processing function specified by the user.

Now that we know how the function should work, let's look at how the user will call it. When thinking about higher-order functions, one of the first aspects to consider is the type. Here's the signature of the function we're going to implement compared with a function for processing lists (we're using DP as an abbreviation for DocumentPart):

```
List.map    : ('a -> 'b) -> list<'a> -> list<'b>
mapDocument : (DP -> DP) -> DP        -> DP
```

There's an interesting difference between these two functions. In lists, the function specified as the first parameter processes a single element of a list. The second parameter and the result are both lists of elements. In documents, we don't distinguish between a single part and the whole document. The processing function specified as the first parameter will usually work with only the root part of the input it gets, and it won't process the nested parts recursively. The `mapDocument` function complements the function for processing a single part with code that recursively traverses the document tree. As a result we'll recursively process the whole document using the function for transforming single document part. See listing 7.15.

Listing 7.15   `map` operation for documents (F#)

```
let rec mapDocument f docPart =
  let processed =                              ⟵──┐ Processes nested
    match docPart with                            │ parts recursively
    | TitledPart(tx, content) ->
      TitledPart(tx, mapDocument f content)    ❶
    | SplitPart(orientation, parts) ->
      let mappedParts = parts |> List.map (mapDocument f)  ❷
      SplitPart(orientation, mappedParts)
    | _ -> docPart                             ⟵──┐ Runs specified
  f(processed)                                     │ function
```

As you recall, the function first recursively processes each subpart of the current part and after that runs the specified processing function. The recursive processing is quite simple. We use pattern matching to handle the two kinds of parts that contain children. For a titled part ❶, we process the body and return a new `TitledPart` with the original title. For a split part ❷, we use `List.map` to obtain a new version of each of the columns or rows, and use the result to construct a new `SplitPart`. Once we have the recursively processed part, we give it as an argument to the specified processing function and return the result.

Now that we have a higher-order function, let's look at how to use it for merging of text elements. This would be useful in an adaptive document layout: on a wide screen we want to view several columns, but on a narrow screen a single column is more readable. Listing 7.16 shows how to shrink a split part containing only text into a single part.

Listing 7.16   Shrinking split part containing text (F#)

```
let isText(part) =                                      │ Tests whether
  match part with | TextPart(_) -> true | _ -> false   │ part is a TextPart

let shrinkDocument part =
  match part with
  | SplitPart(_, parts) when List.forall isText parts ->    ❶
    let res =                                      ┌── Concatenates
      List.fold (fun st (TextPart(tx)) ->    ❷    │ text, returns font
        { Text = st.Text + " " + tx.Text
          Font = tx.Font } )                       ┌── Starts with empty
        { Text = ""; Font = null } parts    ⟵──────┘ string and null font
    TextPart(res)
  | part -> part    ⟵── Ignores other cases

let doc = loadPart(XDocument.Load(@"C:\...\document.xml").Root)
let shrinkedDoc = doc |> mapDocument shrinkDocument
```

In the processing function, we need to check whether the given part is a `SplitPart` containing only text parts. The first condition can be checked directly using pattern matching, and the second one is specified in a `when` clause of the pattern. We write a utility function `isText` that tests whether a part is a `TextPart` and then use it from `List.forall` to test whether all parts fulfill the condition ❶.

Next, we use `fold` to aggregate all the parts in the list into a single part. We already know that each subpart is a `TextPart`, so we can use it directly as a pattern when we write the lambda function to aggregate the result ❷. The compiler can't verify that this is correct, so it gives a warning. You should be always careful when you spot a warning, but in this case we can safely ignore it. In larger projects where you want to eliminate all compiler warnings, you'd probably rewrite the code using the `match` construct and call the `failwith` function in the unreachable branch. The aggregation uses the `TextContent` type as the state and specifies an initial value with no text content and unset font. During every step, we concatenate the existing string with the value in the current part, and use the current font. We don't process fonts in a sophisticated manner, so we'll end up with the font used by the last part.

You can see the final result of this operation in figure 7.5.

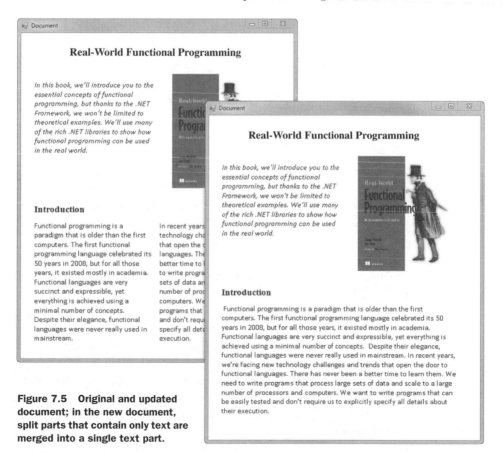

Figure 7.5 Original and updated document; in the new document, split parts that contain only text are merged into a single text part.

We mentioned earlier that this map-like operation is one of several useful operations that we can provide for our documents. In the next section, we'll look at another one, which aggregates the document into a single value.

7.4.2 *Calculating using an aggregate operation*

The idea behind aggregation is that we maintain some state that will be passed around over the course of the operation. We start with an initial state and calculate a new one using the given processing function for each part in the document. This idea is reflected in the signature of the function:

```
val aggregateDocument :
  ('a -> DocumentPart -> 'a) -> 'a -> DocumentPart -> 'a
```

The reason we've used the broad notion of "some state" is that the state can be anything. The type of the state in the function signature is a type parameter `'a`, so it depends on the user of the function. The last two arguments of the function specify a document part to process (which also represents the whole document) and an initial value of the state. The first argument of `aggregateDocument` is a function for processing document parts. It calculates the new state based on the old state and a single document part. Listing 7.17 shows the complete (and perhaps surprisingly brief) implementation.

Listing 7.17   Aggregation of document parts (F#)

```
let rec aggregateDocument f state docPart =
  let state = f state docPart                        ❶
  match docPart with
  | TitledPart(_, part) ->
    aggregateDocument f state part                   ❷
  | SplitPart(_, parts) ->
    List.fold (aggregateDocument f) state parts      ❸
  | _ -> state
```

The code needs to walk over all the parts in the document. It calls the function on the current part and then recursively processes all subparts. The ordering is relevant here: we *could* have designed the function to process all the subparts first and then the current part. The difference is that in listing 7.17, the function is called on the "root" node of the tree, while in the other case it would first be called on the "leaf" nodes. For our purposes, both options would work fine, but for some advanced processing we'd have to consider what kind of traversal we wanted.

When we call the aggregation function with the current part ❶, we use the same name for the value to hold the new state. The new value hides the old one, and in this case that's a useful safety measure: it means we can't accidentally use the old state by mistake after we've computed the new state. Next, we process the parts that can contain subparts. For a titled part, we recursively process the body ❷. When we get a split with a list of subparts, we aggregate it using normal aggregation on lists with the `List.fold` function ❸.

Aggregation can be useful for a variety of things. The following snippet shows how to use this operation for counting a number of words in the whole document:

```
let totalWords =
  aggregateDocument (fun count part ->
    match part with
    | TextPart(tx) | TitledPart(tx, _) ->        Processes both parts
      count + tx.Text.Split(' ').Length            containing text
    | _ -> count) 0 doc
```

The function that we use as an argument only cares about parts that contain text. We have two parts like this, and both contain the text as a value of type `TextContent`. F# pattern matching allows us to handle both cases using only a single pattern. This syntax is called an *or-pattern,* and it can be used only when both patterns bind value to the same identifiers with the same type. In our case, we only need a single identifier (`tx`) of type `TextContent`. In the body for the pattern matching, we split the text into words using a space as the separator and add the length of the returned array to the total count.

NOTE   Here are a few ideas that you'll find solved on the book's website, http://www.functional-programming.net or http://www.manning.com/Real-WorldFunctionalProgramming.

- You can use `mapDocument` to split text parts with more than 500 characters into two columns.
- You can use aggregation to collect a list of images used in the document.
- You can implement a filter-like operation that takes a function of type (`DocumentPart -> bool`) and creates a document containing only parts for which the function returns `true`. Using this function, you can remove all the images from a document.

We've seen that the second representation is convenient for various operations with the document, especially if we implement useful higher-order functions first. Now we'll get back to C#. We'll discuss which of the ideas that we've just seen are applicable to C# programming and also how they relate to well-known concepts in OOP.

7.5   *Object-oriented representations*

Standard design patterns are divided into three groups: creational, structural, and behavioral. In this section we'll look at a few patterns from the last two groups and we'll see that they're similar to some constructs that we used in F# earlier in this chapter. The functional version of the patterns won't be the same as object-oriented, because OOP puts more emphasis on adding new types and FP puts more emphasis on adding new functionality, but the structure will be very similar.

TIP   This section assumes that you know a bit about some of the design patterns. You can find links to introductory articles on the book's website. We don't have space to show all the data structures in C#, but you can find the full implementation online.

We'll start by discussing two structural patterns, and later we'll look at one behavioral.

7.5.1   *Representing data with structural patterns*

If we talk about programs in terms of data structures instead of objects, we can say that structural patterns describe common and proven ways to design data structures. Design patterns are more concrete and specify how to implement these structures in object-oriented languages using objects. In this chapter, we've seen functional ways to represent data. In the first representation we used a simple list of records, which is easy to write in any language, but the second representation (using a discriminated union) is more interesting. The first related pattern that we'll look at is the *composite* pattern.

THE COMPOSITE DESIGN PATTERN

The composite pattern allows us to compose several objects into a single composed object and work with it in the same way as we do with primitive objects. Figure 7.6 shows the usual object-oriented way to implement this pattern.

The composed object is represented by the Composite class. The program then works with objects using the AbstractComponent class, so it doesn't need to understand the difference between primitive and composed objects. You can also see an example of a virtual method, which is called Operation. In the CompositeComponent class, it iterates over all objects from the components collection and invokes the Operation method on them. You can find a similar case in our document representation. When a part is split into multiple columns or rows using SplitPart, we treat it as an ordinary document part in exactly the same way as other parts. The part is composed from other parts that are stored in a list. We can rewrite the general example from figure 7.6 in the same way using the recursive discriminated union type in F#:

```
type AbstractComponent
  | CompositeComponent of list<AbstractComponent>
  | ConcreteComponent of (...)
  | (...)
```

In this example, the composite value is represented as one of the alternatives besides other primitive components. It recursively refers to the AbstractComponent type and stores values of this type in a list representing the composed object. When working

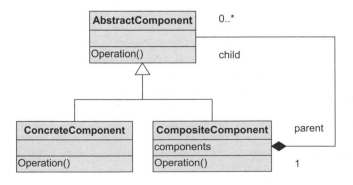

Figure 7.6
CompositeComponent is a class that contains a collection of other components; it inherits from AbstractComponent, so it can be used in place of primitive components in the same way as other components, such as ConcreteComponent.

with values of the `AbstractComponent` type, we don't need to treat composed and primitive values separately, which is the primary aim of this design pattern.

In functional programming the composition is the public aspect of the type. As a result, any user of the type knows there's a component created by composition and can use this fact when writing primitive processing functions, as we did when implementing the `mapDocument` operation.

When using functional data structures, the focus is on the ability to add new functionality to existing types, so making the composition public is a valid design decision. This means that the functional version of the code also doesn't need to define the `Operation` method, which was part of the `AbstractComponent` type in the object-oriented representation. Any operation that uses the type can be implemented independently of the type as a processing function.

F# has an advanced feature called *active patterns* that allows us to encapsulate the composition to some extent. This enables us to publicly expose the composition, but not the whole discriminated union type, which can be useful for evolving F# libraries. We don't discuss details of this feature in the book, but you'll find more information on the book's website.

THE DECORATOR DESIGN PATTERN

Another pattern that's closely related to composite is the *decorator* pattern. The goal of this pattern is to allow us to add a new behavior to an existing class at runtime. As you can see in figure 7.7, the structure looks similar to the composite pattern.

The patterns look similar but their purposes are completely different. While the composite pattern allows us to treat composed values in the same way as primitive values, the purpose of the decorator pattern is to add a new feature to the existing object. As you can see, the `DecoratedComponent` class in figure 7.7 wraps a single other component that's decorated and can carry additional state (such as the `decoration` field). The decorated component can also add behavior that uses the additional state in the `Operation` method.

Again we can see a correspondence between this pattern and one of the parts in our document representation. The part that adds some decoration to another part in our application is `TitledPart`. The decoration is the title, and the added state is the

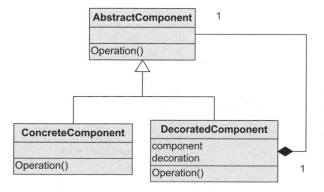

Figure 7.7
The `DecoratedComponent` class wraps a component and adds a new state to it; the `Operation` method in the decorated component calls the wrapped functionality and adds a new behavior that uses the state of the decorated component.

text and font of the title. The F# type that represents the same structure as the one illustrated in figure 7.7 is similarly simple as in case of the composite pattern:

```
type AbstractComponent =
    | DecoratedComponent of AbstractComponent * (...)
    | ConcreteComponent of (...)
    | (...)
```

In this case, the data carried by the decorator alternative is a single decorated component (instead of a list of components in the case of composite) and also the additional state, which can vary between different decorators. We symbolized this using (...) syntax in the previous listing, but this is only pseudo-code. In real F# code you would specify the type of the actual state here, such as `TextContent` in our titled part. Just as with the composite pattern, the code that implements operations on the decorated component is located in the processing functions that we implement for our data structure. The code for the `DecoratedComponent` case in the processing function would call itself recursively to process the wrapped component and execute the behavior added by the decorator, such as drawing a title of the document part.

The F# implementation of both of the patterns in this section relied on using a recursive discriminated union type. In the next section, we'll work with it again, but in a different way. We'll look at the object-oriented way for adding new operations to existing data types.

7.5.2   *Adding functions using the visitor pattern*

Adding new operations to an existing data structure is the primary way of implementing any code that works with data in a functional language. In object-oriented languages, this is more difficult to do, but it's also needed less frequently. In this section we'll talk about the *visitor* pattern that's designed for this purpose, and we'll sketch how we could use it to add operations to our representation of document. Figure 7.8 shows the basic classes that we'll use in this section.

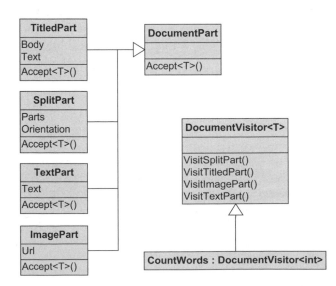

Figure 7.8   A class hierarchy that represents a document and a generic visitor class with state as a generic type parameter (T); all parts support the visitor via the Accept method.

The hierarchy of classes that inherit from an abstract class DocumentPart is a usual way to represent alternatives in OOP, and it corresponds to the discriminated union type that we've used in F#.

The main class of the visitor pattern is a generic DocumentVisitor<T> class. We're using a variant of the pattern that allows working with state, so the type parameter T represents the kind of state we need to maintain, such as arguments or the result of some computation performed by the visitor pattern. The pattern also requires adding a virtual Accept method and implementing it in each of the derived classes. The method takes the visitor pattern as an argument and calls its appropriate Visit method, depending on which part it is. You can find the complete source code at the book's website, but let's look at the code of the Accept method in ImagePart:

```
public override T Accept<T>(DocumentPartVisitor<T> visitor, T state) {
  return visitor.VisitImagePart(this, state);
}
```

The method only delegates the processing to the visitor object. Because it's implemented in every derived class, it can call VisitImagePart, whose argument is a concrete class (in this case ImagePart). This means that when we implement a concrete visitor, we'll have an easy and type-safe way to access properties of the different types that represent the document.

Listing 7.18 shows how we can add an operation that counts words in the document to the object-oriented representation using the visitor pattern.

> **Listing 7.18 Counting words in the document using the visitor pattern (C#)**

```
class CountWords : DocumentPartVisitor<int> {
  public override int VisitTitledPart(TitledPart p, int state) {        ❶ Recursively
    return p.Text.Text.Split(' ').Length +                                counts
        p.Body.Accept(this, state);                                       words of
  }                                                                       body
  public override int VisitSplitPart(SplitPart p, int state) {
    return p.Parts.Aggregate(state, (n, p) =>                            Aggregates
        p.Accept(this, n));                                              count over
  }                                                                      all subparts
  public override int VisitTextPart(TextPart p, int state) {
    return p.Text.Text.Split(' ').Length + state;                       Counts words
  }                                                                    ❷ in each part
  public override int VisitImagePart(ImagePart p, int state) {
    return state;
  }
}
```

This code corresponds to writing a recursive F# function that uses pattern matching to test which of the parts we're currently processing. In an object-oriented way, this choice is done in the Accept methods from the visitor pattern. The CountWords class inherits from the visitor and uses a single int value as the state. Methods that process different types of document parts add the number of words to the current state, and there are two methods (❶, ❷) that have to recursively invoke the visitor on certain subparts. The invocation is done by calling the `Accept` method on the subpart, similar to the code that we need to run the processing on the entire document:

```
int count = doc.Accept(new CountWords(), 0);
```

Here we call the `Accept` method and give it a new instance of the visitor as an argument. If we wanted to add another operation, we'd implement a new class similarly as `CountWords` and execute it by giving it as an argument to the `Accept` method.

7.6   *Summary*

Working with data and designing data structures in a way that matches how we want to *use* the data is an important part of functional program design. In this chapter, we completed our toolset of basic functional data types by looking at the F# record type. We used records, lists, and recursive discriminated unions together to design and implement an application for working with documents.

Functional programs often use multiple representations of data during processing, and our application provided an example of this. One representation (a flat list of elements) allowed us to draw the document simply, whereas another (a hierarchy of parts) proved more useful for constructing and manipulating documents. We implemented a translation between these two representations, so the application could read the document from an XML file, process it in the hierarchical form, and then draw it using the flat form.

We also looked at design patterns that you'd probably use if you wanted to implement the same problem in C#. In particular, you saw that the composite and decorator patterns correspond closely with the alternative values we used in the document data structure. Finally, we discussed a C# way to add a new "function" for processing an existing data structure using the visitor pattern.

This chapter was primarily about data-centric programs, where we design the data structures first. There are also programs primarily concerned with behavior. Of course, in more complex applications these two approaches are combined. In the next chapter, we'll turn our attention to behavior-centric applications.

8

Designing behavior-centric programs

This chapter covers

- Representing behaviors as functions
- Extending program behavior
- Working with functions and closures
- Testing clients using decision trees

In chapter 7, we discussed data-centric applications, and you learned that the first step to designing functional programs is to define the relevant data structures. There are also cases where the data structure contains some form of behavior. One case might be a command that the user can invoke or tasks that the program executes at some point. Instead of hard-coding every behavioral feature, we want to work with them uniformly, so we need to keep them in a data structure that can be easily modified, either before the compilation or at runtime.

An example of a behavior-centric application that we discussed in chapter 7 is one that processes images using graphical filters. The application needs to store the filters and add or remove them depending on what filters you want to apply. When representing this in the program, we could use a list for the actual collection of filters to apply; the harder question is what data structure we should use to represent the filters themselves. Clearly, a filter isn't really *data*, although it may be parameterized in some fashion. Instead, it denotes *behavior*, and the simplest way for representing behavior in a functional language is to use a function.

As you learned in chapter 5, functions can be treated as values, so we can work with them as with any other data types. This means that a list of functions is a perfectly reasonable data structure for representing graphical filters. The difference between behavior-centric and data-centric is more conceptual than technical. Understanding what kind of application you're designing is a helpful hint for creating a proper design. If any of the following is true for your application, you're probably designing behavior-centric application:

- You don't (and can't) know the exact set of required features in advance.
- The user or the programmer should be able to add new behaviors easily.
- The program can be extended using external add-ins.
- The user can create tasks by composing simple features.

The design of functional data-centric applications from the previous chapters relied heavily on functional data types, most importantly discriminated unions. These aren't particularly idiomatic in C#, so we mostly talked about F#. On the other hand, using functions for representing simple behavior is perfectly possible in C# 3.0. Thanks to the Func delegate, which represents a function in C#, most of the examples you'll see in this chapter will be written in both C# and F#.

NOTE In applications of a significant size, both approaches are usually combined. A larger graphical editor that supports vector graphics as well as raster graphical filters might use a data-centric approach for representing shapes and a behavior-centric approach for applying graphical filters to the image. Implementing graphical processing is beyond the scope of this chapter, but you can find a sample application for graphical processing at http://www.functional-programming.net.

In this chapter, we'll use a single example that we'll keep extending to demonstrate the look and feel of behavior-oriented applications. We're going to develop an application for testing the suitability of a client for a loan offer.

8.1   Using collections of behaviors

First, we'll write several conditions for testing whether a bank should offer a loan to the client, and we'll store these conditions in a collection. This way, it's very easy to add new conditions later during the development, because we'd just implement the condition and add it to the collection. One of the key aspects of behavior-oriented programs is the ability to add new behavior easily.

8.1.1   Representing behaviors as objects

We'll start with the C# version, because working with collections of behaviors in a functional way is supported in C# 3.0 to a similar extent as in F#. Before we look at the functional version, it's useful to consider how the same pattern might be written using a purely object-oriented style.

We'd likely start by declaring an interface with a single method to execute the test and return whether or not it failed. In our loan example, a return value of true would indicate that the test suggests the loan offer should be rejected. Later we'd implement the interface in several classes to provide concrete tests. Listing 8.1 shows the interface and a simple implementation.

Listing 8.1   Loan suitability tests using object-oriented style (C#)

```
interface IClientTest {
  bool IsClientRisky(Client client);      ❶            Implements
}                                              ◄────    single test
class TestYearsInJob : IClientTest {
  public bool IsClientRisky(Client client) {
    return client.YearsInJob < 2;         ❷
  }
}
```

When working with tests implemented like this, we'd create a collection containing elements of the interface type ❶ (for example, List<IClientTest>) and then add an instance of each class implementing the interface to this collection. We have to create a separate class for every test, even though the condition itself is a simple compact expression ❷.

8.1.2 *Representing behaviors as functions in C#*

We mentioned earlier that an object-oriented way to understand a function is to think of it as an interface with a single method. If we look at the code from listing 8.1, we can see that IClientTest is declared exactly like this. That means the test can easily be represented as a simple function. In C#, we can write tests using lambda functions:

```
Func<Client, bool> isRiskyYearsInJob =
  client => client.YearsInJob < 2;
```

Instead of using the interface type, we now use a type Func<Client, bool>, which represents a function that takes the Client as an argument and returns a Boolean value. By writing the code in this fashion, we have significantly reduced the amount of boilerplate code around the expression that represents the test.

Just as we could store objects that implement some interface in a collection, we can also create a collection that stores function values, and you'll see how to do this using the List<T> type in listing 8.2. Note that we're creating a completely standard collection of objects—we can iterate over all the functions in the collection or change the collection by adding or removing some of the function values.

When initializing the collection, we can easily write the code to specify the default set of tests in a single method. We can add the tests using the lambda function syntax without the need to declare the functions in advance; we can also use a C# 3.0 feature called *collection initializer* that makes the syntax even more concise.

Listing 8.2   Loan suitability tests using a list of functions (C#)

```
class Client {
  public string Name { get; set; }              ──
  public int Income { get; set; }                 ❶  Stores information
  public int YearsInJob { get; set; }                about client
  public bool UsesCreditCard { get; set; }
  public bool CriminalRecord { get; set; }
}
                                                      Returns list
static List<Func<Client, bool>> GetTests() {  ──      of tests
  return new List<Func<Client, bool>> {
    client => client.CriminalRecord,             ❷  Creates list of tests using
    client => client.Income < 30000,                collection initializer
    client => !client.UsesCreditCard,
    client => client.YearsInJob < 2
  };
}
```

Listing 8.2 uses many of the new C# 3.0 features, and thanks to them it's quite similar to the F# implementation we're about to write. First we declare a class to store information about the client using automatic properties ❶. Next, we implement a method that returns a collection of tests. The body of the method is a single return statement that creates a .NET `List` type and initializes its elements using the collection initializer ❷. This allows you to specify the values when creating a collection in the same way as for arrays. Under the cover, this calls the `Add` method of the collection, but it's clearer.

The values stored in the collection are functions written using the lambda function syntax. Note that we don't have to specify the type of the `client` argument. This is because the C# compiler knows that the argument to the `Add` method is the same as the generic type argument, which in our case is `Func<Client, bool>`.

NOTE   One frequent requirement for behavior-centric programs is the ability to load new behaviors dynamically from a library. For our application that would mean that someone could write a .NET class library with a type containing a `GetTests` method. This would return a list of tests as in the earlier code; our program would call the method to get the tests at execution time, and execute the tests without needing to know anything more about them.

This can be done using the standard .NET classes from the `System.Reflection` namespace. The typical scenario is to load an assembly dynamically, find all appropriate classes inside the assembly, and create their instances at runtime. You can find more information about using reflection on the book's website.

Now that we have a class for representing clients and a collection of tests that advises us whether or not to offer a loan to the client, let's look how we can run the tests.

8.1.3   *Using collections of functions in C#*

When considering a loan for a client, we want to execute all the tests and count the number of tests that returned true (meaning a high risk). If the count is zero or one, the program will recommend the loan. The normal imperative solution would be to declare a variable and enumerate the tests using a `foreach` statement. In the body of the loop, we'd execute the test and increment the variable if it returned `true`. This can be implemented more elegantly using the LINQ extension method `Count` (listing 8.3).

Listing 8.3   Executing tests (C#)

```
void TestClient(List<Func<Client, bool>> tests, Client client) {
  int issuesCount = tests.Count(f => f(client));            ❶
  bool suitable  = issuesCount <= 1;
  Console.WriteLine("Client: {0}\nOffer a loan: {1}",
    client.Name, suitable ? "YES" : "NO");
}

var john = new Client {
    Name = "John Doe", Income = 40000, YearsInJob = 1,
    UsesCreditCard = true, CriminalRecord = false
  };
TestClient(GetTests(), john);
```

❶ **Prints results of testing**

◁─── **Creates client using object initializer**

◁─── **Offer a loan to the client?**

In functional terminology, `Count` is a higher-order function. It takes a predicate as an argument and counts the number of elements for which the predicate returns `true`. We're using it to count how many tests consider the client to be unsuitable for a loan ❶. The element of the collection in our case is a function, so our predicate has to take a function and return a Boolean. The lambda function we wrote executes the function passed as *its* parameter, specifying the client as the argument, and returns the result of the test as the predicate result. Once we count the tests that failed, calculating and printing the result is easy. Describing how it works (even in this relatively simple case) is complicated, but if you think about what you're trying to do with each element, it's not that hard to understand.

We mentioned earlier that the F# version of the example will be essentially the same. This is because all the necessary features such as higher-order functions, lambda functions, and the ability to store functions in a collection are now available in C# 3.0 as well. Let's see what the F# code looks like.

8.1.4   Using lists of functions in F#

First, we'll declare a type to represent information about the client. A client has quite a lot of properties, so the most natural representation will be an F# record type that we've seen in the previous chapter. Listing 8.4 shows the type declaration and code that creates the sample client.

Listing 8.4   Client record type and sample value (F# Interactive)

```
> type Client =
    { Name : string; Income : int; YearsInJob : int
      UsesCreditCard : bool; CriminalRecord : bool };;
type Client = (...)

> let john =
```

```
{ Name = "John Doe"; Income = 40000; YearsInJob = 1
  UsesCreditCard = true; CriminalRecord = false };;
val john : Client
```

There's nothing new here: we're declaring a type and creating an instance of it. To make the listing shorter, we haven't used a separate line for each property, either when declaring the type or when creating the value. This is valid F#, but we have to add semicolons between the properties. In the lightweight syntax, the compiler adds them automatically at the end of the line (when they're needed), but they have to be written explicitly when the line breaks aren't there to help the compiler.

Listing 8.5 completes the example. First it creates a list of tests and then decides whether or not to recommend offering a loan to the sample client (John Doe) from the previous listing.

Listing 8.5   Executing tests (F# Interactive)

```
> let tests =                                    ◁── Creates list of tests
    [ (fun cl -> cl.CriminalRecord = true);
      (fun cl -> cl.Income < 30000);
      (fun cl -> cl.UsesCreditCard = false);
      (fun cl -> cl.YearsInJob < 2) ];;
val tests : (Client -> bool) list          ❶

> let testClient(client) =
    let issues = tests |> List.filter (fun f -> f (client))      ❷
    let suitable = issues.Length <= 1
    printfn "Client: %s\nOffer a loan: %s (issues = %d)" client.Name
            (if (suitable) then "YES" else "NO") issues.Length;;
val testClient : Client -> unit                              Counts issues,
                                                             prints result
> testClient(john);;
Client: John Doe
Offer a loan: YES (issues = 1)
```

This uses the normal syntax for creating lists to initialize the tests which are written using lambda function syntax. We don't have to write any type annotations and F# still infers the type of the list correctly ❶. F# type inference is smart enough to use the names of the accessed members to work out which record type we want to use.

In the C# version, we used the Count method to calculate the number of tests that failed. F# doesn't have an equivalent function; we could either implement it or combine other standard functions to get the same result. We've taken the second approach in this case. First we get a list of tests that considered the client to be unsafe; these are the tests that return true using List.filter ❷. Then we get the number of issues using the Length property.

In this section, you learned how to design and work with basic behavior-oriented data structures—a list of functions—in both C# and F#. In the sidebar "Point-free programming style," we look at an important functional technique that we could use in listing 8.5. In the next section, we'll continue our discussion of common practices as we look at two object-oriented design patterns and related functional constructs.

Point-free programming style

We've seen many examples where we don't have to write the lambda function explicitly when calling a higher-order function, so is this possible in listing 8.5? This way of writing programs is called *point-free*, because we're working with a data structure that contains values (such as a list), but we never assign any name to the value (a particular "point") from that structure. Let's demonstrate this concept using examples that we've seen already:

```
[1 .. 10] |> List.map ((+) 100)
places |> List.map (snd >> statusByPopulation)
```

In the first case, we're working with a collection of numbers, but there's no symbol that would represent values from the list. The second case is similar, except we're working with a list of tuples. Again, there are no symbols that would represent either the tuple or any element of the tuple.

The point-free style is possible thanks to several programming techniques. The first line uses partial function application, which is a way to create a function with the required number of parameters based on a function with larger number of parameters. In our example, we also treat an infix operator (plus) as an ordinary function. The second line uses function composition, which is another important technique for constructing functions without explicitly referencing the values that the functions work with.

Now, let's see how we could rewrite the example from listing 8.5. First, we'll rework the lambda function to use the pipelining operator.

Instead of:

```
(fun f -> f client)
```

We'll write:

```
(fun f -> client |> f)
```

These two functions mean the same thing. We're almost finished, because the pipelining operator takes the client as the first argument and a function as the second argument. If we use partial application to specify just the first argument (client), we'll obtain a function that takes a function (f) as an argument and applies it to the client:

```
tests |> List.filter ((|>) client)
```

Point-free programming style should be always used wisely. Even though it makes the code more succinct and elegant, it's sometimes harder to read and the reasoning that we've demonstrated here isn't trivial. The point-free style is important for some areas of functional programming, and in chapter 15 we'll see how it can be useful when developing a domain-specific language.

8.2   Idioms for working with functions

In the previous chapter, we talked about data structures and related design patterns. We've seen two examples of structural patterns that are related to the problem of designing functional data structures and we've explored a behavioral pattern that describes how objects communicate, which corresponds to how functions call each other in functional terminology.

In this chapter, we're talking about behavior-oriented applications, so it seems natural that the relevant patterns will be behavioral ones. The first one is called the strategy pattern.

8.2.1 The strategy design pattern

The *strategy* pattern is useful if the application needs to choose among several algorithms or parts of an algorithm at runtime. One of the common situations is when several tasks that our application needs to perform differ only in a smaller subtask. Using the strategy pattern, we can write the common part of the task just once and parameterize it by giving it the subtask (primitive operation) as an argument. Figure 8.1 shows an object-oriented representation of the strategy pattern.

The idea of parameterizing a task by giving it a subtask as an argument has probably made it fairly clear what the strategy pattern looks like in functional programming: it's just a higher-order function. The `Strategy` interface in figure 8.1 has a single method, which suggests that it's a simple function; the two classes that implement it are effectively concrete functions that can be created using lambda functions.

In a language that supports functions, we can replace the `Strategy` interface with the appropriate function (a `Func` delegate in C# or a function type in F#). Usually, we pass the strategy directly to the `Operation` method as an argument. Using the abstract names from figure 8.1, we could write

```
Context.Operation(arg => {
  //Implements the specific strategy
});
```

We've already seen a practical example of this pattern when filtering a list. In this case, the function that specifies the predicate is a concrete strategy (and we can use various strategies to write different filters), and the `List.filter` function or the `Where` method is the operation of the context. This means that in a language that supports higher-order functions, you can always replace the strategy pattern with a higher-order function.

Our next pattern is somewhat similar, but more related to our earlier discussion of behavior-centric applications that work with a list of behaviors.

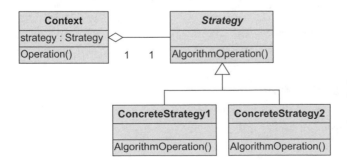

Figure 8.1 `Strategy` is an interface with a method representing the primitive operation. Two concrete strategies implement that operation differently, and the `Context` class can choose between the implementations.

8.2.2 *The command design pattern*

The *command* pattern describes a way to represent actions in an application. As opposed to the previous pattern, which is used to parameterize a known behavior (such as filtering of a list) with a missing piece (predicate), the command pattern is used to store some "unit of work" that can be invoked at a later point. We often see collections of commands that specify steps of a process or operations that the user can choose from. Looking at figure 8.2, you'll recognize an interface that looks like a good candidate for replacement with a single function.

The type that can be easily replaced with a function is the Command interface. Again, it has a single method, which acts as a hint. The classes that implement the interface (such as ConcreteCommand) can be turned into functions, either constructed using the lambda function syntax or, when they are more complex, written as ordinary functions.

We mentioned that the difference between the command and strategy patterns is that the Invoker works with a list of commands and executes them as and when it needs to, very similar to the client loan example. We had a collection of tests for checking the suitability of the client, but instead of declaring the Command interface, our functional version used the Func<Client, bool> delegate in C# and a function type, Client -> bool, in F#. The invoker was the TestClient method, which used the tests to check a client.

NOTE We explained that a Receiver class, shown in figure 8.2, usually represents some state that's changed when the command is invoked. In a typical object-oriented program, this might be a part of the application state. In a graphical editor we could use commands to represent undo history. In that case, the state would be the picture on which the undo steps can be applied.

This isn't the way you'd use the pattern in a functional programming. Instead of modifying state, the command usually returns some result (such as the Boolean value in our client checking example). In functional programming, the Receiver can be a value captured by the lambda function.

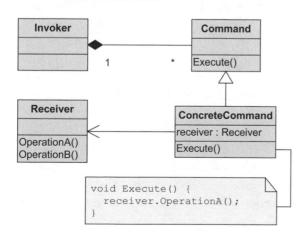

Figure 8.2 Invoker **stores a collection of classes implementing the** Command **interface. When invoked, the** concrete command **uses a** Receiver **object, which usually carries and modifies some state.**

Although mutable state should usually be avoided in functional programming, there's one example where it's useful, even in F#. We'll see that a technique similar to the command pattern can help us to hide the state from the outside world, which is important if we still want to keep most of the program purely functional. First look at a similar idea in C#,then study the usual implementation using lambda functions in F#.

CAPTURING STATE USING THE COMMAND PATTERN IN C#

As we've explained, the command pattern often works with mutable state, encapsulated in something like the `Receiver` class of our example. Listing 8.6 shows an example of this, creating a more flexible income test for our financial application. The goal is to allow the test to be configured later without updating the collection of tests.

Listing 8.6   Income test using the command pattern (C#)

```
class IncomeTest {
  public int MinimalIncome { get; set; }           Corresponds to
  public IncomeTest() {                        ❶ Receiver component
    MinimalIncome = 30000;
  }
  public bool TestIncome(Client client) {
    return client.Income < MinimalIncome;
  }
}

var incomeTest = new IncomeTest();
Func<Client, bool> command =                     Creates ConcreteCommand
  client => incomeTest.TestIncome(client);   ❷ as function

tests.Add(command)     ◁── Registers command with Invoker
```

We start by creating a class that carries the mutable state and corresponds to the `Receiver` component from the command design pattern ❶. The state is a recommended minimal income and the class has a mutable property for modifying it. The next method implements the test itself and compares whether the income of the given client is larger than the current minimal value stored in the test.

The next part of listing 8.6 shows how we can create a new test. First we create an instance of the `IncomeTest` class containing the state, then we create a lambda function that calls its `TestIncome` method ❷. This function corresponds to the `ConcreteCommand` component, and we add it to the collection of tests. We've replaced the abstract `Command` type with a function value, so instead of implementing an interface we're creating a function with appropriate type using lambda function syntax. Listing 8.6 creates the function explicitly with lambda syntax, to demonstrate that it corresponds to the design pattern, but we can write it more concisely:

```
IncomeTest incomeTest = new IncomeTest();
tests.Add(incomeTest.TestIncome);
```

The C# compiler automatically creates a delegate instance that wraps the `TestIncome` method and can be added to the collection if the method has the right signature. Once we add the test to the collection, we can configure the test using the `Minimal-Income` property:

```
TestClient(tests, john);
incomeTest.MinimalIncome = 45000;
TestClient(tests, john);
```

(The result in the first line is yes. The result in the last line is no.)

This is a common pattern that's widely used in imperative OOP. From a functional point of view, it should be used carefully: the code and comments should clearly document what calls can affect the mutable state. In the example, the state is modified using the incomeTest object, and this explains why the same line of code can give different results when called at different times. In the next section, we'll see how to implement similar functionality in a simpler way using F#.

8.2.3 Capturing state using closures in F#

In this section we're going to talk about *closures*, which is an important concept in functional programming. Closures are very common, and most of the time they aren't used with mutable state. Still, working with mutable state is sometimes needed for the sake of pragmatism, and closures give us an excellent way to limit the scope of the mutable state.

First let's look at a simple piece of F# that we saw in chapter 5:

```
> let createAdder num =
    (fun m -> num + m);;
val createAdder : int -> int -> int
```

In our earlier discussion, we didn't see any difference between a function written like this and a function called add taking two parameters and returning their sum. This is because we can call the add function with a single argument: thanks to partial application, the result is a function that adds the specified number to any given argument.

If you carefully analyze what's returned in the previous example, it isn't just the code of the function! The code is a bunch of instructions that add two numbers, but if we call createAdder twice with two different arguments, the returned functions are clearly different because they're adding different numbers. The key idea is that a function isn't just code, but also a *closure* that contains the values that are used by the function but aren't declared inside its body. The values held by the closure are said to be *captured*. In the previous example, the only example of capturing is the num parameter.

Closures may sound complicated, but they're quite simple. The F# compiler uses the abstract class FastFunc<int, int> to represent a function value that takes an integer as an argument and returns an integer as a result. Listing 8.7 shows the generated code for the createAdder function translated to C#.

Listing 8.7 Closure class generated by the F# compiler (C#)

```
class createAdder : FastFunc<int, int> {
  public int num;                           ◁──┐ Stores captured
                                      ❶      │ values
  internal createAdder(int num) {           ──┘
    this.num = num;
  }
}
```

```
    public override int Invoke(int m) {        ◁──┐ Runs constructed
        return this.num + m;                        │ function
    }
}

static FastFunc<int, int> createAdder(int num) {        ❷
    return new createAdder(num);
}
```

The compiler produces a static method `createAdder` ❷ that corresponds to the F#
function. The method constructs a function value that consists of the function code
and stores values captured by the closure. The generated closure class takes captured
values as parameters, so in our example it has a single parameter `num` ❶. When executing the function value using virtual method `Invoke`, the code has access to the values stored in the closure.

   Of course, we've been using closures when creating functions since we started talking about lambda functions. We didn't talk about them explicitly, because usually you
don't need to think about them—they just work. However, what if the closure captures
some value that can be mutated?

MUTABLE STATE USING REFERENCE CELLS

To answer this question, we'll need to be able to create some state to capture. One way
is to use `let mutable`, but that doesn't work in this situation because that kind of
mutable value can be used only locally—it can't be captured by a closure.

   The second way to create mutable values is by using a type called `ref`, which is a
shortcut for a *reference cell*. This is a small object (actually declared as an F# record
type) that contains a mutable value. To understand how the `ref` type works, let's
define the same type in C#. As you can see, it's fairly simple:

```
class Ref<T> {
    public Ref(T value) { Value = value; }
    public T Value { get; set; }
}
```

The important point here is that the `Value` property is mutable, so when we create an
immutable variable of type `Ref<int>`, we can still mutate the value it represents. Listing 8.8 shows an example of using reference cells in F# and shows the corresponding
C# code using the `Ref<T>` type. In F#, we don't access the type directly, because there's
a function—again called `ref`—that creates a reference cell, along with two operators
for setting and reading its value.

   On the first line, we create a reference cell containing an integer. Just like the
`Ref<T>` type we've just declared in C#, the F# `ref` type is generic, so we can use it to

Listing 8.8 Working with reference cells in F# and C#	
F# Interactive	**C#**
`let st = ref 10`	`var st = new Ref<int>(10);`
`st := 11` `printfn "%d" (!st)`	`st.Value = 11;` `Console.WriteLine(st.Value);`

store values of any type. The next two lines demonstrate the operators that work with reference cells: assignment (:=) and dereference (!). The F# operators correspond to setting or reading values of the property but give us a more convenient syntax.

CAPTURING REFERENCE CELLS IN A CLOSURE

Now we can write code that captures mutable state created using a reference cell in a closure. Listing 8.9 shows an F# version of the configurable income test. We create a createIncomeTests function that returns a tuple of two functions: the first changes the minimal required income, the second is the test function itself.

> **Listing 8.9 Configurable income test using closures (F# Interactive)**

```
> let createIncomeTest () =
    let minimalIncome = ref 30000        ❶
    (fun (newMinimal) ->
      minimalIncome := newMinimal),              Sets new
                                                 minimal income
    (fun (client) ->
      client.Income < (!minimalIncome))          Tests client using
                                                 current minimum
  ;;
val createIncomeTest : unit -> (int -> unit) * (Client -> bool)    ❷

> let setMinimalIncome, testIncome = createIncomeTest();;    ❸
val testIncome : (Client -> bool)
val setMinimalIncome : (int -> unit)

> let tests = [ testIncome; (* more tests... *) ];;
val tests : (Client -> bool) list
```

Let's look at the signature of the createIncomeTest function ❷ first. It doesn't take any arguments and returns a tuple of functions as a result. In its body, we first create a mutable reference cell and initialize it to the default minimal income ❶. The tuple of functions to be returned is written using two lambda functions, and both of them use the minimalIncome value. The first function (with the signature int -> unit) takes a new income as an argument and modifies the reference cell. The second one compares the income of the client with the current value stored in the reference cell and has the usual signature of a function used to testing a client (Client -> bool).

When we later call createIncomeTest ❸, we get two functions as a result. We created only one reference cell, which means it is shared by the closures of both functions. We can use setMinimalIncome to change the minimal income required by the testIncome function.

Let's look at the analogy between the F# version and the command pattern with the C# implementation discussed earlier. In F#, the state is automatically captured by the closure while in C# it was encapsulated in an explicitly written class. In some senses, the tuple of functions and the closure correspond to the receiver object from the object-oriented pattern. As we've seen in listing 8.7, the F# compiler handles the closure by generating .NET code that's similar to what we explicitly wrote in C#. The intermediate language (IL) used by .NET doesn't directly support closures, but it has classes for storing state.

Listing 8.10 completes the example, demonstrating how to modify the test using the setMinimalIncome function. The example assumes that the testClient function now uses the collection of tests declared in listing 8.9. To achieve that in F# Interactive, you need to select and evaluate the value binding that declares the tests value, then evaluate the testClient function so that it references the previously evaluated collection.

Listing 8.10   Changing minimal income during testing (F# Interactive)

```
> testClient(john);;
Client: John Doe
Offer a loan: YES (issues = 1)

> setMinimalIncome(45000);;
val it : unit = ()

> testClient(john);;
Client: John Doe
Offer a loan: NO (issues = 2)
```

Just as in the C# version, we first test the client using the initial tests (which the client passes), then modify the income required by one of the tests. After this change, the client no longer fulfills the conditions and the result is negative.

Closures in C#

In the previous section we used C# for writing object-oriented code and F# for writing functional code because we wanted to demonstrate how the concepts relate—how closures are similar to objects and in particular to the Receiver object in the command design pattern.

Closures are essential for lambda functions and the lambda expression syntax in C# 3.0 also supports the creation of closures. This was present in C# 2 in the form of anonymous methods. The following example shows how to create a function that, when called several times, will return a sequence of numbers starting from zero:

```
Func<int> CreateCounter() {
    int num = 0;
    return () => { return num++; };
}
```

The variable num is captured by the closure and every call to the returned function increments its value. In C#, variables are mutable by default, so be extremely careful when you change the value of a captured variable like this. A common source of confusion is capturing the loop variable of a for loop. Assume you capture the variable in multiple iterations. At the end of the loop, all of the created closures will contain the same value, because we're working just with a single variable.

In this section, we talked about object-oriented patterns and related functional techniques. In some cases, we used a function instead of an interface with a single method.

Next we'll look at an example showing what we can do when the behavior is very simple but can't be described by only one function.

8.3 Working with composed behaviors

In this chapter, we're talking about applications or components that work with behaviors and allow new behaviors to be added later in the development cycle or even at runtime. The key design principle is to make sure that adding new behaviors is as easy as possible. After we implement the new functionality, we should be able to register the function (for example, by adding it to a list) and use the application without any other changes in the code.

To simplify things, it's better to minimize a number of functions that need to be implemented. Often, a single function is sufficient to represent the functionality, but in some cases it may not be enough; we may need to include some additional information or provide a few more functions. Of course, in a functional program another function *is* only "additional information," information we can *run* to provide richer feedback.

An example of the first case may be a filter in a graphical editor. The filter itself is a function that works with pictures, but we could also provide a name of the filter (as a string). The user of the editor would rather see a "friendly" name and description than whatever we happened to call our function, with all the inherent naming restrictions.

In the next section, we're going to look at the second case, where more functions are required. We'll improve our loan application so that a test can report the details of why it's recommending against a loan, if the client "fails" the test. This will be implemented using a second function that does the reporting.

8.3.1 Records of functions

We've already seen a way of working with multiple functions. In the previous example, we returned a tuple of functions as a result and we could use the same technique to represent our application with the new reporting feature. Let's say the reporting function takes the client, prints something to the screen, and returns a unit as a result. Using this representation, the type of the list of behaviors would be

```
((Client -> bool) * (Client -> unit)) list
```

This starts to look a bit scary. It's complicated and the functions don't have names, which makes the code less readable. In the previous example, it wasn't a big problem, because the function was used only locally, but this list is one of the key data structures of our application, so it should be as clear as possible. A simple solution that makes the code much more readable is to use a record type instead of a tuple. We can define it like this:

```
type ClientTest =
  { Check  : Client -> bool
    Report : Client -> unit }
```

This code defines a record with two fields, both of which are functions. This is just another example of using functions in the same way as any other type. The declaration resembles a very simple object (or interface); we'll talk about this similarity later. First, let's look at listing 8.11, which shows how we can create a list of tests represented using the record declared earlier.

Listing 8.11   Creating tests with reporting (F#)

```
let checkCriminal(client) = client.CriminalRecord = true
let reportCriminal(client) =
  printfn "Checking 'criminal record' of '%s' failed!" client.Name

let checkIncome(client) = client.Income < 30000
let reportIncome(client) =
  printfn "Checking 'income' of '%s' failed (%s)!"
          client.Name "less than 30000"

let checkJobYears(client) = client.YearsInJob < 2
let reportJobYears(client) =
  printfn "Checking 'years in the job' of '%s' failed (%s)!"
          client.Name "less than 2"

let testsWithReports =
  [ { Check = checkCriminal; Report = reportCriminal };
    { Check = checkIncome;   Report = reportIncome };
    { Check = checkJobYears; Report = reportJobYears };
    (* more tests... *) ]
```

Checks criminal record

Checks minimal income

Checks years in the current job

❶ Creates list of records

Listing 8.11 is a series of `let` bindings. To make the code more readable, rather than using lambda functions we've define all the checks as ordinary F# functions. For each test, we've defined one function with the prefix `check` and one with the prefix `report`. If you enter the code in F# Interactive, you can see that the function types correspond to the types from the `ClientTest` record type. The last operation is creating a list of tests ❶. We need to create a record for each criterion to store the two related functions, and create a list containing the record values.

We also have to update the function that tests a particular client. We'll first find those tests that fail (using the `Check` field) and then let them print the result (using the `Report` field). Listing 8.12 shows the modified function, as well as the output when we run it against our sample client.

Listing 8.12   Testing a client with reporting (F# Interactive)

```
> let testClientWithReports(client) =
    let issues =
      testsWithReports
      |> List.filter (fun tr -> tr.Check(client))
    let suitable = issues.Length <= 1
    for i in issues do
      i.Report(client)
    printfn "Offer loan: %s"
            (if (suitable) then "YES" else "NO")
  ;;
val testClientWithReports : Client -> unit
```

❶ Gets list of tests that failed

Calculates overall result

❷ Reports all found issues

```
> testClientWithReports(john);;
Checking 'years in the job' of 'John Doe' has failed (less than 2)!
Offer loan: YES
```

The testClient function has only changed slightly since listing 8.5. The first change is in the lines that select which tests have failed ❶. The list is now a collection of records, so we have to test the client using a function stored in the Check field. The second change is that earlier, we were interested only in a number of failing tests. This time, we also need to print the detailed information about the failure ❷. This is implemented using an imperative for loop, which invokes the Report function of all the failing tests.

One problem in the current version of the code is that we had to write very similar functions when creating some tests. Let's fix that, reducing unnecessary code duplication.

8.3.2 Building composed behaviors

In listing 8.11 there's obvious duplication in the testing and reporting functions that verify the minimal income and minimal years in the current job. The tests have a similar structure: both test whether some property of the client is smaller than a minimal allowed value.

Identifying commonality is only the first step toward removing duplication. The next step is to look at which parts of the checkJobYears and checkIncome functions (together with their reporting functions) are *different*:

- They check different properties.
- They use different minimal values.
- They have slightly different messages.

To write the code more succinctly, we can create a function that takes these three different parts as its arguments and returns a ClientTest record. When we create the list of tests, we'll call this new function twice with different arguments to create two similar tests. Listing 8.13 shows both the extra function (lessThanTest) and the new way of creating the list of tests.

Listing 8.13 Creating similar tests using a single function (F# Interactive)

```
> let lessThanTest readFunc minValue propertyName =
    let report client =
      printfn "Checking '%s' of '%s' failed (less than %d)!"    ❶
              propertyName client.Name minValue
    { Check = (fun client -> readFunc(client) < minValue)       ❷
      Report = report };;
val lessThanTest : (Client -> int) -> int -> string -> ClientTest    ❸

> let tests =
    [ (lessThanTest (fun client -> client.Income) 30000 "income")
      (lessThanTest (fun client -> client.YearsInJob)
                    2 "years in the job")
      (* more tests... *) ];;
val tests : ClientTest list
```

Creates
two similar tests
with reporting

As usual, the type signature ❸ tells us a lot about the function. The `lessThanTest` function returns a value of type `ClientTest`, which contains the testing and reporting functions. The test is built using three arguments which:

1   Read a numeric property of the client
2   Specify a minimal required value (in our case, representing either an income or a number of years)
3   Describe the property (used in the reporting test)

The code first declares a nested function called `report` ❶, which takes a `Client` as the argument and prints a reason why the test failed. The function uses the arguments of the `lessThanTest` function as well which means that when `report` is returned as a part of the result, all these parameters will be captured in a closure. When constructing a record value that will be returned ❷, we specify `report` as one of the function values, and the second one is written inline using a lambda function.

Working with tuples or records of functions is common in functional programming, and it reflects the F# development style. But in C#, we'd use a different approach to implement this example. Let's look back at the development process and also consider how we'd implement the example in C# and improve the current F# version.

8.3.3   *Further evolution of F# code*

In the previous section, we moved from a simple piece of F# that stored a list of functions to a more sophisticated version that uses a list of records. This is a part of the F# development process that we discussed in chapter 1. You learned that F# programs often start as very simple scripts and evolve into code that follows standard .NET programming guidelines and benefits from the .NET object model.

We started with the most straightforward way to solve the problem using only what we knew at the beginning. When we later realized that we needed to add reporting using another function, we made relatively small adjustments to the code (because this is quite easy to do in F#), resulting in a version with more features. The transition wasn't just in terms of features, but also in a sense of readability and maintainability.

When extending the initial version, we mentioned that we could have used a list containing tuples of functions. Representations like this are more likely to be used in the initial prototype than in a finished application, and using F# record types clearly make the code more readable. Even though we went straight to a record type, bear in mind that there's nothing wrong with using a simple representation when you start writing an application that should turn into a complex product. This kind of change is quite easy to make in F#, and when you develop an initial version, you usually want to get it running with useful features as soon as possible rather than writing it in a robust way.

Even though we've already made a few transitions on the road to the robust version of the application, there are still improvements to consider. Because F# is a language for .NET, we can use several object-oriented features to make the code more .NET-friendly. We'll return to this topic in the next chapter, where you'll see how to turn our record into an F# *interface type*, which corresponds to C# interfaces.

COMPOSED BEHAVIORS IN C#

We began this chapter with an example of C# code that declared an interface with a single method representing the test, but then we used functions (and the Func delegate) as a more convenient way to write the code. If we wanted to implement a program that works with two functions, as we now have in F#, we'd probably turn immediately back to interfaces. Using interfaces in C# is definitely more convenient and more reasonable than using a tuple or a class with functions as its members. Having said that, in C# we have two options: functions for simple behaviors or an interface for anything more complicated.

In F#, the transition between the representations is easier. Most importantly, thanks to the type inference, we don't have to change the types everywhere in the source code. Also, turning a lambda function into a class is a larger change than adding another function. In chapter 9, we'll see that we can represent composed behaviors in F# using .NET interfaces too. Even when using interfaces, there's an easy way to turn a lambda function into something you can think of as a "lambda object." The name for this feature is *object expression,* and we'll talk about it in the next chapter.

In this chapter, we've primarily focused on behavior-centric applications, but in the introduction we explained that data-centric and behavior-centric approaches are often used together. We're going to see that in action now, combining functions with the discriminated union type that was so important for representing data in chapter 7.

8.4 *Combining data and behaviors*

Our original algorithm for testing whether a client is suitable for a loan offer used only the count of the tests that failed. This isn't very sophisticated: if the client has a large income, we may not be interested in other aspects, but we may want to ask additional questions of a client with a smaller income. In this section, we're going to implement an algorithm using *decision trees.* We'll also explore the declaration of a more interesting F# data structure.

8.4.1 *Decision trees*

Decision trees are one of the most popular algorithms in machine learning. They can be used for making decisions based on some data or for classifying input into several categories. The algorithm works with a tree that specifies what properties of the data should be tested and what to do for each of the possible answers. The reaction to the answer may be another test or the final answer.

Machine learning theory provides sophisticated ways for building the tree automatically from the data, but for our example we'll create the tree by hand. Figure 8.3 shows a decision tree for our problem.

We're going to start by implementing the F# version. In F#, it's usually very easy to write the code if we have an informal specification of the problem—in this case, a data structure to work with. The specification for a decision tree could look like this:

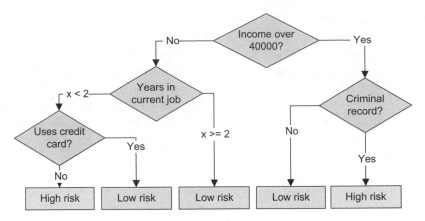

Figure 8.3   A decision tree for testing loan suitability; each diamond represents a question to ask, and the links are possible answers that lead to another question or to a conclusion (shown in a rectangle).

DECISION TREE   A decision tree is defined by an initial query that forms the root of the tree. A query consists of the name of a test and a function that executes it and can return several possible answers. In our implementation, we'll limit the answer to just `true` or `false`. For each answer, the node also contains a link to the next query or the final decision for this path through the tree.

Equipped with this specification, we can start writing the F# code. Before we see how to implement key parts of the problem in C# we'd like to demonstrate how easy it is to rewrite a specification like this into F#.

8.4.2   Decision trees in F#

From the last sentence in the specification you can see that a link leads either to a query or a final result. In F#, we can directly encode this using a discriminated union type with two options. The specification also talks about the query in more detail—it says that the query contains various fields, which suggests that we can represent it as an F# record type.

We'll define an F# record type (`QueryInfo`) with information about the query and a discriminated union (called `Decision`), which can be either another query or a final result. These data types reference each other. In functional terminology, we'd say that the types are *mutually recursive*. Listing 8.14 shows what this means for the F# source code.

Listing 8.14   Mutually recursive types describing decision tree (F#)

```
type QueryInfo =              ❶
  { Title    : string
    Check    : Client -> bool      ❷
    Positive : Decision           |  Refers to second type
    Negative : Decision }
```

```
and Decision =               ❸
  | Result of string
  | Query of QueryInfo    ◁── Refers to first type
```

When writing type declarations in F#, we can only refer to the types declared earlier in the file (or in a file specified earlier in the compilation order or located higher in the Visual Studio solution). Obviously that's going to cause problems in this situation, where we want to define two types that reference each other. To get around this, F# includes the and keyword. The type declaration in the listing starts as usual with the type keyword ❶, but it continues with and ❸, which means that the two types are declared simultaneously and can see each other.

The QueryInfo declaration combines data and behavior in a single record. The name of the test is a simple data member, but the remaining members are more interesting. The Check member ❷ is a function—that is, a behavior. It can return a Boolean value that we'll use to choose one of the two branches to continue with. These branches are composed values that may store a string or can recursively contain other QueryInfo values, so they can store both data and behavior. Alternatively we could return the Decision value as a result from the function, but then we couldn't that easily report whether or not the checking failed—we'd only know what the next test to run is. In listing 8.15 we create a value representing the decision tree shown in figure 8.3.

Listing 8.15 Decision tree for testing clients (F#)

```
let rec tree =                           ❶
  Query({ Title = "More than $40k"
          Check = (fun cl -> cl.Income > 40000)
          Positive = moreThan40; Negative = lessThan40 })
and moreThan40 =                         ❷
  Query({ Title = "Has criminal record"
          Check = (fun cl -> cl.CriminalRecord)
          Positive = Result("NO"); Negative = Result("YES") })
and lessThan40 =                         ❸
  Query({ Title = "Years in job"
          Check = (fun cl -> cl.YearsInJob > 1)
          Positive = Result("YES"); Negative = usesCredit })
and usesCredit =                         ❹
  Query({ Title = "Uses credit card"
          Check = (fun cl -> cl.UsesCreditCard)
          Positive = Result("YES"); Negative = Result("NO") })
```

There's one new thing about listing 8.15 that we haven't seen before. When declaring values, we're using the rec keyword in conjunction with the new and keyword. This isn't exactly the same use of the keyword as when we declared two *types* together in the previous listing, but the goal is similar. The and keyword allows us to declare several *values* (or functions) that reference each other. For example, this is how we can use the value moreThan40 ❷ in the declaration of tree ❶, even though it's declared later in the code.

The declaration order is the main reason for using let rec in this example, because this allows us to start the root node of the tree ❶, then create values for the two possible options on the second level (❷, ❸) and finally declare one additional question for one case on the third level ❹). We used `let rec` earlier for declaring recursive *functions*, which are functions that call themselves from their body (before they're declared). In general, F# also allows the declaration of recursive *values*, which can simplify many common tasks.

Initialization using recursive let bindings

We've seen several examples of recursive functions, but what would recursive value look like? One example might be code to create a UI using Windows Forms. Using a simplified API, it could look like this:

```
let rec form = createForm "Main form" [ btn ]
and btn = createButton "Close" (fun () -> form.Close())
```

The first line creates a form and gives it a list of controls to be placed on the form as the last argument. This list contains a button, which is declared on the second line. The last argument to the `createButton` function is a lambda function that will be invoked when the user clicks the button. It should close the application, so it needs to reference the `form` value, which is declared on the first line.

What's so difficult about this? We could easily write code to do the same thing in C#, and we wouldn't think of it as being particularly recursive. In C# we'd be adding an event handler to the button after creating the form, or adding the button to the form after creating it. Either way, we're mutating the objects. It's easy for two values to refer to each other via mutation, but the tricky part comes when you want to make the values immutable.

Using recursive `let` bindings, we can create values that reference other values and the whole sequence is declared at once. Even recursion has its limitations, as shown in the following code snippet:

```
let rec num1 = num2 + 1
and num2 = num1 + 1
```

In this case, we'd have to evaluate `num1` in order to get the value of `num2`, but to do this we'd need a value of `num1`. The difference that made the first example correct is that the value `form` was used inside a lambda function, so it wasn't needed immediately. Luckily, the F# compiler can detect code like this that can't possibly work, and generates a compilation error.

We've shown you how to declare a record that mixes data with behaviors and how to create a value of this record type using lambda functions. In listing 8.16, we'll finish the example by implementing a function that tests the client using a decision tree.

Listing 8.16   Recursive processing of the decision tree (F# Interactive)

```
> let rec testClientTree(client, tree) =          ❶
    match tree with
    | Result(message) ->                          ❷
      printfn "  OFFER A LOAN: %s" message
```

```
   | Query(qinfo) ->            ❸
     let result, case =
       if (qinfo.Check(client)) then "yes", qinfo.Positive
       else "no", qinfo.Negative
     printfn "  - %s? %s" qinfo.Title result
       testClientTree(client, case)
  ;;
val testClientTree : Client * Decision -> unit

> testClientTree(john, tree);;
  - More than $40k? no
  - Years in job? no
  - Uses credit card? yes
  OFFER A LOAN: YES
val it : unit = ()
```

Depends on test result (annotation pointing to the `if`/`else` lines)

Processes subtree recursively (annotation pointing to `testClientTree(client, case)`)

Tests code interactively (annotation pointing to `> testClientTree(john, tree);;`)

The program is implemented as a recursive function ❶. The decision tree can be either a final result ❷ or another query ❸. In the first case, it prints the result. In the second case it first runs the test and chooses one of the two possible subtrees to process later based on the result. It then reports the progress to the console, and calls itself recursively to process the subtree. In listing 8.16, we also immediately test the code and which path in the decision tree the algorithm followed for our sample client.

In this section, we've developed a purely functional decision tree in F#. As we've seen before, rewriting functional constructs (particularly discriminated unions) in C# can be quite difficult, so in the next section we'll implement a similar solution by mixing object-oriented and functional style in C# 3.0.

8.4.3 Decision trees in C#

In chapter 5 we discussed the relationship between discriminated unions in F# and class hierarchies in C#. In this example, we'll use another class hierarchy to represent a node in a decision tree, deriving two extra classes to represent the two different cases (a final result and a query).

In the functional version, all the processing logic was implemented separately in the testClientTree function. Even though we can do this in object-oriented style too—using the visitor pattern (discussed in chapter 7)—that isn't a particularly object-oriented solution. In this case, we don't need to implement functions for working with the decision tree separately, so we can use the more normal object-oriented technique of inheritance and virtual methods.

Listing 8.17 shows the base class (Decision) and the simpler of the two derived classes (ResultDecision), which represents the final result.

Listing 8.17 Object-oriented decision tree (C#)

```
abstract class Decision {
  public abstract void Evaluate(Client client);     ❶
}
class ResultDecision : Decision {
  public bool Result { get; set; }
  public override void Evaluate(Client client) {     ❷
```

```
        Console.WriteLine("OFFER A LOAN: {0}", Result ? "YES" : "NO");
    }
}
```

This part of the code is quite simple. The base class contains only a single virtual method ❶, which will be implemented in the derived classes and that will test the client and print the result. Its implementation in the class representing the final result ❷ prints the result to the console.

The more interesting part is the implementation of the class representing a query. The problem is that we need to provide different code for each of the concrete queries (testing the income, the number of years in the current job, and so on). We could create a new derived class for each of the query with a similar implementation of the Evaluate method—but that doesn't feel like a good solution, as it involves code duplication. A somewhat better way for implementing this is to use the *template method* design pattern.

THE TEMPLATE METHOD PATTERN

In general, the template method pattern allows us to define the skeleton of an algorithm or a class and fill in the missing pieces later, by implementing them in an inherited concrete class. The base class defines operations to be filled in later and uses them to implement more complicated operations. Figure 8.4 shows this in diagram form.

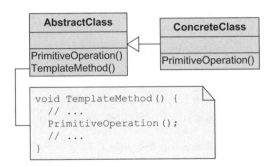

The abstract class from the template method corresponds to our representation of the query (let's call the class QueryDecision). The primitive operation that needs to be supplied by the

Figure 8.4 The base class contains the abstract method PrimitiveOperation, which is used in the implementation of TemplateMethod. This missing piece is filled in by the inherited class ConcreteClass.

derived classes is the testing method, which would take a Client as an argument and return a Boolean value. The template method would be our Evaluate method, which would contain code to print the result to the console and recursively process the selected branch. We'd still have to implement a new concrete class for each of the specific queries, which would make the code quite lengthy. Using functions, we can simplify the pattern and remove this need.

FUNCTIONAL IMPLEMENTATION

Instead of representing the primitive operation as a virtual method that can be filled in by deriving a class, we'll represent it as a property, where the type of the property is the function type Func<Client, bool>. The function is then supplied by the user of the class. Listing 8.18 shows an implementation of the QueryDecision class as well as an example of how we can create a simple decision tree.

Listing 8.18 Simplified implementation of the `Template` method (C#)

```
class QueryDecision : Decision {
  public string Title { get; set; }
  public Decision Positive { get; set; }
  public Decision Negative { get; set; }
  public Func<Client, bool> Check { get; set; }        ❶

  public override void Evaluate(Client client) {
    bool res = Check(client);                          ❷
    Console.WriteLine(" - {0}? {1}", Title, res ? "yes" : "no");
    Decision next = res ? Positive : Negative;
    next.Evaluate(client);                   │ Selects branch to follow
  }
}

                          ┌─ Constructs tree
var tree =                │   with a root query
  new QueryDecision {  ◄──┘
    Title = "More than $40k",
    Check = (client) => client.Income > 40000,       ❸
    Positive = new ResultDecision { Result = true },     │ Specifies ResultDecision or
    Negative = new ResultDecision { Result = false } };  │ QueryDecision as subtree
```

The `QueryDecision` class represents a case where we want to perform another test regarding the client. If we'd followed the template method pattern strictly, the test would be a virtual method, but we instead specified it as a property ❶. The type of the property is a function that takes a client and returns a Boolean value. This function is invoked when testing a client ❷, and depending on the result, the code follows one of the two possible branches. When creating a decision tree, we don't have to write an extra class for every test, because we can simply provide the primitive testing functionality using lambda functions ❸.

This example demonstrates how we can very effectively mix object-oriented and functional concepts. The types we created could be easily made immutable, which would make the example even more functional. The only reason we didn't do so is that using automatic properties makes the code a bit more compact. We started with a standard object-oriented design pattern and simplified it using lambda functions that are now available in C# 3.0. The solution is somewhere between the traditional object-oriented solution and the functional version we implemented in F#.

8.5 Summary

In this chapter we finished our exploration of the core functional concepts. After exploring basic principles such as functional values and higher-order functions, we moved to a higher-level perspective and discussed the architecture of functional applications. We divided applications (or components) into two groups: data-centric and behavior-centric.

In this chapter we discussed behavior-centric programs. You saw how to develop an application where behaviors aren't hard-coded and new behavior can be added easily later, either during development or at runtime, simply by using a list of functions.

Later, we investigated several ways to extend the data structure to combine functions and other functional data types to develop a decision tree, which combines data and behaviors in a single data type.

We also talked about design patterns that are related to behavior-centric programs. In particular, you learned how the strategy pattern corresponds to higher-order functions and how the command pattern relates to closures capturing mutable state in functional programming. Finally, we looked at how the template method pattern can be simplified using functions in C# 3.0.

In part 3, we'll focus on language features specific to F# and on advanced functional concepts. Chapter 9 starts with F# features that allow us to take the next step of the iterative development style. You'll see how to turn conceptually simple data types such as tuples of functions or discriminated unions into types that follow most of the .NET design guidelines. This means that the types follow standard F# and .NET development guidelines, are easy to document, and could be distributed in a commercial F# or .NET library. This also means that the library will be easily accessible from a C# application.

Part 3

Advanced F# programming techniques

In part 2, we talked about functional concepts common to most functional languages. You could now say that you understand functional programming in the same way you can say you're familiar with OOP after reading about encapsulation, inheritance, and polymorphism. You'd still need to learn a few other things before you'd be an effective object-oriented developer, and functional programming in F# is no different.

In the same way that there are specific features in every object-oriented language, there are useful features in F# that aren't commonly available in other functional languages. The first example of this is in chapter 9 when we talk about object types and members. F# is a first-class citizen in the .NET world and allows us to both use and declare standard .NET objects. We'll look at how to encapsulate standard functional code into objects, which is often the next step in the iterative development style. Objects provide a better way to structure your code, and make it easy to use F# functionality from C#.

We'll also discuss best practices that apply to functional F# code. In chapter 10, we'll explore ways to optimize F# programs. We'll explain how to guard against stack overflows when using recursion, and also provide techniques for improving program performance. In chapter 11, we'll look at refactoring and unit testing, two practices that are now regarded as essential in virtually any language or programming paradigm. In particular, we'll see the effect that immutability has on both areas.

In chapter 12 we'll discuss better ways for working with sequences or collections of values, and about *monads,* a most mysterious term in the programming language word, but you'll see that they're not so complicated in reality. In some senses it's a design pattern for composing code from simpler pieces so that the author of the monad can specify an additional aspect or behavior that's added to the pieces written by the user. You'll see that we've been already using this pattern; we didn't explicitly call it out.

After finishing this part of the book, you'll be able to write efficient functional programs in general, but also take advantage of many language features specific to F#. You'll also know how to use functional programming on the .NET platform. This includes the ability to combine functional, object-oriented, and imperative style, but also using standard techniques when writing and testing code. After finishing this part, you could successfully start looking for a job as an F# programmer. We're certainly not suggesting that you skip part 4—it will show examples of how to combine all functional tricks that we talk about in this book.

Turning values into F# object types with members

This chapter covers
- Declaring types with members
- Using interfaces in a functional way
- Writing class and interface types
- Using F# code from C#

When we introduced F# in chapter 1, we described it as a multiparadigm language that takes the best elements of several worlds. Most importantly, it takes ideas from both functional and object-oriented languages. In this chapter, we're going to look at several features inspired by OOP or that allow fluent integration with object-oriented .NET languages like C# and Visual Basic .NET (VB.NET).

This chapter is particularly important for the later steps in the F# development process. As we've mentioned, functional simplicity allows us to write a program quickly and provides great flexibility. OOP in F# is valuable because it gives the code a solid structure, encapsulates related functionality, and allows painless integration with other systems or .NET programming languages. In this chapter, we'll see how to take F# code that we developed earlier and evolve it to make it easier to use in a team or in a larger project.

9.1   *Improving data-centric applications*

Let's go over a few elements of data-centric applications that we covered in the previous chapters. In chapter 7 we saw that the key aspect of data-centric application design is creating the data structures that will be used by the application. Functional languages give us very simple and conceptually clear constructs for thinking about data structures. We've seen all basic data types, namely tuples, discriminated unions, and records. We've also seen how to declare generic types that can be reused by many applications, and we've discussed some available in the F# libraries, such as the option type and the functional list.

So far we've implemented operations separately from the data types. This is the usual approach in functional application design, unlike in OOP, where the operations are a part of type declaration. We discussed the motivation for this approach in chapter 7, but let's briefly review the key benefits for functional programs:

- It allows us to easily add operations when working with discriminated unions.
- Writing code in this way in F# makes the syntax very succinct, so the code can be written faster and we can easily prototype different solutions.
- We can take the full advantage of the F# type inference. As we've seen when working with .NET objects, we often needed type annotations, because the compiler cannot infer the type based on the members that we call.
- This programming style also better supports functional techniques such as partial function application and pipelining.
- The lightweight functional style makes it easier to run the code interactively using the F# Interactive shell.

TIP   If we keep operations separately from the type, the data structure changes less frequently. Once you define the data structure, you can create values of that type and keep them "alive" in F# Interactive. Then you can write the first version of the function, test it using F# Interactive, correct possible errors, improve it, and test it again on the same data. If we were updating the data structure together with all its operations, this process would be a lot more difficult.

There are many reasons *in favor of* keeping operations as part of the data structure; you probably know most of them from experience with C#. Let's demonstrate this using an example. In chapter 7, we wrote a simple `Rect` type and two functions to work with it. You can see the code repeated in listing 9.1. The example uses some types from the `System.Drawing` namespace, so if you're creating a new project, you'll need to add a reference to the `System.Drawing.dll` assembly.

Listing 9.1   Rect type with processing functions (F#)

```
open System.Drawing

type Rect =
  { Left: float32; Top:   float32
```

```
        Width: float32; Height: float32 }                          Shrinks
                                                                    rectangle
let deflate(rc, wspace, hspace) =
    { Left = rc.Left + wspace; Width = rc.Width - (2.0f * wspace)
      Top = rc.Top + hspace;  Height = rc.Height - (2.0f * hspace) }

let toRectangleF(rc) =                                    Converts to System.Drawing
    RectangleF(rc.Left, rc.Top, rc.Width, rc.Height)     representation
```

First we declare the type, then define two operations for working with rectangle values. The operations are implemented independently as F# functions, but, if we implement them as methods instead, it's easier to discover them when writing the code. Instead of remembering the function name, you type a dot after the value name and Visual Studio's IntelliSense pops up with a list of operations. The code is also better organized, because you know what operations belong to which type. The obvious conundrum is how to get the best from both of the approaches in F#.

9.1.1   Adding members to F# types

This is where the F# iterative style of development comes in handy. The ability to debug and test the code interactively is more important during the early phase of the development. As the code becomes more polished and we start sharing the project with other developers, it's more important to provide the common operations as members that can be invoked using dot notation.

This means that in F#, encapsulation of data types with their operations is typically one of the last steps of the development process. This can be done using *members*, which can be added to any F# type and behave just like C# methods or properties. Listing 9.2 shows how to augment the Rect type with two operations using members.

Listing 9.2   Rect type with operations as members (F#)

```
type Rect =                      ❶
    { Left   : float32
      Top    : float32
      Width  : float32
      Height : float32 }

    /// Creates a rectangle which is deflated by 'wspace' from the      ❷
    /// left and right and by 'hspace' from the top and bottom
    member x.Deflate(wspace, hspace) =                                  ❸
        { Left = x.Left + wspace
          Top = x.Top + hspace
          Width = x.Width - (2.0f * wspace)
          Height = x.Height - (2.0f * hspace) }

    /// Converts the rectangle to representation from 'System.Drawing'
    member x.ToRectangleF() =
        RectangleF(x.Left, x.Top, x.Width, x.Height)
```

To create an F# data type with members, you write the member declarations after the normal F# type declaration. As you can see in the example, the member declarations have to be indented by the same number of spaces as the body of the type declaration.

In listing 9.2, we started with a normal F# record type declaration ❶ then added two different methods as members.

The member declaration starts with the keyword member. This is followed by the name of the member with a value name for the current instance. For example, x.Deflate means that we're declaring a method Deflate and that, inside the body, the value x will refer to the current instance of the record. This acts in a similar way to the C# this keyword—think of it as a way of being able to call this anything you like. F# doesn't reserve this as a keyword, so you can name the value this (by writing for example this.Deflate) and then refer to the current instance using the same keyword as in C#. In this book, we'll mostly use the name x, which is often used by the F# community for its brevity. Another name aside from this and x that's also not an F# keyword is self.

The first member ❸ takes a tuple as an argument and creates a rectangle, which is made smaller by subtracting the specified length from its vertical and horizontal sides. When creating types with members, F# developers usually declare a member's parameters as a tuple. Done this way, they're compiled as standard methods usable from C#. If you specify the parameters without parentheses, you can use standard functional techniques such as partial function application with members.

Also note in the example that the comment preceding the member ❷ now starts with three slashes (///). This is a kind of comment that specifies documentation for the member, analogous to C# XML comments. In F#, you can use similar XML-based syntax if you want, but if you write plain non-XML text, the comment is automatically treated as a summary.

Now let's see how we can use the members we've declared. After you select the code and run it in F# Interactive, you'll see the type signature of the Rect type, which includes available members and their types. Listing 9.3 demonstrates calling both members.

Listing 9.3   Working with types and members (F# Interactive)

```
> let rc = { Left = 0.0f; Top = 0.0f              Creates
            Width = 100.0f; Height = 100.0f };;    Rect value
val rc : Rect

> let small = rc.Deflate(10.0f, 30.0f);;           ❶
val small : Rect = { Left = 10.0f; Top = 30.0f
                     Width = 80.0f; Height = 40.0f }

> small.ToRectangleF();;                            ❷
val rcf : RectangleF = {X=10, Y=30, Width=80, Height=40} { ... }
```

We start by creating a value of the Rect type. This hasn't changed; we still specify a value for each of the record type properties. The next command ❶ invokes the Deflate member. As you can see, we can do this using standard object-oriented dot notation that we've already seen when working with .NET objects. In this case, the arguments are specified using a tuple, but if we specified them without parentheses in the declaration, the call would also use the F# function call syntax with parameters separated by a space. The last command ❷ converts the rectangle into a value of the RectangleF object from System.Drawing. The example looks now very much like object-oriented code, but that doesn't mean that we're turning away from the functional programming style in any sense.

NOTE   The code is still purely functional (as opposed to imperative), which means that there are no side effects, despite its more object-oriented *organization*. If you implemented this in the imperative style, the Deflate method would probably modify the properties of the rectangle it was called on. Our implementation doesn't do this. The Rect data type is still immutable: the property values can't be changed once the instance has been created. So, instead of modifying the value, the member returns a new Rect value with modified properties. This is the same behavior that the original deflate function had, but it's important to keep in mind that we can very nicely combine functional concepts (like immutability) with the object-oriented concepts (in this case, encapsulation). This isn't an alien concept in an imperative object-oriented world, of course—look at the System.String type, which takes the same approach.

We've already mentioned that one of the benefits when using members instead of functions is that you can easily discover operations for working with the value using IntelliSense. In figure 9.1 you can see the Visual Studio editor working with Rect type.

Another important benefit is that types with members are naturally usable from other .NET languages like C#. The Deflate member would look just like an ordinary method of the type if we were using it from C#, as you'll see in section 9.5. We have to design the members carefully in order to make all of them compatible with C#, but it's always possible. Some tricky cases include higher-order functions discussed in section 9.5 and events that we'll look at in chapter 16.

When we turned functions into members in listing 9.2, we converted functions declared using let bindings into members declared using the member keyword. This worked, but we had to make quite large changes in the source code. Fortunately, we can avoid this and make smoother the transition from a simple F# style to a more idiomatic .NET style.

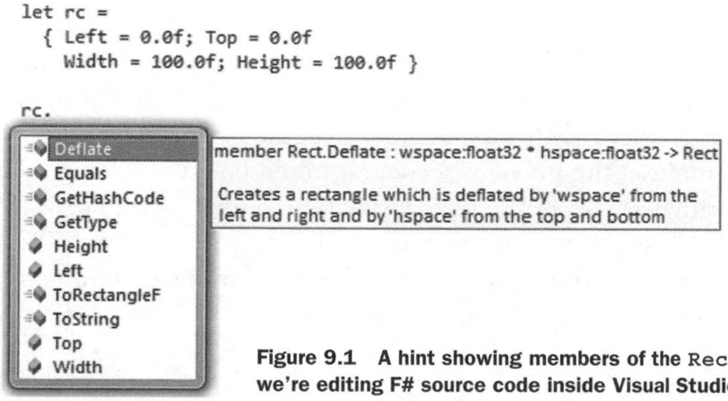

```
let rc =
  { Left = 0.0f; Top = 0.0f
    Width = 100.0f; Height = 100.0f }

rc.
```

Figure 9.1   A hint showing members of the Rect type when we're editing F# source code inside Visual Studio IDE

9.1.2 *Appending members using type extensions*

In the previous section, we mentioned that you can add members to any F# data type. This time, we'll demonstrate it using a discriminated union. We'll use a technique that allows us to add members without making any changes to the original code. This means that we'll be able to leave the original type and original function declarations unmodified and add members to them later.

We'll extend an example from chapter 5 where we declared a schedule type. The type can represent events that occur once, repeatedly, or never. As well as the data type itself, we created a function calculates the next occurrence of the event. Listing 9.4 shows a slightly modified version of the code. We've made the code more compact and also refactored the Once branch of the pattern matching to use a simple utility function. The original code was in listing 5.5, if you want to compare the two.

> **Listing 9.4   Schedule data type with a function (F#)**

```
type Schedule =                              ◁─── ❶ Declares original type
  | Never
  | Once of DateTime
  | Repeatedly of DateTime * TimeSpan           ❷ Implements
                                                  helper calculation
let futureOrMaxValue(dt) =                   ◁───┘
  if (dt > DateTime.Now) then dt else DateTime.MaxValue

let getNextOccurrence(schedule) =            ◁───   Specifies public
  match schedule with                            ❸ behavior
  | Never -> DateTime.MaxValue
  | Once(eventDate) -> futureOrMaxValue(eventDate)
  | Repeatedly(startDate, interval) ->
    let secondsFromFirst = (DateTime.Now - startDate).TotalSeconds
    let q = max (secondsFromFirst / interval.TotalSeconds) 0.0
    startDate.AddSeconds
      (interval.TotalSeconds * (Math.Floor(q) + 1.0))
```

The most interesting change is that we added the utility function futureOrMaxValue ❷. The change doesn't improve readability very much; we made it only to demonstrate the choices available. In a more complicated project you'd definitely have several large utility functions.

The point is that in a typical F# source file, we start with the type declaration ❶, then have a bunch of utility (private) functions, then a couple of functions that we want to expose as members ❸. If we wanted to turn the last function into a member using the technique from the previous section, it would be quite difficult. The members have to be written as part of the type declaration, but we usually want to put several utility functions between the type and its members!

The solution is to use *intrinsic type extensions*, which allow us to add members to a type declared earlier in the file. Listing 9.5 shows how we can use extensions with our schedule type.

Listing 9.5 Adding members using intrinsic type extensions (F#)

```
type Schedule =
  | Never
  | Once of DateTime
  | Repeatedly of DateTime * TimeSpan

let futureOrMaxValue(dt) =
  (...)
let getNextOccurrence(schedule) =            ❶
  (...)

type Schedule with                                       ❷
  member x.GetNextOccurrence() = getNextOccurrence(x)   ❸
  member x.OccursNextWeek =                                    ❹
    getNextOccurrence(x) < DateTime.Now.AddDays(7.0)
```

Most of the code hasn't changed since listing 9.4, so we've omitted it for brevity. We've added only the last four lines of code. The first one ❷ defines a type extension, which tells the F# compiler to add the following members to a type with the specified name. This is followed by the usual member declarations. As we've already implemented the core functionality as a function ❶, the member implementations are simple ❸. Aside from getting the next occurrence, we added one property ❹ that uses the private function to test whether the next occurrence happens during the next week.

If you come from C# 3.0, you can see similarities between type extensions and extension methods. You can use type extensions to add methods and properties to existing types from other assemblies. The case in the previous listing was different, because we used the *intrinsic type extension*. This is a special case when we declare both the original type and the extension in a single file. In that case, the F# compiler merges both parts of the type into a single class and also allows us to access private members of the type in the type extension.

Listing 9.6 demonstrates calling the members from listing 9.5. Members added using type extensions behave in the same way as other members, so the listing shouldn't contain any surprises.

Listing 9.6 Working with `Schedule` using members (F# Interactive)

```
> let sch = Repeatedly(DateTime.Now, TimeSpan(2, 0, 0, 0));;
val sch : Schedule

> sch.OccursNextWeek();;        ◁──┐ Tests using
val it : bool = true                │ repeated event

> let sch = Never;;
val sched : Schedule                  Tests behavior for
                                      unscheduled event
> sch.OccursNextWeek();;        ◁──┘
val it : bool = false
```

Just as when we were working with records, we create the F# value in the usual way. For the discriminated union in our example, this means using the Repeatedly or Never discriminator. (We could have used the `Once` discriminator as well.) Once we have the value, we can invoke its members using the object-oriented dot notation.

As you've just seen, members are very useful when writing mature code, because they wrap the code into well-structured pieces and they make it easier to use the types. In the F# development process, we don't usually *start* by writing code with members, but we add them once the code is well tested and the API design is fixed. We've discussed two ways of adding members:

- Append members directly to the type declaration, when the type is simple enough.
- Use intrinsic type extensions, which require fewer changes to the code, for more complex types.

Type extensions have the additional benefit that we can test the type and its processing functions in the F# Interactive tool before augmenting it, because we don't have to declare the whole type in one go.

You know that members are important for turning data-centric F# code into a real-world .NET application or component. Now we'll turn our attention to behavior-centric applications.

9.2   *Improving behavior-centric applications*

In previous chapters, we've shown that functional programming is based on several basic concepts, which are then composed to get the desired result. We've seen this when discussing the ways to construct data types, with examples of tuples, functions, discriminated unions, and record types.

When creating behavior-centric applications, we used a function type to represent the behavior and we composed it with other types. For example, we used a record type to store two related functions in a single value.

9.2.1   *Using records of functions*

Using records that store functions is a common technique in OCaml and to some extent also in F#. Before looking at possible improvements, listing 9.7 provides a reminder of the original solution in chapter 8.

> **Listing 9.7   Testing clients using records of functions (F#)**

```
type ClientTest =                    ⟵── Represents test
  { Check : Client -> bool
    Report : Client -> unit }

let testCriminal(client) = client.CriminalRecord = true
let reportCriminal(client) =
  printfn "'%s' has a criminal record!" client.Name

let tests =
  [ { Check = testCriminal
      Report = reportCriminal };        Creates record value
    (* more tests... *) ]
```

The code first creates a record type that specifies types of functions that form the checking and reporting part of the test. It then creates two functions and combines them to form a value of the record type. Using records of functions is conceptually very simple, and it's easy to refactor code using individual functions into a design using records. If we want to evolve this code into a more traditional .NET version, we can take one more step.

We mentioned earlier that the function type is similar to an interface with a single method. It's not surprising that a record consisting of two functions is quite similar to an interface with two methods. In C# you'd almost certainly implement this design using an interface, and F# lets us do the same thing.

Similarly to members, interfaces are more important when creating robust applications or reusable .NET libraries. If we use an interface, we don't say how it should be implemented. This gives us a lot of flexibility when we write the application. We'll talk about ways to implement an interface in F# later in this chapter. Interfaces are also useful when developing a .NET library that should be callable from C#. If we declare an interface in F#, the C# code will see it as an ordinary interface. On the other hand, an F# record type with functions as members looks like a class with properties of some hard-to-use type. Let's see how we can adapt our record type into an interface while still using it in a natural way from F#.

9.2.2 Using interface object types

Just like records and discriminated unions, interfaces types are declared using the `type` construct. Listing 9.8 shows our earlier test record type converted to an interface type.

> **Listing 9.8 Interface representing client test (F#)**

```
type ClientTest =
  abstract Check : Client -> bool
  abstract Report : Client -> unit
```

The declaration in listing 9.8 says that any type implementing the `ClientTest` interface will need to provide two members. In the interface declaration, the members are written using the `abstract` keyword, which means that they don't yet have an implementation. The declaration specifies the names and type signatures of the members. We didn't explicitly say that we're declaring an interface, but the F# compiler is smart enough to deduce that. If we, for example, provided implementation of one of the members, the compiler would realize that we want to declare an abstract class. In the usual F# programming practice, we'll need abstract classes and implementation inheritance very rarely, so we'll focus on working with interfaces in this chapter.

One point to note before we move on to look at the implementations: in F#, we didn't use the I prefix when declaring the interface; F# has ways to declare a type and attempts to unify all of them (for example, we don't use D prefix when declaring discriminated unions and so on). We can break the >NET rules when writing purely F#

code, but when writing an F# library that's supposed to be used from other .NET languages, you should always follow all the standard .NET coding conventions in all public API (for example, by using the I prefix for interfaces).

 If we wanted to create a test that checks, say, the criminal record of the client in C#, we'd have to write a new class implementing the interface. F# supports classes as well, but provides another solution called *object expressions*. This is inspired by functional programming and is often more elegant, because we don't have to write any class declarations before creating useful values.

Object expressions and lambda functions

The analogy between interface and function types is useful when explaining what an object expression is. The signature of a function type describes it in an abstract sense. It specifies that the function takes arguments and returns a result of some type. The concrete code of the function is provided when we're creating a function value. This can be done using a lambda function, which is an expression that returns a function, or a let binding, which creates a named function.

An interface is an abstract description of an object. It (1) defines that the object should have some members and (2) specifies their types. Again, we provide the actual code for the members when creating a concrete value. One option is to write a named class that implements the interface, which is similar to creating a named function. Object expressions are similar to lambda functions. They can be used anywhere in the code and create a value that implements the interface without specifying the name of the type providing the actual code. If you're familiar with Java, object expressions in F# are essentially the same as *anonymous classes* in Java.

In listing 9.9, we'll create tests to check the client's criminal record and his income, and create a list of interface values just like our earlier lists of records.

Listing 9.9   Implementing interfaces using object expressions (F# Interactive)

```
> let testCriminal =
    { new ClientTest with                                    ❶
      member x.Check(cl) = cl.CriminalRecord = true
      member x.Report(cl) =
        printfn "'%s' has a criminal record!" cl.Name };;     ❷
val testCriminal : ClientTest                                 ❸

> let testIncome =
    { new ClientTest with
        member x.Check(cl) = cl.Income < 30000
        member x.Report(cl) =
          printfn "Income of '%s' is less than 30000!" cl.Name };;
val testCriminal : ClientTest
> let tests = [ testCriminal; testIncome ];;
val tests : ClientTest list
```

❶❷ Implements testing of client

❷ Implements reporting

Creates list of interface values

The code creates two values implementing the `ClientTest` interface type using object expressions. Each object expression is enclosed in curly braces and starts with an initial header ❶ that specifies what interface we're implementing. This is followed by the `with` keyword, then by the member declarations ❷. Syntactically, this is quite similar to the type extensions that we discussed in the previous section. Member declarations give an implementation for the members specified by the interface, so the expressions in listing 9.9 implement members `Check` and `Report`.

The whole object expression fulfills the normal definition of an F# expression: it does a single thing, which is returning a value. If we look at the output from F# Interactive ❸, we can see that it returns a value of type `ClientTest`. This is the interface type, so the object expression returns a concrete value implementing the interface, just like a lambda function returns a function value implementing an abstract function type.

NOTE   Technically, the F# compiler creates a class that implements the interface and object expression returns a new instance of this class. However, the declaration of the class is only internal, so we can't access this class directly. The only thing we need to know about it is that it implements the specified interface.

This is similar to anonymous types in C# 3.0, where the compiler also creates a hidden class behind the scenes that we can't access directly. In C#, we know what the properties of the class are, but this information about properties is available only locally inside the method. On the other hand, in F# we know which interface the class implements, so we can work with it without any such limitations. We can write methods that return well-known interface types and implement them using object expressions.

In this section, you learned how to use interface types to make one final step in the iterative development of behavior-oriented applications in F#. Interfaces give us an idiomatic .NET solution, but F# provides features to allow us to work with interfaces in a natural way that's consistent with its functional style. Thanks to the object expressions, it's easier to implement the interface than to construct a record of functions.

Later in this chapter you'll learn that using interfaces makes it possible to call F# code comfortably from C#. We haven't yet talked about class declarations in F#, because ordinary classes aren't used that frequently in pure F# projects, but we'll look at them briefly in section 9.4. Before that, let's see how we can take advantage of object expressions when using some common types from the .NET libraries.

9.3   *Working with .NET interfaces*

The .NET Framework is fully object-oriented, so we'll often work with interfaces when using .NET libraries from F#. In this section we'll explore how to implement an interface that can be used to customize equality of keys stored in the `Dictionary` object and we'll work with the well-known interface for resource management: `IDisposable`.

9.3.1   *Using .NET collections*

So far, we've mostly used the built-in F# list type for storing collections of data although, in some cases, it's useful to work with other .NET types such as the `Dictionary` class from the `System.Collections.Generic` namespace. This type is particularly useful when we need fast access based on keys, because immutable types providing similar functionality (such as `Map` from the F# library) are less efficient.

Note that the `Dictionary` type is a mutable type. This means that methods like `Add` change the state of the object instead of returning a new, modified copy. This means we have to be careful when working with it in scenarios where we want to keep our code purely functional.

Listing 9.10 shows how to create a simple lookup table using `Dictionary` and how to specify a custom way for comparing the keys by providing an implementation of the `IEqualityComparer<T>` interface.

Listing 9.10   Implementing the `IEqualityComparer<T>` interface (F# Interactive)

```
> open System
  open System.Collections.Generic;;

> let noSpaceComparer =
    let replace(s:string) = s.Replace(" ", "")    ◁——| Removes spaces from string
    { new IEqualityComparer<_> with          ❶
        member x.Equals(a, b) =
          String.Equals(replace(a), replace(b))     Compares strings, ignoring spaces
        member x.GetHashCode(s) =
          replace(s).GetHashCode() };;

> let scaleNames = new Dictionary<_, _>(noSpaceComparer)    ❷
  scaleNames.Add("100", "hundred")
  scaleNames.Add("1 000", "thousand")
  scaleNames.Add("1 000 000", "million");;

> scaleNames.["10 00"];;
val it : string = "thousand"

> scaleNames.["1000000"];;
val it : string = "million"
```

This example demonstrates that object expressions can be quite useful when we need to call a .NET API that accepts an interface as an argument. In this case, the constructor of the `Dictionary` type ❷ accepts an implementation of the `IEqualityComparer<T>` interface as an argument. The interface is then used to compare keys when accessing elements stored in the dictionary. We created a value called `NoSpaceComparer`, which implements the interface ❶. Our implementation compares strings and ignores any spaces in the string. We did that by creating a utility function that removes spaces from any given string and then comparing the trimmed strings. We also implemented a method that calculates the hash code of the string, which is used by the `Dictionary` type to perform the lookup efficiently.

F# type inference helped us again in this listing. We used an underscore (_) instead of the actual type when writing the object expression as well as when creating an instance of the `Dictionary` class. When the compiler sees the underscore, it uses other information to figure out what the actual type parameter is, and in this example it had enough information from other parts of the code.

Another familiar interface for a .NET programmer is `IDisposable`, which is used for explicit cleaning of resources. Let's see how we can use it from F#.

9.3.2 *Cleaning resources using IDisposable*

We've already worked with several types that implement `IDisposable`, like `Graphics` and `SolidBrush`. We wanted to make the code as easy to follow as possible, so when we finished using the object, we explicitly called the `Dispose` method.

C# contains syntactic sugar for this in the form of the `using` statement, which makes sure that `Dispose` is called even if an exception is thrown within the body of the statement. F# has a similar construct with the `use` keyword. Listing 9.11 shows a simple example that works with files.

Listing 9.11 Working with files and the `use` keyword (F# Interactive)

```
> open System.IO;;
> let readFile() =
    use reader = new StreamReader("C:\\test.txt")      ❶
    let text = reader.ReadToEnd()
    Console.Write(text)
 ;;                                                     ❷
val readFile : unit -> unit

> readFile();;
Hello world!       │ Prints content
Ahoj svete!        │ of sample file
```

When creating a `StreamReader` (which implements the `IDisposable` interface), we declare it using the `use` keyword ❶. Note that the syntax is similar to the `let` keyword in a usual `let` binding. The difference is that the F# compiler automatically adds a call to the `Dispose` method at the end of the function ❷, so the `StreamReader` is automatically disposed after we finish working with it. The compiler also inserts a `try-finally` block to make sure that the cleanup is run even when an exception occurs.

An important difference between the `using` construct in C# and the `use` keyword in F# is that in C# we have to specify the scope explicitly using curly braces. In F# the `Dispose` method is called at the end of the scope where the value is visible. This is usually what we need, so it makes a lot of code snippets easy to write. Listing 9.12 shows the C# and F# versions.

Listing 9.12 Cleaning up resources in F# and C#

```
// F# version
let test() =
  use reader = new StreamReader("C:\\test.txt")
```

```
  let text = reader.ReadToEnd()
  Console.Write(text)              ❶

// C# version
void Test() {
  using(var reader = new StreamReader("C:\\test.txt")) {
    var text = reader.ReadToEnd();
    Console.Write(text);
  }                                  ❷
}
```

In both languages, the object is disposed when the execution leaves the scope where the value `reader` is accessible ❶ ❷. In F#, this happens at the end of the function by default, which is often what we need. When the function continues with code that can run for a long time, it's better to make sure that the resource is disposed earlier. Let's say that we'd like to close the file and print the content to the console after it's closed. In C#, we'd have to create a local variable inside the function and assign it a value inside the `using` block. In F#, this can be done more easily, because we can specify the scope explicitly using whitespace:

```
let test() =
  let text =
    use reader = new StreamReader("C:\\test.txt")
    reader.ReadToEnd()
  Console.Write(text)
```

The syntax may be somewhat surprising, but it becomes clear once we realize that in F# every block of code is an expression. In the previous code, we're specifying the way in which the expression is constructed in the same way as when we write `(1 + 2) * 3` instead of the default `1 + (2 * 3)`. This way, we can limit the scope of the `reader` value to the expression that initializes the value of `text`.

Even though the `use` keyword is primarily useful when working with .NET objects that keep some resources, it can be used for a wider range of scenarios. Let's look at an example.

PROGRAMMING WITH THE USE KEYWORD

As we've seen, if we create a value using the `use` keyword, the compiler will automatically insert a call to its `Dispose` method at the end of the function where it's declared. This is useful for resources, but there are other situations where we need to enclose a piece of code between two function calls.

Suppose we want to output text to a console in a different color and then restore the original color. Traditionally, we'd have to store the original color, set the new one, send the output to the console, and restore the original color.

The same thing can be done rather elegantly thanks to the `use` keyword. We can write a function that changes the color of the console and returns an `IDisposable` value. This value contains a `Dispose` method, which restores the original color when called, and thanks to the `use` keyword, the method will be called automatically. Listing 9.13 shows the function and a demonstration of its use.

Listing 9.13   Setting console color using IDisposable (F# Interactive)

```
> open System;;

> let changeColor(clr) =
    let orig = Console.ForegroundColor           ❶
    Console.ForegroundColor <- clr               ❷
    { new IDisposable with                       ❸
        member x.Dispose() =
           Console.ForegroundColor <- orig };;    ❹
val changeColor : ConsoleColor -> IDisposable

> let hello() =
    use clr = changeColor(ConsoleColor.Red)       ❺
    Console.WriteLine("Hello world!")
    ;;                                            ❻
val hello : unit -> unit
```

The most interesting part of the code is the changeColor function. We can imagine that it contains two pieces of code. The first part is executed immediately when the function is called, and the second part is returned and executed at a later time. The first part of the code first stores the original color ❶ and then sets the new one ❷.

The second part needs to be returned as a result. We could return it as a function (possibly using lambda function syntax), but then the caller would have to call it explicitly. Instead, we create an IDisposable value using an object expression ❸ and place the code that restores the original color in the Dispose method ❹.

When the changeColor function is used, the first part (which sets the new color) is executed immediately ❺. We store the result using the use keyword, so at the end of the function ❻ the Dispose method is called and the original color is restored. You can see the result of running this code in the F# Interactive console window in figure 9.2. Note that we have to use the standalone console version of F# Interactive and not the integrated Visual Studio window, which doesn't support changing the text color.

The same idea is useful in other contexts, such as temporarily changing the cursor in a GUI to an appropriate "please wait" indicator, or temporarily changing the current thread's culture to a specific value when unit-testing culture-specific code. The clue here is the word *temporarily*, which suggests the "change something, do some work, restore the original value" pattern—ideal for the use keyword!

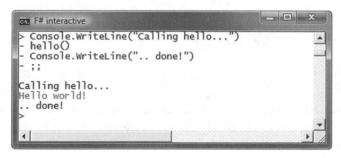

Figure 9.2   Changing the color of the console text using the changeColor function. You can see that the color is changed only inside the hello function and then the original color is restored.

In all the examples showing object-oriented features, we used the standard F# types, interfaces, and object expressions. This is quite normal when using F# in a functional way, but the language supports other object-oriented features as well. As this book is primarily about functional programming we won't discuss all of them, but we'll look at a couple of the most important examples.

9.4   Concrete object types

The most important construct of OOP is a class declaration. In F#, this is valuable when you're writing a library that can be used from C#, because an F# class declaration looks just like a normal class when referenced from C#. Conceptually, classes are a bit like records with members, because they store values in fields and provide members for accessing them. Classes have additional features. In F#, you can typically use classes in the following scenarios:

- When you need to encapsulate data and behavior.
- In a later phase of the iterative development process when turning simple tuples or records into a more evolved type that hides internal implementation.
- When the type needs to run some computation inside the constructor.

Classes aren't used when you need to design an extensible type that supports adding of operations. Implementation inheritance and virtual methods are used only rarely.

Let's start with the simplest possible example. Listing 9.14 shows a class declaration with a constructor, several properties, and a method.

Listing 9.14   Class with client information (F# Interactive)

```
> type ClientInfo(name, income, years) =          ❶
    let loanCoefficient = income / 5000 * years          Executes during
    do printfn "Creating client '%s'" name               construction

    member x.Name = name
    member x.Income = income          ❷
    member x.Years = years

    member x.Report() =                                                    ❸
      printfn "Client: %s, loan coefficient: %d" name loanCoefficient
  ;;
type ClientInfo = (...)                                Creates class,
                                                       runs constructor
> let john = new ClientInfo("John Doe", 40000, 2);;   ◀
val john : ClientInfo
Creating client 'John Doe'          Invokes method
                                    of class
> john.Report();;                ◀
Client: John Doe, q=16
val it : unit = ()
```

The declaration starts with the class name and constructor arguments ❶. The next couple of lines before the first member declaration are executed during construction. This part of code forms an *implicit constructor*. The arguments to the constructor (such as name and others) and values declared in the initialization code (like `loanCoefficient`) are accessible from anywhere inside the class. This is quite useful, because a C# constructor often only copies its arguments to private fields, so they can be accessed from other places. If you use the parameter only inside the code of the constructor, it isn't stored as a field, because the compiler knows that we won't need it.

Next, the class contains three member declarations that expose constructor arguments as properties of the client ❷ and a single method ❸. Just like when adding members to F# data types, the `x.` prefix means that the current instance of the class can be accessed using the `x` value. We might use it to call another method or read other properties.

> **NOTE** F# provides a richer set of features for declaring classes than what we've seen in this example. The goal of the F# language is to be a first-class .NET citizen, so nearly everything you can write in C# can also be translated to F#. However, in the usual F# programming, we don't need advanced .NET object model features such as overloaded constructors and overloaded methods or, for that matter, publicly accessible fields.
>
> The goal of this book is to introduce functional concepts and not to explain every F# feature, so we'll look only at the most useful object-oriented constructs that F# provides and how they work with the functional style. You can find more information about class declarations on the book's website and also in the [F# Documentation] and [F# Language Specification] in the Resources section at the end of this book.

The class from the previous example is still purely functional, in the sense that it doesn't have any mutable state. This demonstrates how object-oriented and functional paradigms can work very well together.

9.4.1 *Functional and imperative classes*

Just like the `let` bindings we've seen in other F# code, a `let` binding in a class or an argument to a class constructor is an immutable value. Also, a property declaration using the `member` keyword creates a read-only property (with only a getter). This means that if the class references only values of other immutable types, it will also become immutable.

Let's say that we want to allow changes of the client's income in the previous example. This can be done in two ways:

- In a purely functional style, the object will return a new instance with updated income and the original values of all other properties.
- Using the imperative style, the income will be a mutable field.

Listing 9.15 shows the functional version of the class (named `ClientF`) together with the imperative class named `ClassI`.

Listing 9.15   Functional and imperative version of `Client` type (F#)

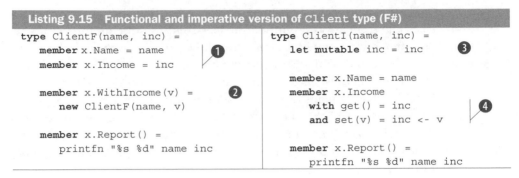

```
type ClientF(name, inc) =                    type ClientI(name, inc) =
    member x.Name = name            ❶            let mutable inc = inc        ❸
    member x.Income = inc

                                                member x.Name = name
    member x.WithIncome(v) =        ❷            member x.Income
        new ClientF(name, v)                         with get() = inc
                                                     and set(v) = inc <- v   ❹

    member x.Report() =                         member x.Report() =
        printfn "%s %d" name inc                     printfn "%s %d" name inc
```

In the functional version, all properties remain read-only ❶. When we want to change the income of a client, we have to create a new instance of the client. This can be done easily using the `WithIncome` ❷ method, which returns a copy of the object with the income set to the new value.

The imperative version declares an updatable field for storing the income using the `mutable` keyword ❸. When declaring the field, we use the same name for both the value and the constructor parameter. The new value hides the original one, meaning that we can no longer access the original value. This may seem strange at first, but it prevents you from accidentally using the initial value when you intend to use the current (possibly changed) one.

The next notable thing in the imperative version is the read/write property ❹ for changing income of the client. The property is composed from two members, similar to method declaration. The `get` member doesn't have any parameters and returns the value, while the `set` member has a single parameter for the new value and should return `unit` as the result. Even though the syntax is slightly different from that of a C# property declaration, the principles are the same.

When we're changing the income of a client, each of the two classes is used differently, but we can use both versions to get the same result. You can see an F# Interactive session demonstrating how to use the classes in listing 9.16.

Listing 9.16   Programming functional and imperative `Client` type (F# Interactive)

```
> let joeOriginal = new ClientF("Joe", 30);;
val joeOriginal : ClientF                         ❶ Creates new
                                                     client instance
> let joeUpdated = joeOriginal.WithIncome(40);;   ⟵
val joeUpdated : ClientF

> joeUpdated.Income;;
val it : int = 40

> let joeMutable = new ClientI("Joe", 30);;
val joeMutable : ClientI

> joeMutable.Income <- 40;;      ⟵   Mutates existing
val it : unit = ()            ❷     instance

> joeMutable.Income;;
val it : int = 40
```

When using the immutable version ❶, we store the returned client as a value with a new name. This means that we can still access the original value. We could use value hiding and use the same name for the value if we didn't want to access the original instance later in the code. In the imperative version, we can update the income using the read/write property ❷. We're using the <- operator just like when working with any other object declared in standard .NET library.

Even though we're concentrating on functional programming, it's sometimes useful to know how to write a mutable class like this. If you need to expose a larger piece of F# code to a C# client, you'll probably wrap your code in at least one class, because this makes it easier to use from C#. At this point, you can choose which style to follow: an imperative one with some mutable types, or a purely functional one where everything is mutable. The second solution is cleaner from the F# point of view, but developers who aren't accustomed to dealing with libraries composed entirely of immutable types may find it easier to use a wrapper with mutable state.

We're nearly ready to show a complete example of calling F# code from C#, but we need to finish our tour of object-oriented F# features first.

9.4.2 *Implementing interfaces and casting*

We've discussed how to declare an interface in F# and how to create a value that implements the interface using object expressions. This is a very lightweight solution similar to lambda functions. Just as lambda syntax isn't always the appropriate choice for creating functions, it sometimes makes sense to implement an interface in a named class.

We're going to work with the same example as earlier in the chapter. We'll look at implementing interfaces in both C# and F#, so let's recap the declaration of the interface in both languages:

```
// C# interface declaration
interface IClientTest {
  bool Check(Client client);
  void Report(Client client);
}
// F# Interface declaration
type ClientTest =
  abstract Check : Client -> bool
  abstract Report : Client -> unit
```

The interface has two methods: one that tests the client and one that prints a report to the screen. Let's suppose we want to implement the interface using a coefficient calculated from several properties. Earlier we created similar tests using object expressions, but when the code becomes more complex it's better to move it into a separate class declaration or possibly into a separate source file.

Listing 9.17 shows the C# implementation testing a client's income and how many years he's been in his current job using weightings and a threshold, all specified in the constructor. The class uses *explicit interface implementation*, which is slightly unusual—but we'll see why when we look at the F# implementation.

Listing 9.17   Client test using explicit interface implementation (C#)

```
class CoefficientTest : IClientTest {            ← Implements IClientTest
  readonly double incomeCoeff, yearsCoeff, minValue;

  public CoefficientTest(double ic, double yc, double min) {
    this.incomeCoeff = ic;                          Stores
    this.yearsCoeff = yc;                           arguments in
    this.minValue = min;                            private field
  }
  public void PrintInfo() {
    Console.WriteLine("income * {0} + years * {1} >= {2}",
      incomeCoeff, yearsCoeff, minValue);
  }
  bool IClientTest.Check(Client client) {            Implements   ❶
    return client.Income * incomeCoeff +          interface methods
      client.YearsInJob * yearsCoeff < min;
  }
  void IClientTest.Report(Client client) {
    Console.Write("Coeffficient {1} less than {0} ", minValue,
      client.Income * incomeCoeff + cl.YearsInJob * yearsCoeff);
  }
}
```

To implement an interface member using the explicit syntax in C#, we include the name of the interface when writing the method ❶ and remove the access modifier. This is a minor change, but the more important difference is how the class can be used. The methods from the interface (in our case `Test` and `Report`) aren't directly accessible when using the class. To call them, we first have to cast the class to the interface type. Let's look at an example:

```
var test = new CoefficientTest(0.001, 5.0, 50.0);
test.PrintInfo();

var cltest = (IClientTest)test;
if (cltest.Check(john)) cltest.Report(john);
```

We can't simply write `test.Check(john)`, because `Check` isn't directly available as a public method of the class. It's only usable as a member of the interface, so we can access it using the `cltest` value, which has a type `IClientTest`. We used an explicit cast and the `var` keyword in the code, because that will help our understanding how interface implementations work in F#. Another option is to declare the variable type as `IClientTest` and then assign the `test` value to it, because the C# compiler would use implicit conversion to the interface type.

Other than using explicit interface implementation, the class is wholly unremarkable. We're using it as a point of comparison with the F# code. Speaking of which…

IMPLEMENTING INTERFACES IN F#

Listing 9.17 uses explicit interface implementation in C# because that is the *only* style of interface implementation that F# allows. In the functional programming style, this is often adequate. If you *really* need to expose the functionality directly from the class, you can add an additional member that invokes the same code. Listing 9.18 shows an F# version of the previous example.

Listing 9.18 Implementing interface in a class (F#)

```
type CoefficientTest(incomeCoeff, yearsCoeff, minValue) =        ❶

  let coeff(client) =
    float(client.Income) * incomeCoeff +
    float(client.YearsInJob) * yearsCoeff                          ❷
  let report(client) =
    printfn "Coefficient %f less than %f" (coeff(client)) minValue

  member x.PrintInfo() =
    printfn "income*%f + years*%f > %f"
            incomeCoeff yearsCoeff minValue

  interface ClientTest with
    member x.Report(client) = report(client)                       ❸
    member x.Check(client) = coeff(client) < min
```

Listing 9.18 uses so-called *implicit class syntax*, which means that it specifies parameters of the constructor directly in the declaration ❶. It takes three arguments specifying coefficients for the calculation. Since we're referring to these parameters later in the members, the F# compiler will automatically store them in class fields.

Next, we defined two local helper functions using the standard `let` binding syntax ❷. These aren't visible from outside of the class, and we use them only for other members later in the code. When implementing an interface ❸, we group all members from a single interface together using the `interface ... with` syntax and implement them using usual members. If we also wanted to expose some of the same functionality as a public method, we could add another member to the class declaration and call the local helper function. Alternatively, we could implement the functionality in the public member and call that member from the interface implementation.

Working with the class is very much like the previous C# version, which was using explicit interface implementation. You can see the F# version of the code in listing 9.19.

Listing 9.19 Working with F# classes and interfaces (F# Interactive)

```
> let test = new CoefficientTest(0.001, 5.0, 50.0);;     ◁─┐ Creates instance
val test : CoefficientTest                                 │ of class

> test.PrintInfo();;                                     ◁─┐ Uses method
income*0.001000 + years*5.000000 > 50.000000               │ of class

> let cltest = (test :> ClientTest);;       ❶
val cltest : ClientTest
                                                           ┐ Uses methods
> if (cltest.Check(john)) then cltest.Report(john);;   ◁─┘ of interface
Coefficient 45.000000 is less than 50.000000.
```

Most of listing 9.19 should be quite straightforward. The only exception is the code that casts the value to the interface type ❶, because we haven't yet talked about casts. In F#, there are two kinds of casts. In this case, the compiler knows at the compilation that the cast will succeed, because it knows that the class (`CoefficientTest`) implements the interface (`ClientTest`). This is called an *upcast*. In the next section, we'll look at both of the casts in detail.

UPCASTS AND DOWNCASTS IN F#

When the conversion between the types can't fail, it's called an upcast. We've seen that this is the case when converting a type to an interface implemented by that type. Another example is casting a derived class to its base class. In this case the compiler can also guarantee that the operation is correct and won't fail.

If we have a value of a base type and we want to cast it to an inherited class, the operation can fail because the value of the base class may or may not be a value of the target class. In this case, we have to use a second type of casting, which is called a *downcast*. Let's demonstrate this using an example. We'll use the standard `Random` class, which is (just like any other .NET class) derived from the `Object` class:

```
> open System;;
> let rnd = new Random();;
val rnd : Random

> let rndObject = (rnd :> Object);;          Succeeds--operation
val obj : Object                             can't fail

> let rnd2 = (rndObject :> Random);;         Invalid use
stdin(4,12): error: Type constraint mismatch.   of upcast
The type 'Object' is not compatible with the type 'Random'

> let rnd2 = (rndObject :?> Random);;        Succeeds--but
val rnd2 : Random                            could fail

> (rndObject :?> String);;
System.InvalidCastException: Unable to cast object of type
   'System.Random' to type 'System.String'.
```

As you can see, if we accidentally try to use an upcast inappropriately, the F# compiler reports this as an error. The error message says that `Object` isn't compatible with `Random`, which means that the compiler can't guarantee that the value of type `Object` can be casted to the `Random` type. Finally, the listing shows that a downcast can fail and throws an exception if we try to cast an object to the wrong inherited class.

A good way to remember the F# syntax for upcasts (`:>`) and downcasts (`:?>`) is to realize that there's some uncertainty when using downcasts, because the operation can fail. This uncertainty is the reason why the downcast operator contains the question mark symbol and upcast doesn't. The F# language also provides an equivalent to the `is` operator known from C# that returns a Boolean value specifying whether an object instance can be casted to the specified type. To test whether `obj` can be casted to `String`, we'd write `obj :? String`.

It's worth thinking about the differences between F# and C# here. In C#, we didn't even *need* the cast in listing 9.17: when the compiler knows the conversion can succeed and it's not needed for disambiguation, you can let it occur implicitly. F# doesn't perform any conversions implicitly, so it makes sense for it to have a language construct expressing conversions that are guaranteed to succeed. In C# it wouldn't make sense as you'd use it so rarely—it's simpler to use the same syntax for both kinds of conversion. The programming style where you specify conversions explicitly makes type inference possible, but it also often helps to clarify what code actually does.

It would be impossible to review all the object-oriented features of F# in a single (reasonably sized!) chapter, but we've seen that the ones that are most important in order to evolve functional applications into real-world .NET code.

We've said several times that these changes make our F# code more easily accessible from C#, and it's time to provide proof of that, and show how the interoperability hangs together.

9.5 *Using F# libraries from C#*

Like C#, F# is a statically typed language, which means that the compiler knows the type of every value as well as signatures of class methods and properties. This is very important for interoperability with C#, because the compiler can generate code that looks just like an ordinary .NET library.

Interoperability with other .NET languages

The interoperability between F# and C# or VB.NET is very smooth compared to dynamically typed languages that have a .NET implementation like Python, Ruby, or JavaScript. Compilers for these languages don't know whether a method takes an argument of type int or, for example, Customer, so using code written in these languages is more difficult when using C# 3.0. Often you don't even know whether an object contains a method with a particular name, so the C# code has to look like this:

```
obj.InvokeMethod("SayHello", new object[] { "Tomas" });
```

This example specifies the name of the method as a string and passes the arguments to the method in an array. This is an important problem for many languages, so C# 4.0 introduces the dynamic type, which allows you to write something like this:

```
obj.SayHello("Tomas");
obj.SaiHello("Tomas");
```

The syntax is the same as for normal method calls, but there's an important difference. We intentionally added another method call, but with a misspelled method name. This will compile correctly, because the method name is internally represented as a string just as in the previous example. The problem only comes to light at runtime. The fact that F# is statically typed means we don't have to worry about this: we can rely on the compiler to spot the same kinds of errors it would when calling into other C# code.

When creating F# libraries that should be usable from C#, we need to distinguish between two kinds of F# constructs. The first kind includes classes or records with members, which appear as standard C# classes and can be used without any trouble. The second kind includes values or higher-order functions that are compiled in a nonstandard way and are harder to use from C#. Let's start by looking at an example of the first kind.

9.5.1   *Working with records and members*

We'll start with a basic example. In the first section of this chapter, we saw how to add members to the `Rect` type that represents a rectangle. Now we're going to use the type from C#. First we need to create a new F# "Library" project and add a source file (for example, export.fs) containing the code from listing 9.20.

> **Listing 9.20   Compiling F# types into a library (F#)**

```
namespace Chapter09.FSharpExport        ❶

open System
open System.Drawing

type Rect =
    { Left : float32; Width : float32         ❷
      Top : float32; Height : float32 }

  member x.Deflate(wspace, hspace) =
    { Top = x.Top + wspace; Height = x.Height - (2.0f * hspace)
      Left = x.Left + hspace; Width = x.Width - (2.0f * wspace) }    ❸
  member x.ToRectangleF () =
    RectangleF(x.Left, x.Top, x.Width, x.Height)
```

As you can see, we've added a single line to specify the .NET namespace ❶. This namespace will contain all the type declarations from the file (in our case, there's only a single type called `Rect`). This type will be easy to use from C# because the fields of the record ❷ will become properties and members ❸ will appear as methods.

Next we're going to add a new C# project to the solution. Adding a reference to the F# project is done exactly as if you were referencing another C# class library, although you should also add a reference to the `FSharp.Core.dll` assembly. This is an F# redistributable library that contains the F# core functions and types. After configuring the projects, you should see something similar to figure 9.3. The figure also shows how other F# types from this chapter appear in IntelliSense from C#.

If you experiment with IntelliSense, you'll see that the F# type is present in the namespace we specified in its source code. IntelliSense also shows what properties and methods the type has, so you'd surely be able to use it without any further help. For completeness, listing 9.21 gives an example.

> **Listing 9.21   Using types from the F# library (C#)**

```
using System;
using Chapter09.FSharpExport;

class Program {
  static void Main(string[] args) {
    var rc1 = new Rect(0.0f, 100.0f, 0.0f, 50.0f);       ❶
    var rc2 = rc1.Deflate(20.0f, 10.0f);                 ❷
    Console.WriteLine("({0}, {1}) - ({2}, {3})",
      rc2.Left, rc2.Top, rc2.Width, rc2.Height);
  }
}
```

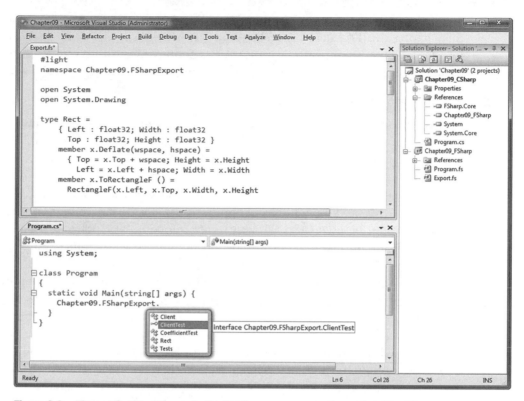

Figure 9.3   After adding a reference to the F# library, we can see types from the F# project in IntelliSense. The F# record type Rect is compiled as an ordinary class.

The code listing 9.21 first creates an instance of the Rect type. It uses a constructor that was automatically generated by the F# compiler ❶ and corresponds to the F# code for creating a record. We have to specify values for all the fields of the record at construction time—we can't change them later, as the type is immutable. The next step is to invoke the Deflate method ❶. This is a perfectly ordinary method, although it's implemented in a purely functional style so it returns a new Rect value instead of mutating the existing one. Finally, we print the information about the returned rectangle. This is also easy, because record fields are exposed as .NET properties.

NOTE   We've looked at referencing F# projects from C# because this is a common scenario and we wanted to explicitly show how nicely the two languages play together when the F# code uses object types. You can also reference F# libraries from F# applications. The steps to do this would be the same: specify a namespace for the F# library, add a reference in Visual Studio, and add an appropriate open directive to your F# application. It's worth noting that when referencing an F# library from F#, the compiler will recognize that the library is authored in F# and all constructs (such as discriminated unions or functions) will be accessible in the normal F# way.

Using the Rect type from C# is quite simple, and figure 9.3 shows other types from this chapter. An F# Interface declaration (ClientTest) shows as an ordinary .NET interface, so the interoperability works very smoothly. What if we wanted to export a higher-order function or a value? What would these two constructs look like in C#?

9.5.2   *Working with values and delegates*

In this section, we're going to look at using two more typical F# constructs from C#. We'll see how to export a value and a higher-order function. The latter is tricky, because F# uses quite a sophisticated internal representation for functions.

If a function took int -> int -> int as an argument, a C# developer would see this as FastFunc<int, FastFunc<int, int>>. It's possible to work with this type, but it isn't very convenient; we'll use a different approach. If we're writing a higher-order function that should be used from C#, we can use standard .NET delegates. This isn't as natural as using normal functions in F#, but the library will be much simpler to use from C#.

Another problem crops up when we want to export a value or function directly: methods (and fields) don't appear on their own in .NET, or even as part of a namespace—they're always part of a type. The very idea of a method existing with no containing type to love and nurture it is enough to make a compassionate C# developer distraught. Help is at hand in the form of F# *modules*. Listing 9.22 shows how a value and a utility function can be exported so they can be used from C#, and also demonstrates the previous point about using delegates for higher-order functions.

> **Listing 9.22   Exporting values and higher-order functions (F#)**

```
namespace Chapter09.FSharpExport
open System

type Client =
  { Name : string; Income : int; YearsInJob : int
    UsesCreditCard : bool; CriminalRecord : bool }

module Tests =                                          ❶
    let John =
      { Name = "John Doe"; Income = 25000; YearsInJob = 1
        UsesCreditCard = true; CriminalRecord = false }

    let WithIncome (f:Func<_, _>) client =             ❷
      { client with Income = f.Invoke(client.Income) } ❸
```

The module declaration ❶ tells the F# compiler to enclose the values and functions into a class with static methods (when compiling functions) and static properties (for values). We've chosen to follow the C# naming conventions here (using Pascalcase) as the reason for creating the module in the first place is to expose the values to C#.

The next point to note is the WithIncome function. It's a higher-order function, but instead of taking a normal F# function as an argument, it takes a .NET delegate Func with two generic arguments ❷. We're using an underscore so the F# compiler infers the actual types for us. When we need to invoke the delegate later in the code ❸, we use its `Invoke` method. This is somewhat inelegant compared with normal F# function calling, but it means the C# client can work with it in an idiomatic manner using lambda functions:

```
var client = Tests.John;
client = Tests.WithIncome(income => income + 5000, client);
Console.WriteLine("{0} - {1}", client.Name, client.Income);
```

The module that we called `Tests` is compiled into a class, so the value `John` becomes a static property of this class and `WithIncome` becomes a method. As you can see, it takes an argument of type `Func<int, int>`, so anyone who knows C# 3.0 can use it even though the code is actually written in F#. In reality, we could make `WithIncome` a member of the `Client` type and the C# user would call it using the familiar dot notation. However, we wanted to demonstrate that even basic F# functions can be used from C# with no problems.

9.6   *Summary*

In the last few chapters, we've talked about functional programming and implemented several sample applications in the functional style. We started with simple functional ideas such as combining values into "multiple values" or "alternative values," then we discussed ways of working with functions. In chapters 7 and 8 we talked about the design of functional programs. This wasn't a haphazard decision: the structure of the book corresponds to the iterative F# development style. We started with simple concepts that allowed us to solve problems succinctly and quickly. In this chapter we took the final step of the iterative development process, exposing our code in familiar .NET terms.

We've seen members that allow us to encapsulate functionality related to a type with the type itself and intrinsic type extensions that can be used if we already have the code as ordinary functions. Next, we looked at abstract types (interfaces) that are quite useful when writing behavior-centric applications. We also discussed classes, which are particularly important in interoperability scenarios.

There are still many things that we haven't covered. In the next few chapters, we're going to turn our attention from architectural aspects back to the core functional programming techniques. In the upcoming chapter, we're going to revisit lists and simple recursive functions, and you'll see essential techniques for writing efficient functional code. This is an important aspect that we skipped earlier to make the introduction as simple as possible. You've already mastered all the basic functional ideas, so we're now ready to dive into important advanced techniques.

Efficiency of
data structures

This chapter covers
- Optimizing and improving recursive functions
- Using tail-recursion and continuations
- Working efficiently with lists and arrays

So far in this book, we've used functional techniques such as recursion and functional data structures like immutable lists. We've written the code in the most straightforward way we could, using the basic F# collection type (a list) and expressing our intentions directly. This works very well in many situations, but when it comes to processing large data sets, "obvious" code sometimes leads to performance problems. In this chapter, we'll look at techniques for writing code that work regardless of the size of the input and examine ways to optimize the performance of functions working with data. We'll still strive to keep the code as readable as possible.

If you've been developing for any significant length of time, you've almost certainly written a program that caused a stack overflow exception. In functional programming this error can easily be caused by a naïvely written recursive function, so we'll explore several ways of dealing with functions that can cause this error when processing large amounts of data. This will be our starting topic, and we'll return to it at the end of the chapter.

In between these discussions on recursion, we'll discuss functional lists and arrays. When working with functional lists, it's important to understand how they work so you can use them efficiently. F# also supports arrays that can give us better performance in some situations. Even though arrays are primarily imperative data types, you'll see that we can use them in a very functional way.

10.1 *Optimizing functions*

In earlier chapters, you learned that recursion is the primary control flow mechanism for functions in F#. We first used it for writing simple functions that perform some calculation, such as adding up numbers in a specified range or working out a factorial. Later we found it invaluable while working with recursive data structures—most importantly lists.

You may be familiar with several limitations of recursion, and the possibility of stack overflow is the most obvious one. As you'll see, some recursive computations can be very inefficient too. In imperative languages, you'd often use nonrecursive functions to avoid problems. Functional languages have developed their own ways of dealing with these problems and can work with recursion efficiently. First let's concentrate on correctness: it's no good being really efficient with up to 1 KB of data if an extra byte blows your stack...

10.1.1 *Avoiding stack overflows with tail recursion*

For every function call, the runtime allocates a *stack frame*. These frames are stored on a stack maintained by the system. A stack frame is removed when a call completes; if a function calls another function, then a new frame is added on top of the stack. The size of the stack is limited, so too many nested function calls leave no space for another stack frame, and the next function can't be called. When this happens in .NET, a `StackOverflowException` is raised. In .NET 2.0 and higher, this exception can't be caught and will bring down the whole process.

Recursion is based on nested function calls, so it isn't surprising that you'll encounter this error most often when writing complex recursive computations. (That may not be true. The most common cause in C# is *probably* writing a property that accidentally refers to itself instead of its backing field. We'll ignore such typos and only consider *intentional* recursion.) Just to show the kind of situation we're talking about, let's use the list-summing code from chapter 3, but give it a really big list.

> **Listing 10.1   Summing list and stack overflow (F# Interactive)**

```
> let test1 = [ 1 .. 10000 ]          Creates lists
  let test2 = [ 1 .. 100000 ];;        for testing
val test1 : int list
```

```
val test2 : int list

> let rec sumList(lst) =
    match lst with
    | [] -> 0                          ❶
    | hd::tl -> hd + sumList(tl);;          ❷
val sumList : int list -> int

> sumList(test1)              ❸
val it : int = 50005000

> sumList(test2)              ❹
Process is terminated due to StackOverflowException.
```

Just like every recursive function, sumList contains a case that terminates the recursion ❶ and a case where it recursively calls itself ❷. The function completes a certain amount of work before performing the recursive call (it performs pattern matching on the list and reads the tail), then it executes the recursive call (to sum the numbers in the tail). Finally, it performs a calculation with the result: it adds the value stored in the head with the total sum returned from the recursion. The details of the last step are particularly important, as you'll see in a moment.

As we might have predicted, there's a point when the code stops working. If we give it a list with tens of thousands of elements ❸, it works fine. For a list with hundreds of thousands of elements, the recursion goes too deep and F# Interactive reports an exception ❹. Figure 10.1 shows what's happening: the arrows above the diagram represent the first part of the execution, before and during the recursive call. The arrows below the diagram represent the recursion returning the result.

We used a notation [1..] to denote a list containing series that begins with 1. In the first case, F# Interactive starts executing sumList with a list from 1 to 10000 as its argument. The figure shows how a stack frame is added to the stack for each call. Every step in the process takes the tail of the list and uses it as an argument for a recursive call to sumList. In the first case, the stack is a sufficient size, so we eventually reach a case where the argument is an empty list. In the second case, we use up all of the space after roughly 64,000 calls. The runtime reaches the stack limits and raises a StackOverflowException.

Executing sumList test1:

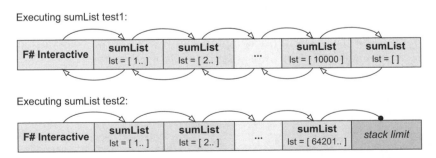

Executing sumList test2:

Figure 10.1   Stack frames when summing numbers in a list. In the first case, the stack frames fit within the limit, so the operation succeeds. In the second case, the calculation reaches the limit and an exception is thrown.

Both arrows from the left to the right and back again do some work. The first part of the operation is executed before the recursive call and decomposes a list into head and tail components. The second part, executed after the recursive call completes, adds the value from the head to the total.

Now we know why it's failing, what can we do about it? The essential idea is that we only need to keep the stack frame because we need to do some work after the recursive call completes. In our example, we still need the value of the head element so we can add it to the result of the recursive call. If the function didn't have to do anything after the recursive call completed, it could jump from the last recursive call back, directly to the caller, without using anything from the stack frames in between. Let's demonstrate this with the following trivial function:

```
let rec foo(arg) =
  if (arg = 1000) then true
  else foo(arg + 1)
```

As you can see, the last operation that the `foo` function performs in the `else` branch is a recursive call. It doesn't need to do any processing with the result; it returns the result directly. This kind of recursive call is called *tail recursion*. Effectively, the result of the deepest level of recursion—which is a call to `foo(1000)`—can be directly returned to the caller.

Figure 10.2 The recursive function `foo` doesn't do anything after the recursive call. The execution can jump directly to the caller (F# Interactive) from the last recursive call, which is `foo(1000)`.

In figure 10.2, you can see that the stack frames created during the computation (while jumping from the left to the right) are never used on the way back. This means that the stack frame is only needed before the recursive call, but when we recursively call `foo(2)` from `foo(1)`, we don't need the stack frame for `foo(1)`. The runtime can simply throw it away to save the space. Figure 10.3 shows the actual execution of the tail-recursive function `foo`.

Figure 10.3 shows how F# executes tail-recursive functions. When a function is tail recursive, we need only a single slot on the stack. This makes the recursive version as efficient as an iterative solution.

You may be wondering whether every recursive function can be rewritten to use tail

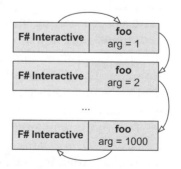

Figure 10.3 Execution of a tail-recursive function. The stack frame can be dropped during the recursive call, so only a single frame is needed at any point during the execution.

Tail recursion in the .NET ecosystem

When compiling function that uses tail recursion, the F# compiler uses two techniques. In cases when the function calls itself (such as `foo` in the previous example), it translates the recursive code to equivalent code that uses imperative loops. Tail calls also occur when several functions recursively call each other. In this case the compiler cannot easily rewrite the code and uses a special `tailcall` instruction that is directly supported by the Intermediate Language (IL).

In the debug configuration, the second optimization is turned off by default, because it complicates debugging. In particular, the stack frames are dropped during a tail call, so you can't see them in the stack trace window. You can turn this feature on in the project properties using the "Generate tail calls" check.

Since tail calls are directly supported by IL, the C# compiler could also spot tail-recursive calls and make use of this optimization. At the moment, it doesn't do so, because C# developers normally design code in imperative fashion where tail recursion isn't needed.

That's not to say that the runtime won't use tail call optimizations with code written in C#. Even if the IL doesn't contain explicit hints that it wants to use a tail call, the just-in-time compiler (JIT) may notice that it can do so safely and go ahead. The rules for when this happens are complicated, and vary between the x86 and x64 JIT compilers. They're subject to change at any time. In .NET 4.0 the JIT was improved in many ways, so it uses tail recursion more often. Also it never ignores the `tailcall` instruction, which was occasionally the case in .NET 2.0, especially in the x64 version.

recursion. The answer is yes, but the general technique, which we'll discuss in section 10.3, is a bit complicated. The rule of thumb is that if a function executes a single recursive call in each branch, we should be able to use a relatively straightforward trick.

USING AN ACCUMULATOR ARGUMENT

Let's think about how we'd make the `sumList` function tail recursive. It only performs the recursive call once in the branch where the argument is a cons cell (a nonempty list). Our rule of thumb suggests that it shouldn't be difficult—but at the moment it does more than return the result of the recursive call: it adds the value from the head to the total number.

To turn this into a tail-recursive function, we can use a technique that supplies an *accumulator argument*. Instead of calculating the result as we jump from the right to the left (in the earlier figures, as we're coming back toward the original function call), we can calculate the result as part of the operation that runs before the recursive call. We'll need to add another parameter to the function to provide the current result. Listing 10.2 shows this technique.

Listing 10.2   Tail-recursive version of the `sumList` function (F# Interactive)

```
> let rnd = new System.Random()
  let test1 = List.init 10000 (fun _ -> rnd.Next(-50, 51))
  let test2 = List.init 100000 (fun _ -> rnd.Next(- 50, 51));;    ❶
val rnd : Random
val test1 : int list = [1; -14; -35; 34; -1; -39; ...]
val test2 : int list = [29; -44; -1; 25; -33; 36; ...]

> let sumList(lst) =
    let rec sumListUtil(lst, total) =         ❷
      match lst with
      | [] -> total                           ❸
      | hd::tl ->
        let ntotal = hd + total               ❹     Makes
        sumListUtil(tl, ntotal)                      recursive call
    sumListUtil(lst, 0);;                      ◄     Calls helper
val sumList : int list -> int                        with total=0

> sumList(test1);;
val it : int = -2120            Both calls
                                compute
> sumList(test2);;              the result!
val it : int = 8736
```

Listing 10.2 begins by generating two lists containing random numbers ❶. We're using a function `List.init` that takes the required length of the list as the first argument and calls the provided function to calculate value of the element at the specified index. We're not using the index in the computation, so we used "_" to ignore it. The reason we need better testing input is that if we added all numbers between 1 and 100,000, we'd get incorrect results, because the result wouldn't fit into a 32-bit integer. We're generating random numbers between –50 and +50, so in principle the sum should be very close to zero.

The most interesting part of the listing is the `sumList` function. When we use an accumulator argument, we need to write another function with an additional parameter. We don't usually want this to be visible to the caller, so we write it as a local function ❷. The accumulator argument (in our example, `total`) stores the current result. When we reach the end of the list, we already have the result, so we can just return it ❸. Otherwise, we add the value from the head to the result and perform a recursive call with the accumulator set to the new value ❹. Figure 10.4 shows how the new computation model works. Both the call to the utility function and the recursive call inside it return the result immediately, so they can be executed using the tail call.

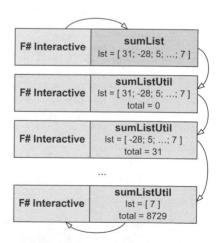

Figure 10.4 Execution of the tail-recursive `sumList` function. The first call invokes the utility function, which keeps track of the current result of summing all preceding elements using an accumulator argument (`total`).

The sumList example isn't difficult, but it demonstrates the idea of using an accumulator. We add another parameter to the function and use it to calculate a temporary result before making the recursive call. When you're trying to make a function tail recursive, look at the information you're currently using *after* the recursive call, and try to find a way to pass it *into* the recursive call instead.

We'll see some trickier examples when we talk about list processing, but we'll take a detour first, via another important optimization technique: *memoization*.

10.1.2 *Caching results using memoization*

Memoization, described as caching the results of a function call, may sound complicated, but the technique is very simple. As we mentioned earlier, most functions in functional programming do not have side effects. This means that if we call a function with the same argument twice, we'll get the same result.

If we're going to get the same result we got last time, why would we want to go to all the trouble of executing the function again? Instead, we can cache the results. If we store the result of the first call in some dictionary, we won't need to recompute the value for the second call. We can read the result from the dictionary and return it right away. Listing 10.3 shows a function that adds two integers.

Listing 10.3   Adding numbers with memoization (F# Interactive)

```
> open System.Collections.Generic;;

> let addSimple(a, b) =                ❶
    printfn "adding %d + %d" a b              <--- Prints debugging info
    a + b
  ;;
val addSimple : int * int -> int

> let add =                            ❷
    let cache = new Dictionary<_, _>()              Creates function
    (fun x ->                                       that uses cache
      match cache.TryGetValue(x) with
      | true, v -> v                        Reads value
      | _ -> let v = addSimple(x)           from cache or
          cache.Add(x, v)                   calculates it
          v)
  ;;
val add : (int * int -> int)

> add(2,3);;
adding 2 + 3                Executes
val it : int = 5           addSimple
                           only once
> add(2,3);;
val it : int = 5
```

The first part of listing 10.3 is a normal addition function ❶ with the slight twist that it logs its execution to the console. Without this we wouldn't see any obvious differences between the original and memoized version, because the change in efficiency is really small for this example.

The function that implements addition with caching is called add ❷. It uses the .NET `Dictionary` type to store the cached results. The cache is declared as a local value and is used from the lambda expression that's assigned to the add value. We used a similar pattern in chapter 8 when we were talking about capturing mutable state using closures. Here, the cache value is also mutable (because `Dictionary` is a mutable hash table) and is also captured by a closure. The point is that we need to use the same cache value for all calls to the add function, so we have to declare it before the function, but we don't want to make it a global value.

The last part of the function is the lambda itself. It only uses the addSimple function when the result isn't cached already. As you can see from the F# Interactive session, the function that does the calculation is executed only for the first time.

This technique is more widely applicable than tail recursion. It can be applied to any function that doesn't have any side effects.[1] This means that we can use it successfully from C# 3.0 as well. In the next subsection, we're going to use C# 3.0 to write a more generic version of the code.

REUSABLE MEMOIZATION IN C# AND F#

If you look at the code that builds the add value from listing 10.3, you can see that it doesn't really know about addition. It happens to use the addSimple function, but it could just as well work with any other function. To make the code more general, we can turn this function into a parameter.

We're going to write a function (or method in C#) that takes a function as an argument and returns a memoized version of this function. The argument is the function that does the actual work and the returned function is augmented with caching capability. You can see the C# version of the code in listing 10.4.

Listing 10.4   Generic memoization method (C#)

```
Func<T, R> Memoize<T, R>(Func<T, R> func) {          ❶
  var cache = new Dictionary<T, R>();          ⟵  Captures cache
  return arg => {                                    by closure
    R val;
    if (cache.TryGetValue(arg, out val)) return val;  ⟵  Returns
    else {                                                cached value
      val = func(arg);              Calculates value,
      cache.Add(arg, val);          adds it to cache
      return val;
    } };
}
```

The code is similar to the addition-specific function in listing 10.3. Again, we first create a cache, then return a lambda function that captures the cache in the closure. This means that there will be exactly one cache for each returned function, which is just what we want.

---

[1] This may be somewhat confusing, because the function in the previous listing had a side effect (printing to the screen). This is a "soft side effect" that we can safely ignore. The core requirement is that the result should depend only on the arguments passed to the function.

The method signature ❶ indicates that it takes a function Func<T, R> and returns a function of the same type. This means that it doesn't change the structure of the function; it wraps it into another function that does the caching. The signature is generic, so it can be used with any function which takes a single argument. We can overcome this limitation with tuples. The following code shows the C# version of the memoized function for adding two numbers:

```csharp
var addMem = Memoize((Tuple<int, int> arg) => {
  Console.Write("adding {0} + {1}; ", arg.Item1, arg.Item2);
  return arg.Item1 + arg.Item2; });

Console.Write("{0}; ", addMem(Tuple.Create(19, 23)));       ❶
Console.Write("{0}; ", addMem(Tuple.Create(19, 23)));

Console.Write("{0}; ", addMem(Tuple.Create(18, 24)));       ❷
```

If you run the code, you'll see that the second block of code prints "adding 19+23" only once ❶ and the third block prints "adding 18 + 24" ❷. This means that the first addition executed only once, because when the cache compares two tuple values, it will find a match when their elements are equal. This wouldn't work with our first implementation of Tuple because it didn't have any implementation of value equality; the Tuple type in .NET 4.0 as well as the version in the source code for this chapter overrides the Equals method to compare the component values. This is called structural comparison, and you'll learn more about it in chapter 11. Another option to make the Memoize method work with functions with multiple parameters would be to overload it for Func<T1, T2, R>, Func<T1, T2, T3, R> and so on. We would still use tuple as a key in the cache, but this would be hidden from the user of the method.

The same code in F# shows how easy it is to make code generic. We'll take the code we wrote for addition in listing 10.3 and make the function that does the computation parameter of the memoization function. You can see the F# version in listing 10.5.

Listing 10.5 Generic memoization function (F# Interactive)

```fsharp
> let memoize(f) =
    let cache = new Dictionary<_, _>()       ◁─┐ Initializes cache
    (fun x ->                                   │ captured by closure
      match cache.TryGetValue(x) with
      | true, v -> v
      | _ -> let v = f(x)
             cache.Add(x, v)
             v);;
val memoize : ('a -> 'b) -> ('a -> 'b)       ❶
```

In the F# version, the type signature is inferred ❶, so we don't have to make the function generic by hand. The F# compiler uses generalization to do this for us; the inferred signature corresponds to the explicit one in the C# code.

This time, we'll use a more interesting example to demonstrate how effective memoization can be. We'll go back to the world's favorite recursion example: the factorial function. Listing 10.6 attempts to memoize this, but it doesn't quite go according to plan…

Listing 10.6 Difficulties with memoizing recursive function (F# Interactive)

```
> let rec factorial(x) =                    ❶
    printf "factorial(%d); " x
    if (x <= 0) then 1 else x * factorial(x - 1);;   ❷
val factorial : int -> int

> let factorialMem = memoize factorial      ❸
val factorial : (int -> int)

> factorialMem(2);;                                  ┐ Calculates 2!
factorial(2); factorial(1); factorial(0);  <────────┘ for first time
val it : int = 1

> factorialMem(2);;    ┐ Uses cached
val it : int = 1   <───┘ value

> factorialMem(3);;                                       ❹ Why is the value
factorial(3); factorial(2); factorial(1); factorial(0)  <──┘  of 2! recalculated?
val it : int = 2
```

At the first glance, the code seems correct. It first implements the factorial computation as a straightforward recursive function ❶ and then creates a version optimized using the `memoize` function ❸. When we test it later by running the same call twice, it still seems to work. The result is cached after the first call and it can be reused.

The last call ❹ doesn't work correctly—or more precisely, it doesn't do what we'd like it to. The problem is that the memoization covers only the first call, which is `factorialMem(3)`. The subsequent calls made by the `factorial` function during the recursive calculation call the original function directly instead of calling the memoized version. To correct this, we'll need to change the line that does the recursive call ❷ to use the memoized version (`factorialMem`). This function is declared later in the code, so we could use the `let rec...` and `...` syntax to declare two mutually recursive functions.

A simpler option is to use lambda functions and only expose the memoized version as a reusable function. Listing 10.7 shows how we can do this with just a few lines of code.

Listing 10.7 Correctly memoized factorial function (F# Interactive)

```
> let rec factorial = memoize(fun x ->
    printfn "Calculating factorial(%d)" x
    if (x <= 0) then 1 else x * factorial(x - 1));;    ❶
warning FS0040: This and other recursive references to the
object(s) being defined will be checked for initialization-     ❷
soundness at runtime through the use of a delayed reference...

val factorial : (int -> int)

> factorial(2);;                                  ┐ Computes first
factorial(2); factorial(1); factorial(0);  <──────┘ few values
val it : int = 2

> factorial(4);;              ┐ Computes only
factorial(4); factorial(3);  <┘ missing value
val it : int = 24
```

The `factorial` symbol in this example refers to a value. It's not syntactically defined as a function with arguments; instead it's a value (which happens to have a function type) returned by the `memoize` function. This means that we're not declaring a recursive *function* but a recursive *value*. We used `let rec` to declare recursive values in chapter 8 when creating the decision tree, but we only used it for writing nodes in a more natural order—there weren't any recursive calls within the code.

This time, we're creating a truly recursive value, because the `factorial` value is used within its own declaration ❶. The difficulty with recursive values is that if we're not careful, we can write code that refers to some value during the initialization of that value, which is an invalid operation. An example of incorrect initialization looks like this:

```
let initialize(f) = f()
let rec num = initialize (fun _ -> num + 1)
```

Here, the reference to the value `num` occurs inside a lambda function, which is invoked during the initialization when the `initialize` function is called. If we run this code, we'll get a runtime error at the point where `num` is declared. When using recursive functions, the function will always be defined at the time when we'll perform a recursive call. The code may keep looping forever, but that's a different problem.

In our declaration of `factorial` the reference to the `factorial` value occurs in a lambda function, which is *not* called during initialization, so it's a valid declaration. The F# compiler can't distinguish these two cases at compile time, so it emits a warning ❷ and adds runtime checks. Don't be too scared by this! Just make sure that the lambda function containing the reference won't be evaluated during the initialization.

Since the declaration of `factorial` uses the memoized version when it makes the recursive call, it can now read values from the cache for any step of the calculation. For example, when we calculate factorial of 4 after we've already calculated the factorial of 2, we only need to compute the two remaining values.

NOTE   So far we've seen two optimization techniques used in functional programming. Using tail recursion, we can avoid stack overflows and write better recursive functions. Memoization can be used for optimizing any functions without side effects.

Both techniques fit perfectly with the iterative development style that we consider an important aspect of F# programming. We can start with a straightforward implementation—often a function, possibly recursive, with no side effects. Later in the process, we can identify areas of code that need to be optimized. Just as we saw how it's easy to evolve the structure of the code earlier and add object-oriented aspects, the changes required for optimization are reasonably straightforward to make. The iterative process helps us to pay the small additional price in complexity only in places where the benefit is actually significant.

So far we've seen general-purpose tricks for writing efficient functions. There's one type of data structure that lends itself to very specific optimizations: collections. In the next section we'll talk about functional lists and also look at how we can use .NET arrays in a functional way.

10.2 Working with large collections

We mentioned that we'd come back to tail recursion and show some slightly more complicated situations involving lists. Hopefully by now any recursion-induced headaches will have worn off, and after a fresh cup of coffee you should be ready for the upcoming examples.

As well as making sure our programs don't blow up with stack overflow exceptions, we want them to run in a reasonable amount of time as well. (What is it with employers making such unrealistic demands?) Functional lists are fabulously useful and *can* be used very efficiently, but if you use them in the *wrong* way you can end up with painfully slow code. We'll show you how to avoid these problems.

10.2.1 Avoiding stack overflows with tail recursion (again!)

Our naïve list processing functions in chapter 6 weren't tail recursive. If we passed them very large lists, they would fail with a stack overflow. We'll rewrite two of them (map and filter) to use tail recursion, which will remove the problem. Just for reference, we've included the original implementations in listing 10.8. To avoid name clashes, we've renamed them to mapN and filterN.

Listing 10.8 Naïve list processing functions (F#)

```
// Naïve 'map' implementation
let rec mapN f list =
  match list with
  | []     -> []
  | x::xs -> let xs = (mapN f xs)          <┐
            f(x) :: xs                      ◄┐
                                              │
// Naïve 'filter' implementation             │
let rec filterN f list =           ❶      ❷
  match list with
  | []     -> []
  | x::xs -> let xs = (filterN f xs)       <┘
            if f(x) then x::xs else xs      ◄┘
```

Both functions contain a single recursive call ❶, which isn't tail recursive. In each case the recursive call is followed by an additional operation ❷. The general scheme is that the function first decomposes the list into a head and a tail. Then it recursively processes the tail and performs some action with the head. More precisely, mapN applies the f function to the head value and filterN decides whether the head value should be included in the resulting list. The last operation is appending the new head value (or no value in case of filtering) to the recursively processed tail, which has to be done after the recursive call.

To turn these into tail-recursive functions, we use the *same* accumulator argument technique we saw earlier. We collect the elements (either filtered or mapped) as we iterate over the list and store them in the accumulator. Once we reach the end, we can return elements that we've collected. Listing 10.9 shows the tail-recursive implementations for both mapping and filtering.

Listing 10.9   Tail recursive list processing functions (F#)

```
// Tail-recursive 'map' implementation
let map f list =
  let rec map' f list acc =
    match list with
    | []     -> List.rev(acc)
    | x::xs -> let acc = f(x)::acc
               map' f xs acc
    map' f list []

// Tail-recursive 'filter' implementation
let filter f list =
  let rec filter' f list acc =
    match list with
    | []     -> List.rev(acc)
    | x::xs -> let acc = if f(x) then x::acc else acc
               filter' f xs acc
    filter' f list []
```

As usual when implementing tail-recursive functions, both functions contain a local utility function that has an additional accumulator parameter. This time, we added a single quote (') to the name, which may look strange at first. F# treats this single quote as a standard character that can be used in the name, so there's no magic going on.

Let's start by looking at the branch that terminates the recursion ❶. We said that we just return the collected elements, but we're actually reversing their order first by calling List.rev. This is because we're collecting the elements in the "wrong" order. We always add to the accumulator list by prepending an element as the new head, so the *first* element we process ends up as the *last* element in the accumulator. The call to the List.rev function reverses the list, so we end up returning the results in the right order. This approach is more efficient than appending elements to the end as we'll see in section 10.2.2.

The branch that processes a cons cell is now tail recursive. It processes the element from the head and updates the accumulator as a first step ❷. It makes the recursive call ❸ and returns the result immediately. The F# compiler can tell that the recursive call is the last step, and optimize it using tail recursion.

We can easily spot the difference between the two versions if we paste them into F# Interactive and try to process a large list. For these functions, the depth of the recursion is the same as the length of the list, so we run into problems if we use the naïve version:

```
> let large = [ 1 .. 100000 ]
val large : int list = [ 1; 2; 3; 4; 5; ...]

> large |> map (fun n -> n*n);;
val it : int list = [1; 4; 9; 16; 25; ...]

> large |> mapN (fun n -> n*n);;
Process is terminated due to StackOverflowException.
```

As you can see, tail recursion is an important technique for recursive processing functions. Of course, the F# libraries contain tail-recursive functions for working with lists, so you don't really have to write your own map and filter implementations as we have here. In chapters 6, 7, and 8 we saw that designing our own data structures and writing functions that work with them is the key to functional programming.

Many of the data structures that you'll create will be reasonably small, but when working with a large amount of data, tail recursion is an essential technique. Using tail recursion, we can write code that works correctly on large data sets. Of course, just because a function won't overflow the stack doesn't mean it will finish in a reasonable amount of time—which is why we need to consider how to handle lists efficiently, too.

10.2.2 *Processing lists efficiently*

Tail-recursive functions usually improve efficiency slightly to start with, but usually the choice of algorithm is much more important than micro-optimization of its implementation. Let's demonstrate with an example, where we want to add elements to an existing list.

ADDING ELEMENTS TO A LIST

So far we've seen how to append elements to the front of an existing (functional) list. What if we wanted to append elements at the end of the list? This sounds like a reasonable requirement, so let's try to implement it. Listing 10.10 shows the difference in performance between inserting at the front of a list and a naïve attempt to insert at the end.

> **Listing 10.10   Adding elements to a list (F# Interactive)**

```
> let prepend el list = el::list;;            ❶
val prepend : 'a -> 'a list -> 'a list

> let rec append el list =                    ❷
    match list with
    | []    -> [el]          ←──┐  Appends to
    | x::xs -> x::(append el xs) ←─  empty list
val append : 'a -> 'a list -> 'a list   Appends to the
                                         rest recursively
> #time;;                                      ❸
> let l = [ 1 .. 30000 ];;
val l : int list

> for i = 1 to 100 do ignore(prepend 1 l);;
Real: 00:00:00.000, CPU: 00:00:00.000        Shows that
                                             append is
> for i = 1 to 100 do ignore(append 1 l);;   much slower
Real: 00:00:00.434, CPU: 00:00:00.421
```

The implementation of prepend is trivial ❶, because we can simply construct a new list cell using the cons operator (::). Appending an element to the end of the list requires writing a recursive function ❷. This follows the normal pattern for recursive list processing, with one case for an empty list and another for a cons cell.

Next, we enter a very useful F# Interactive command, `#time`, which turns on timing ❸. In this mode, F# will automatically print the time taken to execute the commands that we enter. We can see that appending an element at the end of large list is much slower. We run this one hundred times in a `for` loop and the time needed for appending to the front is still reported as zero, but appending elements to the end takes a significant amount of time. Any "simple" operation that takes half a second for only a hundred iterations is a concern.

Our appending function isn't tail recursive, but that's not a problem here. Tail recursion helps us to avoid stack overflow, but it only affects performance slightly. The problem is that functional lists are not suitable for the operation that we're trying to execute.

Figure 10.5 shows why this operation can't be implemented efficiently for functional lists. Appending an element to the front is easy. Because a list is an immutable data structure, we can create a single cell and reference the original list. Immutability guarantees that nobody can mutate the original list later, changing the contents of the "new" list behind our back. Compare that with appending an element to the end, which requires changing the last element. Previously the last element "knew" it came last, whereas we need it to have the new element following it. The list is immutable so we can't change the information stored in the last element. Instead, we have to clone the last element, which also means cloning the previous element (so it knows that it's followed by the cloned last element) and so on.

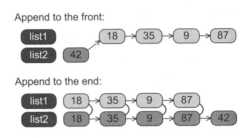

Figure 10.5   When appending an element to the front, we create a new cons cell and reference the original list. To append an element to the end, we need to iterate over and clone the whole list.

Of course, there are various data structures and each of them has different operations that can be executed efficiently. There's always a trade-off and that's why it's important to choose the right data structure for your problem.

Complexity of algorithms

Computer scientists use very precise mathematical terms to talk about complexity of algorithms, but the concepts behind these terms are important even when we use them informally. In general, the complexity of an operation tells us how the number of "primitive" steps the algorithm requires depends on the size of the input. It doesn't predict the exact number of steps—just its relationship to the size of the input.

Let's analyze our previous example. Appending an element to the front of the list always involves a single step: creating a new list cons cell. In the formal notation this is written as O(1), which means that the number of steps is constant, no matter how large the list. Adding an element to the start of a list with a million elements is as cheap as adding an element to the start of a list with just one element!

(continued)

Appending an element to the end of the list is trickier. If the list has N elements at the beginning, we'll need to process and duplicate N cons cells. This would be written as O(N), which means that the number of steps is roughly proportional to the size of the list: adding an element to the end of a list of size 1000 is roughly twice as expensive as adding an element to the end of a list of size 500.

If we wanted to append, for example, M new elements to the list, the complexity would be multiplied by M. This means that appending to the front would require O(M) steps, because 1 * M = M. Using similar reasoning, appending to the end would require O(N*M) steps, which could be bigger by an order of magnitude.

So far we've talked about functional lists, the most important collections in functional programming. Let's take a big leap and look at the collection that exists in almost all imperative programming languages: the humble array. F# is a .NET language, so it can use normal .NET arrays too.

10.2.3 Working with arrays

Arrays correspond closely to a simple model of computer memory—essentially a sequence of numbered boxes, where you can read or change the value in any box cheaply if you know the number. Arrays form continuous blocks of memory, so the overheads are small and they are useful for storing larger data sets. Arrays are allocated in advance: once they are created, the size is fixed; we can't add a new value to an existing array.

Arrays are mutable data structures, so we can easily update them. This is sometimes useful, but for a functional programmer, it means that we're losing many guarantees about the program state. First let's look at the basic F# syntax for arrays, as shown in listing 10.11.

Listing 10.11   Creating and using arrays (F# Interactive)

```
> let arr = [| 1 .. 5 |];;            ❶
val arr : int array = [|1; 2; 3; 4; 5|]

> arr.[2] <- 30;;          ❷
val it : unit = ()

> arr;;
val it : int array = [|1; 2; 30; 4; 5|]

> let mutable sum = 0
  for i in 0 .. arr.Length - 1 do      ❸
    sum <- arr.[i] + sum;;
val mutable sum : int = 42
```

Arrays in F# support all basic operations that we'd expect from an array. We start by initializing arr using syntax very similar to list initialization ❶. Next, we use the assignment operator to mutate the array and set the value at the specified index ❷.

Note that when accessing an element in F#, we have to write a dot (.) before the square braces that specify the index. The next couple of lines show how we can process an array in an imperative style ❸. It uses a for loop to iterate over all the elements and a mutable value to store a sum of them.

Don't worry if you feel slightly dirty looking at listing 10.11. It means you're becoming accustomed to the functional style. We wouldn't normally write code like this—it's only for the sake of demonstrating the syntax.

Even though arrays are typically used in imperative programming, we can work with them in a functional style. Aside from the basic operations we've just seen, F# provides several higher-order functions similar to those for working with lists. Let's see how we can use arrays *without* feeling dirty.

USING ARRAYS IN A FUNCTIONAL WAY

We'll start by looking at an F# example that shows a couple of useful higher-order functions for working with arrays from the F# library and then implement the same functionality in C#. Listing 10.12 shows a script that first initializes an array with random numbers, then calculates their squares.

Listing 10.12   Functional way of working with arrays (F# Interactive)

```
> let rnd = new System.Random();;
val rnd : System.Random

> let numbers = Array.init 5 (fun _ -> rnd.Next(10));;          ❶
val numbers : int array = [|1; 0; 7; 2; 2|]

> let squares = numbers |> Array.map (fun n -> (n, n*n));;      ❷
val squares : (int * int) array = [| ... |]

> for sq in squares do                    | Prints tuples from
    printf "%A " sq;;                      | resulting array
(1, 1) (0, 0) (7, 49) (2, 4) (2, 4)
```

The first higher-order function that we're working with is Array.init ❶, which is similar to List.int that we discussed in listing 10.2. It initializes the array using the specified function. The second function is Array.map ❷, which does the same thing as the familiar List.map function. In this example we use it to create an array of tuples where each element of the result contains the original integer and its square.

The interesting thing about this example is that we don't use the assignment operator anywhere in the code. The first operation constructs a new array. The second one doesn't modify it, but instead returns another newly created array. Even though arrays are mutable, we can work with them using higher-order functions that never mutate them in our code. This example would have worked in a similar fashion if we had used functional lists.

Our previous examples have shown us how to use some of the basic operations that are available for arrays although we'll often need to write some similar operations ourselves. Listing 10.13 shows a function that works with arrays in a functional style: it takes one array as an argument and returns a new one calculated from the inputs. The func-

Choosing between arrays and lists

We've seen that arrays and lists can be used in similar ways, so you need to know when to pick which option. The first point to consider is whether or not the type is mutable. Functional programming puts a strong emphasis on immutable data types, and we'll see practical examples showing why this is valuable in the next chapter and in chapter 14. We can work with arrays in a functional way, but lists give us much stronger guarantees about the correctness of our programs.

Another point is that some operations are easier or more efficient with one data type than the other. Appending an element to the front of a list is much easier than copying the contents of one array into a slightly bigger one. On the other hand, arrays are much better for random access. Operations that process arrays are often somewhat faster. We can see this with a simple example using the #time directive:

```
let l = [ 1 .. 100000 ]
let a = [| 1 .. 100000 |];;        Takes
for i in 1 .. 100 do           ⟵   885ms
    ignore(l |> List.map (fun n -> n));;
for i in 1 .. 100 do                        ⟵
    ignore(a |> Array.map (fun n -> n));;   Takes 109ms
```

In general, arrays are useful if you need to work efficiently with large data sets. In most situations you should use aim for clear and simple code first, and functional lists usually lead to greater readability.

tion is used to "smooth" or "blur" an array of values, so that each value in the new array is based on the corresponding value in the original *and* the values either side of it.

Listing 10.13   Functional implementation of blur for arrays (F#)

```
let blurArray (arr:int[]) =
  let res = Array.create arr.Length 0
  res.[0] <- (arr.[0] + arr.[1]) / 2
  res.[arr.Length-1] <- (arr.[arr.Length-2] + arr.[arr.Length-1]) / 2      ❶
  for i in 1 .. arr.Length - 2 do
    res.[i] <- (arr.[i-1] + arr.[i] + arr.[i+1]) / 3      ❷
  res
```

The function starts by creating an array for storing the result, which has the same size as the input. It then calculates the values for the first and the last element ❶ of the new array (these are average values over two elements). These values are calculated separately from the rest of the array because they're edge cases that don't quite fit the rest of the pattern. Finally, it iterates over the elements in the middle of the array, taking the average of three values and writing the results to the new array ❷.

The function uses mutation internally. It creates an array filled with zeros at the beginning and later writes the calculated values to this array. This mutation isn't visible from outside: by the time the caller is able to use the array, we've finished mutating it. When we use this function, we can safely use all the normal functional techniques:

```
> let ar = Array.init 10 (fun _ -> rnd.Next(20));;     ◁──┐ initializes
val ar : int [] = [|14; 14; 4; 16; 1; 15; 5; 14; 7; 13|]      │ random array

> ar |> blurArray;;                 ◁──┘ Blurs array once
val it : int [] = [|14; 10; 11; 7; 10; 7; 11; 8; 11; 10|]     ◁──┐ Blurs 3 times
                                                                 │ using pipelining
> ar |> blurArray |> blurArray |> blurArray;;     ◁──┘
val it : int [] = [|7; 8; 9; 9; 9; 9; 9; 9; 8; 8|]
```

The `blurArray` function has type `int[] -> int[]`, which makes it compositional. In the second command, we use the pipeline operator to send a randomly generated array to this function as an input and the F# Interactive console automatically prints the result. The final command shows that we can also call the function several times in a sequence in the same way we would use `map` or `filter` operations on a list.

You can probably imagine extending this example to process images, turning our `blurArray` function into a real blur filter working with bitmaps. If you want to try this out, you'll need to use the `Array2D` module, which has functions for working with 2D arrays, and the .NET `Bitmap` class with functions such as `GetPixel` and `SetPixel` for reading and writing graphical data. We'll get back to this problem in chapter 14 where we'll also discuss how to use parallelism to perform the operation more efficiently.

Having seen how we can use arrays neatly in F#, we'll turn our attention back to C#. All C# programmers already know the basics of how to use arrays—what we're interested in is how we can write C# code that uses arrays in a functional style.

USING ARRAYS IN A FUNCTIONAL WAY IN C#

You can already use many functional constructs with arrays in C# 3.0 thanks to LINQ to Objects. Most LINQ operators don't return arrays: if you call `Enumerable.Select` on an array, it will return the result as `IEnumerable<T>`. In some situations we'd prefer to keep the results in an array, and we may wish to avoid the overhead of calling `Enumerable.ToArray` to copy the result sequence back into an array.

Some common functional operations for arrays are already available as static methods of the `System.Array` class. They use different naming conventions than F# and LINQ, so you'll find, for example, the `map` operation under name `ConvertAll`. We'll implement our version with the standard name to demonstrate how the operation looks. Listing 10.14 also adds method similar to F# `Array.int` function.

Listing 10.14   Methods for functional array processing (C#)

```
static class ArrayUtils {
  public static T[] int<T>(int length, Func<int, T> init) {       ❶
    T[] arr = new T[length];
    for (int i = 0; i < length; i++) arr[i] = init(i);
    return arr;
  }
  public static R[] Select<T, R>(this T[] arr, Func<T, R> map) {   ❷
    R[] res = new R[arr.Length];
    for (int i = 0; i < arr.Length; i++) res[i] = map(arr[i]);
    return res;
  }
}
```

The int method is a normal static method ❶. It takes a function init as an argument and uses it to initialize the elements of the array. The Select method is an extension method that applies a mapping function to each element in the original array, and returns the result as a new array. It hides the standard Select operation provided by LINQ. We can use these methods in a similar way to the earlier corresponding F# functions:

```
var rnd = new Random();
var numbers = ArrayUtils.int(5, n => rnd.Next(20));
var squares = numbers.Select(n => new { Number = n, Square = n*n });

foreach (var sq in squares)
  Console.Write("({0}, {1}) ", sq.Number, sq.Square);
```

Just like in the F# version, we don't modify the array once it's created. From a high-level perspective, it's a purely functional code working with an immutable data structure. Of course, we're actually performing mutations—but only within the ArrayUtils class, and only on collections that haven't been exposed to any other code yet. The mutation isn't observable to the outside world. This way of writing code is even more valuable in C#, where functional lists are harder to use than they are in F#.

Our final topic in the chapter deals with *continuations*. These can be somewhat hard to wrap your head around, but once you understand them there are some amazing possibilities. The good news is that if you've ever written any asynchronous code in .NET, you've already been using continuations in some sense—but F# makes them a lot easier. We'll look at them in more detail in chapter 13, but using continuations is an interesting optimization technique for recursive functions, which is the aspect we'll concentrate on here.

10.3 *Introducing continuations*

We began this chapter with a discussion about recursive calls. We've seen an important technique called tail recursion that allows us to perform a recursive call without allocating any space on the stack. Thanks to tail recursion, we can write functional list processing functions that can handle large data sets without breaking into a sweat.

We've seen how to rewrite many functions to use tail recursion using an accumulator argument, but not every function can be rewritten to use it. If a function needs to perform two recursive calls, then it clearly can't be written in this way. (They can't *both* be the very last thing to be executed before returning, after all.)

10.3.1 *What makes tree processing tricky?*

Let's take a simple example working with trees. Listing 10.15 declares a type representing a tree of integers, and shows a recursive function that sums all the values in the tree.

Listing 10.15 Tree data structure and summing elements (F# Interactive)

```
> type IntTree =                      ❶
    | Leaf of int
    | Node of IntTree * IntTree;;
type IntTree = (...)
```

```
> let rec sumTree(tree) =          ❷
    match tree with
    | Leaf(n)    -> n
    | Node(l, r) -> sumTree(l) + sumTree(r);;
val sumTree : IntTree -> int
```

Recursively sums
values in subtrees

The IntTree type ❶ used for representing the tree is a discriminated union with two options. Note that this is actually quite similar to the list type! A tree value can represent either a leaf that contains an integer or a node. A node doesn't contain a numeric value, but it has two subtrees of type IntTree. The recursive function for calculating sum ❷ uses pattern matching to distinguish between these two cases. For a leaf, it returns the numeric value; for a node, it needs to recursively sum the elements of both the left and right subtrees and add the two values together.

If we look at the sumTree function, we can see that it isn't tail recursive. It performs a recursive call to sumTree to sum the elements of the left subtree and then needs to perform some additional operations. More specifically, it still has to sum the elements of the right subtree and finally it has to add these two numbers. We don't know how to write this function in a tail-recursive way, because it has two recursive calls to perform. The last of these two calls could be made tail recursive with some effort (using some sort of accumulator argument), but we'd still have to do one ordinary recursive call! This is annoying, because for some kinds of large trees, this implementation will fail with a stack overflow.

We need to think of a different approach. First let's consider what trees might actually look like. Figure 10.6 shows two examples.

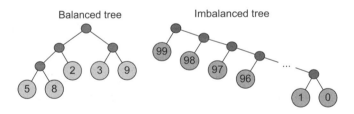

Figure 10.6 An example of balanced and imbalanced trees. Dark circles correspond to the Node case and light circles containing values correspond to the Leaf case

The balanced tree in figure 10.6 is a fairly typical case where the elements of the tree are reasonably divided between the left and the right subtrees. This isn't too bad, as we never end up recursing particularly deeply. (With our current algorithm, the maximum recursion depth is the longer path that exists between the root of the tree and a leaf.) The imbalanced example is much nastier. It has many Node elements on the right side, so when we process it recursively we'll have to make a large number of recursive calls. The difference between the handling of these two trees is shown in listing 10.16.

Listing 10.16 Summing tree using naïve recursive function (F# Interactive)

```
> let tree = Node(Node(Node(Leaf(5), Leaf(8)), Leaf(2)),
              Node(Leaf(2), Leaf(9)))
  sumTree(tree);;
val it : int = 26
```

```
> let numbers = List.init 100000 (fun _ -> rnd.Next(- 50, 51));;
val numbers : int list = [29; -44; -1; 25; -33; 36; ...]

> let imbalancedTree =
    numbers |> List.fold (fun currentTree num ->
      Node(Leaf(num), currentTree)) (Leaf(0));;
val imbalancedTree : IntTree

> sumTree(imbalancedTree);;
Process is terminated due to StackOverflowException.
```

❶ Creates node with current tree on right

The first command creates a simple tree and sums the leaf values. The second command uses the `fold` function to create a tree similar to the imbalanced example in figure 10.6 but bigger. It starts with a leaf containing zero and in each step appends a new node with a leaf on the left and the current tree on the right ❶. It takes the numbers from the list that we created in listing 10.2 and that contains 100,000 random numbers between –50 and +50. As a result, we'll get a tree with a height of 100,000 nodes. When we try to sum the leaves of this tree, we get a stack overflow. This isn't a particularly typical situation, but we can still encounter it in our tree-processing code. Luckily, continuations give us a way to write functions that work correctly even on trees like this one.

10.3.2 Writing code using continuations

The problem is that we want to make a tail-recursive call, but we still have some code that we want to execute after the tail-recursive call completes. This looks like a tricky problem, but there's an interesting solution. We'll take all the code that we want to execute after the recursive call completes and provide it as an argument to the recursive call. This means that the function we're writing will contain just a single recursive call.

Think of this as another sort of accumulator argument: instead of accumulating values, we're accumulating "more code to run later." Now, how can we take the remaining code and use it as an argument to a function? This is possible thanks to first class functions, and this last argument is called a *continuation* because it specifies how the execution should continue.

This will all become much clearer after looking at some practical examples. Listing 10.17 shows a simple function implemented first in the normal style and then using continuations. We're using C# here so that there's only one new concept to understand, but bear in mind that C# doesn't support tail recursion: this technique can't be used as an optimization for recursion in C#. (Continuations are still useful in C#, just not for recursion.)

Listing 10.17 Writing code using continuations (C#)

```
// Reports result as return value
int StringLength(string s) {
  return s.Length;
}
void AddLengths() {                          ❶
  int x1 = StringLength("One");
```

```
    int x2 = StringLength("Two");
    Console.WriteLine(x1 + x2);
}

// Reports result using continuations
void StringLengthCont(string s, Action<int> cont) {
    cont(s.Length);                                    ❷
}
void AddLengthsCont() {
    StringLengthCont("One", x1 =>         ❸
        StringLengthCont("Two", x2 =>       ❹
            Console.WriteLine(x1 + x2)
    ));
}
```

In both versions, we first declare a function that calculates the length of the string. In the usual programming style, it gives the result as a return value. When using continuations, we add a function (a continuation) as the last argument. To return the result, the StringLengthCont function invokes this continuation ❷. We're using a function instead of the usual return statement, which means that the value is given as an argument to a function instead of storing it as a result on the stack.

The next function, called AddLengths, ❶ calculates the length of two strings, adds these values, and prints the result. In the version using continuations, it includes only a single top-level call to the StringLengthCont function ❸. The first argument to this call is a string, and the second one is a continuation. The top-level call is the last thing that the function does, so in F# it would be executed using a tail call and it wouldn't occupy any stack space.

The continuation receives the length of the first string as an argument. Inside it, we call StringLengthCont for the second string. Again, we give it a continuation as a last argument and once it's called, we can sum the two lengths and print the result. In F#, the call inside the continuation ❹ would be again a tail call, because it's the last thing that the code in the lambda function does. Let's now look how we can use this style of programming to optimize our previous function for summing elements of a tree.

TREE PROCESSING USING CONTINUATIONS

To change our previous implementation of the sumTree function into a version that uses continuations, we'll first add an additional argument (a continuation) to the function. We'll also need to update how the function returns the result. Instead of simply returning the value, we'll call the continuation given as the argument. The final version of the code is shown in listing 10.18.

Listing 10.18   Sum elements of a tree using continuations (F# Interactive)

```
> let rec sumTreeCont tree cont =
    match tree with
    | Leaf(num) -> cont(num)
    | Node(left, right) ->
        sumTreeCont left (fun leftSum ->        ❶
            sumTreeCont right (fun rightSum ->    ❷
                cont(leftSum + rightSum)));;        ❸
val sumTreeCont : IntTree -> (int -> 'a) -> 'a
```

Modifying the branch for the leaf case is quite easy, because it previously returned the value from the leaf. The second case is far more interesting. We're using a pattern similar to the one in the previous C# example. We call the function to sum the elements of the left subtree ❶ (this is a tail recursion) and give it a lambda function as the second argument. Inside the lambda we do a similar thing for the right subtree ❷ (again, a tail-recursive call). Once we have sums of both subtrees, we invoke the continuation that we originally got as the argument ❸ (which is once more a tail-recursive call).

Another interesting thing about the function that we've just written is its type signature. As usual, we didn't write any types explicitly and F# inferred the types for us. The function takes the tree as the first argument and the continuation as the second one. The continuation now has a type `int -> 'a` and the overall result of the function is `'a`. In other words, the return type of the whole function is the same as the return type of the continuation.

Earlier we mentioned that all recursive calls in the code are now tail recursive, so we can try this function on the imbalanced tree that failed in the previous version:

```
> sumTreeCont imbalancedTree (fun r ->
    printfn "Result is: %d" r);;
Result is: 8736
val it : unit = ()

> sumTreeCont imbalancedTree (fun a -> a);;    ⟵  Returns sum from
val it : int = 8736                                the continuation
```

As you can see, the code now works on very large trees without any trouble. In the first example, we print the result directly in the continuation and the continuation doesn't return any value, so the overall result of the expression is `unit`. In the second case, we give it an *identity function* (a function that just returns its argument) as the continuation. The identity function is already available in F# libraries, so we could write `id`. The return type of the continuation is `int`, and the value returned from the call to `sumTreeCont` is the sum of all the elements in the tree.

10.4   Summary

In this chapter, we explored topics related to the efficiency of functional programs, and we discussed how to deal with large amounts of data in a functional way. Since most of the functional programs are implemented using recursion, a large part of the chapter was dedicated to this topic.

You saw that when using recursion we have to write our code carefully to avoid errors caused by the stack overflowing if the recursion level becomes too deep. In the beginning of the chapter, we looked at a technique called tail recursion that allows us to rewrite familiar list processing functions (such as `map` and `filter`) in a way that makes them immune to stack overflow. Tail recursion alone can't help us in every situation, so we also looked at continuations and used them to write a robust version of a simple tree-processing function.

We also explored techniques for optimizing the performance of processing functions. In particular, we looked at memoization, which allows us to cache results of functions without side effects. Effective optimization relies on complexity analysis, so we looked at functional data structures and their performance characteristics. We have to be careful when choosing algorithms and operations, as some differences that look small—such as whether we add elements to the head or tail of functional lists—can have a significant impact on performance. We also talked about arrays, which aren't primarily functional data structures but can be used functionally if we're careful.

In the next chapter, we'll continue our exploration of common tricks for implementing algorithms in a functional language. Many of the topics from the following chapter are related to the use of immutable data types and mathematical clarity of functional programming.

Refactoring and testing functional programs

This chapter covers

- Refactoring functional programs
- Reasoning about code using immutability
- Writing unit tests for F# programs
- Caching results using lazy values

One theme of this book is that functional programming makes it easier to understand code just by reading it. This is particularly important when you need to modify an unfamiliar program or implement behavior by composing existing functions or when refactoring existing code. Functional programming makes refactoring easier thanks to both clarity and modularity: you can make improvements to the code and be confident that the change doesn't break other parts of the program.

As with many things in functional programming, the idea of modifying code without changing its meaning is closely related to math, because operations that don't change the meaning of an expression are the basis of many mathematical tasks. We can take a complex equation and *simplify* it to get an equation that's easier to read but means the same thing. Let's take the following equation: $y = 2x + 3(5 - x)$. If we multiply the expression in parentheses by 3, we can write it as $y = 2x + 15 - 3x$, which in turn can be simplified to: $y = 15 - x$.

Another technique we can learn from math is *substitution*. If we have two equations, $y = x/2$ and $x = 2z$, we can substitute the right-hand side of the second one into the first one and we'll get (after simplification) $y = z$. The important point is that by substituting the correct equation into another one, the substituted equation can't suddenly become incorrect. This technique appears in functional programming as composition.

Functional programming is closely related to mathematics, so it's not surprising that some of the techniques used in algebra can be applied to functional programs, too. In the programming world, the simplification of equations corresponds to *refactoring*, which is the centerpiece of this chapter. In particular, we'll look at reducing code duplication and discuss code dependencies.

Substitution is also a form of refactoring, but you'll learn that it has other important practical benefits, particularly when unit testing. Substitution allows us to focus on testing primitive functions and spend much less time testing functions that are composed from simple building blocks, because the composition can't break already tested components.

We'll also examine a topic that's closely related to refactoring. When a program lacks side effects, we should get the same result regardless of the order in which the individual parts are executed. A value can be calculated as soon as it's declared, or we can delay execution until the value is really needed. This technique is called *laziness (or lazy evaluation)*, and we'll show you some of the practical benefits when we explore potentially infinite data structures and caching of computer values.

11.1 *Refactoring functional programs*

Refactoring is an integral part of many modern development methodologies. In some languages, this technique is also supported by IDEs such as the C# editor in Visual Studio. Most of the refactoring techniques have been developed for the object-oriented paradigm, but we'll be looking at it from a functional point of view.

REFACTORING   Refactoring is the process of modifying source code to improve its design without changing its meaning. The goal of refactoring is to make the code more readable, easier to modify or extend in the future, or to improve its structure. A simple example of refactoring is renaming a method to make the name more descriptive; another is turning a block of code into a method and reusing it to avoid code duplication.

Refactoring allows us to write code that works first, and then make it "clean." Performing these two tasks separately simplifies testing because refactoring shouldn't affect the behavior of the application. While some changes such as renaming are fairly simple (particularly with help from tools), others can involve more thoughtful consideration.

If you switch the order of two statements, will the code behave the same way afterward? With imperative code using side effects, you'd have to look carefully at the two statements. Functional programming makes reasoning about the code easier, so refactoring becomes easier too. We'll take a look at several examples in this section, but let's start with a common functional refactoring that removes code duplication.

11.1.1 Reusing common code blocks

One of the best programming practices is to avoid duplicating the same code in multiple places. If you have two routines that look similar, it's worth considering how they could be merged into one. The new routine would take a new argument that specifies what code path to follow in the part that was originally different.

In functional programming, we have one powerful weapon: the ability to use function values as arguments. This makes it much easier to parameterize a function or method. To demonstrate, let's say we have a database with information about cities and we want to generate several reports from the data.

We'll start by writing a function that loads the data. To make the example simpler, we won't look at working with databases. You could do that yourself by using standard .NET database API, which works smoothly with F#. Instead, we'll use the following function, which simply returns a list that we create by hand:

```
let loadPlaces() =
  [ ("Seattle", 594210);  ("Prague", 1188126)
    ("New York", 7180000); ("Grantchester", 552)
    ("Cambridge", 117900) ]
```

The data structure is simple, but it's close to what we could use in a real-world application. Instead of using tuples for storing the name and the population, we'd probably use records or object types. Listing 11.1 shows two functions that generate reports from the data: one prints a list of cities with more than one million inhabitants, and the other prints all the locations in alphabetical order. In a real application this might generate an HTML report, but we'll keep things simple and print it to the console as plain text.

Listing 11.1 Printing information about places (F#)

```
let printBigCities() =
  let places = loadPlaces()
  printfn "===== Big cities ====="                              ❶ Prints report title
  let selected = List.filter (fun (_, p) -> p > 1000000) places
  for name, population in selected do
    printfn " - %s (%d)" name population

                                                                Lists cities with
                                                                population over
                                                                1 million ❷

let printAllByName() =
  let places = loadPlaces()                     ❸ Prints report
  printfn "===== All by name ====="                title
  let selected = List.sortBy fst places
  for name, population in selected do           Sorts cities by
    printfn " - %s (%d)" name population         ❹ their name
```

The two functions have very similar structure, but there are some differences. The most important one is that they select the list of places to print in different ways. The printBigCities function filters places using List.filter ❷, while printAllNames uses `List.sortBy` to reorder them ❹. They also differ in terms of the report title that's printed ❶ ❸.

They share many common aspects. Both functions first call `loadPlaces` to obtain the collection of places, then process this collection in some way and finally print the result to the screen.

When refactoring the code, we want to write a single function that can be used for both tasks. We also want to make the code more extensible. It should be possible to use the printing function with a completely different strategy. If we were creating a crossword, we might look for cities with the specified length starting with a particular letter. This means that we should be able to provide almost any strategy as an argument. Functional programming gives us a great way to do this kind of parameterization using functions.

Listing 11.2 shows a higher-order function, `printPlaces`, and we'll soon see that we can use it to replace both of the functions from the previous listing.

Listing 11.2   Reusable function for printing information (F# Interactive)

```
> let printPlaces title select =
    let places = loadPlaces()
    printfn "== %s ==" title        ❶
    let sel = select(places)        ❷
    for name, pop in sel do
      printfn " - %s (%d)" name pop
  ;;
val printPlaces : string ->
    ((string * int) list -> #seq<string * int>) -> unit     ❸
```

Our new function has two parameters. These specify what to do in places where the original two functions were different from each other. The first is the report title ❶, and the second is a function that selects the places to be printed ❷. We can learn more about this function by looking at its type in the printed type signature ❸.

The argument of the function is a list of tuples, each of which contains a string and an integer. This is our data structure for representing places. We'd expect the return type of the function to be the same, because the function returns a collection of places in the same data format, but the type inferred by F# is `#seq<string * int>`. The difference is that instead of `list` it inferred the `#seq` type.

This choice is interesting for two reasons.

- `seq<'a>` is a common interface implemented by all collections and is an alias for the standard .NET `IEnumerable<T>` type. This means that the function *can* return a list, but could equally return an array, because the only thing we need is the ability to iterate over all the elements in the collection. We'll go into more detail about sequences in the next chapter, but if you know LINQ to Objects this should be familiar territory: most of the common operators work with (and return) `IEnumerable<T>`.

- The hash symbol means that the returned collection doesn't have to be upcast to the `seq<'a>` type explicitly. This means we can provide a function that's actually typed to return a `list<'a>`, for example. In the strictly typed sense, this is a different type of function, but the hash symbol adds some valuable flexibility. Most of the time you don't need to worry about this very much; it just means that the compiler inferred that the code can be more generic.

Now that we have the function, we need to show that it can really be used in place of the two functions that we started with. Listing 11.3 shows arguments we can supply to get the same behavior as the original functions.

Listing 11.3 Working with 'printPlaces' function (F#)

```
// Writing lambda function explicitly
printPlaces "Big cities" (fun places ->          ❶
  List.filter (fun (_, s) -> s > 1000000) places)

// Using partial function application
printPlaces "Big cities" (List.filter (fun (_, s) -> s > 1000000))   ❷
printPlaces "Sorted by name" (List.sortBy fst)    ❸
```

The only interesting aspect of the first example ❶ is the lambda function that we use as the second parameter. It takes the data set as an argument and filters it using `List.filter` to select only cities with more than one million inhabitants. The next example ❷ shows that we can write the call more succinctly using partial function application. In the last example ❸ we use `List.sortBy` to sort the collection.

As you can see in listing 11.3, using the function that we created during refactoring is quite easy. It could be used to print different lists just by specifying another function as the second argument.

The refactoring we performed in this section relied on the ability to use functions as arguments. C# has the same ability, so the same kind of refactoring can be applied effectively there, using delegates. We could specify the data transformation argument either as a lambda expression or by creating the delegate from another method with an appropriate signature.

Another functional principle that's very valuable when refactoring code is the use of immutable data. The impact here is slightly more subtle than simply being able to express differences in behavior using functions, but it's no less important.

11.1.2 *Tracking dependencies and side effects*

One of the many benefits of immutability is the clarity it provides. If a function takes a collection as an argument and returns a number, you can safely assume that it calculates the result based on the collection content, but does *not* modify the collection. We don't have to look at any code to reach that conclusion; we don't have to examine the implementation *or* any other functions that it calls. Let's start by looking at an example that demonstrates how easy it is to introduce errors when using mutable objects.

USING MUTABLE DATA STRUCTURES

In listing 11.4 you can see two functions that work with a collection storing names of places from the previous example. This time, we're using C# and storing the names in the standard List<T> type, which is mutable.

Listing 11.4   Working with places stored in List<T> (C#)

```
List<string> LoadPlaces() {                              ❶
  return new List<string> { "Seattle", "Prague",
    "New York", "Grantchester", "Cambridge" };
}
void PrintLongest(List<string> names) {         ❷
  var longest = names[0];                    <—— Starts with first place
  for(int i = 1; i < names.Count; i++)
    if (names[i].Length > longest.Length) longest = names[i];
  Console.WriteLine(longest);
}
void PrintMultiWord(List<string> names) {       ❸
  names.RemoveAll(s => !s.Contains(" "));        <—
  Console.WriteLine("With space: {0}", names.Count);
}
```

Remembers new longest name

Removes all single-word names

The code first shows a function that loads sample data ❶. It's like our loadPlaces function from earlier, but without the population values. Next, we implement two processing functions. The first one ❷ finds the place with the longest name; the second ❸ determines how many names contain more than one word by removing any name that doesn't contain a space. Even though the method uses lambda function syntax, it's definitely not functional: the RemoveAll method modifies the names collection. If we wanted to use these functions later in our program, we could write the following code:

```
PrintMultiWord(LoadPlaces());  // Prints '1'
PrintLongest(LoadPlaces());    // Prints 'Grantchester'
```

This gives the correct results although, we're calling the LoadPlaces function twice, which seems to be unnecessary. If the function loaded data from a database, it would be better to retrieve the data only once for performance reasons. A simple refactoring is to call the function once and store the places in a local variable:

```
var places = LoadPlaces();
PrintMultiWord(places);        // Prints '1'
PrintLongest(places);          // Prints 'New York'
```

After this simple change we get incorrect results! If you've been following the source code carefully, you've probably spotted the problem: List<T> is a mutable data structure and the function PrintMultiWord accidentally mutates it when it calls RemoveAll. When we call PrintLongest later in the code, the collection places contains only a single item, which is "New York." Now let's see why we couldn't make a similar mistake if we used immutable data structures.

USING IMMUTABLE DATA STRUCTURES

To demonstrate how to write the same code in an immutable fashion, we don't necessarily have to use a functional list. We can avoid mutating the collection even when using the standard List<T> type. Then it's unfortunately our responsibility to ensure that we're not modifying the list accidentally, which can be difficult.

A better approach is to work with a type that doesn't allow mutation. We could use a truly immutable type such as FuncList<T> from chapter 3 or the ReadOnly-Collection<T> available in .NET Framework. We can get a good safety guarantee even when working with IEnumerable<T>. It can be used for enumerating elements of any collection type (including both mutable and immutable), but it doesn't give us any direct way for modifying the underlying collection. If we were mutating the collection from another thread, we could still get unexpected results, but that's not the case in this example.

Let's implement the same example using IEnumerable<T>. The LoadPlaces and PrintLongest methods don't change very much, so we've omitted them here. The PrintMultiWord method is more interesting: we can't use our previous strategy of using RemoveAll, because the IEnumerable<T> type is immutable. Earlier we used this method to remove all single-word names from the collection. This side effect made the method harder to reason about. If we want the same kind of results using immutable types we have to be more explicit about it, as shown in listing 11.5.

Listing 11.5   Implementation of `PrintMultiWord` using `IEnumerable<T>` (C#)

```
IEnumerable<string> PrintMultiWord(IEnumerable<string> names) {
  var namesSpace = names.Where(s => s.Contains(" "));            ❶
  Console.WriteLine("With space: {0}", namesSpace.Count());
  return namesSpace;                                             ❷
}
```

We can't modify a collection when we're working with immutable data structures, so the method first creates a new collection that contains only multiword names ❶. We've also made the side effect from the previous implementation explicit, so the method now returns the new collection. Of course, it isn't really a side effect at all now—it's a return value. It achieves the same result of making the multiword names list available to the caller if they want it ❷.

Our first example was searching for the longest name from all the names and our second example (which printed "New York") returned the longest name containing a space. Listing 11.6 shows how both of these examples can be implemented using our new function.

Listing 11.6   Printing the longest and the longest multiword name (C#)

```
IEnumerable<string> places =            IEnumerable<string> places =
   LoadImmutablePlaces();                  LoadImmutablePlaces();


PrintMultiWord(places);                 var placesSpace =
PrintLongest(places);         ❶            PrintMultiWord(places);    ❷
                                        PrintLongest(placesSpace);    ❸
```

Now that we've made the mutation more explicit, it won't surprise you that the results will differ. The version on the left side prints "Grantchester" ❶, while the version where we select the longest name containing a space prints "New York" ❸.

Listing 11.6 also demonstrates that using immutable data types makes it easier to reason about the program and decide which refactorings are valid. In the example on the left side, we could change the order of `PrintMultiWord` and `PrintLongest` and they'd still print the same results (in the opposite order). We can't change the order of the calls in the right side of listing 11.6, because the value `placesSpace` is the result of the first call ❷.

This means that when refactoring functional code, we can track dependencies of the computations more easily. We can see that a function depends on other calls if it takes a result of these calls as an argument. Because this is explicitly visible in the code, we can't make accidental refactoring errors because incorrectly modified code won't compile. This is also useful when testing the code using unit tests.

11.2   *Testing functional code*

Neither functional programming nor any other paradigm can eliminate bugs entirely or prevent us from introducing bugs when making changes to existing code. This is one reason behind the widespread adoption of unit testing. The good news is that most of the unit-testing techniques that you already use when testing C# code can be applied to F# programs as well. Additionally, functional programming and F# make testing easier in many ways.

> **Choosing a unit-testing framework for F#**
>
> As we saw in chapter 9, we can write standard classes in F#, so any of the unit-testing frameworks for .NET works as normal. Why should we write unit tests in F# as members of a class rather than simply using functions declared with `let` bindings? Classes certainly have some benefits, such as enabling sophisticated setup and teardown code. However, most of the unit tests that we'll write benefit from using the simplest possible syntax.
>
> In this chapter we'll use the xUnit.net framework. This works with standard F# functions as well as F# classes. F# functions written using `let` bindings are compiled into static methods of a class. When we wrap the code inside a module, the module name is used as the name of the static class. Otherwise, F# generates a class based on the name of the file. The xUnit.net framework supports unit tests that are implemented as static methods without applying a special attribute (such as `TestFixture`) to the class, which makes it friendlier to F# programmers. If you don't have xUnit.net installed, you can get the latest version from http://www.codeplex.com/xunit. Other unit-testing frameworks should work in a similar way, but xUnit.net was the first one to provide smooth integration with F#.

When we've discussed testing so far, we've usually talked about checking whether the code works immediately after writing it in the F# Interactive shell. If you're a veteran of unit testing, you may well have been thinking to yourself that a test which can't be reproduced later on is hardly worth running. Well, let's see how this kind of test can evolve into a unit test.

11.2.1 *From the interactive shell to unit tests*

Testing code interactively is valuable when you're writing the initial implementation, but we'd also like to make sure that the code keeps giving the same results even if you change it. This can be done easily by turning the one-off interactive test code into a solid unit test that we keep alongside our production code and run repeatedly. You may be surprised at how small a change is required to achieve this.

TESTING PROGRAMS IN F# INTERACTIVE

Let's demonstrate the whole process from the beginning. We'll use two functions similar to `PrintLongest` and `PrintMultiWord` from the previous section, but this time we'll implement them in F#. As you can see in listing 11.7, we'll use the interactive shell slightly differently.

Listing 11.7 Testing code interactively using xUnit.net (F# Interactive)

```
> #if INTERACTIVE
  #r @"C:\Program Files\xUnit\xunit.dll"          ❶ Refers to
  #endif                                             xUnit.net library
  open Xunit;;

> let getLongest(names:list<string>) =            ❷ Returns
    names |> List.maxBy (fun name -> name.Length);;   longest name
val getLongest : list<string> -> string

> let test = [ "Aaa"; "Bbbbb"; "Cccc" ];;
val test : string list = ["Aaa"; "Bbbbb"; "Cccc"]
                                                  ❸ Tests function
> Assert.Equal("Bbbbb", getLongest(test));;          using xUnit.net
val it : unit = ()
```

First, we need to place the code into a file with an extension of .fs such as Program.fs (as opposed to .fsx files that represent interactive scripts) because we want to compile the program into a .NET assembly. Also, we need to add a reference to the xUnit.net core library . This is simply a matter of using the Add Reference dialog box in Visual Studio. We also want to run the code interactively, so we have to load the library in F# Interactive. We'd usually do that using the #r directive, but this directive is allowed only in F# scripts (FSX files). Fortunately, F# supports conditional compilation and defines the INTERACTIVE symbol when running the code from the command shell, which mean the initial part of the listing ❶ will work whether or not we're running it interactively.

Next we implement the function for finding the longest name from a given list ❷. The code is quite simple because it uses a higher-order function from the F# library. This function selects the element for which the given function returns the largest value. Once we have the function, we test it in the next two lines. The most interesting line is the one ❸, where we use the Assert.Equals method. This is imported from the Xunit namespace and verifies that the actual value (given as the second argument) matches the expected value (the first argument). The method throws an exception if that's not the case—the fact that it returned unit as the result means the test passed.

WRITING UNIT TESTS IN F#

If we write our immediate testing code in this manner, it's easy to turn it into a unit test and make it part of a larger project. We'll discuss how to do that using xUnit.net soon, but first let's write another call that should be definitely covered by the unit tests: calling the getLongest function with a null value as the argument:

```
> getLongest(null);;
Program.fs(24,12): error FS0043: The type 'string list'
does not have 'null' as a proper value
```

We haven't tried that before, and as you can see F# Interactive reports a compile-time error rather than an exception. This means that we can't even *write* code like that, which means that if we're only using the function from F# we don't need to test that possibility. Values of types that were declared in F# (including discriminated unions, records, but also F# class declarations) simply aren't allowed to be null. They always have to be initialized to a valid value. As you learned in chapter 5, the right way to represent a missing value in F# is to use the option type. This rule is used only for types declared in F# and used in F#. When calling a usual .NET method that takes an existing .NET type as a parameter, you can specify null as a valid argument value.

NOTE   Other languages such as C# don't understand the restriction to disallow null as a value for an F# type. This means that an F# function such as get-Longest still can receive null as an argument if it's called from C#. We can check this case inside the function by using the generic Unchecked.defaultof<'T> value, which gives us an *unsafe* way to create a null value of any reference type in F# or to get the default value of a value type. In other words, it's the equivalent of default(T) in C#. Then we should also use this trick to write unit tests to verify the behavior of the function. This isn't necessary very often because public API of F# libraries tend to use standard .NET types such as seq<'T>, which have null as a valid value, and so we can write the unit test for the API in the usual manner.

We only intend to use our simple function from F#, so we don't have to handle the case when a C# user calls it with a null argument. Listing 11.8 shows several other tests that we can add. Note that a large part of the listing is a slightly modified version of the code that we wrote in listing 11.7 when testing the function interactively. The most notable differences are that we've wrapped the testing code inside functions and added an attribute that marks it as an xUnit.net test.

> **Listing 11.8   Function with unit tests to verify its behavior (F#)**

```
#if INTERACTIVE
#r @"C:\Programs\Development\xUnit\xunit.dll"
#endif
open Xunit
```

```
let getLongest(names:list<string>) =
  names |> List.maxBy (fun name -> name.Length)

module LongestTests =                       ❶ Marks tests
  [<Fact>]                                       using attribute
  let longestOfNonEmpty() =
    let test = [ "Aaa"; "Bbbbb"; "Cccc" ]   Adjusted
    Assert.Equal("Bbbbb", getLongest(test)) interactive test

  [<Fact>]
  let longestFirstLongest() =
    let test = [ "Aaa"; "Bbb" ]             ❷ Requires first of the
    Assert.Equal("Aaa", getLongest(test))       longest elements

  [<Fact>]
  let longestOfEmpty() =
    let test = []                           ❸ Requires empty string
    Assert.Equal("", getLongest(test))          for an empty list
```

In addition to wrapping every test into a function, we've also created a module to keep all the unit tests together in a single class. This isn't technically necessary, but it's a good idea to keep the tests separated from the main part of the program. Depending on your preferences, you can move the tests to the end of the file, to a separate file in a single project, or even to a separate project.

The xUnit.net framework uses an attribute called Fact to mark methods that represent unit tests ❶. We can apply this to F# functions declared with let bindings, as they're compiled as methods. The first test in the module is an adjusted version of the code we wrote when testing the code interactively, but we've also added two new tests.

The second test ❷ verifies that the getLongest function returns the first of the elements that have the maximal length when there are several of them. The maxBy function from the F# libraries follows this rule, but it isn't documented so it may depend on the implementation; testing it explicitly is a good idea. The last test ❸ checks that the function returns an empty string when we pass it an empty list. This is one of the corner cases that are worth considering. Returning an empty string may be the desired behavior when you're displaying the result in a UI, for example. As you've probably guessed, our original implementation doesn't follow this rule. If you run the xUnit.net GUI on the compiled assembly, you'll get a result similar to the one in figure 11.1.

Now that we've clarified the required behavior of the getLongest function, we can fix it easily by adding a pattern to match the empty list:

```
let getLongest(names:list<string>) =
  match names with
  | [] -> ""
  | _ -> names |> List.maxBy (fun name -> name.Length)
```

All three unit tests pass after this change. So far, the tests have been quite simple and we've only had to check whether the returned string matched the expected one. Often unit tests are more involved than this. Let's look at how we might test a more complicated function and in particular how to compare an actual value with an expected one when a function returns a list.

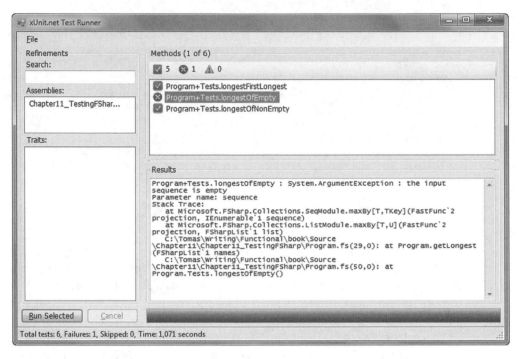

Figure 11.1   **Instead of returning an empty string, the tested function throws an exception when given an empty list as its argument.**

11.2.2 *Writing tests using structural equality*

Testing for equality with complicated data structures can be tricky in C#. If we construct a new object with the same properties and compare the two using the == operator, the result is likely be false, because we'd be comparing two distinct *instances*.

The == operator can be overloaded in C#, and Object.Equals can be overridden, but both should usually only be done for value types or immutable data structures. When you compare two different instances of mutable types, it's important to distinguish between them, because the data can change later on. On the other hand, if we have two immutable types storing the same values, we can treat them as equal. The data can't change in the future, so the two objects will always be equal.

STRUCTURAL EQUALITY AND COMPARISON

As most of the types that we can declare in F# are immutable, the F# compiler automatically implements the IComparable<T> interface and overrides the Equals method if we don't provide an explicit implementation. It does this using a comparison for *structural equality*. This isn't done automatically for F# classes—just for simple functional types like records and discriminated unions, and tuples, which don't have to be declared explicitly.

Values of types that use this comparison are considered equal if they're equal simple types, such as integers or strings, or they're composed from the same values, using structural equality recursively. Listing 11.9 demonstrates structural equality with records containing tuples and primitive values.

Listing 11.9   Comparing records with structural equality (F# Interactive)

```
> type WeatherItem =
    { Temperature : int * int;
      Text : string }
  let winter1 = { Temperature = -10, -2; Text = "Winter" }      Creates records con-
  let winter2 = { Temperature = -10, -2; Text = "Winter" };;    taining same values
(...)

> System.Object.ReferenceEquals(winter1, winter2);;      ◁──┐  Values represented
val it : bool = false                                       ❶  by different instances

> winter1.Equals(winter2);;
val it : bool = true                    ❷  ...but considered
                                            as equal
> winter1 = winter2;;
val it : bool = true
```

First we declare an F# record type, which contains two fields. The first field type is a tuple of two integers, and the second is a string. We create two values of the record type using the very same value for each corresponding field.

We can see that we genuinely have two instances: a test for reference equality ❶ returns `false`. If we use an overridden `Equals` method or the standard F# operator for testing equality ❷, the runtime will use structural equality, and it will report that the values are equal. First the two tuple values are compared for structural equality, then the two strings are compared.

As we said earlier, this technique works for records, tuples, discriminated unions, and arrays. Since immutable F# lists are declared as discriminated unions, they receive the same treatment. We'll use this feature when writing a unit-test expectation, but first let's look at one more feature of the automatically generated functionality. We've seen how to use structural equality to test whether values are equal, but F# also provides *structural comparisons* for ordering:

```
> let summer = { Temperature = 10, 20; Text = "Summer" };;
(...)

> summer = winter1;;
val it : bool = false

> summer > winter1;;
val it : bool = true
```

This snippet creates a new value of the record type declared in listing 11.9 and compares it with the value from the previous listing. The first result isn't surprising: the two values are different. The second one deserves an explanation. Why should the `summer` value be considered to be *larger than* the `winter1` value? The reason is that the F# compiler also generates a default comparison for the `WeatherItem` type. The comparison uses the values of the fields in the order in which they're declared: a tuple value (10, 0) is larger than a tuple (9, 100), for example. This default behavior can be useful, particularly if you take it into consideration when you design your type, but for the rest of this chapter we'll be focusing on structural equality.

WRITING TESTS FOR LISTS

The function we're going to test is a generalized version of the one that printed names consisting of multiple words. The difference is that instead of printing the names, the function will return them as a result. The result will be a tuple of two lists: one containing the multiword names, and one containing the single-word names. In functional terminology this operation is called *partitioning*, and we can easily implement our function using the List.partition function from the standard F# library:

```
> let partitionMultiWord(names:list<string>) =
    names |> List.partition (fun name -> name.Contains(" "));;
val partitionMultiWord : string list -> string list * string list
```

The partition function takes a predicate as an argument and divides the input list into two lists. The first list contains elements for which the predicate returned true, and the second contains the remaining elements. Listing 11.10 shows two unit tests for the function declared earlier.

Listing 11.10   Unit tests for the partitioning operation (F#)

```
module PartitionTests =
  [<Fact>]
  let partitionKeepLength() =
    let test = ["A"; "A B"; "A B C"; "B" ]              ❶ Verifies length
    let multi, single = partitionMultiWord(test)          of returned
    Assert.True(multi.Length + single.Length = test.Length)  ◁─┘ lists

  [<Fact>]
  let partitionNonEmpty() =
    let test = ["Seattle"; "New York"; "Reading"]
    let expected = ["New York"], ["Seattle"; "Reading"]   ❷ Tests result using
    Assert.Equal(expected, partitionMultiWord(test))    ◁─ structural equality
```

Listing 11.10 shows two unit tests implemented as functions marked with the Fact attribute. The first test ❶ checks that the lengths of the two lists returned as results add up to the same number as the length of the original input. This is a simple way to partially verify that no elements are lost by the partitioning. We're using only a single input (the value test) in the listing, but we could simply extend the test to use multiple input lists.

The second test is more interesting, because it uses the structural equality feature we discussed earlier. It declares a value with the test input and a value that represents the expected output of the tests. The expected value is a tuple of two lists. The first list contains a single element, which is the only name composed from multiple words. The second list contains single-word names in the same order in which they occur in the input list. If you run the test, the assertion ❷ succeeds, because the runtime uses structural equality to compare the tuples and the lists contained in the tuple. This means that it compares all the individual strings in the lists.

As we've seen, structural equality is a simple but valuable feature that streamlines unit testing, even though it's not a fundamental aspect of functional programming. A more important and more inherently functional technique that aids testing is function composition.

11.2.3 Testing composed functionality

In section 11.1.2 when we discussed tracking dependencies in code, we used C# methods similar to the two F# functions from the last two examples to demonstrate how functional programming makes it easier to recognize what a function does and what data it accesses. This is useful when writing the code, but it's also extremely valuable when testing it.

In section 11.1, we wrote an imperative method for printing names consisting of multiple words, but with the side effect of removing elements from the mutable list passed to it as argument. This didn't cause any problems as long as we weren't using the same list later. Any unit tests for that method that checked the printed output would have succeeded.

What made the method tricky was that if we used it in conjunction with another method that was also correct, we could get unexpected results. This makes it hard to test imperative code thoroughly. In principle we should test that every method does exactly what it's supposed to do and nothing more. Unfortunately, the "and nothing more" part is really hard to test, because any piece of code can access and modify any part of the shared mutable state.

In functional programming we shouldn't modify any shared state, so we only need to verify that the function returns correct results for all the given inputs. This also means that when we're using two tested functions together, we only have to test that the combination has the appropriate result: we don't need to verify that the functions don't tread on each other's data in subtle ways. Listing 11.11 shows the kind of test that looks completely pointless—but imagine what it might show if we were working with List<T> instead of immutable F# lists.

> **Listing 11.11 Testing calls to two side effect–free functions (F#)**

```
[<Fact>]
let partitionThenLongest() =
  let test = ["Seattle"; "New York"; "Grantchester"]
  let expected = ["New York"], ["Seattle"; "Grantchester"]

  let actualPartition = partitionMultiWord(test)          ❶
  let actualLongest = getLongest(test)

  Assert.Equal(expected, actualPartition)                 ❷
  Assert.Equal("Grantchester", actualLongest)
```

As you can see, the unit test runs the two functions in sequence ❶, but only uses the results in the section where we verify whether the results match our expectations ❷. This means that the function calls are independent, and if they don't contain any side effects we can reorder the calls freely. In a functional world, this unit test isn't needed at all: we've already written unit tests for the individual functions and this test doesn't verify any additional behavior.

However, if we'd written similar code using the mutable List<T> type, this test could catch the error we found in section 11.1. If the partitionMultiWord function modified the list referenced by the value test, removing all single-word names, the result of the second call wouldn't be "Grantchester," as expected by the test. This is an important general observation about functional code: if we test all the primitive pieces properly and test the code that composes them, we don't need to test whether the primitive pieces will still behave correctly in the new configuration.

So far we've talked about refactoring and testing functional programs. We've seen that first-class functions allow us to reduce code duplication and immutable data structures help us to understand what the code does as well as reduces the need to test how two pieces of code might interfere with each other.

The remainder of this chapter discusses when (and if) code is executed, and how we can take advantage of this to make our code more efficient. First we need to get a clear idea of when some flexibility is available, and how F# and C# decide when to execute code.

11.3   *Refactoring the evaluation order*

We've looked at how to track dependencies between functions in code that uses immutable data structures. Once we know what the dependencies are, we can sometimes reorder operations to make the program more efficient but keep the original meaning. Listing 11.12 shows a simple example of this kind of optimization.

Listing 11.12   Reordering calculations in a program (C#)

```
var num = Calculate1(10);        ❶
var test = TestCondition();
if (test == true)
    return Calculate2(num);
else return 0;
```

```
var test = TestCondition();
if (test == true) {
    var num = Calculate1(10);    ❷
    return Calculate2(num);
} else return 0;
```

In the first version, we call the Calculate1 function at the beginning of the program ❶. The result of this call is used only if TestCondition returns true. If that's not the case, we executed the Calculate1 function without any reason and we're wasting our CPU time! In the second version, we moved this computation inside the if condition ❷, so it will be calculated only if the result will be needed.

This was a simple modification and you'd probably have written the more efficient version without even thinking about it. As a program grows larger, optimizations like this become more difficult to spot. Listing 11.13 shows a slightly trickier example.

Listing 11.13   Passing a computed result to a function (C#)

```
int TestAndCalculate(int num) {
    var test = TestCondition();      ❶
    if (test == true)
```

```
        return Calculate2(num);          ❷
    else return 0;
}
TestAndCalculate(Calculate1(10));     ⬅─┘
```

❸ **Used later in the program**

The function in this example takes a value num as an argument—but this value may not be needed by the function at all. If the condition ❶ evaluates to false, the function returns 0 and the value of num isn't relevant. When calling this function ❸, the function Calculate1 is executed even if we later find out that we don't need its result.

In Haskell (another popular functional language) this code wouldn't call Calculate if it didn't need the result, because Haskell uses a different *evaluation strategy*. Let's look at a few options before we return to optimizing listing 11.13.

11.3.1 *Different evaluation strategies*

Haskell is a purely functional language. One of its interesting aspects is that it doesn't allow any side effects. There are techniques for printing to a screen or working with file systems, but they're implemented in a way that they don't actually look like side effects to the programmer. In a language like that, it's possible to reorder expressions when evaluating them, so Haskell doesn't evaluate a function unless it needs the result. This doesn't affect the program's result because the function can't have side effects.

Both C# and F# functions can have side effects. They're discouraged in F# and the language supports many ways to avoid them, but they can still be present in the program. Both languages specify the order in which the expressions will run, as otherwise we couldn't tell which side effect would occur first, making reliable programming impossible!

EAGER EVALUATION IN C# AND F#

In most mainstream languages, the rule that specifies evaluation order is quite simple: to make a function call, the program evaluates all the arguments, then executes the function. Let's demonstrate using our previous example:

```
TestAndCalculate(Calculate(10));
```

In all mainstream languages, the program will execute Calculate(10) and then pass the result as the argument to TestAndCalculate. As we've seen in the previous example, this is unfortunate if the function TestAndCalculate doesn't need the value of the argument. In that case, we just wasted some CPU cycles for no good reason! This is called an *eager evaluation strategy*.

The benefit of eager evaluation is that it's easy to understand how the program executes. In C# and F# this is clearly important, because we need to know the order in which side effects (such as I/O and UI manipulation) will run. In Haskell this is controlled by arguments and the return values of functions, so we don't need to know that much about the order.

LAZY EVALUATION STRATEGY IN HASKELL

In a lazy evaluation strategy, arguments to a function aren't evaluated when the function is called, but later when the value is needed. Let's return to the previous example:

```
TestAndCalculate(Calculate(10));
```

Here, Haskell jumps directly into the body of `TestAndCalculate`. The name of the argument is `num`, so Haskell remembers that if it needs the value of `num` later, it should run `Calculate(10)` to get it. Then it continues to execute by getting the result of `TestCondition`. If this function returns `true`, it needs the value of `num` and executes `Calculate(10)`. If `TestCondition` returns `false`, the `Calculate` function is never called.

11.3.2 *Comparing evaluation strategies*

We can demonstrate different evaluation strategies using the computation by calculation technique described in chapter 2. This shows how the program runs step by step, so you can clearly see the difference between lazy and eager evaluation. Listing 11.14 shows evaluation of an expression that uses two functions: `PlusTen(a)` returns a + 10 and `TimesTwo(a)` returns a * 2.

Listing 11.14   Lazy evaluation and eager evaluation

Lazy evaluation	Eager evaluation
`PlusTen(TimesTwo(4))`	`PlusTen(TimesTwo(4))`

`// Start calculating PlusTen:`
`TimesTwo(4) + 10` ❶
	`// To get values of all arguments,`
	`// calculate result of TimesTwo:`
	`PlusTen(8)` ❸

`// Calculate TimesTwo, because`
`// we need its result now:`
`8 + 10` ❷
	`// Evaluate PlusTen next:`
	`8 + 10` ❹

`// Calculate the result:` `18`	`// Calculate the result:` `18`

The lazy evaluation strategy starts by evaluating `PlusTen` and doesn't evaluate the argument first. In the next step it will need to add 10 to the argument ❶, but the argument hasn't been evaluated yet. Since the value of the argument is needed to make further progress, the call to `TimesTwo` is executed ❷ and we get the final result.

The eager evaluation strategy starts by evaluating the argument, so in the first step it evaluates `TimesTwo(4)` to obtain the value 8 ❸. All arguments to the function `PlusTen` have now been evaluated, so it can continue by evaluating this function ❹ and calculating the result.

So far we've only looked at one motivation for using a lazy evaluation strategy, but it seems useful already. Why have we brought it up at all if it only exists in Haskell? Similar effects can be achieved in F# and C# 3.0.

11.3.3 *Simulating lazy evaluation using functions*

The evaluation order in F# and C# is eager: expressions used as arguments to a function are evaluated before the function itself starts to execute. In both C# and F#, we can simulate lazy evaluation using function values, and F# even supports lazy evaluation via a special keyword.

But first, there's one exception from the eager evaluation rule. You definitely know about it and use it frequently, but it's so common that you may not realize that it's doing something special. Certain C# operators such as logical or (||), logical and (&&), the conditional operator (?:), and the null-coalescing operator (??) implement short-circuiting behavior and evaluate only those operands that they need for computing the result. This means that we can't, for example, easily implement an Or method that would have the same behavior as the || operator:

```
if (Foo(5) || Foo(7))
  Console.WriteLine("True");
if (Or(Foo(5), Foo(7)))
  Console.WriteLine("True");
```

Let's say that the Foo method returns true when the parameter is less than 10. This means that when the value of Foo(5) is evaluated, the built-in || operator already knows that the overall result will be true and so it doesn't evaluate the result of Foo(7). On the other hand, when calling the Or method, both of the arguments will be evaluated prior to the method call. Is there any way to write the code so that the Foo(7) expression isn't evaluated if the Foo(5) expression evaluates to true?

One possible answer is to use function values. Instead of having a method with a parameter of type bool, we'll make it take Func<bool>. When we need the value later in the code, we can execute the function, which will in turn evaluate the value of the expression. You can see how to write the or operator (now called LazyOr) using this trick in listing 11.15.

Listing 11.15 Lazy or operator using functions (C#)

```
bool Foo(int n) {
  Console.WriteLine("Foo({0})", n);        ❶
  return n <= 10;
}
bool LazyOr(Func<bool> first, Func<bool> second) {    ❷
  if (first()) return true;        ◁──── Evaluates first
  if (second()) return true;       ◁──── argument
  return false;                    Evaluates second
}                                  argument
if (LazyOr(() => Foo(5), () => Foo(7)))    ◁──── Prints Foo(5) only
  Console.WriteLine("True");
```

We're demonstrating the problem using a Foo method that writes to the screen ❶ so we can track how it's being called. The original arguments to the or operator are now wrapped inside lambda functions. When the method is called, its arguments are eagerly evaluated, but the value of the argument is a function. The expression *inside* the lambda function isn't evaluated until the function is called.

Look at the LazyOr method ❷. In the places where we need to access the Boolean value that we're calculating with, we call the function provided by that argument. If the function first returns true, then the LazyOr method immediately returns true and the second function never gets called. This means that the code behaves just like the built-in logical or operator.

Suppose we needed to access the argument value more than once. Should we invoke the function multiple times? That doesn't sound like a very efficient solution, so we'd probably want to store the result locally. In F#, this is made simpler using a feature called *lazy values*. First we'll look at some F# code, and then we'll implement the same behavior in C#. After that, we'll look at a sample application that may give you some ideas for places to use this technique in your own code.

11.3.4 *Lazy values in F#*

A lazy value in F# is a way to represent delayed computation—this means a computation that's evaluated only when the value is needed. In the previous section, we implemented a similar thing using functions in C#, but lazy values automatically calculate the value only once and remember the result.

The best way to explore this feature is to play with it inside F# Interactive. A script that demonstrates how to use it is in listing 11.16.

Listing 11.16   Introducing lazy values (F# Interactive)

```
> let foo(n) =
    printfn "foo(%d)" n
    n <= 10;;
val foo : int -> bool

> let n = lazy foo(10);;                        ❶
val n : Lazy<bool> = Value is not created.

> n.Value;;                         Calls foo to get
foo(10)                      ❷     the result
val it : bool = true

> n.Value;;                         Returns
val it : bool = true         ❸     immediately
```

We start by writing a function similar to our C# Foo method. This lets us track when the computation is evaluated by writing to the console. The second command uses the F# lazy keyword ❶. If you mark an expression with lazy, the expression won't be evaluated immediately and will be wrapped in a lazy value. As you can see from the output, the foo function hasn't been called yet and the created value has type Lazy<bool>. This represents a lazy value that can evaluate to a Boolean value.

On the next line, you can see that lazy values have a member called Value ❷. This property evaluates the delayed computation. In our case, this means calling the foo function. The last command shows that accessing Value again ❸ doesn't reevaluate the computation. If you look at the output, you can see that the `foo` function wasn't called. That said, we can clearly see that `Lazy<'T>` is a mutable type. If we used a purely functional function without side effects as its argument we wouldn't be able to observe that.

In the earlier chapters, we've emphasized the functional way of looking at data types, and we've seen that it's useful to know what kind of operations are needed to work with a type. Let's look at lazy values using this point of view.

Specifying lazy values using operations

If the F# language didn't have the `lazy` keyword and didn't allow us to write objects with properties, we'd need two operations—one to construct the lazy value and one to extract the actual value:

```
val create : (unit -> 'T) -> Lazy<'T>
val force : Lazy<'T> -> 'T
```

As you can see, the argument of the `create` operation is a function that's wrapped inside the `Lazy<'T>` value. In functional programming, other types exist that represent delayed computations, so when a function takes a function of type `unit -> 'T` as an argument and returns some generic type, the type likely represents a delayed computation. The signature of the `force` operation is even more straightforward. It simply extracts the actual value from the type that wraps it. The signature doesn't tell us how the actual value is wrapped, but since we have the `force` operation, we can always extract it.

As we'll see in the next chapter, this abstract description of a type in terms of basic operations that we can use for working with it is useful in functional programming. Even though F# provides a more convenient way to work with lazy values than using functions, it's still helpful to realize what the *primitive operations* are.

Our motivation when we started talking about lazy values was that we couldn't write our own implementation of the logical or operator that would only evaluate the argument on the right-hand side if and when it needed to. Let's try again now, armed with our new knowledge of lazy values.

IMPLEMENTING OR AND LAZY OR

Since we're implementing an operator, we're going to define it as a true operator rather than just as a normal function. As you learned in chapter 6, we can introduce our own operators in F#, so listing 11.17 shows two different variations of the or operator.

Listing 11.17   Comparing eager and lazy or operators (F# Interactive)

```
let (||!) a b =            ❶          let (||?) (a:Lazy<_>) (b:Lazy<_>) =
   if a then true                        if a.Value then true         ❷
   elif b then true                      elif b.Value then true
   else false                            else false
```

Listing 11.17   Comparing eager and lazy `or` operators (F# Interactive) *(continued)*

```
// Using in F# Interactive
> if (foo(5) ||! foo(7))        ❸
    then printfn "True";;
foo(5)
foo(7)
True
```

```
> if lazy foo(5) ||? lazy foo(7)    ❹
    then printfn "True";;
foo(5)
True
```

Arguments of the eager version of the operator ❶ are Boolean values, so we can use them directly in the `if` condition. The lazy version takes lazy values wrapping a computation that returns a Boolean value. To read the value, we use the `Value` property ❷.

When using the eager operator ❸, we specify the arguments as normal. As the output shows, both of the arguments are evaluated. In fact, they're evaluated even before the body of our custom operator executes. When using the lazy version ❹ we add additional `lazy` keywords to delay both arguments. The result is that only one expression is evaluated, because that's enough to calculate the final result.

In many ways this example was only a curiosity, but it was useful to demonstrate how we can programmatically achieve an element of laziness that's already familiar through language constructs. Next we'll implement lazy values as a type we can use from C#. It's not quite as syntactically compact, but even in this form it can be useful.

11.3.5   *Implementing lazy values for C#*

In section 11.3.3 we represented delayed computation in C# using functions. The `Lazy<T>` type that we've just explored in F# adds the ability to cache the value when its value is calculated. Since Visual Studio 2010, the type is available in the core .NET libraries under the name `System.Lazy<T>`, so we don't have to implement it ourselves.

Listing 11.18 shows a simple implementation of the `Lazy<T>` class. The code is simplified, because it isn't thread-safe and doesn't handle exceptions in any way, but it shows the core idea.

Listing 11.18   Class for representing lazy values (C#)

```
public class Lazy<T> {
  readonly Func<T> func;
  bool evaluated = false;      │ Represents state
  T value;                     │ of the cache

  public Lazy(Func<T> func) {      ❶
    this.func = func;
  }
  public T Value {      ❷
    get {
      if (!evaluated) {
        value = func();          │ Computes value,
        evaluated = true;        │ modifies state
      }
      return value;
    }
```

```
    }
  }
}
public class Lazy {
  public static Lazy<T> Create<T>(Func<T> func) {        ◁─┐  Enables type inference
    return new Lazy<T>(func);                                │  when creating values
  }
}
```

The first important part of the class is a constructor ❶ that takes a function and stores it inside a `readonly` field. The function doesn't take any arguments, but evaluates the value when it's called, so we're using the `Func<T>` delegate. There's also a static method in a nongeneric type to make it easier to use C#'s type inference when we create lazy values.

The lazy value uses a flag to specify whether the value has already been evaluated. Note that we're using generics, so we can't easily represent this using the `null` value, and even if we added a restriction to force `T` to be a reference type, we need to allow for the possibility that the function could return `null` as the computed value.

Most of the code that uses the cached value is in the `Value` property ❷ getter. From the user's perspective this is the second important part of the class. First it tests whether we've already evaluated the function. If we have, we can use the value we computed earlier. If not, it calls the function and marks a flag so that we don't evaluate it multiple times.

Let's look at a simple code snippet that shows how we can work with this type:

```
var lazy = Lazy.Create(() => Foo(10));
Console.WriteLine(lazy.Value);        // Prints 'Foo(10)' and 'True'
Console.WriteLine(lazy.Value);        // Prints only 'True'
```

If you try this code, you should see exactly the same behavior as in the F# version. When creating the lazy value, we give it a function: the `Foo` method won't be called at this point. The first call to `Value` evaluates the function and calls `Foo`; any subsequent call to `Value` uses the cached value computed earlier, so the last line prints the result.

So far, our motivation for exploring lazy values was the difficulty with implementing lazy version of the or operator. In the next section we'll look at two more complicated examples of using lazy values in practice.

11.4   *Using lazy values in practice*

Lazy values are useful when we have a set of computations that can take a long time and we need to calculate the value (or values) on demand. In that case, we can benefit from the caching that we've implemented in C# in the previous section and use lazy values as a cache that's populated on demand.

Another important use of laziness is when expressing some concept that's hard to encode in other ways. We'll start our discussion about practical uses of lazy values with a couple of examples that are motivated by Haskell—the fact that Haskell uses lazy evaluation everywhere makes it a very expressive language.

11.4.1 *Introducing infinite lists*

The heading of this section may sound a little odd (or insane), so we'll offer a word of explanation. One of the data structures that we've used quite a lot is the functional list. We might also want to represent logically infinite lists, such as a list of all prime numbers. In reality we wouldn't *use* all the numbers, but we can work with a data structure like this without worrying about the length. If the list is infinite, we know that we'll be able to access as many numbers as we need.

Aside from mathematical challenges, the same concept can be useful in more mainstream programming. When we drew a pie chart in chapter 4, we used random colors, but we could instead use an *infinite* list of colors generated in a way that makes the chart look clear. We'll see all these examples in the next chapter, but now we'll show you how the idea can be represented using lazy values.

Storing an infinite list of numbers in memory seems like a tricky problem. Obviously we can't store the whole data structure, so we need to store part of it and represent the rest as a delayed computation. As we've seen, lazy values are a great way to represent the delayed computation part.

We can represent a simple infinite list in a similar way to an ordinary list. It is a cell that contains a value and the rest of the list. The only difference is that the rest of the list will be a delayed computation that gives us another cell when we execute it. We can represent this kind of list in F# using a discriminated union, as shown in listing 11.19.

Listing 11.19 Infinite list of integers (F#)

```
type InfiniteInts =
  | LazyCell of int *          ❶
              Lazy<InfiniteInts>     ❷
```

This discriminated union has only a single discriminator, which means it's similar to a record. We could have written the code using a record instead, but discriminated unions are more convenient for this example, because we can use the nice pattern-matching syntax to extract the carried values. The only discriminator is called `LazyCell`, and it stores the value stored in the current cell ❶ and a reference to the "tail" ❷. The tail is a lazy value, so it will be evaluated on demand. This way, we'll be able to evaluate the list cell by cell and when a cell is evaluated, the result will be cached.

Lazy lists in F# and Haskell

As mentioned earlier, Haskell uses lazy evaluation everywhere. This means that a standard list type in Haskell is automatically lazy. The tail isn't evaluated until the value is accessed somewhere from the code.

In F#, lazy lists aren't used very frequently. We'll see a more elegant way of writing infinite collections in F# and also in C# 2.0 in the next chapter. F# provides an implementation of lazy lists similar to the type we've implemented in this section. You can find it in the FSharp.PowerPack.dll library as `LazyList<'a>`.

Now that we've got our type, let's use it to create a simple infinite list that stores integers 0, 1, 2, 3, ... Listing 11.20 also shows how to access values from the list.

Listing 11.20   Creating a list containing 0, 1, 2, 3, 4, ... (F# Interactive)

```
> let rec numbers(num) =                      ❶    ┐ Creates next cell as
    LazyCell(num, lazy numbers(num + 1));;       ◄──┘ delayed computation
val numbers : int -> InfiniteInts

> numbers(0);;                                                              ❷
val nums : InfiniteInts = LazyCell(0, Value is not created.)

> let next(LazyCell(hd, tl)) =    ❸     ┐ Evaluates lazy value
    tl.Value;;                      ◄──┘ representing next cell
val next : InfiniteInts -> InfiniteInts
                                              ┐ Accesses sixth
                                              │ value from list
> numbers(0) |> next |> next |> next |> next |> next;;   ◄──┘
val nums : InfiniteInts = LazyCell(5, Value is not created.)
```

We begin by writing a recursive function numbers ❶ that returns an infinite list of integers starting with the number given as an argument and continuing to infinity. It returns a cell that contains the first value and a tail. The tail is a lazy value that (when evaluated) recursively calls numbers to get the next cell.

If we call the function with 0 as an argument, we'll get an infinite list starting from 0 ❷. The output from the F# Interactive isn't particularly readable, but you can spot that the first value is 0 and that the tail is a value of type Lazy<InfiniteInts>. The subsequent command declares a function next, which gives us the next cell of the list ❸. We use pattern matching in the declaration to decompose the only argument. This looks a bit unusual, because you don't typically use discriminated unions with only a single discriminator, but it's the same principle as decomposing a tuple into its components. In the body of the function, we read the Value property, which evaluates the next cell. Finally, the last line uses the next function several times to read the sixth value from the list.

There are many more things that we could do with lazy lists, but we won't go into them here as we'll see a more idiomatic F# technique in the next chapter. There are situations where the LazyList<'a> type is quite useful. Even though we haven't worked with the F# library type directly, you won't have problems using it now that you understand the principles.

In this introduction to infinite data structures, we've focused more on the functional style without even showing a C# example. It would be possible to write the same type in C# now that we know how to write a lazy value in C#, but in the next chapter we'll see a more natural way for representing infinite structures or streams of values in C#.

The lazy lists in this example had one very interesting aspect. Once we evaluated the list to some point, the evaluated values remained available in memory, and we didn't have to recalculate them each time. As we'll see in the next section, this aspect of lazy values can be used as a simple but elegant caching mechanism.

Writing functions for working with infinite lists

When working with the standard list type, we can use functions like `List.map` and `List.filter`. We can implement the same functions for infinite lists as well, but of course, not all of them. For example, `List.fold` and `List.sort` need to read all the elements, which isn't possible for our lazy list. As an example of what *is* possible, here's an implementation of the `map` function:

```
let rec map f (LazyCell(hd, tl)) =
    LazyCell(f(hd), lazy map f tl.Value)
```

The structure is similar to the normal `map` function. It applies the given function to the first value in the cell, then recursively processes the rest of the list. The processing of the tail is delayed using the `lazy` keyword. Other common list-processing functions would look similar.

11.4.2   *Caching values in a photo browser*

In our next example, we're going to write an application that finds all the photos in a specified folder and displays a list of them. When the user selects a photo, the application resizes it and shows it in a window. (For simplicity, we won't allow the user to resize the window.) When we draw the photo, we'll need to resize it to fit the screen and show the resized image.

Obviously, we don't want to resize all photos when the application starts: it could take an enormous amount of time for a large set of photos. We also don't want to resize the photo every time we draw it because we'd have to resize the same photo again and again. From the description it's fairly obvious that lazy values can help us. We'll demonstrate how to write the application in F#, but you can find the equivalent C# version on the book's website.

CACHING USING LAZY VALUES

The most interesting part of the application is the code that's executed when the application starts. It finds all the files in the specified directory and creates an array with information about each file. This information contains the name of the file and the lazy value that will evaluate to the resized preview. Listing 11.21 shows how we can create this data structure.

Listing 11.21   Creating a collection of photo information (F#)

```
open System.IO
open System.Drawing

type ImageInfo = { Name : string; Preview : Lazy<Bitmap> }      ❶

let dir = @"C:\My Photos"                                          ⟵  Specifies the
let createLazyResized(file) =                   ❷                      directory with
  lazy( use bmp = Bitmap.FromFile(file)     ⟵  Manages                 your photos
        let resized = new Bitmap(400, 300)      disposal
        use gr = Graphics.FromImage(resized)    automatically
```

```
    let dst = Rectangle(0, 0, 400, 300)
    let src = Rectangle(0, 0, bmp.Width, bmp.Height)
    gr.InterpolationMode <- Drawing2D.InterpolationMode.High
    gr.DrawImage(bmp, dst, src, GraphicsUnit.Pixel)
    resized)

let files =
  Directory.GetFiles(dir, "*.jpg") |> Array.map (fun file ->
    { Name = Path.GetFileName(file)
      Preview = createLazyResized(file) })
```

Draws resized bitmap to target

❸

❹

We start by declaring a record type **❶** that represents information about the photo. As you can see, the type of the preview is Lazy<Bitmap>, which is a delayed computation that will give us a Bitmap when we'll need it. Next, we implement a function that returns a lazy value representing the resized bitmap **❷**. To draw the preview, we write the usual code to resize a Bitmap object and wrap the entire body using the lazy keyword.

Next, we create the data structure that contains information about photos **❸**. We obtain an array of files using a normal .NET method call and use the Array.map function to create an ImageInfo value for every photo. Inside the lambda function, we create a record value containing the name and the lazy preview returned by the createLazyResized function **❹**.

One interesting property of the program is that we could delete all uses of the lazy keyword, change all types from Lazy<'T> to 'T, and delete all uses of the Value property, and the code would still work correctly, except everything will be evaluated eagerly.

IMPLEMENTING THE USER INTERFACE

Now that we have all the data we need about the photos, we can add a simple GUI using Windows Forms. In listing 11.22, we'll create a couple of controls to show the data and code that shows the selected photo.

Listing 11.22 Adding a user interface for the photo browser (F#)

```
open System
open System.Windows.Forms

let main = new Form(Text="Photos", ClientSize=Size(600,300))
let pict = new PictureBox(Dock=DockStyle.Fill)
let list = new ListBox(Dock=DockStyle.Left, Width=200,
                       DataSource=files,
                       DisplayMember = "Name")
list.SelectedIndexChanged.Add(fun _ ->
  let info = files.[list.SelectedIndex]
  pict.Image <- info.Preview.Value)
main.Controls.Add(pict)
main.Controls.Add(list)

[<STAThread>]
do Application.Run(main)
```

❶ Displays Name property from files array

Handles change of selection

❷ Evaluates lazy value

❸ Runs application

To show the list of photos in the ListBox control, we use data binding **❶**, which is a feature used in many .NET controls. We simply specify that the DataSource for the control is our array of files. To specify what should be displayed, we set the DataMember property to the name of the record member that we want to display (Name).

Next, we register a lambda function as a handler for the `SelectedIndexChanged` event of the `ListBox`. When this is triggered, we choose the selected `ImageInfo` value and use the `Value` property to get the resized bitmap. If this is the first time that particular bitmap has been shown, it will be resized at that point; if we've seen it before, we can immediately use the cached result. Listing 11.22 shows the code as a standalone application, which means that we run it using the `Application.Run()` method ❸. In F# Interactive, you'd use `main.Show()` to display the form instead. You can see how the application looks in figure 11.2.

If you run the application using a folder containing large photos, the difference made by lazy values is obvious. Selecting a "new" photo can take some time, but if you revisit a photo you've already seen, it will be rendered immediately.

NOTE   You may be wondering if we could improve this application using multiple threads. There are two areas where using multiple threads could help here. First, we could start the computation when a user selects a file without blocking the UI. Currently, the application is frozen until the image is resized. To this end, we could use asynchronous programming techniques such as the F# asynchronous workflows discussed in chapter 13.

Another possibility is that the application could precompute the resized bitmaps in the background. Instead of doing nothing, it could resize some images in advance so that the user wouldn't have to wait when clicking on the photo. In chapter 14, we'll see that this is quite easy—we'll look at the `Task<T>` type, which is like `Lazy<T>`, except that it isn't as lazy and computes the value on a background thread.

We're sure you have a pretty good idea how you'd implement the same application using our `Lazy<T>` class in C#, so we won't discuss that in this book. You can find the source code of the application at the book's website. One of the interesting things in

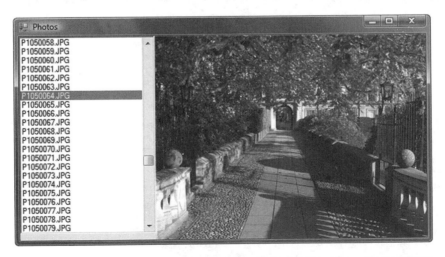

Figure 11.2   Photos can be selected from the list on the left side. The resized version is cached automatically thanks to the use of lazy values.

the C# version is that you can use C# 3.0 anonymous types for representing information about photos if you write the code inside a single method.

11.5 Summary

The general theme of this chapter was refactoring of functional programs, even though we've seen a larger number of examples and concepts. We started by talking about the equivalent of refactoring in mathematics, and you saw that in mathematics, we can more easily reason about the "code," so we can see when a particular change is correct. Thanks to its roots in mathematics, functional programming often has the same property.

We first explored how we can use the function type to reduce code duplication, which is the simple case of refactoring. Then we've seen how functional programming makes it easier to track dependencies in the code, and as a result, we can see whether or not a particular refactoring is correct.

Next we focused on unit testing of functional programs using xUnit.net. You learned how to combine unit testing and interactive testing using F# Interactive, so if you were worried about interactive testing in one of the earlier chapters, you now know that interactive tests are only a part of a larger testing story. In addition, we demonstrated how immutability makes it simpler to test code, because we only need to test that a function gives the expected result: we don't need to worry about side effects.

Then we turned our attention to laziness. We've seen that laziness can be used to cache the results of a computation, so that the code runs more efficiently next time we access the value. As long as we work only with immutable data structures, this modification doesn't change the result of the program, so we can view it as just another form of useful refactoring. You also learned that laziness can be used to express interesting functional concepts such as infinite data types. In fact, this was only a teaser for the next chapter, where we'll talk about C# iterators and F# sequence expressions, both of which allow us to express a sequence of values in a much more natural way. This is just one example of a bigger idea, so we'll also look at how we can change or extend the meaning of code in general.

Sequence expressions and alternative workflows

> **This chapter covers**
> - Processing and generating sequences of values
> - Working with F# sequence expressions
> - Understanding monads and LINQ expressions
> - Implementing F# computation expressions

Before we can start talking about sequence expressions, you must know what a *sequence* is. This is another F# term that comes from mathematics, where a sequence is an ordered list containing a possibly infinite number of elements. Don't worry if that all sounds a bit abstract; you're already familiar with the type that expresses the same idea in .NET: IEnumerable<T>.

The primary reason for having the IEnumerable<T> type in the .NET Framework is it gives us a unified way to work with collections of data such as arrays, dictionaries, mutable lists, and immutable F# lists. In F# we'll be talking about sequences, because this is a more general term. A sequence can represent a finite number of elements coming from a collection, but it can be also generated dynamically and retrieved on an on-demand basis. You'll learn that infinite sequences, which sound somewhat academic, can still be useful in real applications.

We'll begin by looking at ways to create and process sequences. The traditional functional technique is to use higher-order functions, but modern languages often provide an easier way. In C#, we can use iterators to generate a sequence and LINQ queries to process an existing one. The F# language unifies these two concepts into one and allows us to write most of the operations using *sequence expressions.*

The syntax used for writing sequence expressions in F# isn't a single-purpose language feature designed only for sequences. That is just one (very useful!) application of a more general construct called *computation expressions.* Computation expressions can be used for writing code that looks like ordinary F# but behaves differently. In the case of sequence expressions, a sequence of results is generated instead of just one value, but we'll look at other examples. We'll show you how to use computation expressions for logging, and how they can make option values easier to work with.

NOTE   Computation expressions can be used for customizing the meaning of the code in many ways, but some limits exist. In particular, the code written using computation expressions has to be executed as compiled .NET code and we can customize only a few primitives inside it. It can't be used to manipulate the code and execute it in a different environment, in the way that LINQ to SQL does, for example. To do similar things in F#, we have to combine ideas from this chapter with a feature called *F# quotations,* which isn't discussed in this book. You'll find resources about quotations on the book's website.

We'll start by talking about sequences, and once you become familiar with sequence expressions, we'll look at computation expressions and how they relate to LINQ queries in C#. Let's take our first steps with sequences. Before we can start working with them, we need to know how to create them.

12.1   *Generating sequences*

There are several techniques for generating sequences, so let's look at our options. The direct way is to implement the `IEnumerator<T>` interface, providing a `Current` property and a `MoveNext` method, which moves the enumerator object to the next element. This forces us to explicitly create an object with mutable state, which obviously goes against the functional style. Normally we can apply techniques that hide the mutation and give us a more declarative way of expressing the generated sequence's contents. This is similar to using lazy values that we've seen in the previous chapter. Using mutable state explicitly (for example, to implement caching) doesn't look like a good functional style, but when we hide the mutation into a `Lazy<'T>` type, we'll get a perfectly reasonable functional code.

As usual in functional programming, we can use higher-order functions. The F# library supports quite a few of these for working with sequences, but we'll look at only one example. As we'll see later, both C# and F# give us a simpler way to generate sequences. In C#, we can use *iterators* and F# supports a general-purpose sequence-processing feature called *sequence expressions.*

12.1.1 *Using higher-order functions*

The functions used to work with sequences in F# are in the Seq module, and we'll examine one very general function called Seq.unfold. You can see it as an opposite to the fold function, which takes a collection and "folds" it into a single value. unfold takes a single value and "unfolds" it into a sequence. The following snippet shows how to generate a sequence containing numbers up to 10 formatted as strings:

```
> let nums = Seq.unfold (fun num ->
    if (num <= 10) then Some(string(num), num + 1) else None) 0
 ;;
val nums : seq<string> = seq ["0"; "1"; "2"; "3"; ...]
```

The num value represents the state used during the generation of the sequence. When the lambda function is called for the first time, the value of num is set to the initial value of the second parameter (zero in our example). The lambda function returns an option type containing a tuple. The value None marks the end of the sequence. When we return Some, we give it two different values in a tuple:

- A value that will be returned in the sequence (in our case, the number converted to a string).
- A value that is the new state to use when the lambda function is next called.

As you can see from the output, the type of the returned value is seq<string>. This is an F# type alias for the IEnumerable<string> type. It's a different way of writing the same type, in the same way that float is a C# alias for System.Single, so you can mix them freely. The output also shows the first few elements of the sequence, but since the sequence can be infinite, the F# Interactive shell doesn't attempt to print all of them.

The standard .NET library doesn't contain a similar method for C#. One of the few methods that generate sequences in C# is Enumerable.Range (from the System.Linq namespace), which returns an ascending sequence of numbers of the specified length (second argument) from the specified starting number (the first argument). We could implement a function like Seq.unfold in C# as well, but we'll see that similar results can be easily achieved using C# iterators, which we'll look at next.

12.1.2 *Using iterators in C#*

When iterators were first introduced in C# 2.0, the most common use for them was to simplify implementing the IEnumerable<T> interface for your own collections. The programming style used in C# has been evolving, and iterators are now used together with other functional constructs for a variety of data processing operations.

Iterators can be used for generating arbitrary sequences. We'll start with a simple example that generates a sequence of factorials that are less than 1 million, formatted as strings. Listing 12.1 shows the complete source code.

Listing 12.1   Generating factorials using iterators (C#)

```
static IEnumerable<string> Factorials() {
    int factorial = 1;                              ❶
    for(int num = 0; factorial < 1000000; num++) {
```

```
        factorial = factorial * num;                              ❷
        yield return String.Format("{0}! = {1}", num, factorial);
    }
}
```
Returns next string

The C# compiler performs a rather sophisticated transformation on the iterator code to create a "hidden" type that implements the IEnumerable<T> interface. The interesting thing about listing 12.1 is how it works with the local state. We declare one local variable to store some mutable state ❶, and a second mutable variable is declared as part of the for loop. The algorithm is implemented inside a loop, which is executed every time we want to pull another value from the iterator. The loop body updates the local state of the iterator ❷ and yields the newly calculated value.

The code is very imperative, because it heavily relies on mutation, but from the outside iterators look almost like functional data types, because the mutable state is hidden. Let's look at the *sequence expression*, which is the general F# mechanism for generating, but also for processing, sequences.

12.1.3 *Using F# sequence expressions*

Iterators in C# are very comfortable, because they allow you to write complicated code (a type that implements the IEnumerable<T>/IEnumerator<T> interfaces) in an ordinary C# method. The developer-written code uses standard C# features such as loops, and the only change is that we can use one new kind of statement to do something nonstandard. This new statement is indicated with yield return (or yield break to terminate the sequence), and the nonstandard behavior is to return a value as the next element of a sequence. The sequence is then accessed on demand (end evaluated element-by-element) using the MoveNext method. Sequence expressions in F# are similar: they use a construct that's equivalent to yield return.

WRITING SEQUENCE EXPRESSIONS

In C#, we can use iterators automatically when implementing methods that return IEnumerable<T>, IEnumerator<T>, or their nongeneric equivalents. F# sequence expressions are marked explicitly using the seq identifier, and don't have to be used as the body of a method or function. As the name suggests, sequence expressions are a different type of expression, and we can use them anywhere in our code. Listing 12.2 shows how to create a simple sequence using this syntax.

Listing 12.2   Introducing sequence expression syntax (F# Interactive)

```
> let nums =
    seq { let n = 10          ❶
          yield n + 1         ❷
          printfn "second.."       ❸
          yield n + 2 };;
val nums : seq<int>          ❹
```

When writing sequence expressions, we enclose the whole F# expression that generates the sequence in a seq block ❶. The block is written using curly braces and the seq identifier[1] at the beginning denotes that the compiler should interpret the body of the block as a sequence expression. There are other possible identifiers that specify other alternative workflows, as you'll see later. In the case of seq, the block turns the whole expression into a lazily generated sequence. You can see this by looking at the inferred type of the value ❹.

The body of the sequence expression can contain statements with a special meaning. Similarly to C#, there's a statement for returning a single element of the sequence. In F# this is written using the yield keyword ❷. The body can also contain other standard F# constructs, such as value bindings, and even calls that perform side effects ❸.

Similar to C#, the body of the sequence expression executes lazily. When we create the sequence value (in our previous example, the value nums), the body of the sequence expression isn't executed. This only happens when we access elements of the sequence, and each time we access an element, the sequence expression code only executes as far as the next yield statement. In C#, the most common way to access elements in an iterator is using a foreach loop. In the following F# example, we'll use the List.ofSeq function, which converts the sequence to an immutable F# list:

```
> nums |> List.ofSeq;;
second..
val it : int list = [11; 12]
```

The returned list contains both of the elements generated by the sequence. This means that the computation had to go through the whole expression, executing the printfn call on the way, which is why the output contains a line printed from the sequence expression. If we take only a single element from the sequence, the sequence expression will only evaluate until the first yield call, so the string won't be printed:

```
> nums |> Seq.take 1 |> List.ofSeq;;
val it : int list = [11]
```

We're using one of the sequence processing functions from the Seq module to take only a single element from the sequence. The take function returns a new sequence that takes the specified number of elements (one in the example) and then terminates. When we convert it to an F# list, we get a list containing only a single element, but the printfn function isn't called.

When you implement a sequence expression, you may reach a point where the body of the expression is too long. The natural thing to do in this case would be to split it into a couple of functions that generate parts of the sequence. If the sequence uses multiple data sources, we'd like to have the code that reads the data in separate functions. So far, so good—but then we're left with the problem of composing the sequences returned from different functions.

---

[1] You may be surprised that we're referring to seq as an identifier instead of a keyword, but you'll see later that it's an identifier (that we could even define ourselves) rather than a special keyword built into the F# language. The seq identifier also isn't defined automatically by the seq<'a> type. The name is the same, but seq identifier here is a different symbol defined by the F# library.

COMPOSING SEQUENCE EXPRESSIONS

The yield return keyword in C# only allows us to return a single element, so if we want to yield an entire sequence from a method implemented using iterators in C#, we'd have to loop over all elements of the sequence using foreach and yield them one by one. This would work, but it would be inefficient, especially if we had several sequences nested in this way. In functional programming, composability is a more important aspect, so F# allows us to compose sequences and yield the whole sequence from a sequence expression using a special language construct: yield! (usually pronounced *yield-bang*). Listing 12.3 demonstrates this, generating a sequence of cities in three different ways.

Listing 12.3   Composing sequences from different sources (F# Interactive)

```
> let capitals = [ "Paris"; "Prague" ];;      ⟵── Lists capital cities
val capitals : string list          ┌─ Returns name and
> let withNew(name) =           ⟵──┘  name with prefix
    seq { yield name
          yield "New " + name };;
val withNew : string -> seq<string>

> let allCities =
    seq { yield "Oslo"       ❶
          yield! capitals              ❷
          yield! withNew("York") };;         ❸
val allCities : seq<string>
                                              All data composed
                                                    together
> allCities |> List.ofSeq;;
val it : string list = ["Oslo"; "Paris"; "Prague"; "York"; "New York"]    ⟵──┘
```

Listing 12.3 starts by creating two different data sources. The first one is an F# list that contains two capital cities. The type of the value is list<string>, but since F# lists implement the seq<'a> interface, we can use it as a sequence later in the code. The second data source is a function that generates a sequence containing two elements. The next piece of code shows how to join these two data sources into a single sequence. First, we use the yield statement to return a single value ❶. Next, we use the yield! construct to return all the elements from the F# list ❷. Finally, we call the function withNew ❸ (which returns a sequence) and return all the elements from that sequence. This shows that you can mix both ways of yielding elements inside a single sequence expression.

Just like yield, the yield! construct also returns elements lazily. This means that when the code gets to the point where we call the withNew function, the function gets called, but it only returns an object representing the sequence. If we wrote some code in the function before the seq block it would be executed at this point, but the body of the seq block wouldn't start executing. That only happens after the withNew function returns, because we need to generate the next element. When the execution reaches the first yield construct, it will return the element and transfers the control back to the caller. The caller then performs other work and the execution of the sequence resumes when the caller requests another element.

We've focused on the syntax of sequence expressions, but they can sound quite awkward until you start using them. There are several patterns that are common when using sequence expressions; let's look at two of them.

12.2 *Mastering sequence expressions*

So far, we've seen how to return single elements from a sequence expression and also how to compose sequences in F#. We haven't yet examined the F# version of the previous factorial example using mutable state. Somewhat predictably, the F# code will be quite different.

12.2.1 *Recursive sequence expressions*

The primary control flow structure in functional programming is recursion. We've used it in many examples when writing ordinary functions, and it allows us to solve the same problems as imperative loops but without relying on mutable state. When we wanted to write a simple recursive function, we used the let rec keyword, allowing the function to call itself recursively.

The yield! construct for composing sequences also allows us to perform recursive calls inside sequence expressions, so we can use the same functional programming techniques when generating sequences. Listing 12.4 generates all factorials under 1 million just like the C# example in listing 12.1.

> **Listing 12.4 Generating factorials using sequence expressions (F# Interactive)**

```
> let rec factorialsUtil(num, factorial) =            ❶
    seq { if (factorial < 1000000) then
              yield sprintf "%d! = %d" num factorial      ❷
              let num = num + 1
              yield! factorialsUtil(num, factorial * num) };;   ❸
val factorialsUtil : int * int -> seq<string>

> let factorials = factorialsUtil(0, 1)       ❹
val factorials : seq<string> =
  seq ["0! = 1"; "1! = 1"; "2! = 2"; "3! = 6"; "4! = 24 ...]
```

Listing 12.4 begins with a utility function that takes a number and its factorial as an argument ❶. When we want to compute the sequence of factorials later in the code, we call this function and give it the smallest number for which a factorial is defined to start the sequence ❹. This is zero, because by definition the factorial of zero is one.

The whole body of the function is a seq block, so the function returns a sequence. In the sequence expression, we first check whether the last factorial is smaller than 1 million, and if not, we end the sequence. The else branch of the if expression is missing, so it won't yield any additional numbers. If the condition is true, we first yield a single result ❷, which indicates the next factorial formatted as a string. Next, we increment the number and perform a recursive call ❸. This returns a sequence of factorials starting from the next number; we use yield! to compose it with the current sequence.

Note that converting this approach to C# is difficult, because C# doesn't have an equivalent of the yield! feature. We'd have to iterate over all the elements using a foreach loop, which could cause stack overflow. Even if it worked, it would be inefficient due to a large number of nested loops. In F#, there's an optimization for tail-recursive calls using yield!, similar to the usual function calls. This means that when a sequence expression ends with the yield! call and there's no subsequent code (like in the previous example), the call won't add any inefficiency even if we use several nested yield! calls.

This example shows that we can use standard functional patterns in sequence expressions. We used the if construct inside the sequence expression and recursion to loop in a functional style. F# allows us to use mutable state (using reference cells) and imperative loops such as while inside sequence expressions as well, but we don't need them very often. On the other hand, for loops are used quite frequently, as we'll see when we discuss sequence processing later in this chapter.

List and array expressions

So far, we've seen sequence expressions enclosed in curly braces and denoted by the seq identifier. This kind of expression generates a lazy sequence of type seq<'a>, which corresponds to the standard .NET IEnumerable<T> type. F# also provides support for creating immutable F# lists and .NET arrays in a simple way. Here's a snippet showing both collection types:

```
> let cities =
    [ yield "Oslo"
      yield! capitals ]
;;
val cities : string list =
  [ "Oslo";
    "London"; "Prague" ]
```

```
> let cities =
    [| yield "Barcelona"
       yield! capitals |]
;;
val cities : string array =
  [| "Barcelona";
     "London"; "Prague" |]
```

As you can see, we can also enclose the body of the sequence expression in square brackets just as we normally do to construct F# lists, and in square brackets followed by the vertical bar symbol (|) to construct arrays. F# treats the body as an ordinary sequence expression and converts the result to a list or an array, respectively.

When we use array or list expressions, the whole expression is evaluated eagerly, because we need to populate all the elements. Any side effects (such as printing to the console) will be executed immediately. Although sequences may be infinite, arrays and lists can't: evaluation would continue until you ran out of memory.

Take another look at listing 12.4, where we generated factorials up to a certain limit. What would happen if we removed that limit (by removing the if condition)? In ordinary F# we'd get an infinite loop, but what happens in a sequence expression?

The answer is we'd create an infinite sequence, which is a valid and useful functional construct.

12.2.2 *Using infinite sequences*

In the previous chapter, we briefly demonstrated how to implement a lazy list using lazy values. This data structure allowed us to create infinite data structures, such as a list of all integers starting from zero. This was possible because each evaluation of an element was delayed: the element's value was only calculated when we accessed it, and each time we only forced the calculation of a single element.

Sequences represented using seq<'a> are similar. The interface has a MoveNext method, which forces the next element to be evaluated. The sequence may be infinite, which means that the MoveNext method will be always able to calculate the next element and never returns false (which indicates the end of sequence). Infinite sequences may sound just like a curiosity, but we'll see that they can be quite valuable and give us a great way to separate different parts of an algorithm and make the code more readable.

In chapter 4, we talked about drawing charts. We used random colors to fill the individual parts, which didn't always give the best result. You can represent colors of the chart as an infinite sequence. In listing 12.5, we'll start by generating sequence of random colors, but we'll look at other options soon.

Listing 12.5   Generating an infinite sequence of random colors in C# and F#

```
// C# version using loops
IEnumerable<Color> RandomColors(){
  var rnd = new Random();
  while(true) {                                                       ❶
    int r = rnd.Next(256), g = rnd.Next(256), b = rnd.Next(256);
    yield return Color.FromArgb(r, g, b);                            ❷
  }
}

// F# version using recursion
let rnd = new Random()
let rec randomColors = seq {                                         ❸
  let r, g, b = rnd.Next(256), rnd.Next(256), rnd.Next(256)
  yield Color.FromArgb(r, g, b)                                      ❹
  yield! randomColors }          ❺
```

Both implementations contain an infinite loop that generates colors. In C#, the loop is achieved using while(true) ❶. The functional way to create infinite loops is to use recursion ❺. In the body of the infinite loop, we yield a single randomly generated color value. In F# we use the yield construct ❹ and in C# we use yield return ❷.

If you compile the F# version of the code, you'll get a warning on the line with the recursive call ❺. The warning says that the recursive reference will be checked at runtime. We saw this warning in chapter 8. It notifies us that we're referencing a value inside its own definition. In this case, the code is correct, because the recursive call will be performed later, after the sequence is fully initialized.

Listing 12.5 also uses a different indentation style when enclosing F# code in a `seq` block ❸. Instead of starting on a new line and indenting the whole body, we added the `seq` identifier and the opening curly brace to the end of the line. We'll use this option in some listings in the book, to make the code more compact. In practice, both of these options are valid and you can choose whichever you find more readable.

Now that we have an infinite sequence of colors, let's use it. Listing 12.6 demonstrates how infinite sequences allow a better separation of concerns. Only the F# code is shown here, but the C# implementation (which is very similar) is available at the book's website.

Listing 12.6 Drawing a chart using sequence of colors (F#)

```
open System.Drawing
open System.Windows.Forms

let dataSource = [ 490; 485; 450; 425; 365; 340; 290; 230; 130; 90; 70; ]
let coloredSequence = Seq.zip dataSource randomColors            ❶
let coloredData = coloredSequence |> List.ofSeq       ❷

let frm = new Form(ClientSize = Size(500, 350))
frm.Paint.Add(fun e ->
  e.Graphics.FillRectangle(Brushes.White, 0, 0, 500, 350)
  coloredData |> Seq.iteri(fun i (num, clr) ->        ❸      Calculates
    use br = new SolidBrush(clr)                                    location of bar
    e.Graphics.FillRectangle(br, 0, i * 32, num, 28) )   ◁──      using index
  )
frm.Show()
```

To provide a short but complete example, we've just defined some numeric data by hand. We use the `Seq.zip` function to combine it with the randomly generated colors ❶. This function takes two sequences and returns a single sequence of tuples: the first element of each tuple is from the first sequence, and the second element comes from the second sequence. In our case, this means that each tuple contains a number from the data source and a randomly generated color. The length of the returned sequence is the length of the shorter sequence from the two given sequences, so it will generate a random color for each of the numeric value and then stop. This means that we'll need only limited number of colors. We could generate, say, one hundred colors, but what if someone gave us 101 numbers? Infinite sequences give us an elegant way to solve the problem without worrying about the length.

Before using the sequence, we convert it to a list ❷. We do this is because the sequence of random colors isn't pure and returns different colors each time we reevaluate it. This means that if we didn't convert it to a list before using it, we'd get different colors during each redraw of the form. Once we have the list of data with colors, we need to iterate over its elements and draw the bars. We're using `Seq.iteri` ❸, which calls the specified function for every element, passing it the index of the element in the sequence and the element itself. We immediately decompose the element using a tuple pattern into the numeric value (the width of the bar) and the generated color.

What makes this example interesting is that we can easily use an alternative way to generate colors. If we implemented it naïvely, the color would be computed in the drawing function ❸. This would make it relatively hard to change which colors are used. However, the solution in listing 12.6 completely separates the color-generation code from the drawing code, so we can change the way chart is drawn just by providing a different sequence of colors. Listing 12.7 shows an alternative coloring scheme.

Listing 12.7   Generating a sequence with color gradients (C# and F#)

```
// C# version using loops
IEnumerable<Color> GreenBlackColors() {
  while(true) {                              ❶
    for(int g = 0; g < 255; g += 25)
      yield return Color.FromArgb(g / 2, g, g / 3);
  }
}

// F# version using loop and recursion
let rec greenBlackColors = seq {
  for g in 0 .. 25 .. 255 do                 ❷
    yield Color.FromArgb(g / 2, g, g / 3)
  yield! greenBlackColors }                  ❸
```

The code in listing 12.7 again contains an infinite loop, implemented either using a while loop ❶ or recursion ❸. In the body of the loop, we generate a color gradient containing 10 different colors. We're using a for loop to generate the green component of the color and calculating the blue and red components from that. This example also shows the F# syntax for generating a sequence of numbers with a specified step ❷. The value of g will start off as 0 and increment by 25 for each iteration until the value is larger than 250. Figure 12.1 shows the end result.

As you can see, infinite sequences can be useful in real-world programming, because they give us a way to easily factor out part of the code that we may want to change later. Infinite sequences are also curious from the theoretical point of view. In Haskell, they're often used to express numerical calculations.

So far we've mostly examined *creating* sequences. Now we're going to have a look at some techniques for *processing* them.

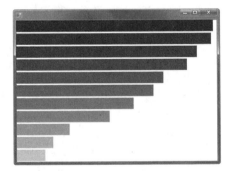

Figure 12.1   A chart painted using color gradient generated as a sequence of colors

Infinite lists in Haskell and sequence caching in F#

As we mentioned in chapter 11, Haskell uses lazy evaluation everywhere. We've seen that Lazy<'a> type in F# can simulate lazy evaluation for values when we need it, and sequences enable us to emulate some other Haskell constructs in the same way.

(continued)

Let's look at one slightly obscure example, just to get a feeling for what you can do. In Haskell, we can write the following code:

```
let nums = 1 : [ n + 1 | n <- nums ]
```

Once we translate it into F#, you'll understand what's going on. The standard functional lists in Haskell are lazy (because everything is) and the `:` operator corresponds to the F# `::` operator. The expression in square brackets returns all the numbers from the list incremented by 1. In F#, we could write the same thing using sequence expressions:

```
let rec nums =
  seq { yield 1
        for n in nums do yield n + 1 };;
```

The code constructs a sequence that starts with 1 and recursively takes all numbers from the sequence and increments them by 1. This means that the returned sequence will contain numbers 1, 2, 3, and so on. The F# version is horribly inefficient, because in each recursive call, it starts constructing a new sequence from the first element. To evaluate the sequence of length 3, we create one instance of `nums` of length 3, one of length 2, and one of length 1.

The idiomatic version of the code in F# would look differently. Just like when generating factorials in listing 12.4, we could implement a utility function that generates sequence from the given number. Then we'd recursively call it using the optimized `yield!` primitive. In Haskell, the situation is different because evaluated values are cached. This means that it doesn't have to recalculate the sequence from the beginning. We can get similar behavior in F# using a function `Seq.cache`:

```
let rec nums =
  seq { yield 1
        for n in nums do yield n + 1 } |> Seq.cache;;
```

The `Seq.cache` function returns a sequence that caches values that have already been calculated, so this version of the code performs a lot more sensibly. Accessing the 1000th element is about 100 times faster with the caching version than with the original. Combining caching and sequence expressions gives us some of the same expressive power as the more mathematically oriented Haskell. However, it's usually a better idea to look for an idiomatical F# solution, in this case using `yield!`.

12.3 Processing sequences

When processing sequences, we have a wide variety of options ranging from low-level techniques where we can control all the details, but that make it difficult to express more complicated but common processing patterns, to higher-level techniques that can't express everything we may want, but the rest can be expressed very elegantly.

In C#, the lowest level (aside from implementing the IEnumerable<T> interface directly) is to use iterator blocks and read the input sequence using either foreach or the enumerator object. At the higher level, we can use predefined (or our own) higher-order methods such as Where and Select, and if the processing involves only certain operations, we can use the C# 3.0 query syntax.

The most common approach for processing sequences in F# is similar to those for other collection types. We've seen that lists can be processed with functions like List.filter and List.map, and that similar functions are available for arrays in the Array module. It should come as no surprise that the same set of functions exists for sequences as well, in the Seq module. The F# language doesn't explicitly support any query syntax, but we'll see that sequence expressions to some point unify the ideas behind lower-level iterators and higher-level queries.

12.3.1 Transforming sequences with iterators

So far, we've only used iterators to generate a sequence from a single piece of data (if any). However, one common use of iterators is to transform one sequence into another in some fashion. As a simple example, here's a method that takes a sequence of numbers and returns a sequence of squares:

```
IEnumerable<int> Squares(IEnumerable<int> numbers) {
  foreach(int i in numbers)
    yield return i * i;
}
```

We're using the familiar foreach construct, but keep in mind that foreach, which contains the yield return statement, has a different meaning. It doesn't run the loop eagerly and instead evaluates it on demand. The foreach statement allows us to write code that generates some elements for every iteration of the loop, which corresponds to pulling a single element from the input sequence and pushing zero or more elements to the output sequence (in the previous case, we always generate exactly one element). We'd use the very same approach if we wanted to implement generic Where and Select methods from LINQ to Objects.

As a more complicated example, let's implement a Zip method with the same behavior as the Seq.zip function in F#. We'll give it two sequences and it will return a single sequence containing elements from the given sequences joined in tuples. This method is available in the .NET 4.0 libraries, but we'll look at it, because it shows an interesting problem. We can't use foreach to simultaneously take elements from two source sequences. As you can see in listing 12.8, the only option we have is to use the IEnumerable<T> and IEnumerator<T> interfaces directly.

Listing 12.8 Implementing the Zip method (C#)

```
public static IEnumerable<Tuple<T1, T2>> Zip<T1, T2>
    (IEnumerable<T1> first, IEnumerable<T2> second) {
  using(var firstEn = first.GetEnumerator())          ❶
  using(var secondEn = second.GetEnumerator()) {
```

```
    while (firstEn.MoveNext() && secondEn.MoveNext()) {          ❷
      yield return Tuple.Create(firstEn.Current, secondEn.Current);   ❸
    }
  }
}
```

Looking at the signature of the method, we can see that it takes two sequences as arguments. The method is generic, with each input sequence having a separate type parameter. We're using a generic C# tuple, so the returned sequence contains elements of type Tuple<T1, T2>. In the implementation, we first ask each sequence for an enumerator we can use to traverse the elements ❶. We repeatedly call the Move-Next method on each enumerator to get the next element from both of the sequences ❷. If neither sequence has ended, we yield a tuple containing the current element of each enumerator ❸.

This example shows that sometimes, processing methods need to use the IEnumerator<T> interface explicitly. The foreach loop gives us a way to pull elements from a single source one by one, but once we need to pull elements from multiple sources in an interleaving order, we're in trouble. If we wanted to implement Seq.zip in F#, we'd have to use the same technique. We could use either a while loop inside a sequence expression or a recursive sequence expression. Most of the processing functions we'll need are already available in the .NET and F# libraries so we'll use these where we can, either explicitly or by using C#'s query expression syntax.

12.3.2 *Filtering and projection*

The two most frequently used sequence processing operators are filtering and projection. We used both of them in chapter 6 with functional lists in F# and the generic .NET List<T> type in C#. The Where and Select extension methods from LINQ libraries already work with sequences, and in F# we can use two functions from the Seq module (namely Seq.map and Seq.filter) to achieve the same results.

USING HIGHER-ORDER FUNCTIONS

Working with the Seq module in F# is the same as with List, and we've already seen how to use LINQ extension methods in C#. There's one notable difference between working with lists and sequences: sequences are lazy. The processing code isn't executed until we take elements from the returned sequence, and even then it only does as much work as it needs to in order to return results as they're used. Let's demonstrate this using a simple code snippet:

```
var nums1 =                          let nums1 =
  nums.Where(n => n%3 == 0)            nums |> Seq.filter (fun n -> n%3=0)
     .Select(n => n * n)                   |> Seq.map (fun n -> n * n)
```

When we run this code, it won't process any elements; it only creates an object that represents the sequence and that can be used for accessing the elements. This also means that the nums value can be an infinite sequence of numbers. If we only access the first 10 elements from the sequence, the code will work correctly, because both filtering and projection process data lazily.

You're probably already familiar with using higher-order processing functions after our extensive discussion in chapter 6, and we've provided many examples throughout the book. In this chapter, we'll instead look at other ways to express alternative workflows.

USING QUERIES AND SEQUENCE EXPRESSIONS

In C# 3.0, we can write operations with data that involve projection and filtering using the new query expression syntax. Query expressions support many other operators, but we'll stick to only projection and filtering in order to demonstrate functional techniques and F# features.

Although F# doesn't have specific query expression support, we can easily write queries that project and filter data using sequence expressions. This is due to the way that sequence expressions can be used anywhere in F#, rather than just as the implementation of a function returning a sequence. Listing 12.9 shows how we can implement our earlier example using a query in C# and a sequence expression in F#.

Listing 12.9   Filtering and projecting sequences in C# and F#

C#	F#
```var nums1 = from n in nums where n%3 == 0 select n * n;```	```let nums1 = seq { for n in nums do if (n%3 = 0) then yield n * n }```

In C#, query expressions and iterators are quite different, but sequence expressions in F# show how they're conceptually related. Each part of the query expression has an equivalent construct in F#, but it's always more general: the `from` clause is replaced by a simple `for` loop, the `where` clause is replaced by an `if` condition, and the `select` clause corresponds to the `yield` statement with the projection expressed as a normal calculation.

C# query expression syntax supports several other operators that aren't easily expressible using F# sequence expressions. This means that the C# version is more powerful, but the F# implementation is more uniform.

Note how both C# query expressions and F# sequence expressions work internally. A C# query expression is translated in a well-defined way into a sequence of calls such as `Where`, `Select`, `SelectMany`, `Join`, and `GroupBy` using lambda expressions. These are typically extension methods but they don't have to be—the compiler doesn't care what the query expression *means*, only that the translated code is valid. This "data source agnosticism" is essential for data processing technologies such as LINQ to Objects and LINQ to SQL, but we'll use it shortly to show how the query syntax can be used for working with other kinds of values.

On the other hand, sequence expressions can be used to express more complicated and general-purpose constructs. We could duplicate the `yield` construct to return two elements for a single item from the data source. This would be easy enough to achieve in C# using iterators, but it's not possible to express the transformation "inline" using the query syntax.

Additional query operators in LINQ

Query expression syntax in C# 3.0 is tailored for retrieving and formatting data from various data sources, so it includes operations beyond projection and filtering. These operators are mostly present for this single purpose, and there's no special syntax for them in F#. All these standard operators are available as regular higher-order functions operating on sequences. For instance, take ordering data:

```
var q =                          let q =
   from c in customers              customers
   orderby c.Name                   |> Seq.sortBy (fun c -> c.City)
   select c;
```

The function that we give as the first argument to the `Seq.sortBy` operator specifies which property of the processed element should be used when comparing two elements. In the C# query syntax, this corresponds to the expression following the `orderby` clause. The C# compiler transforms this expression into a call to a standard `OrderBy` method using a lambda function. Another operation that is available only as a higher-order function in F# is grouping:

```
var q =                          let q =
   from c in customers              customers
   group c by c.City;               |> Seq.groupBy (fun c -> c.City)
```

To group a sequence we need to specify a function that returns the key that identifies the group in which the element belongs. Again, C# has special syntax for this, but in the F# snippet we're using a standard lambda function.

In these examples, both versions of the code look reasonable. However, when we need to write F# code that mixes projection and filtering together with some operations that can only be written using higher-order functions, the equivalent C# query expression will be easier to understand.

The implementation of sequence expressions in the F# compiler is optimized, but without these optimizations, it would work similarly to the C# query expressions. An arbitrary sequence expression could be translated into a sequence of standard function calls. Similar to C#, we can provide our own implementation of these functions, so it's wise to look deeper and understand how the translation works in F#. The F# language uses a smaller number of operations and heavily relies on a single operation called flattening projection.

12.3.3 Flattening projections

A *flattening projection* allows us to generate a sequence of elements for each element from the source collection and merges all the returned sequences. As we'll soon see, it's an essential operation that can be used to define other processing operations including projection and filtering. The unique thing about flattening projection is that it lets us generate multiple output elements for each input element.

NOTE   In LINQ libraries, this operation is called `SelectMany`. In query expressions it's represented by having more than one `from` clause. The name reflects the fact that it's similar to the `Select` operation with the exception that we can return many elements for each item in the source. The F# library's equivalent function is `Seq.collect`. Here, the name suggests the implementation—it's like calling the `Seq.map` function to generate a sequence of sequences and then calling `Seq.concat` to concatenate them.

We'll start off by looking at an example where this is needed, which means that we couldn't write the example just using higher-order functions from the previous section. We'll start by looking at the implementation that uses F# sequence expressions, then we'll gradually change the code to use flattening projection.

FLATTENING PROJECTIONS IN SEQUENCE EXPRESSIONS

Suppose we have a list of tuples, each of which contains a city's name and the country it's in, and we have a list of cities selected by a user. We can represent sample data for this scenario like this:

```
let cities = [ ("New York", "USA"); ("London", "UK");
               ("Cambridge", "UK"); ("Cambridge", "USA") ]
let entered = [ "London"; "Cambridge" ]
```

Now suppose we want to find the countries of the selected cities. We could iterate over the entered cities and find each city in the `cities` list to get the country. You can probably already see the problem with this approach: there is a city named Cambridge in both the United Kingdom and the United States, so we need to be able to return multiple records for a single city. You can see how to write this using two nested `for` loops in a sequence expression in listing 12.10.

Listing 12.10   Joining collections using sequence expressions (F# Interactive)

```
> seq { for name in entered do          ❶
          for (n, c) in cities do        ❷
            if (n = name) then           ❸
              yield sprintf "%s (%s)" n c };;
val it : seq<string> =
  seq [ "London (UK)"; "Cambridge (UK)"; "Cambridge (USA)" ]
```

Both countries returned for Cambridge

The outer `for` loop iterates over the entered names ❶, and the nested loop iterates over the list of known cities ❷. This means that inside the body of the nested loop, we'll get a chance to compare whether the name of each entered city is equal to a name of each of the known cities. The code that's nested in these two loops ❸ uses the `yield` statement to produce a single item if the names are the same. If the names aren't the same, it doesn't yield any elements.

In database terminology, this operation could be explained as a join. We're joining the list of entered names with the list containing information about cities using the name of the city as the key. Writing the code using sequence expressions is quite easy, and it's the preferred way for encoding joins in F#.

We mentioned that any sequence expression can be encoded using the flattening projection operation, so let's see how we can rewrite the previous example using `Seq.collect` explicitly. You wouldn't do this in practice, but it will be invaluable when we explore defining our own alternative workflows similar to sequence expressions.

USING FLATTENING PROJECTIONS DIRECTLY

First, let's see what the flattening projection looks like. As usual, the initial step in understanding how the function works is to examine its type signature. Figure 12.2 compares the signatures of `Seq.map` (ordinary projection) and `Seq.collect` (flattening projection).

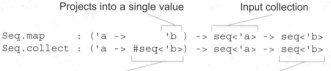

Figure 12.2 Projection returns a single element for each input element while flattening projection can return any collection of elements.

As a reminder, the # symbol in the part of the type signature describing the projection function passed to `collect` means that the return type of the function doesn't have to be exactly the `seq<'b>` type. We talked about types declared using the # symbol in the previous chapter—the actual type used in place of the `#seq<'b>` can be any type implementing the `seq<'b>` interface. This means that we can return a sequence, also an F# list, an array, or even our own collection type.

Now, let's see how we can rewrite the previous example using the `Seq.collect` function. The general rule is that we can replace each use of the `for` loop inside a sequence expression with a single call to `Seq.collect`. This is exactly how the F# compiler compiled sequence expressions in early versions. Since our example has two nested loops, we'll do the transformation in two steps. In listing 12.11, we start by replacing the outer loop.

Listing 12.11 Replacing the outer loop with flattening projection (F# Interactive)

```
> entered |> Seq.collect (fun name ->          ❶
    seq { for (n, c) in cities do              ❷
          if (n = name) then
            yield sprintf "%s (%s)" n c });;
val it : seq<string> =
  seq [ "London (UK)"; "Cambridge (UK)"; "Cambridge (USA)" ]
```

We replaced the outer loop with a flattening projection, so listing 12.11 calls `Seq.collect` and gives it a list of cities entered by the user as input ❶. The lambda function we provide takes the name of a single city and iterates over the collection of all known cities to find the country or countries containing that city ❷. The searching is implemented using a sequence expression from listing 12.10 with the outer loop deleted. The lambda function we use returns a sequence with information about cities with the specified name, and the `Seq.collect` function concatenates all of these to return a single sequence with results.

Now we have a combination of function call and a sequence expression, so let's see how we can replace the inner `for` loop to complete the translation. We could implement the nested part with `Seq.filter` and `Seq.map`, or, even better, with `Seq.choose`, which lets us combine the two operations into one. We're showing what the compiler would do and it would naïvely follow the rule to replace every `for` loop with a flattening projection. Listing 12.12 shows the same processing code again, but using only `Seq.collect` calls.

Listing 12.12   Replacing both loops with flattening projection (F# Interactive)

```
> entered |> Seq.collect (fun name ->
    cities |> Seq.collect (fun (n, c) ->        ❶
      if (n = name) then
        [ sprintf "%s (%s)" n c ]               ❷
      else [] ));;
val it : seq<string> =
  seq [ "London (UK)"; "Cambridge (UK)"; "Cambridge (USA)" ]
```

The outer call is the same as in listing 12.11, but inside the lambda function we now perform another call to `Seq.collect` ❶. The nested call iterates over all the cities and for each city returns either an empty list if the name of the city doesn't match the entered name or a list containing a single element when the name matches. As you can see, we've replaced the use of `yield` with code that returns a list containing a single element. If the code contained multiple yields, we'd return a longer list. It's also worth noting that we had to add an `else` clause that returns an empty list; inside sequence expressions this is implicit.

Even though the `Seq.collect` function is sometimes useful when writing sequence-processing code using higher-order functions, its real importance is that it can be used to translate arbitrary sequence expression into function calls. As we'll see shortly, sequence expressions are one specific example of a more general F# construct and the flattening projection is the primitive operation that defines how sequence expressions work. We'll also see that the translation we demonstrated in this section works in a similar way for other computations that we can define for our own values.

We mentioned earlier that we could use projection and filtering to implement the nested loop ❷, but as you can see, `for` loops in sequence expressions are expressive enough to implement the projection, filtering, and joins we've seen in this section. Now, let's examine the same operation in C#.

USING FLATTENING PROJECTIONS IN C#

The LINQ operator analogous to the `collect` function is called `SelectMany`. Differences exist between the two versions, because LINQ has different requirements. While F# sequence expressions can be expressed using just the `collect` function, LINQ queries use many other operators, so they need different ways for sequencing operations.

Let's again start by looking at the usual syntax and then examine how it's translated to the explicit syntax using extension methods. We'll use the same data as in the previous F# example. The list of cities with the information about the country contains instances of a class `CityInfo` with two properties, and the list of entered names contains only strings. Listing 12.13 shows a LINQ query that we can write to find countries of the entered cities.

Listing 12.13 Searching for country of entered cities using a query (C#)

```
var q =
  from e in entered          ❶
  from known in cities        ❷
  where known.City == e
  select string.Format("{0} ({1})", known.City, known.Country);   ❸
```

The query expresses exactly the same idea as we did in the previous implementations. It iterates over both of the data sources (❶ and ❷), which gives us a cross join of the two collections and then yields only records where the name entered by the user corresponds to the city name in the "known city" list; finally it formats the output ❸.

In C# query expression syntax, we can also use the `join` clause, which directly specifies keys from both of the data sources (in our case, this would be the value e and the `known.City` value). This is slightly different: `join` clauses can be more efficient, but multiple `from` clauses are more flexible. In particular, the second sequence we generate can depend on which item of the first sequence we're currently looking at.

As we said earlier, query expressions are translated into normal member invocations. Any `from` clause in a query expression after the first one is translated into a call to `SelectMany`. Listing 12.14 shows the translation as it's performed by the C# compiler.

Listing 12.14 Query translated to explicit operator calls (C#)

```
var q = entered
  .SelectMany(
    e => cities,                        ❶
    (e, known) => new { e, known })      ❷
  .Where(tmp => tmp.known.City == tmp.e)
  .Select(tmp => String.Format("{0} ({1})",     Filters, formats
    tmp.known.City, tmp.known.Country));        output
```

Unlike in F#, where the `if` condition was nested inside the two `for` loops (flattening projections), the operations in C# are composed in a sequence without nesting. The processing starts with the `SelectMany` operator that implements the join; the filtering and projection are performed using `Where` and `Select` at the end of the sequence.

The first lambda function ❶ specifies a collection that we generate for every single item from the source list. This parameter corresponds to the function provided as an argument to the F# `collect` function. In the query, we return all the known cities, so the operation performs only joining, without any filtering or further processing. The second parameter ❷ specifies how to build a result based on an element from the original sequence and an element from the newly generated sequence returned by the function. In our example, we build an anonymous type that contains both items so we can use them in later query operators.

In F#, all the processing is done inside the filtering projection, so we return only the final result. In C# most of the processing is done later, so we need to return both elements combined into one value (using an anonymous type), so that they can be accessed later. In general, the first `from` clause specifies the primary source of the query, and if we add more `from` clauses, they're joined with the original source using the `SelectMany` operator. Any further operators such as `where` and `select` are appended to the end and work with the joined data source. This is different from the F# translation, because in F# both filtering and projection are nested in the innermost call to `Seq.collect`.

Understanding how the translation works isn't that important, but we'll need to know a little bit about the translation in the next section. We'll see that F# sequence expressions represent a more general idea that can be also partly expressed using LINQ queries. The flattening projection we've just been looking at plays a key role.

12.4 *Introducing alternative workflows*

Computation expressions is an F# feature that has been partly inspired by Haskell *monads*. Monads have an unfortunate reputation for being brain-bustingly difficult—but don't worry. We'll look at implementing an interesting set of techniques that let us work with `Option<T>` values nicely in C#. We'll see how to do a similar thing in F# and also how to write simple logger with a nice syntax in F#.

We could do all of this without even mentioning the word monad. Since the book is about functional programming in a more general sense, we want to give you more than an overview of all F# features. We'll occasionally explain some of the underlying terminology, which can be helpful if you want to look at other programming languages. You can always skip the part that sounds complicated and move on to the next example. You may be surprised to know we've already explained monads in this chapter. In fact, you've probably used them before even picking up this book: LINQ is based on monads too.

In section 6.7 we looked at the `bind` function for option values, and you learned that a similar operator makes sense for lists as well. Its name in the standard F# libraries is `List.collect`, so you won't be surprised to hear that `Seq.collect` is also a form of *bind* operator, but this time working with sequences. In this chapter, we've seen that this operation is important in LINQ queries and F# sequence expressions. Again, here are the type signatures of the three operations:

```
Option.bind  : ('a -> option<'b>) -> option<'a> -> option<'b>
List.collect : ('a -> list<'b>)    -> list<'a>   -> list<'b>
Seq.collect  : ('a -> #seq<'b>)    -> seq<'a>    -> seq<'b>
```

The function provided as the argument specifies what to do with each value (of type `'a`) contained in the value given as the second argument. For lists and sequences, that means the function will be called for each element of the input sequence. For option values, the function will be executed at most once, only when the second argument is `Some` value. Just a reminder: the option value can be viewed as a list of either zero or one elements.

You may already know that you can create your own implementation of LINQ query operators and use them to work with your own collection types. Nothing limits us to using the query syntax only for working with collections.

12.4.1 *Customizing query expressions*

In principle, we can use queries to work with any type that supports the *bind* operation. This is the standard name used in functional programming for functions with type signatures of the form shown in the previous section. Technically speaking, we need to implement methods that are used by the C# compiler when translating the query expression into standard calls. We'll implement these for the `Option<T>` type in section 12.6. The type doesn't implement `IEnumerable<T>`, so the standard query operators can't be used.

Let's first consider what the meaning of a query applied to option types would be. Listing 12.15 shows two queries. The one on the left one works with lists and the one on the right works with option types. We're using two simple functions to provide input: the `ReadIntList` function reads a list of integers (of type `List<int>`) and `TryReadInt` returns an option value (of type `Option<int>`).

Listing 12.15   Using queries with lists and option values (C#)

```
var list =                          var option =
    from n in ReadIntList()             from n in TryReadInt()
    from m in ReadIntList()             from m in TryReadInt()
    select n * m;                       select n * m;
```

The queries are the same with the exception that they work with different types of data, so they use different query operator implementations. Both read two different inputs and return multiples of the entered integers. Table 12.1 gives examples of inputs to show what the results would be.

Table 12.1   Results produced by queries working with lists and option values for different possible inputs

Type of values	Input #1	Input #2	Output
Lists	[2; 3]	[10; 100]	[20; 200; 30; 300]
Options	Some(2)	Some(10)	Some(20)
Options	Some(3)	None	None
Options	None	Not required	None

For lists, the query performs a cross join operation (you can imagine two nested `for` loops as in the F# sequence expression). It produces a single sequence consisting of a single entry for each combination of input values. For option values there are three possibilities.

- When the first input is a value, we need to read the second one. Then, the following two cases can occur depending on the second input:
  - If the second input is also a value, the result is again `Some` value containing the result of the multiplication.
  - If the second input is `None` we don't have values to multiply, so the query returns `None`.
- When the first input is `None`, we know the result without needing the second input. The whole query is executed lazily, so we don't have to read the second input: the `TryReadInt` function will be called only once.

As you can see, query expressions give us a convenient way of working with option values. Listing 12.15 is definitely easier to write (and read) than the equivalent code we saw in chapter 6, where we used higher-order functions explicitly. We'll see how to implement all the necessary query operators later in this chapter, but let's first look at similar syntax in F#.

12.4.2 *Customizing the F# language*

So far, we've talked about sequence expressions, which were denoted using the `seq` identifier preceding the block of code enclosed in curly braces. However, F# allows us to create our own identifiers that give a special meaning to a block of code. In general, this feature is called *computation expressions* and sequence expressions are a single special case that's implemented in the F# core and optimized by the compiler.

We've seen that computation expressions can contain standard language constructs such as `for` loops, but also additional constructs like `yield`. The identifier that precedes the block gives the meaning to these constructs in the same way query operators (such as `Select` and `Where` extension methods) specify what a LINQ query does. This means that we can create a customized computation expression for working with option values. We could work with option values using the `for` construct, but F# gives us a nicer way to customize the expression. You can see these alternative approaches in listing 12.16. The first version uses syntax similar to sequence expressions; the second is a more natural way of writing the same thing.

Listing 12.16 Computation expressions for working with option values (F#)

```
// Value binding using customized 'for' primitive
option {
  for n in tryReadInt() do
    for m in tryReadInt() do
      yield n * m
}

// Value binding using special 'let!' primitive
option {
  let! n = tryReadInt()
  let! m = tryReadInt()
  return n * m
}
```

The behavior of all custom primitives that occur inside the computation expression (such as `for`, `yield`, and `let!`) is determined by the `option` identifier that defines what kind of computation expression we're writing. Now you can see that a sequence expression is just a special case that's defined by the `seq` identifier. We'll see how to define identifiers in section 12.5, but first let's look at the two examples in listing 12.16.

The first version closely resembles the LINQ query in listing 12.15. Each `for` loop can be executed at most once. When the option value contains a value, it will be bound to the symbol n or m, respectively, and the body of the loop will execute. Developers have an expectation that loops work with collections and not option values, so the constructs `for` and `yield` are usually only used with sequences. When we create a computation expression that works with other types of values, we'll use the later syntax. The second version uses two more computation expression primitives. The first one is `let!`, which represents a customized value binding.

In both versions, the type of values n and m is `int`. The customized value binding unwraps the actual value from the value of type `option<int>`. It may fail to assign the value to the symbol when the value returned from `TryReadInt` is `None`. In that case, the whole computation expression will immediately return `None` without executing the rest of the code. The second nonstandard primitive in the expression is `return`. It specifies how to construct an option value from the value. In listing 12.16, we give it an `int` value and it constructs the result, which has a type `option<int>`.

The concepts we've just seen can be regarded as a functional design pattern. We can use F# computation expressions without understanding all the details of the pattern. If you want to learn how to define your own computation expressions, it's useful to learn about the background concepts and terminology. The sidebar "Computation expressions and monads" discusses the pattern in more detail and explains how it relates to Haskell monads.

Computation expressions and monads

As we mentioned earlier, computation expressions in F# are an implementation of an idea called monads that has proven useful in Haskell. Monad refers to a term from mathematics, but F# uses a different name that better reflects how the idea is used in the F# language.

When defining a computation expression (or monad), we always work with a generic type such as `M<'a>`. This is often called a *monadic type*, and it specifies the meaning of the computation. This type can augment the usual meaning of the code we write. For example, the `option<'a>`, which we've just seen, augments the code with the possibility of returning an undefined value (`None`). Sequences also form a monad. The type `seq<'a>` augments the code with the ability to work with multiple values.

Each computation expression (or monad) is implemented using two functions—`bind` and `return`. `bind` allows us to create and compose computations that work with values of the monadic type. In listing 12.16, the `bind` operation was used whenever we used the `let!` primitive. `return` is used to construct a value of the monadic type.

> **(continued)**
> It's worth noting that sequence expressions are also an instance of a monad. For sequences, the bind operation is `Seq.collect`, even though in sequence expressions we don't use the `let!` syntax and instead use the more comfortable `for` loop syntax. Listing 12.16 shows that these two are closely related. The `return` operation for sequences is creating a sequence with a single element. Inside sequence expressions, this can be written using a more natural `yield` primitive.

In the next section, we'll look at the simplest possible custom computation. We'll implement it in both C# and F# to explain what the monadic type is and how the `bind` and `return` operations look.

12.5 *First steps in custom computations*

The example in this section doesn't have any real-world benefit, but it demonstrates the core concepts. The first task in designing a custom computation is to consider the type that represents the values produced by the computation.

12.5.1 *Declaring the computation type*

The type of the computation (the monadic type in Haskell terminology) in this example will be called `ValueWrapper<T>`, and it will simply store the value of the generic type parameter `T`. It won't augment the type with any additional functionality. This means that the computation will work with standard values, but we'll be able to write the code using query expressions in C# and computation expressions in F#.

Listing 12.17 shows the type declaration in both C# and F#. In C#, we'll create a simple class, and in F# we'll use a simple discriminated union with only a single case.

> **Listing 12.17   Value of the computation in C# and F#**

```
// C# class declaration
class ValueWrapper<T> {
  public ValueWrapper(T value) {
    this.Value = value;
  }
  public T Value { get; private set; }      ❶
}

// F# discriminated union type
type ValueWrapper<'a> =
  | Value of 'a                             ❷
```

The C# class is a simple immutable type that stores the value of type `T` ❶. The use of a discriminated union with a single case ❷ in F# is also interesting. It allows us to create a named type that is easy to use. As we'll see shortly, we can access the value using pattern matching (using the `Value` discriminator). Pattern matching with this type can never fail because there's only a single case. This lets us use it directly inside value bindings, which will prove useful when we implement the computation algorithm. First let's examine the kinds of computation we'll be able to write with this new type.

12.5.2 Writing the computations

C# query expressions and F# computation expressions allow us to use functions that behave in a nonstandard way (by returning some monadic value) as if they returned an ordinary value. The computation type we're using in this section is `ValueWrapper<T>`, so primitive functions will return values of type `ValueWrapper<T>` instead of only T.

These functions can be implemented either using another query or computation expression, or directly by creating the value of the computation type. Some computation expressions can encapsulate complicated logic, so it may be difficult to create the value directly. In that case, we'd typically write a small number of primitives that return the computation type and use these primitives to implement everything else. However, constructing a value of type `ValueWrapper<T>` is not difficult. The following code shows how to implement a method in C# that reads a number from the console and wraps it inside this computation type:

```
ValueWrapper<int> ReadInt() {
    int num = Int32.Parse(Console.ReadLine());
    return new ValueWrapper<int>(num);
}
```

The method reads a number from the console and wraps it inside the `ValueWrapper<T>` type. The F# version is equally simple, so we won't discuss it here. The important point is that these primitive functions are the only place where we need to know anything about the underlying structure of the type. For the rest of the computation, we'll need to know only that the type supports all the primitives (most importantly `bind` and `return`) needed to write a query or computation expression.

Once we define the value identifier that denotes a computation expression in F# (section 12.5.3) and implement the necessary extension methods in C# (section 12.5.4), we'll be able to work with values of the type easily. Note that the type we're working with doesn't implement the `IEnumerable<T>` interface. The query syntax and computation expression notation works independently from sequences. We'll define the meaning of the code by implementing a couple of methods for working with the `ValueWrapper<T>` type. Listing 12.18 shows a snippet that reads two integers using the primitive and performs a calculation with them.

Listing 12.18 Calculating with computation values in C# and F#

C#	F#
```var v =```	```value {```
``` from n in ReadInt()``` ①	``` let! n = readInt()``` ②
``` from m in ReadInt()```	``` let! m = readInt()```
``` let add = n + m```	``` let add = n + m```
``` let sub = n - m```	``` let sub = n - m```
``` select add * sub;``` ③	``` return add * sub }``` ④

In C# we're using the from clause to unwrap the value ❶. In F#, the same thing is achieved using the customized value binding ❷.

Once the calculation is done, we again wrap the value inside the computation type. In C#, we're using a select clause ❸, and in F# we're using the return primitive ❹.

As you can see, the structure of the code in C# and F# is quite similar. The code doesn't have any real-world use, but it will help us understand how nonstandard computations work. The only interesting thing is that it allows us to write the code in C# as a single expression using the let clause, which creates a local variable. This clause behaves very much like the F# let binding, so the whole code is a single expression.

In the following discussion, we'll focus more on the F# version, because it will make it simpler to explain how things work. The query expression syntax in C# is tailored to writing queries, so it's harder to use for other types of computations. We'll get back to C# once we've implemented the F# computation expression.

You can see that listing 12.18 is using only two primitives. The bind primitive is used when we call the computation primitives ❷, and the return primitive is used to wrap the result in the ValueWrapper<int> type. The next question you probably have is how the F# compiler uses these two primitives to interpret the computation expression and how can we implement them.

12.5.3 *Implementing a computation builder in F#*

The identifier that precedes the computation expression block is an instance of a class that implements the required operations as instance members. Numerous operations are available: we don't have to support them all. The most basic operations are implemented using the Bind and Return members. When the F# compiler sees a computation expression such as the one in listing 12.18, it translates it to F# code that uses these members. The F# example is translated to the following:

```
value.Bind(ReadInt(), fun n ->
  value.Bind(ReadInt(), fun m ->
    let add = n + m
    let sub = n - m
    value.Return(n * m) ))
```

Whenever we use the let! primitive in the computation, it's translated to a call to the Bind member. This is because the readInt function returns a value of type Value-Wrapper<int>, but when we assign it to a symbol, n, using the customized value binding, the type of the value will be int. The purpose of the Bind member is to unwrap the value from the computation type and call the function that represents the rest of the computation with this value as an argument.

You can compare the behavior of the let! primitive with the standard value binding written using let. If we wrote let n = readInt() in listing 12.18, the type of n would be ValueWrapper<int> and we'd have to unwrap it ourselves to get the integer. In this case, we could use the Value property, but there are computations where the value is hidden and the only way to access it is via the Bind member.

The fact that the rest of the computation is transformed into a function gives the computation a lot of flexibility. The `Bind` member could call the function immediately, or it could return a result without calling the function. For example, when we're working with option values and the first argument to the `Bind` member is the `None` value, we know what the overall result will be (`None`) regardless of the function. In this case, the `bind` operation can't call the given function, because the option value doesn't carry an actual value to use as an argument. In other cases, the `bind` operation could effectively remember the function (by storing it as part of the result) and execute it later. We'll look at an example of this in the next chapter.

Our example also shows that multiple `let!` constructs are translated into nested calls to the `Bind` member. This is because the function given as the last argument to this member is a continuation, meaning that it represents the rest of the computation. The example ends with a call to the `Return` member, which is created when we use the `return` construct.

Understanding the type signatures of bind and return

The types of the two operations that we need to implement for various computation expressions will always have the same structure. The only thing that will vary in the following signature is the generic type `M`:

```
Bind   : M<'T> * ('T -> M<'R>) -> M<'R>
Return : 'T -> M<'T>
```

In our previous example, the type `M<'T>` is the `ValueWrapper<'T>` type. In general, the `bind` operation needs to know how to get the value from the computation type in order to call the specified function. When the computation type carries additional information, the `bind` operation also needs to combine the additional information carried by the first argument (of type `M<'T>`) with the information extracted from the result of the function call (of type `M<'R>`) and return them as part of the overall result. The `return` operation is much simpler, because it constructs an instance of the monadic type from the primitive value.

In the previous example, we used an identifier `value` to construct the computation. The identifier is an ordinary F# value and it is an instance of object with specific members. The object is called a *computation builder* in F#. Listing 12.19 shows a simple builder implementation with the two required members. We also need to create an instance called `value` to be used in the translation.

Listing 12.19 Implementing computation builder for values (F#)

```
type ValueWrapperBuilder() =
  member x.Bind(Value(v), f) = f(v)      ❶
  member x.Return(v) = Value(v)          ❷
let value = new ValueWrapperBuilder()        ◁──
```

❸ **Creates instance
of builder**

The `Bind` member ❶ first needs to unwrap the actual value from the `ValueWrapper<'T>` type. This is done in the parameter list of the member, using the `Value` discriminator of the discriminated union as a pattern. The actual value will be assigned to the symbol v. Once we have the value, we can invoke the rest of the computation f. The computation type doesn't carry any additional information, so we can return the result of this call as the result of the whole computation. The `Return` member is trivial, because it wraps the value inside the computation type.

Using the `value` declared in this listing, we can now run the computation expression from listing 12.18. F# also lets us use computation expressions to implement the `readInt` function as well. We need to wrap the result in an instance of `ValueWrapper<int>` type, which can be done using the `return` primitive:

```
> let readInt() = value {
    let n = Int32.Parse(Console.ReadLine())
    return n };;
val readInt : unit -> ValueWrapper<int>
```

This function doesn't need the `bind` operation, because it doesn't use any values of type `ValueWrapper<'T>`. The whole function is enclosed in the computation expression block, which causes the return type of the function to be `ValueWrapper<int>` instead of just `int`. If we didn't know anything about the `ValueWrapper<'T>` type, the only way to use the function would be to call it using the `let!` primitive from another computation expression. The important point is that computation expressions give us a way to build more complicated values from simpler values by composing them. The monadic value is then a bit like a black box that we can compose, but if we want to look inside, we need some special knowledge about the monadic type. In the case of `ValueWrapper<'T>`, we need to know the structure of the discriminated union.

Writing a function like `readInt` in C# using query syntax isn't possible, because queries need to have some input for the initial `from` clause. There is a `let` clause inside the query syntax, which roughly corresponds to a `let` binding in a computation expression, but a query can't start with it. Nevertheless, as we've seen in listing 12.15, there are many useful things that we can write using queries, so let's look at adding query operators for our `ValueWrapper<'T>` type.

12.5.4 *Implementing query operators in C#*

We've seen how the C# queries are translated to method calls in listing 12.14 when we were talking about sequences and when we analyzed the `SelectMany` operation. We'll support only queries that end with the `select` clause and ignore cases that are useful only for collections such as grouping. This means that we'll need to implement the `Select` extension method.

We said earlier that the second and subsequent `from` clauses are translated into a call to the `SelectMany` method. When writing computations using queries, we use the `from` clause in a similar way to the F# `let!` construct to represent a nonstandard value binding, so we'll use it quite often. This means that we'll need to implement the `SelectMany` operation for our `ValueWrapper<'T>` type as well.

You already know that the `SelectMany` method corresponds to the `bind` function, but it's slightly more complicated because it takes an additional function that we'll need to run before returning the result. The `Select` method is simpler, but we'll talk about that after looking at the code. Listing 12.20 shows the implementation of both of the primitives.

Listing 12.20 Implementing query operators (C#)

```
static class ValueWrapperExtensions {
  public static ValueWrapper<R> Select<T, R>
      (this ValueWrapper<T> source,
       Func<T, R> selector) {
    return new ValueWrapper<R>(selector(source.Value));
  }
  public static ValueWrapper<R> SelectMany<T, V, R>
      (this ValueWrapper<T> source,
       Func<T, ValueWrapper<V>> valueSelector,
       Func<T, V, R> resultSelector) {
    var newVal = valueSelector(source.Value);
    var resVal = resultSelector(source.Value, newVal.Value);
    return new ValueWrapper<R>(resVal);
  }
}
```

Projects value using given function ←

1
2
3

Both methods are implemented as extension methods. This means that C# will be able to find them when working with values of type `ValueWrapper<T>` using the standard dot notation, which is used during the translation from the query syntax. The `Select` operator implements projection using the given function, so it only needs to access the wrapped value, run the given function, then wrap the result again.

The `SelectMany` operator is confusing at first, but it's useful to look at the types of the parameters. They tell us what arguments we can pass to what functions. The implementation starts off like the F# `Bind` member by calling the function given by the second argument after unwrapping the first argument ❶. We also need to combine the value from the source with the value returned by the first function. To obtain the result, we call the second function ❷, giving it both of the values. Finally, we wrap the result into the computation type ❸ and return from the method.

After implementing the operators, the query expression in listing 12.18 will compile and run. The computation type that we created in this section doesn't augment the computation with any additional aspects. The very fact that it was so simple makes it a good template for the standard operations. We can implement more sophisticated monadic types by starting with this template and seeing where we need to change it. We'll put this idea into practice now by implementing similar operators for the option type.

12.6 *Implementing computation expressions for options*

We used option values as an example in section 12.4 when we introduced the idea of creating nonstandard computations using LINQ queries and F# computation expressions. The code we wrote worked with option values as if they were standard values, with a customized value binding to read the actual value. Now that we've seen how computation expressions are translated, we know that our `Bind` member will receive a value and a lambda function. With our option type computation expression, we only want to execute the lambda expression if the value is `Some(x)` instead of `None`. In the latter case, we can return `None` immediately.

To run the earlier examples, we'll need to implement LINQ query operators in C# and the `option` computation builder in F#. Again we'll start with the F# version. Listing 12.21 shows an F# object type with two members. We've already implemented the `Option.bind` function in chapter 6, but we'll reimplement it here to remind you what a typical `bind` operation does.

Listing 12.21   Computation builder for option type (F#)

```
type OptionBuilder() =
  member x.Bind(opt, f) =
    match opt with                        ❶
    | Some(value) -> f(value)       ❷
    | _           -> None           ❸
  member x.Return(v) = Some(v)      ◁——— Wraps actual
                                          value
let option = new OptionBuilder()
```

The `Bind` member starts by extracting the value from the option given as the first argument. This is similar to the `Bind` we implemented earlier for the `ValueWrapper<'T>` type. Again we're using pattern matching ❶, but in this case, the value may be missing so we're using the `match` construct. If the value is defined, we call the specified function ❷. This means that we bind a value to the symbol declared using `let!` and run the rest of the computation. If the value is undefined, we return `None` as the result of the whole computation expression ❸.

The `Return` member takes a value as an argument and has to return a value of the computation type. In our example, the type of the computation is `option<'a>`, so we wrap the actual value inside the `Some` discriminator.

To write the corresponding code in C# using the query syntax, we'll need to implement `Select` and `SelectMany` methods for the `Option<T>` type we defined in chapter 5. Listing 12.22 implements the two additional extension methods so that we can use options in query expressions. This time we'll use the extension methods we wrote in chapter 6 to make the code simpler.

Listing 12.22   Query operators for option type (C#)

```
static class OptionExtensions {
  public static Option<R> Select<S, R>
      (this Option<S> source, Func<S, R> selector) {
    return source.Map(selector);                           ❶
  }
  public static Option<R> SelectMany<S, V, R>
      (this Option<S> source,
        Func<S, Option<V>> valueSelector,
        Func<S, V, R> resultSelector) {
    return source.Bind(sourceValue =>                      ❷
```

```
        valueSelector(sourceValue).Map(resultValue =>      ③
          resultSelector(sourceValue, resultValue)));
    }
}
```

The `Select` method should apply the given function to the value carried by the given option value if it contains an actual value. Then it should again wrap the result into an option type. In F# the function is called `Option.map`, and we used an analogous name (`Map`) for the C# method. If we'd looked at LINQ first, we'd probably have called the method `Select` from the beginning, but the simplest solution is to add a new method that calls `Map` ❶.

`SelectMany` is more complicated. It's similar to the `bind` operation, but in addition it needs to use the extra function specified as the third argument to format the result of the operation. We wrote the C# version of the `bind` operation in chapter 6, so we can use the `Bind` extension method in the implementation ❷. To call the formatting function `resultSelector`, we need two arguments: the original value carried by the option and the value produced by the binding function (named `selector`). We can do this by adding a call to `Map` at the end of the processing, but we need to place this call inside the lambda function given to the `Bind` method ❸. This is because we also need to access the original value from the source. Inside the lambda function, the original value is in scope (the variable named `sourceValue`), so we can use it together with the new value, which is assigned to the variable `resultValue`.

This implementation is a bit tricky, but it shows that many things in functional programming can be composed from what we already have. If you tried to implement this on your own, you'd see that the types are invaluable helpers here. You might start just by using the `Bind` method, but then you'd see that the types don't match. You'd see what types are incompatible and if you looked at what functions are available, you'd discover what needs to be added in order to get the correct types. At the risk of repeating ourselves: the types in functional programming are far more important and tell you much more about the correctness of your program.

Using the new extension methods, we can run the examples from section 12.3. In F#, we didn't provide an implementation for the `yield` and `for` primitives, so only the version using `return` and `let!` will work. This is intentional, because the first set of primitives is more suitable for computations that work with sequences of one form or another. We still need to implement the `TryReadInt` method (and the similar F# function). These are really simple, because they need to read a line from the console, attempt to parse it, and return `Some` when the string is a number or `None` otherwise.

> **The identity and maybe monads**
>
> The two examples that we've just seen are well known in the Haskell world. The first one is the *identity monad*, because the monadic type is the same as the actual type of the value, just wrapped inside a named type. The second example is the *maybe monad*, because `Maybe` is the Haskell type name that corresponds to the `option<'a>` type in F#.

> **(continued)**
> The first example was mostly a toy example to demonstrate what we need to do when implementing computations, but the second one can be useful when you're writing code that's composed from a number of operations, each of which can fail. When you analyze the two examples, you can see how important the *monadic type* is. Once you understand the type, you know what makes the computation nonstandard.

So far the examples have been somewhat abstract. Our next section is a lot more concrete; we'll add automatic logging into our code.

12.7 Augmenting computations with logging

Logging can be usually implemented using global mutable state. However, what if we wanted to avoid using global mutable state and keep the program purely functional? One option we'd have is to pass the state of the logger as an additional argument to every function we call. Implementing that would be quite difficult. (And imagine if we decided to add another parameter to the state!)

To solve this problem, we can create a custom computation type that enables logging and hides the state of the logger inside the computation type. This is similar to a technique that Haskell uses to embed working with state (such as filesystems) in a purely functional language without any side effects. The example that we'll implement relies on the fact that we can surround any piece of standard F# code with the computation expression block. As such, it's not feasible to use C# for this example. We'll start off by designing the computation type (monadic type) we need to allow simple logging.

12.7.1 Creating the logging computation

The computation will produce a value and will allow us to write messages to a local logging buffer. This means that the result of the computation will be a value and a list of strings for the messages. Again we'll use a discriminated union with a single discriminator to represent the type:

```
type Logging<'T> =
  | Log of 'T * list<string>
```

This type is quite similar to the `ValueWrapper<'a>` example we discussed earlier, but with the addition of an F# list of the messages written to the log. Now that we have the type, we can implement the computation builder. As usual, we'll need to implement the `Bind` and `Return` members. We'll also implement a new member called `Zero`, which enables us to write computations that don't return any value. We'll see how that's used later.

The implementation of the builder is shown in listing 12.23. The most interesting is the `Bind` member, which needs to concatenate the log messages from the original value and the value generated by the rest of the computation (which is the function given as an argument to the `Bind` member).

Listing 12.23 Computation builder that adds logging support (F#)

```
type LoggingBuilder() =
  member x.Bind(Log(value, logs1), f) =            ❶
    let (Log(newValue, logs2)) = f(value)          ❷
    Log(newValue, logs1 @ logs2)                   ❸
  member x.Return(value) =
    Log(value, [])                                      Augments value
  member x.Zero() =                                      with empty log
    Log((), [])
                                                    Returns no value
let log = new LoggingBuilder()                      with empty log
```

As with our other examples, the most difficult part is implementing the `Bind` member. Our logging type follows all the normal steps, including a third one that was missing for both the `option` and `ValueWrapper` types:

1 We need to unwrap the value. Since we're using a single case discriminated union, we can use pattern matching in the argument list of the member ❶.

2 We need to call the rest of the computation if we have a value to do that. In listing 12.23, we always have the value, so we can run the given function ❷. We don't immediately return the result; instead we decompose it to get the new value and the log messages produced during the execution.

3 We've collected two buffers of log messages, so we need to wrap the new value and augment it with the new logger state. To create that new state, we concatenate the original message list with the new list that was generated when we called the rest of the computation ❸. This is written using a list concatenation operator (@).

The `Return` and `Zero` members are simple. `Return` needs to wrap the actual value into the `Logging<'T>` type, and the `Zero` represents a computation that doesn't carry any value (meaning that it returns a unit). In both cases, we're creating a new computation value, so the primitives return an empty logging buffer. All the log messages will be produced in other ways and appended in the `Bind` member. If you look at the code we have so far, there's no way we could create a nonempty log! This means that we'll need to create one additional primitive to create a computation value containing a log message. We can write it as a simple function:

```
> let logMessage(s) =
    Log((), [s])
val logMessage : string -> Logging<unit>
```

The function creates a computation value that contains a `unit` as the value. More importantly, it also contains a message in the logging buffer, so if we combine it with another computation using `Bind`, we get a computation that writes something to the log. Now we can finally write code that uses the newly created logging computation.

12.7.2 *Creating the logging computation*

Listing 12.24 begins by implementing two helper functions for reading from and writing to the console. Both will also write a message to the log, so they'll be enclosed in the `log` computation block. We then use these two functions in a third function, to show how we can compose nonstandard computations. In our previous examples, we used the let! primitive, but listing 12.24 introduces do! as well.

Listing 12.24   Logging using computation expressions (F# Interactive)

```
> let write(s) = log {                         ①  Writes string to
    do! logMessage("writing: " + s)               console and to log
    Console.Write(s) }
val write : string -> Logging<unit>

> let read() = log {
    do! logMessage("reading")
    return Console.ReadLine() }
val read : unit -> Logging<string>

> let testIt() = log {                ②  Calls primitive
    do! logMessage("starting")           logging function   ③  Calls another
    do! write("Enter name: ")                                   computation expression
    let! name = read()              ④  Uses customized
    return "Hello " + name + "!" }      value binding
val testIt : unit -> Logging<string>

> let res = testIt();;
Enter name: Tomas

> let (Log(msg, logs)) = res;;
val msg : string = "Hello Tomas!"
val logs : string list = ["starting"; "writing: Enter name:"; "reading"]
```

If you run the code in the listing, it waits for a console input. This doesn't always work perfectly in the F# Interactive add-in in the Visual Studio, so you may want to run the code in the standalone console version of the shell. We use the new do! primitive in several places to call functions that return Logging<unit>. In this case, we want to write a nonstandard binding that executes the Bind member, because we want to concatenate logging messages. We can ignore the actual value, because it's unit. That's the exact behavior of the do! primitive. In fact, when we write do! f(), it's shorthand for writing let! () = f(), which uses the customized binding and ignores the returned unit value.

When implementing the computation builder, we added a member called Zero. This is used behind the scenes in listing 12.24. When we write a computation that doesn't return anything ①, the F# compiler automatically uses the result of Zero as the overall result. We'll see how this member is used when we discuss how the compiler translates the code into method calls.

If you look at the type signatures in the listing, you can see that the result type of all the functions is the computation type (Logging<'T>), which is the same as the result type of the logMessage function we implemented earlier. This demonstrates that we have two ways of writing functions of a nonstandard computation type. We can build the computation type directly (as we did in the logMessage function) or use the computation expression. The first case is useful mostly for writing primitives; the second approach is useful for composing code from these primitives or other functions.

You can see the composable nature of computation expressions by looking at the testIt function. It first uses the do! construct to call a primitive function implemented directly ❷. Writing to the screen (and to the log) is implemented using a computation expression, but we call it in exactly the same way ❸. We're calling a function that returns a value and writes to the log, so we're using the customized binding with the `let!` keyword ❹.

In practice it isn't necessary to understand how the compiler translates the computation expression into method calls, but if you're curious, listing 12.25 shows the translation of the code from the previous listing, including the use of `Zero` member and the translations of `do!` primitive.

Listing 12.25   Translated version of the logging example (F#)

```
let write(s) =
  log.Bind(logMessage("writing: " + s), fun () ->
    Console.Write(s)
    log.Zero())              ⬅  Automatically uses
                          ❶  zero as result
let read() =
  log.Bind(logMessage("reading"), fun () ->
    log.Return(Console.ReadLine()))

let testIt() =
  log.Bind(logMessage("starting"), fun () ->
    log.Bind(write("Enter name: "), fun () ->     ❷  Translates multiple
      log.Bind(read(), fun name ->                   bindings into nested calls
        log.Return("Hello " + name + "!"))))
```

The `Zero` primitive is used only in the `write` function ❶ because this is the only place where we aren't returning any result from the function. In the other two functions, the innermost call is to the `Return` member, which takes a simple value as an argument and wraps it into a `LoggingValue<'T>` type that doesn't contain any log messages.

As you can see, when translating the computation expression, each use of `do!` or `let!` is replaced with a call to the `Bind` member ❷. If you recall our earlier discussion about sequence expressions, you can see the similarity now. In sequence expressions, every `for` loop was translated into a call to `Seq.collect`. We could take this analogy even further, because the `Return` primitive corresponds to creating a sequence containing a single element and the `Zero` primitive for sequence expressions would return an empty sequence.

There's one other interesting point that we want to highlight. If you look at the original code in listing 12.24, you can see that it looks just like ordinary F# code with a couple of added `!` symbols, which makes it easy to wrap an ordinary F# code into a computation expression.

12.7.3 *Refactoring using computation expressions*

In the previous chapter, we saw ways of refactoring functional programs. The last topic was laziness, which changes the way code executes without affecting the outcome of the program. In one sense, adding laziness can be also viewed as a refactoring technique. Computation expressions are similar in that they augment the code with an additional aspect without changing its core meaning.

TIP   There's a close relationship between computation expressions and lazi-ness. It's possible to create a computation expression that turns code into a lazily evaluated version, with a computation type of Lazy<'T>. You can try implementing the computation on your own: the only difficult part is writing the Bind member. We won't talk about this anymore here, but you can find additional information on the book's website.

The interesting thing is how easy it is to turn standard F# code into code that has non-standard behavior. We have to enclose the code in a computation expression block and add calls to the primitives provided for the computation expression, such as the logMessage function we just implemented. When the code we're implementing is split between several functions, we have to change the calls to these functions from a usual call or usual value bindings into customized value bindings using either let! or do! primitives. When writing code that uses computation expressions in F#, the typical approach is to start with the standard version of the code, which is easier to write and test, then refactor it into an advanced version using computation expressions.

12.8   *Summary*

In the first part of the chapter, we talked about .NET sequences, as represented by the IEnumerable<T> type, also known as seq<'a> in F#. We started by looking at tech-niques for generating sequences, including higher-order functions, iterators, and F# sequence expressions. We saw that sequences are lazy, which allows us to create infi-nite sequences. We looked at a real-world example using an infinite sequence of col-ors to separate the code to draw of a chart from the code that generates the colors used in the chart.

Next we discussed how to process sequences. We wrote the same code using higher-order functions, the corresponding LINQ extension methods, C# query expressions, and F# sequence expressions. This helped us to understand how queries and sequence expressions work. One most important operation is the *bind* operation, which occurs in sequences as the collect function in F# and the SelectMany method in LINQ.

The same conceptual operation is available for many other types, and we saw how to create F# computation expressions that look like sequence expressions but work with other types. We provided two practical examples, implementing computation expressions for working with option types and storing log messages during execution. The same idea can be implemented in C# to some extent, with query expressions used in the place of computation expressions. The F# language features are more general, while C# query expressions are tailored to queries.

Perhaps the most difficult thing about using computation expressions is to identify when it's beneficial to design and implement them. In the next chapter, we'll look at one of the most important uses of F# computation expressions. It allows us to execute I/O operations without blocking the caller thread. This is particularly important when performing slow I/O such as reading data from the internet. Later we'll see how F# enables us to interactively process and visualize data, which is becoming an important task in the today's increasingly connected world.

Part 4

Applied
functional programming

Although functional programming is certainly elegant, you're probably more interested in it for practical purposes: it's useful as a general-purpose style, and it positively excels in certain problem domains. We've already seen examples, such as the pie chart drawing application in chapter 4 and the simple photo browser in chapter 11, but the main purpose of these examples was to demonstrate specific concepts and techniques.

Part 4 is different. In each chapter we'll spend most of the time talking about one real-world problem, using the most appropriate features of F# and functional programming to solve it. The code will use many of the features we've seen so far and will be relatively complicated given the space limitations we have for a single chapter.

There are two related areas where functional programming offers obvious advantages: asynchronous and concurrent programming.

In chapter 13, we'll talk about asynchronous programming, but in the larger context of modern data-driven programming. We'll obtain data asynchronously, explore its structure interactively, and visualize the results using Excel.

In chapter 14, we'll turn our attention to parallel programming, an area where functional programming shines: immutability sidesteps the issue of modifying shared state, so programs written in a functional style are much easier to parallelize.

In chapter 15, we'll explore developing functional libraries using the *composition* principle. Many of the functional features that we've seen so far are built using this principle. The idea is that we can provide a small number of easy-to-understand primitives that can be combined in very rich ways. Then we can use the primitives to build complex results without specifying any implementation details. To demonstrate how you can design libraries that follow this principle, we'll create a library for describing animations, but we'll also briefly sketch another example from the financial world.

In chapter 16, we'll talk about applications that need to react to various events. This is a broad topic: the events in question could be generated from a UI, or from background tasks that need to collect and present data to the user.

In chapters 13 and 16 we'll use F# features that are quite difficult to write in C#, so the examples will use F# exclusively. Chapters 14 and 15 build only on top of the standard aspects of functional programming, such as immutability, higher-order functions, or a focus on writing composable code. This means that we'll be able to write most of the code in both F# and C#. Unlike in earlier parts of the book where we often used C# just to demonstrate specific concepts, this time it will be closer to the real code you'd write to solve a business problem using functional ideas to inspire the design.

Asynchronous and
data-driven programming

13

This chapter covers
- Programming asynchronous workflows
- Exploring data using F# Interactive
- Defining meaning of types using units of measure
- Processing and visualizing data

We'll begin with a quote from an interview with Bill Gates in which he talks about the type of programming tasks that he's interested in and describes the typical scenario when writing the application:

> *Go grab data from the web, don't just think of it as text, bring structure into it and then [...] try out different ways of presenting it, but very interactively. [...] Write a little bit of code that may have your specific algorithm for processing that data. [Gates, 2008]*

This describes exactly what we're going to do in this chapter, and as you'll see, the F# language and its interactive shell are excellent tools for solving this kind of task. We'll call this approach *explorative programming*, because the goal is to explore a massive amount of data and find a way to gather useful information from it. We'll spend most of the chapter working with F# Interactive, because it gives us a great way to "write a little bit of code" with our "specific algorithm for processing that data" and immediately execute it to see the results.

The F# language and libraries support this type of programming in many ways, and we'll look at all the important technologies involved. To obtain the data, we can use asynchronous workflows based on the computation expression syntax that we introduced in the previous chapter. Then we'll look at "bringing a structure" to the data using F# types. We'll also use units of measure that allow us to specify that a certain value isn't just a floating-point number but that it has a unit such as square kilometers.

> **TIP**   In this chapter, we'll use data provided by the World Bank. The first half of the chapter covers, in some detail, how to obtain all the data we need in the right format.
>
> If you're more interested in processing and visualization, you can go directly to section 13.4. Instead of downloading the data step-by-step from the World Bank as described in the first part, you can get all the data directly from the book's website.

Finally, we'll look at "trying out different ways of presenting the data." In particular, we'll see how to export the structured data to Excel using its .NET API, and programmatically visualize the data as a chart.

13.1   Asynchronous workflows

There are many areas where we can use asynchronous operations. When we're working with disks, calling web services, or connecting to the database, asynchronous workflows can give us a notable performance benefit. When an application performs an asynchronous operation, it's not easy to predict when the operation will complete. If we don't handle asynchronous operations properly, the application will be inefficient and may become unresponsive.

Writing the code that performs asynchronous operations without blocking the calling thread is essential to avoid problems, but difficult to implement using the current techniques. In F#, this is largely simplified thanks to *asynchronous workflows*. Before we'll look at using them, let's explain what the problem is.

13.1.1   Why do asynchronous workflows matter?

Assume we want to download the content of a web page so that we can use it in our application. We could use the `WebClient` class from the `System.Net` namespace, but that wouldn't demonstrate the problems we have when we need to run complicated, long-running operations. Instead, we'll create an HTTP request explicitly as a first step, then download the data as the second step:

```
var req = HttpWebRequest.Create("http://manning.com");      Initializes
var resp = req.GetResponse();                          ◄──── connection
var stream = resp.GetResponseStream();
```

```
var reader = new StreamReader(stream);        ┐ Downloads
var html = reader.ReadToEnd();         ◄───────┘ web page
Console.WriteLine(html);
```

This code will work, but it's far from perfect. It performs HTTP communication in two places. In the first, it needs to initialize the HTTP connection with the server; in the second, it downloads the web page. Both operations could potentially take a long time and each could block the active thread, thus causing our application to become unresponsive.

To solve this, we could run the download on a separate thread, but using threads is expensive, so this approach would limit the number of downloads we can run in parallel. Also, most of the time the thread would be waiting for the response, so we'd be consuming thread resources for no good reason. To solve the problem properly, we should use an asynchronous API that allows us to trigger the request and call a callback that we provide when the operation completes:

```
var req = HttpWebRequest.Create("http://manning.com");   ┐ Starts
req.BeginGetResponse(asyncRes1 => {        ◄───────────────┘ operation
  var resp = req.EndGetResponse(asyncRes1);
  var stream = resp.GetResponseStream();
  var reader = new StreamReader(stream);        ┐ Doesn't
  reader.BeginReadToEnd(asyncRes2 => {    ◄──────┘ exist!
    var html = reader.EndReadToEnd(asyncRes2);
    Console.WriteLine(html);
  });
});
```

This version of code is quite difficult to write. Even if we use lambda functions from C# 3.0, the code still looks complicated. We had to change its structure; instead of writing sequential code, we're writing a sequence of nested callbacks.

The previous snippet has one more problem. The `BeginReadToEnd` method isn't available in the .NET Framework, so we'd have to implement the asynchronous download ourselves. Unfortunately, this can't be done using a simple sequential code, because we need to download the page in a buffered way. If we want to write this in an asynchronous style (using nested callbacks), we can't use any of the built-in constructs such as `while` loops.

As we'll see, asynchronous workflows solve all the problems we had when writing the download. They allow us to write code in the usual sequential way using standard control structures such as recursion or even `while` loops. The code executes asynchronously, which means that the workflow waits for an operation to complete without using a dedicated thread. In the next section, we'll look how to use F# asynchronous workflows to implement the example we've just discussed.

13.1.2 Downloading web pages asynchronously

Before we can use asynchronous workflows to fetch web content, we'll need to reference the FSharp.PowerPack.dll library that contains asynchronous versions of many .NET methods. When developing a standalone application, you'd use the Add Reference command. In this chapter we're using the interactive development style, so we'll create a new F# script file and use the #r directive (listing 13.1).

Listing 13.1   Writing code using asynchronous workflows (F# Interactive)

```
> #r "FSharp.PowerPack.dll";;

> open System.IO
  open System.Net;;

> let downloadUrl(url:string) = async {          ❶
    let request = HttpWebRequest.Create(url)
    let! response = request.AsyncGetResponse()     ❷
    use response = response                         ❸
    let stream = response.GetResponseStream()
    use reader = new StreamReader(stream)
    return! reader.AsyncReadToEnd() };;            ❹
val downloadUrl : string -> Async<string>
```

After opening all the required namespaces, we define a function that's implemented using the asynchronous workflow. It uses the async value as a computation builder ❶. You can easily prove that it's an ordinary value; if you type a dot (.) immediately after the value in Visual Studio, IntelliSense shows that it contains all the usual computation builder members such as Bind and Return, and also a couple of additional primitives that we'll need later. The printed type signature shows that the type of the computation is Async<string>. We're going to look at this type in more detail later.

The code in listing 13.1 uses the let! construct once when executing a primitive asynchronous operation AsyncGetResponse ❷ provided by the F# library. The return type of this method is Async<WebResponse>, so the let! construct composes the two asynchronous operations and binds the actual WebResponse value to the response symbol. This means that we can work with the value once the asynchronous operation completes.

The next line ❸ uses the use primitive, which disposes of the given object once it is out of scope. We already discussed use in the context of ordinary F# programs, and inside asynchronous workflows it behaves similarly. It will dispose of the HTTP response when the workflow completes. We're using value hiding to hide the original response symbol and declare a new one that will be disposed. This is a common pattern, so F# provides a convenient way to write this using the use! primitive, which is simply a combination of let! and use. Now that we know about it, we can replace the two lines with the following:

```
use! response = request.AsyncGetResponse()
```

On the last line of listing 13.1, we're using a primitive that we haven't seen before: return! ❹. This allows us to run another asynchronous operation (just like using the let! primitive) but returns the result of the operation when it completes rather than assigning it to some symbol. Like the do! primitive, this is simply syntactic sugar. The computation builder doesn't have to implement any additional members; the compiler could also treat the code as if it were written like this (the actual translation is simpler):

```
let! text = reader.AsyncReadToEnd()
return text
```

Now that we have the `downloadUrl` function that creates the asynchronous computation, we should also determine how we can use it to download the content of a web page. As you can see in listing 13.2, we can use functions from the `Async` module to execute the workflow.

Listing 13.2   Executing asynchronous computations (F# Interactive)

```
> let downloadTask = downloadUrl("http://www.manning.com");;     ◁──────    Builds asynchronous
val downloadTask : Async<string>                                            workflow  ❶

> Async.RunSynchronously(downloadTask);;       ◁──────
val it : string = "<!DOCTYPE html PUBLIC "-//W3C//DTD XHTML 1.0            Runs
    Transitional//EN" "http://www.w3.org/TR/xhtml11/DTD/xhtml1-tr          workflow,
    ansitional.dtd"><html><head> (...)"                                    waits for
                                                                     ❷     result
> let tasks =
    [ downloadUrl("http://www.tomasp.net");
       downloadUrl("http://www.manning.com") ];;
val tasks : list<Async<string>>

> let all = Async.Parallel(tasks);;     ◁──────    Combines several
val all : Async<string[]>                     ❸    workflows into one

> Async.RunSynchronously(all);;
val it : string[] = [ "..."; "..." ]
```

Code written using asynchronous workflows is delayed, which means that when we execute the `downloadUrl` function on the first line, it doesn't start downloading the web page yet ❶. The returned value (of type `Async<string>`) represents the computation that we want to run, just as a function value represents code that we can later execute. The `Async` module provides ways of running the workflow, some of which are described in table 13.1.

Table 13.1   Selected primitives for working with asynchronous workflows that are available in the `Async` module in the standard F# library

Primitive	Type of primitive and description
RunSynchronously	`Async<'T> -> 'T` Starts the given workflow on the current thread. When an asynchronous operation is used in the workflow, the workflow resumes on the thread used for invoking the asynchronous callback. This operation blocks the caller thread and waits for the result of the workflow.
Start	`Async<unit> -> unit` Starts the given workflow in the background (using a thread pool thread) and returns immediately. The workflow executes in the parallel with the subsequent code of the caller. As indicated in the signature, the workflow can't return a value.

Table 13.1   Selected primitives for working with asynchronous workflows that are available in the Async module in the standard F# library *(continued)*

Primitive	Type of primitive and description
CreateAsTask	`Async<'T> -> Task<'T>` The method is available only on .NET 4.0. It wraps the asynchronous workflow into a `Task<'T>` object that can be used for executing it. The task can be started using `Start` or `RunSynchronously` methods that behave similarly to the `Async` primitives. To get the result of the workflow, we can use the `Result` property, which blocks if the workflow hasn't completed yet.
Parallel	`seq<Async<'a>> -> Async<array<'a>>` Takes a collection of asynchronous workflows and returns a single workflow that executes all of the arguments in parallel. The returned workflow waits for all the operations to complete and then returns their results in a single array.

In listing 13.2 we initially use `Async.RunSynchronously` ❷, which blocks the calling thread. This is useful for testing the workflow interactively. In the next step, we create a list of workflow values. Again, nothing starts executing at this point. Once we have the collection, we can use the `Async.Parallel` method ❸ to build a single workflow that will execute all workflows in the list in parallel. This still doesn't execute any of the original workflows. To do that, we need to use `Async.RunSynchronously` again, which will start the composed workflow and wait for its result. The composed workflow starts all the workflows and will wait until all of them complete.

The code still blocks to wait for the overall result, but it runs efficiently. It uses the .NET thread pool to balance the maximal number of running threads. If we created hundreds of tasks, it wouldn't create hundreds of threads, because that would be inefficient. Instead a smaller number of threads would be used. When the workflow reaches a primitive asynchronous operation called using the `let!` construct, it registers a callback in the system and releases the thread. Because .NET manages threads using a thread pool, a thread that finished its work can be reused for starting another asynchronous workflow. When we use asynchronous workflows, the number of tasks running in parallel can be significantly larger than when using threads directly.

In this chapter, we need to obtain the data interactively, so we're interested in running workflows in parallel rather than in developing responsive GUI applications. The latter class of applications (also called *reactive* applications) is important, and chapter 16 will focus solely on this topic. Now we've seen what code *using* asynchronous workflows looks like, let's see how they're implemented.

13.1.3 *Understanding how workflows work*

In the previous chapter we saw that F# code written using a computation expression is translated into an expression that uses the primitives provided by the appropriate computation builder. For asynchronous workflows, this means that the `let!` construct is translated into a call to `async.Bind`, and `return` is translated into `async.Return`. In addition, asynchronous workflows are delayed. This means that the computation itself needs to be wrapped in an additional primitive to make sure that the whole code will be enclosed in a function. The function can then be executed later when we start the workflow. Listing 13.3 shows the translated version of the workflow from listing 13.2.

Listing 13.3 Asynchronous workflow constructed explicitly (F#)

```
async.Delay(fun () ->
  let request = HttpWebRequest.Create(url)
  async.Bind(request.AsyncGetResponse(), fun response ->
    async.Using(response, fun response ->
      let stream = response.GetResponseStream()
      async.Using(new StreamReader(stream), fun reader ->
        reader.AsyncReadToEnd() )
    )
  )
)
```

The `Delay` member wraps a function into a workflow value that can be executed later. The body of the lambda function used as an argument creates an HTTP request and assigns a value to the `resp` symbol using customized asynchronous value binding. The compiler translated each use binding into a call to the Using member, which is another primitive that can be optionally provided by the computation expression builder. It takes care of disposing of objects at the end of the workflow in case of both success and an error.

The `Delay` member is one of the computation builder members that we can provide when implementing a computation expression. In listing 13.3, it takes a function that returns the asynchronous workflow (the type is `unit -> Async<'a>`) and returns a workflow value (`Async<'a>`) that wraps this function. Thanks to this primitive, the whole computation is enclosed inside a function, and it isn't executed when we create the `Async<'a>` value. This is an important difference from the examples in the previous chapter such as the `option<'a>` type. An option represents a value, so the computation expression runs immediately, performing the computation and returning a new option value, but a workflow represents a computation. It will become clearer what this means when we look at the `Async<'a>` type in detail.

The other primitive that occurs in listing 13.3 is the `Bind` member. As you learned in the previous chapter, this is crucial for all computation expressions. In asynchronous workflows, `Bind` allows us to start an operation without blocking the caller thread. The following list summarizes the steps that take place when we execute the workflow using a primitive such as `Async.RunSynchronously`:

1 The function given as an argument to the `Delay` primitive starts executing. It synchronously creates the object that represents the HTTP request for the given URL.

2 `AsyncGetResponse` is called. The result is a primitive asynchronous workflow that knows how to start the request and call a specified function when the operation completes.

3 We execute the `Bind` member and give it the workflow from step 2 as the first argument and a function that takes the HTTP response as an argument and should be executed when the workflow completes. This function is called a *continuation*, which is a term we've seen already. (We used it when discussing recursion in chapter 10 as an accumulator parameter to accumulate more code that we want to run later.)

4 The `Bind` member runs the workflow created by `AsyncGetResponse`, passing it the specified continuation. The primitive workflow then calls the .NET `Begin-GetResponse` method that instructs the system to start downloading the response and call the given continuation when the operation completes. At this point, the `Bind` member returns and the thread that was executing the operation is freed to continue doing other work, or it's returned to the thread pool.

5 When the response is ready, the system will call the continuation. The workflow gets the response object using the `EndGetResponse` .NET method and executes the continuation given to the `Bind` member, which represents the rest of the workflow. Note that the system again picks a thread from the thread pool, so the rest of the workflow may be executed on a different thread each time we use the `let!` primitive.

The key point is that when we execute an asynchronous workflow, we don't wait for the result. Instead, we give it a continuation as an argument; this continuation will be executed when the corresponding step in the workflow has completed. The great thing about asynchronous workflows is that we don't have to write the code using continuations explicitly. The compiler translates `let!` primitives into the calls to the `Bind` member, creating the continuation automatically.

Investigating the asynchronous workflow type

You can use asynchronous workflows without understanding all the details, but you may be interested in a bit of information about how they're implemented. We've seen that asynchronous workflows are similar to functions in that they represent a computation that we can execute later. The type is represented as a function in the F# library. The type is a bit more sophisticated, but the simplest asynchronous computation could be represented using the following:

```
type Async<'T> = (('T -> unit) * (exn -> unit) * (unit -> unit)) -> unit
```

This is a function that takes three arguments as a tuple and returns a unit value. The three arguments are important, because they are continuations—functions that can be called when the asynchronous workflow completes. The first one is called success continuation. Its type is `'T -> unit`, which means that it takes the result of the workflow. This continuation will be called when the workflow completes. It can then run another workflow or any other code. The second one is exception continuation. It takes an `exn` value as an argument, which is the F# abbreviation for the .NET `Exception` type. As you can guess, it's used when the operation that the workflow executes fails. The third function is called cancellation continuation and can be triggered when the workflow is being canceled.

Even though the precise implementation details of asynchronous workflows aren't essential, it's useful to be able to create your own primitive workflows—the equivalent of the `AsyncGetResponse` method used in listing 13.3. You can then use the rest of the building blocks to run your code asynchronously with a minimum of fuss.

13.1.4 *Creating primitive workflows*

The F# PowerPack library contains asynchronous versions for many important I/O operations, but it can't include all of them. For that reason, the F# library also provides methods for building your own primitive workflows. If the operation you want to run inside the workflow uses a standard .NET pattern and provides `BeginOperation` and `EndOperation` methods, you can use the `Async.FromBeginEnd` method. If you give it these two methods as an argument, it'll return an asynchronous workflow.

Other operations are available that can be executed without blocking the thread. For example, we may want to wait for a particular event to occur and continue executing the workflow when it's triggered. Listing 13.4 creates a primitive that waits for the specified number of milliseconds using a timer and then resumes the workflow.

> **Listing 13.4   Implementing asynchronous waiting (F# Interacitve)**

```
> module MyAsync =
    let Sleep(time) =
      Async.FromContinuations(fun (cont, econt, ccont) ->          <--┐
        let tmr = new System.Timers.Timer(time, AutoReset = false)
        tmr.Elapsed.Add(fun _ -> cont())    <--┐
        tmr.Start()              Resumes computation  ❷
      );;                                                   Suspends
(...)                                                       workflow for
                                                            specified time  ❶
> Async.RunSynchronously(async {
    printfn "Starting..."
    do! MyAsync.Sleep(1000.0)   <--┐  Waits without
    printfn "Finished!"         ❸  blocking thread
  });;
Starting...
Finished!
val it : unit = ()
```

The same functionality is already available in the F# library, so it isn't only a toy example. It's implemented by `Async.Sleep`, and we'll need it later in the chapter. Of course, we could block the workflow using the synchronous version, `Thread.Sleep`, but there's an important difference. This method would block the thread, while our function creates a timer and returns the thread to the .NET thread pool. This means that when we use our primitive, the .NET runtime can execute workflows in parallel without any limitations.

The `Sleep` function ❶ takes the number of milliseconds for which we want to delay processing and uses the `Async.FromContinuations` method to construct the workflow. This method reflects the internal structure of the workflow quite closely. The argument is a lambda function that will be executed when the workflow starts. The lambda takes a tuple of three continuations as an argument. The first function should be called when the operation completes successfully, and the second should be called when the operation throws an exception. Similarly to the declaration of the `Async<'T>` type from an earlier sidebar, there's a third continuation that can trigger cancellation of the workflow. In the body of the lambda, we create a timer and specify the handler for its `Elapsed` event. The handler simply runs the success continuation ❷.

Having created our new primitive, listing 13.4 shows a simple snippet that uses it. Because it returns a unit value, we're using the `do!` primitive rather than `let!` ❸. When the code is executed, it constructs the timer with the handler and starts it. When the specified time elapses, the system takes an available thread from the thread pool and runs the event handler, which in turn executes the rest of the computation (in our case, printing to the screen).

Asynchronous workflows in C#

There have been numerous attempts to simplify asynchronous programming in C#, but none of the available libraries works quite as neatly as the asynchronous workflow syntax. The F# syntax is extremely simple from the end-user point of view (just wrap the code in an `async` block), which is quite difficult to achieve in C#.

We've seen that LINQ queries roughly correspond to F# computation expressions, so you might be tempted to implement `Select` and `SelectMany` operations. In principle, it would be possible to write asynchronous operations using query expressions, but the syntax we can use inside queries is limited. Interestingly, C# iterators can be also used for this purpose. This approach is described in the article "Asynchronous Programming in C# Using Iterators" (available at http://tomasp.net/blog/csharp-async.aspx). The most real-world library that uses this technique is Jeffrey Richter's PowerThreading library [Richter, 2009].

One of the most complex libraries based on C# iterators is the Concurrency and Coordination Runtime (CCR) [Chrysanthakopoulos and Singh, 2005]. This library was developed as part of Microsoft Robotics studio, where responsiveness and asynchronous processing is essential for any application. You can find more information about this library in Jeffery Richter's "Concurrency Affairs" article [Richter, 2006].

It's time to start using asynchronous workflows for more practical purposes. In the next section, we'll look at the data services provided by the World Bank, and see how we can call them using asynchronous workflows.

13.2   Connecting to the World Bank

It's no accident that our discussion on asynchronous workflows is located in a chapter about explorative programming. Many of the interesting data sources you'll work with today are available online in the form of a web service or other web-based application. As we've seen, asynchronous workflows are the essential F# feature for obtaining the data.

Downloading the data efficiently isn't our only problem. The data sources usually return the data in an untyped format (such as a plain text or XML without a formally defined schema), so we first need to understand the structure. Also, remote data sources can be unreliable, so we have to be able to recover from failure. This means that even before we write the code to obtain the data, we need to explore the data source. As we'll see, the F# Interactive tools give us a great way for doing that.

13.2.1 Accessing the World Bank data

The data source we'll use in this chapter is the service provided by the World Bank, an international organization that provides funding and knowledge to developing countries. As part of its job, the organization needs to identify what type of support is the most efficient, determine where it's needed, and evaluate whether it had an impact on the economy, quality of life or the environment of the developing country. The World Bank has a data set called *World Development Indicators* that contains information about many countries, and it makes the data available online. In this chapter, we'll work with information about the environment and more specifically about the area covered by forests. The data provided by the World Bank is available for free, but you need to register on the bank's website first.

TIP To register, first go to http://developer.worldbank.org. Once you fill in the form and get the confirmation email, you can return to the website and obtain an API key, which is used when sending requests to the World Bank services. The website also provides documentation and a brief tutorial about the service. You can look at it there, but we'll explain everything we use in this chapter. One interesting feature on the web page is Query Generator, which allows you to run and configure queries interactively and shows the URL that we can use to request the data programmatically.

The World Bank exposes the data using a simple HTTP-based service, so we can use the `downloadUrl` function we created earlier. If you look at the documentation or experiment with the Query Generator for some time, you'll quickly learn the structure of the request URLs. The address always refers to the same page on the server, and all the additional properties are specified in the URL as key-value pairs. In listing 13.5, we'll start by creating a function that constructs the request URL from an F# list containing the key-value pairs so that we can access the data more easily.

Listing 13.5 Building the request URL (F#)

```
open System.Web
                                          Specify your World
let worldBankKey = "xxxxxxxxxx"     ◁──┐  Bank key here!
let worldBankUrl(functions, props) =
  seq { yield "http://open.worldbank.org"
      for item in functions do                                    ❶
        yield "/" + HttpUtility.UrlEncode(item:string)
      yield "?per_page=100"
      yield "&api_key=" + worldBankKey
```

```
    for key, value in props do
        yield "&" + key + "=" + HttpUtility.UrlEncode(value:string) }     ❷
    |> String.concat "&"
```

The function `worldBankUrl` contains a sequence expression that generates a collection of strings and then concatenates them into a single URL.

In the sequence expression, we first return the base part of the URL. Next, we add a path to the required function provided by the server. The function can be for example "/keywords/Wood", so we take a list that specifies parts of the function name and concatenate all of them using "/" as the separator ❶. Once we specify the function, we add the API key and page length, which are another parts shared by all the requests we'll need in this chapter. Finally, we process additional properties specified by the user. We iterate over all the key-value pairs specified as the `props` argument and return a `"&key=value"` string ❷.

To make sure that the URL is well formed, we're using the `HttpUtility` class from the `System.Web` namespace. If you're compiling the file as part of a project, you'll need to add reference to the System.Web assembly, which isn't referenced by default. The utility encodes an arbitrary string into a string that can be contained in a URL. As there are various overloads of the `UrlEncode` method, we're using a type annotation to specify that the type of the `value` argument is a string.

In this chapter, we're creating an F# script file rather than a traditional application, so the next step is to write a couple of F# Interactive commands that we can execute immediately to see whether the function we just wrote works correctly. This "test request" is also useful to see the data format used by the bank, so we know what we need to do later to parse the data.

The statistics provided by the World Bank are available for individual countries, but they can also be grouped based on region or income. These aggregated statistics make it easier to see overall trends. The first thing we need to do is get the information about all the available groups. You can try this on the website using the Query Generator. First select the Countries option on the Country Calls tab and enter your API key. To get a list of aggregated country groups, you can choose Aggregates from the Region list and then run the request. Listing 13.6 shows how to run the same request using F# Interactive.

Listing 13.6 Testing the World Bank data service (F# Interactive)

```
> let url =
    worldBankUrl(["countries"],                    ❶ Builds URL with
                 ["region", "NA"];;                   specified properties
val url : string =
    http://open.worldbank.org/countries?per_page=100&          ❷ Downloads
    api_key=hq8byg8k7t2fxc6hp7jmbx26&region=NA"                   page as
                                                                  string
> Async.RunSynchronously(downloadUrl(url));;
val it : string = "<?xml version=\"1.0\" encoding=\"utf-8\" (...)"
```

We start by creating the URL using the function we just implemented ❶. We give it `countries` as the name of the function we want to invoke. The additional region parameter specifies what types of countries we want to list. The NA value means that we're interested in the aggregated country information. As we're using F# Interactive, we immediately see the composed URL. It contains all the specified parameters, the World Bank key, and a flag specifying that we want to return up to 100 records per page. We'll talk about paging of the output later when we need to obtain a larger number of indicators.

Once we have the URL, we can copy it into a web browser to see what data the World Bank returns. To download the page programmatically, we can use our download-loadUrl function ❷ (from listing 13.1). As with any network operation, the download may fail. This doesn't matter if we're running the request manually, but when we're executing a bulk operation to download data from URLs in parallel, we need to write the code in a way it can recover from nonfatal failures.

13.2.2 Recovering from failures

The World Bank service allows us to make only a limited number of requests each day for a single user key, and it also limits the frequency of requests. This means that if we run a large number of requests at once, some of them may return an error. The workaround is to catch the exception and retry the request later.

Listing 13.7 implements a loop that executes a request repeatedly until either it succeeds or we've tried 20 times. The failure is reported using exceptions, and we're using the F# try ... with construct to catch the exception.

Listing 13.7 Running the web request repeatedly (F# Interactive)

```
> let worldBankDownload(properties) =
    let url = worldBankUrl(properties)
    let rec loop(attempts) = async {          ❶
      try
        return! downloadUrl(url)              ❷
      with _ when attempts > 0 ->                        ❸
        printfn "Failed, retrying (%d): %A" attempts properties
        do! Async.Sleep(500.0)
        return! loop(attempts - 1) }          ❹
    loop(20);;
val worldBankDownload : seq<string * string> -> Async<string>

> let props = ["countries"], ["region", "NA"];
val props : string list * (string * string) list

> Async.RunSynchronously(worldBankDownload(props))
Failed, retrying (20): [("countries"); ("region", "NA")]
val it : string = "<?xml version=\"1.0\" encoding=\"utf-8\" (...)"
```

This code implements a recursive and asynchronous loop function ❶, which attempts to run the actual download ❷. If the download fails, an exception can be thrown. When an exception occurs and the remaining number of attempts isn't zero ❸, we suspend the workflow for some time and then retry the download ❹.

The normal functional way to create a loop is to write a recursive function that takes the number of remaining attempts as an argument and decrements this number on each iteration. Listing 13.7 uses this pattern with a twist. The `loop` function **①** is implemented using an asynchronous workflow, so we're creating a recursive asynchronous workflow. The recursive call is in the exception handler **④**, and it uses the `return!` primitive to run the next iteration of the asynchronous loop. The body of the workflow attempts to download the page, but it does this in a `try … with` block that catches possible exceptions.

The `try … with` block in F# is similar to the `try … catch` in C#, but it has some additional features. It allows us to distinguish between exceptions using pattern matching, which makes the `with` construct **③** very similar to the `match` expression that we're already familiar with. In listing 13.7, we're simply catching all exceptions, but we've added a `when` clause **②**. This means the exception will be caught only when the number of attempts is less than 20. It's worth noting that we're handling exceptions inside the asynchronous workflow in the same way you can handle exceptions in normal F# code. This is possible thanks to additional primitives called `TryWith` and `TryFinally` that the asynchronous workflow provides under the hood; these primitives tell F# how to deal with exceptions that occur during asynchronous operations.

On the last few lines of listing 13.7, you can see how to use the function to get data from the World Bank. Note that the parameter properties of the function is a tuple containing both function and additional properties. We didn't write that explicitly as a tuple in the implementation, but the compiler knows that `theworldBankUrl` function expects a tuple value. You can simulate a failure in the connection by disconnecting your computer from the network for a short time, and you'll see that the code is able to recover from the failure. Now that we have a reliable function for downloading data, we can move forward and download all data we want to work with.

13.3   Exploring and obtaining the data

As we've seen in the last couple of examples, the World Bank data service returns the data as XML documents, so before we can write any code to process the data in a meaningful way, we'll need to convert it to an F# type. In chapter 7, we converted between XML and our own custom discriminated union type, but in this case we're going to use tuples and sequences. This is because the data structure will be quite simple, and when we work with data interactively we need to modify the code frequently, either to tweak how we're using the existing values or to download different information. Tuples are more flexible for this task—we won't end up constantly renaming values.

We'll use LINQ to XML again, just as we did in chapter 7, but this time, we won't use the whole file. Instead, we'll just pick out the nodes that are relevant. First, we need a few helper functions.

13.3.1   Implementing XML helper functions

LINQ to XML is primarily designed for C# and VB, and working with it from F# can be cumbersome. For example, F# doesn't support implicit type conversions (because it would complicate type inference), so every time we specify an element name, we have to use XName.Get instead of simply using a string. Alternatively, we could write a simple utility function or a custom operator to do this for us.

We can easily implement a couple of F# functions to wrap the most commonly used parts of LINQ to XML and give us a very "F#-friendly" way to work with the data. As you can see in listing 13.8, most of the functions are straightforward. The listing is created using F# Interactive, so you can use the inferred type signatures to understand what a function does. One notable aspect is that each function takes the input element as its last argument, which means that we'll be able to compose the functions using the pipelining operator.

> **Listing 13.8 Helper functions for reading XML (F# Interactive)**

```
> #r "System.Xml.dll"
  #r "System.Xml.Linq.dll"
  open System.Xml.Linq;;

> let wb = "http://www.worldbank.org";;
val wb : string = "http://www.worldbank.org"
> let xattr s (el:XElement) =                    ❶
    el.Attribute(XName.Get(s)).Value
  let xelem s (el:XContainer) =                   ❷
    el.Element(XName.Get(s, wb))
  let xvalue (el:XElement) =                      ❸
    el.Value
  let xelems s (el:XContainer) =                  ❹
    el.Elements(XName.Get(s, wb));;
val xattr : string -> XElement -> string
val xelem : string -> XContainer -> XElement
val xvalue : XElement -> string
val xelems : string -> XContainer -> seq<XElement>

> let xnested path (el:XContainer) =             ❺
    let res = path |> Seq.fold (fun xn s ->
      let child = xelem s xn
      child :> XContainer) el            ◁──┘  Upcasts element
    res :?> XElement                               to container
  ;;                                           ◁──  Downcasts result
val xnested : seq<string> -> XContainer -> XElement   back to element
```

Most of the helper functions are quite simple. xattr ❶ returns value of the specified attribute; xelem ❷ returns child element with the specified name; xvalue ❸ reads text inside the element; and xelems ❹ returns all child elements with the specified name. xnested ❺ is more interesting and returns a child node specified by a path given as a sequence of element names. When accessing elements, we specify the XML namespace used in the documents returned from the World Bank. When we'll use our helper functions later in the chapter, we'll only need to provide the local name of the element.

Listing 13.8 first references the necessary assemblies for LINQ to XML and opens the namespace containing classes such as XElement. The first group of functions is used to access child nodes, attributes, or the value of any given element. Note that the xelem function takes XContainer as an argument, which means that we can use it for both ordinary elements, but also with an object that represents the whole document.

This is possible because F# allows implicit conversion to a base class or an implemented interface when passing instance as an input argument to a function or method. No implicit conversions are done in other locations, such as when returning a result from a lambda function. This makes the xnested function slightly more complicated, and we need to add a couple of explicit casts.

The xnested function takes a sequence of names as an argument and follows this path to find a deeply nested element. It's implemented with Seq.fold and uses the input element as the initial state. The lambda function is executed for each name in the path. It finds a child of the current element with the specified name and returns it as a new child element. We want the type of the input to be XContainer, so the folding operation uses this type to represent the current state. As a result, we need to upcast the returned element to XContainer inside the lambda function and downcast the final result to XElement.

Equipped with these helper functions, we can easily extract all the information we want from the downloaded XML documents. If you're unsure about what any of the new functions do, don't worry: everything will become clearer once we start using them with real data.

13.3.2 *Extracting region codes*

The result of our download function is a string, so we need to parse this string as an XML document. We'll need this operation frequently, so we'll write a simple wrapper function that downloads the data using worldBankDownload and returns the result as an XDocument object. The download executes asynchronously, so we'll implement the function using asynchronous workflows:

```
let worldBankRequest(props) = async {
  let! text = worldBankDownload(props)
  return XDocument.Parse(text) }
```

The code first invokes the asynchronous download using let!. When it completes, it parses the XML data and returns the XDocument object. Once we execute the download using Async.RunSynchronously, we can query the returned XML document using the helper functions from the previous section. Listing 13.9 shows an example of this; it downloads the aggregated information about countries and then accesses some values we'll need later.

Listing 13.9   Exploring the region information (F# Interactive)

```
> let doc =
    worldBankRequest(["countries"], ["region", "NA"])
    |> Async.RunSynchronously;;
val doc : XDocument = (...)

> let c = doc |> xnested ["countries"; "country" ];;      ❶
val c : XElement

> c |> xattr "id";;      ❷
val it : string = "EAP"

> c |> xelem "name" |> xvalue;;      ❸
val it : string = "East Asia & Pacific"
```

We start by accessing the first `country` element in the returned document. This is a child element of the root element named `countries`. To walk down the XML tree, we use the `xnested` function ❶ and specify the path to the element we want to select.

Now we can look at the content of the element to see what information we want to extract. First, we demonstrate how to get the ID of the region. This is stored in the `id` attribute, so we can read it using the `xattr` function ❷. We'll also need the name of the region so we can display the data in a user-friendly format. This is the value of the `name` element ❸.

Now that we've explored the structure and made sure we know how to access all the region information we need for a single region, we can loop over all the regions. Listing 13.10 uses the same functions, but in a sequence computation.

Listing 13.10   Creating sequence with region information (F# Interactive)

```
> let regions =
    seq { let countries = doc |> xnested [ "rsp"; "countries" ]
          for country in countries |> xelems "country" do        ❶
            yield country |> xelem "name" |> xvalue };;           ❷
val regions : seq<string * string> = seq
  [ ("East Asia & Pacific";
    ("Europe & Central Asia";
    ("European Monetary Union";
    ("Heavily indebted poor countries (HIPC)"; ...]
```

The only important change from the previous listing is that we're now processing all the `country` nodes in the data. We access these elements as a sequence using the `xelems` function ❶, and iterate over them using a `for` loop. As we're using a sequence expression, we can generate result elements using the `yield` keyword. We use parts of the code that we tried in listing 13.9 to get the user-friendly name of the country, and return it as the element of the sequence ❷.

In this section, we've seen how to get a list of regions that we want to further study. The important aspect isn't the exact code we've used but the general process. We created helper functions to make data access easy, checked that we understood the document structure by fetching information interactively, and we wrapped the code inside a function. As a next step, we'll download the indicators that we want to show, such as the area occupied by forests.

13.3.3 *Obtaining the indicators*

To obtain the data about countries or regions, we'll use a different function of the World Bank service. The path to the function is `/countries/indicators` and you can find it in the Query Generator on the Data Calls tab. This allows us to request indicator data about a specific country for a given time period. Instead of downloading the data individually for each region that we're interested in, we'll fetch the information for all countries at once and process them in memory. Even though we'll download more data in this way, we'll use a smaller number of requests, because we won't have to create requests for every region.

We'll follow the same pattern as before; we'll start by downloading a sample portion of the data, then examine it using our XML querying functions. Listing 13.11 shows how to download indicators specifying the proportion of a country covered by forests as a percentage. The key for this indicator is AG.LND.FRST.ZS, which is best discovered by simulating the query in the Query Generator. We'll download the data for 1990 and request the first page of the data set.

Listing 13.11   Obtaining area covered by forests (F# Interactive)

```
> let ind = "AG.LND.FRST.ZS"        Specifies first page
  let date = "1990:1990"            of forest area data
  let page = 1                      from 1990
  let props =
   [ "countries", "indicators"; ind ]
   [ "date", date; "page", string(page) ];;
(...)

> let doc = Async.RunSynchronously(worldBankRequest(props))      ❶ Gets data,
  printfn "%s..." (doc.ToString().Substring(0, 301));;              prints preview
val doc : XDocument
<wb:data xmlns:wb="http://www.worldbank.org"
  page="1" pages="3" per_page="100" total="231">
 <wb:data>
  <wb:indicator id="AG.LND.FRST.ZS">Forest area (% ...</wb:indicator>
  <wb:country id="AW">Aruba</wb:country>
  <wb:value></wb:value>
  <wb:date>1990</wb:date>
 </wb:data>...

> doc |> xnested [ "data" ]          ❷ Reads number
     |> xattr "pages" |> int;;          of pages
val it : int = 3

> doc |> xnested [ "data"; "data"; "country" ]      ❸ Reads ID of
     |> xvalue;;                                        first country
val it : string = "Aruba"
```

Listing 13.11 first defines a couple of properties that we need to specify in order to create the request. It then creates a list with the properties that we need for the worldBankRequest function. After downloading the document, we want to explore its structure, so we convert it back into string and print the first few lines ❶. The output shows us that the total data set has three pages. Information for each country is nested in data elements, which contain the country name and ID, information about the data, and the actual value. The value is missing for the first country, so we'll have to be careful and handle this case when parsing the data.

Next we'll write two simple expressions that we'll need very soon. First we need to read the number of pages ❷ so that we can download all the data. The next expression ❸ reads the name of the first country. This will be needed later, because we'll want to match it with the name of the region that we collected in the previous section.

Now that we have a pretty good idea about the structure of the data, we can write a function to download everything we need. Listing 13.12 shows an asynchronous workflow which runs in a loop until it gets all the pages. We're not downloading pages in parallel, because that would be slightly harder to write, but we're going to run the same function in parallel for different indicators and years, so there will be enough parallelism in the end.

Listing 13.12 Downloading all indicator data asynchronously (F#)

```
let rec getIndicatorData(date, indicator, page) = async {
  let args = [ "countries"; "indicators"; ind ],
            [ "date", date; "page", string(page)]
  let! doc = worldBankRequest args

  let pages =
    doc |> xnested [ "data" ]              ① Gets number
        |> xattr "pages" |> int              of pages
  if (pages = page) then
    return [doc]            ← Returns
  else                    ② last page              ③ Downloads
    let page = page + 1                              remaining
    let! rest = getIndicatorData(date, indicator, page)  ←┘ pages
    return doc::rest }
```

The function takes the date, indicator, and the required page number as parameters. We use them to build the list of arguments for the `worldBankRequest` function. When we receive the XML, we read the attribute that specifies the total number of pages of the data set ①. If the page we're currently processing is the last one, we return a list containing only the current page ② as a single-element list. Otherwise, we need to download the remaining pages. Note that the function is declared with `let rec`, so we can invoke it recursively to get the remaining pages ③. This is done using `let!` because we're inside an asynchronous workflow. Once we get the list of remaining pages, we append the page we just downloaded and return all the pages as the result.

Before moving on, you can verify that this function works correctly using F# Interactive. Make a request for the indicator `AG.LND.FRST.ZS`, year range `1990:1990`, and page number `1`. When you run the workflow using `Async.RunSynchronously`, you should get three pages containing data about all the countries and regions.

Now let's introduce some parallelism, downloading all the indicators for all the years that we're interested in. We'll be using the `Async.Parallel` primitive, so we need to create a sequence of asynchronous workflows. The code in listing 13.13 does this using a simple sequence expression that calls the `getIndicatorData` function for all the combinations of parameters. Don't forget that calling `getIndicatorData` doesn't perform the fetch—it returns a workflow that *can* perform the fetch.

Listing 13.13 Downloading multiple indicators for multiple years in parallel (F#)

```
let downloadAll = seq {
  for ind in [ "AG.SRF.TOTL.K2"; "AG.LND.FRST.ZS" ] do
    for year in [ "1990:1990"; "2000:2000"; "2005:2005" ] do  ①
      yield getIndicatorData(year, ind, 1) }
let data = Async.RunSynchronously(Async.Parallel(downloadAll))  ②
```

The script first generates a workflow for each combination of indicator and a year we're interested in ❶. Then it combines all workflows into a single one running in parallel and runs it synchronously to download all the data ❷.

The sequence expression first iterates over two indicators. The first represents the total surface of the country or region in square kilometers, and the second is the percentage of forest area, as we've already seen. If you look at the data on the World Bank website, you can see that the forest area indicator is only available for three different years, so the nested loop iterates over these. For each combination of these parameters, we create (and yield) a workflow that runs the download starting from the first page.

This means that we'll get in total six tasks, each of which may download multiple pages. We combine the tasks into a workflow that returns an array of these six results and run the combined workflow using `Async.RunSynchronously`. The download can take some time, and you may see that some of the requests failed and were restarted, as we discussed earlier. The type of the `data` value that we get as a result is `array<list<XDocument>>`. The array contains a list of pages that were returned for each indicator-year combination.

Since we're writing an F# script, we don't have to worry about putting the settings such as years and indicators into a configuration file. We're writing the code only for a single purpose at the moment. We can modify it later to be generally useful, but that would happen later in development. Now that we've retrieved the data, we need to do something useful with it.

13.4   *Gathering information from the data*

The amount of data that we can download from the internet is enormous, but the difficult part is gathering useful information from it. So far in this chapter, we've downloaded a list of regions and converted it into a sequence containing the name of each region. Then we downloaded a bunch of XML documents that contain information about all regions and countries. In this section, we'll take this untyped XML data and convert it into a typed data structure that contains information we can easily display to the user.

13.4.1   *Reading values*

The first thing we need to do is to extract the data in which we're interested from the XML. We're going to write a function that takes a list of `XDocument` objects (one for each page of the data set) and returns a sequence where each element contains the value of the indicator, the name of the region, and the year in which the value was measured.

Listing 13.14 shows this in the form of the `readValues` function, as well as a helper function that reads data from an XML node representing a single record. Each function has a parameter named `parse`, which is a function used to parse the actual string value. We'll soon see the reason behind this parameter.

Listing 13.14 Reading values from the XML data (F#)

```
let readSingleValue parse node =
  let value = node |> xelem "value" |> xvalue
  let country = node |> xelem "country" |> xvlue
  let year = node |> xelem "date" |> xvalue |> int
  if (value = "") then []
  else [ (year, country), parse(value) ]

let readValues parse data = seq {
  for page in data do
    let root = page |> xnested [ "data" ]
    for node in root |> xelems "data" do
      yield! node |> readSingleValue parse }
```

❶ Returns list with zero or one elements

Finds all dataPoint elements for all pages

We start by writing the utility function that takes the formatting function and an XML node that contains a single data element. It reads values from child nodes and attributes, converting the year to an integer. If you look at the data we downloaded, you can see that the `value` element is sometimes empty. We handle this by returning an empty list if the value is missing and a list containing a single element otherwise. Note that we could have used an `option` type instead, but a list makes the second function more elegant: we don't have to distinguish between the two cases; we simply return all the elements (either none or one) using the `yield!` primitive.

The second function takes the entire input data as a sequence of XDocument objects. It finds all the XML elements containing data entries, formats them, and returns a sequence. The type of the element in the returned sequence is `(int * string) * 'a`. The first tuple contains the year and the name of the country. We'll use this as a key later on when searching for the data, which is why we're using a nested tuple. The second element is the value formatted using the `parse` function, so the type will be the same as whatever the function returns.

As usual, we can try the function immediately. The key input for the function is the data source, which is written as the last argument so we can use the pipelining operator. The simplest parser we can use (for test purposes) is one that returns whatever string it's given, without processing it. The following snippet shows how to process the first data set, which contains the total surface area of all the countries in the year 1990. We're parsing the input using identity function `id`, so the values will be formatted simply as strings:

```
> data.[0] |> readValues id;;
val it : seq<(int * string) * string> =
  seq [ ((1990, "ABW"), "180"); ((1990, "ADO"), "470");
        ((1990, "AFG"), "652090"); ((1990, "AGO"), "1246700");
        ...]
```

You can see we're getting closer to what we need: we can now read the data directly from the sequence. The only remaining irritation is that the values are clearly numbers, but we're treating them just as strings. Fortunately this is easy to fix.

13.4.2 *Formatting data using units of measure*

When reading the values of many of the indicators from the XML data, we *could* just convert them to `float` values. That would work, because both the surface area and forestation percentages are numbers, but it wouldn't tell us much about the data. The purpose of converting the data from untyped XML into a typed F# data structure is to annotate it with types that help us understand the meaning of the values. To make the type more specific, we can use units of measure, which we mentioned in chapter 2. Using this feature, we can specify that surface is measured in square kilometers and the area covered by forests in percentage of the total area. Let's start by looking at a couple of examples that introduce units of measure.

USING UNITS OF MEASURE

Working with units of measure in F# is very easy, which is why we've introduced them as a brief digression in this chapter. We can declare a measure using the `type` keyword with a special attribute. Strictly speaking, a measure isn't a type, but we can use it as part of another type. Let's start by defining two simple measures to represent hours and kilometers:

```
[<Measure>] type km
[<Measure>] type h
```

As you can see, we're using the `Measure` attribute to specify that the type is a measure. This is a special attribute that the F# compiler understands. Instead of defining units ourselves, we could also use the standard set in the FSharp.PowerPack.dll library, but for now we'll use our own declarations. Now that we have units `km` and `h`, we can create values that represent kilometers or hours. Listing 13.15 shows how to create values with units and how to write a function that calculates with them.

Listing 13.15   Writing calculations using units of measure (F#)

```
> let length = 9.0<km>;;            ❶
val length : float<km> = 9.0

> length * length;;                 ❷
val it : float<km^2> = 81.0

> let distanceInTwoHours(speed:float<km/h>) =    ❸
    speed * 2.0<h>;;
val distanceInTwoHours : float<km/h> -> float<km>    ❹

> distanceInTwoHours(30.0<km/h>);;
val it : float<km> = 60.0
```

When we want to specify units of a numeric constant, we append the unit in angle brackets to the value ❶. We started by defining a value that represents a length in kilometers. If we write a calculation using value with units, F# automatically infers the units of the result, so we can see that multiplying two distances gives us an area in square kilometers ❷. When specifying units, we can use the conventional notation, so `^` represents a power, `/` is used for division, and multiplication is written by juxtaposing the units.

The next example shows that we can write functions with parameters that include information about the units. Our sample function takes a speed and returns the distance traveled in two hours ❸. We want the parameter to be specified in kilometers per hour, so we add a type annotation that contains the unit. This is written by placing the unit in angle braces in the same way we do when specifying type arguments of a type such as list<int>. The F# compiler infers the return type for us ❹ just as it does when working with ordinary types. As usual, this provides a useful clue to understanding what a function does when you're reading it. It's also a valuable check to avoid making simple mistakes when writing the function—if we were trying to calculate a distance but ended up with a return type using a unit of time, we'd know something was wrong.

In our World Bank data, we'll use the unit km^2 to represent the total area of a country. So far, so good—but the second indicator that we obtained is provided as a percentage. How can we specify the unit of a percentage? Even though units of measure are primarily used to represent physical units, we can use them to represent percentages as well:

```
[<Measure>] type percent
let coef = 33.0<percent>
```

This code creates a unit for specifying that a number represents a percentage and then defines a constant coef, which has a value of 33 percent. Strictly speaking, the value in percents doesn't have a unit, because it's a coefficient, but defining it as a unit is quite useful. To demonstrate, let's try to calculate 33 percent of a 50 kilometer distance. Since coef represents a coefficient, we can simply multiply the two values:

```
> 50.0<km> * coef;;
val it : float<km percent> = 1650.0
```

This is obviously wrong. We want the result to be in kilometers, but if you look at the inferred type, you can see that the result is in kilometers multiplied by our new percent unit. Since we're running the code interactively, we can also see that the number is too high, but the great thing about units of measure is that we can spot the error during the type checking without actually running the program. So what went wrong? The problem is that a percentage value represents a coefficient multiplied by 100. To write the calculation correctly, we need to divide the value by 100 percent:

```
> 50.0<km> * coef / 100.0<percent>;;
val it : float<km> = 16.5
```

As you can see, this is much better. We divided the result by 100 percent, which means that we don't have the percent unit in the result. F# automatically simplifies the units, and it knows that km percent/percent is the same thing as km. This example demonstrates a significant reason for using units of measure: just like other types, they help us catch a large number of errors as early as possible.

NOTE   There are many other interesting aspects of units of measure that we haven't covered in this introduction. For example, you can define derived units such as N (representing a force in newtons), which is in fact just kg m/s^2. It's also possible to use units as generic type parameters in functions or types. For more information about units of measure, consult the F# online documentation and the blog of the feature's architect, Andrew Kennedy (http://blogs.msdn.com/andrewkennedy).

Let's get back to our main example and convert the data that we downloaded into a typed form that includes information about units. We'll use the percent atomic unit for representing the portion of the area covered by forests and the km^2 unit for representing the area.

FORMATTING THE WORLD BANK DATA

When we declared the readValues function to read the values from XML documents, we included a parsing function as the final parameter. This is used to convert each data point into a value of the appropriate type. The array we downloaded contains three data sets of surface areas in square kilometers and three data sets of the forest area percentages. Listing 13.16 shows how we can turn the raw documents into a data structure from which we can easily extract the important information.

Listing 13.16   Converting raw data into a typed data structure (F#)

```
let areas =
  Seq.concat(data.[0..2])                              ❶
    |> readValues (fun a -> float(a) * 1.0<km^2>)      ❷
    |> Map.ofSeq                                       ❸
let forests =
  Seq.concat(data.[3..5])
    |> readValues (fun a -> float(a) * 1.0<percent>)
    |> Map.ofSeq
```

The processing pipeline first concatenates data from all pages for the first indicator ❶, converts each value from string to a number in square kilometers ❷, then builds a map from the data ❸. The second command processing area covered by forests is similar.

The main part of the data processing is written using pipelining. It uses a new feature that we haven't yet introduced to get the first three elements from the data set. This is called *slicing*, and the syntax data.[0..2] gives us a sequence containing the array items with indices 0 to 2 ❶. We concatenate the returned sequence using Seq.concat, so we'll get a single sequence containing data for all the years. The next step in the pipeline is to read the values and convert them to the appropriate type using units of measure ❷. This turns out to be the easiest part—just a simple lambda expression! Note that the World Bank uses dot as a delimiter, so the number is, for example, 1.0. The built-in float function always uses the invariant culture, so it will parse the string correctly on any system.

We use the Map.ofSeq function to build an F# map type from the data ❸. This function takes a sequence containing tuples and uses the first element as a key and the second element as the value. In listing 13.16, the key has a type int * string and contains the year and the region name. The value in the first case has a type `float<km^2>` and in the second case `float<percent>`. We've converted the data into a map so that we can easily look up the indicators for different years and regions.

13.4.3 *Gathering statistics about regions*

Our goal is to show how the forested area has changed in different regions since 1990. We'll need to iterate over all the regions that we have, test whether the data is available, and find the value of the indicators we downloaded. This can be done quite easily using the maps we created, because they have the year and the region ID as the key.

We have to be careful because some data may be missing, so we'll filter out any region for which we don't have data for all the years we're interested in. Also, we want to display the total area of forests rather than the percentage, so we need a simple calculation before returning the data. Even though it may sound difficult, the code isn't very complicated. Listing 13.17 shows the final few commands that we need to enter to the F# Interactive to get the data we wanted to gather.

Listing 13.17 Calculating information about forested area (F# Interactive)

```
> let calculateForests(area:float<km^2>, forest:float<percent>) =      ◁───┐
    let forestArea = forest * area                          Calculates total
    forestArea / 100.0<percent>                               forest area    ❶
  ;;
val calculateForests : float<km ^ 2> * float<percent> -> float<km ^ 2>

> let years = [ 1990; 2000; 2005 ]
  let dataAvailable(key) =                    ◁───┐   Is the value available
    years |> Seq.forall (fun y ->                 ❷  for the specified key?
      (Map.contains (y, key) areas) &&
      (Map.contains (y, key) forests));;
val years : int list
val dataAvailable : string -> bool      ❸  Gets value
                                            for each year
> let getForestData(key) =                      ◁───┘
    [| for y in years do
        yield calculateForests(areas.[y, key], forests.[y, key]) |];;
val getForestData : string -> float<km ^ 2> array

> let stats = seq {                 ◁───┐   Finds available
    for name in regions do               ❹  data for all regions
        if dataAvailable(name) then
            yield name, getForestData(name) };;
val stats : seq<string * float<km ^ 2> array>
```

Listing 13.17 defines a couple of helper functions that work with the data we downloaded and defines a single value named `stats` that contains the final results. Thanks to units of measure, you can easily see what the first function ❶ does. It calculates the total area of forests in square kilometers from the total area of the region and the forested area in percentage.

The second function ❷ tests whether the data we need is available for the specified region ID for all the three years that we're interested in. It uses the function `Map.contains`, which tests whether an F# map (specified as the second argument) contains the key given as the first argument. The last utility function ❸ looks similar to the second one. It assumes that the data is available and extracts that data from the maps using the year and the region name as the key for all the monitored years. It then calculates the forest area from the raw data using the first function.

Equipped with the last two functions, we can collect statistics for all the regions ❹. The returned value is a sequence of tuples containing the title of the region as the first element and an array as the second element. The array will always have three elements with the values for the three years that we're monitoring.

Once we get the data into F# Interactive, we can make observations about it, but it's difficult to see any patterns by printing the data in the interactive window. To get the most from the data we gathered, we have to visualize them in a more user-friendly way, such as using Microsoft Excel.

13.5   *Visualizing data using Excel*

F# gives us an almost unlimited number of ways to visualize the data. We can use the standard .NET libraries such as Windows Forms or WPF to create the visualization ourselves, we can implement a sophisticated visualization using DirectX, or we can use one of the many existing libraries available for .NET. In this chapter, we'll use a slightly different approach, presenting the data using Excel. As you'll see, this is relatively easy to do, because Excel can be accessed using a .NET API. There are also many benefits to using Excel. Some operations are easier to do using a GUI, so once we obtain the data, we can perform the final processing in Excel. Also, Excel is used throughout the world, which makes it a useful distribution format.

NOTE   The .NET Framework 4.0 (a version that matches Visual Studio 2010) includes a new library for drawing charts that can be used in Windows Forms, server-side Web applications and also Silverlight. The library is fully managed, so it can be used directly from F# as any other .NET library. If you need to display charts in your standalone F# applications, this library is definitely worth a look; you'll find examples of its uses on this book's website. In this chapter we're focusing on the interactive and explorative approach, so we'll use Excel, which is a great tool for interactive programming.

The Excel API for .NET is exposed via the *Primary Interop Assemblies* (PIA) installed with Visual Studio 2008. They can be also obtained as a separate download, so if you run into any issues with them, you can find a link on the book's website. Let's take our first steps into the world of the Office API.

13.5.1   *Writing data to Excel*

The Excel interop assemblies are standard .NET assemblies that we can reference from F# Interactive using the #r directive. Once we do this, we can use the classes to run Excel as a standalone (visible or invisible) application and script it. Listing 13.18 shows how to start Excel, create a new workbook with a single worksheet, and write data to the worksheet.

Listing 13.18   Starting Excel and creating worksheet (F#)

```fsharp
#r "office.dll"
#r "Microsoft.Office.Interop.Excel.dll"
open System
open Microsoft.Office.Interop.Excel

let app = new ApplicationClass(Visible = true)                              ❶
let workbook = app.Workbooks.Add(XlWBATemplate.xlWBATWorksheet)            ❷
let worksheet = (workbook.Worksheets.[1] :?> _Worksheet)                   ❸

worksheet.Range("C2").Value2 <- "1990"
worksheet.Range("C2", "E2").Value2 <- [| "1990"; "2000"; "2005" |]         ❹
```

In listing 13.18, we create a new instance of the `ApplicationClass` ❶. This type comes
from the Excel namespace and represents the application. After you run this line, a new
Excel window should appear. The next line ❷ creates a workbook, so after running it,
you should see the usual Excel grid. Next we fetch an object that represents the first
sheet from the workbook (sheets are displayed at the bottom left of the application). As
you can see, we need to cast the object to a `Worksheet` class ❸, because the Excel API
is weakly typed in many places. Once we get the worksheet, we can start writing data to
the grid. This can be done using the `Range` indexer and the `Value2` property ❹. The type

of this property is `object`, so we can use
it in various ways. The first example
writes a single string value to a single column, and the second one fills a range (a
single row containing three columns)
with values from a .NET array. You can
see the Excel worksheet created by running the code in figure 13.1.

So far we've created headers for the
table we want to display, so the next step
is to fill in all the remaining informa-

**Figure 13.1   An Excel application started from an
F# Interactive with programmatically entered data.**

tion and, most importantly, the matrix containing the forested area in different years.
Listing 13.19 converts the data into a two-dimensional array, which is also a valid data
source for the `Value2` property.

Listing 13.19   Exporting data to Excel worksheet (F#)

```fsharp
let statsArray = stats |> Array.ofSeq
let names = Array2D.init statsArray.Length 1 (fun index _ ->          ❶
  let name, _ = statsArray.[index]
  name )

let dataArray = Array2D.init statsArray.Length 3 (fun index year ->
  let _, values = statsArray.[index]
  let yearValue = values.[year]
  yearValue / 1000000.0 )

let endColumn = string(statsArray.Length + 2)
```

❶ Gets names of regions as 2D array

◁— Displays millions of square kilometers

```
worksheet.Range("B3", "B" + endColumn).Value2 <- namesVert
worksheet.Range("C3", "E" + endColumn).Value2 <- tableArr
```
Writes data to worksheet

When writing data to Excel worksheets, we can use a primitive value, an array, or a two-dimensional array. One-dimensional arrays can be used for writing rows of data, as we saw in the first example, but if we want to fill a matrix or a column with data, we have to use a 2D array. In listing 13.19, we start by creating a 2D array that stores the names of the regions vertically. To do this, we create a simple array containing the names and then use the `Array2D.init` function to convert it to a 2D array ❶. The init function takes width and height of the array as the first two arguments, followed by a function that's run to generate a value for every coordinate. The resulting array contains only a single column, so we can ignore the second coordinate in the initialization.

The next step is to generate a 2D array with the data about the regions. We convert the input sequence into an array, so that we can index it when generating the 2D array using the `Array2D.init` function again. In the lambda function, which is executed for every array cell, we first get the information about the region, then find the value for the specified year and divide it by 1 million to display the output in a more readable form. Finally, we calculate the right ranges in the Excel worksheet (depending on the number of regions) and set the data using the same approach as in the previous example.

After running the code, the data should appear in Excel. We can work with it at the same time as we execute our F# script, so if you tweak the design of the table we just generated, you'll see something similar to figure 13.2.

Understanding the data is much easier now that we have it in Excel. We can take one additional step and create a chart with the data. You could do this by hand, but generating a complete Excel file that includes a chart is quite easy in F#.

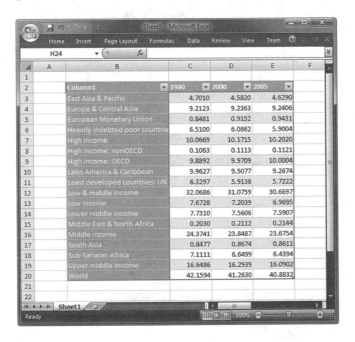

Figure 13.2   An Excel table generated by our F# script showing the changes in the area covered by forests in regions all over the world during the last 20 years.

13.5.2 *Displaying data in an Excel chart*

To create a chart, we need to specify quite a few properties. Fortunately the Excel API provides the `ChartWizard` method to make it easier. This method takes all the important attributes of the chart as optional parameters, so we can specify only those we need. The F# language supports optional parameters, so the code in listing 13.20 that creates the chart is very straightforward.

Listing 13.20 Generating Excel chart (F#)

```
let chartobjects = (worksheet.ChartObjects() :?> ChartObjects)
let chartobject = chartobjects.Add(400.0, 20.0, 550.0, 350.0)

chartobject.Chart.ChartWizard
  (Title = "Area covered by forests",
   Source = worksheet.Range("B2", "E" + endColumn),
   Gallery = XlChartType.xl3DColumn,
   PlotBy = XlRowCol.xlColumns,
   SeriesLabels = 1, CategoryLabels = 1,
   CategoryTitle = "", ValueTitle = "Forests (mil km^2)")
chartobject.Chart.ChartStyle <- 5
```

❶ Configures chart using wizard

❷ Uses predefined graphical style

First we need to create a new chart in the worksheet. We do this by adding a new element to the collection of charts. Again the weakly typed API means we have to cast it to the appropriate type (`ChartObjects`) before we can call the `Add` method. This method gives us a new chart that we can configure using the `ChartWizard` method ❶. We mentioned that the method takes optional parameters, so the code uses the F# syntax to specify them. For each parameter that we want to set, we include the name of the parameter and the value. Most of the parameter names are self-explanatory, but it's worth noting that we specify the range including the text labels and then set `Series-Labels` and `CategoryLabels` to 1, which tells Excel that the first row and column contain data labels.

The last line sets a `ChartStyle` property to specify the predefined green color scheme of the chart ❷. Note that this property is available only in Office 2007, so if you're using an older version of Excel, you'll have to remove this line and Excel will use the default colors. After you run the code, you should see a chart like the one in figure 13.3.

The chart in Excel gives us a perfect way to understand and examine the data that we obtained from the World Bank. If you look at the chart carefully, you can see that the area covered by forests is very slightly increasing in Europe and Central Asia and high-income countries, but decreasing more significantly almost everywhere else in the world.

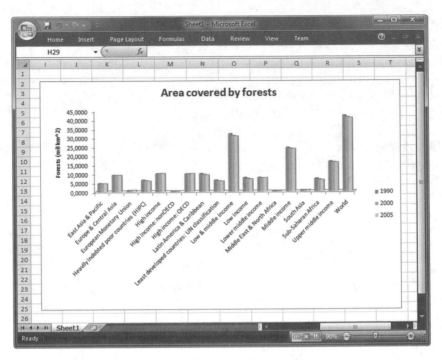

Figure 13.3   A chart generated from F# showing the changes in the forested area

13.6   *Summary*

The "big picture" of this chapter was to demonstrate a typical lifecycle of *explorative programming* in F#. We also introduced some F# language and library features that are very important in other development processes.

We started by obtaining data from the web. To do this, we used asynchronous workflows, an F# computation expression implemented in the standard F# library. Asynchronous workflows can be used for efficiently implementing I/O and other time-consuming operations without blocking the caller thread and wasting resources. Once we downloaded the data, we used the LINQ to XML library to explore its structure before parsing it and converting it into a typed F# representation. All of this was done in an interactive fashion, often alternating between writing a couple of lines of code to try something with one piece of data, and then writing a function to apply the same logic to all the information we'd downloaded.

We used many advanced features such as sequence expressions when processing collections, and we also used units of measure to specify the precise nature of the data. Finally, we looked at how to control Excel from the F# Interactive shell. This shows a general principle that can be used when working with any Office application or with other applications that expose COM interfaces.

We'll return to F# asynchronous workflows when we talk about reactive programming in chapter 16. The next chapter is on closely related topic, and for many people it's the most convincing reason for considering functional programming. We're going to look at parallelizing functional programs to get the most out of multicore processors.

Writing parallel functional programs

We've already seen many arguments in favor of functional programming. One reason it's becoming increasingly important these days is parallelism. Writing code that scales to a large number of cores is much easier in the functional style compared to using the typical imperative approach.

The two concepts from the functional world that are essential for parallel computing are the declarative programming style and working with immutable data structures. These two are closely related. The code becomes more declarative when using immutable data, because the code is more concerned with the expected result of the computation than with the details of copying and changing data. Both concepts are important in different ways when it comes to parallelization.

The declarative style allows most code that works with collections to be parallelized very simply, because the declarative style doesn't specify how the code runs. This means that we can replace the sequential implementation by a parallel implementation with minimal effort. Immutable data structures and side effect-free functions are important, because when code doesn't contain side effects, we can easily identify which pieces of code don't depend on each other. Once we do that, we can use task-based parallelism to run the pieces in parallel. Both C# and F# allow us to use mutable data types as well. In chapter 10, you learned that we can hide this mutable state and make the overall program functional. In some cases, such as when processing an array in some way, these hidden imperative islands of code can be easily parallelized too.

As you can see, there's a lot to explore. We'll begin with a brief overview to demonstrate all these techniques and explain when each is useful. After this introduction, we'll look at two more complex sample applications that show how parallel functional programming works on a larger scale. There isn't room to show all the code for two complete real-world examples in a single chapter, so we'll omit some of the less interesting details in the book. We'll focus particularly on the architectural aspects and areas directly related to parallelism. You can obtain the complete source code, which fills in the missing pieces, from the book's website.

14.1 *Understanding different parallelization techniques*

In this section, we'll look at three techniques and use a simple example to demonstrate each. We're going to use Parallel Extensions to .NET, which is a library for parallel programming. It's part of the standard .NET Framework 4.0, but unfortunately isn't available for earlier versions of .NET. If you want to experiment with Parallel Extensions using Visual Studio 2008, you can still download a CTP version, but there are a few naming changes.

Parallel Extensions to .NET

The library consists of two key parts that we're going to use in this chapter.

- Task Parallel Library (TPL) includes underlying constructs that can execute *tasks* (primitive units of work) in parallel. Another component of TPL allows creating of tasks for common computations such as `for` loops.
- Parallel LINQ (PLINQ), which can be used for writing *data parallel* code. This is code that processes a large amount of data using the same algorithm.

The underlying technology used to execute tasks in parallel is implemented in fully managed code and uses advanced techniques originating from Microsoft Research (MSR). It uses dynamic work distribution, which means that tasks are divided between worker threads depending on the availability of the threads. Once a thread completes all its own assigned tasks, it can start "stealing" tasks from other threads, so the work will be evenly distributed among all the available processors or cores. The tasks are stored in queues for each worker thread, which also minimizes the needed synchronization and locking in the implementation.

Let's start with a specific technique we mentioned in the introduction: parallelizing imperative code that works with arrays. This isn't relevant for pure functional languages that don't allow any side effects, but as we saw in chapter 10, working with arrays in a functional style is a useful technique in C# and F#.

14.1.1 *Parallelizing islands of imperative code*

The most common construct in imperative programming that can easily be parallelized is the for loop. When the iterations of the loop are independent, we can execute them on separate threads. By *independent*, we mean that no iteration can rely on a value computed by any earlier iterations.

For example, when summing the elements in an array, we need the sum of all the previous elements to calculate the next one. (This can be still parallelized, but not quite so simply.) Recall the function for "blurring" an array, which we implemented in chapter 10. This is a good candidate for parallelization: even though each iteration uses multiple elements from the *input* array, it doesn't rely on anything in the *output* array. Listing 14.1 shows a simple for loop based on the earlier example, in both C# and F#.

Listing 14.1   for loop for calculating blurred array (C# and F#)

C#	F#
```for(int i=1; i<inp.Length-1; i++){ var sum = inp[i-1] + inp[i] + inp[i+1]; res[i] = sum / 3;}```	```for i in 1 .. inp.Length - 2 do let sum = inp.[i-1] + inp.[i] + inp.[i+1] res.[i] <- sum / 3```

Even though it is imperative code, it can still be part of a pure functional program. The inp array is an input that isn't modified anywhere in our code and res is the output array, which shouldn't be modified after it's calculated by the loop.

To parallelize the loop, we can use the Parallel.For method. The class is available only on .NET 4.0 and lives in the System.Threading.Tasks namespace. The Parallel. For method takes an Action<int> delegate argument, which we can supply using a lambda function. Using the method directly in F# feels a bit heavyweight, so we'll define a simple function that makes the code more succinct:

```
let pfor nfrom nto f =
  Parallel.For(nfrom, nto + 1, Action<_>(f)) |> ignore
```

This code wraps the function f (which has a type int -> unit) in a delegate type and runs the parallel for loop. The method returns information on whether the loop completed successfully, which we don't need, so we ignore it. Note that we also add 1 to the upper bound, because the upper bound is inclusive in the F# for loop but exclusive in C# for loops and the Parallel.For method. Listing 14.2 shows the parallelized versions of the previous example.

Listing 14.2 Parallelized for loop (C# and F#)	
C#	F#

``
Parallel.For(1,inp.Length-1,i => {
    var sum = inp[i-1] +
        inp[i] + inp[i+1];
    res[i] = sum / 3;
});
``
	``
	pfor 1 (inp.Length-2) (fun i ->
	    let sum = inp.[i-1] +
	                inp.[i] + inp.[i+1]
	    res.[i] <- sum / 3
	)
	``

As you can see, this is nearly as simple as the original sequential version. Again, this shows the power of functional constructs: thanks to lambda functions, the only thing you have to do when you want to convert a sequential for loop into a parallel one is to use the Parallel.For method (or pfor function in F#) instead of the built-in language construct.

NOTE Aside from the For method, the Parallel class also contains ForEach, which can be used to parallelize the foreach construct in C# or the for ... in ... do construct in F#. Both methods have overloads available to let you customize the iteration. There are overloads allowing you to change the step used to increment the index in the For method, or stop the parallel execution (similar to break in a C# loop). If you ever feel you need a little more control, consult the documentation to see if one of these overloads can help you.

The Parallel.For method is particularly useful when working with arrays and other imperative data structures. We'll use it in one of the larger sample applications later in this chapter (section 14.2.5), where we'll once again work with arrays in a functional way. First, let's finish our overview. The other two techniques we'll look at are purely functional.

14.1.2 *Declarative data parallelism*

The key idea behind the declarative style of programming is that the code doesn't specify how it should be executed. Execution is provided by a minimal number of primitives such as select and where in LINQ or map and filter in F#, and these primitives can behave in a sophisticated way.

In chapter 1, we demonstrated how you can change an ordinary LINQ query into a query that runs in parallel using PLINQ. We showed this using C# query expressions, but to understand how it works, it's better to examine the translated version using method calls and lambda functions. We'll use a trivial example here, but we'll look at something more complicated later. Listing 14.3 counts the number of primes between 1 million and 2 million. It shows the C# code using method calls, and also an F# version.

Listing 14.3 Counting the number of primes (C# and F#)

C#	F#
```bool IsPrime(int n) { if (n <= 1) return false; int top = (int)Math.Sqrt(n); for (int i = 2; i <= top; i++) if (n%i == 0) return false; return true; }```	```let isPrime(n) = let top = int(sqrt(float(n))) let rec isPrimeUtil(i) = if i > top then true elif n % i = 0 then false else isPrimeUtil(i + 1) (n > 1) && isPrimeUtil(2)```

```
// Count the primes (C# version)
var nums = Enumerable.Range(1000000, 2000000);
var primeCount = nums.Where(IsPrime).Count();        ❶

// Count the primes (F# version)
let nums = [1000000 .. 3000000]
let primeCount = nums |> List.filter isPrime |> List.length        ❷
```

The listing starts with typical imperative and functional solutions for testing whether a number is a prime. We implemented them differently in order to use the most idiomatic code for each language. As you surely know already, a number is prime if it can be divided without a remainder only by 1 and itself. We test divisibility only by numbers from 2 to square root of the given number, because this is sufficient.

In C#, the code is implemented using an imperative `for` loop. In F#, we use a recursive function; thanks to tail recursion, this is an efficient implementation. Also note that the F# version is using a keyword that we haven't seen so far: the `elif` keyword, which is simply a shortcut for `else` followed by another `if` expression.

The second part of the listing is more interesting. To count the number of primes in the given range, we select only numbers that are primes and then count them. In C# ❶, we generate a range of integers (`nums`) of type `IEnumerable<int>`. LINQ provides extension methods `Where` and `Count` for this type, so we use these to calculate the result. In F# ❷, we specify the functions explicitly. We're working with a list, so we implemented the code using functions from the `List` module.

Now let's modify the code to run in parallel. In C# this means adding a call to the `AsParallel` extension method. In F#, we could access LINQ methods directly, but a more idiomatic way is to use the pipelining operator. To do this, we'll use a few functions that wrap calls to the .NET PLINQ classes similarly to the `pfor` function from the previous section. These functions are available in a module called `PSeq`.

Getting parallel extensions for F#

Before we'll continue, you'll need to obtain a file with a couple of extensions that make parallel programming in F# easy. The file contains `PSeq` module with a collection of simple wrappers and also `pseq` computation builder that we'll use shortly. A file like this may eventually become part of the F# library or F# PowerPack, so we won't show how to implement it.

(continued)

For now, you can download functions that we'll need from the book's website. To reference the file from the F# script, you can use the `#load` directive and specify the path of the fs file.

Listing 14.4 shows the parallelized queries in both C# and F#. The "prime testing" function hasn't been repeated, as it doesn't need to change.

Listing 14.4   Counting primes in parallel (C# and F#)

C#	F#

`var primeCount =`
`  nums.AsParallel()`
`      .Where(IsPrime)`
`      .Count();`
	`let primeCount =`
	`  nums |> PSeq.ofSeq`
	`       |> PSeq.filter isPrime`
	`       |> PSeq.length`

The F# sample is consistent with all other collection processing examples we've seen already. Functions for parallel data processing follow the same pattern as functions for working with lists and arrays. This means that we first have to convert the data to a parallel data structure using `PSeq.ofSeq` (which is just like `Array.ofSeq`), and then we can use various processing functions. The parallel data structure is another type of sequence, so if we needed to, we could convert it to a functional list using the `List.ofSeq` function.

The C# version requires more careful examination—ironically, because it's changed less than the F# version. In chapter 12 we saw how to implement custom LINQ query operators, and PLINQ uses a similar technique. The return type of the `AsParallel` method is `ParallelQuery<T>`. When the C# compiler searches for an appropriate `Where` method to call, it finds an extension method called `Where` that takes `ParallelQuery<T>` as its first argument, and it prefers this one to the more general method that takes `IEnumerable<T>`. The parallel `Where` method returns `ParallelQuery<T>` again, so the whole chain uses the methods provided by PLINQ.

Measuring the speedup in F# Interactive

In chapter 10 we measured performance when discussing functions for working with lists. To quickly compare the parallel and sequential version of our samples, we can use F# Interactive and the `#time` directive. Once we turn timing on, we can select one of the versions and run it by pressing Alt+Enter:

```
> #time;;
> nums |> List.filter isPrime |> List.length;;        ⟵  Uses List module
Real: 00:00:01.606, CPU: 00:00:01.606                     functions
val it : int = 70501

> nums |> PSeq.ofSeq |> PSeq.filter isPrime            Uses PSeq
      |> PSeq.length;;                                  module functions
val it : int = 70501
Real: 00:00:00.875, CPU: 00:00:01.700
```

> **(continued)**
>
> The `Real` time is the elapsed time of the operation, and as you can see, running the operation in parallel gives us a speedup of about 180 to 185 percent on a dual-core machine. This is impressive when you bear in mind that the maximum theoretical speedup is 200 percent (on a dual-core machine we've used for testing), but of course, we've been testing it using only a toy example. The CPU time shows the total time spent executing the operation on all cores, which is why it's higher than the actual time in the second case.
>
> Unfortunately, measuring the performance in C# isn't as easy, because we can't use any interactive tools. We'll write some utility functions to measure performance of the compiled code later in this chapter.

The last topic we'll look at in this introduction to declarative data parallelism is how to simplify the F# syntax. In chapter 12, we learned how to write sequence expressions to perform computations with numeric collections. Creating a computation expression to work with sequences in parallel is the natural next step.

PARALLEL SEQUENCE EXPRESSIONS IN F#

The nice thing about the C# version of the code was that switching between the sequential and parallel versions was a matter of adding or removing the `AsParallel` call. In the F# example, we explicitly used functions like `List.xyz` or `PSeq.xyz`, so the transition was less smooth.

If we rewrite the code using sequence expressions, we can parallelize a large part of the code by touching the keyboard only once. You can see both of the versions in listing 14.5.

Listing 14.5   Parallelizing sequence expressions (F#)

```fsharp
// Sequence expression          // Parallel sequence expression
seq {                           pseq {
   for n in nums do                for n in nums do
      if (isPrime n) then             if (isPrime n) then
         yield n }                       yield n }
   |> Seq.length                   |> PSeq.length
```

The parallel sequence expression is denoted by the `pseq` value, which is available in the F# parallel extensions file. It changes the meaning of the `for` operation inside the expression from a sequential version to a parallel one. The syntax is more flexible than C# query expressions, because you can return multiple values using the `yield` and `yield!` keywords, but the performance may be slightly lower. The reason is that the F# compiler treats the expression differently than the C# compiler. Parallel sequence expressions are implemented using computation expressions, and as you learned in chapter 12, the translation of sequence processing code relies on a single primitive that corresponds to a `for` loop in general. This tells the framework less information about the algorithm than when we explicitly use `PSeq.filter` and `PSeq.map`, so it can't be as clever when parallelizing the code. Interestingly, implementing the `pseq` construct for F# is easier than you might think.

PARALLELISM USING LINQ AND COMPUTATION EXPRESSIONS

In chapter 12 we implemented our own set of LINQ operators and learned how to write computation expressions in F#. These two concepts are based on the same principles: we implemented a set of basic operators and the LINQ query or F# computation expression is then executed using these operators.

The PLINQ library implements virtually all operators supported by the C# query syntax, including Select, SelectMany, Where, OrderBy, and many others. So, what members have to be implemented in the pseq expression?

In chapter 12, we saw a couple of primitives that we can provide when implementing computation expression, most importantly the Bind member, which corresponds to let! and the Return member that's used when we write return. We also talked about sequence expressions and the for construct. We've seen that a sequence expression that includes for can be translated into a call to the flattening projection operation. If we want to support for inside computation expressions, we can implement a member named For. The implementation for parallel sequence expression can use the SelectMany operator from the Parallel LINQ library, because this operator implements a flattening projection in LINQ.

There are other primitives that we haven't seen and that we'll need to use when implementing parallel sequence expressions, but they are quite simple. First of all, we'll need to support yield, which generates a value. This can be done by adding Yield, which will return a sequence containing the single element that it gets as an argument. Since you can have multiple yields in the expression, we'll also need the Combine member, which will take two sequences and concatenate them into one. Finally, the Zero member (which allows us to write an if condition without an else branch) will return an empty sequence. For detailed information about the F# implementation of the pseq computation expression, read more on the book's website.

Parallelizing declarative code that works with large amounts of data is perhaps the most appealing aspect of functional programming, because it's very easy and gives great results for large data sets. However, often we need to parallelize more complicated computations. In functional programming, these would be often written using immutable data structures and recursion, so we'll look at a more general technique in the next section.

14.1.3 *Task-based parallelism*

In chapter 11 we saw that you can easily track dependencies between function calls in a functional program. The only thing that a function or a block of code can do is take values as arguments and produce a result. If we want to find out whether one call depends on some other call, we can check whether it uses the output of the first call as part of its input. This is possible thanks to the use of immutable data structures. If the first call could modify shared state and the second call relied on this change, we couldn't change the order of these calls, even though this wouldn't be obvious in the calling code. The fact that we can see dependencies between blocks of code is vital for *task-based parallelism.* We've seen data-based parallelism, which performs the same task on different inputs in parallel; task-based parallelism performs (possibly different) tasks concurrently.

Listing 14.6 shows an F# script that recursively processes an immutable data structure. We'll look at a simple example here but show a more complicated scenario in section 14.3.5. The code uses the binary tree type we designed in chapter 10 and implements a function to count the prime numbers in the tree. This isn't the most typical example for task-based parallelism, because we'll be creating two similar tasks, but it nicely introduces the technique that we can use.

Listing 14.6   Counting primes in a binary tree (F# Interactive)

```
> type IntTree =                              Represents
    | Leaf of int                             binary tree
    | Node of IntTree * IntTree;;
type IntTree = (...)

> let rnd = new Random()
  let rec tree(depth) =                        ❶
    if depth = 0 then Leaf(rnd.Next())
    else Node(tree(depth - 1), tree(depth - 1));;
val rnd : Random
val tree : int -> IntTree

> let rec count(tree) =            ❷
    match tree with
    | Leaf(n) when isPrime(n) -> 1
    | Leaf(_) -> 0
    | Node(left, right) -> count(left) + count(right);;
val count : IntTree -> int
```

Listing 14.6 starts by declaring a binary tree data structure that can store values of type int. Then we implement a function ❶ that generates a tree containing randomly generated numbers. The function is recursive and takes the required depth of the tree as an argument. When we generate a node that's composed of two subtrees, the function recursively generates subtrees with a depth decremented by 1.

We implement a count function ❷ which uses pattern matching to handle three cases:

- For a leaf node with a prime value, it returns 1.
- For a leaf node with a nonprime value, it returns 0.
- For a node with two subtrees, it recursively counts the primes in these subtrees.

Note that the tasks of counting primes in the left and the right subtree are independent. In the next section, we'll see how to run these calls in parallel.

TASK-BASED PARALLELISM IN F#

In the previous section, we were using the PLINQ component from the Parallel Extensions to .NET. To implement task-based parallelism, we'll use classes from the TPL. This is a lower-level library that allows us to create tasks that will be executed in parallel by the .NET runtime. In this section, we'll work with a generic class, `Task<T>`.

As you'll see, working with this class in F# is quite easy. When creating tasks, we use the `TaskFactory<T>` class, which has a method called `StartNew`; to get the instance of the factory, we can use the static property `Task.Factory`. Now, let's look how we can use tasks to parallelize the `count` function from listing 14.6. The most interesting part of listing 14.7 is the case when a tree is a node with two subtrees that can be processed recursively.

Listing 14.7   Parallel processing of a binary tree (F#)

```
let pcount(tree) =
  let rec pcountDepth(tree, depth) =        ❶
    match tree with
    | _ when depth >= 5 -> count(tree)      ❷
    | Leaf(n) when isPrime(n) -> 1
    | Leaf(_) -> 0
    | Node(left, right) ->
      let countLeft = Task.Factory.StartNew(fun() ->
        pcountDepth(left, depth + 1))       ❸
      let countRight = pcountDepth(right, depth + 1)   ❹
      countLeft.Result + countRight         ❺
  pcountDepth(tree, 0)
```

We need to store an additional argument during the recursion, so we've created a local function called `pcountDepth` ❶. The additional argument (named `depth`) specifies the depth within the tree that we're currently processing. This allows us to use the nonparallel version of the function (`count`) after we've created a number of tasks that run in parallel. If we created a separate task for every tree node, the overhead of creating new tasks would exceed the benefit we get from running the computations in parallel. Creating thousands of tasks on a dual-core machine isn't a good idea. The overhead isn't as bad as creating an extra thread for each task, but it's still nonzero.

The `depth` argument is increased in every recursive call. Once it exceeds a threshold, we process the rest of the tree using the sequential algorithm. In listing 14.7, we test this with pattern matching ❷ and the threshold is set to 5 (which means that we'll create roughly 31 tasks).

When we process a nonleaf tree node, we create a value of type `Task<int>` and give it a function that processes the left subtree ❸. The `Task` type represents a computation that will start executing in parallel when it's created and will give us a result when we need it at some point in the future. It's worth noting that we don't create a task for the other subtree ❹. If we did that, the caller thread would have to wait to collect both results and wouldn't do any useful work. Instead we immediately start recursively processing the second subtree. Once we finish the recursive call, we need to sum the values from both subtrees. To get the value computed by the task, we can use the `Result` property ❺. If the task hasn't completed, the call will block until the value is available. The execution pattern can be tricky to understand, but figure 14.1 shows it in a graphical way.

Just like with the data parallelization example in section 14.1.2, we're interested in the performance gains we get from the parallelization of tasks. Again we can measure the speedup easily using #time in F# Interactive:

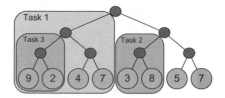

```
> let t = tree(16);;
> count(t);;
Real: 00:00:00.591, CPU: 00:00:00.561

> pcount(t);;
Real: 00:00:00.386, CPU: 00:00:00.592
```

Figure 14.1 In the root node, we create `Task 1` to process the left subtree and immediately start processing the right subtree. This is repeated for both subtrees, and two more tasks are created.

As you can see, the statistics look good. Like our previous example, the speedup is between 180 and 185 percent. One of the reasons we get such good results is that the tree was balanced; it had the same depth for all leaf nodes. If we didn't know in advance whether that was the case, it would have been wise to generate more tasks to make sure that the work would be evenly distributed among processors. In our example, we'd do that by increasing the threshold.

So far we've only shown code for task-based parallelism in F#, because implementing the binary tree is easier in F#, but of course it's feasible in C# too. Rather than showing all of the code here, we'll look at the key parts of the C# version. The full code is available on the book's website.

TASK-BASED PARALLELISM IN C#

In C#, we'll first need to implement classes that represent the binary tree. We've implemented an `IntTree` class with two methods that allow us to test whether the tree is a leaf or a node:

```
bool TryLeaf(out int value);
bool TryNode(out IntTree left, out IntTree right);
```

These methods return `true` if the tree is a leaf or a node, respectively. In that case, the method also returns details about the leaf or the node using `out` parameters. Listing 14.8 shows how to implement sequential and parallel versions of the tree-processing code in C#.

Listing 14.8 Sequential and parallel tree processing using tasks (C#)

```
static int Count(IntTree tree) {      ⏴── Sequential version
  int value;
  IntTree left, right;

  if (tree.TryLeaf(out value)) return IsPrime(value) ? 1 : 0;      ❶
  else if (tree.TryNode(out left, out right)
    return Count(left) + Count(right);      ❷
  throw new Exception();
}
                                                  ❸ Parallel
static int CountParallel(IntTree tree, int depth) {   ⏴─┘  version
  int value;
  IntTree left, right;
```

```
    if (depth >=5) return Count(tree);                              ④
    if (tree.TryLeaf(out value)) return IsPrime(value) ? 1 : 0;
    else if (tree.TryNode(out left, out right)) {
      var countLeft = Task.Factory.StartNew(() =>        ⑤
        CountParallel(left, depth + 1));
      var countRight = CountParallel(right, depth + 1);      ⑥
      return countLeft.Result + countRight;              ⑦
    }
    throw new Exception();
}
```

For a node, the sequential version recursively processes the left and the right subtree ❷. When processing a leaf, it tests whether the number is prime and returns 1 or 0 ❶. The tree is always a node or a leaf, so the last line of the method should never be reached.

In the parallel version, we have an additional argument that represents the depth ❸. When the depth exceeds the threshold, we calculate the result using the sequential Count method ❹.

When processing the node in parallel, we create a task to process the left subtree ❺ and process the right subtree immediately ❻. The program waits for both operations to finish and adds the results ❼.

This is almost a literal translation of the F# code. The `Task<T>` type from the `System.Threading.Tasks` namespace can be used from both F# and C# in a similar fashion. The only important thing is that the computation that's performed by the task shouldn't have (or rely on) any side effects. The `Task<T>` type is surprisingly similar to the `Lazy<T>` type that we implemented in chapter 11.

Tasks and lazy values

When we discussed lazy values in chapter 11, we highlighted the fact that we can use them when we don't need to specify when the value should be executed. This is the case for tasks as well. Both evaluate the function exactly once. A lazy value evaluates the result when it's needed for the first time, whereas a future value performs the computation when a worker thread becomes available.

Another way to see the similarity between `Task<T>` and `Lazy<T>` is to look at the operations that we can do with them. When constructing a task or lazy value, we create them from a function that calculates the value. The F# type signature for this would be `(unit -> 'a) -> T<'a>`, where `T` is either `Lazy` or `Task`. The second operation is to access the value. This simply takes a lazy or future value and gives us the result of the computation, so the type signature is `T<'a> -> 'a`.

In this section, we looked at the last of the three techniques for parallelizing functional programs that we're discussing in this chapter. Task-based parallelism is particularly useful when we're recursively processing large immutable data structures. This kind of computation is common in functional programming, so task-based parallelism is a great addition to our toolset, along with declarative data processing.

Now we're going to return in more depth to our first topic: parallelizing imperative code that's hidden from the outside world to keep the program functional. We'll demonstrate this using a larger application that applies graphical filters to images.

14.2 *Running graphical effects in parallel*

To demonstrate the first technique, we'll develop an application that needs to process large arrays in parallel. One of the simplest examples of large arrays is image data represented as a two-dimensional array of colors. We used the same example in chapter 8 when we discussed behavior-centric applications, but this time we'll be focusing on different aspects.

The user will be able to open an image, select one of the filters from a list, and apply it to the image. First we'll develop a few filters, then work out how to run a single effect on different parts of the image in parallel.

14.2.1 *Calculating with colors in F#*

To implement graphical effects such as blurring or grayscaling, we need to perform calculations with colors. We can do this by working with the standard `Color` type in `System.Drawing`, but we'd have to treat the red, green, and blue components separately, which isn't always convenient.

There's a more natural way to perform these calculations in both F# and C#. We can use operator overloading and implement our own color type. When we blur the image later, we'll be able to simply add colors together and divide the resulting color by the number of pixels. You probably already know how to do this in C#, but you can find an implementation in the downloadable source code at the book's website. Listing 14.9 shows the F# version.

> **Listing 14.9   Implementing color type with operators (F#)**

```
[<Struct>]                                              ❶
type SimpleColor(r:int, g:int, b:int) =
  member x.R = r
  member x.G = g
  member x.B = b
  member x.ClipColor() =                                ❷
    let check(c) = min 255 (max 0 c)
    SimpleColor(check(r), check(g), check(b))
  static member (+) (c1:SimpleColor, c2:SimpleColor) =  ❸
    SimpleColor(c1.R + c2.R, c1.G + c2.G, c1.B + c2.B)
  static member (*) (c1:SimpleColor, n) =               ❹
    SimpleColor(c1.R * n, c1.G * n, c1.B * n)
  static member DivideByInt (c1:SimpleColor, n) =       ❺
    SimpleColor(c1.R / n, c1.G / n, c1.B / n)
  static member Zero = SimpleColor(0, 0, 0)             ❻
```

The type is annotated using a .NET attribute named `Struct` ❶. This is a special attribute that instructs the F# compiler to compile the type as a value type; it corresponds to the C# `struct` keyword. In this example, it's important to use the value type, because we'll create an array of these values and allocating a new object on the heap for every pixel would be extremely inefficient.

The type provides a constructor that takes red, green and blue components of the color and exposes them via members. Note that when declaring value types, we have to explicitly provide types of all parameters. The parameters specify fields of the type and define the structure of value types, so it is useful to see them. The type then provides a member that clips the values of components if they are less than 0 or exceed 255 ❷. This can be used for creating valid color values with all components in range 0-255. Next, the type provides overloaded operators for component-wise addition of colors ❸ and for multiplying components by an integer ❹.

Just like in C#, overloaded operators are implemented as static members of the type. We've already seen another way to implement operators in F# (in chapter 6), where we declared them like functions using `let` bindings. Overloaded operators are more suitable if the operator is an intrinsic part of the type. The pipelining operator (`|>`) doesn't logically belong to any type, whereas our operators are specific to `SimpleColor`.

Some F# library functions can work with any types that provide basic operators and members. That's also the reason why we provided the member `Zero`, which returns a black color ❻. When a type has the plus operator and the `Zero` member, it should be true that `clr = clr + T.Zero` for any `clr`. We can see that this is true for our type. The `DivideByInt` member is another name expected by some F# library functions, as we'll see later. It performs division of the color value of an integer ❺. We could provide this functionality as the `/` operator, but it's more common for the `/` operator to have the same types of operands, so we'd use it if we wanted to implement division that takes two colors as its arguments.

Another important aspect of the type is that it's immutable. None of the operations modify the existing value; instead they return a new color (even the instance member `ClipColor`). Even if you're not programming in a functional style, this is good practice when you write your own value types. Mutable value types can cause headaches in all kinds of subtle ways.

Now that we have a type to represent colors, let's see how to represent graphical filters and how to run them. We won't parallelize the operation yet—it's generally worth writing code that works correctly when run sequentially before trying to parallelize it, while bearing parallelization in mind.

14.2.2 *Implementing and running color filters*

First we'll look at one special type of effect: color filters. Later, we'll extend the application to work with any effect, implementing blurring as an example. A color filter only changes the coloration of the image, so it's simpler. The filter calculates a new color for each pixel without accessing other parts of the image. As we saw in chapter 8, this is a behavior that's naturally represented as a function.

Filters for adjusting colors can be represented as a function that takes the original color and returns a new color. The F# type signature would be `SimpleColor -> SimpleColor`. In C# we can represent the same thing using the `Func` delegate. The code that runs the filter will apply this function to every pixel of the image. When we process the bitmap, we'll represent it as a 2D array.

Converting bitmaps to arrays

The .NET representation for images is the `Bitmap` class from the `System.Drawing` namespace. This class allows us to access pixels using `GetPixel` and `SetPixel`, but these methods are inefficient when you need to access lots of pixels—they're the graphical equivalent of reopening a file each time you want to read a byte of data. That's why we're going to represent the bitmap as a 2D array instead.

We still need to convert the bitmap to an array and back. This can be done efficiently using the `LockBits` method. This gives us a location in unmanaged memory that we can address directly. Writing and reading to the memory can then be done using the .NET `Marshal` class. In our application, we need two functions to do the conversion. These functions are implemented in the `BitmapUtils` module and are called `ToArray2D` and `ToBitmap`. While they're of some interest in themselves, they're not directly relevant to the topic of parallelization. You can find the full implementation in the online source code at this book's website.

The implementation of the filters themselves will be similar in C# and F#, but the code to execute the filter sequentially will be different. The F# library includes higher-order functions for working with 2D arrays, but .NET doesn't, so we'll need to implement those first. We won't make the code fully general as the functions in the F# `Array2D` module. Let's start by implementing a couple of filters in C#.

CREATING AND APPLYING COLOR FILTERS IN C#

Even though we're going to represent color filters using the `Func` delegate, we'll implement them as ordinary methods that we can convert to delegates when we need to, such as to store them in a collection of filters. Listing 14.10 shows two simple color filters. The first converts the color to grayscale and the second lightens the image.

Listing 14.10 Grayscale and lighten filters (C#)

```
class Filters {
  public static SimpleColor Grayscale(SimpleColor clr) {
    var c = (clr.R*11 + clr.G*59 + clr.B*30) / 100;          ❶
    return new SimpleColor(c, c, c);
  }

  public static SimpleColor Lighten(SimpleColor clr) {
    return (clr * 2).ClipColor();                            ❷
  }
}
```

To calculate the grayscale color, we use a weighted average ❶ because the human eye is more sensitive to green light than to red or blue. The implementation of the second filter is even simpler, but this time it uses the overloaded operators of the `Simple-Color` type. It uses component-wise multiplication to multiply the color by 2. This may create colors with components outside the normal range of 0–255, so we use the `ClipColor` method ❷ to limit each component appropriately.

Now that we have our filter methods, let's apply them to the 2D array representation of an image. Listing 14.11 does this by implementing an extension method on the array type itself. At the moment we're still performing all the computation in a single thread.

Listing 14.11 Sequential method for applying filters (C#)

```
public static SimpleColor[,] RunFilter
    (this SimpleColor[,] arr, Func<SimpleColor, SimpleColor> f) {
  int height = arr.GetLength(0), width = arr.GetLength(1);
  var result = new SimpleColor[width, height];                    ❶
  for(int y = 0; y < height; y++)
    for(int x = 0; x < width; x++)                                ❷
      result[y, x] = f(arr[y, x]);
  return result;
}
```

The `RunFilter` method first creates a new array that will be returned as a result ❶. We're writing the application in a functional way, so the method won't modify the array given as the input. In the body of the method, we imperatively iterate over all the pixels in the array and apply the color filter function to every pixel ❷. Note that we specify Y as the first coordinate of the array. This can make some operations on images more efficient, because a single horizontal scan line in this setting is just a block of memory.

Given our earlier experience with `Parallel.For` you can probably already see how to parallelize this code. Before we get onto that, we'll finish up the single-threaded version by looking at the F# code.

CREATING AND APPLYING COLOR FILTERS IN F#

In chapter 10, when we wanted to apply a function to all elements of an array and collect the results in a new array, we used the `Array.map` function. This is exactly what our method `RunFilter` from listing 14.11 did, with the exception that it worked on 2D arrays. It may not surprise you that the F# library contains a module `Array2D` for working with 2D arrays, which is similar to the one-dimensional `Array` module. This module also contains a `map` function, which makes the F# implementation of `runFilter` trivial. You can see it together with the two color filters in listing 14.12.

Listing 14.12 Applying filters and two simple filters (F# Interactive)

```
> let runFilter f arr = Array2D.map f arr       ❶

  module ColorFilters =                         ❷
    let Grayscale(clr:SimpleColor) =
      let c = (clr.R*11 + clr.G*59 + clr.B*30) / 100
      SimpleColor(c, c, c)
    let Lighten(clr:SimpleColor) =
      (clr * 2).ClipColor()
  ;;
```

```
val runFilter : ('a -> 'b) -> 'a [,] -> 'b [,]

module ColorFilters =
  val Grayscale : SimpleColor -> SimpleColor
  val Lighten : SimpleColor -> SimpleColor
```

❸

The runFilter function calls Array2D.map to do the work ❶; in fact, we could just use Array2D.map in our later code. Wrapping Array2D.map into another function makes the code more readable and self-explanatory. Also, if we eventually decided to change the representation of the bitmap, we could update the runFilter function without touching the code that uses it.

We also use F# modules to organize the code in a more structured fashion. All the graphical filters are encapsulated in a module called ColorFilters ❷. The listing shows that you can enter the entire module in the F# Interactive to see the inferred type signature ❸. The implementation of our two sample filters is almost the same as in C#, but we'll see later that F# allows us to do a little more with custom types that provide standard overloaded operators.

Before we look at how to parallelize the application, we need to wrap all the code we've written so far into an application that we can run. This will allow us to test our filters and measure the performance. You'll do this in the next section. We'll only show you the C# version, and not in much detail; the full source code is available at the book's website. We'll focus on the interesting bits.

14.2.3 Designing the main application

So far, we've only created color filters, but we want our final application to cater for more general graphical effects. A color filter such as grayscaling or lightening applies a function to each pixel based only on that pixel's value. Other effects may be much more general—they could do anything with the image, such as geometrical transformations or blurring. We'll use blurring as an example later on, just to show that it's possible. We'll take this goal into account as we build the application.

The application allows you to open an image file, select an effect from a list, and apply it to the image. We'll create a sequential and parallel version of each of the effect, so that we can measure the performance. After running the effect, the application automatically displays how long it took to apply. Figure 14.2 shows a screenshot of the finished application.

In C#, we can create the UI for the application using the Windows Forms designer. The application uses the ToolStrip control to create the toolbar with the necessary commands, and uses a ToolStripComboBox control for the list of available effects. A PictureBox control wrapped in a TabControl shows the image, so we can easily switch between the original image and the processed version.

Once we've created the GUI in the designer, we can use the filter we've already implemented. As we said earlier, the application will be flexible enough to work with general effects beyond just filters, so let's look at how we want to represent these effects in code.

Figure 14.2   Completed image-processing Application after first running the grayscale and then the lighten filter on a sample image

Creating Windows applications in F#

Unfortunately the F# support in Visual Studio doesn't include a Windows Forms designer. We've seen how easy it is to create simple GUIs by hand in F#, but for this kind of application a designer would be useful. Fortunately, F# can easily reference C# libraries, and vice versa, so several options are available to us.

If you only need to create forms, you can create a C# class library project that contains the graphical elements such as forms and user controls, then reference the library from your F# application and use the GUI components from F#. This is the approach we used to create the F# version of this application, so you can see exactly how it works if you download the source code.

An alternative approach is to implement the user interaction in C# and reference an F# library that contains all the data processing code. If we wanted to use this approach, we'd wrap the graphical effects in an F# object type (as discussed in chapter 9) and compile the F# code as a library. The C# application would then use the types in the library to run the graphical effects.

REPRESENTING EFFECTS

A color filter was a function that took a color and returned the new color. Effects are functions too; however, the parameter and result type is different. An effect can process the entire image, so it needs to take the whole image as the input. In the C# GUI application, we also need to store the name of the effect. Later when we'll look how to parallelize the processing, we're going to add a separate item for the parallel version of the effect. Listing 14.13 shows all of this information wrapped up into an `EffectInfo` type.

Listing 14.13   Representation of graphical effect (C#)

```
class EffectInfo {
  public Func<SimpleColor[,], SimpleColor[,]> Effect { get; set; }
  public string Name { get; set; }
}
```

The class is simple, with just two properties. We've created it in the most straightforward way possible, with mutable properties. We're only going to use this type within the GUI itself, so while that may leave us feeling a little uncomfortable, we won't worry about it too much. The first property of the class is a function that runs the effect and the second is a name. This is similar to an F# record containing a function and a string; that's the design we'll use in the F# version of the application. Next we'll look at how we can create `EffectInfo` instances to represent the color filters we implemented earlier.

14.2.4   *Creating and running effects*

In section 14.2.2, we implemented a couple of color filters, but our application contains a list of more general graphical effects. It appears that we still have a lot of work to do, but actually, we already have everything we need to create graphical effects from a simple color filter. Everything should start making sense in the next section, where you'll learn how to create an effect from a color filter.

CREATING EFFECTS FROM COLOR FILTERS IN C#

To create a general effect based on a color filter, we can apply the filter to all the pixels in the image. We've already implemented the sequential form of this as the `Run-Filter` method. Let's start by writing a simple function that uses `RunFilter` to create an effect that runs the given filter sequentially, and we'll look at the parallelized version shortly. As you can see in listing 14.14, to construct an effect we use a lambda function and return a delegate from the method.

Listing 14.14   Creating graphical effect from a color filter (C#)

```
Func<SimpleColor[,],SimpleColor[,]> MakeEffect
    (Func<SimpleColor, SimpleColor> filter) {
  return arr => Filters.RunFilter(arr, filter);       ❶
}
```

The method has only a single argument, which is the color filter that we want to convert into an effect. The effect should apply this filter to each pixel of an image, but how can we do this when we don't have the image yet? The answer is that we'll get the image later as an argument for the function that represents the effect, so the body of the method returns the effect via a lambda function ❶.

The lambda function takes only a single argument: the image to process. Once we have this information, we can call the `RunFilter` method. If you remember our discussion about closures in chapter 8, you know that the `filter` argument to the method will be captured by a closure that's associated with the returned function.

It's important to note that the return type is exactly the same as the type of the function stored in `EffectInfo`, so we can use it immediately when we're building our drop-down list of effects for the toolbar. When we'll look at the parallelization of image filters later, we'll implement a parallelized version of the processing method called `RunFilterParallel`, and we'll also need to add a parallelized version of the `MakeEffect` method, but this will be just another three-line method that only adapts the method signature.

Here's an example of how to create effects from our two existing color filters and add them to the `listFilter` control. When we finish the parallelized version of `Make-Effect`, we'll be able to add parallelized versions of the effects as well:

```
var effects =
  new List<EffectInfo> {
    new EffectInfo {
      Name = "Grayscale (sequential)",
      Effect = MakeEffect(Filters.Grayscale) },
    new EffectInfo {
      Name = "Lighten (sequential)",
      Effect = MakeEffect(Filters.Lighten) }
  };
listFilters.ComboBox.DataSource = effects;
listFilters.ComboBox.DisplayMember = "Name";
```

Converts grayscale, lighten filters to effects

Shows effects in drop-down list

We're using a C# 3.0 collection initializer to create a `List<EffectInfo>` containing information about the two color filters that we created so far. When we call `MakeEffect`, we give it a method group from the `Filters` class as an argument. The method group is automatically converted into a `Func` delegate by the C# compiler. The last two lines set the list as the data source for the drop-down control and use the `DisplayMember` property to specify that the displayed text should be the name of the effect.

The corresponding code in the F# version of the application is quite interesting, so even though we won't look at the full source code, we'll discuss this part.

USING PARTIAL FUNCTION APPLICATION IN F#

The F# solution to this problem will be a lot easier. The method that we've just implemented in C# only changes the way we provide arguments to the `RunFilter` method. It's called `MakeEffect`, to better reflect what it does return, but aside from the name, it isn't really too different. To understand this better, let's look at the types. Here's the type signature of the `MakeEffect` method using the F# notation:

```
(SimpleColor -> SimpleColor) -> (SimpleColor[,] -> SimpleColor[,])
```

Let's recall the `runFilter` function that we've implemented as an F# alternative to the `RunFilter` method in C#. We've seen that it's a generic function for working with 2D arrays. If we replace the type parameter with the actual type we're using to represent pixels, we'll get the following signature:

```
(SimpleColor -> SimpleColor) -> SimpleColor[,] -> SimpleColor[,]
```

The only difference between these two signatures is that the first returns a function as the result while the second one takes two arguments and returns the processed array.

As we've learned in chapter 5, the F# compiler treats these two functions as if they were exactly the same. This means that if we call the F# function `runFilter` using partial application and specifying only the first argument (color filter function), we'll get a function representing an effect as the result:

```
> let effect = runFilter ColorFilters.Grayscale;;
val effect : (SimpleColor[,] -> SimpleColor[,])
```

As you can see, thanks to the partial function application, we don't need any F# function that would correspond to the `MakeEffect` method and we get conversion from filters to effects for free. We could write the C# `RunFilter` method in a way that it would behave the same as `MakeEffect`, but that wouldn't be a natural way to write C# code, so we've chosen to add one simple method to serve as a simple façade. As the description suggests, this form of conversion isn't in any way dissimilar to the façade design pattern.

Now let's get back to the user interface, and look at what the event handler for the Apply button has to do.

EXECUTING GRAPHICAL EFFECTS

When we apply the effect, we need to measure the time it takes. We could remember the time before running the effect, then run the effect and subtract the original time from the current time. However, this mixes the calling aspect with the timing aspect. If we wanted to measure the time in different places, we'd have to copy and paste the code, which isn't a good practice. Functional programming gives us a better way to approach the problem.

We can implement time measurement as a higher-order function, taking another function as an argument and measuring the time taken to run it. The return value is a tuple containing the result of the function and the elapsed time in milliseconds. Listing 14.15 shows this implemented in both F# and C#.

Listing 14.15 Measuring the time in C# and F#

C#	F#
```using System.Diagnostics;```	```open System.Diagnostics```

```csharp
Tuple<T, long> MeasureTime<T>
    (Func<T> f) {
  var st = Stopwatch.StartNew();
  var res = f();
  var t = st.ElapsedMilliseconds;
  return Tuple.Create(res, t);
}
```

```fsharp
let measureTime(f) =
  let st = Stopwatch.StartNew()
  let res = f()
  let t = st.ElapsedMilliseconds
  (res, t)
```

The function first initializes the `Stopwatch` class to measure the time and then runs the specified function. We don't want to throw away the result, so we store it locally and count the elapsed time. Since we need to return multiple values from the function, we use a tuple value. The first element of the tuple is the result of the function we passed in, which can be any type, depending on the function. The second element will contain the time taken in milliseconds.

Listing 14.16 uses this new method in the event handler for the `Click` event of the Run button.

Listing 14.16   Applying the selected effect to a bitmap (C#)

```
var info = (EffectInfo)listFilters.SelectedItem;
var effect = info.Effect;
var arr = loadedBitmap.ToArray2D();                    ◁── Runs effect,
var res = MeasureTime(() => filter(arr));                   measures time

pictProcessed.Image = res.Item1.ToBitmap();
lblTime.Text = string.Format("Time: {0} ms", res.Item2);
```

The available effects are in the drop-down list, stored as `EffectInfo` instances, so we start by accessing the selected item from the list. Once we have the effect, we can perform the bitmap processing. We first convert the bitmap to a 2D array and then apply the filter. The operation is wrapped in a call to the `MeasureTime` method, so the type of `res` is `Tuple<SimpleColor[,], long>`. We first convert the returned array into a bitmap, display it, and show the time taken to apply the effect.

We're currently concerned only with the performance of the effect itself, but it would be possible to parallelize the conversion between a bitmap and an array as well. We'll leave that as an exercise if you're interested, but for the moment let's get on with parallelizing the effect.

14.2.5 *Parallelizing the application*

Because this chapter is really about parallelization, this is the most interesting part of the application. We're going to discuss the code in both languages; we'll begin by implementing the C# version in the simplest way possible.

RUNNING FILTERS IN PARALLEL IN C#

To implement the C# version, we'll take the `RunFilter` method from listing 14.11 and replace the `for` loop with a call to the `Parallel.For` method. Thanks to lambda functions in C# 3.0, this is just a syntactic transformation. We'll also write a parallel variant of the `MakeEffect` method from listing 14.14 that returns graphical effect (as a function) that executes the color filter. You can see the parallel versions in listing 14.17.

Listing 14.17   Applying color filter in parallel (C#)

```
public static SimpleColor[,] RunFilterParallel
    (this SimpleColor[,] arr, Func<SimpleColor, SimpleColor> f) {
  int height = arr.GetLength(0), width = arr.GetLength(1);
  var result = new SimpleColor[height, width];
  Parallel.For(0, height, y => {                ◁── Parallelizes outer loop
    for(int x = 0; x < width; x++)         ◁┐  Leaves inner
      result[y, x] = f(arr[y, x]);            │  loop sequential
  });
  return result;
}

public static Func<SimpleColor[,], SimpleColor[,]> MakeParallelEffect
```

```
    (Func<SimpleColor, SimpleColor> filter) {
  return arr => RunFilterParallel(arr, filter);
}
```
Returns effect as function ◄────┘

The original code contained two nested `for` loops, but we're only parallelizing the outer loop. For most images this will give the underlying library enough flexibility to parallelize the code efficiently, without creating an unnecessarily large number of tasks. Making the filter run in parallel involved changing only two lines of code. Changing `for` loops to `Parallel.For` method calls isn't always as simple as it looks. You always have to look carefully at the code and consider whether parallelization could introduce any problems.

For instance, we have to be careful if the loop modifies any mutable state. In listing 14.17, we avoided this problem by using only local mutable state. The `result` array can't be accessed from outside this function, which makes the overall method functional. Also, each iteration only uses a separate part of the array (a single horizontal line).

Additionally, many .NET types aren't thread-safe, which means that when you start accessing a single instance from several threads, their behavior may be undefined. In section 14.3, we'll see that this is a problem even for simple-looking types such as `Random`; we'll also see how to solve this problem by using locks. First, let's look at the F# version of the previous code.

PARALLEL ARRAY PROCESSING IN F#

The source code for the F# version will be almost a direct translation of what we've seen in the previous C# listing—but at the same time, it'll be a much more general function. If you reimplemented the previous C# listing in F#, one of the changes you'd probably make would be to delete all the unnecessary type annotations. After doing that, you'd see that the code doesn't explicitly mention the `SimpleColor` type anywhere and it doesn't need to know that it's working with colors. If you hover over the function translated from C# in Visual Studio, you'd see the following inferred type:

```
('a -> 'b) -> 'a[,] -> 'b[,]
```

Just by deleting type annotations, we've made the function more generic. The type of the function is the same as the type of `Array2D.map`, which we used earlier in this chapter. The change in type signature also suggests that the name should be generalized too—after all, we're performing a mapping operation, just in parallel. The result of these changes is shown in listing 14.18.

Listing 14.18 Parallel map function for the 2D array (F#)

```
module Array2D =
  module Parallel =                                  ❶
    let map f (arr:_ [,]) =
      let height, width = arr.GetLength(0), arr.GetLength(1)
      let result = Array2D.zeroCreate height width
      pfor 0 (height - 1) (fun y ->            ◄────┐ Parallelizes
        for x = 0 to width - 1 do                   │ outer loop
```

```
        result.[y, x] <- f(arr.[y, x]))
    result

let runFilterParallel f arr  = Array2D.Parallel.map f arr        ❷
```

The fact that the simple act of translation has revealed a deeper aspect of our original code is quite a strange phenomenon. The new function does the very same thing as `Array2D.map` but executed in parallel, so we've named the function `map` and placed it inside a module called `Array2D.Parallel` ❶ to make it more reusable. To implement the parallelization, we're using our utility function `pfor` from section 14.1.1.

After we've noticed this generalization in F#, we could change the C# version to match it, changing the method declaration to something like this:

```
public static TResult[,] ParallelMap<TSource, TResult>
    (this TSource[,] arr, Func<TSource, TResult> f) {
```

We'd then have to propagate the type parameters appropriately through the code, substituting `SimpleColor` for either `TSource` or `TResult`, depending on the context. Type inference would then take care of providing the type arguments where we call the method.

The final line of listing 14.18 creates an alias for the parallel `map` function ❷. Our original goal was to write a function to run a graphical filter in parallel, and this alias makes the code more readable, because the name provides a better clue as to how the function can be used.

Now that we've parallelized simple color filters, we're going to implement a single, more general effect: blurring the image. This will wrap up our coverage of the application, but you may want to experiment with more effects.

14.2.6 *Implementing a blur effect*

Our final effect won't be just a color filter. The process of blurring an image relies on computing a new pixel value based on *multiple* original pixels. We can still perform a pixel-by-pixel transformation of the image. However, the transformation will need to access the whole image, as well as the coordinates of the pixel we want to transform.

We've left the implementation of `RunEffect` and `RunEffectParallel` as an exercise for you, but it's fairly straightforward; it's simply a matter of changing the details of the loop and giving the transformation function more information. Converting the sequential form into a parallel form is the same for this effect as for color filters. If you get stuck, look at the full source code on this book's website.

The blurring transformation itself is quite interesting, as shown in listing 14.19. It's not particularly difficult, but it does provide a nice demonstration of declarative programming.

Listing 14.19   Implementing the `Blur` effect (F#)

```
let blur(arr:SimpleColor[,], x, y) =                              ❶
    let height, width = arr.GetLength(0) - 1, arr.GetLength(1) - 1
    let checkW x = max 0 (min width x)                            ❷
    let checkH y = max 0 (min height y)
```

```
[ for dy in -2 .. 2 do
    for dx in -2 .. 2 do
      yield arr.[checkH(y + dy), checkW(x + dx)] ]
|> List.average
```
③
④

The blur function takes three parameters that specify the image and X, Y coordinates of the pixel that we want to calculate ❶. If you were implementing blur in an imperative style, you'd create a mutable variable, initialize it to 0, and add the colors of all the nearby pixels. Divide the result by the number of pixels to get the average color.

In F#, we can use a more declarative approach and write that we want to calculate the average color. We first declare utility functions for checking that the index is in the range of the array ❷. Next, we use a sequence expression to create a list containing colors of all the nearby pixels ❸ and calculate the average value from this using List.average ❹.

Exploring List.average

To calculate the average value, the List.average function needs to know three things:

- What a "zero" value is for the particular type.
- How to add values together.
- How to divide value of the particular type by integer.

The first two bullets are enough to sum the list. Then it needs to divide the result by the number of elements in the list and here we need the third item. In our effect, we're working with values of the SimpleColor type, and this type implements the plus operator. We also added the special members Zero and DivideByInt. The average function uses these members. It's a generic function, but it requires the type to implement the appropriate members. A constraint like this one can't be expressed using .NET generics. Constraints available for generic types can require parameterless constructor or an interface, but not a specific member.

For this reason, F# implements its own mechanism for compile-time member constraints. In this case, the constraint is resolved by the F# compiler at compile time (as opposed to constraints for .NET generics, which are also checked by the .NET runtime). The following example demonstrates how to use this feature to define a function that calculates half of any value that supports division by integers:

```
> let inline half (num: ^a) : ^a =
    LanguagePrimitives.DivideByInt< (^a) > num 2
 ;;
val inline half : ^a -> ^a
  when ^a : (static member DivideByInt : ^a * int -> ^a)

> half(42.0);;
val it : float = 21.0

> half(SimpleColor(255, 128, 0));;
val it : SimpleColor = SimpleColor {B = 0; G = 64; R = 127;}

> half("hello");;
error FS0001: The type 'string' does not
support any operators named 'DivideByInt'
```

> **(continued)**
>
> The function is called `half` and we use explicit type annotations to specify that the type of the parameter `num` and the type of the results is a generic parameter `^a`. Note that we're using a type parameter starting with a hat (`^`) instead of the usual apostrophe (`'`). In the body, we invoke the `DivideByInt` function from the `LanguagePrimitives` module. This is one of primitive functions with member constraint that divides numeric type by an integer or uses the `DivideByInt` member if available.
>
> As you can see, the member constraint is present in the inferred type signature. Now that we have the function, we can use it with various numeric types, but also with our `SimpleColor` type. If we try to call it with an argument that doesn't support the `DivideByInt` operation, we'll get a compile-time error.

In this example, we've looked at key parts of a larger application. You can get the complete source code from the book's website and see how the parts we implemented in this chapter are connected. Even though the most important parts of the application use mutable arrays, we've designed the whole application in a functional way, including using the arrays in the functional style as described in chapter 11. This approach allowed us to parallelize the core algorithms easily and safely.

This has been an example of a behavior-centric application. Our main concern was how to parallelize individual behaviors. Another way to parallelize a behavior-centric application is to run different behaviors in parallel. We might want to process a series of images in a batch, applying multiple effects to each image. In the next section, we'll turn our attention to data-centric applications.

14.3 *Creating a parallel simulation*

Our next sample application is going to be a simulation of a world containing animals and their predators. The goal of predators is to move close to animals to hunt them, and the aim of animals is to run away within the area of the world. Just like our image-processing example, we'll only show the most interesting aspects here, but the full source code is available at this book's website.

This is a data-centric application, so the first task is to identify the primary data structure involved. In this case, it's the representation of the "current" state of the world. The world effectively has a single operation: make time "tick," moving all the animals and predators. In a data-centric application, we can either run multiple operations in parallel or focus on parallelizing individual operations. In our simulation, we'll obviously have to parallelize the tick operation. The operation isn't that simple, so there's enough room for parallelization. We'll use the normal techniques involved in data-centric functional programs, with a combination of declarative and task-based parallelism.

As usual when creating data-centric applications, we'll start by designing a data structure to represent our world. The parallelization will come later when we'll be writing operations to manipulate with that data structure.

14.3.1 Representing the simulated world

Our simulated world is quite simple. It contains only animals and predators, so we can represent it using two lists. In principle, we should also include the width and height of the world area, but we'll use a fixed size to make things simpler. You can get a better picture about the world we're trying to represent by looking at figure 14.3, which shows a screenshot of the running simulation.

We'll look at the interesting elements of the simulation in both languages, just as we did for the image application. We'll start with the F# version to illustrate a typical functional approach.

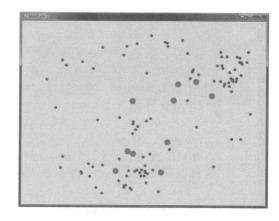

Figure 14.3   Running simulation with 10 predators (larger circles) hunting 100 animals (small circles)

REPRESENTING THE SIMULATION STATE IN F#

As we've mentioned, the state of the simulation will be two lists with the locations of animals and predators. We'll need to perform calculations with locations, such as calculating several locations on a path between two locations. To make this easier, we'll implement our `Vector` type and use it to represent the location of the animal (relatively to the origin). We'll also implement a couple of operators for adding and subtracting vectors as well as for multiplying the vector by a scalar floating point number.

We'll implement our vector as a simple immutable value type, and the state of the simulation will be an F# record type with two fields. You can see the data structure declaration in listing 14.20.

Listing 14.20   Representing the state of the world (F#)

```
[<Struct>]                                              ❶
type Vector(x:float, y:float) =
  member t.X = x
  member t.Y = y
  static member (+) (vect1:Vector, vect2:Vector) =
    Vector(vect1.X + vect2.X, vect1.Y + vect2.Y)       ❷
  static member (*) (vect:Vector, f) =
    Vector(vect.X * f, vect.Y * f)                     ❸
  static member (-) (vect1:Vector, vect2:Vector) =
    vect1 + (vect2 * -1.0)                             ❹

type Simulation =                 ❺
{ Animals : list<Vector>
  Predators : list<Vector> }
```

The location is a simple object marked using the `Struct` attribute ❶. It contains the X and Y coordinates as immutable properties, set in the constructor. It supports operations for component-wise addition ❷, multiplication by a scalar value ❸ and subtraction of vectors ❹. Note that the subtraction is implemented by using the two other operators. All the operators return new values, as you'd expect. The type that represents the simulation is also straightforward ❺. This type is immutable too, so in order to work with it, we'll need to construct a new Simulation value for each step of the simulation.

Now let's look at our C# representation. We're mostly going to use standard .NET types, but we'll work with them in a functional way.

REPRESENTING SIMULATION STATE IN C#

In C#, the simplest approach is to represent some of the state using mutable types, because that's what the C# language and the standard .NET libraries provide the most support for. In particular, .NET doesn't provide a functional list type. We could have used our FuncList<T> type from earlier chapters, which would have made the two representations similar. However, functional programming is a style and not a technology, so we can write functional code even with the classes that we already have; we'll just have to be more careful to do it correctly.

Listing 14.21 shows the class we're going to use to represent the simulation in C#. We've omitted the implementation of the Vector type because it's a simple immutable struct with overloaded operators, exactly the same as the F# version.

Listing 14.21 Representing the state of the world (C#)

```
public class Simulation {
  private readonly IEnumerable<Vector> animals;                    Creates new      ❶
  private readonly IEnumerable<Vector> predators;              simulation state

  public Simulation(List<Vector> animals, List<Vector> predators) {
    this.animals = animals;
    this.predators = predators;
  }

  public IEnumerable<Vector> Animals       ❷  Exposes properties as
  { get { return animals; } }                  immutable sequence
  public IEnumerable<Vector> Predators
  { get { return predators; } }  ❷
}
```

We use two different collection types here; one for the constructor arguments ❶ when we're creating the simulation state and a different one for the properties ❷. In the constructor, we use List<T>, to ensure that we get a fully evaluated collection that contains all the locations. Since IEnumerable<T> is a lazy sequence, we wouldn't know if the locations were evaluated already or whether they'll be evaluated later when we'll need them somewhere later in the code. This isn't a big problem, but it would make it difficult to measure the performance because we wouldn't know when the code executed. Also, if we ran the tick operation multiple times without forcing the evaluation of the sequence, it would create a lazy sequence that would perform the work later, which might be confusing in this kind of application.

We don't want to expose the state as List<T>, because that's a mutable type and someone could modify it. Instead, we use IEnumerable<T> so client code can iterate over the animals and predators but can't directly modify the existing state.

Now that we have the data structures to represent the state, we should also look at what we can do with it. In a typical functional design, that's always the next thing to do.

14.3.2 *Designing simulation operations*

In this section we'll consider the operations that we need to implement for the simulation. We won't implement all the difficult operations now, because we only want to design the structure of the application. Our first goal is to get the application running with minimal effort and then we can get back to the interesting parts, such as the algorithms describing the movements of animals and predators.

In a typical functional fashion, we'll start with some initial state, and in each step we'll create a new state based on the previous one. This means that we'll need an operation to create an initial state, and another to run a single step of the simulation. Both are logically related to the simulation state, so in C# we'll add them to the Simulation class. In F#, we'll add them to the Simulation type using intrinsic type extensions, which we discussed in chapter 9. The following snippet shows the types of these operations using C# syntax:

```
class Simulation {
  public static Simulation CreateInitialState();
  public Simulation Step();
}
```

If you're writing the sample code as you read the book, you can implement these on your own in some simple way. For now, the Step method can return the original state or it can move all the animals by one pixel in some direction, so that we can tell that the simulation is running. The CreateInitialState method should generate a couple of randomly located animals and predators. We'll get back to these methods after we finish implementing the machinery that runs the simulation.

Next we need the ability to draw the simulation state. In C#, we'll make this part of the MainForm class. In F#, the form is a global value, so we can implement the drawing code as a simple function. The operation will iterate over all the animals and predators in the current simulation state and draw them on the form using System.Drawing classes. The C# method has this signature:

```
bool DrawState(Simulation state);;
```

We won't present the full code here, but now you'll recognize it when we call it. One notable thing about the method is that it returns a Boolean value, which specifies whether the form is still visible. We'll use this result shortly to stop the simulation whenever the user closes the form.

At this point, we have everything we need to run the simulation, even though we haven't implemented any interesting algorithms for animal and predator movement. Let's put everything together, so we can test it before we start making the animals behave more intelligently.

RUNNING THE SIMULATION

We'll run the simulation as fast as the computer is able to, so we'll implement it as a loop that runs the Step method, redraws the form, then starts again and runs until the form is closed. We don't want to block the main application thread, because that would make the application unresponsive, so we'll run the simulation as a background process. The F# and C# versions are implemented in different ways, so we'll look at both of them. Listing 14.22 shows the C# code, which explicitly creates a thread.

Listing 14.22   Running simulation on a thread (C#)

```
private void MainForm_Load(object sender, EventArgs e) {
  var th = new Thread(() => {
    var state = Simulation.CreateInitialState();        ❶
    bool running = true;                                ❷
    while(running) {
      state = state.Step();                             ❸
      running = (bool)this.Invoke(new Func<bool>(() =>
        DrawState(state)));                             ❹
    }
  });
  th.Start();
}
```

This method is the only part of the C# version of the simulation where we need to use mutable state. In particular, we create a variable that holds the current state of the simulation ❶ and a variable that specifies whether the simulation form is still opened ❷. We run the simulation on a thread in a `while` loop, and we calculate the new state. We store this state in the same local variable for each iteration and update the form. In C#, we can't write the code without mutation, but we won't need this in F#.

Another notable point is the way we update the form ❸. In Windows Forms, we can only access controls from the main GUI thread. We use the `Invoke` method that takes a delegate and runs on the GUI thread. Earlier we said that the `DrawState` method ❹ returns a flag whether the form is still opened, so we wrap the method call into a `Func<bool>` delegate. When it returns a Boolean as the result, we update the running flag.

We don't use threads explicitly in the F# version, because we can start the simulation using asynchronous workflows. Also, we can replace the mutable variable and imperative `while` loop using recursion as shown here:

Listing 14.23   Running simulation using recursion and `async` (F#)

```
let rec runSimulation(state:Simulation) =
  let running = form.Invoke(new Func<bool>(fun () ->       | Triggers redraw
    drawState(state))) :?> bool                            | of form
  if (running) then
    runSimulation(state.Step())          ❶

Async.Start(async {
    runSimulation(Simulation.CreateInitialState())        ❷
  })
```

The loop that runs the simulation is implemented as a recursive function. We don't need to worry about running out of stack space, because the recursive call is tail recursive ❶. The lack of tail recursion in C# is the only thing that prevents us from using the same technique there.

The function is an ordinary function that loops in a blocking way while the form is visible, but we can still use asynchronous workflows to launch it in the background ❷. This isn't related to the typical asynchronous programming as we discussed it in the previous chapter; `Async.Start` is a simple way to start executing the function on a separate thread. The workflow calls the recursive function that blocks the thread and runs the simulation loop.

If you've implemented the `Step` method and added the code to draw the simulation, you should have a working application by now. Now that we have the skeleton in place, we can work on making the animals and predators behave intelligently, but first we'll need a couple of helper functions.

14.3.3 *Implementing helper functions*

Before we look at the code that calculates locations of the animals, we'll digress slightly. We'll need to implement a couple of functions that will be used by the algorithm for determining animal and predator locations. These functions need to use random numbers for various purposes, and to generate random numbers correctly, we first need to discuss how to safely access objects that aren't thread-safe. This can be problem when we're dealing with objects with mutable state, which is often the case with .NET types.

ACCESSING SHARED OBJECTS SAFELY

The `Random` class is a commonly used .NET class that's not thread-safe. In our application, we'll need to generate random locations to choose where the animal or predator should move to; this functionality can be called from several threads simultaneously. However, `Random` needs to be initialized once, then used again and again. (If you create a new `Random` instance for each call, you'll often get repeated numbers as the initial "seed" for the random number generator is taken from the system time.) If you call the `Next` method on the same instance from multiple threads, the behavior of the method is undefined. Actually, it will eventually start returning zero. We're responsible for making sure that only a single thread will access one object at a time.

To avoid this problem we can use locking, which blocks other threads from executing code guarded by the same lock until the operation completes. This makes the code less efficient. Listing 14.24 provides a solution that's safe but allows us to be efficient.

Listing 14.24 Safe way for generating random numbers (F# and C#)	
F#	**C#**

```fsharp
module SafeRandom =
    let private rnd =              ❶
        new Random()

    let New() =
        lock rnd (fun () ->
            new Random(rnd.Next())   ❷
        )
```

```csharp
static class SafeRandom {
    static Random rnd =            ❶
        new Random();
    public static Random New() {
        lock (rnd)
            return new              ❷
                Random(rnd.Next());
    }
}
```

We created a module in F# and a static class in C#, both of which serve the same purpose: they can be used for generating random number generators. These generators are created using a random seed that's obtained from a single global random number generator ❶ that's safely accessed within a lock ❷. Thanks to this approach, we don't have to use locks every time we'll need to create a random number. We only need to create a new generator every time we execute an operation that can be executed in parallel with other tasks. Within a single thread, we can reuse the same instance safely, knowing that no other thread will have access to it.

The F# equivalent of C#'s `lock` keyword is the `lock` function that takes a simple function as its argument. It acquires the lock using the `Monitor` class, runs the specified function, then releases the lock. We'll make good use of `SafeRandom` in the next section, where we'll need to generate random locations somewhere in the simulation world.

WORKING WITH LOCATIONS

When generating locations of animals, we'll need to generate random locations as possible targets; then we'll need some way of measuring which of the locations is the best choice. This can be done depending on how close other predators and animals are. To write these algorithms, we'll need a couple of functions. We'll look at their type signatures, which should give you enough information to understand how they work and also to implement them on your own if you want to. The following snippet shows their commented F# type signatures:

```
/// Returns the distance between two specified locations
val distance : Vector -> Vector -> float

/// Returns specified number of check-points
/// on the path between the specified locations
val getPathPoints : int * Vector * Vector -> seq<Vector>

/// Returns the specified number of randomly generated locations
val randomLocations : int -> seq<Vector>
```

The first function can be implemented using `Math.Pow` and `Math.Sqrt`. Note that we've given the function several parameters, which allows us to use partial application. This is convenient in F# when we want to calculate the distance of a collection of locations from one specific point. The second and third functions can be implemented using sequence expressions in F# and iterators in C#.

We'll need to call the `randomLocations` function from multiple threads running in parallel, so we need to use the `SafeRandom` module we created earlier. Each call to `randomLocations` first creates a new random number generator using `SafeRandom.New()` and then uses this generator repeatedly to build the result. The result is a lazy sequence, so it will be actually generated on demand. As it happens, we'll need all the items in the sequence to calculate the location of animal, so this doesn't make a big difference.

These three helper functions are relatively simple, but we'll use them all the time when implementing the simulation. Thanks to the rich standard F# library and these three functions, the algorithms for movement can be written in a concise way.

14.3.4 *Implementing smart animals and predators*

The algorithms that compute the new locations of animals and predators look quite similar in C# and F#, because we can implement them using the same collection processing functions. In F# and other standard functional languages, these are part of standard libraries and in C# 3.0 they're available using LINQ. We'll look at these algorithms in the next two sections, showing each in a single language.

MOVING ANIMALS IN F#

Let's start with a function that takes the location of a single animal and the current state as arguments and returns the animal's new location. We'll have around 100 animals in the simulation, and we'll have to calculate the new location for all of them. This means it's probably not worth making the function run its logic in parallel within a single call. Instead, we'll just parallelize the many calls to the function later. Working out where to split the computation is an important part of parallelizing an application.

Listing 14.25 implements an animal's behavior by generating 10 random locations in the world and working out which is the safest. It does this by looking at the direct path to the location and calculating how close the nearest predator is.

Listing 14.25   Implementing the animal behavior (F#)

```
let moveAnimal (state:Simulation) (animPos:Vector) =
  let nearestPredatorDistanceFrom(pos) =          ◁─┐   Gets distance of
    state.Predators                                 ❶ nearest predator
    |> Seq.map (distance pos) |> Seq.min

  let nearestPredatorDistanceOnPath(target) =     ◁─┐   Checks safety of
    getPathPoints(10, animPos, target)              ❷ path to the target
    |> Seq.map nearestPredatorDistanceFrom |> Seq.min

  let target =
    randomLocations(10)                                  ❸ Chooses best
    |> Seq.maxBy nearestPredatorDistanceOnPath              location...

  animPos + (target - animPos) *              ❹ ...moves in that
    (20.0 / (distance target animPos))          direction by 20 points
```

Listing 14.25 starts by implementing two local utility functions. The first one ❶ uses `Seq.map` to calculate the distance between each predator and the specified location, then uses `Seq.min` to get the shortest of those distances. The second one ❷ looks for the nearest predator on the path between the animal's current location and a specified destination by checking several points on the path between them.

Next we choose a target location for the animal. We generate 10 random locations and choose the one the animal can reach while staying as far away from predators as possible ❸. We do this with `Seq.maxBy`, which returns the element for which the given function returns the largest value. In our case, the function returns the shortest distance between the predators and the path from the animal's current location to the randomly generated target. Finally, we use the overloaded operators of the `Vector` type to calculate and return a new location of the animal. Each time the function is called, the animal moves 20 points in the best generated direction ❹.

We'll use a similar algorithm to move the predators—but obviously with a different aim. The predator will also generate random locations, then move in the best possible direction. The following section shows the C# version of the code.

MOVING PREDATORS IN C#

The algorithm for determining the best target for a predator is a bit more difficult. We're going to make the predator follow a path to the largest number of animals and the smallest number of other predators. The C# method that implements the algorithm is shown in listing 14.26. It's a part of the `Simulation` class, which lets us access other predators and animals easily. (This is why we don't need to take the current state as a parameter as we did in the F# animal behavior function; the current state is available as `this`.)

Listing 14.26   Implementing the predator behavior (C#)

```
int CountCloseLocations(IEnumerable<Vector> an, Vector pos) {          ← Counts
  return an.Where(a =>                                                    locations
    Distance(a, pos) < 50).Count();                                      close to
}                                                              ❶ given point

int CountCloseLocationsOnPath(IEnumerable<Vector> an,
    Vector pfrom, Vector ptarget) {              ←  Counts locations close
  return GetPathPoints(10, pfrom, ptarget)       ❷ to specified path
    .Sum(pos => CountCloseLocations(an, pos));
}

Vector MovePredator(Vector predPos) {                         ❸ Selects path
  var target = RandomLocations(20).MaxBy(pos =>                 with many
    CountCloseLocationsOnPath(Animals, predPos, pos) -          animals, few
    CountCloseLocationsOnPath(Predators, predPos, pos) * 3);    predators

  return predPos + (target - predPos) *        | Moves predator
    (10.0 / Distance(target, predPos));        | by 10 points
}
```

In the F# code for animal movement, we started by implementing two local helper functions. In C#, we implement similar helpers as ordinary methods. In principle, we could also use local lambda functions, but we decided to use a more typical C# approach to make the code simpler.

The first method ❶ takes a collection of vectors (which can be our collection of animals or predators) and counts how many are close to the specified point. The second helper ❷ sums how many predators are close to a selected point on the whole path. This is done by generating a collection of points on that path, calling the first method on each point and summing the results. This can count a single predator multiple times if it's close to multiple points on the path. In practice this isn't a problem, because if a predator is close to multiple points, it's probably more dangerous.

To implement the predator behavior, we generate 20 random locations and choose the one with the largest number of animals and smallest number of predators ❸ close to the path between the predator's current location and the target. For each random location, we compute this "score" with two calls to `LocationsOnPath`. We multiply the count of nearby predators by a constant to make it more significant, because the number of predators in the whole simulation is smaller. The MaxBy extension method returns the location with the largest score. This method isn't a standard LINQ operator, but you can find its implementation in the complete simulation source code at this book's website.

Now that we have functions for calculating new locations for both animals and predators, we can finally implement the larger step function of the simulation. It will need to calculate new locations of all the animals and predators, so this will be the best place to introduce parallelism into the simulation.

14.3.5 *Running the simulation in parallel*

To run the simulation in parallel, we'll use a combination of task-based parallelism using Task and declarative parallelism using PLINQ (and the PSeq module in F#). To calculate the new state of the simulation, we need to perform two basic tasks: move all the animals and move all the predators. With the algorithms from section 14.3.4, these two tasks take roughly the same time, so this would be enough on a dual-core machine.

Splitting the work into just two tasks isn't the best option if we have a machine with more than two processors, or if one of the tasks takes longer than the other. At this point, we can use declarative data parallelism, because we can calculate the new location of each animal and predator independently: we can view it as a list-processing operation. Listing 14.27 uses both of these techniques to implement an F# function that runs the simulation.

> **Listing 14.27 Generating random state and running a simulation step (F#)**

```
let simulationStep(state) =
  let futureAnimals = Task.Factory.StartNew(fun () ->      ❶
    state.Animals
      |> PSeq.ofSeq
      |> PSeq.map (moveAnimal state)
      |> List.ofSeq)
  let predators =                    ❷
    state.Predators
      |> PSeq.ofSeq
      |> PSeq.map (movePredator state)
      |> List.ofSeq
  { Animals = futureAnimals.Result; Predators = predators }

type Simulation with
  member x.Step() = simulationStep(x)      ❸
  static member CreateInitialState() =
    { Animals = randomLocations(150) |> List.ofSeq
      Predators = randomLocations(15) |> List.ofSeq }
```

The listing implements the simulation step as an F# function and makes this function part of the Simulation type using type extension ❸. It adds the CreateInitial-State method that generates 150 random locations for animals and 15 randomly located predators.

The simulation step starts processing collection of animals using a `Task` in background ❶, then processes predators on the current thread ❷, so we only need a single `Task` value. This is similar to the tree-processing code we discussed earlier. Each task creates a new list with locations for the next simulation step. The list processing is further parallelized using the `PSeq` module.

TIP   Tweaking the code to get the maximal performance is always difficult and requires a lot of experimentation. If you run the simulation with either parallelization technique, you should get a reasonable speedup. On our dual core machine, it's about 155 percent times the speed of a sequential implementation when we just use `Task`, and 175 percent when using both PLINQ and `Task`. You can try various configurations to find the best performance on your system.

The C# implementation of the `Step` method is similar to the F# version, as you can see next.

Listing 14.28   Running the simulation step in parallel (C#)

```
public Simulation Step() {
    var futureAnimals = Task.Factory.StartNew(() =>     ❶
        Animals.AsParallel()
            .Select(a => MoveAnimal(a))
            .ToList());                     ❷
    var predators =
        Predators.AsParallel()              ❸
            .Select(p => MovePredator(p))
            .ToList();
    return new Simulation(futureAnimals.Result, predators);     ❹
}
```

Just as in the F# version, we create a single `Task` value to process animals ❶ and run the code that processes predators on the primary thread ❷. Each list-processing task uses the `AsParallel` method ❸ so the query operators are executed in parallel. We only need the `Select` operator to get a new location for every animal or predator, so we use the extension method directly rather than writing a query expression. Finally we create a new `Simulation` object ❹ that holds the new state.

As you can see, running the simulation in parallel wasn't difficult because we used functional techniques in our application design. The data structure representing the state is immutable, and in every step of the simulation we create a new state. This means that we can't run into race conditions while updating the state from multiple threads running concurrently.

14.4 *Summary*

In this chapter, we reviewed three approaches for writing parallel applications in a functional style, two of which are based on essential aspects of functional programming.

Declarative programming lends itself to data parallelization, and PLINQ makes this particularly easy. We can use this from both C# and F#, and a wrapper module makes the F# code more idiomatic than working with PLINQ directly. Both C# and F# use higher-order functions to represent the work to be done, either directly or through C# query expressions.

The second technique is task-based parallelism. This is made simpler by using the immutable data structures we're used to in functional programming. We can spawn multiple tasks to calculate different parts of the result and then just assemble these subresults; immutability guarantees that tasks can work independently and won't corrupt one another.

You also learned how to parallelize applications that use mutable state but keep the mutation local. This is a valid and useful approach that allows us to use arrays in a functional way. When we create a new array the result of an operation, we can initialize the array in parallel. We saw how helper functions can make this even simpler, and we implemented a parallel version of array mapping in the `Array2D.Parallel` module.

Code is only useful when it's part of an application, so we looked at two complete applications in this chapter. When an application is designed in a functional manner from the start, the changes needed to introduce parallelism are relatively straightforward. In fact, we could use the techniques from this chapter to parallelize all the applications we created when talking about functional architecture in chapters 7 and 8.

In the next chapter, we're going to leave the realm of asynchronous and parallel computing and look at how we can express logic and behavior as clearly as possible. Some of the aspects of F# that make it so expressive can also be applied in C# 3.0 thanks to features such as lambda functions and extension methods. We're going to look at a famous functional approach for creating animations as our main example, but the same ideas can also be used in other domains.

Creating composable functional libraries

A design principle that arises in many aspects of functional programming is *compositionality*. This means building complex structures from a few primitives using composition operations. We're describing compositionality in a general sense because it can appear in countless forms. Let's look at two examples you're already familiar with.

We'll begin with the F# type system: there are a few primitive types, such as integer and Boolean, as well as ways of combining them, such as using the * type constructor to build a tuple of type int * bool. If we leave out the object-oriented features of F#, we have only three ways of composing them: multiple values using tuples, alternative values using discriminated unions, and functions. We can use them to build incredibly rich types.

A second example of composable design is the F# library for working with lists. We can use this library as inspiration to teach us how to write good functional libraries. This time the primitives involved are the operations to create lists from scratch, and those we can apply to existing lists such as List.filter, List.length, and so on. We can use primitives individually, but more often we've composed them into a single list-processing unit using the pipelining operator (|>). This composable design is also an essential element of the declarative style. We can describe what we want to achieve by composing primitives or derived components that we built earlier.

Our main example in this chapter will be a library for creating animations. We'll use a bottom-up approach when describing the library. This means that for most of the chapter we'll be talking about very simple things. We'll look at a couple of primitives for representing values that change with the time and a simple representation of drawings. The beauty of a composable library is that each piece is easy to build, understand, and test. The power is demonstrated when we start putting these building blocks together. In this case we'll not only combine primitives from the same domain, but we'll bring two domains together: a drawing that varies over time is practically the definition of an animation. This is a bit like using LINQ to XML, which is an XML API designed to work well with LINQ to Objects. When libraries can be combined in a natural way, it can lead to readable and flexible code.

To show that this approach works just as well in the world of business as in toy examples like animation, we'll close the chapter with an example that specifies financial contracts in a composable and functional way.

15.1 Approaches for composable design

Let's begin by reviewing how we can put the idea of composable design into practice. The idea of composing complex structures from a couple of primitives has been used for a long time in the LISP language. We'll analyze one example in LISP, which will give us a good background for further discussion on composable libraries in both F# and C#.

15.1.1 Composing animations from symbols

Among other things, the LISP language is famous for its simple yet powerful syntax. When writing any sophisticated program, you always end up defining your own primitives and then specifying what they mean. The following example shows how we could define a simple animation using the LISP syntax. The code creates two moving discs: a green one with a diameter of 50 and a smaller red one with a diameter of 20. The green one is rotating around the point (0, 0) with a 100 pixel radius and the red one is moving between two specified points:

```
(compose
  (disc 50 green (rotating 0 0 100))
  (disc 20 red (linear -100 0 100 0))
)
```

In LISP, everything is either a symbol or a list. In the previous snippet, all the identifiers (such as `compose` or `red`) as well as all the numeric constants are symbols. A list is created using parentheses, so the code (`rotating 0 0 100 2`) constructs a list containing five elements, all of them symbols. A list can consist of primitive symbols, but it can also contain nested lists. At the top level our example is a list consisting of the `compose` symbol and two nested lists.

If we look at the symbols that occur in the code snippet, we can identify several primitives. For example, `disc` is used for creating a visible shape, and we have two primitives (`rotating` and `linear`) to specify primitive shape movements. Then we have a symbol `compose` that builds a single animated object from other shapes. This is an example of an operation that composes primitives: we can use the result in exactly the same way as other shapes. We could specify the movement of the whole composed animation just as easily as we did for the individual shapes.

From a syntactic perspective, the previous example creates a list containing one symbol and two other lists, so it's natural to ask how we specify what our code actually means.

15.1.2 *Giving meaning to symbols*

The LISP code is quite readable and a human can easily understand what it means. The code doesn't reveal any technical details. We can't tell whether we're creating an object that will represent the animation as a tree-like data structure that we can process or whether we're creating a function that knows how to draw the animation. This is the nice thing about declarative programming. When we *use* the library, the technical details are abstracted away from us.

Of course, the technical details have to be present somewhere. We provide them when implementing the library. The options we have when creating composable libraries in F# and C# are very similar to the following two ways that we can follow in LISP:

- The code can build a tree-like data structure that stores all the primitives and how they're composed. In the previous LISP example, this closely corresponds to the syntax of the code. We'll get a list containing symbols and other lists. This option means we implement all the functionality (such as drawing of the animation) as a separate function that takes the data structure as a parameter.[1]
- We can interpret the code as an executable computation. When executed, the computation builds a function value or an object type that performs the required operation, such as drawing the animation at the specified time. In this case, primitives are simple function values or objects. Operations for composing primitives are functions that take function values or objects as their arguments and build a composite.

---

[1] The terminology used to describe these approaches isn't uniform. In Expert F# [Syme, Granicz, and Cisternino, 2007], this approach is called *abstract syntax representation* to highlight the point where the data structure corresponds to the syntax. Martin Fowler [Fowler, 2008] calls similar constructs *literal collection expressions*, because they're constructed as collections of literals (like lists of symbols in LISP).

Both techniques can be used to develop composable libraries in C# and F#. The first one is more suitable when we know exactly which primitives and which operations for composing them we'll need. The second approach is appropriate if we know how we'll want to use the composed entity. In section 15.2, we'll use the second one. When designing our animations library, we know that we want to be able to draw the animation at the specified time and we don't need to do anything else.

Another interesting point about composable functional libraries is that the code often doesn't look like LISP, F#, or even C#, but looks as if it were written in language for solving problems from the specific problem domain (such as a language for creating animations).

Language-oriented programming in F#

Language-oriented programming refers to writing code that somehow resembles a programming language, extends the language in some way, modifies its meaning, or changes its execution environment. In LINQ we can use it to describe what LINQ to SQL does when it executes a query written in C# 3.0 on the SQL Server. This is language-oriented programming, because it changes the execution environment of the C# code by translating the expression tree to an SQL statement. In F#, it's used when talking about F# quotations (which correspond to C# expression trees) or computation expressions. In this case, we're changing the meaning of standard F# code. Instead of running sequentially and blocking a thread, we modify it to run asynchronously.

The term can be also used when talking about composable libraries that we're discussing in this chapter. In some sense, we're designing a *language* for solving problems from a particular domain. In this chapter, the domain is creating animations, but other examples include processing collections of data (using functions for working with lists) or specifying business rules. These libraries are sometimes called *embedded domain-specific languages* (DSL). *Embedded* refers to the fact that we're not creating a standalone programming language, but that we're instead extending the host language (C# or F#) in some way.

In the functional programming tradition, the term DSL means the same thing as declarative functional libraries, but in recent years the term DSL is gaining more popularity and has been used in numerous programming languages with various meanings. In this book, we'll focus on creating well-designed declarative libraries. As we mentioned in the introduction, the key to this goal is to write the library in a compositional way. We'll follow the language-oriented programming style in many ways, because we'll try to make the syntax as nice as possible. You'll see many techniques that are useful for creating DSLs in F# and C#, but this isn't the primary goal of this chapter.

Our goal in this chapter will be to create a declarative functional library. We listed the options we have earlier, so let's now look at the first option from the list: creating a library so the code builds a data structure.

15.1.3 *Composing values*

Describing the problem as a value is the simplest way of embedding a "language" in F#. This only works for simple problems: we shouldn't have to specify any complicated behavior (such as the predicate of a filtering function), and most problems should be de-scribed just by combining primitive objects or collections and specifying their properties.

When the code effectively describes values, we can implement it in F# by creating types that allow us to create values specifying all the properties we want. The most common F# type for this kind of problem is a discriminated union, but you can also use lists (to represent collections of items) or records for primitives with a large number of properties. Listing 15.1 shows a simple type declaration for the same sort of animation example as the one shown earlier in LISP.

> **Listing 15.1   Specifying animations using discriminated unions (F#)**

```
type AnimatedLocation =                      ⊲──┐   Movement
  | Static of PointF                             │   of object
  | Rotating of PointF * float32
  | Linear of PointF * PointF
                                              ┌──   Shapes with
type Animation =                        ⊲─────┘     animated location
  | Disc of Brush * int * AnimatedLocation
  | Compose of Animation * Animation
```

Using this type, we can now create values describing simple animations. In some sense, the types in listing 15.1 specify the syntax when using the library for creating animations, because it specifies what a valid animation value is. The following snippet shows the same animation as the LISP example:

```
let animation =
  Compose(
    Disc(Brushes.Green, 50, Rotating(PointF(0.f,0.f), 100.f)),
    Disc(Brushes.Red, 20, Linear(PointF(-100.f,0.f), PointF(100.f,0.f)))
  )
```

This creates a value with a tree-like structure describing an animation composed from two discs. It specifies how the location of each object changes over time and the F# data structure `AnimatedLocation` allows us to create objects that are static, rotating, or moving along a line.

When using this approach in C#, we can rewrite the discriminated union type as a class hierarchy. Then we'll get similar results by creating an object tree. In C# 3.0 this is further simplified by object and collection initializer features:

```
var animation = new Compose(
  new Disc { Brush = Brushes.Green, Diameter = 50, Movement =
    new Rotating(new PointF(0.0f,0.0f), 100.0f) },
  new Disc { Brush = Brushes.Red, Diameter = 20, Movement =
    new Linear(new PointF(-100.0f, 0.0f), new PointF(100.0f, 0.0f) } }
);
```

The principle is the same: the declarative library is used to create values that describe the problem. The choice between discriminated unions or collections and objects is largely influenced by what syntax creates the most natural code in the host language.

This has been a passive way of describing the animation—we were basically constructing data structure. Let's look at a technique that gives a more active feeling to the code.

15.1.4 Composing functions and objects

The second option that we can use for creating composable libraries is to build some function or an object that represents the declarative specification and that can execute it. This limits the operations we can do with the composed object, because the operation is an intrinsic part of every primitive. In fact, it's often used when we need to perform a single operation, such as drawing an animation frame or calculating trades of a financial contract. We can easily add new primitives and implement new ways for composing the primitives. In functional languages, libraries written in this ways are called *combinator libraries*.

USING COMBINATOR LIBRARIES IN F#

When developing a combinator library, we'll create a couple of primitives implemented as functions or simple object values. To build more sophisticated specifications, we'll add combinators: functions or operators used to compose primitive values. This approach is flexible, because we can declare new primitives by composing core primitives provided by the library. We can also create more sophisticated functions to compose primitives by using several combinators together.

We'll use this programming style to create the F# version of the animation library. It's worth having a look at an example of the final result, so you can see what we're aiming for. The following snippet shows an animation with a sun and two rotating planets:

```
let planets =
    sun -- (rotate 150.0f 1.0f earth)
        -- (rotate 200.0f 0.7f mars)
```

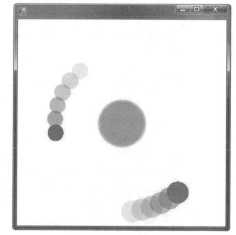

The animation is composed from three primitives using a single combinator: --. We're using three solar objects. These aren't a core part of the animation library, but we defined them using other available primitives. The example also uses a `rotate` primitive, which gives us a way to specify how an object rotates. This looks like a basic primitive, but again, it's derived from the only single primitive available for specifying the movement of an object. Figure 15.1 shows the result of running this animation.

Figure 15.1 Planet simulation with Mars and Earth rotating around the sun

Parser combinators

Combinator libraries are popular in the functional programming community and have been used for numerous tasks. The best-known example may be the Parsec library for creating parsers [Leijen, Meijer, 2001]. In that case, we're building functions that take a list of characters as an argument and return a parsed value, which can be, for example, an XML document loaded in a tree-like hierarchy. The primitives that we're starting with are extremely simple, such as a parser that returns a character if it matches a predicate specified by the user (for example, a function that returns `true` when the character is +) and fails in all other cases. The combinators let us run two parsers in parallel and return values returned by the one that succeeded or run them in a sequence.

The following example shows how to write a simple parser that can parse trivial numeric expressions, such as addition with numbers and variables (5+10 and x-12). We're using a primitive `parse` that creates a parser from a predicate and a primitive `repeated` that applies the parser one or more times in a sequence. Next, we use two custom operators that compose parsers. The `<|>` operator builds a parser that succeeds when any of the two parsers succeed and the `<+>` operator composes parsers in a sequence:

```
let argument = parse Char.IsLetter <|> repeated (parse Char.IsDigit)
let operator = parse ((=) '+') <|> parse ((=) '-')
let simpleExpression = argument <+> operator <+> argument
```

We start by defining a parser `argument` that succeeds when the input contains a letter, representing a variable name, or when it contains one or more digits, representing a number (it can parse strings like "x" or "123", but not for example "1x3"). Next we build a parser named `operator` that succeeds when the input contains a plus or minus symbol. Note that we're using partial function application to build a predicate that returns true when the input is the specified character. Finally, we compose the two parsers in a sequence using the `<+>` operator to build a parser that parses the whole expression.

We can implement something like a combinator library in C# too. Instead of using function calls and custom operators, we'll use the most elementary expression that object-oriented languages like C# have: a method call.

USING METHOD CHAINS IN C#

We've talked about immutable objects in numerous places in the book, so you understand the basic axiom: all operations of an immutable object return a new instance of the object with modified values. This changes the way we work with the type, but it also changes the syntax we can use. When each method call returns a new object, we can sequence operations by creating a method chain. We'll demonstrate this using a LINQ query as an example. As you already know, all LINQ operators return a new sequence, keeping the original one unchanged, so we can elegantly chain operations like this:

```
var q = data.Where(c => c.Country == "London")
          .OrderBy(c => c.Name)
          .Select(c => c.Name);
```

Usual code written using a composable functional library is written as a single expression. In F#, the expression can be factored into pieces using `let` bindings, but that's only a way to make the expression more readable. The code written using method chains in object-oriented languages is no different. We're writing a single expression that looks like a declarative specification of what results we want to get.

Now, let's return to our example with animations. We can easily imagine that the values representing solar objects (`sun`, `earth`, and `mars`) are some immutable objects. Then we can write the same declarative specification of the solar system like this:

```
var planets =
  sun.Compose(earth.Rotate(150.0f, 1.0f))
     .Compose(mars.Rotate(200.0f, 0.7f));
```

All solar objects are values of the same type that could be called `AnimShape`. (This isn't the representation we'll implement later in the chapter, but we can use it to describe the code snippet.) The `Rotate` method can be invoked on any `AnimShape` value. It takes parameters for the rotation as arguments and creates a new animated shape, with additional rotation.

The code is very compositional, because all the operations of `AnimShape` return a new `AnimShape` value as the result. The first call to the `Compose` method creates a new shape that consists of the sun and the rotating earth. The second call combines the composed shape with rotating Mars, so we'll get a single `AnimShape` value representing three solar objects, each of them with a different movement. Movements are compositional too. If we chain a call to the `Rotate` method with a call to `MoveFromTo` (representing movement between two specified points), the object will be rotating and the center of the rotation will be moving between the specified points.

As a benefit of method chaining, we can write declaratively looking code. In functional programming, this doesn't require additional effort, because we get the syntax for free thanks to immutability. Similar constructs can be used when working with mutable objects as well.

Method chains for mutable objects

In imperative programming languages, providing the same syntax is a bit more difficult. If we were writing code to build a solar system animation using mutable objects, the methods for configuring objects would return `void` and we couldn't use method chaining. A typical imperative code to create and configure objects looks like this:

```
var planets = new AnimShape();
earth.SetRotation(150.0f, 1.0f);
mars.SetRotation(200.0f, 0.7f);
planets.Children.AddRange(new AnimShape[] { sun, earth, mars });
```

> **(continued)**
>
> Once you become accustomed to using the declarative composable style, you'll find this less readable than the previous snippet. You can use various techniques to get the same syntax, even when working with mutable objects. In the context of OOP, the programming style is also called a *fluent interface*, and it has many supporters because of the enhanced readability.
>
> When using this style, you create a wrapper type that configures a mutable object created under the hood. Martin Fowler calls the construct *Expression Builder* and describes how to do this [Fowler, 2008]. This is one of the nice benefits of using functional programming style in C#: you'll often end up creating a readable fluent interface even if you're not doing that intentionally. Be careful when using an API like this. A class that uses fluent interfaces may look like immutable even though it's not!

The example we've just seen shows that composition is a powerful principle, so you're probably eager to know how we can implement the library that enables this. In the next few sections, we'll implement F# and C# libraries for describing animations, and we'll also see how combinators and method chains work.

15.2 *Creating animated values*

The idea of expressing animations in a functional language using a combinator library comes from a Haskell project called Fran, created by Conal Elliott and Paul Hudak in 1997 [Elliot, Hudak, 1997]. Fran (which stands for *functional reactive animations*) allows you to create animations and specify how the animation reacts to events such as mouse clicks.

15.2.1 *Introducing functional animations*

The library that we'll implement in this chapter is largely motivated by Fran. We'll focus on the animations alone and we won't talk in detail about reacting to events. We'll look at how the library could be extended to support this in the next chapter, where we'll talk about reactive GUI programming. Animations can be elegantly modeled using time-varying values. In Fran, these values are called *behaviors*, and we'll use the same name.

NOTE   In our animation system, a behavior is a time-varying value. It can be represented as a composite value, whose actual value may be different depending on the time. We talked about composite values earlier. `Option<int>` is a simple example: it can have an integer value or a special value of `None`. Similarly, we'll have a type `Behavior<int>`, whose actual integer value can be different depending on the time.

Behaviors are an essential part of our animation framework, because we can use them to specify the locations of objects. We'll create an application that counts the time and redraws the content repeatedly. During each redraw, we'll get the locations of all objects at the current time and we'll draw them, which means that the whole scene will be animated. We'll focus on behaviors now and come back to their place in the animation library later. At that point you'll see that once we have behaviors, the rest of the framework falls into place easily.

15.2.2 Introducing behaviors

Behaviors are largely independent from the animation library. They represent a value that varies according to time: it may not be related to graphics or drawing. A behavior could model network traffic flow, tidal movement, a stock price, the value of sensory input of a robot such as the temperature, or any other time-varying measurement.

This means that we can start by implementing behaviors without restricting ourselves to animation. In a typically functional manner, we'll first think about how we want to represent behaviors, then we'll implement some simple ones. Once we've created the behaviors, we'll be able to apply them to animation; we'll develop more sophisticated behaviors using composition toward the end of the chapter.

We've already described a behavior as a composite type; let's make that concrete and give it a name: `Behavior<'T>`. It's generic so that it can represent any kind of time-varying measurement: a temperature behavior might return a `float32`, whereas an ad rotator in a web application might return a `Uri` for the ad to display at the given time. From the user's perspective, the internal representation isn't interesting. Our library will provide basic functions to create behaviors, and the user will build behaviors using these functions. Since we're going to implement even the simple behaviors, we'll need to work at a lower level.

REPRESENTING BEHAVIORS IN F#

One possible representation would be to store the initial value and some difference that specifies how the value changes over time. If we had an initial value of 10 and a "difference per second" of 1, the value after 15 seconds would be 25. This isn't very flexible and we could represent only limited kinds of animated values. We'll use a more general representation: a function that returns the value if we give it the time as an argument. This allows us to represent any kind of time-based value. Here are the F# type declarations.

Listing 15.2 Representing behaviors using functions (F#)

```
type BehaviorContext =
  { Time : float32 }
type Behavior<'T> =
  | BehaviorFunc of (BehaviorContext -> 'T)
```

The `BehaviorContext` type represents arguments for evaluating time-varying values. The `Behavior` type is declared as a single-case discriminated union, and it consists of a function that evaluates the value of behavior. The simplest possible representation of the behavior would be an F# function type `float32 -> 'T`, and in that case we wouldn't have to declare a type `Behavior<'T>`.

TIP   In this chapter, we're storing a time in behaviors as a value of type
       float32. The reason is that we'll use behaviors primarily with graphics,
       and the System.Drawing namespace uses this numeric type. There are
       other options as well. Most interestingly, we could use units of measure
       and store the time as float<s> representing time in seconds. Units of
       measure would make the code more self-explanatory. We could define a
       pixel unit (px) and represent locations as float<px>. You can try aug-
       menting the code with units yourself, or you can find a version that uses
       units on the book's website.

It's generally a good idea, to name the types that are important. Listing 15.2 has taken
this guideline two steps further, so it will be easier to use and extend behaviors in the
future.

- We're using a simple record type to wrap the current time. This allows us to add
  new information that can be used by the behavior, beyond just the time.
- We're using a single-case discriminated union to wrap the function. This gives a
  name to the type and allows us to hide the internal representation of the type.

The user of our library could then see Behavior<int> without knowing that internally
it's just a function. The fact that we're using single-case discriminated union also
means we can use pattern matching to access the function value. Now that we've got
the F# type declaration, let's look at its equivalent in C#.

REPRESENTING BEHAVIORS IN C#

We have fewer options to choose from in C#, although there are possibilities other than
creating a class. We could represent the behavior directly using a delegate such as
Func<float, T> but we're going to follow the F# model and hide the internal representation. Listing 15.3 shows a simple implementation that's quite similar to the F# code.

Listing 15.3   Representing behaviors (C#)

```
internal struct BehaviorContext {          ◁─┐    Represents
  public BehaviorContext(float time) {      ❶   animation state
    this.time = time;
  }
  private readonly float time;
  public float Time { get { return time; } }◁─┐  Stores
}                                             ❷ current time
public class Behavior<T> {
  internal Behavior(Func<BehaviorContext, T> f) {
    this.f = f;
  }
  private readonly Func<BehaviorContext, T> f;
  internal Func<BehaviorContext, T> BehaviorFunc      ❸   Wraps function that
  { get { return f; } }                                   calculates value
}
```

We're using a simple immutable value type to store the current time ❶. We'll pass its
values as arguments to various functions, so we want to make sure it can't be modified.
In this case, making the type immutable is as simple as creating a read-only field and

property ❷. The representation of the behavior itself is a generic class with a single immutable property of type Func<DrawingContext, T> ❸, which corresponds to the function value wrapped inside an F# discriminated union.

To hide the representation of the Behavior type from the user, we've marked the property as internal. Similarly, the BehaviorContext type is also internal. Instead of constructing the behaviors directly, the user will create them using the primitive functions that we provide. Let's look at those primitives now, starting with the C# version.

15.2.3 *Creating simple behaviors in C#*

We'll begin with just a few basic functions for creating behaviors. Once we have a nice way for visualizing behaviors, we'll return to this topic and add interesting constructs.

The simplest method that creates a behavior will take a function that we can directly use as the underlying representation of the behavior. This will be an internal method used for implementation of other primitives. Since we're going to wrap the creation of the object in a method, we can create a generic method in a nongeneric class and use C#'s type inference to make the calling code simpler. This resembles the helper methods we implemented earlier, such as Option.Some. Here's the code for this trivial creation method.

Listing 15.4 Creating behavior from a function (C#)

```
internal static class Behavior {
  internal static Behavior<T> Create<T>(Func<BehaviorContext, T> f) {
    return new Behavior<T>(f);
  }
}
```

Listing 15.4 creates a new instance of the immutable Behavior<T> class. We'll see that we can create most of the behaviors without using this method directly from the user's code, so we can mark it as internal. This means that the internal representation of behaviors can stay fully hidden.

Next, we can use the Behavior.Create method to create a couple of primitive constructs that we'll make available to the user. In C#, we'll expose them as static methods and properties in a static class. You can see this class in listing 15.5.

Listing 15.5 Primitive behaviors (C#)

```
public static class Time {
  public static Behavior<float> Current {              ❶
    get { return Behavior.Create(ctx => ctx.Time); }
  }
  public static Behavior<float> Wiggle {               ❷
    get { return Behavior.Create(ctx =>
          (float)Math.Sin(ctx.Time * Math.PI)); }
  }
  public static Behavior<T> Forever<T>(T v) {          ❸
    return Behavior.Create(ctx => v);
  }
```

```
    public static Behavior<float> Forever(this float v) {        4
      return Behavior.Create(ctx => v);
    }
}
```

The first three constructs are quite straightforward. The `Current` property returns a behavior that represents the current time ❶. The property named `Wiggle` calculates the sine function of the time ❷. This will be quite useful in the animation—sine can be used for creating circular movements, and we'll use it later to create rotating drawings. The `Forever` method creates a behavior that always has the same value, which is specified as an argument ❸. This method is generic, so we can use it to create constant behaviors of any type. The nongeneric overload of the method ❹ makes it possible to use a nicer syntax when creating constant behaviors of floating-point numbers.

We'll use behaviors for creating animations later, but there's another way to visualize them: we can draw a graph of a numeric value against time in the obvious way. Figure 15.2 shows the three primitive behaviors we just implemented. The function that draws the screenshot is available as part of the source code available at this book's website, so you can use it to experiment with behaviors yourself.

The last construct in listing 15.5 is an extension method for the C# `float` type ❹. The C# syntax allows us to call methods directly on numeric literals, so we can use this method to write expressions such as `0.5f.Forever()`. This is syntactically very simple, which makes our library look a bit like DSL. In later examples, this construct will be used frequently; calling the `Time.Forever` method directly would definitely make the code less readable.

Why didn't we create a single generic method that was also an extension method? That would work, but we'd add a `Forever` method to each and every single .NET type.

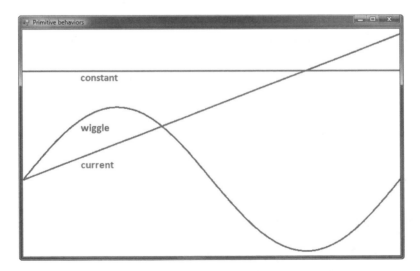

Figure 15.2 Primitive behaviors during the first two seconds. The value of `current` ranges from 0 to 2 and `wiggle` oscillates between +1 and –1. The `constant` behavior has a value of 1.5.

This looks like overkill, because we won't need to create behaviors from most of the .NET types. On the other hand, this extension method makes sense for floats, since we'll need to create constant behaviors from floating-point numbers relatively often.

Now we know what behaviors we want to implement, it's easy to do the same thing in F#. After that, we'll experiment with them in F# Interactive to learn how we can use them later in this chapter.

15.2.4 Creating simple behaviors in F#

We'll begin by duplicating the functionality we've just implemented in C#. Listing 15.6 implements two behavior values (called `wiggle` and `time`) and a function for creating constant behaviors (called `forever`).

Listing 15.6 Primitive behavior functions and values (F#)

```
> open System;;
> let sample(a) = BehaviorFunc(a);;                        ◁─┐   Builds behavior
val sample : (BehaviorContext -> 'a) -> Behavior<'a>      ❶   directly

> let forever(n) = sample(fun _ -> n)
  let time        = sample(fun t -> t.Time)
  let wiggle      = sample(fun t -> sin(t.Time * float32 Math.PI))
  ;;
val forever : 'a -> Behavior<'a>              ┌─  Declares generic
val time : Behavior<float32>               ❷   function, two values
val wiggle : Behavior<float32>
```

Listing 15.6 starts by creating a utility function called `sample` ❶, which is similar to the previous `Behavior.Create` method. We could use the discriminated union constructor `BehaviorFunc` directly, but we want to make sure that the internal representation isn't unnecessarily exposed. In case we later wanted to change the representation from a function to, say, a list of values, we could still provide a reasonable implementation of the `sample` function. The name `sample` reflects the fact that the function can be used to get individual observations at selected times (called *sampling* in statistics).

Once we have the utility function, we create three primitives just as we did in listing 15.5. You can also see the type signatures inferred by F# Interactive ❷. We have a generic function (`forever`) and two simple values (`time` and `wiggle`). The one aspect of the C# code that we haven't implemented yet is a syntactically friendlier way to construct constant numeric behaviors. Using the `forever` function, we could write (`forever 0.5f`), which isn't as elegant as it could be. We can use the same approach as in C# and define a type extension for the type `float32`:

```
type System.Single with
  member x.forever = forever(x)
```

To implement an extension member, we have to use the full .NET name of `float32`, which is `System.Single`. Extension members in F# aren't limited to methods, so we've implemented this extension as a property. It's used like this:

```
> let v = 123.0f.forever;;
val v : Behavior<System.Single>
```

As you can see, this is syntactically very elegant. If we strictly followed .NET naming, the name of the property would start with an uppercase F. However, we're writing a library that attempts to look like a language. In that case, the syntax is important and lowercase single-word identifiers are often used as keywords of DSL. Now that we know how to create primitive behaviors, we'll explore working with them. The best tool for explorative programming like this is F# Interactive.

15.3 Writing computations with behaviors

In this section, we'll write a few utility functions to help us work with behaviors. Even though we're experimenting at this stage, most of the code in this section will be useful when we implement our animation sample. We'll implement the functions in F# first and test them in F# Interactive, then reimplement the most important ones in C#.

The first thing we'll need to implement in order to test any code using behaviors is a function that reads the value of a behavior at the specified time.

15.3.1 Reading values

Calculating the value of a behavior at the given time is easy. The internal representation is a function that gives us the value when it gets the time as an argument, so we need to execute this function. Listing 15.7 shows a function called readValue, which takes a time and a behavior and returns the value. Once we have this function, we use it to read values from the primitive behaviors we created earlier.

Listing 15.7   Reading values of behaviors at the specified time (F# Interactive)

```
> let readValue time (BehaviorFunc bfunc) =
    bfunc { Time = time };;
val readValue : float32 -> Behavior<'a> -> 'a

> 42.0f.forever |> readValue 1.5f;;
val it : System.Single = 42.0f

> time |> readValue 1.5f;;
val it : float32 = 1.5f

> wiggle |> readValue 1.5f;;
val it : float32 = -1.0f
```

The function in listing 15.7 takes a behavior as the second parameter, which makes it possible to call the function elegantly using the pipelining operator. We use pattern matching to extract the function carried by the behavior passed into the function. Next we construct a BehaviorContext value to wrap the given time, and pass it as an argument to the function, which calculates the value of the behavior at the specified time.

The rest of listing 15.7 shows values calculated by the primitive behaviors we implemented earlier. The constant behavior works as expected, the time primitive returns 1.5f after one and half seconds, and the value of wiggle in the lowest peak is –1.0f. The interactive development style once again helped us make sure that we're starting with correct code. Reading values of primitive behaviors is a good start, but how can we create behaviors that are more sophisticated? Suppose we wanted to create behavior that represents the square of the current time. We could write this using `sample`, but that's quite complicated—and we're hoping to hide that from the end user anyway. Ideally, we want to apply the `square` function to a behavior.

15.3.2 Applying a function to a behavior

When describing behaviors earlier, we explained that a behavior is a composite value and that a similarity exists between `Behavior<int>` and `Option<int>`. Both are composite values that contain another value, but in some special way. The option type is unusual because it may be empty, and behavior is unusual because the value depends on the time.

This analogy suggests a way forward for behaviors. We've seen the `Option.map` function in a few different contexts now, and its ability to apply the specified function to the value carried by the option is exactly what we're looking for in our behavior system. Listing 15.8 creates a similar `map` function for behaviors and demonstrates it with a simple "time squared" behavior.

Listing 15.8   Implementing `map` for behaviors (F# Interactive)

```
> module Behavior =
    let map f (BehaviorFunc bfunc) =
      sample(fun t -> f(bfunc(t)));;        ❶
module Behavior =
  val map : ('a -> 'b) -> Behavior<'a> -> Behavior<'b>

> let squared = time |> Behavior.map (fun n -> n * n);;    ❷
val squared : Behavior<float32>

> squared |> readValue 9.0f;;    ❸
val it : float32 = 81.0f
```

The `map` function is declared inside a module to follow the standard naming pattern. The first argument of `Behavior.map` is a function (`f`) that we want to apply to values of the behavior. The second argument is the behavior itself, and we again extract the underlying function that represents it (`bfunc`) using pattern matching. To build the result ❶, we need to create a new behavior, so we construct its underlying representation, which is a function. We use a lambda function that takes the time as the argument. It first runs `bfunc` to get the value of the original behavior at that time, then runs the `f` function to get the final result. In fact, the body is just composing the functions, so we could also write `sample(bfunc >> f)` as the implementation. In listing 15.8, we used a lambda function to make the code more explicit, but after working with functional code for some time, you'd probably find function composition easier to use and more readable in this case.

We can now use `Behavior.map` to perform any calculation with the values carried by the behavior. The second command ❷ shows that we can calculate the square of other primitive behaviors. The behavior that we get as a result doesn't execute the square function until we ask it for an actual value at the specified time. When we do this ❸, it executes the function that we returned as a result from `map`. This function then gets the current time by evaluating the value of the original behavior (in this case the `time` primitive). Then it runs the square function that we provided.

The general goal of combinator libraries is to provide a way to describe the problem by composing other primitives rather than writing a program to solve the problem. Functions like `Behavior.map` play a key role in this approach, because they represent a well-understood idea (such as *projection*) that we can use when writing a declarative description of the problem. As we'll see shortly we can employ the `map` function in one very useful way that we didn't think of when designing it.

We've made a lot of progress: we can now take a primitive behavior and construct a more complex behavior using almost any calculation. We could now implement the `wiggle` primitive just by applying the sine function to the `time` primitive using `map`. There are still things that we can't do easily. What if we wanted to add two behaviors? Is there a more elegant way to do this than using the `sample` primitive?

15.3.3 *Turning functions into "behavior functions"*

The `Behavior.map` function takes two arguments and we specified both in listing 15.8. Partial function application allows us to call the function with a single argument. Using the function in this way will give us an interesting insight. In listing 15.9, we only specify the first argument (a function); we'll use the `abs` function, which returns the absolute value of an integer.

Listing 15.9   Using `Behavior.map` with partial application (F# Interactive)

```
> abs;;
val it : (int -> int)

> let absB = Behavior.map abs;;
val absB : (Behavior<int> -> Behavior<int>)
```

The first line shows the type of the `abs` function, and the second line shows what happens if we call `Behavior.map` with `abs` as the first and only argument. The type of the result is a function that takes a `Behavior<int>` and returns a `Behavior<int>`. This means that we used `Behavior.map` to create a function that calculates the absolute value of a behavior. We can use this trick to turn any function that takes a single parameter into a function that does the same thing for behaviors.

LIFTING OF OPERATORS AND FUNCTIONS

The construct that we've just seen is a well-known concept in functional programming, usually called *lifting*. In some senses, we could even call it a functional design pattern. The Haskell wiki [HaskellWiki, 2009] defines lifting as a concept that allows us to transform a function that works with values into a function that does the same thing in a different setting. Lifting is used in one C# 2.0 language feature, so we can demonstrate it using familiar code. If we want to create a primitive value such as `int`, which can have a `null` value, we can use C# 2.0 nullable types:

```
int? num1 = 14;
int? num2 = null;
```

So far, there's nothing out of the ordinary. We've declared two nullable `int` values. One contains a real integer value and the other doesn't have a value. You may not know that you can write following:

```
int? sum1 = num1 + num2;
int? sum2 = num1 + num1;
```

The result of the first calculation will be `null`, because at least one of the arguments is `null`. The result of the second expression will be 28, because both arguments of the + operator have a value. In this example, the C# compiler takes the + operator, which works with integers, and creates a lifted + operator that works with nullable types. This operation is similar to what we want to do with behaviors.

`Behavior.map` implements lifting for functions with a single argument, but we'd like to implement the same functionality for other functions. Listing 15.10 shows helpers to allow functions with up to three arguments to be lifted.

Listing 15.10   Lifting functions of multiple arguments (F#)

```
> let lift1 f behavior =
    map f behavior
  let lift2 f (BehaviorFunc bf1) (BehaviorFunc bf2) =
    sample(fun t -> f (bf1(t)) (bf2(t)))
  let lift3 f (BehaviorFunc bf1) (BehaviorFunc bf2) (BehaviorFunc bf3) =
    sample(fun t -> f (bf1(t)) (bf2(t)) (bf3(t)))
  ;;
val lift1 : ('a -> 'b)              -> B<'a> -> B<'b>
val lift2 : ('a -> 'b -> 'c)        -> B<'a> -> B<'b> -> B<'c>
val lift3 : ('a -> 'b -> 'c -> 'd) -> B<'a> -> B<'b> -> B<'c> -> B<'d>
```

We're placing all functions to the `Behavior` module, but the listing doesn't repeat the module declaration. Our example first shows how to implement the lifting functions and, separately, shows their signatures. Note that we've abbreviated `Behavior` as `B` in the printed type signatures.

The implementation of lifting function with one parameter is trivial, because it does the same thing as `Behavior.map`. This is possible only thanks to partial function application, so the C# implementation will be different. The implementations of `lift2` and `lift3` are similar to the `map` function we saw earlier, and the same pattern could clearly be applied to functions with more than three arguments.

At this point, we can implement general computations for behaviors without using the low-level `sample` primitive. Any computation you can think of can be implemented using the `time` primitive and one of the lifting functions. Here's the solution to our earlier problem of adding two behaviors:

```
> let added = Behavior.lift2 (+) wiggle time;;
val added : Behavior<float32>
```

This example uses the `lift2` function, passing in the + operator and two primitive behaviors. If we read the value of the returned behavior, it will get the values of the two behaviors used as arguments and add them together. We can visualize this behavior in

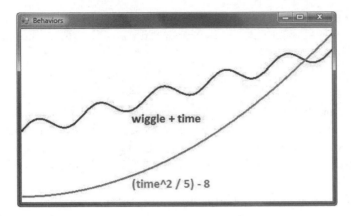

Figure 15.3   Graph showing values of two complex behaviors during the first 10 seconds

the same way as before. Figure 15.3 shows this behavior and a version of the "squaring" behavior, modified slightly to avoid it going off the top of the screenshot too quickly.

You may be wondering if that's the best we can do in terms of syntax—it's still a little clumsy, after all. Indeed, later on we'll see what's required to allow us to write just `wiggle + time`, but first let's implement `Behavior.map` and the lifting functions in C#.

15.3.4 *Implementing lifting and map in C#*

Lifting functions and a `map` operation are essential for constructing behaviors, so we'll need them in the C# version of the project as well. After the previous discussion about the F# version, you have some idea of what these functions should do, so we won't discuss everything in detail. The C# version has interesting differences from the F# code.

Whenever we've seen a `map` function in F#, we've used the name `Select` in C#. This is the standard terminology used in LINQ, so we'll stay consistent and implement a `Select` extension method for behaviors. Earlier we mentioned that in C# there's a difference between the `Select` method and the lifting methods. The best way to understand the difference is to look at the function signatures for `Select` and the simplest lifting method:

```
// Apply the function 'f' to values of 'behavior'
Behavior<R> Select<T, R>(Behavior<T> behavior, Func<T, R> f);
```

```
// Returns a function that applies 'f' to the given behavior
Func<Behavior<T>, Behavior<R>> Lift<T, R>(Func<T, R> f);
```

In C#, we can create an overloaded method, so the lifting method for different types of functions will be called `Lift`. The version in the previous code snippet takes one argument (a function) and returns a function (as a `Func` delegate). The `Select` method takes the function to apply and also the behavior, so it can immediately construct a new behavior using this function. The implementation of these functions will be similar, so we can still see that they're related, but we can't implement them easily using the same code. (It's possible to implement each of these functions using the other one. If you want to practice your functional thinking skills, you can try to do that.) Listing 15.11 shows the implementation of `Select`, and two overloads of `Lift`.

Listing 15.11 Lifting methods and `Select` (C#)

```csharp
public static Behavior<R> Select<T, R>
    (this Behavior<T> behavior, Func<T, R> f) {
  return Create(ctx => f(behavior.BehaviorFunc(ctx)));     ❶
}

public static Func<Behavior<T>, Behavior<R>>
    Lift<T, R> (Func<T, R> f) {
  return behavior => Create(ctx => f(behavior.BehaviorFunc(ctx)));   ❷
}

public static Func<Behavior<T1>, Behavior<T2>, Behavior<R>>
    Lift<T1, T2, R>(Func<T1, T2, R> f) {
  return (b1, b2) => Create(ctx =>                          ❸
    f(b1.BehaviorFunc(ctx), b2.BehaviorFunc(ctx)));
}
```

We've added all the extension methods to the static, nongeneric `Behavior` class, which already contained the internal `Create` method. The implementation of `Select` ❶ is a direct translation of the F# version. It constructs a behavior and gives it a function that calculates the value at the specified time using the original behavior (`behavior`) and the provided function.

The second method ❷ is more interesting, because it returns a function. We implement this with a lambda function that takes the behavior as an argument and does the same thing as the previous method. Finally, we implement one more overload, which is similar but works with functions of two arguments ❸. Using these methods, we can construct the same behaviors as we did in F#. The best way to create a behavior representing the squared time is to use the `Select` extension method. To add two primitive behaviors, we'll create a lifted addition function and then use it:

```csharp
var squared = Time.Current.Select(t => t * t);
```

```csharp
var plusB = Behavior.Lift((float a, float b) => a + b);
var added = plusB(Time.Current, Time.Wiggle);
```

The first example should be fairly straightforward. It uses the `Select` method to specify a function that will be used for calculating values of the `squared` behavior. The second example first declares a value `plusB`, which is a function that can add two behaviors of type float. The overall type of this function is quite long:

```csharp
Func<Behavior<float>, Behavior<float>, Behavior<float>>
```

Fortunately we can use an implicitly typed local variable to avoid cluttering up the source code. Once we have this lifted + operator, we can use it to add two behaviors together. In this case we add behaviors representing the current time and the `wiggle` primitive, with the result being another behavior (more specifically `Behavior<float>`).

Behaviors are essential to our animation framework and are the most difficult aspect of it. The next step is to decide how we're going to draw our shapes. We're not animating them yet—we're drawing an individual frame.

Behaviors and LINQ

The signature of the `Select` method in listing 15.11 has the same structure as the `Select` method used in LINQ when writing queries. This isn't accidental, and it means you can use C# query expressions to create behaviors. Here's another way of creating the squaring behavior:

```
var squared = from t in Time.Current select t * t;
```

This means the same thing as the earlier version: the compiler translates the query expression into the same code. This type of query is interesting because the source of the values (`Time.Wiggle`) effectively contains a potentially infinite set of values. The "query" is only evaluated when we need a value from the new behavior for a specific time. We won't discuss LINQ queries for behaviors in any more detail here, but we could also implement the `SelectMany` query operator, which would allow us to combine behaviors like this:

```
var added = from a in Time.Current
            from b in Time.Wiggle
            select a + b;
```

This is definitely an interesting alternative to using lifting explicitly. In F#, we could implement a computation expression builder too. You can find implementations of these interesting extensions on this book's website.

15.4 *Working with drawings*

If we're going to work with a drawing, first we must ask ourselves, what *is* a drawing? What do we want it to represent in a general sense? What do we want to be able to do with it? What's the best way to represent graphics in our animations?

We'll think about these questions in a moment, but we already know some of the answers—in particular, we know that we want to be able to *compose* our drawings. The animation will be described in terms of drawings that are moving and that are composed to form a single drawing. In the future, we could also support other geometrical transformations such as scaling and skewing.

15.4.1 *Representing drawings*

In chapter 2 we used the concept of a shape to demonstrate discriminated unions. This would be a good choice for a diagramming application, where the application needs to understand the structure of shapes. It wouldn't be particularly flexible for our animation library, so we'll use a more extensible representation. In C#, a drawing will be an interface with a method to draw with a `Graphics` object. This could be represented more simply as a function, but again we want to hide the internal representation.

The F# version will follow the C# style and use an interface too. The reason is that the code will be using a lot of .NET functionality, and interfaces are more consistent with standard .NET programming than F#-specific types. Another reason is that it's a good chance for us to exercise working with F# object types. As the representations are so similar, we can discuss them together. Listing 15.12 shows the first steps in implementing drawings.

> **Listing 15.12   Representing drawings in C# and F#**

```csharp
// C# version
using System.Drawing;

interface IDrawing {          ❶
  void Draw(Graphics gr);
}

class Drawing : IDrawing {          ❷
  private readonly Action<Graphics> f;
  public Drawing(Action<Graphics> f) {
    this.f = f;
  }
  public void Draw(Graphics gr) {
    DrawFunc(gr);
  }
}
```

```fsharp
// F# version
open System.Drawing

type Drawing =          ❸
  abstract Draw : Graphics -> unit

let drawing(f) =          ❹
  { new Drawing with
      member x.Draw(gr) = f(gr) }
```

Even though the architectural idea is the same in both languages, the implementation uses different techniques. In both C# and F#, we first define an interface ❶ ❸. In F# we don't say that we're declaring an interface—the compiler infers that because the type contains only abstract members. As we mentioned in chapter 9, we can omit the I prefix from the F# interface name as long as it's used only from F#, because F# unifies all type declarations.

Next we need to decide how we're going to create a drawing. It's specified by the drawing function, so we want to be able to specify a lambda function. In C#, we create a simple class ❷ that implements the interface and takes a function of type Action<Graphics> as the argument of its constructor. The argument represents the function that is called when the drawing is asked to draw itself. In F#, we could use object expressions every time we need to create a Drawing value, but we implement a utility function to simplify this task. The function drawing ❹ takes a function that does the drawing as an argument and returns a Drawing value that will use this function. This allows us to use a lambda function, which is syntactically simpler than an object expression.

Listing 15.12 shows that object-oriented and functional concepts can be used effectively together. The interface declaration uses a conventional object-oriented idea, because the sample we're discussing in this chapter is already a more evolved application. However, for the implementation, we can still use the simplicity of functional style. We'll see this in the next section as we implement our first concrete drawing.

15.4.2 *Creating and composing drawings*

We're going to keep things simple by drawing a circle. We could implement many other types in a similar way, but we'll look at one example and you can add additional drawings yourself. The exact shapes aren't particularly important, but we need something concrete before we can discuss the more interesting topic of composition.

CREATING AND MOVING CIRCLES

Creating a drawing is a matter of providing a function to draw on the Graphics object, which is given to the function as an argument. The Graphics type has a FillEllipse method, so the implementation shouldn't be tricky at all. It's worth noting that the listing contains a small amount of additional noise: adding another drawing would only take a few lines of code. Listing 15.13 shows both the C# and F# implementations.

Listing 15.13   Creating circle in F# and C#

```
// C# version
public static class Drawings {                                ①
  public static IDrawing Circle(Brush brush, float size) {
    return new Drawing(gr =>                                   ②
      gr.FillEllipse(brush, -size/2.0f, -size/2.0f, size, size)
    );
  }
}

// F# version
module Drawings =                 ③
  let circle brush size =
    drawing(fun g ->                                          ④
      g.FillEllipse(brush, -size/2.0f, -size/2.0f, size, size))
```

To better structure the code, we've placed the functionality inside an organizational unit named Drawings. In C# it's implemented as a static class ①, while in F# we're using a module ③. The C# code that implements the Circle method creates a new Drawing object ①, giving it the drawing function as an argument. The lambda function calls FillEllipse with the specified brush and size. In F#, we implement circle as a simple function that takes the brush and the size as two arguments.

   In the traditional functional design, this is the preferred way of writing functions unless there's some logical reason for using tuples (such as when a tuple represents a point with two coordinates). We've been using tupled parameters more often in F#, to conform with the usual .NET coding style, but in this case, we'll use the functional approach. Using the functional style when developing combinator libraries is generally a good idea—we'll see shortly how this design makes it easier to create an animated circle.

The function uses the higher-order function `drawing` that we implemented earlier and gives it a lambda function to draw the circle ❹. We'll use `circle` as the only primitive drawing for now, and see what we can do with it.

If we created two circles, the center of both would be the point `(0,0)`. This means that if we composed two circles, we wouldn't get very interesting results. The code in listing 15.13 allows us to specify a circle's size, but it appears we forgot to specify a location! Actually this was deliberate, because we're going to use a different approach to specify the location. We'll create a circle with the center at `(0,0)` and move it to any point we'll need.

We'll implement movement of a drawing as a function (or method) that takes a drawing and a pair of coordinates as arguments. It then returns a new drawing that draws the original one translated by the given offset. How can we implement this functionality? We could draw the original drawing to a bitmap and then draw the bitmap to the specified coordinates, but there's a simpler solution. The `Graphics` type that we're using to do the drawing supports the translation transformation directly. Listing 15.14 shows the implementation for both languages.

Listing 15.14   Translating drawings in F# and C#

```
// F# version
let translate x y (img:Drawing) =
  drawing(fun g ->
    g.TranslateTransform(x, y)        ❶
    img.Draw(g)                       ❷
    g.TranslateTransform(-x, -y) )    ❸

// C# version
public static IDrawing Translate(this IDrawing img, float x, float y) {   ❹
  return new Drawing(g => {
    g.TranslateTransform(x, y);
    img.Draw(g);
    g.TranslateTransform(-x, -y); }
  );
}
```

The combinator returns a new translated drawing value. The implementation uses the same creation pattern as the code to draw a circle. The F# function uses the `drawing` primitive to specify how to draw the translated image, while in C# we create a new `Drawing` object directly and specify the drawing function. The C# version implements `Translate` as an extension method ❹, so that we can call it using dot notation. Note that we're adding a method to an interface `IDrawing`. This wouldn't be possible without extension methods, because interfaces can contain only abstract members.

The implementation is slightly more interesting this time. It changes the origin of the coordinate system used when drawing on the graphics using the `TranslateTransform` method ❶. This means that if we run the original drawing code (drawing a circle, for example), it will still draw at `(0,0)`, but the point will actually be somewhere else on the graphics surface. Once we configure the translation, we run the original drawing ❷ and reset the transform ❸. Strictly speaking, we should run the code that restores the original settings in a `finally` block, but we wanted to keep the code simple.

Now that we can move drawings around, we can finally create something other than circles drawing on top of each other. However, we don't want to work with a collection of drawings all the time. How can we create a single drawing from two other drawings?

COMPOSING DRAWINGS

If we composed drawings by storing all the drawings in a collection, we'd have to duplicate many functions. We might want to move all the drawings in a collection, but `translate` only works with a single drawing. Instead, we want to create a single drawing that will draw all the composed values. We're going to create a composition function to achieve this. To understand how the function works, we can look at its type signature:

```
val compose : Drawing -> Drawing -> Drawing
```

The function takes two drawing values as arguments and returns a single drawing. We don't need to specify any offsets to define the positions of drawings, because we can translate the arguments before calling `compose` using the `translate` function from the previous section. The implementation is quite simple, as you can see here.

Listing 15.15   Creating composed drawing in F# and C#

```
// F# version
let compose (img1:Drawing) (img2:Drawing) =
  drawing(fun g ->
    img1.Draw(g)           ❶ Draws both
    img2.Draw(g) )            composed drawings

// C# version
public static IDrawing Compose(this IDrawing img1, IDrawing img2) {
  return new Drawing(g => {
    img1.Draw(g);
    img2.Draw(g); }
  );
}
```

Listing 15.15 once again repeats the pattern that we've been using to create drawings. This time, the lambda function used for the new drawing invokes the `Draw` method of both of the original drawings that we're composing together ❶.

Using the three functions we've just implemented, we can create drawings containing multiple colorful circles at different locations. Implementing other primitive drawings would be simple but wouldn't teach us anything new: we'll stick with circles for this chapter.

So far we've seen the code used to implement the drawings, but we haven't used any of it. Before we explore animations, let's look at some code to create a simple drawing. We won't create a full application yet, because that will be easier to demonstrate when we start animating the drawings, so for now we'll look at only the code. Figure 15.4 shows a simple drawing that we want to create.

We'll just look at the F# version of the code. There will be more interesting C# samples once we turn everything into animations.

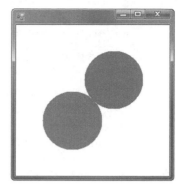

```
open Drawings          ◁——⌐ Opens module with
                              drawing functions
let greenCircle = circle Brushes.OliveDrab 100.0f
let blueCircle = circle Brushes.SteelBlue 100.0f

let greenAndBlue =
  compose (translate -35.0f 35.0f greenCircle)
          (translate 35.0f -35.0f blueCircle)
```

Composes two translated circles

Figure 15.4 Two circles moved using `translate` **and composed using** `compose`

The code starts by opening the `Drawings` module, which contains all the functions for working with drawings. Next, we create one green and one blue circle of size 100 pixels. We move these circles in different directions by about 50 pixels and then compose the two translated drawings to create a single drawing value.

NOTE In this section, we've only implemented a couple of basic drawing features, but there are many other ideas you may want to try. You could create new primitives such as squares or bitmaps, and also new transformations such as rotating and scaling. The `Graphics` type makes it easy to implement these using `RotateTransform` and `ScaleTransform`. You may want to finish the chapter first, so you can see how everything runs as an animation.

Now that we've implemented the separate concepts of drawings and time-varying values, implementing animation is simply a matter of combining the two.

15.5 *Creating animations*

We began this chapter by promising you a library for animations, and here we are, many pages later, without a single animation to be seen. It should be fairly clear that all the foundations we've been building will make it pretty easy to animate our drawings.

Let's briefly recap what we've done so far. We created a type `Behavior<'T>` to represent a value that changes over time, as well as functions to create new behaviors based on old ones. We've also created a drawing type (`Drawing` in F#, `IDrawing` in C#) along with construction and manipulation functions. How can we use these two components to create an animation?

ANIMATION You might describe the concept of an animation as a drawing that changes over time. We've seen that we can represent a value changing over time as a behavior, so animation is a behavior of a drawing. This means that we can represent animations using the `Behavior<Drawing>` type.

By that definition, we've already implemented a library for creating animations! Let's see how to create an animation using our existing types. We ended the previous section by creating a simple drawing in F# (a value called `greenAndBlue`). We can turn it into an animation by using a function that creates a constant behavior:

```
> let animDrawing = forever greenAndBlue;;
val animDrawing : Behavior<Drawing>
```

The type of the result is `Behavior<Drawing>`, which is the type that we'll use to represent animations. This is only an animation in the weakest possible sense: the drawing always stays the same but it's enough to let us at least try to display animations. It's at last time to create the application to run the animations.

15.5.1 *Implementing the animation form in F#*

In this section, we'll implement a form for displaying animations. This is particularly interesting in F#, because we'll use it from F# Interactive to create and experiment with animations. At this point, the typical style of development in F# is very different from C#. In C#, we'll implement the form, create the animation, compile our application, and run it. In F#, we'll implement the form, load it into F# Interactive, and then try to write some animations, injecting them into the existing form to see how they work.

Listing 15.16 shows the F# implementation of the form. The C# version is essentially the same and you can find it at this book's website. We won't discuss the C# code needed to display the animation, because we'd have to compile the whole application, but we'll continue to show all the interesting parts of the code (such as creating some nice animations) in both C# and F#.

Listing 15.16   Implementing a form for showing animations (F#)

```
open System.Windows.Forms

type AnimationForm() as this =
  inherit Form()                                        ❶
  let emptyAnim = forever(drawing(fun _ -> ()))
  let mutable startTime = DateTime.UtcNow               ❷
  let mutable anim = emptyAnim

  do
    this.SetStyle(ControlStyles.AllPaintingInWmPaint |||
                  ControlStyles.OptimizedDoubleBuffer, true)
    let tmr = new Timers.Timer(Interval = 25.0)
    tmr.Elapsed.Add(fun _ -> this.Invalidate() )         ❸
    tmr.Start()

  member x.Animation           ❹
    with get() = anim
    and set(newAnim) =
      anim <- newAnim                                    ❺
      startTime <- DateTime.UtcNow

  override x.OnPaint(e) =                                 ❻
    let w, h = x.ClientSize.Width, x.ClientSize.Height
    e.Graphics.Clear(Brushes.White)
    e.Graphics.TranslateTransform(float32(w) / 2.0f), float32(h) / 2.0f))
```

```
let elapsed = (DateTime.UtcNow - startTime).TotalSeconds
let currentDrawing = anim |> readValue (float32(elapsed))
currentDrawing.Draw(e.Graphics)
```

The type inherits from the .NET Form class ❶ and uses mutable value bindings to store the state of the object ❷. Inside the constructor, we create a timer to redraw the animation form every 25 ms ❸.

The class exposes animation as a mutable property ❹ that gets or sets the local mutable value. In the setter, we also reset the starting time of the animation ❺.

The drawing is implemented inside the overridden OnPaint method ❻. It uses the readValue function to get the drawing at the given time ❼.

The class declaration contains a few advanced aspects of OOP in F# that we'll need to explain. The form inherits from the .NET class Form. This is written using the inherit Form() construct directly following the type declaration. The body of the class starts with a few ordinary let bindings. The first one declares an empty animation: a constant behavior containing a drawing (created using the drawing primitive) that doesn't draw anything. We use this as the initial animation displayed on the form. In order to experiment with animations, we'll create one form in F# Interactive and use mutation to imperatively change the animation to display. This is a common and perfectly valid use of mutable state when using interactive development in F#.

The mutation is performed using a property named Animation. To create a read/write property, we use the with keyword and specify the getter and setter as two blocks of code using syntax that's similar to a normal function declaration. In the setter, we set the new animation and reset the starting time.

The declaration of the form also contains the as this construct directly following the implicit constructor. This allows us to use the reference to the form in the constructor code. We use it to call the SetStyle method to avoid flickering (the ||| operator is the F# bitwise or operator, which can also be used for working with enumerations). The this reference is also used when we create the timer that forces redrawing of the form.

The most interesting part is the OnPaint member. This overrides the default OnPaint method of a .NET form and draws the animation. It's called repeatedly, due to the timer that invalidates the form using the Invalidate method. After we've cleared the window, drawing the animation is easy. We use the helper function readValue, which we declared earlier when experimenting with behaviors. The function gives us the appropriate drawing for the current time in the animation. Once we have the drawing, we invoke its Draw method, which paints it on the graphics object provided by the system.

This was the only complex piece of code we had to write in order to start creating animations. Now, we can instantiate the form in F# Interactive and set its Animation property to the simple drawing we created earlier (the value we called animDrawing). At this point you should see a circle. It's theoretically animated, but you won't see any movement because the drawing is always the same. To show a real animation, we'll need to use more interesting behaviors.

15.5.2 Creating animations using behaviors

Now that we have all the underlying machinery to create animations and a form to display them in, we can start creating animations. We'll start with the drawing of two colorful circles we created in F# earlier and create an animation that moves it. We'll only use F# in this section as we'll be using F# Interactive to experiment. You'll see that the primitives we've already written provide quite a lot of flexibility, and we'll consider what other operations we might want to do with animated graphics. After that we'll go back to implementing everything in both F# and C#. Listing 15.17 creates the form and displays our first animation.

Listing 15.17   Creating simple animation (F# interactive)

```
> let translate x y img = Behavior.lift3 Drawings.translate x y img;;
val translate :
    Behavior<float32> -> Behavior<float32> ->
    Behavior<#Drawing> -> Behavior<Drawing>
```
Translates animation using behaviors **❶**

```
> let wiggle100 = Behavior.lift2 (*) wiggle 100.0f.forever;;
val wiggle100 : Behavior<float32>
```
Oscillates in range -l00 … l00 **❷**

```
> let af = new AnimationForm(ClientSize = Size(750, 750), Visible = true);;
val af : AnimationForm

> af.Animation <- translate wiggle100 0.0f.forever animDrawing;;
```

Listing 15.17 begins by creating a version of the translate primitive that works with animations using lifting **❶**. The original function created a new *drawing* by translating an existing drawing in a fixed way. This version creates a new *animation* by translating an existing animation in a *variable* way. Whenever the form wants to draw a frame of the animation, the animation will ask the two float32 behaviors what their values are at that point, to work out how to translate the drawing. It will then ask the original animation to draw itself (again, for the specified time), but translated appropriately.

The implementation uses the Behavior.lift3 primitive, which turns a function with three arguments into a function that works with behaviors. As you can see from the inferred type signature, the function now takes two behaviors specifying the offset and one specifying an animation (the use of #<type> isn't important here, so we can read it as a type Behavior<Drawing>); the return type is another animation.

Don't worry if you find this a bit confusing to start with:[2] just think of it as combining three entirely separate time-varying values. One specifies a horizontal offset, one specifies a vertical offset, and one specifies what the drawing would look like if we weren't translating it at all. On the next two lines, we use this primitive to create an animation, which you can see in figure 15.5.

To define the animation, we first need to create a behavior that will give us reasonably large X and Y offsets. We do this by multiplying the wiggle primitive by a constant

---

[2]   Both of the authors certainly did: Tomas when understanding the Haskell Fran library and Jon when reading the code presented here. We're confident you'll be able to get your head around it.

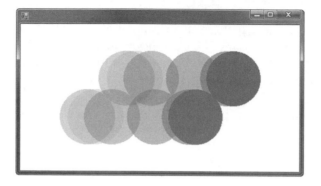

Figure 15.5   Two circles from figure 15.4 moving from the left to the right (shadows are added, so you can see how objects move)

behavior that always returns 100. This means that the value of `wiggle100` ❷ will oscillate between −100 and +100. Next, we create and display an animation of an appropriate size. Finally, we use the new `translate` function that takes behaviors as its arguments. We give it the `wiggle100` value as the X coordinate and a behavior that's always 0.0f as the Y coordinate. The result is an animation that sets the coordinates of the drawing to values ranging between `(-100,0)` and `(100,0)`.

NOTE   Presenting animations in a book is somewhat challenging, for obvious reasons. To give you an indication of how the animations move, we added shadows that show earlier locations of the objects. Implementing this attractive effect was rather easy: all we need to do is to draw the animation repeatedly, passing different times to the behaviors and using .NET's drawing features to make older animations more and more transparent. We won't look at the implementation in the book, but you can find it at the book's website (as an additional type of form that presents the animation). It's another example of the power of composition.

Listing 15.17 suggests that we're going to need two kinds of operations quite often when creating animations. We need lifted versions of primitive functions such as `translate` or `compose` applied to animations, and it would also be nice if we could perform simple arithmetic on behaviors without using explicitly lifted operators as we did here to create `wiggle100`. Let's see what we can do.

15.5.3 Adding animation primitives

Our goal is to make the code that constructs animations as declarative and simple as possible. For this reason, we want to provide primitives that are specifically designed for creating animations. We've seen that we can already do anything we need just using the existing functions for working with behaviors and drawings, but the code would look more elegant if we could use specialized primitives for creating animations rather than using lifting explicitly. Let's start by looking at functions for working with drawings.

CREATING DRAWING PRIMITIVES FOR ANIMATIONS

In listing 15.17, we created a `translate` primitive that works with animations by lifting the `Drawings.translate` function. Now we need to do the same thing for the other drawing primitives, `circle` and `compose`. Listing 15.18 shows the F# declarations for a composition operator and a primitive that creates an animated circle. We've included the C# version of composition (this time as an extension method) to demonstrate how to use lifting in C#. The C# implementation of the other lifted operations is essentially the same, so it isn't included in the listing.

Listing 15.18   Creating animation primitives using lifting in F# and C#

```
// F# version
> let circle brush size =
    Behavior.lift2 Drawings.circle brush size
  let ( -- ) anim1 anim2 =                              ❶
    Behavior.lift2 Drawings.compose anim1 anim2
 ;;
val circle : Behavior<#Brush> -> Behavior<float32> -> Behavior<Drawing>
val (--) : Behavior<#Drawing> -> Behavior<#Drawing> -> Behavior<Drawing>   ❷

// C# version
public static class Anims {
  public static Behavior<IDrawing> Compose
      (this Behavior<IDrawing> anim1, Behavior<IDrawing> anim2) {   ❸
    return Behavior.Lift<IDrawing, IDrawing, IDrawing>
      (Drawings.Compose)(anim1, anim2);                            ❹
  }
}
```

Using lifting in F# is quite easy thanks to its advanced type inference. We created the `translate` primitive earlier, so in this listing we add the `circle` function and a custom operator `--` ❶ for composing animations. Both have two arguments, so we can use the `Behavior.lift2` function to take a function that works with drawings and turn it into a variant that works with animations. As you can see from the inferred type signature ❷, the resulting function (or an operator) takes two behaviors as arguments and returns a behavior (more specifically, the type `Behavior<Drawing>`, which represents an animation). The `circle` function now takes both the brush and the size as behaviors, so we can create circles that change color and size over time.

In the C# version, we've created a static `Anims` class for all the operations. In chapter 6 we compared custom operators in F# with extension methods in C#, which suggests that we should implement `Compose` as an extension method ❸. In the body of the method, we use lifting to get a lifted version of the `Drawings.Compose` method. The `Lift` method returns a function that we call immediately. We give it two animations as arguments and return the result, which is the composed animation ❹. Before we look at how to use the new functionality, let's make two more improvements that will allow us to do interesting things with behaviors.

CALCULATING WITH BEHAVIORS

Another operation that we'll need quite frequently is to multiply or add numeric behaviors. In the sample animation, we wanted to multiply the `wiggle` value by the constant behavior `100.0f.forever`. Instead of using lifting explicitly, it's more convenient to provide overloaded operators that work with numeric behaviors. Listing 15.19 shows how to implement two operators for addition and multiplication in F#.

Listing 15.19 Extension operators for calculating with behaviors (F#)

```
type Behavior<'T> with                                        ❶
  static member (+) (a:Behavior<float32>, b) =
    Behavior.lift2 (+) a b
  static member (*) (a:Behavior<float32>, b) =
    Behavior.lift2 (*) a b                                    ❷
```

In F#, we can add operators to a type using intrinsic type extensions ❶. It adds two static members to the type; each member takes two arguments of type `Behavior<float32>`. Adding generic operators that work with any numeric type would be more difficult, so we only create operators for the numeric type we're using in this chapter. The implementation of the operator is easy, because we can express it using the appropriate lifting function ❷. The C# implementation is almost the same, so we won't talk about it.

We've already applied the concepts of addition and multiplication to locations, but the other dimension our animations work with is time. What can we do with that? Well, we might want to speed up an animation, or delay it for a period of time. If we had two rotating circles, we may want to rotate one twice as fast as the other. We could create a new primitive behavior, but there's a more elegant way. We can create a function that takes a behavior as an argument and returns a new behavior that runs faster or that's delayed by a specified number of seconds. You can see the F# version in listing 15.20.

Listing 15.20 Speeding up and delaying behaviors (F#)

```
let wait shift (BehaviorFunc bfunc) =
  sample(fun t -> bfunc { t with Time = t.Time + shift })
let faster q (BehaviorFunc bfunc) =
  sample(fun t -> bfunc { t with Time = t.Time * q })
```

Functions in listing 15.20 work with any kind of behavior, not just animations. Each takes a floating-point number as the first argument and an original behavior as the second. To create a new behavior, we have to use the low-level `sample` primitive. We create a new behavior that calls the function extracted from the original behavior and gives it a different time as the argument. In the first case, the time is shifted by the specified number of seconds, and in the second case it's multiplied by the provided coefficient. To explain what this means, let's look at the second function and say we're running a behavior twice as fast. When the actual time is 3 seconds, the returned behavior will invoke the original one with a time of 6 seconds, which means that the animation will do the movements it would usually perform in 6 seconds in just 3 seconds.

We could write an entirely general function for manipulating with the time. The more general version would specify the time adjustment as a behavior—a function that returns the adjusted time given the original time. The simple functions we've created will be easier to use and understand.

As a final demonstration, we'll create an animation of the sun, the moon, and the earth. It will use everything we implemented so far to create a complicated and interesting animation, and we'll use it to demonstrate how composable and reusable our solution is.

15.5.4 *Creating a solar system animation*

At this point, we implemented all types and functions of the animations library. Even though we're using F# Interactive, it's a good idea to save the core part of the library into a separate file (for example, Animations.fs). Then we can load the entire library using the #load directive, which takes the filename as an argument. This way, you also ensure that intrinsic type extensions (including the operators we added to behaviors) are loaded correctly, because intrinsic type extensions have to be processed in the same command as the type they extend.

The key part of the animation will be the rotation of objects around each other. The library we've just created allows us to compose the existing primitives into higher-level ones for a particular problem. We can then encapsulate rotation inside a reusable function (or C# method) that we'll later use to describe the simulation. This is an important property of a well-designed functional library; functions that work with sequences are composable in the same way.

Our new primitive will rotate an animation around the point (0,0) at a specified distance and speed. Listing 15.21 shows the implementation. Considering the complexity of what we're doing, very little code is required.

Listing 15.21   Implementing rotation in F# and C#

```
// F# function
let rotate (dist:float32) speed img =          Oscillates between
  let pos = wiggle * dist.forever     ◀──      -dist and +dist
  img |> translate pos (wait 0.5f pos)  ❶
      |> faster speed                   ❷

// C# extension method
public static Behavior<IDrawing> Rotate
    (this Behavior<IDrawing> img, float dist, float speed) {
  var pos = Time.Wiggle * dist.Forever();
  return img.Translate(pos, pos.Wait(0.5f))       ❸
            .Faster(speed);
}
```

Somewhat surprisingly, we can implement the rotation just using the translate function. The movement created using the wiggle primitive is sinusoidal, which means that it gives us values for one coordinate of the rotating object. To get the second coordinate, we need to delay the phase by half a second. This gives us the same value we'd get if we created a similar primitive using a cosine function. To delay the behavior, we can use the wait function we just implemented ❶.

We can use pipelining to specify sequence of operations that should be done with an animation. After specifying the rotation, we also apply the faster function ❷ to specify the required speed of the rotation. In C#, we can use the same programming style thanks to the use of extension methods ❸ that take the animation as a first argument and return a new one as the result. This is similar to applying multiple operators (filtering, projection, grouping) in a LINQ query.

Using the primitive to describe rotation, we can now create our solar system animation quite easily. We'll start by creating three circles to represent the sun, the earth, and the moon and then describe how they rotate around each other. Figure 15.6 shows the running animation, so you can see what we're creating.

Let's now look at the code. Listing 15.22 shows the implementation in both languages, so we can see how the relevant constructs in F# and C# correspond to each other.

The code that constructs planets is quite simple. The only notable thing is that we're using a circle primitive for creating animations, so we have to

Figure 15.6 Running solar system simulation; the moon is rotating around the earth and both of them are rotating around sun.

provide both the brush and the size as a behavior. This means we could make interesting effects, such as creating a sun that grows bigger and changes color over time.

Listing 15.22 Creating solar system animation in F# and C#

```
// F# version
let sun   = circle (forever Brushes.Goldenrod) 100.0f.forever
let earth = circle (forever Brushes.SteelBlue) 50.0f.forever
let moon  = circle (forever Brushes.DimGray)   20.0f.forever

let planets =
  sun --
    (earth -- (moon |> rotate 40.0f 12.0f)          ❶
         |> rotate 160.0f 1.3f)                      ❷
   |> faster 0.2f                                    ❸
```

```
// C# version
var sun = Anims.Circle(Time.Forever(Brushes.Goldenrod), 100.0f.Forever());
var earth = Anims.Circle(Time.Forever(Brushes.SteelBlue),50.0f.Forever());
var moon  = Anims.Circle(Time.Forever(Brushes.DimGray), 20.0f.Forever());

var planets =
  sun.Compose(
    earth.Compose(moon.Rotate(50.0f, 12.0f))        ❶
        .Rotate(150.0f, 1.0f))                       ❷
    .Faster(0.2f);                                   ❸
```

Composing the animation from rotating objects is more interesting. We'll start explaining it from the middle. We use the `rotate` function to create a moon that rotates around the center at a distance of 50 pixels. We compose this animation with the earth, which isn't rotating ❶, so the result is the moon rotating around the earth. The type of this result is an animation, so we can again start, this time rotating it at a distance of 150 pixels ❷. When we compose the resulting animation with a sun (that isn't moving), we get the animation where the earth is rotating around the sun. Finally, we use the `faster` primitive to change the speed of the animation ❸. We actually slow it down, because the multiplicator we use is less than 1. Note that in F#, we can use the pipelining operator to write the animated object first and then various transformations.

We've animated only three objects here, but it's easy to see how you'd add the remaining planets. The composable nature of the framework means that incremental changes remain simple, even as the overall result becomes increasingly elaborate.

Taking the animation library further

There are many interesting additions that we could make to the library. We already mentioned that we could add more primitive drawings and transformations. Adding lifted versions of the new primitives would allow us to use them easily when creating animations. There are other even more interesting options.

We could implement behaviors that used additional contextual information. We've already encapsulated the context in the `BehaviorContext` type, so adding extra information would be quite simple. We could add the current cursor location to the context, enabling us to create animations where shapes either chased the cursor or ran away from it.

A more sophisticated extension could allow us to create nonlinear dynamic systems. We could add a primitive that tells us how quickly is a certain behavior value changing, and we could then use it to create a system that depends on how quickly its state is changing.

The animation library provides an example of a library implemented in a functional programming style. You may be wondering how this style translates to more traditional business application development. Let's take a quick romp through another example—we won't cover it in nearly as much detail as our animation library, but it should give you an idea of what a business declarative library (or DSL) might *feel* like.

15.6   *Developing financial modeling language*

So far in this chapter, we've seen most of the concepts that you need to know if you plan to design your own functional library or a DSL. To give you some idea how this could be done for a more business-oriented problem, we'll sketch a library that can be used for modeling financial contracts. This example is motivated by an article by Simon Peyton Jones et al., "Composing Contracts: An Adventure in *Financial Engineering*" [Jones, Eber, Seward, 2000]. In this section, we'll implement only the most basic parts of the library: the original article contains much more information, and is well worth reading.

15.6.1 Modeling financial contracts

The financial industry uses a large number of types of contracts including swaps and futures. A contract generally specifies what commodity is bought or sold, when, and for what price. When creating an application for working with contracts, we could hard-code the support for each of the known types of the contract directly. Unfortunately, there's a huge number of options, so this solution wouldn't be very flexible.

Instead, we'll create a language that allows us to describe contracts in general. The most elementary component of a contract is a trade, so we'll provide primitives for saying that we're willing to make some trade—either purchasing or selling some amount of some commodity. For example, we could say that we're willing to buy 1,000 shares of Google stock.

Contracts typically also specify when or under what conditions the trade can take place, so to support that in our language, we'll add primitives for limiting the date when the offer is valid. Using these, we'll be able to specify that we're selling, say, 500 Yahoo! shares from the next week but only until the end of the month.

In the example with animations, we could also define our own primitives, such as `rotate`, in terms of more basic primitives, like `translate`. In the financial modeling language, the users should be able to do exactly the same thing. In particular, they'll be able to define primitives for creating standard types of contracts such as swaps and futures. Let's now start by taking the usual first step when creating a library: creating a couple of basic primitives.

15.6.2 Defining the primitives

We first need to define the type of value we're working with and then implement a few primitives that can be composed later. Our primitive data type will be called `Contract` and will represent trades that can occur at a particular date and time.

DECLARING THE CONTRACT TYPE

As you can see in listing 15.23, the `Contract` type is quite similar to the behavior type from the animation example. It's a discriminated union with a single discriminator named `ContractFunc`. This is a trick we've been using already when defining behaviors, and it gives us a way to create simple, named, and encapsulated function values.

Listing 15.23 Type representing financial contracts (F# Interactive)

```
> type Contract =
    | ContractFunc of (DateTime -> seq<string * int>);;       ❶
(...)
> let eval (ContractFunc f) dt = f(dt) |> List.ofSeq;;         ❷
val eval : Contract -> DateTime -> (string * int) list
```

The function that represents the actual contract takes a single argument and returns a sequence of tuples ❶. When we call it with a particular date, it will generate all the trades that can occur on that date. Each trade is represented as a tuple containing the name of the stock and the number of shares that we want to buy or sell. We'll use positive numbers to represent buying stocks and negative values for selling.

The second part of listing 15.23 implements an `eval` function ❷ that evaluates the contract at a given time and returns the list of trades. We're using a sequence to represent the trades in the contract, because that makes the code more general. We've seen how easy it is to generate sequences dynamically and compose them. The `eval` function returns a list, because that will be easier to work with from the caller's point of view.

IMPLEMENTING COMBINATORS

Once we have the data type representing the values of our language, we need to implement a couple of primitive functions for creating and composing these values. For behaviors, we created primitive values such as `wiggle` and lifted operators for composing them. In our language for contracts, we'll start with a function `trade` that creates a contract representing a single purchase that can occur at any time. To compose contracts, we'll provide a function `combine`, which joins the trades of two other contracts.

Listing 15.24 shows the implementation of these two functions as well as functions for restricting the dates on which contracts can occur and a function for creating trades where we're selling the stocks represented by a contract.

Listing 15.24 Combinators for creating and composing contracts (F# Interactive)

```
> let trade what amount = ContractFunc(fun _ ->       ❶
    seq { yield what, amount })
  let combine (ContractFunc a) (ContractFunc b) =
    ContractFunc(fun now ->                            ❷
      Seq.concat [ a(now); b(now) ])
  ;;
val trade : int -> string -> Contract
val combine : Contract -> Contract -> Contract

> let after dt (ContractFunc f) = ContractFunc(fun now ->    ◁─┐
    seq { if now >= dt then yield! f(now) })                   │ ❸
  let until dt (ContractFunc f) = ContractFunc(fun now ->    ◁─┘
    seq { if now <= dt then yield! f(now) })
  let sell (ContractFunc f) = ContractFunc(fun now ->     ❹
    seq { for itm, am in f(now) -> itm, -am })
  ;;
val after : DateTime -> Contract -> Contract
val until : DateTime -> Contract -> Contract
val sell : Contract -> Contract
```

A single trade that can occur at any time is represented as a function that ignores its parameter (the date on which we're evaluating the contract) and returns a sequence with a single element ❶. Composition is also easy ❷, because we concatenate all trades of the two underlying contracts that can occur at the given date.

The next two primitives let us limit the dates for which a contract is active ❸. We implemented them by creating a function that tests whether the given date matches the condition of the primitive. When the test succeeds, it returns all underlying trades using the `yield!` primitive; otherwise it returns an empty sequence. The final primitive can be used to change whether a contract is a sale or a purchase ❹. We iterate over all the underlying trades of a contract, changing positive amounts to negative, and vice versa.

Even though we're only sketching out the library, the few primitives we've implemented already allow us to describe many interesting scenarios.

15.6.3 *Using the modeling language*

Perhaps the most valuable thing about composable libraries is that we can use the basic primitives provided by the library designer to create more complicated functions using composition. This gives the library flexibility, because the users of the library (in our case financial experts) can create the primitives that they need. As the designers of the core library, we only need to provide primitives that are rich enough to allow users to build more.

Listing 15.25 demonstrates this with two functions that are defined in terms of the primitives we've just built. First we define a function that builds a trading window: a time interval within which a trade can occur. A second function provides a particular kind of trading window: one that allows the trade to occur only on a single date.

> Listing 15.25 **Implementing derived financial contract functions (F# Interactive)**

```
> let between dateFrom dateTo contract =
    after dateFrom (until dateTo contract);;
val between : DateTime -> DateTime -> Contract -> Contract

> let tradeAt date what amount =
    between date date (trade what amount);;
val tradeAt : DateTime -> int -> string -> Contract
```

The first function is composed from the two primitives that we defined for restricting the date of the contract. It takes the start and end dates along with the contract to restrict, and returns a contract that can't happen before or after the specified interval. The original contract can include trades that are already restricted in some other way. The second function creates a primitive trade that can occur only at the precisely specified date. It uses the `trade` function to construct an elementary trade and then limits its validity using the `between` function. Note that the `after` and `until` functions use operators that allow equality (`>=` and `<=`), so the use of `between` with the same value twice doesn't create an impossible trade.

Equipped with these functions for creating and composing contracts, let's try to write some contracts and evaluate which trades can occur as part of the contract at two distinct dates. Listing 15.26 shows a contract where we're willing to sell 500 shares of Google on one particular date and we can buy 1000 shares of Microsoft at any time within a specific 10-day period.

> Listing 15.26 **Creating and evaluating sample contract (F# Interactive)**

```
> let dfrom, dto = DateTime(2009, 4, 10), DateTime(2009, 4, 19)
  let itstocks =
    combine (sell (tradeAt (DateTime(2009, 4, 15)) "GOOG" 500))      ❶
            (between dfrom dto (trade "MSFT" 1000));;
val itstocks : Contract = ContractFunc <fun:trade@6>
```

```
> eval itstocks (DateTime(2009, 4, 14));;
val it : (string * int) list = [("MSFT", 1000)]

> eval itstocks (DateTime(2009, 4, 15));;
val it : (string * int) list = [("GOOG", -500); ("MSFT", 1000)]
```

2

Listing 15.26 begins by creating values that represent two dates between which we're willing to purchase Microsoft shares. Then we define a value, `itstocks`, that represents our contract. We're using the `combine` primitive to merge two possible trades **1**. The first one is the sale of Google shares. One way to construct a sale is to create a contract that represents a stock purchase (using the `tradeAt` function implemented in listing 15.25) and then use the `sell` primitive to change purchase into a sale. This way, we can create reusable trades and use them to write both sales and purchases. Alternatively, we could have used `tradeAt (DateTime(2009, 4, 15)) "GOOG" -500`. The second trade is the purchase of Microsoft shares within the 10-day period.

Once we've defined the contract, we can evaluate it. The contract represents a specification of trades that can occur at some specified date, so we can evaluate by providing that date. As you can see in the output, the result for the first date is a purchase of Microsoft shares; for the second date, we'll get both trades.

Representing contracts as abstract values

In this example, we represented contracts in a way that is quite similar to our language for behaviors. We essentially used a function to calculate the trades, and then wrote combinators that compose these functions. This is one of the two basic techniques that we mentioned in the beginning of the chapter.

Another option would be to design a discriminated union representing the contract as data rather than as a computation. We could use different options covering our different primitives. It might look something like this:

```
type Contract =
    | Exchange of string * int
    | After of DateTime * Contract
    | Until of DateTime * Contract
    | Combine of Contract * Contract
```

The type is recursive, so we can compose the elementary value `Exchange` that represents a single trade with other trades using `Combine`, limit their validity using `After` and `Until`, and so on.

One difference between these two techniques is that when we're using abstract value representations, we can write all sorts of processing functions for the language that are aware of the specific restrictions. We could add a function that takes a `Contract` value and evaluates its overall value. On the other hand, when we use a function type under the hood, we can't observe many properties of the value once it's created: we can only execute it. In reality, it would probably be more practical to represent contracts using abstract values, but we wanted to demonstrate how you can use the technique we saw earlier with animations to create a language in a very different domain.

Clearly, the domain-specific language that we've described here is limited and simplistic, but it demonstrated that the approach is applicable to a variety of problem domains. Hopefully you're already thinking about situations in your own development where it may be applicable.

15.7 Summary

We began the chapter by talking about the language-oriented programming style, and in particular about techniques for creating internal DSLs. We briefly mentioned techniques like abstract value representations, in which case we usually design a data type (in particular discriminated unions) to represent the combinators. Next, we looked at fluent interfaces, which are particularly useful in C#, and combinator libraries, which are used in functional programming languages.

We spent the bulk of this chapter creating a language to describe animations. Most of the work went into developing separate concepts of behaviors and drawings. In each of these areas we created primitives (such as `wiggle`, `time`, and `circle`) and then operations for composition and transformation. It's amazing how much flexibility can be achieved with relatively few of these, if you choose them appropriately.

The next level of composition is at the library level; just as we can compose two primitives to create something more complex, we can combine two well-designed but orthogonal libraries to create a rich result—in our case, animations. We wrapped up the chapter with a quick look at a different problem domain, representing stock trades. The same techniques we used for behaviors and drawings are applicable in this and other domains.

In the next chapter, we'll turn our attention back to the asynchronous workflows we saw in chapter 13, but we're going to use them differently. We'll look at developing applications that react to external events, including events from the user interface. In general, we'll talk about writing *reactive applications* and related techniques in F#.

Developing reactive
functional programs

This chapter covers

- Reacting to events and declaring them in F#
- Working with events as first-class values
- Programming GUIs using asynchronous workflows
- Using message passing concurrency

This final chapter is about reacting to external events, such as user input. We're also going to discuss another F# feature that can be used for creating concurrent programs. Although these sound like unrelated topics, we'll see similarities as we explore them. All of the libraries and examples we'll see in this chapter share a similar architecture, so let's first look at the reactive architecture in general.

A lot of the code we write (in both imperative and functional programming) assumes that it's in the driving seat—that we're in control of what happens at each step. This model often breaks down for UIs. A Windows application needs to handle a variety of UI events; it may also have to respond to the completion of an asynchronous web service request or background task. The execution of this type of application is controlled by the events, and the application is concerned with *reacting* to them. For this reason, this principle is sometimes called *inversion of control* and is sometimes lightheartedly referred to as *the Hollywood Principle*.[1]

The standard .NET mechanism for reactive code is an event. Subscribers add event handlers which are called when the event is triggered. Event handlers require mutable state to keep track of the subscriptions, which is somewhat antithetical to functional principles, but it's the most straightforward way, and it's the one used by many existing .NET classes. We've seen how to use it in Windows Forms applications, so our coverage here will be fairly brief. Instead, we'll focus on some of the more functional alternatives that F# offers.

We'll start by looking at the declarative way to handle events, which is somewhat similar to declarative list processing. We'll then look at using asynchronous workflows for event handling, which gives us a way to reverse the inversion of control, writing the code in a way where we at least *appear* to control what the application is doing. Finally, we'll consider state management in reactive applications and message-passing concurrency, which is a powerful technique for writing multithreaded applications.

16.1 Reactive programming using events

At this point, you know how to write an application that reacts to events in C#, and we've seen that the same technique can be used in F# as well. The pattern is to register a callback function (or a method) with the event; when the event occurs, the callback function is executed. This can react to the event, perhaps updating the state of the application or making changes to the UI.

Let's first review this approach with an example. The code in listing 16.1 monitors changes in the filesystem using the `FileSystemWatcher` class. Once initialized, the watcher triggers an event every time a file is created, renamed, or deleted.

> **Listing 16.1   Monitoring filesystem events (F#)**

```
open System.IO
let fileWatcher = new FileSystemWatcher(@"C:\Test")        ◁──┐ Provide a path
fileWatcher.EnableRaisingEvents <- true                        │ for testing

let isNotHidden(fse:RenamedEventArgs) =
  let hidden = FileAttributes.Hidden                           ❶
  (File.GetAttributes(fse.FullPath) &&& hidden) <> hidden

fileWatcher.Renamed.Add(fun fse ->        ❷
  if isNotHidden(fse) then
    printfn "%s renamed to %s" fse.OldFullPath fse.FullPath)
```

Listing 16.1 begins by creating the `FileSystemWatcher` object for a folder where we can easily create and rename some files to test the code. The next few lines ❶ show a simple function that checks whether a file is not marked as hidden. The argument to this function is a class derived from `EventArgs` that carries information about the event triggered by the watcher. We'll use this function to demonstrate one interesting

---

[1] "Don't call us, we'll call you."

feature in declarative event handling shortly. We're using binary and operator (&&&) to check whether a flag of .NET enumeration type is set.

The last part of the code ❷ registers an event handler that will be called when a file is renamed. Events are represented in a different way in F# compared to other .NET languages. In C#, an event is a special member of a class, and you can only work with it through the operators for adding (+=) or removing (-=) event handlers. In F#, events appear as standard members of type IEvent<'T>, where the T parameter specifies the value carried by the event (usually derived from EventArgs). This type has an Add method that we can use for registering a callback function. It also supports methods called AddHandler and RemoveHandler, so you can still use delegates if you want to be able to remove the registered callback later.

The example in listing 16.1 uses the Add method and gives it a lambda function as an argument. The lambda function takes only a single parameter and doesn't include the usual "sender" parameter. The reason is that in F#, you can easily access the sender object by capturing it in a closure, so it doesn't have to be passed explicitly as an argument. The callback reacts to the event by printing information about the renamed file, but we don't want to react to every event. Instead we want to display the message only when the affected file is not marked as hidden. To do this, we write an if condition inside the callback function.

This works fine, but F# allows us to write the filtering of events in a more declarative way, which makes the program easier to read and promotes a cleaner separation of concerns. Later we'll see that the same principles can be used in C#, at least to some extent.

16.1.1 *Introducing event functions*

Working with events by explicitly providing a callback function isn't very declarative. We're imperatively adding the event handler and the whole behavior is wrapped inside the callback function. How can we think of events in a more declarative way? We've seen that one important technique in declarative code is the use of higher-order functions. The best examples are functions for working with lists such as List.filter, List.map, or List.fold. If we had a list of events from the filesystem watcher (called watcherEvents), we could split the code into two parts. The first one would transform the events from the source format to the format suitable for printing. This part would be written in a declarative way using higher-order functions for working with lists. The second part would be simple imperative code to print the information. The key benefit of this approach is that most of the code is written in the declarative style. In particular, the filtering code would look like this:

```
let renamedVisible =
  watcherEvents |> List.filter isNotHidden
```

This snippet uses the isNotHidden function as an argument to the function that filters the list. The second part could use List.iter to print each item in the list. This was just familiar working with lists, but listing 16.2 shows a complete example that uses exactly this pattern with events. We can think of events as similar to lists: both represent a sequence of values, with the difference that the values from an event aren't available immediately. A new value appears every time the event is triggered. This sequence of event arguments can be filtered in a similar way to collections. The `Observable.filter` function creates an event that's triggered when the source event produces a value that matches the given predicate.

Listing 16.2 Filtering events using the `Observable.filter` function (F# Interactive)

```
> let renamedVisible =
    fileWatcher.Renamed |> Observable.filter isNotHidden     ①
 ;;
val renamedVisible : System.IObservable<RenamedEventArgs>     ②

> renamedVisible |> Observable.add (fun fse ->     ③
    printfn "%s renamed to %s" fse.OldFullPath fse.FullPath);;
val it : unit
```

The first command ① filters the event in much the same way we filtered a list of values. The returned event listens to the event of the filesystem watcher, and when a file is renamed it uses the specified filtering function to test whether or not the value carried by the event should be ignored. If the filtering function returns `true`, the resulting event is triggered; otherwise the current occurrence of the event is ignored.

The type that represents the returned event value ② requires more explanation. We get a value of a new .NET 4.0 type `System.IObservable<'T>`. It has been added as a uniform way of working with objects that need to notify other objects of state changes. In the previous section, I wrote that events in F# appear as values of the `IEvent<'T>` type, so you may be wondering why we're not seeing `IEvent<'T>` here as well. We'll first look at the rest of the listing, then discuss the relation between these two types in detail.

The last command in the listing registers a lambda function that prints information about the renamed file using the filtered event ③. We're using another function for working with events called `Observable.add`. This function behaves similarly as the `Add` method of the `IEvent<'T>` type, which we used earlier. When using `IObservable<'T>`, we'll write the whole event-processing code as a single pipeline using higher-order functions. Now, let's take a look at the way events and event values are represented in F# in more detail.

16.1.2 Using events and observables

So far, we've seen two types for representing events. The relation between them is fairly straightforward: the `IEvent<'T>` interface inherits from the `IObservable<'T>` interface. The `IEvent<'T>` type is more specific and is used primarily by F# to represent standard .NET events instead of making them a special language feature.

We've also seen the `Observable` module with higher-order functions for working with events. Functions in the module take values of the `IObservable<'T>` interface as parameters, but since `IEvent<'T>` is inherited from `IObservable<'T>`, we can use the functions for working with standard F# events as well. For completeness, there is also an `Event` module with functions similar to those from the `Observable` module. These functions take only values of type `IEvent<'T>` and produce event values of the same type. Deciding which interface and module to use may sound complicated, but we can decide using four simple facts and rules:

- `IObservable<T>` has a method called `Subscribe`. It is used for registering an observer that will be called when the state of the observable object changes.

- `IEvent<T>` adds a couple of methods that make it possible to use the usual coding patterns for working with standard events. It provides `Add` method as an easy way for registering handler and `AddHandler`/`RemoveHandler` pair, which is useful when we want to use delegates.

- We can use the `IEvent<'T>` type, as we'll see in section 16.1.5, when declaring C# compatible events in F#. If you want to construct an event like this from another event using higher-order function, you'll need to use the `Event` module.

- In the rest of the chapter, we'll prefer functions from the `Observable` module, because these functions work better with the `Async.AwaitObservable` primitive that we'll see in section 16.3. Combining functions from the `Event` module with the approach we'll use later can introduce leaks where event handlers aren't correctly removed.

Now that we know we'll use mostly the `Observable` module, look at the table 16.1, which shows what functions the module provides. The structure of the `Event` module is very similar, except for the type signatures. As you can see, many of the functions correspond closely to functions working with sequences.

Table 16.1   Overview of the most important functions of the `Observable` module

Function	Type and description
filter	`('T -> bool) -> IObservable<'T> -> IObservable<'T>` Returns an event that's triggered when the source event occurs, but only if the value carried by the event matches the specified predicate. This function corresponds to `List.filter` for lists.
map	`('T -> 'U) -> IObservable<'T> -> IObservable<'U>` Returns an event that's triggered every time the source event is triggered. The value carried by the returned event is calculated from the source value using the specific function. This corresponds to the `List.map` function.
add	`('T -> unit) -> IObservable<'T> -> unit` Registers a callback function for the specified event. The given function is called whenever the event occurs. This function is similar to `List.iter`.
scan	`('U -> 'T -> 'U) -> 'U -> IObservable<'T> -> IObservable<'U>` This function creates an event with internal state. The initial state is given as the second argument and is updated every time the source event occurs using the specified function. The returned event reports the accumulated state every time the source event is triggered, after recomputing it using the source event's value.

Table 16.1 Overview of the most important functions of the `Observable` module *(continued)*

Function	Type and description
`merge`	`IObservable<'T> -> IObservable<'T> -> IObservable<'T>` Creates an event that's triggered when either of the events passed as arguments occurs. Note that the type of the values carried by the events (`'T`) has to be the same for both events.

`partition`	`('T -> bool) -> IObservable<'T>`
	`                 -> IObservable<'T> * IObservable<'T>`
	
	Splits an event into two distinct events based on the provided predicate. When the input event fires, the `partition` function runs the predicate and triggers one of the two created events depending on the result of the predicate. The behavior corresponds to `List.partition` function.

Most of the functions from table 16.1 should be easy to understand, because we've seen similar functions working with lists. The only difference is `Observable.scan`, which looks a bit more complicated than the others. The `scan` function that works with lists exists as well, but we haven't discussed it. The signature also resembles `List.fold`, which we know very well already.

Both functions take an initial state and a function that knows how to calculate a new state from the original one and an element from the list or value carried by the event. The difference is that the `fold` function returns the result of accumulating all the elements of the list. This is impossible for events, because we don't know when the event will take place for the last time. Instead of waiting for the last element, the `Observable.scan` function returns an event that's triggered every time the internal state is recalculated, with the aggregated value so far. We'll see an example of this function in section 16.1.3.

The biggest benefit of using higher-order functions for events is that we can write the code in a more declarative way. In our example, we replaced an imperative `if` in the body of the event handler with a filter, but we can take the example even further. If we create a function (we'll call it `formatFileEvent`) that formats the information carried by `RenamedEventArgs`, we can write the whole event handling as a single, succinct expression, as shown next.

Listing 16.3 Declarative event handling (F#)

```
fileWatcher.Renamed
  |> Observable.filter isNotHidden
  |> Observable.map formatFileEvent
  |> Observable.add (printfn "%s")
```

Listing 16.3 implements the same functionality as listing 16.2, using two helper functions and the functions from the `Observable` module. Once you start thinking of an event as a series of values, the code is easy to read. Instead of imperatively specifying what to do when the event occurs, we declaratively specify aspects of the required result. The first line specifies what kind of events we're interested in, the second one specifies what information is important for us, and the last line displays the formatted information.

Initially, we're starting with an event carrying values of type RenamedEventArgs. The filtering operation doesn't change the type; it doesn't trigger the returned event in some cases. The projection can change the type and the formatFileEvent function returns a string value, so we end up with events carrying strings. This means that the last primitive expects a function taking a string as an argument and returning a unit. As you can see, we can easily create a function like this using partial function application. The printfn function with the %s format specifier creates a function that prints the given string.

This way of handling events also gives us a richer way to split the code into reusable elements. We could omit the last line to create an event that can be used in several other places in the application. We could then use Observable.add in conjunction with MessageBox.Show to display the notifications in a graphical form, and use the same event to append to a log file. Let's look at a slightly more complicated example.

16.1.3 Creating a simple reactive application

We're going to build a small Windows Forms application to demonstrate the power of this type of event processing. Figure 16.1 shows the main form of the application; the intended behavior should be fairly obvious from the figure.

Figure 16.1   We change the number displayed in the label by clicking the buttons.

One way to implement this application in the normal way is to create a mutable field (or mutable ref cell in F#) and an event handler to be called when either button is clicked. The event handler would test which of the buttons was clicked, and would increment or decrement the mutable state and display it on the label. There are many other possible approaches, but in most we'd have to explicitly declare some mutable state.

Now, how can we implement the same behavior using the functions we introduced in the previous section without explicitly relying on a mutable state? One of the nice things about declarative coding is that in many cases the code can be visualized easily. This is true for events; figure 16.2 shows a diagram demonstrating our solution.

The idea is that we'll take the click events and turn them into events carrying an integer value. We'll do this using a helper function named always. It returns a function

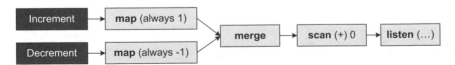

Figure 16.2   An event-processing pipeline used in the sample application; the two boxes on the left represent source events, and the lighter boxes represent events created using processing functions.

that ignores its argument and always returns the same value. We'll use it to create events that will carry either +1 or –1 depending on which button was clicked. Then we can merge these two events and use the `Observable.scan` function to sum the values carried by the events.

The code required to build the UI isn't very interesting, so listing 16.4 only shows the part that sets up the event processing.

Listing 16.4 Pipeline for handling events (F#)

```
let always x = (fun _ -> x)            ❶

let incEvent = btnUp.Click |> Observable.map (always 1)      ⎤
let decEvent = btnDown.Click |> Observable.map (always -1)   ⎦ ❷

Observable.merge incEvent decEvent         ❸
  |> Observable.scan (+) 0
  |> Observable.add (fun sum ->
      lbl.Text <- sprintf "Count: %d" sum)       ❹
```

We start by declaring a utility function `always` that returns a function that ignores its argument and returns the value specified as an argument ❶. Next, we start implementing the event processing code. To make it more readable, we don't encode the whole pipeline as a single expression. Instead, we first declare two helper values that represent events ❷.

The type of both `incEvent` and `decEvent` is `IObservable<int>`, which means that they represent events carrying integers. The value carried by the event raised by the Increment button is always +1, and the value of the other event is always –1. To generate the value, we're using the `always` helper function that returns a function ignoring the argument and always returning the same value. The value being ignored in listing 16.4 is the `EventArgs` argument of the `Click` event.

We merge these events ❸ to create an event that will be triggered every time either button is clicked. The event carries integer values, so we can use `Observable.scan` to sum the values starting with 0 as an initial value. We're using the plus operator for aggregation, so for each click the function will add +1 or –1. Finally, we use the `Observable.add` function ❹ to specify a handler that displays the current sum of clicks.

The ability to work with .NET events as values of type `IEvent<'T>` (which makes it possible to process them with higher-order functions) is a special feature of F#. F# automatically wraps .NET events into this type, so we can work with events as standard values. Using the same idea in C# is tricky, but it's possible with a bit of effort, and it nicely demonstrates the power of the declarative programming style and LINQ.

16.1.4 Declarative event processing using LINQ

To use events as first-class values in C#, we can use the .NET 4.0 `IObservable<T>` type, but we'll need a few additions. First, there must be a way of creating an `IObservable<T>` value from a standard .NET event. Second, we'll need C# versions of the functions from the `Observable` module that we used in the previous section.

NOTE The project that adds LINQ support to IObservable<T> is called .NET Reactive Framework, and it's expected to become part of the .NET Framework. It's discussed in a video interview "Inside .NET Rx and IObservable/ IObserver in the BCL (VS 2010)" [Hamilton, Dyer, 2009]. In this chapter, we're using an early preview of this framework, so there may be several differences. You can also find examples of using LINQ queries to process events in C# in Reactive LINQ, which is a project by one of the authors. You can find more information about it in a series of online articles starting with "Introducing Reactive LINQ" [Petricek, 2008]. You can find the latest version of the source code, as well as links to download the Reactive Framework, on the book's website.

Even though you may not use the code from this section in the exact form in the final version of Reactive Framework, it will give you a good idea of how declarative programming makes it easy to process events. As we'll see shortly, LINQ provides an elegant way for writing the code we implemented in section 16.1.3 using higher-order functions in F#.

USING REACTIVE LINQ IN C#

Let's see how we could implement the Windows Forms example in C#. Reactive LINQ gives us a couple of extension methods for doing the same things as Observable.filter, Observable.map, and others. The library follows the standard LINQ naming convention, so the corresponding extension methods are called Where and Select.

The problem that we have to work around in C# is that events (such as btnUp. Click) aren't first-class values; they can't be passed as an argument to a method. First we have to convert them into the IObservable<T> representation. Reactive Framework provides a method called Observable.Attach that takes the event publisher and the name of the event as a string and creates an event value of type IObservable<T>. The method is also available as an extension method for all Windows Forms controls, because this is a common scenario.

We mentioned that the methods for working with events are called Where and Select. This is important, because it means we can use the syntactic sugar available in C# query expressions to write the event-processing code instead of calling the methods explicitly. Listing 16.5 uses Reactive Framework to create an application with buttons for incrementing and decrementing the displayed number, just like in the previous F# version.

Listing 16.5 Processing WinForms events using LINQ (C#)

```
var upEvent = Observable.FromEvent<EventArgs>(btnUp, "Click");      ❶
var downEvent = Observable.FromEvent<EventArgs>(btnDown, "Click");

var up = from clickArgs in upEvent select +1;       ❷
var down = from clickArgs in downEvent select -1;

Observable.Merge(up, down)           ❸
  .Scan(0, (state, num) => state + num)        ❹
  .Subscribe(sum =>
    lblCount.Text = string.Format("Count: {0}", sum));
```

The code in listing 16.5 is an initialization of the whole event-processing chain, so we need to run it exactly once when the application starts. In C#, this is easily done by placing it in the handler for the OnLoad event. We use the FromEvent method to turn two Click events into a first-class value ❶ represented using the IObservable<IEvent<EventArgs>> interface. In Reactive Framework, the IEvent groups the event argument as well as the sender. The method takes a single argument, which is the name of the event. It uses reflection under the hood, so we have to be careful to specify the name correctly. This is unfortunately the only way, because the only way to work with btnUp.Click event directly is to use the += or -= operators.

Next, we write two simple queries to create events carrying numeric values ❷. The clickArgs variable represents the event arguments and the sender that we get when the event is triggered. In this case, it has a value of type IEvent<EventArgs>, so it doesn't carry any useful information, but if it carried, say, mouse location, we could use it in the where clause to filter certain events. Keep in mind that the C# compiler translates the queries into ordinary calls to the Select extension method using lambda expressions, so there's nothing magical going on.

Once we have the two primitive event values, we merge them into a single event that carries +1 or −1 as the value depending on which button caused it ❸. Then we can use the Scan method to construct an event that uses the specified lambda function to calculate a new state each time the event occurs ❹. The state is calculated based on the current state and a value carried by the event.

The cover of this book says it includes examples in F# and C#. The sidebar "Using Reactive LINQ in Visual Basic" makes one exception. It shows how to use a Visual Basic 9 feature that's not available in C# 3.0 when working with events.

Using Reactive LINQ in Visual Basic

Similarly to C#, Visual Basic contains a special language support for writing LINQ queries. The syntax is a bit more flexible and supports a few additional constructs, but the principle is the same. The interesting thing is that Visual Basic supports aggregation directly. This means that we don't have to call the Scan method explicitly and we can instead use the special syntax it provides. The following shows the core parts of listing 16.5 in Visual Basic 9:

```
Dim upEvent = Observable.FromEvent(Of EventArgs)(btnUp, "Click")
Dim downEvent = Observable.FromEvent(Of EventArgs)(btnUp, "Click")

Dim sumEvent = _
  Aggregate num In Reactive.Merge( _
    (From clickArgs1 In upEvent Select +1), _          Merges events,
    (From clickArgs2 In downEvent Select -1)) _        calculates sum
  Into MovingSum(num)
```

This time, we've written the whole event-processing code inside a single query. This would be possible in C# as well, but we wanted to show one more complicated query demonstrating how declarative event processing looks in action. As you can see, we use nested queries to create events carrying numbers and then merge them just like in the previous version. Then we use a query written using the Aggregate clause. The query specifies that we're aggregating num values coming from the source sequence (in our case, the merged event stream) using an operation specified after the Into keyword.

> **(continued)**
> The query is translated to a call to the MovingSum extension method. This is a very simple extension method that we implement for the IObservable<int> type so the listing corresponds to simpler C# code than the one we saw in listing 16.5. It's still interesting to see that LINQ queries intended for aggregating collections can be used for counting button clicks and reacting to them.

In the last few sections, you've learned how to construct new events based on existing ones using higher-order functions or LINQ queries. We still haven't discussed how to declare a new event. In C# this is done using the event keyword, but F# is slightly different.

16.1.5 Declaring events in F#

To declare a new event, we need two things. First we must create an event value that we can publish so that others can subscribe to our newly created event. This time, we'll need to use the F# specific IEvent<'T> interface instead of the .NET IObservable<'T>. We also need a way to trigger the event. In C#, the event can be triggered using the method invocation syntax, but only from the class where it was declared. When we create a new event in F#, we'll get a function used to trigger it as well.

All of this is clearer with an example. Listing 16.6 shows a simple concrete object type (a class) that exposes one event and one method that sometimes triggers it.

Listing 16.6   Declaring an event as a class member (F# Interactive)

```
> type Counter() =
    let mutable num = 0
    let changedEvt = new Event<_>()            ❶ Creates event

    member x.SignChanged = changedEvt.Publish  ❷ Publishes IEvent value
    member x.Add(n) =
      let original = num
      num <- num + n
      if (sign(original) <> sign(num)) then
        changedEvt.Trigger(num);;              ❸ Triggers event
> let c = Counter()
  c.SignChanged |> Observable.add (printfn "Number: %d");;
type Counter = (...)

> c.Add(10);;        Changes sign from 0 to I
Number: 10

> c.Add(10);;
> c.Add(-30);;       Changes sign to – I
Number: -10
```

The Counter class contains a single mutable field that stores the current number. The Add method changes this field, and we want to trigger the SignChanged event when the sign of the stored number changes. To declare a new event, we use the Event<'T> class from the F# library. This class contains a Publish member that returns the corresponding `IEvent<'T>` value that can be listened to and a `Trigger` member for running the event.

Listing 16.6 shows the typical way of working with events in a type declaration. We store the instance of the `Event` class as a local value ❶ and we expose the event value returned by the `Publish` member as a public member of the class ❷, so that the users can listen to the event but can't trigger it. When the appropriate condition is met, we raise the event using the `Trigger` member ❸.

Declaring C#–compatible events

The technique we've used in this section creates events that can be used very naturally from F#, but they won't appear as standard C# events. The F# compiler doesn't treat properties of the `IEvent<'T>` type in any special way, so it will compile the `SignChanged` member as a standard property. We could use the `AddHandler` method of the interface from C#, but that would be confusing.

Luckily, F# compiler provides an easy way to fix that. If you want to declare a standard .NET event in F#, we can use the `CLIEvent` attribute. This attribute is understood by the compiler, and in this case, the compiler creates an event that can be accessed using `+=` and `-=` operators in C#:

```
type Counter() =
  [<CLIEvent>]
  member x.SignChanged = ev.Publish
```

Another difference between F# events that we've created so far and the usual C# event is that F# uses its own generic delegate type (`Handler<T>`). If you want to use some other delegate, you can create the event using a class `Event<'TDel, 'T>`, which allows you to specify the type of the delegate as the first argument. For example, in a typical Windows programming, you'd create events using the `Event<EventHandler, EventArgs>` type.

So far, we've examined some of the benefits of using events as first-class values. The most important concept is probably the ability to use higher-order functions for working with events, treating them as sequences of values to an extent. Now we'll extend our animation example from the previous chapter to allow the user to interact with the animations.

16.2 *Creating reactive animations*

When we implemented the animation library in the previous chapter, we mentioned that its design was largely influenced by functional reactive programming. We were concentrating on the part that implements animations, so the examples couldn't react to events such as mouse clicks. Implementing a complete library for functional reactive programming is outside of the scope of this book, but we can look at one example that shows the relationship between behaviors (from the previous chapter) and the events we've seen so far.

As you may remember from the previous chapter, a behavior is a value that can vary over time. In this section, we'll create a function called switch that allows us to create behaviors that change when an external event occurs. We'll use switch to create an animation that starts as a static image and animates faster each time the user clicks on the form.

16.2.1   *Using the switch function*

We'll start by looking at the example, then describe the implementation of the switch function. Here's its type, which gives us a good starting point for understanding it:

```
val switch : Behavior<'T> -> IObservable<Behavior<'T>> -> Behavior<'T>
```

The result of the function is a behavior that represents a value of 'T varying in time. This means that the function somehow constructs a behavior using the first two arguments. The first argument represents an initial behavior. Before the event occurs, the returned behavior will be the same as the one provided as the first argument.

The most interesting aspect is the second argument. It's an event that carries values of type Behavior<'T>. This means that each time the event is triggered, it will give us a new behavior that we can use instead of the previous (or initial) behavior. Each time the event occurs, the switch function will (behind the scenes) replace the behavior it returns with the one obtained from the event. You may be thinking that an event carrying a behavior as a value sounds a bit complicated. If we wanted to build such an event from scratch it would indeed be tricky—but as always, we can create a complex value by composing simpler ones.

Now that we know what the switch function is going to do, let's try using it. Listing 16.7 first creates a simple rotating circle similar to the ones we saw in chapter 15. It then constructs an event that's triggered when the user clicks on the form, and carries a new behavior: the same animation running a bit faster. Finally, it uses the switch function to construct a behavior that changes with every click.

Listing 16.7   Animation with changing speed (F#)

```
let af = new AnimationForm(ClientSize = Size(400, 400), Visible=true)

let greenCircle = circle (forever Brushes.OliveDrab) 100.0f.forever      ❶
let rotatingCircle = rotate 100.0f 1.0f greenCircle

let circleEvent =        ❷
  af.Click
  |> Observable.map (always 0.1f)                            ❸
  |> Observable.scan (+) 0.0f
  |> Observable.map (fun x -> faster x rotatingCircle)       ❹

let init = faster 0.0f rotatingCircle
af.Animation <- switch init circleEvent         ❺
```

Listing 16.7 first creates a standard behavior, rotatingCircle, that represents an animated green circle that's rotating using a constant speed ❶. Next, it constructs the event that yields new behaviors ❷. We're using the same trick that we did when counting the number of clicks on a button to create an event that will yield a number specifying the speed, which increments with every click ❸. The last call to Observable.map in the pipeline ❹ turns the event carrying the speed into an event that carries a behavior. It changes the speed of the original rotating circle each time by calling the faster function with the new speed as the first argument.

Once we have the event, we can finally use the switch function. First we create an initial behavior, which is the circle with the rotation speed set to zero. Then we use this behavior and the event declared earlier to create the final animation ❺. Figure 16.3 shows the final animation in action; the left side is the result of 3 clicks, and the right is after 13 clicks.

Thanks to the combination of first-class events and behaviors, we can write quite interesting animations in a fully declarative way. Now it's time to look at the implementation of the switch function, which makes it all possible.

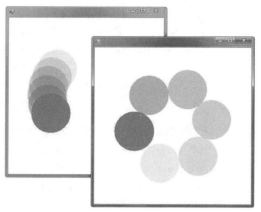

Figure 16.3 Two forms showing the animation running using different speeds after several mouse clicks

16.2.2 Implementing the switch function

We described how the switch function behaves in the previous section, and the implementation isn't much more than a direct translation of that description into code, as shown in listing 16.8. The key idea is that the function will return a behavior that uses an actual behavior stored in a mutable variable. Each time the event occurs, we'll update the mutable variable, so that any subsequent requests for the behavior's value use the new result. Note that this use of mutable state is hidden from the user, so the end-user code can be declarative and free from any visible side effects.

Listing 16.8 Implementing the switch function (F#)

```
let switch initialBehavior behaviorEvent =
  let current = ref initialBehavior
  behaviorEvent |> Observable.add (fun newBehavior ->      ❶
    current := newBehavior)
  sample(fun ctx ->
    let (BehaviorFunc f) = !current      ❷
    f(ctx))
```

The function in listing 16.8 first declares a mutable variable using an F# ref cell (as we discussed in chapter 8). The initial value of the ref cell is set to the initial behavior. Next, we set up a handler for the event that can yield a new behavior ❶. When the event occurs, we set the value of the ref cell to the new behavior that we obtained from the event. We're not worrying about thread-safety in this example, because when we use the `switch` function from Windows Forms, the state is only accessed from the (single) GUI thread. The behavior that's returned from the function is constructed using the `sample` primitive from the previous chapter ❷. When the lambda function is called to retrieve the value of the behavior at the specified time, we simply dereference the current behavior and use it to process the request.

The functions from the `Observable` module are useful if the logic of the event handling isn't complicated. If the reaction to an event is always the same and if you need to filter the event or combine it with other events, then the declarative style is useful. Describing more complex logic declaratively using events isn't always simple. In the next section we'll look at another technique that uses the asynchronous workflows we saw in chapter 13 to handle GUI events.

16.3   *Programming UIs using workflows*

When designing applications that don't react to external events, you have lots of control flow constructs available, such as `if-then-else` expressions, `for` loops and `while` loops in imperative languages, or recursion and higher-order functions in functional languages. Constructs like this make it easy to describe what the application does. The control flow is clearly visible in the source code, so drawing a flowchart to describe it is straightforward.

Understanding reactive applications is much more difficult. A typical C# application or GUI control that needs to react to multiple events usually involves mutable state. When an event occurs, it updates the state and may run more code in response to the event, depending on the current state. This architecture makes it quite difficult to understand the potential states of the application and the transitions between them. Using asynchronous workflows, we can write the code in a way that makes the control flow of the application visible even for reactive applications.

16.3.1   *Waiting for events asynchronously*

The reason why we can't use standard control flow constructs to drive reactive applications is that we don't have any way of waiting for an event to occur. Writing a function that runs in a loop and checks whether an event has occurred is not only difficult to implement, it's also very bad practice: it would block the executing thread. As you learned in chapter 13, asynchronous workflows allow us to write code that looks sequential, but which can include waiting for external events (such as the completion of an asynchronous I/O operation) but is executed asynchronously without blocking the thread.

So far, we've seen only asynchronous methods that perform I/O operations, but we can also define a primitive that stops the asynchronous workflow and resumes it when the specified event occurs. The primitive, called `AwaitObservable`, is available in the online source code for the book as an extension for the `Async` type.[2] Let's start by looking at its type signature:

```
val AwaitObservable : IObservable<'T> -> Async<'T>
```

---

[2]   The `Async.AwaitObservable` primitive may eventually become part of F# core or F# PowerPack library.

The type shows us that the function is quite simple. It takes event as an argument and returns a value that we can use inside an asynchronous workflow using the `let!` keyword. One important difference between events and `Async<'T>` values is that an asynchronous workflow can be executed at most once, while events can be triggered multiple times. This means that the `AwaitObservable` function has to wait only for the *first occurrence* of the event and then resumes the asynchronous workflow. Let's take a look at how we can use `AwaitObservable` in a GUI application.

COUNTING MOUSE CLICKS

We'll start by implementing an example similar to the counter increment/decrement application we used to demonstrate higher-order functions from the `Observable` module. This will be simpler: it counts the number of clicks that take place and displays the count on a label. This behavior could be implemented using `Observable.scan` and the source code would be shorter, but as we'll see later `AwaitObservable` is a far more powerful construct. Listing 16.9 shows how to write event handling code using asynchronous workflows.

Listing 16.9   Counting clicks using asynchronous workflows (F#)

```
let frm, lbl = new Form(...), new Label(...)          Creates user
                                                       interface (omitted)
let rec loop(count) = async {                    ❶
  let! args = Async.AwaitObservable(lbl.MouseDown)    ❷
  lbl.Text <- sprintf "Clicks: %d" count
  return! loop(count + 1) }                      ❸

do
  Async.StartImmediately(loop(1))                ❹
  Application.Run(frm)
```

The essential part of the application that implements the counting is a single recursive function that's implemented as an asynchronous workflow ❶. The function appears to create an infinite loop, which sounds suspicious to start with. The construct is completely valid, because it starts by waiting for a `MouseDown` event ❷. This is done asynchronously, which means that the workflow will install the event handler and the rest will only be executed when the user clicks the label. Once the event occurs, we update the text and loop with the incremented counter ❸.

Earlier we mentioned that the `AwaitObservable` primitive waits for the first occurrence of the event, because asynchronous workflows can yield only a single value. As you can see in this example, if we want to handle every occurrence of the event, we can simply use a recursive loop to wait for the next occurrence. Using recursion also allows us to store the current state in the function parameters. In fact, this technique for expressing computations is similar to the primitive recursive functions we saw earlier in the book.

When working with Windows Form controls, we're required to access them only from the GUI thread, which is the main thread of the application. When you try to use property from other threads, the behavior is undefined and the application could crash. This means that we need to make sure that the asynchronous workflow will be executed only on the GUI thread. So far, we didn't really care where the workflow executes, but F# libraries provide a mechanism to control that.

First, most of the asynchronous operations return to the calling thread after completion. This means that when you invoke an operation such as `AsyncGetResponse`, `AsyncRead`, or `Async.Sleep`, the operation will release the calling thread and start executing in the background. When it completes (usually on some background thread), it will use the .NET `SynchronizationContext` class to return to the thread where it was started.

When we start the workflow on the GUI thread, it will continue running on the GUI thread even if the workflow includes some operations that involve background threads. Thanks to this behavior, we can safely access Windows Forms controls from any part of the workflow. The only remaining question is how we can start workflow on the GUI thread. In listing 16.9, we use the `Async.StartImmediate` primitive ❹, which runs the workflow on the current thread. When the application starts, the current thread will be the main GUI thread.

Figure 16.4 shows what happens when we use the `StartImmediate` primitive to run a workflow that contains a call to `AsyncGetResponse`. The most important fact is that when we run an asynchronous operation (using the `let!` primitive), the GUI thread is free to perform other work. When the workflow running on a GUI thread spends most of the time waiting for completion of an asynchronous operation, the application won't become unresponsive.

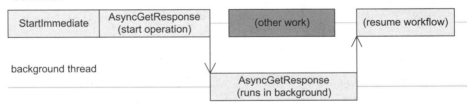

Figure 16.3 `StartImmediate` **starts the workflow on a GUI thread. The** `AsyncGetResponse` **operation runs in the background, while the GUI thread can perform other work. When the background operation completes, the workflow returns to the GUI thread.**

As we said earlier, we could easily have implemented this example using `Observable.scan`; let's look at a slightly more complicated problem.

LIMITING THE SPEED OF CLICKS

Let's say that we'd like to limit the rate of clicks. We want the count to stay the same at least for one second after it gets incremented by the user clicking on the label. One way for implementing this is to add another parameter to the `loop` function of type `DateTime` that will store the last time of a successful click. When the event occurs inside the loop, we could then check the difference from the current time and the last time and increase the count only when the difference is larger than the limit.

There's a much simpler way of achieving this. In chapter 13 we discussed the `Async.Sleep` method, which allows us to stop the workflow for a specified time. If we use it somewhere in the loop function, it will sleep for one second before reacting to the next event, which is exactly what we wanted. All we have to do is to add the following single line before the line that last line that runs the recursion:

```
do! Async.Sleep(1000)
```

This is already something that would be quite difficult to do using the functions from the `Observable` module. If you're curious, you can find the solution using `Observable` functions in the source code at this book's website; it's about 8 lines long and a bit tricky to understand. The control flow of this example was still pretty simple. In the next section, we'll explore a more sophisticated example that better demonstrates the capabilities of using asynchronous workflows for GUI programming.

16.3.2 *Drawing rectangles*

One problem that's surprisingly difficult to solve in a functional way is the user interaction when drawing graphical objects on a Windows Forms control. Suppose we want to draw a rectangle so that the user starts by pressing the mouse button in one of the corners, moves the cursor to the opposite corner, then releases the button. While moving the cursor with the button pressed, the application should draw the current shape of the rectangle, and when the button is released, it should be finally applied to a bitmap or stored in the list of vector shapes.

A typical imperative implementation would use a mutable flag specifying whether we're currently drawing and a mutable variable to store the last location where the user pressed the mouse button. Then we'd handle `MouseDown` and `MouseMove` events and modify the state appropriately when one of them fired. We can check whether the drawing is finished in the handler for the `MouseMove` event, because it also carries information about the state of mouse buttons. Alternatively, we could use the `MouseUp` button, but the first version will be easier to start with. If we think of the control flow of the application, we can see that it's quite simple. You can see a flowchart that shows it in figure 16.5.

We're almost ready to convert this state machine into an F# program using asynchronous workflows, but first we need a form to draw on and a utility function to help us with the basic task of drawing a rectangle.

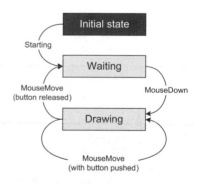

Figure 16.5 When the application is `Waiting`, we can press the button to start `Drawing`. In this state, we can either continue `Drawing` by moving the mouse or complete the task and change the state of the application back to `Waiting` by releasing the button.

IMPLEMENTING PROGRAM FUNDAMENTALS

We'll improve this application later, but let's start with an empty form on which we can draw rectangles. Listing 16.10 shows the code required to create the form and a function, `drawRectangle`, that draws a rectangle on the form using the specified color and two of any corner points of the rectangle.

Listing 16.10   Creating a user interface and drawing utility (F#)

```
open System
open System.Drawing
open System.Windows.Forms

let form = new Form(ClientSize=Size(800, 600))

let drawRectangle(clr, (x1, y1), (x2, y2)) =        ⟵ Passes points as tuples
  use gr = form.CreateGraphics()
  use br = new SolidBrush(clr)
  let left, top = min x1 x2, min y1 y2              | Specifies upper-left
  let width, height = abs(x1 - x2), abs(y1 - y2)    | point, rectangle size
  gr.Clear(Color.White)
  gr.FillRectangle(br, Rectangle(left, top, width, height))
```

Listing 16.10 is very straightforward. The function `drawRectangle` takes all its arguments as a tuple, so it can be used in a way that's consistent with calling .NET methods. In addition, its second and third parameters are nested tuples that represent the X and Y coordinates of the corners of the rectangle. This makes the rest of the code easier.

IMPLEMENTING THE STATE MACHINE

Now that we have all the basics of the application, we can implement our user interaction. We're going to follow the state machine described in figure 16.5, with two states (`Waiting` and `Drawing`) that have various transitions between them. Asynchronous workflows allow us to translate this directly, representing each state with a single function. The transitions can be encoded as function calls or by returning a value from a function.

For our example this means that we'll have two functions called `drawingLoop` and `waitingLoop`. The first of these also needs to remember some state, which we represent using the function's parameters. Listing 16.11 shows both functions.

Listing 16.11   Workflow for drawing rectangles (F#)

```
let rec drawingLoop(clr, from) = async {
  let! move = Async.AwaitObservable(form.MouseMove)                   ❶
  if (move.Button &&& MouseButtons.Left) = MouseButtons.Left then
    drawRectangle(clr, from, (move.X, move.Y))                        ❷
    return! drawingLoop(clr, from)
  else
    return (move.X, move.Y) }          ❸

let waitingLoop() = async {
  while true do                                         ❹
    let! down = Async.AwaitObservable(form.MouseDown)
    let downPos = (down.X, down.Y)
    if (down.Button &&& MouseButtons.Left) = MouseButtons.Left then
      let! upPos = drawingLoop(Color.IndianRed, downPos)              ❺
      do printfn "Drawn rectangle (%A, %A)" downPos upPos }
```

The most direct way to encode the state machine would be to use recursive calls between the two functions using the `return!` keyword. Listing 16.11 makes a minor change to this, to aid readability. The `waitingLoop` function contains an infinite `while` loop ❹ that waits until the user clicks the left button, then transfers control to the drawingLoop function. When drawingLoop completes, it returns the end position of the rectangle ❸ and transfers the control back to waitingLoop ❺. We can then print the information about the drawn rectangle and wait for another MouseDown event.

The function that runs while the user is drawing a rectangle is looping using recursive calls, because it needs to keep some state. It starts by waiting for the MouseMove event, which is also triggered when the button is released ❶. It then tests whether the button is currently pressed; if that's the case, it refreshes the view of the form ❷. This transition corresponds to the arc looping in the Drawing state. When the button is released, it returns the last location as a result ❷, which is the transition back to the Waiting state.

That's almost everything we need to run the application. All that remains is to start the asynchronous workflow that handles drawing of rectangles and run the application. We'll use the Async.StartImmediately primitive to start the workflow on the GUI thread:

```
[<STAThread>]
do
  Async.StartImmediately(waitingLoop())
  Application.Run(form)
```

In this simple application, we need only a single asynchronous workflow that handles all the interaction with the application, but multiple workflows can be combined easily. If we wanted to allow polygons to be drawn using the right mouse button, we could implement that without making any changes to the existing code. We'd simply create another workflow for drawing polygons and start it independently using Async.StartImmediately. This way of writing the UI code gives us a modular way of splitting complex interactions into separate processes.

Running workflows on the GUI thread

The application we just implemented consists of a single running process, but it's important to realize that a process in the sense we're using here doesn't correspond to a thread. Even if we had multiple processes waiting for GUI events, the application would still be single-threaded.

When we run the Async.StartImmediately method in the earlier example, it starts running the workflow and doesn't complete until the workflow reaches a point where it waits for a completion of an asynchronous operation (such as waiting for an event). Both Async.Sleep and Async.AwaitObservable, which we've used so far, return to the caller thread after completion, so the workflow will continue running exclusively on the GUI thread.

Even if we add multiple processes that wait for UI events, this technique doesn't introduce any parallelism. All the code runs on the GUI thread, and if a single event causes state transition in multiple processes, the bits of workflows are executed sequentially. Using asynchronous workflows to write UIs gives us an easier way to write our single-threaded GUI processing.

> **(continued)**
>
> Later on, we'll see a technique that allows us to integrate this form of GUI processing with other processes that can potentially run in parallel. However, code for user interface interaction like this should be simple and shouldn't perform any complicated computations, so there's no need for parallelism. Even when we need to perform some time-consuming computations for the GUI, it's still a good idea to move all this work to a background worker thread.

The code we've written so far isn't a drawing application, because it doesn't store the rectangles we've drawn. Once a rectangle has been completed by the user releasing the button, it prints information to the console and forgets the rectangle. We could store a list of rectangles as a parameter of the `waitingLoop` function (if we made it a recursive function), but that would cause other problems. The list would be private to the drawing loop, so it couldn't be accessed from other parts of the application. We need a different approach to handle global state that's used by the whole application.

16.4   *Storing state in reactive applications*

The asynchronous workflow we used to draw rectangles can be viewed as a lightweight process that runs inside the application to handle a specific task. In this chapter, the task was a GUI interaction, but we could just as easily add other asynchronous workflows that perform other tasks, such as downloading the content of a website as we saw in chapter 13. This means there can be multiple processes like this running in parallel. An asynchronous workflow doesn't correspond to a thread. Unless we explicitly limit it to run on the GUI thread using the `StartImmediately` method, we can have numerous workflows running in parallel.

Structuring the code using workflows allows us to split the code into small pieces nicely, but we haven't discussed one essential aspect yet: how these processes can communicate.

16.4.1   *Working with state safely*

In a single-threaded application like the drawing of rectangles we've implemented so far, we could use global mutable variables. This may not be the most elegant solution from the pure functional point of view, but it's a pragmatic choice, because using mutation in .NET programming is easy. You could no doubt write the code using, for example, the mutable `List<T>` type to store the rectangles yourself, so we'll look at an alternative solution that's more important once we introduce parallelism and makes the code clearer from a functional point of view.

In this book, we won't introduce parallelism in the demo, but you can get a more evolved version of the sample from the book's website. In that version we make the application online and allow multiple users to connect to a single server and collaborate on drawing a single image. In that case, the state can be modified by the user, but also *concurrently* by a message coming from a network communication. If we decided to use mutable state, we'd have to carefully use locking, which would complicate the code. When we store the state using the technique we'll introduce in this section we won't have to do a single change—the code as we'll write it is perfectly thread-safe, which is quite important nowadays.

The technique we're going to use instead is called *message passing*. In a message-passing application, the processes can send messages to each other and exchange all the state they need just by sending or replying to messages.

16.4.2 Creating a mailbox processor

Let's look at using message passing in practice. We'll extend the application from the previous section and add a process that will store the current state of the application: the currently selected color (we'll add an option to change the color) and a list of all the rectangles that we've drawn so far. The application will handle messages that will be sent from the process for drawing rectangles or from other event handlers that we'll add to the application. In the extended version of the demo that we mentioned in the section introduction, the messages can also be sent concurrently from a component handling the network communication. In F#, the processes that can receive messages are also called *mailbox processors*. Before we can start implementing the mailbox processor, we need to know what a message is.

IMPLEMENTING THE MESSAGE TYPE

Each process can handle messages of a single known type, so we'll begin by declaring the type that represents the message. We'll use a discriminated union, because that way we can represent multiple kinds of messages as discriminators of a single union type. As you can see in listing 16.12, discriminated union is the right F# type for this purpose.

> ### Listing 16.12 The type representing messages (F#)

```
type RectData = Color * (int * int) * (int * int)

type DrawingMessage =
  | AddRectangle of RectData
  | SetColor of Color
  | GetRectangles of AsyncReplyChannel<list<RectData>>
  | GetColor of AsyncReplyChannel<Color>
```

Listing 16.12 starts by declaring a type alias called `RectData`, which is a tuple containing all the information that we need to store about a single rectangle. The discriminated union itself then contains two types of messages. The first two messages are used to change the current state. In the case of `AddRectangle`, the processor will add the information about the newly created rectangle to an internal list; in the case of `Set-Color`, it will change the currently selected color.

The next two messages look a bit trickier, because the value they carry has a type `AsyncReplyChannel<'T>`. This type allows us to create messages that send a reply back to the caller. In our case, it means that when the process receives one of these messages, it will send a reply back containing either a list of all the rectangles or the currently selected color.

Now that we've got the message, we need to know how to implement the mailbox processor, and how to send and receive messages. Let's start with the mailbox processor.

IMPLEMENTING THE PROCESSOR

In general, mailbox processors can be quite complicated. They can perform calculations in reaction to the messages they receive; they can send messages to other processors and collect the replies; they can even start new mailbox processors. Our example is simple: the mailbox processor stores the current state of the application and handles the messages to read or update this state.

Listing 16.13 implements the processor in much the same way as our earlier state machine code. Most of the code is a recursive function written using asynchronous workflows that maintains the current state using function parameters.

Listing 16.13   Creating the mailbox processor (F#)

```
let state = MailboxProcessor.Start(fun mbox ->          ❶
  let rec loop(clr, rects) = async {
    let! msg = mbox.Receive()          ❷
    match msg with
    | SetColor(newClr) ->
      return! loop(newClr, rects)                 ◁─┐
    | AddRectangle(newRc) ->                          ❸
      form.Invalidate()
      return! loop(clr, rects@[newRc])            ◁─┘
    | GetColor(chnl) ->
      chnl.Reply(clr)                   ◁─┐
      return! loop(clr, rects)             ❹
    | GetRectangles(chnl) ->
      chnl.Reply(rects)                 ◁─┘
      return! loop(clr, rects) }
  loop(Color.IndianRed, []) )          ❺
```

To create a mailbox processor, we use the `Start` member of the `MailboxProcessor` type. It initializes the mailbox for the messages and runs the specified function ❶ to start processing messages. The function returns an asynchronous workflow that can wait for messages using the `Receive` method ❷ of the mailbox that we get as an argument during the initialization.

We've implemented the workflow using a recursive function called `loop` that takes two parameters. The parameter `clr` represents the currently selected color and `rects` is a list of rectangles. To return the workflow from the lambda function, we call `loop` with a red color and an empty list as the initial state ❺.

Now let's have a look at the body of the `loop` function. It starts by receiving the next message from the mailbox ❷. The mailbox internally stores a queue, so if a message is already in the queue it will be returned immediately. If the queue is empty, the `Receive` method will block the workflow (without blocking the actual thread) and resume it once a message is sent to the processor. Once we receive a message, we use pattern matching to decide how to handle it. The first two messages modify the state of the processor, so we call the `loop` function recursively with the updated state using the `return!` keyword ❸. Note that when we get a new rectangle, we want to add it to the end of the list to make sure that it will be displayed on the top, so we use the `@` operator for concatenating lists.

The last two messages ❹ are used for reading the state of the processor and carry a reply channel as an argument. When the processor receives the message, it uses the `Reply` method of the channel to send the list of rectangles or the current color back as a result to the caller, and then loops without altering the state.

> **NOTE** When you're writing mailbox processors, it's important to understand how they're executed with respect to threads. The thread that's executing the body can change when the workflow waits for an asynchronous operation, but the body of a single mailbox processor instance will never run on multiple threads concurrently. If a new message is received while we're processing an existing one, it's just queued and handled later. Our example doesn't perform any complicated computations, so it will almost always process the message immediately. Mailbox processors are thread-safe by design, so when we use them to store state that's accessed concurrently, we don't have to worry about race conditions.

Now that we have the mailbox processor ready, let's see what changes we need to make in order to use and update the state stored in the processor.

16.4.3 *Communicating using messages*

Listing 16.13 created a mailbox processor called `state`, which has a type `MailboxProcessor<DrawingMessage>`. Note that the `Start` method we used to create it was a member of a nongeneric class of the same name. This is the same pattern we've used in C# to take advantage of type inference. Before we start integrating this into our code, we'll see what operations are supported by mailbox processors. Table 16.2 shows the most important instance methods of the generic type.

Table 16.2 The most important methods provided by the `MailboxProcessor<'Msg>` type

Mailbox function	Description of the function
Post	Sends a message to the mailbox processor without waiting for any reply. If the mailbox processor is busy, the message is stored in the queue.
PostAndReply	Sends a message that expects `AsyncReplyChannel<'T>` as an argument to the mailbox processor and blocks the calling thread until the mailbox processor invokes the `Reply` method of the channel. It then returns the value sent to the channel by the processor.
PostAndAsyncReply	Similar to `PostAndReply` with the exception that it runs asynchronously. This is usually invoked from an asynchronous workflow using `let!` so that the calling thread isn't blocked while the message is waiting to be processed.

Table 16.2   The most important methods provided by the `MailboxProcessor<'Msg>` type *(continued)*

Mailbox function	Description of the function
Receive	We used this method when creating the mailbox processor to asynchronously receive the next message from the queue, so that we can process it inside workflow. This method shouldn't be used outside the mailbox processor.
Scan	Like `Receive`, this method shouldn't be used outside the mailbox processor. It can be used when the processor is in a state when it can't process all types of messages. The provided lambda function returns an option type, and it can return `Some` containing asynchronous workflow to process the message or `None` when the message can't be processed. Unprocessed messages remain in the queue to be processed later.

We've seen how to use `Receive`, and we'll talk about `Scan` later on. The remaining three methods can be used from any thread. Although it's occasionally useful for a processor to send a message to itself, the more typical scenario is for a message to be sent to a processor from a different process (for example, an asynchronous workflow implementing the GUI interaction or a background worker thread).

IMPROVING THE DRAWING PROCESS

Now we know what's available, we can change the drawing process to keep all the rectangles the user has drawn, and to allow the user to select a different color. First we need to change the drawing code. The `drawRectangle` function originally erased the whole screen, which isn't appropriate if we want to draw multiple rectangles. We still need to clear the screen, but just once rather than for every rectangle. Listing 16.14 shows a new function that draws all the rectangles in a specified list. The `drawRectangle` function isn't shown, but the only change is to remove the first call to `Clear`.

Listing 16.14   Utility function for drawing rectangles (F#)

```
let redrawWindow(rectangles) =
  use gr = form.CreateGraphics()
  gr.Clear(Color.White)
  for r in rectangles do
    drawRectangle(r)
```

The function clears the content of the form and iterates over all the elements of the given list, drawing each individual rectangle using `drawRectangle`. The list stores rectangles as tuples with three elements (the color and two opposite corners), which is compatible with the tuple expected by the `drawRectangle` function.

Now we're finally ready to modify the process that handles the user interaction. Because the whole code is implemented as an asynchronous workflow, we can use the asynchronous method `PostAndAsyncReply` when we need to get information from the mailbox processor that stores the state. This is the preferred option when it's possible to use it, because it doesn't block the calling thread. Most of the code in listing 16.15 is the same as it was in listing 16.11, so we've highlighted the lines that have changed.

Listing 16.15 Changes in the drawing process (F#)

```
let rec drawingLoop(clr, from) = async {
  let! move = Async. AwaitObservable(form.MouseMove)
  if (move.Button &&& MouseButtons.Left) = MouseButtons.Left then
    let! rects = state.PostAndAsyncReply(GetRectangles)          ❶
    redrawWindow(rects)                                          ❷
    drawRectangle(clr, from, (move.X, move.Y))
    return! drawingLoop(clr, from)
  else
    return (move.X, move.Y) }

let waitingLoop() = async {
  while true do
    let! down = Async. AwaitObservable(form.MouseDown)
    let downPos = (down.X, down.Y)
    if (down.Button &&& MouseButtons.Left) = MouseButtons.Left then
      let! clr = state.PostAndAsyncReply(GetColor)              ❸
      let! upPos = drawingLoop(clr, downPos)
      state.Post(AddRectangle(clr, downPos, upPos)) }           ❹
```

Let's begin by looking at the changes we did in the drawingLoop function, at the point where we update the window. Originally, we needed to erase whatever was there before and draw the new rectangle, but now we also need to draw all the rectangles that were drawn earlier. We obtain the list of rectangles from the mailbox processor by sending it the GetRectangles message ❶. The message takes an argument of type AsyncReplyChannel<'T> that will be used by the mailbox processor to reply to the caller, but we don't specify the channel explicitly in the code. The F# compiler treats the discriminated union constructor (GetRectangles) as a function that takes a single argument. We could write the same thing like this:

```
let! rects = state.PostAndAsyncReply(fun chnl -> GetRectangles(chnl))
```

If we write the code in this longer form, it's easier to see what's going on in detail. The PostAndAsyncReply method creates a channel for the reply and uses the specified lambda function to create the message that carries the channel. The message is then sent to the mailbox processor and the workflow is suspended until a reply is sent to the channel. Once we receive the reply with a list of rectangles, we can draw them. We then draw the new rectangle that the user is drawing right now ❷. Note that the reply can be sent from a background thread. The PostAndAsyncReply method returns to the caller thread after completion, so the rest of the workflow will execute on the GUI thread.

The second change is in the waitingLoop function, at the point where the user starts drawing a new rectangle. First we read the currently selected color ❸. We haven't implemented the UI aspect of selecting a different color yet, but that will come soon, so we might as well be ready for it. We have to retrieve the color *after* the call to AwaitObservable completes; otherwise the user could change the color after we fetch it but before we start drawing. Once we've got the color, we can call the draw-ingLoop function to handle the period of time when the user is still pressing the mouse button. We use the `Post` method to send all the information about the newly created rectangle to the mailbox processor **❹**.

ADDING THE USER INTERFACE

The UI of the application will be quite simple, but we'll need to call the mailbox processor from various places to work with the current application state. First we'll add a handler for the `Paint` event, so the application redraws the rectangles when any part of the window is invalidated. This could happen if the application is resized, or if another window is moved in front of it. Second, we'll add a toolbar with a single button that allows the user to change the current color. Figure 16.6 shows an example of the application in action.

Listing 16.16 shows the most interesting parts of the remaining application code. We've omitted the code that creates the toolbar and the button, but the full source is on this book's website.

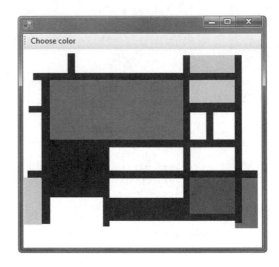

Figure 16.6   Running the application with a drawing consisting only of rectangles.

Listing 16.16   Implementing the user interface (F#)

```
let btnColor = new ToolStripButton(...)          ⊲─┐ Creates user
                                                    │ interface (omitted)
btnColor.Click.Add(fun _ ->
  use dlg = new ColorDialog()
  if (dlg.ShowDialog() = DialogResult.OK) then   ⊲─┐ Shows dialog for
    state.Post(SetColor(dlg.Color)) )      ❶       │ color selection

form.Paint.Add(fun _ ->
  let rects = state.PostAndReply(GetRectangles)   ❷
  redrawWindow(rects) )

[<STAThread>]
do                                               ⊲─┐ Starts rectangle-
  Async.StartImmediate(waitingLoop())              │ drawing workflow
  Application.Run(form)
```

Most of the code is fairly straightforward. We create the UI and register a handler for two events. We don't need to do anything complicated with these events, so we're calling the `Add` method instead of using functions from the `Observable` module. The first handler displays a `ColorDialog` so the user can select a new color. If a color is selected, we post a message with the new color to the mailbox processor **❶**. We don't need to wait for any reply to this message, so this operation is performed without blocking the thread.

The second event handler is for the Paint event. First it needs to obtain the list of existing rectangles, which it does using the PostAndReply method ❷. This constructs the message with a reply channel and then waits until the mailbox sends a reply. This method blocks the thread, so it should be used only when we can't complete the operation asynchronously. Updating the window of the application based on the Windows Forms request is definitely one of these situations, so this use is correct.

So far, we've been using the mailbox processor object directly. That's okay in the early stages of development, but once the application becomes larger, or if we want to turn part of the application into a separate library, it would be better to encapsulate the mailbox processor in an object. Even though we're not going to extend our drawing application much further, it's worth taking a look at what this involves.

16.4.4 *Encapsulating mailbox processors*

To encapsulate the mailbox processor, we'll change the global value representing the processor into a local field within a normal object type. We'll add methods that send the messages to the private mailbox, which is also good for encapsulation: we don't have to expose all of the messages that the mailbox can respond to, if some of them are only intended for internal use.

Making this change doesn't require any modification to the message-processing code. You can see the declaration of the concrete object type in listing 16.17; the processing code itself is omitted because it hasn't changed.

Listing 16.17   Encapsulating mailbox processor into a type (F#)

```
type DrawingState() =
  let mbox = MailboxProcessor.Start(fun mbox ->       ◁─┐  Creates private
    let rec loop(clr, rects) = async {                 ❶  mailbox processor
      let! msg = mbox.Receive()
      // Message processing code as before
    }
    loop(Color.Black, []) )

  member x.SetColor(clr) =
    mbox.Post(SetColor(clr))              ❷  Updates state
  member x.AddRectangle(rc) =                without blocking
    mbox.Post(AddRectangle(rc))

  member x.AsyncGetRectangles() =
    mbox.PostAndAsyncReply(GetRectangles))   ❸  Reads state
  member x.AsyncGetColor() =                     asynchronously
    mbox.PostAndAsyncReply(GetColor))

  member x.GetRectangles() =
    mbox.PostAndReply(GetRectangles)       ❹  Reads state
  member x.GetColor() =                         with blocking
    mbox.PostAndReply(GetColor)

let state = new DrawingState()
```

To create a local mailbox processor inside the class declaration, we use a local let binding ❶. This becomes a part of the constructor of the class, which means that the mailbox will be started when the instance is created. Values declared using local `let` bindings are turned into fields, so they're accessible from anywhere inside the class.

The members of the type are mostly boilerplate code. Members that update the state of the mailbox processor and don't wait for any return value ❷ send their messages using the `Post` method. The second group of members ❸ read state asynchronously, using the `PostAndAsyncReply` method. Note that we're using the `Async` prefix in the name of these members. This is a standard notation used across the entire F# library to denote members that can only be accessed from asynchronous workflows. The final two methods ❹ are simple blocking methods that use the synchronous `PostAndReply` method.

Once we've encapsulated the mailbox processor inside a class, we need to modify the rest of the code where it's accessed. Instead of sending a message explicitly, we simply call one of the methods. For instance, the calls in the asynchronous workflow to get and set the selected color turn into these lines:

```
let! clr = state.AsyncGetColor()
state.SetColor(clr)
```

Now that we've encapsulated the mailbox processor in a class, it can be compiled into an F# library and distributed as a reusable component. Unfortunately it's hard to use methods that return asynchronous workflow objects (`Async<'T>`) from C#, so if you want to be able to use the component from C#, you should also provide methods that take a delegate to act as a callback, and run that when the asynchronous operation completes.

In the next section we'll add one more feature to our application to show another aspect of event handling using the `AwaitObservable` primitive inside asynchronous workflows.

16.4.5 *Waiting for multiple events*

In all the `AwaitObservable` examples so far, we've only been waiting for a single event to occur. The rectangle drawing application first waits for the `MouseDown` event and then repeatedly waits for `MouseMove`. What if we wanted to wait until *either* the `Mouse-Move` event *or* some other event occurred? We might want to be able to cancel drawing the new rectangle in some way. We'll implement exactly this scenario, using a key press as our cancellation event.

We're going to need to change the return type of the `drawingLoop` function. There are now two possibilities when the function returns: either the user has drawn a rectangle (in which case the calling function needs to know the details of it) or the user canceled the drawing. This is a perfect match for an option type: the return type was originally `Async<int * int>`, and after the change it will become `Async<option<int * int>>`. Of course we won't need to explicitly change the return type: the F# compiler can infer it as normal.

When the user hits the Esc key, we'll stop the `drawingLoop` and return `None` as the result. To do this, we need to wait for the `MouseMove` or the `KeyDown` event and handle the one that occurs first. You can find the modified code for the `drawingLoop` function in listing 16.18.

Listing 16.18 Drawing rectangle with cancellation using the Esc key (F#)

```
let rec drawingLoop(clr, from) = async {
  let! args = Async.AwaitObservable(form.MouseMove, form.KeyDown)    ◁┐ Waits
  match args with                                                    ┆ for any
  | Choice1Of2(move) when                                           ❶ event
      MouseButtons.Left =
      (move.Button &&& MouseButtons.Left) ->       ◁┐ Continues
    let! rects = state.AsyncGetRectangles()        ❷ drawing
    redrawWindow(rects)
    drawRectangle(clr, from, (move.X, move.Y))
    return! drawingLoop(clr, from)              ❸ Returns
  | Choice1Of2(move) ->                          ◁   rectangle
    return Some(move.X, move.Y)
  | Choice2Of2(key) when key.KeyCode = Keys.Escape ->    ◁┐ Cancels drawing,
    form.Invalidate();                                   ┆ returns None
    return None
  | _ -> return! drawingLoop(clr, from) }
```

In all the previous examples, we used the `AwaitObservable` method, which takes just one event as an argument. However, the source code for the book also implements an overload, which allows us to specify multiple events and waits for the first occurrence of any of the specified events, ignoring any subsequent occurrences. In our case, this means that the call ❶ will block until either a mouse is moved or a key is pressed; it will run the processing code. If the processing ends with a recursive call, then `Await-Observable` will be called again to wait for the next event, but otherwise the next occurrence will be ignored. To better understand how the overload taking two parameters works, let's look at its type signature:

```
AwaitObservable : IObservable<'T> * IObservable<'U> -> Async<Choice<'T * 'U>>
```

When `AwaitObservable` returns, we need to know which of the events occurred and what argument it carried. Also, the values carried by the events can be different for all the provided events. In this situation, the method can't simply return the carried argument, so let's look at the type of the returned value. The type `Choice` is a generic discriminated union and can represent one of several choices. The type is overloaded by the number of type parameters. In listing 16.18, we have two different choices, so the type of the `args` value is `Choice<MouseEventArgs, KeyEventArgs>`.

When the `MouseMove` event occurs first, the returned value will use the discriminated union constructor `Choice1Of2` carrying information about the mouse event; otherwise the constructor `Choice2Of2` will be used with a value of type `KeyEventArgs`. If you wanted to wait for more events, you'd use a name such as `Choice1Of3` and so on.

Responding to multiple events appropriately is a task that lends itself to pattern matching. The first branch ❷ is called when the mouse moves while the user is still pressing the left button. In that case we update the window and continue drawing. If the mouse button has been released, the next case ❸ will be called. This means that the user finished drawing, so we can return the end location of the rectangle.

The last two cases respond to the `KeyDown` event. Again we use a `when` clause, this time to determine whether the key being pressed was Esc. If that's the case, we cancel the drawing process and return `None` as the result; otherwise we ignore the keyboard event and continue waiting for another event.

Having changed the `drawingLoop` function, the final step is to tweak the `waiting-Loop` function so that it sends the `AddRectangle` message only when a rectangle is actually drawn. This is a simple change that doesn't introduce any new concepts, so you can find it in the full source code on the book's website.

We started this section by discussing how to use a mailbox processor to store the state of the application in a scenario where we need to handle various events. In all our examples so far, we've limited ourselves to events coming from the UI. An important feature of mailbox processors is that they can be also used in scenarios involving concurrency. We'll take a look at this topic in the next section.

16.5   *Message passing concurrency*

When we discussed developing concurrent programs in chapter 14, we focused on techniques where we could avoid using mutable state. Without mutable state, we can run several parts of a computation in parallel, because they can't interfere with each other. This works very well for many data processing problems that can be implemented in a functional way, but there are also problems when the processes need to exchange information more frequently.

The most widely known solution is using the *shared memory* and protecting access to the shared state using locks. The problem with this technique is that using locks correctly is quite difficult. You have to make sure that all the shared memory is properly locked (to avoid *race conditions* when multiple threads write to the same location). Another difficulty is that when we don't use caution when acquiring locks we can cause a *deadlock*, where two threads become blocked forever, each waiting for the other to complete.

The `MailboxProcessor<'Msg>` type in F# can be used to implement concurrent programs using a technique called *message passing* concurrency. This approach isn't as widely used, but is the basis of concurrency in a functional language called Erlang [Armstrong et al., 1996], which is known for its scalability. We've already seen this approach when we stored the state of our rectangle-drawing application in a mailbox, but that scenario was designed to explore asynchronous logic and event handling more than true concurrency.

In this section, we'll look at using a mailbox processor from multiple threads to demonstrate this approach. We'll use an example with a single mailbox processor and multiple asynchronous workflows (running on multiple threads) that access it. More sophisticated programs that use message-passing concurrency often use multiple mailbox processors that communicate with each other.

16.5.1 Creating a state machine processor

The mailbox processor we created earlier was quite simple. It was able to process four different messages and it maintained some local state, but it was always able to process any message that it received immediately. This may not always be the case. If a single mailbox processor sends a message to two other processors, it may need to collect the replies from these processors before reacting to any other message.

We can write mailbox processors that represent a state machine in a similar way to our event-handling state machine for drawing rectangles using asynchronous workflows. A full application demonstrating this is beyond the scope of this book, but we'll create a simple example that shows the concepts involved.

Our message processor will store an integer that can be modified by a message, and have the ability to block and resume operation. While it's blocked, no further modification messages will be processed. To keep things simple, we're not going to provide any way of retrieving the stored integer: when we modify the state we'll print a message to the console so we can see what's going on. With this goal in mind, it's easy to design the message type:

```
type Message =
  | ModifyState of int
  | Block
  | Resume
```

The individual messages are simple, and we've already explained what `ModifyState` will do. The two other messages are worth considering in more detail. If the process is in the initial state and it receives `Block`, it stops processing all the `ModifyState` messages and waits for `Resume`. Messages sent to the processor when it's in the blocked state aren't lost: the processor has an internal queue where the messages are stored, so once we resume it again, it will process all the messages it received while it was blocked.

Listing 16.19 implements this mailbox processor. We're encoding the state machine using recursive asynchronous workflow functions, just like we did for our drawing state machine: one function is used to respond to messages in the `active` state, and one function responds to (or ignores) messages in the `blocked` state. The two functions call each other when the mailbox changes from one state to the other.

Listing 16.19 Mailbox processor using state machine (F#)

```
let mbox = MailboxProcessor.Start(fun mbox ->
  let startTime = DateTime.UtcNow
  let rec active(n) = async {
    printfn "[%A] Processing: %d" (DateTime.UtcNow - startTime) n
    let! msg = mbox.Receive()                                        ◁──❶ Processes
    match msg with                                                        any message
    | ModifyState(by) -> return! active(n + by)
    | Resume -> return! active(n)
    | Block -> return! blocked(n) }
  and blocked(n) =
    printfn "[%A] Blocking" (DateTime.UtcNow - startTime)
```

```
mbox.Scan(fun msg ->                        Only processes
  match msg with                     ②       Resume message
  | Resume -> Some(async {                              Returns workflow
      let dt = (DateTime.UtcNow - startTime)   ③        that will be executed
      printfn "[%A] Resuming" dt
      return! active(n) })           ④   Skips given
  | _ -> None)                               message
active(0) )
```

The processor is started by calling the `active` function with zero as the initial state. In this state, we can handle any message, so we simply use the `Receive` primitive ❶ that asynchronously returns the next message. If the message is `ModifyState`, we update the number and continue in the `active` state. The `Resume` message doesn't make much sense in this state (because we haven't received the `Block` message yet), so we can ignore it. When we receive the `Block` message, we need to do something to stop processing all messages other than `Resume`, so we call the `blocked` function that represents the second state.

When the processor is in the blocked state, we have to use the `Scan` primitive ❷, which allows us to specify what messages we can handle and which messages should remain in the queue for later processing. The `Scan` member takes a function that specifies what to do when a message is received. In our example, when the message is `Resume`, we return an asynchronous workflow ❸ that the `Scan` member will run. The workflow prints a message to the console and executes the `active` function to switch back to the active state. When the processor receives any other message in the `blocked` state, the lambda expression executed by `Scan` will return `None` ❹. This means that it can't process the message, so `Scan` adds the message to the queue and waits for another one.

Note that the mailbox processor as we implemented it doesn't work well when we have multiple threads sending the `Block` and `Resume` messages. If it receives a `Block` message when it's already blocked, it doesn't handle it and instead continues processing once it receives the first `Resume` message. To solve this more robustly, we'd have to handle `Block` messages in the blocked state and increment some number representing the count of `Block` messages. The `Resume` message would decrement it and we'd resume the processing only after the number reached zero again. This isn't particularly difficult, but we'll keep the code simple for our example.

16.5.2 *Accessing mailbox concurrently*

The mailbox processor handles only a single message at time, but it can be safely accessed from multiple threads. All the methods for posting message to the processor (such as `Post` and `PostAndReply`) are thread-safe. Let's create a small application that uses our mailbox processor from three threads to demonstrate the concurrency.

Listing 16.20 represents the situation where two threads repeatedly perform a computation and then send a state update to the mailbox processor. To keep the code simple, our threads will just sleep for some time and then generate a random number. A third thread repeatedly sends `Block` and `Resume` messages to the processor, again sleeping in between messages.

Listing 16.20   Sending messages from multiple threads (F#)

```
let modifyThread() =                                              ◁──  Performs
  let rnd = new Random(Thread.CurrentThread.ManagedThreadId)            calculations
  while true do
    Thread.Sleep(500)
    mbox.Post(ModifyState(rnd.Next(11) - 5))    ◁──┐   Sends update
                                                   ❶  to mailbox
let blockThread() =
  while true do
    Thread.Sleep(2000)
    mbox.Post(Block)
    Thread.Sleep(1500)      ┐   ❷  Blocks processing
    mbox.Post(Resume)       │      for I.5 seconds

for proc in [ blockThread; modifyThread; modifyThread ] do
  Async.Start(async { proc() })
```

The code for the threads is quite simple. Both functions contain an infinite loop that would execute useful work in a real application, and both occasionally send messages to the mailbox to synchronize. The first function only uses the ModifyState message ❶, and the second one first sends the message to block the mailbox, then waits for some time and unblocks it ❷. We use Async.Start to start executing the functions in three thread pool threads by creating a list of function values representing the processes to run and then starting each of them in a for loop. The list contains the modifyThread function twice, so we'll have two threads sending updates to the state.

Let's analyze the behavior of the application when we execute it. The application prints the time of an operation, so you can run it and look at the printed times. It starts off by processing the incoming ModifyState messages for about 2 seconds. The blocking/resuming thread then sends the Block message, so nothing will be printed to the console for the next 1.5 seconds, even though new ModifyState messages will still be posted to the mailbox. After that, the mailbox processor will be resumed and it'll process all the queued ModifyState messages, so the state will be updated several times in quick succession. It will continue running, processing messages as they arrive for the next 2 seconds until the next Block message is received.

Even though this example doesn't implement any particularly useful behavior, it should give you a pretty good idea of how to use mailbox processors in a real-world application that needs to synchronize state using message-passing concurrency.

16.6   Summary

In this chapter, we covered techniques to develop reactive applications in a functional way. We started by talking about first-class events in F#, which allow us to use events as standard values that can be passed into or returned from a function. This allows us to use higher-order functions (such as Observable.filter and Observable.map) to process events. This leads to more declarative code in the same way as processing lists using higher-order functions or LINQ queries.

This declarative style doesn't work as well for more dynamic behavior. F# provides a convenient alternative using the asynchronous workflows introduced in chapter 13. These allow us to write flow control that looks similar to synchronous code but that executes based on events occurring. This technique works particularly well for translating a state machine into code, using a natural mapping of states into functions that call each other recursively.

Finally, we faced the problem of managing state in an application that's encoded as asynchronous workflows that handle GUI events. We saw how this can be handled using message passing with the `MailboxProcessor<'T>` type in F#. This type can be also used in concurrent scenarios, so we wrapped up with an example showing how to use it from a multithreaded application.

Unfortunately, most of the examples we've seen in this chapter rely on asynchronous workflows, so they can't really be translated into C# directly. In C#, you can encode similar patterns using the new .NET 4.0 namespace `System.Threading.Tasks`. Various projects are attempting to offer a more elegant syntax, such as the Concurrency and Coordination Runtime [Richter, 2006]. However, none of them provides the same clarity as F#. The message-passing concurrency techniques shown later in this chapter exists in many different forms. The F# implementation is close to the Erlang style of message passing (see, for example, *Concurrent Programming in Erlang* [Armstrong, et al., 1996]), but other alternatives exist. One of them is also available as a library for C# 2.0, so take a look at the Joins Concurrency Library [Russo, 2007].

appendix:
Looking ahead

We could stop at this point by saying "And so, *that* is functional programming," but that wouldn't be accurate for this kind of book. Unlike a programming language or a particular technology, functional programming doesn't have clear borders: there isn't a complete, definitive list of features that we could walk through and then say "So, that's it." We've done our best to explain all the fundamental concepts behind the functional paradigm, so you can certainly say that you understand the foundations of functional programming.

We've combined two different aspects of functional programming in this book. We've looked at concepts that are very different from those you're probably used to, as well as some of the important real-world uses of functional style. We hope you found both ingredients equally interesting: without solid foundations, it's hard to benefit from functional ideas, but even the most beautiful idea is useless until it's applied in the real world. We write that with a degree of sadness, but this book isn't about art, philosophy, or mathematics.

A.1   *What have you learned?*

We began with a chapter titled "Thinking differently" because learning functional programming isn't the same as learning how to use a library or the newest version of your favorite language. It gives you a new way of thinking about problems—a different perspective. The focus on data structures provides an alternative approach to application architecture, and aspects like first-class and higher-order functions offer simpler but more flexible ways to think about implementation.

If we had to choose the most interesting aspect of what we've covered in this book, we'd probably choose F# *type signatures*. It is amazing how much information you can get from so few characters. Thanks to immutability, a function's type signature tells us everything about what it can produce. If it uses higher-order functions, the signature may also suggest the most likely implementation. Given that it usually fits on a single line, that's often much more than you could achieve with a single natural language sentence. We hope that with your newly acquired "functional glasses," you'll see many problems in a much clearer light.

We've seen many real-world scenarios where functional programming can be useful, ranging from parallel programming to composable libraries for writing animations or financial contracts. The final chapter demonstrates reactive applications, using F# in a novel way that the language designers didn't originally anticipate. In fact, most of the ideas in the chapter came into existence while Tomas was doing an internship with Don Syme at Microsoft Research, after the first half of the manuscript was written.

We mention this to show that F# and functional programming in the real-world context are still actively evolving. We believe that within the next few years you can expect to see many interesting frameworks built using functional principles—perhaps with F# itself—that will make you more productive and that will make development more enjoyable. We want to encourage you to try new things with F# and functional programming. Even though the field has a long history, it's gaining a new momentum. There's still a good chance that your idea will turn into the "next big thing."

Don't worry about being drowned in a deluge of new technologies. This book has given you a solid foundation, so understanding any technology built on top of functional ideas shouldn't present any problems.

A.2   *Where do you want to go next?*

As we've mentioned, this book offers one view of functional programming. If you find functional programming interesting and want to see a slightly different approach, you may want to look at other functional languages.

Scheme, a language based on LISP, offers the greatest difference in perspective. It puts strong emphasis on meta-programming—that is, writing programs that generate, modify, or manipulate other programs. This may sound complicated, but Scheme has an extremely simple syntax. This technique is also essential for out-of-process LINQ—the manipulation with expression trees that makes LINQ to SQL possible is a great example of meta-programming. If you want to learn more, *Structure and Interpretation of Computer Programs* [Abelson, Sussman, and Sussman, 1985] is a great starting point.

Another language that definitely deserves attention is Haskell. You may find it interesting if you like the clarity and purity of functional programming, because Haskell takes this approach even further. *The Haskell School of Expression* [Hudak, 2000] explains essential Haskell ideas using many elegant and fun examples working with multimedia. Even though Haskell isn't integrated with a big ecosystem such as .NET or Java, *Real World Haskell* [O'Sullivan, Stewart, and Goerzen, 2008], does a great job of showing how to use pure functional programming to solve a wide range of interesting problems. The book presents a more traditional functional point of view than we've done here, because we've often tried to find a compromise between a purely functional style and the traditional .NET style.

There are several books you may find interesting if you want to learn more about the F# language. In this book we focused more on functional programming, so we didn't cover all the features and details of F#.

The Definitive Guide to F# [Syme, Granicz, and Cisternino 2009] doesn't spend a long time explaining principles, but moves quickly to advanced F# techniques showing most of the language.

Programming F# [Smith, 2009] covers the constructs organized by language features.

F# for Scientists [Harrop, 2008] focuses on advanced numerical computing, visualization, and many other related topics.

F# in Action [Laucher, forthcoming 2010], published by Manning, as is this book, discusses, among other topics, concurrency, service-oriented architecture, and development of F# business rules engines.

resources

All URLs listed here were valid at the time of publishing. No doubt some of these will change over time. Some of the cited works are academic articles that are available only in journals or conference proceedings. Where possible, we also include a URL to the article on the author's website.

Works cited

In print

Abelson, Harold, Gerald Jay Sussman, and Julie Sussman. *Structure and Interpretation of Computer Programs*. MIT Press, 1985.

Armstrong, Joe, Robert Virding, Claes Wikström, and Mike Williams. *Concurrent Programming in ERLANG*, 2nd ed. Prentice Hall International Ltd., 1996. First part available at http://erlang.org/download/erlang-book-part1.pdf.

Dean, Jeffrey, and Sanjay Ghemawat. *MapReduce: Simplified Data Processing on Large Clusters. Proceedings of Operating System Design and Implementation (OSDI)*, 2004, pg. 137–50. http://labs.google.com/papers/mapreduce.html

Elliott, Conal and Paul Hudak. *Functional Reactive Animation*. Proceedings of International Conference on Functional Programming (ICFP), 1997, pp. 263-273. Available at http://conal.net/papers/icfp97/icfp97.pdf .

Harrop, Jon. *F# for Scientists*. Wiley-Interscience, 2008.

Hudak, Paul. *The Haskell School of Expression: Learning Functional Programming through Multimedia*. Cambridge University Press, 2000.

Jones, Simon Peyton, Jean-Marc Eber, and Julian Seward. *Composing Contracts: An Adventure in Financial Engineering*. Proceedings of International Conference on Functional Programming (ICFP), 2000, pp. 280–92. http://research.microsoft.com/en-us/um/people/simonpj/papers/financial-contracts/contracts-icfp.ps.gz

Laucher, Amanda. *F# in Action*, Manning Publications, forthcoming, 2010.

Leijen, Daan and Erik Meijer. *Parsec: A Practical Parser Library. Electronic Notes in Theoretical Computer Science* (41): 1, 2001. http://research.microsoft.com/en-us/um/people/emeijer/papers/parsec.pdf.

O'Sullivan, Bryan, Don Stewart, and John Goerzen. *Real World Haskell*. O'Reilly Media, 2008.

Russo, Claudio. *The Joins Concurrency Library*. Proceedings of Practical Aspects of Declarative Languages (PADL), 2007, pp. 260–74 http:::research.microsoft.com:en-us:um:people:crusso:papers:padl07.pdf. For more information see http://research.microsoft.com/en-us/um/people/crusso/joins

Skeet, Jon. *C# in Depth*, Manning Publications, 2008.

Smith, Chris. *Programming F#*. O'Reilly Media, 2009.

Syme, Don, Adam Granicz, and Antonio Cisternino. *The Definitive Guide to F#*. Apress, 2009.

Online

Bolognese, Luca. *An Introduction to Microsoft F#*. 2008. http://channel9.msdn.com/pdc2008/TL11/

Chrysanthakopoulos, Georgio and Satnam Singh. *An Asynchronous Messaging Library for C#*. Proceedings of Synchronization and Concurrency in Object-Oriented Languages (SCOOL) conference (online), 2005. http://research.microsoft.com/en-us/um/people/tharris/scool/papers/sing.pdf

ECMA, *C# Language Specification* (Standard ECMA-334). 2006. http://www.ecma-international.org/publications/standards/Ecma-334.htm

F# home page, *Microsoft F# Developer Center*. http://msdn.microsoft.com/fsharp

F# Language specification. Search http://msdn.microsoft.com/fsharp for language specification.

F# Documentation. *Visual F#*, MSDN Documentation, Microsoft. http://msdn.microsoft.com/en-us/library/dd233154(VS.100).aspx

Fowler, Martin. *Domain Specific Languages*. 2008 http://www.martinfowler.com/dslwip/

Gates, Bill. *TechEd Keynote interview*. 2008. Interviewed by Dan Fernandez. http://channel9.msdn.com/posts/Dan/Bill-Gates-TechEd-Keynote/

Hamilton, Kim, and Wes Dyer. *Inside .NET Rx and IObservable/IObserver in the BCL (VS 2010)*. Channel 9 Video. 2009. http://channel9.msdn.com/shows/Going+Deep/Kim-Hamilton-and-Wes-Dyer-Inside-NET-Rx-and-IObservableIObserver-in-the-BCL-VS-2010/

HaskellWiki, *Lifting*, Community content. http://www.haskell.org/haskellwiki/Lifting

Hurt, Brian. *The "Hole in the middle" pattern*. 2007. http://enfranchisedmind.com/blog/2007/07/10/the-hole-in-the-middle-pattern/

Hutton, Graham, editor, Frequently Asked Questions for comp.lang.functional. 2002. http://www.cs.nott.ac.uk/~gmh/faq.html

Meijer, Erik, Wolfram Schulte, and Gavin M. Bierman. *Unifying Tables, Objects and Documents*. Proceedings of Declarative Programming in the Context of Object-Oriented Languages (DP-COOL), 2003. http://research.microsoft.com/~emeijer/Papers/XS.pdf

Petricek, Tomas. *Asynchronous Programming in C# Using Iterators*. 2007. http://tomasp.net/articles/csharp-async.aspx

Petricek, Tomas. *Reactive Programming (II) – Introducing Reactive LINQ*. 2008. http://tomasp.net/blog/reactive-ii-csevents.aspx

Richter, Jeffrey. *Concurrency and Coordination Runtime*. 2006. http://msdn.microsoft.com/en-us/magazine/cc163556.aspx

Additional resources

In print

Calvert, Charlie, and Dinesh Kulkarni. *Essential LINQ*. Addison-Wesley, 2009. Discusses the concepts behind LINQ project and presents technologies that build on top of LINQ, including LINQ to Entities, LINQ to XML, and LINQ to SQL.

Gamma, Erich, Richard Helm, Ralph Johnson, John M. Vlissides. *Design Patterns: Elements of Reusable Object-Oriented Software*. Addison-Wesley Professional, 2004. The essential book about design patterns that describes all the patterns referenced in chapters 7 and 8.

Marguerie, Fabrice, Steve Eichert, and Jim Wooley. *LINQ in Action*. Manning Publications, 2008. Presents general-purpose LINQ query facilities in C# 3.0 and Visual Basic 9 and describes how to use LINQ when working with objects, XML documents, and databases.

Mitchell, John C. *Concepts in Programming Languages.* Cambridge University Press, 2003. If you want to learn about different programming paradigms (including object-oriented, imperative, functional, and logic) and their origins, this is a book for you.

Paulson, Lawrence C. *ML for the Working Programmer.* Cambridge University Press, 1996. F# inherits the core principles from the ML language, so if you're interested in learning more about the history of this kind of functional language, this book provides a great overview.

Skeet, Jon. *C# in Depth, 2nd Ed.* Manning Publications, forthcoming 2010. In-depth explanation of all new C# features, including functional features (such as lambda expressions and the query syntax) as well as recent C# 4 additions.

Online

Companion website: http://www.functional-programming.net

Book website: http://www.manning.com/FunctionalProgrammingintheRealWorld.com

Erlang.org: http://erlang.org/

Haskell.org: http://www.haskell.org/

LINQ Developer Center: http://msdn.microsoft.com/en-us/data/cc299380.aspx

Windows Presentation Foundation: http://windowsclient.net/wpf

World Bank–Data: http://www.worldbank.org/data

xUnit.net: http://www.codeplex.com/xunit

index

MORE TITLES FROM MANNING

C# in Depth, Second Edition
by Jon Skeet

ISBN: 978-1-935182-47-4
500 pages
$49.99
Spring 2010

The Art of Unit Testing
with Examples in .NET
by Roy Osherove

ISBN: 978-1-933988-27-6
320 pages
$39.99
May 2009